The Westminster Confession into the 21st Century

Volume 3

'We live in a day of wholesale historical amnesia and theological confusion. The antidote for this crisis is clear – we need a recovery of what has been lost. That is what makes volume 3 of The Westminster Confession into the 21st Century *so important and timely. The Westminster Assembly represents one of the most decisive moments in church history, and this collection of essays brings new light to our understanding of the Westminster divines and their work. Here we find scholarship matched to a deep love for the church. This book is a worthy successor to the first two volumes in this series. I celebrate its publication and commend it to all who love the church.'*

R. Albert Mohler, Jr.,
President and Joseph Emerson Brown Professor of Theology,
The Southern Baptist Theological Seminary, Louisville, Kentucky

The Westminster Confession into the 21st Century

*Essays in Rememberance of the
350th Anniversary of the Westminster Assembly*

Volume 3

General Editor
J. Ligon Duncan, III

Associate Editors
Derek W. H. Thomas
Jerry F. O'Neill
Robert C. "Ric" Cannada, Jr.
W. Duncan Rankin
William McMillan
J. Nicholas Reid

ⅯENTOR

© J. Ligon Duncan III

ISBN 978-1-85792-992-8

10 9 8 7 6 5 4 3 2 1

Published in 2009
in the
Mentor Imprint
by
Christian Focus Publications,
Geanies House, Fearn,
Ross-shire, IV20 1TW, Scotland

www.christianfocus.com

Cover design by Moose77.com

Printed and bound in the USA

Contents

Foreword

Over a decade and a half ago we marked the 350th anniversary of the English Parliament's ordinance calling for the historic Westminster Assembly (1643–1649/52). Reformed Theological Seminary (RTS) has a special interest in the promotion of the study of the Assembly since the Confession serves as our basic doctrinal position. Because we passionately believe these truths, RTS has aimed to produce pastors who believe and promote them in a way that is warmly and winsomely Reformed and biblically ecumenical, spreading the influence of these truths as broadly as possible.

This set of books is published with a view to introducing the student to some of the main issues in the history, theology, and literature of the Assembly, and in hopes of spurring new interest in the work of the Westminster Divines. Our aims, however, are not merely academic. They are also pastoral and devotional. We hope to provide material that will prove both interesting and helpful to the scholars, ministers, elders, candidates, and congregations of the various evangelical churches influenced by the Westminster Assembly.

We catch something of the pastoral and devotional heart of the Assembly in the words of Samuel Rutherford (a Scottish commissioner to the Assembly), speaking of his Savior, Jesus Christ: "I am so in love with His love, that if His love were not in heaven, I should not be willing to go thither." This kind of passionate adoration of Christ is at the heart of Reformed theology at its best, and that is the sort of devotion we seek to promote through the work of Reformed Theological Seminary: love for God, love for his truth, love for Christ, love for people. Our message is "A mind for truth, a heart for God."

There is much indeed to feed our souls (as well as to strengthen our minds) which we can learn from these forefathers in the faith. The Westminster Assembly has provided for us both a profound, reverent, moving exposition of the doctrines of the Bible, and a worthy model of the function of truth in the pursuit of godliness.

Personally, my parents led me to memorize the Westminster Shorter Catechism when I was a young boy. Later I was given a copy of the complete Westminster Standards by my home church, First Presbyterian Church in Jackson, Mississippi, along with all others in that congregation when we completed our secondary education. My parents made sure that copy was packed in my luggage when I left home for undergraduate studies. A number of times as I discussed issues with others at Vanderbilt University, I turned to the Westminster Confession for guidance into the truths of Scripture. In particular the Confession was a great help to me in those days in my understanding and teaching on the subject of assurance of salvation and for my own personal comfort and encouragement in this vital area of the Christian life.

May our Sovereign God use these volumes to reacquaint His people with the rich spiritual heritage bequeathed to them by their Puritan forefathers and to spur them on to further study of their "affectionate, practical" theology.

Dr. Robert C. "Ric" Cannada, Jr.
President, Reformed Theological Seminary
Jackson, Mississippi; Orlando, Florida; Charlotte, North Carolina;
Washington, DC; Atlanta, Georgia, USA
Associate Editor, Westminster Assembly Project

Introduction

LIGON DUNCAN

This volume is the third in a series of what has become four volumes, all part of a larger scholarly initiative known as Reformed Theological Seminary's "Westminster Assembly Project," begun in the early 1990s, with the encouragement of the administration of Reformed Theological Seminary (Jackson, Mississippi; Orlando, Florida; Charlotte, North Carolina; Washington, DC; Atlanta, Georgia). As a part of this project, a group of eminent scholars from around the world was approached to participate in the production of literature (both popular and academic) designed to discuss and debate the most important issues in current post-Reformation studies, as well as promote interest in the Westminster Assembly and its work. For more information about the literary products of this project, the reader is referred to the introduction of the first volume.

For more than a decade and a half, we have been researching, producing literature, and preparing this multi-volume set of scholarly essays on various subjects related to the work of the Westminster Assembly. Our aim has been to produce something of a symposium on the theology of the Assembly. Indeed, prior to the General Assembly of the Presbyterian Church in America each summer, over the past decade, RTS has sponsored a conference on the Westminster Assembly, during which some of the contents of these volumes were first presented. Because this endeavor was a public discussion and debate on the theology and work of the Assembly, not all the contributors are in agreement, though all of us have a high regard for the product and importance of the Assembly.

As an example of the kind of differences and debate we have been willing to allow, I could mention what is, perhaps, the most widely reported and discussed historical claim in these volumes is David Wright's assertion in volume two, that the Westminster Confession teaches a doctrine of "baptismal regeneration." I never thought this claim held water (if I can put it that way!), and Chad Van Dixhoorn's research has now shown, authoritatively, that that assertion is unfounded and incorrect. Nevertheless, out of deference to Dr. Wright (who was, before his recent death, a widely respected patristic and reformation scholar, and who had partnered with Dr. Van Dixhoorn in the important work of producing a new definitive edition of the Minutes of the Assembly, and who was also my own, beloved, PhD supervisor at New College, Edinburgh), we allowed his article and his assertion to stand as submitted as both a professional courtesy and as a normal part of scholarly debate.

Another example of differences represented in this symposium is on the subject of Westminster, Calvin and the Lord's Supper. Dr. Wayne Spear's chapters in this volume take a different approach than my own in volume two. This kind of debate is enriching though for the scholar and student of the Assembly, and so we commend all our contributions to you for your critical assessment and reflection. If we have started and can start healthy discussions in disputed or neglected areas of the Assembly's theology, then we may help clarify these theological and historical issues for generations to come.

That being said, most of the contributors to these volumes both have a positive appreciation of and are in general agreement about the Assembly's theology. For example, all of us would embrace some form of a "continuity view" of how the Westminster theology (and the larger Puritan/Protestant Scholastic stream) relates to the earlier Reformed tradition. Consequently, we argue for the basic continuity between Calvin and Calvinism, without ignoring developments and discontinuities.

As I have said in the introductions to the two previous volumes, our purpose is to **inform, challenge, evaluate**, and **commend**. We aim (1) to inform the reader about the Assembly in is historical, theological, political, and social setting, (2) to challenge inaccurate assertions commonly made about Westminster in its relation to both earlier and later Reformed theology, (3) to provide fresh evaluation of its place in and contribution to the Calvinian tradition, and (4) to commend the Westminster theology as a faithful expression of clear-headed Christian thinking for our own generation.

There are many reasons why it is beneficial for us to study the Westminster Assembly. I have already articulated some of those reasons in the introduction to the first volume. And precisely because such a study is worthwhile, my colleagues and I have assembled contributions from an impressive list of students of Westminster and its context, to provide a window into its work and world.

This volume begins with an essay from Chad Van Dixhoorn on "The Westminster Assembly at Work." Dr. Van Dixhoorn is general editor of the Westminster Assembly Project (a project distinct and different from the RTS Westminster Assembly Project)—an endeavor that focuses on editing and publishing documents from the Westminster Assembly in an effort to greatly expand our knowledge on the work of the Assembly (the appendix to this volume being a case in point). In his chapter, Van Dixhoorn masterfully updates the work of B.B. Warfield and Samuel Carruthers on the everyday work of the Assembly. He also gives a totally new and comprehensive view of the Assembly, in contrast to that of (for instance) Robert Paul, and consequently challenges a reductionistic account of the Assembly.

Professor Robert Cara's essay, "Redemptive-Historical Themes in the Westminster Larger Catechism," sounds a clear note that needs to be heard and appreciated by many in our own time. Whereas some pit union with Christ over and against the *ordo salutis*, redemptive history (or biblical theology) over against systematic theology, Cara refutes these false juxtapositions and shows how the Larger Catechism, in a systematic framework, helpfully depicts redemptive historical/biblical theological themes in its treatment of union with Christ. Bob is a good friend, and the Chief Academic Officer of Reformed Theological Seminary.

Dr. Rowland S. Ward (faithful minister in the Presbyterian Church of Eastern Australia, prolific author and admired colleague) contributes an outstanding overview of the history of confessional subscription in chapter three of this volume. Rowland essay is called "Subscription to the Confession." Few people know the subjects of the history of subscription, and the doctrine, logic and justification of subscription, as well as Rowland. Hence, we are well-rewarded in reading his superb summarization and long-considered reflections on this hotly debated subject.

Dr. Robert Norris' contribution, "The Thirty-Nine Articles at the Westminster Assembly," discusses the early history of the Assembly, presenting his mature reflections on the Assembly's often overlooked debates over the Thirty-Nine Articles. Norris gives a clear argument about the importance of these early discussions for the subsequent work of the Assembly, drawing particular attention to the gathering's debates over the doctrine of justification. Dr. Norris' work was written before Van Dixhoorn's research and so one will want to read him in dialogue with Van Dixhoorn's findings.

"Karl Barth and the Westminster Confession of Faith," Will Traub's chapter, shows Barth's surprisingly high esteem of the Assembly, despite his vigorous disagreements with its theology. Will, a long-time missionary in Germany, and very able scholar walks us through this material critically, but respectfully.

In the twentieth and twenty-first centuries, it has been common to argue that Reformed theology does not embrace natural theology. J. V. Fesko and Guy Richard demonstrate otherwise in their essay, "Natural Theology and the Westminster Confession of Faith." Any assessment of how the epistemology of the Confession relates to post-Kantian reformed epistemology must reckon with the kind of material Fesko and Richard unearth.

Derek Thomas gives us the best concise treatment of the lapsarian issue at the Assembly that I have ever read in his chapter, "The Westminster Consensus on the Decree." This essay, in fact, changed my mind about the issue. I won't say more. That's endorsement enough, except to say that Derek has been my colleague in church and academy for a joyous decade and a half now, and I thank God for him.

In his essay, "The New Perspective: Paul, Luther, and Judaism," Donald Macleod (Principal and Professor of Theology at the Free Church of Scotland College, Edinburgh) assesses the New Perspective from a Westminsterian perspective, especially focusing on N.T. Wright's understanding of justification. Macleod has a way of getting to the heart of things, and he is characteristically insightful and provocative here.

For those who think that Westminster theology does not promote missions or that missions is absent from the Confession because it does not contain a specific chapter on the subject, they may want to think again after considering Valdeci Santos' essay, "A Missiological Analysis of the Westminster Confession of Faith." Valdeci is a former student, now professor and leader in the Brazilian Presbyterian Church.

In the debates on Calvin, the Lord's Supper, and the Reformed tradition, three schools of thought (or at least tendencies) can be detected. One reads into Calvin's views of the presence of Christ and sacramental efficacy positions that he himself did not hold. A second suggests that the Westminster standards and later Reformed orthodoxy had a slightly different view than Calvin, but prefers Calvin's views to those of the later Reformed tradition. A third likewise posits that the Westminster standards and later Reformed orthodoxy had a different view than Calvin, but sides with the later Reformed tradition over against Calvin (William Cunningham, Robert Lewis Dabney and Donald Macleod all fall into this camp). Both of Spears' essays in this volume stand squarely in this third school of thought. His essays are literally stimulating.

Mark Ross' "Improving the Means of Grace: The Larger Catechism on Spiritual Growth" practically and helpfully unfolds the instruction of the Westminster Larger Catechism to improve one's baptism. This is a notion that sounds strange to us in our day, but was once part of normal Christian instruction in the church at an older, wiser, and healthier time. Mark is a cherished friend and Professor of Theology at Erskine Seminary on Columbia, SC.

In his essay, "The Westminster Standards and the Structure of Christian Ethics," now-retired Covenant Seminary professor David C. Jones elaborates on the Westminster Standards' contribution to Christian ethics—a "study of the way of life that conforms to the will of God as revealed in Christ and the Holy Scriptures." He argues that the Standards can be more fully appreciated by relating the threefold fundamentals of ethics—goal, disposition, and norms—to "the thematic unity of covenant theology" and proposes looking at these respectively as covenant purpose, covenant virtue, and covenant practice.

And finally in my essay, "Objections to the Covenant Theology of the Confession," I offer an introductory examination of the objections and responses to classic covenant theology. In general, I am responding to Barthian criticisms of Westminster's covenant theology, but I also rejoin the venerated John Murray (to whom I owe so much, but who, in this area, got some things wrong, I think), and also engage a little bit with the so-called "federal vision."

The magnitude of the Assembly and its work, the quality of its product, and its significance for the English-speaking world and beyond in successive generations should not be underestimated, but often is today. The Assembly's theological formulations are a landmark of pastoral theology, and the work of the Assembly marks the highpoint of Reformed confessionalism, and thus warrants the further study, consideration, discussion and debate that these essays intend to promote.

J. Ligon Duncan, III, BA, MDiv, MA, PhD
General Editor, The Westminster Assembly Project
Senior Minister, First Presbyterian Church (PCA), Jackson, Mississippi, USA
President, Alliance of Confessing Evangelicals
Adjunct Professor, Reformed Theological Seminary
Past Moderator, General Assembly, Presbyterian Church in America

Acknowledgements

LIGON DUNCAN

So many people have been involved in this project that it is impossible in a short space to properly thank them all, but there a few whom I must not fail to thank. First among them, William Mackenzie, our publisher, and Willie Mackenzie, our editor, of Christian Focus Publications (Mentor) both of whom have displayed extraordinary patience with me and have waited in hope for several years now to receive the manuscript of this book. They have been good-natured and intrepid, encouraging and prodding, and I think we are even still friends after it all. I am deeply appreciative of their support and perseverance. Only one more volume to go!

I also wish to express my gratitude to the authors, the associate editors, and my assistants Nick Reid and Jason Grabulis. The material you have written and pulled together will be a benefit not only to scholarship on the Westminster Assembly but for the well-being of the church. And, while I'm at it, on behalf of my fellow editors, we wish to thank Jeremy Smith (who is now Executive Minister at First Presbyterian Church, Jackson, Mississippi) and Jonathan Sherrod (former intern of mine and now medical student) for their help with this project. The whole editorial team also expresses a debt of gratitude to the Chancellor and Executive Committee of RTS for their multifaceted support and encouragement over the years.

Without the financial provision of the Lord, this project would not have been possible. Among those whom the Lord chose to use, three stand out particularly: The First Presbyterian Church, Yazoo City, Mississippi, James R. "Sonny" Peaster (a trustee of the Banner of Truth Trust), and my new and old dear friend, a Ruling Elder at First Presbyterian Church, Jackson, Mississippi, A. William May.

We would also like to thank Dr. Jerry O'Neill, President and Professor of Theology at Reformed Presbyterian Theological Seminary (RPTS), and the dear folk at RPTS for their unfailing assistance and encouragement. RPTS's "Westminister Confession into the 21st Century" conferences have garnered some choice pieces for this volume and the next.

Nothing I undertake would be possible without the support of my wife Anne. Thank you, dear one. Let me also here acknowledge my world-class Executive Assistant, Missye Rhee Breazeale: without you I'd never get anything done! Missye Rhee interfaces with just about everyone involved in these projects, and they all end up both loving and respecting her. And well they should!

Finally, this volume of essays on the work of an assembly of "Old Calvinists" is dedicated to the resurging "New Calvinists." We trust that as you consider the work of the Westminster Assembly, you will be challenged, edified, grown in your understanding of Scripture, and, more importantly stirred, to worship the Living God, through Jesus Christ, our Lord. To his name be all the glory!

Ligon Duncan
The Study, First Presbyterian Church,
Jackson, Mississippi, USA

1

The Westminster Assembly at Work

Chad Van Dixhoorn

Introduction

Defining the Task

Parliament's biggest blunder on the first day of July 1643, hardly hidden by all the fanfare, was its failure to give the Westminster Assembly any specific task to perform. This became immediately apparent to the divines after William Twisse's sermon drew to a close. Sir Simond D'Ewes relates that forty members of the House of Commons, "some of which were of the synod, went with the said prolocutor and the rest of the divines then present into Henry the Seventh's Chapel in Westminster adjoining to the abbey church."[1] But aside from sitting, there was little else to do but "call over the names of the divines appointed to be of this assembly that so it might appear who were absent and who were present."[2]

---

[1] See D'Ewes' account in the British Library (BL) Harleian MS 165, fo. 105r. In this and all other manuscript citations I follow the standard convention of listing place, manuscript collection with volume number, and folio. Historians have not previously referred to D'Ewes' account of the Assembly's opening day. Although he relates only secondhand information, being absent for the morning, D'Ewes provides more detail than does John Lightfoot's better known account (see below). I am thankful for Anne Steele Young's permission to use her transcription of D'Ewes' diary. A copy of her transcript is housed in the History of Parliament which kindly permitted me access to this and other materials.

[2] BL Harl. 165, fo. 105r.

Dr. Cornelius Burges "moved in the assembly that there might be a day appointed for a fast to be held by them as a due preparation to their future consultation."[3] However, since this was the first day of the Assembly and the first opportunity for Parliament to assert itself before the divines, two members of the House of Commons, John Selden and William Pierrepont, were quick to dismiss the motion, providing an interpretation of the summoning ordinance which construed the task of the Assembly in as exact a manner as possible, not even allowing the divines to fast without Parliament's permission. At this point "it was agreed amongst that they should move the two Houses" about the fast "and having appointed a new day for meeting rose awhile after."[4] The appointed meeting day was July 6, and on that day a message was sent by Parliament to the waiting divines in the abbey requiring them to consider the first ten of the Thirty-Nine Articles.[5]

In spite of the restricted task presented in the summoning ordinance, as Selden and Pierrepont saw it, the Assembly's work was almost unimaginably varied. General summaries of this work have, of course, been written.[6] But thus far, only S. W. Carruthers has attempted to describe the variety of the tasks of the Westminster Assembly. His discussions are illuminating, but his use of sources is unsystematic, incomplete, and undocumented.[7] This

---

[3] BL Harl. 165, fo. 105v.

[4] BL Harl. 165, fo. 105v.

[5] That order was passed on July 5 (House of Lords, Main Papers (MP) 5 July 1643). Since the Main Papers of the House of Lords are uncatalogued except by the dates and descriptions provided in Historic Manuscript Commission reports, Appendixes 4-7, I follow the conventional practice of citing each document as "MP" followed by the date.

[6] W. Beveridge, *A Short History of the Assembly* (Edinburgh: T & T Clark, 1904; reprint, Greenville, SC: Reformed Academic Press, 1993), 15-104; F. Higham, *Catholic and Reformed* (London: SPCK, 1962), 213-23; W. R. Spear, "A Brief History of the Westminster Assembly," *Evangel* 11 (1993), 73-76; "Westminster Assembly and documents," in *Dictionary of Scottish Church History and Theology* (Edinburgh: T & T Clark, 1993); C. B. Van Dixhoorn, "Unity and Disunity at the Westminster Assembly (1643-1649)," *The Journal of Presbyterian History* 79:2 (Summer 2001), 103-18.

essay, although briefer than Carruthers' treatment, provides a systematic, quantified account of the whole of the Assembly's work and considers both the material available to Carruthers and more recently discovered manuscripts.[8]

At one level, then, this study supplements Carruthers' account by reporting tasks and documents of which he was unaware or considered uninteresting. And yet this chapter seeks to do more than merely describe what the Westminster Assembly did. It gives for the first time a sense of proportion to the work of the Assembly and seeks to identify the major subject areas which most occupied the Assembly in its reforming efforts. "One of the issues confronting scholarly examination of the late sixteenth and the seventeenth century," Richard Muller writes, "is simply identifying who were the major figures and what were the major issues in debate – and then sufficiently raising the profile of the figures or issues in order to bring about an alteration of the broader surveys of the era."[9] This study sets the stage for such a scholarly examination of the Assembly. To change the metaphor, it maps the intellectual terrain over which the Westminster Divines traveled and logs the amount

---

[7]   S. W. Carruthers, *The Everyday Work of the Westminster Assembly* (Philadelphia: Presbyterians Historical Society [of America] and Presbyterians Historical Society of England, 1943). Carruthers does not mention his sources, but he must have relied on the transcripts of the minutes of the Westminster Assembly, held in New College, University of Edinburgh. Indeed, his distinctive hand can be found in the margins of the transcript.

[8]   A search to find the lost minutes of the Westminster Assembly led instead to my locating and identifying uncatalogued manuscripts of the Assembly in the Bodleian Library, to my identifying six manuscripts of the Westminster Assembly in Westminster College in Cambridge, to my locating most of the remaining manuscripts of the Assembly in the Main Papers of the House of Lords record office, and to the rediscovery of John Lightfoot's journal (see below). Only two of these manuscripts have previously been identified as Assembly texts and used by historians: the *Confession of Faith* in Westminster College (Braye MS, fos. 111r-143r), and the *Shorter Catechism* in the Bodleian (Nalson MS 22, fos. 179r-185r).

[9]   Richard A. Muller, *After Calvin: Studies in the Development of a Theological Tradition* (Oxford: OUP, 2003), 192.

of time spent in each place, helping us to locate sites that were of major interest to the divines.

Thus one operating assumption of this essay is that the importance of a subject area, at least for the Westminster Divines, is often proportional to the quantity of time and effort expended on that subject by the Assembly. Working from the inside out, this study describes the work of the gathering and then allows this description to inform our understanding of what constitutes the major issues and events of the gathering. The description and analysis of the Westminster Assembly at work is divided into two parts. The first part of this essay surveys all surviving accounts of the Assembly's plenary sessions in its minutes[10] and in Lightfoot's journals,[11] Gillespie's journals,[12] and the Journals of both houses

---

[10] I make extensive use of the manuscript records or minutes of the Westminster Assembly. The three-volume folio of the minutes contains approximately 530,000 words and survives in Dr. Williams's Library, London, the pre-eminent library for the study of Puritanism and nonconformity. It spans the years 1643 to 1652, covering the Westminster Assembly's formal debates (1643–1649) and the proceedings of the 'rump' committee which continued to ordain ministers after the Assembly had completed its major tasks (1649–1652). Approximately one third of the Assembly's minutes were printed in the nineteenth century. I cite the text of the Assembly's manuscript minutes (Dr. Williams's Library, London, MS 38.1-3) as 'Minutes' by volume and folio as transcribed in C. B. Van Dixhoorn, "Reforming the Reformation: Theological Debate at the Westminster Assembly, 1643–1652," (unpublished Ph.D. diss., University of Cambridge, 2004), vols. 3-7. I am currently preparing an 880,000 word critical text of *The Minutes and Papers of the Westminster Assembly, 1643–1652* to be published by Oxford University Press. The late Professor David F. Wright(1937–2008) of New College, Edinburgh, was the project's founder, consulting editor, and chair of the advisory board.

[11] In November 2001, I located and identified John Lightfoot's original manuscript in the Cambridge University Library (CUL Dd.XIV.28(4), fos. 1r-62v) and discovered that it is 85 percent longer than the transcript on which the editor of Lightfoot's published journal and subsequent historians of the Assembly have relied. For a discussion of Lightfoot's journal and for a transcription of this newly discovered journal, see Van Dixhoorn, "Reforming the Reformation," vol. 2. In this essay I cite the manuscript journal with foliation as "Lightfoot, MS Journal." I cite Lightfoot's published journal with pagination as "Lightfoot, *Journal*." I hope to introduce and edit this manuscript journal, together with a new edition of Lightfoot's other manuscript journals, and submit it for publication at some point.

of Parliament.[13] With the discovery of Lightfoot's earliest journal, we now, for the first time, have some information on every day that the Assembly met, as can be seen in "An Analysis of the Plenary Sessions of the Westminster Assembly" at the close of this volume. The second part of this essay classifies and briefly describes the Assembly's 210 ad hoc committees.

Subject Classifications

Both parts of this study rely on a subject classification that corresponds with the following key with descriptions:

A: Approving candidates: all matters pertaining to the approval of men for chaplaincies, churches, and university appointments.

B: Business: all business relating to the Assembly, its ordering, regulating, procedures, finances, and members; the welcoming of visitors; correspondence with foreign churches (including the Church of Scotland); works of charity; and relations with politicians.

C: Church government: the practice of ordination, the rights of church government, the structure of the national church, Presbyterianism, Independency, Erastianism, and the establishment of presbyteries.

D: Doctrine: the revision of the Thirty-nine Articles; the formation of confessions, catechisms, the doctrinal and moral standard for admission to the Lord's Supper, and the petitioning against and confuting of heretics.

F: Fast: fast days or discussion about fasting.

W: Worship: all matters having to do with the Directory for Worship, Sabbath observance, and the Psalter.

---

[12] George Gillespie, "Notes of Debates and Proceedings of the Assembly of Divines and Other Commissioners at Westminster," ed. D. Meek, in *Works*, (Edinburgh: Robert Ogle and Oliver and Boyd, 1846), 2:9-100.

[13] *Journals of the House of Lords* (1846), cited as LJ; *Journals of the House of Commons* (1803 –), cited as CJ.

The classification of the work of plenary sessions or committees according to a single subject code is obviously a simplification.[14] Yet, in spite of the interrelatedness of each subject of debate with the other subjects, the Divines themselves tended to class their works in categories similar to those used in this study, and they often distinguished between the types of work in which they were engaged based on, say, the documents which they intended to produce.[15] The category that I have labelled "business" is perhaps the most expansive. It functions as a repository for miscellaneous tasks not associated with the examination of ministers and ministerial candidates, and it often includes those tasks more clearly related to the operation of the Assembly.

In Session: An Analysis of Plenary Sessions of the Westminster Assembly as Described in Lightfoot's Journals and the Minutes of the Assembly

Chronological Analysis

Plenary Sessions and the Record of the Minutes

One reason why church governance has remained the focus of most historians who have used the Assembly's minutes has to do with the character of the minutes themselves. If one takes into account the missing fascicules of Byfield's minutes, the imbalance of material for the early sessions of the Assembly versus the later sessions is dramatic. According to my reconstruction of the text of the minutes, it appears that an amazing 1,050 folios

---

[14] Some debates pertain equally to church government and to doctrine and are thus marked as having two subjects. What is more, 17th century doctrinal systems and confessions would classify church government and worship as doctrinal loci along with the doctrine of God or the doctrine of justification.

[15] One reason why I have followed this pattern of description and have listed A, B, C, D, F, and W as distinct subjects is that they often required the creation of distinct documents. Thus, where worship, fasting, or ecclesiology was debated in the Assembly as doctrinal loci with the Confession or catechisms in view, this study classifies it as doctrine. Similarly, if theology was discussed while writing the Directory for Worship, the subject is classed as worship.

of description (written recto and verso) were expended on the first 325 sessions of the Assembly, whereas only 300 folios are expended for the last 1,000 sessions of the Assembly. For some reason which I cannot yet ascertain, in November of 1644 the scribe abruptly stopped writing full accounts and began to write summaries. Thus, by sheer paper weight, the topics discussed in those first seventeen months are given far greater prominence than those discussed in later years. Furthermore, although 350 of the 1,050 early folios discuss theology and worship, 150 of these 350 folios are missing.[16] The combined effect of Byfield's early scribal enthusiasm and of the 150 missing folios covering theology and worship leaves the impression that ecclesiology was the dominant subject of debate in the Assembly – an impression based not on the time that the Assembly actually spent on the subject (as I shall argue below), but on the time the scribe spent writing about it.

As indicated above, in order to provide a more accurate picture of the Assembly's day-to-day work, I have created "An analysis of the plenary sessions of the Westminster Assembly," found at the end of this volume.[17] In the "Analysis" the main debate(s) of each plenary session of the Assembly are summarized, whether described fully or briefly in the minutes. The "Analysis" cross-references all available sources for each day of the Assembly, and provides the date, day of the week, session number, and a subject classification using the subject key used for the chronological bibliography. It traverses all of the Assembly's meetings from July 1, 1643 to March 25, 1652 and records both numbered and unnumbered sessions. If the conjectural numbering of the sessions in Lightfoot's

---

[16] For more information on the minutes, see C. B. Van Dixhoorn, "Reforming the Reformation: Theological Debate at the Westminster Assembly, 1643–1652," (unpublished Ph.D. diss., University of Cambridge, 2004), 2:xxiv-xlvi; or C. B. Van Dixhoorn and D. F. Wright, eds., *The Minutes and Papers of the Westminster Assembly,* Oxford University Press, in preparation.

[17] Pages 501-536.

journals provided in the "Analysis" is correct,[18] then the sessions of the Assembly total 1333.[19] The "Analysis" also contains a basic subject classification of the debates of each plenary session (the same as that used in this essay). Classifications are provided only for plenary sessions and grand committees of the Assembly and not for other committee meetings or fasts which are mentioned in the table of contents but not identified as plenary sessions either by the scribe or, in the early months of the Assembly, by Lightfoot in his journals. These subject classifications are tallied in Table 1.[20]

---

[18] See "Analysis." Lightfoot records no session numbers in his journals, but if fast days are not counted as sessions and if afternoon plenary sessions are, then the first forty-four sessions of the Assembly are all accounted for in my conjectural numbering in the "Analysis."

[19] The minutes of the Assembly reveal that the gathering held between 1,333 or 1,335 numbered and unnumbered plenary sessions. The ambiguity occurs with session numbers 1,061 and 1,111 where either no scribal record survived for a session that was held or where a simple error in numbering occurred. Other irregularities in the numbering of plenary sessions can be accounted for. Sometimes session numbers are missing: session number 75 is missing but it appears that the scribe counted the fast as a session without recording it as such. The scribe did not usually count fasts as plenary sessions, but he did so for some early fasts such as the ones held on Sept. 25, 1643; Oct. 23, 1644; Oct. 8, 1645; May 6, 1646; and probably, if my conjectural numbering is correct, on Aug. 30, 1643; the fast in the Assembly on May 17,1644; is also considered a session of the Assembly. On other occasions, session numbers are repeated. Such is the case with session numbers 1,066 and 1,067. Curiously, for sessions 601 to 900, the scribe's original records and a polished draft have survived. Session numbers 720, 721, 732, 734, 780, and 834 are repeated in the original "rough" minutes only and not in the revised minutes.

[20] The same subject classification is used in each table and in the "Analysis." Note only the addition of "?" which indicates that no information or insufficient information is available to determine the subject of a session. The column, "Percentage of sessions shared with one or more other subjects," is based on the number of sessions where a subject is a main but not exclusive subject of debate out of the total number of sessions where a subject is a main subject of debate. The column, "Percentage of total number of the 1395 known subject classifications," is based on the number of sessions where a subject is a main subject of the session, including those sessions where there is more than one main subject classification and excluding those sessions where the subject is unknown. Thus there are a total of 1,423 known subject classifications for 1,333 (or 1,335) plenary sessions, minus 28 (or 30), totaling 1,395.

Table 1
Number of plenary sessions of the Westminster Assembly by subject classification
(with sessions containing one or more main subject of debate specified)

Subject	Number of sessions where subject is the only main subject of debate	Number of sessions where subject is a main but not exclusive subject	Total number of sessions where subject is a main subject	Total percentage of the 1395 sessions with known subjects
A	301	44	345	25%
B	52	36	88	6%
C	326	30	356	26%
D	456	52	508	36%
F	14	5	19	1%
W	68	11	79	6%
?	27	1	28	-
Totals	1244	179	1423	100%

Brief Chronology of Plenary Sessions
The "Analysis" is helpful in identifying the overall flow of the
Assembly's work and permits the following chronological summary of each month in the Assembly's history where there is a major
shift in topic:

July 1643 – Thirty-Nine Articles
October 1643 – Directory for Church Government
January 1644 – Directory for the ordination of ministers pro
    tempore
February 1644 – Directory for Church Government
End of May 1644 – Directory for Worship
October 1644 – Directories for Church Government and Worship
January 1645 – Directory for Church Government
June 1645 – Admission to the Lord's Supper

July 1645 – Directory for Church Government and the Confession of Faith

August 1645 – Admission to the Lord's Supper and the examining of ministers

September 1645 – Confession of Faith

April 1646 – Church Government (*jus divinum*)

June 1646 – Church Government (*jus divinum*) and Confession of Faith

July 1646 – Church Government (*jus divinum*)

August 1646 – Confession of Faith

September 1646 – Confession and catechisms

October 1646 – Confession of Faith

December 1646 – Catechisms

January 1647 – Confession

April 1647 – Confession and catechisms

May 1647 – Catechisms and some days spent examining ministers

June 1648 – Assembly business and examining ministers

July 1648 – Examining ministers

March 1652 – Assembly concluded

I do not think it is possible to further summarize the Assembly's work and still maintain an accurate chronology. The "Analysis" itself demonstrates that the work of the Assembly was much more varied and interrupted than this chronology allows. That is to say, this chronology is a summary of the "Analysis," which is itself a summary and reduction of the work of the Assembly on a day-to-day basis. Yet this chronology does provide a much better picture of the Assembly's work over time than does a simple list of documents published by the Assembly, for these published documents were often detained by Parliament.

Topical Analysis of Plenary Sessions

Classifications

The "Analysis" of the Assembly's plenary sessions not only permits chronological observations but topical ones. Of course the debates and the records of some plenary sessions did not allow a straightforward classification. Twenty-eight sessions provide no information or insufficient information to settle conclusively the focus of the plenary session. Since no one subject of debate clearly dominated these sessions, I have provided two or (for one session only) three subject classification marks. In eighty-eight sessions the work of the Assembly roughly divides into two subjects, and in one session the work of the Assembly covered three subjects equally.[21]

In classifying and listing the main subjects of the concisely recorded debates in the third volume of the minutes, I have inferred some correspondence between these tersely described proceedings and the more fully described sessions found in volumes one and two. In the minutes of the first two volumes it is evident that where Assembly debates follow upon committee reports, the debates almost always take up more time than the reports. I assume that this pattern remains constant in the remainder of the plenary sessions where the minutes often record reports and debates but say nothing of the debates themselves. Thus, where debates are explicitly mentioned in the third volume of the minutes, I categorize them as main subjects of discussion in Table 1. Reports are listed as main subjects of discussion only where no debates are mentioned in the sources available for that day.

As was anticipated, the subject classification of these debates is inevitably a simplified one. Deliberations over the Directory for Ordination also involved extended controversy over pastoral theology and worship; days spent discussing sectaries and their doctrines involved both political and theological considerations; debates behind the Confession of Faith, a doctrinal subject, involved drafting chapters on the church, church censures, synods,

---

[21] Thus eighty-eight sessions yield two classification marks, and one session yields three, totaling 179 classification marks in a total of eighty-nine sessions. See the column totaling the "number of sessions where the subject is a main but not exclusive subject of debate."

and councils. Again, in each of these cases I classified the day's work according to the genre of the document being produced. Thus, a debate leading to the production of the *Confession* or catechisms is categorized as doctrine, and a debate about a letter to France is categorized as business.[22] It should also be noted that in almost every session the main subject of debate is not the only subject of debate. On most days items of business were carried out and ministers and ministerial candidates were approved and licensed, and on many days reports from committees were submitted, sometimes occupying a significant, although not primary, part of a plenary session.

Summary Analysis

This examination of the Assembly's work by session and subject reveals that theological concerns took up the greatest part of the Assembly's time. In 508 sessions theology was *the or a* main subject of debate. The preponderance of sessions dedicated to deliberating theology does not in itself indicate that theological debates were of primary importance at the Assembly. But the fact that 36 percent of the Assembly's sessions were spent debating theology suggests that there may be doctrinal issues which the Divines considered both important and difficult to state. Sadly most of these doctrinal debates take place in the later sessions of the Assembly where Adoniram Byfield's record keeping is especially parsimonious. Thus, while we can read that the doctrine of creation was debated for three days in the Assembly, and while we can estimate the relative contentiousness of this topic from the length of its debate compared to other topics of debate, we cannot

---

[22] Classification is more difficult for the debates during the drafting of the ordinance for admittance to the Lord's Supper. The ordinance consisted of a short creed and a reluctantly produced list of scandalous sins that would bar the unrepentant from the Lord's Supper. Although the document was framed as an ecclesiastical tool, the Assembly was not permitted to draft the ecclesiastical portion of the document; thus, for the purposes of this chart, I have labeled the debates over this document as doctrinal and not as ecclesiastical.

specify what the more precise focus of the debate was without further information.[23]

Occupying substantially fewer plenary sessions than theology were the tasks of licensing ministers and of debating church government, with 345 and 356 sessions respectively.[24] Most striking, perhaps, is the quantity of time spent examining ministers, although of the 301 full sessions spent examining ministers, 217 were from June 22, 1648 to March 25, 1652 when the Assembly's work on theology, ecclesiology, and worship was largely completed. Prior to June 1648, most of the hours spent approving and licensing ministers took place before and during the plenary sessions of the Assembly in various ad hoc committees.

Certainly these observations overturn the reigning historiography of the Assembly. It is common to assume that ecclesiological debate dominated the work of the Assembly. The fact is that time spent on ecclesiological debate rivaled the time spent in the examination of ministers, although much of the latter work was carried out after the creed-making tasks of the Assembly had reached completion or termination. More significantly, during the busiest and most productive years of the Assembly, the time required by debates over doctrine dominated and overshadowed the debates over discipline and government. Similar observations can be seen in study of the Assembly's ad hoc committees.

In Committee: The ad hoc Committees of the Westminster Assembly

Standing and ad hoc Committees

The committee work of the Assembly best reflects the diversity of tasks required of and assumed by the Assembly. In fact the days when Selden and Pierrepont could insist on a rigid obedience to

---

[23] See sessions 537-39 and 662 in Minutes 3:111r-v and 3:160v.

[24] In some cases the approving and examining of ministers became the main work of the day simply because the Assembly did not reach quorum.

the mandate spelled out in the Assembly's summoning ordinance did not extend beyond the summer of 1643.

I have written a detailed account of the operation of the Assembly and its committees elsewhere.[25] Here it needs simply to be noted that the work of the Assembly's three standing committees prove almost beyond analysis, although Wayne Spear has carefully produced a basic outline of some of their tasks.[26] The three standing committees typically did not deal with the approving and licensing of ministers, Assembly business, or matters regarding fasting, but they did address matters of doctrine, worship, and church government. Often these committees assigned their own subcommittees to draft documents or reports, thus addressing multiple subjects contemporaneously. Given the multiplicity of tasks apportioned to the standing committees and the absence of information about the content of the individual meetings, the following account concentrates on the ad hoc committees only.

The subject of discussion for each committee was assigned in plenary sessions. The Assembly's ad hoc committees were usually assigned one specific task and after that task was accomplished the committee was usually disbanded. In a few cases these ad hoc committees were called upon to perform subsequent, usually related tasks.

The Assembly's committees were as important as its plenary sessions but are more difficult to describe because of a lack of surviving material. Lightfoot and Gillespie note the transactions of some committees, and the minutes include one seemingly random record of an Assembly committee meeting.[27] No other committee records and almost no committee papers appear to have survived.[28] The major source of information about the committees comes from the orders and resolutions of the plenary sessions,

---

[25] See Van Dixhoorn, "Reforming the Reformation," Chapter Three.

[26] W. R. Spear, "Covenanted Uniformity in Religion" (unpublished Ph.D. diss., University of Pittsburgh, 1976), 64-73.

recorded in the minutes, when the committees were established, supplemented, mentioned, or abolished. Almost nothing is known about the frequency with which the 210 ad hoc committees met, or their duration, although the members of most of these committees are named in the minutes. The descriptions of the committees furnished in the minutes do allow us to ascertain the subject focus of each committee, for which I use the same subject categories as those employed above and in the "Analysis." Tallies of the committees, by subject, allow for some comparison of the main subjects of the Assembly's committee work.

This study covers all committees which are termed as such in the minutes or in Lightfoot's journals. This list may not be exhaustive since there are sessions for which Lightfoot's first journal is the only source of information and Lightfoot rarely mentions the Assembly's business or the process of examining ministers. Furthermore, the Assembly probably considered most, and perhaps all, delegations of divines sent across the street to Parliament to be committees. For the sake of consistency, and because of a lack of evidence that all such delegations were constituted as committees, I record only those which are explicitly referred to as committees in the minutes.[29]

Analysis[30]

Approving and Licensing of Ordinands and Ministers
The Assembly was assigned the responsibility of examining ministers on July 28, 1643 when the House of Commons

---

[27] Minutes 1:242v-245v.

[28] There are a few exceptions to this rule. BL Add. 4276, fo. 166r, March 20, 1647 contains an order for ministers, signed by William Gouge and other divines. And notably, the papers of the committee for examination have survived in the Main Papers of the House of Lords and, to a much lesser extent, elsewhere (see BL Add. 15672, fos. 56v-59r).

[29] See, for example, the delegation mentioned in Minutes 2:201v (17 Sept. 1644).

[30] Throughout this study of committees, I catalogue only the establishment of a committee and those occasions where the committee is supplemented or

appointed it to examine all ministers who had been plundered by the king's forces and who wished to take the place of other ministers who had been sequestered by Parliament.[31] As a result, twenty-six Divines were nominated, "but any five of them might be a Committee."[32] Although the committee began to function immediately, with John Ley evolving into the role of chief examiner, the Assembly did not draw up rules for the committee of examination until September 28, two months after the initial order. The order stated that "noe minister shall be approved of by certificate to the Committee for Plundered Ministers but his name shall be first propounded in the assembly the day before he be examined,[33] and then any 5 of the Assembly, wherof Mr. Ley to be one, may examine him, who are to make report of his sufficiency to the Assembly before the certificate be made unto the

---

re-established. In some instances, the initial constituting of a committee is not mentioned; later references by Lightfoot or elsewhere in the minutes are the only indication of its existence; in each of these cases I state that the committee is "mentioned." For the purposes of enumerating the committees by subject, I count each new committee, even if it is a new committee to replace a former committee, as a separate or distinct committee. Note also that for the 300 sessions of the minutes which are revised, I rely on the revised minutes only. The differences between them are only slight with respect to committees, and the task of collating the folio references to committees in both the 300 unrevised and revised sessions is too time-consuming and unnecessary for the present project. Furthermore, since I am attempting to catalogue the work of the Assembly and determine its major focus, I list only the foliation and not the session numbers and dates of the establishment of these committees. I do not supply the names of committee members. Such a study would be useful, both for biographers of individual divines and for historians of the Assembly.

[31] Lightfoot, MS Journal, fos. 8v-9r; for subsequent legislation, see W. A. Shaw, *A History of the English Church during the civil wars and under the commonwealth 1640–1660* (London: Longmans, Green, and Co., 1900), 2:279-81.

[32] CJ 3:183, Thursday 27 July 1643. The ordinance states that the Committee for Plundered Ministers was to nominate only persons approved by the Assembly, and the Assembly was to establish a committee for this purpose. However, the Committee for Plundered Ministers could eject ministers without consultation. A similar note is recorded in the minutes of the Committee for Plundered Ministers (see BL Add. 15669, fo. 2r).

[33] The first draft of this order refers to the "arti[cles]," suggesting that the Thirty-Nine Articles were used as the standard for examination.

House of Commons. The time of examining to be 9 of the clocke in the morning."[34] If the letters of reference (or certificates) were deemed satisfactory and if the ordinand, minister, or his referees were known to the Assembly-men, the candidate would preach a sermon before the Assembly prior to the commencement of a plenary session.[35] If a certificate was not deemed satisfactory, the candidate was not admitted to examination and was instead asked to produce better letters of recommendation, perhaps from better sources.[36] At Dr. Thomas Temple's request, the committee for examinations was reconstituted on June 4, 1644, some new examiners were proposed, and liberty was granted to any member of the Assembly to join and vote in the committee at any time.[37] That Ley remained the de facto chair appears from a reference on November 7, 1645 to the examination committee as Mr. Ley's committee.[38] Other rules were added on a regular basis. For example, examination was to finish prior to the start of the plenary session at 9:00 a.m.[39]

Further study is needed of the Assembly's practices in its examination of ministers or candidates. Also useful would be a discussion of conflicts between the Assembly and Parliament with regard to the examination process and with regard to candidates favored by

---

[34] Minutes 1:78v.

[35] The minutes do not mention these sermons, and the first sermon mentioned by Lightfoot was preached on Aug. 3, 1643: "This morning we had a Sermon[,] for the Committee for examination of ministers had appointed one to preach upon this text[,] 2 Chron. 16:9." See Lightfoot, MS Journal, fo. 12r.

[36] The assumption seemed to be that a godly man could always find a godly Divine known to the Assembly to approve of him. If he could not, he needed to become acquainted with some godly ministers and prove his good character, or else repent of his sins.

[37] Minutes 2:89r.

[38] Ley's primary role seems to come to an end in late 1647. Beginning with session 993, Jan. 14, 1648, and without explanation, one member of the Assembly was announced as the chairman of the Assembly for the following week, for the duration of one week. See Minutes 3:340v and subsequent Friday sessions.

[39] Minutes 3:114r.

one or other of the Houses but rejected by the Assembly, for the Assembly felt keenly the political or legal liabilities of rejecting candidates.[40] Although the task of examination was not mentioned in the summoning ordinance and slowed the Assembly's progress on other tasks, the significance of the work was not lost upon the divines. For the first time since the birth of English Puritanism, godly clergy were able to design and implement a national filter through which (at least in theory) all ministers appointed to a new charge were to pass.[41] The process of examination was often complex. Twenty-seven times the Assembly appointed special committees to deal with specific candidates or ministers under examination.[42] The examination of ministers was a time-

---

[40] I discuss the Assembly's practices in examining ministers in *The Westminster Assembly and the Pulpit: Foundations of Puritan Preaching.* This work is being reviewed for publication.

[41] Shaw, *History of the English Church*, 2:281, appears to be incorrect in limiting examinations to sequestrations and applications for augmentations only – if this is indeed what he argues, for his account on p. 181 is unclear.

[42] Committee to investigate Mr. Anderson, Minutes 1:170v; Committee concerning Mr. Moulines, Lightfoot, *Journal,* 147; Committee to find a fit man for Hempstead to replace the Anabaptist, Mr. Kendall, Minutes 1:356v; Committee to communicate with Plundered Ministers Committee about Mr. Anthony and Mr. Needham, formerly denied certificates, Minutes 1:357v; Committee to deal with Richard Vines and his refusal to be Master of Pembroke College, Cambridge, Minutes 2:14r; Committee to consider Mr. Bedford's business, Minutes 3:155r; supplemented, Minutes 3:160v; Committee to consider Mr. Reynolds, Minutes 3:157r; Committee to consider Mr. Watts, Minutes 3:157r; Committee for Mr. Gobert mentioned, Minutes 3:163r; Committee for Mr. Greenwood mentioned, Minutes 3:180r; Committee for Mr. Launce, Minutes 3:191r; supplemented, Minutes 3:192r, 346r; Committee for Sidrach Simpson, Minutes 3:193v; Committee to consider the ministers who have gone to Wales, Minutes 3:198v-199r; Committee to consider Mr. Dicks, Minutes 3:200r; Committee for Mr. Bacon, Minutes 3:210r; Committee to consider Mr. Picke, Minutes 3:202v; Committee to consider Mr. Hall, Minutes 3:206r; supplemented, Minutes 3:206r; new committee, Minutes 3:217v; supplemented, Minutes 3:220v; Committee for Mr. Jerom mentioned, Minutes 3:228r; Committee to consider Mr. Lucas, Minutes 3:331v; Committee to consider Mr. Harward's case, Minutes 3:336r; Committee to consider Mr. Wallis, Minutes 3:338r; Committee to consider Mr. Henson, Minutes 3:342v; Committee to consider Mr. Pierce, Minutes 3:343r; Committee to consider Thomas Wilmot, Minutes 3:344v; Committee concerning Mr. Woodward mentioned, Minutes 3:372r; Committee concerning

consuming process, not least because it involved controversial issues and difficult people.[43]

The charge to examine ministers was interpreted broadly, both by Parliament and by the Assembly. One committee was formed to try scholars applying for Cambridge fellowships,[44] and four were created to resolve conflicts in churches.[45] Additional committees were formed to find ministers for Ireland, Wales, the north of England, and the Temple in London.[46] From time to time the Assembly was also required to find preachers for the army and the navy, but it did not summon committees for the purpose. Another eight committees related to the examination of ministers included a committee to investigate ministers who were obtaining livings without the Assembly's permission, a committee to establish a registry to track the institution and induction of ministers, and a committee to examine how the examination committee could be more efficient.[47] Sometimes a committee was called to adjudicate

---

Mr. Wood mentioned, Minutes 3:372v. The names are recorded here as they are in the minutes or Lightfoot's journal; it is beyond the purposes of this study to determine the Christian names of each of these ordinands or ministers.

[43] For example, a preacher had forgotten his Greek – was he now to be barred from the ministry? After hours of debate the Assembly's answer came, as it often did, in the form of a committee commissioned to draft the academic standards required for ministers (Minutes 1:126v, 128r).

[44] Minutes 2:25r.

[45] Committee to consider schism in French church mentioned, Lightfoot, *Journal,* 93; Committee to present a letter from Guernsey to the Commons, Minutes 2:87v; New committee to consider petition and letter from St. Peter's Port, Guernsey, Minutes 3:112r; Committee to hear the differences between Alborough and Waxfield/Watsfield, Minutes 3:84v.

[46] Committee to provide a minister for the Temple, Minutes 2:88r; Committee to consider ministers for York, Minutes 2:163r; supplemented, Minutes 2:169r; Committee of York and Durham, Minutes 2:240r; disputed, Minutes 2:261v; called "the Committee for the North" and supplemented, Minutes 2:292r; supplemented, Minutes 3:78r; supplemented Minutes 3:82v; supplemented, Minutes 3:184v; Committee to consider minister for Ireland, Minutes 3:60r; Committee to consider ministers for Wales, Minutes 3:329r.

[47] Committee to consider the Lords' order and the petition from Wapping, Minutes 2:109v; supplemented, Minutes 3:101v; Committee of the Western men to consider the letter from the commanders of the Lord General, Minutes 2:111v;

disputes and cases of conscience involving Westminster divines and, in most cases, the Assemblyman would get the better deal or the benefit of the doubt. In one such case, the people of Maidstone in Kent asked their godly minister Mr. Smith to find another church so that they could have their old pastor Thomas Wilson back in the pulpit. Wilson persuaded the incumbent to submit to a panel of "six judicious Ministers of the Assembly." The panel decided that Wilson, a member of the Assembly, should get the church and that Smith should move on to a nearby church.[48]

In total, the examination of ministers required the formation of forty-seven different committees from 1643 to 1652 and constituted a continuous and near systematic attempt to purge the Church of England of preachers who were ungodly, unlearned and, on a less firm biblical basis, anti-parliamentarian.

Assembly Business

The Assembly's day-to-day operations and odd-jobs generated forty-five ad hoc committees, one of which (the steering committee) evolved into something like a standing committee.[49] The committee which should have been a standing committee, but was not, was the pay distribution committee. Pay distribution ought to have

---

Committee to attend upon the Committee for Plundered Ministers mentioned and supplemented, Minutes 2:275r; Committee to investigate ministers who have obtained livings without the Assembly's permission, Minutes 3:162r; Committee to petition for a Registry to combat the institution and induction of scandalous ministers, Minutes 3:197r-v; Committee to consider ministers that come to the Assembly for approbation from the enemy's quarters, Minutes 3:199v; Committee to consider the expedition of the examination of ministers, Minutes 3:202r; called the "Committee for the consideration of the examination of ministers" supplemented, Minutes 3:202v; Called the "Committee for Review" of the examination of ministers mentioned, Minutes 3:205r, 228v, 324r, 340v; Committee to consider inconveniences mentioned by Plundered Ministers Committee, Minutes 3:340r-v.

[48] G. S. *The Life and Death of Mr. Tho. Wilson, Minister of Maidstone, in the County of Kent, M. A.* (n.p., 1672), 23-24.

[49] Minutes 3:54v; it appears that the committee was soon referred to as the "committee of the Assembly," Minutes 3:59v and perhaps 3:60r.

been simple: the ordinance summoning the Assembly states not only that the Divines were to be paid four shillings for every day of attendance, as well as for the ten days preceding and following the Assembly, but also that payment would be made "at such time and in such manner as by both Houses of Parliament shall be appointed."[50] However, the time and manner of Parliament's payments were not what the assembled Divines had expected, as a petition for £7,500 of back-pay demonstrates.[51] On the other hand, the ordinance also failed to specify a pay-scale for Divines who arrived late in the morning, who were ill, or who were absent for various reasons. The Assembly established a committee to judge excuses for absence or lateness, with reference to pay.[52] This committee was distinct from two other (ineffective) committees summoned to treat the ongoing problem with attendance at the Assembly, although the lack of attendance may have been pay-related.[53]

The committee for attendance was poorly received by most in the Assembly, but no committee experienced rejection as often as the string of elected payroll committees. These committees were often discarded after one use. In fact, the Assembly dissolved eight different payroll committees before it settled on a committee which everyone thought was fair – and that committee was finally established on December 11, 1646.[54] Even then, for a reason not

---

[50] *An Ordinance of the Lords and Commons Assembled in Parliament. For The Calling of an Assembly* (London: for I. Wright, June 13, 1643), unpaginated.

[51] See Bodleian Library, Nalson 22, fos. 28r-29v; CJ iv.13; Minutes 3:22v.

[52] Minutes 2:125v.

[53] Committee to promote attendance at the Assembly, Minutes 2:91r; supplemented, Minutes 2:121r; sometimes called the "committee apoynted to attend the committee of Plundered ministers," e.g. Minutes 2:125v; New committee, Minutes 3:78v.

[54] First committee for the distribution of £100, Lightfoot, MS Journal, fo. 29v, Minutes 1:24r; New committee for distributing £600, Minutes 2:101r; New committee for distributing £1000, Minutes 3:56r; New committee, a former committee mentioned for distributing £200, Minutes 3:87r; New committee for distribution of £200 "from Haberdashers Hall," Minutes 3:101v; served again

disclosed, the Assembly appointed a committee on May 17, 1647 to audit the accounts of the Assembly. The first draft of the motion proposed that the assessors and scribes form the committee. The final draft removed all the scribes and one assessor (Cornelius Burges) from the committee, and left one assessor (Herbert Palmer) and eight newly appointed Divines in their places.[55]

The most complex committee of the Assembly was its international relations panel which became the Assembly's committee of representatives in Parliament's Grand Committee for Religion. The latter committee was comprised of a delegation of Scottish Commissioners, a committee of the House of Commons, a committee of the House of Peers, and this committee of the Assembly.[56] The Assembly's committee to the Grand Committee began

---

to distribute £1000, Minutes 3:111r; New committee to distribute £400 "from the committee of the Revenew," Minutes 3:149v; New committee to distribute £600, Minutes 3:160r; New committee to distribute £500, Minutes 3:187r; served again to distribute £500, Minutes 3:189v; served again to distribute an unknown sum for payment, Minutes 3:195v; served again to distribute £192, 11 shillings, Minutes 3:225r; served again to distribute £300, Minutes 3:233r; served again to distribute £400, Minutes 3:334r; served again to distribute £400, Minutes 3:337v; served again to distribute £300, Minutes 3:344v; probably served again to distribute £600, Minutes 346r; served again to distribute £100, Minutes 3:346v; served again to distribute £400, Minutes 3:351v; served again to distribute £200, Minutes 3:355v; served again to distribute £300, Minutes 3:360r; served again to distribute £200, Minutes 3:361r; served again to distribute £100, Minutes 3:363r; served again to distribute £300, Minutes 3:365r. The rump Assembly distributed £50 to its members in the last recorded payment, 21 March 1649/50, Minutes 3:369v. This is a comprehensive list of recorded committees, not a catalogue of all payments. For full payment information, see Chapter Three of "Reforming the Reformation."

[55] Minutes 3:214r. Unfortunately, I have not been able to locate the Assembly's financial accounts.

[56] The Grand Committee for Religion was often called simply The Grand Committee. The latter term is not to be confused with the Assembly or the two Houses, each of which sometimes sat *as* a grand committee, that is, every member of the Assembly or House sat together as a committee rather than as a plenary session. The minutes, CJ, and LJ all refer to Grand Committees, but only CJ and LJ distinguish between a Grand Committee as a mode of sitting in the House and the Grand Committee for Religion. For the constitution, membership, and work of the Grand Committee, see Spear, "Covenanted uniformity," 73-82.

as a deputation that was to correspond with the Scots. It was subsequently required to reconcile differences between the Scottish and English Divines with respect to the Solemn League and Covenant, appraise the Solemn League itself, formulate a statement on church government, and compose letters to foreign churches. At times new committees were formed for these tasks, but the former committee was periodically recalled, recommissioned, and occasionally supplemented with new members over the course of the Assembly.[57]

The remaining twenty-two miscellaneous ad hoc committees of the Assembly range far and wide. There was a committee to recommend moving Oxford students to London, a committee defending the Assembly from scandalous reports, and one more mediating between the city of London, the army, and Parliament. One committee recommended the printing of the Septuagint, and another forbade the production and sale of lascivious books and pictures and generated an index of books to be suppressed.[58] Even

---

[57] Committee established to communicate with Scottish commissioners, Lightfoot, MS Journal, fo. 11v; Committee to answer the Scots letter mentioned, Lightfoot, MS Journal, fo. 12r; mentioned and supplemented, Lightfoot, MS Journal, fo. 35r; Committee to reconcile differences with Scots, Minutes 1:39v; to engage in further negotiations, 1:41r; to prepare a declaration about the Solemn League and Covenant, Minutes 1:78v; to treat with Scots commissioners, perhaps becoming a standing committee, Minutes 1:123r; to write a letter to Holland, Minutes 1:215r; supplemented, Minutes 1:378v; to hasten work on Church discipline, Minutes 1:419v; to draft a directory for Church discipline, Minutes 2:21r; to translate and report on letter from Zealand, Minutes 2:90v; to translate and report on letter from Geneva, Minutes 2:95r; to consider letters from classis of Amsterdam, Minutes 2:108v; Committee supplemented, Minutes 3:111r; New committee to write a letter to Scotland, Minutes 3:58r; supplemented, Minutes 3:64v; New committee to consider a letter from the General Assembly of the Church of Scotland, Minutes 3:117v; Former committee to consider a letter from the ministers of London, Minutes 3:117v; New committee to answer letter from Utrecht, Minutes 3:210v; New committee to consider letter from Switzerland, Minutes 3:215v; Assembly's former committee to the Grand Committee summoned, Minutes 3:328v; New committee to write a letter of the Church of Scotland, Minutes 3:351v; supplemented? Minutes 3:352r.

[58] Committee to stir up the people for Parliament, Lightfoot, MS Journal, fo. 11v; Committee to answer Cornelius Burges's petition, Lightfoot, MS Journal, fo.

these examples do not represent all of the Assembly's ad hoc delegations, such as the one of 10 June 1645: in an unparalleled effort to communicate the gravity of the offence, the officers of the Assembly led a delegation to Parliament where prolocutor Twisse and then assessor White spoke of the danger and sin of blasphemy and then assessor Burges revealed the anti-Trinitarian errors of Paul Best.[59]

Part of what is surprising about these committees is the sheer number of miscellaneous tasks which the Assembly took upon itself. Only four of the twenty-two miscellaneous tasks were assigned by Parliament: a committee to stir up the nation to favour Parliament's cause, a committee to give money to Sir Thomas Middleton's forces, a committee to minister to prisoners, and a committee to discuss the merits of a translation of Luther's *Table*

23v; Committee to bring it into Parliament, Lightfoot, MS Journal, fo. 23v; Committee to recommend moving Oxford students to London, Minutes 1:205v; recommissioned? Minutes 1:280r; Committee to move Houses for a more solemn thanksgiving day service, Lightfoot, MS Journal, p. 118; Committee to encourage subscriptions to Sir Thomas Midleton's forces, Minutes 1:339v; Committee for printers and stationers mentioned and supplemented, Minutes 2:88r, Minutes 3:37r; supplemented, Minutes 3:53r, 58v, 111v, 112r; Committee to draw up a petition against the book *Directions of the Lords and Commons*, Minutes 3:88r; Committee to consider Mr Smart's (financial) condition, Minutes 2:89v; Committee to confer about Ireland and Holland, Minutes 2:259v; same committee? Minutes 3:27v; Committee to receive correspondence from English congregations, Minutes 3:64v; Committee to ease godly ministers from immoderate taxes, Minutes 3:69r; Committee to acquire the revenue of the Archbishop of Canterbury on the Assembly, Minutes 3:70r; Committee to consider or engage in ministry to prisoners, Minutes 3:78r; Committee to consider scandalous books written and licensed against the Assembly and Parliament, Minutes 3:149r; Committee to consider a translation of Luther's *Table Talk*, Minutes 3:201r-v; Committee to offer the Assembly's services to the city of London, army, and Parliament, Minutes 3:231r; Committee to consider what the Assembly will do when the Catechism is finished, Minutes 3:334r; Committee to move Parliament to consider the pains of Mr. Young in printing the Septuagint, Minutes 3:336v-337r; Committee to write an answer to the General (unnamed), Minutes 3:340v-341r; Committee about the paper against Mr. Byfield mentioned, Minutes 3:351v; Committee to treat stationer Michael Sparke's petition for suppression of lascivious books and pictures and for a catalogue of books to be suppressed, Minutes 2:94v, Lightfoot, *Journal,* 282.

59   BL Harl. 166 fo. 217b.

Talk. Parliament did use the Assembly for tasks far beyond its original remit, but the Assembly was aggressively proactive in expanding its own role in the establishment of a godly church and nation.

Church Government

Ecclesiological debates and documents compelled the Assembly to form forty-one different ad hoc committees. Ten committees dealt with issues concerning ordination,[60] including one committee charged with determining the place of doctors or teachers in the church, another to write a letter about ordination to the Vice-Chancellor of Cambridge, and one committee to hasten the Directory for Ordination *pro tempore*.[61]

Other committees were assigned specific documents to write, such as the committees designated to draft the directory for excommunication (a part of the Directory for Church Government).[62] Another committee was "to put into method the votes of

---

[60]   Committee to draw up the Assembly's results (or votes) on ordination, Minutes 1:407r; New committee to draw up a directory for ordination, Minutes 1:419v; supplemented, Minutes 1:432v; supplemented, same as the "committee for the summary"? Minutes 2:9r; called the "summary committee," Minutes 2:173r; Committee to explain the Assembly's position on ordination, Minutes 2:102v; New committee, Minutes 2:166r; Committee to finish the parts of the Directory for Ordination, Minutes 2:158r; Committee to deliver directory for ordination to the House of Commons, Minutes 2:163r; Committee to methodize votes concerning Presbytery that relate to ordination, Minutes 1:431v. For a discussion of committees related to ordination, see Spear, "Covenanted Uniformity," 86-89.

[61]   Committee to discuss the propositions of the First committee re: doctor or teacher, Minutes 1:204r, 205v; Committee for speeding the directory for ordination *pro tempore* (three chosen from each committee), Lightfoot, *Journal*, 116; Committee to consider the heads of a letter to the Vice-Chancellor of the University of Cambridge, re: ordination, Minutes 3:122r.

[62]   Committee for drawing up votes mentioned, new task, to draw up a directory for excommunication, Minutes 3:32v; New committee to reach accommodation in a paragraph in the directory, Minutes 3:22v; new task and committee supplemented, Minutes 3:26r; New committee for excommunication and government, Minutes 3:32r; supplemented? Minutes 3:34v; new task and supplemented, Minutes 3:35v. The committee "to draw up the whole businesse

the Assembly concerning government."[63] Still another time the Assembly wanted to assess its progress in its ecclesiological deliberations and summoned a committee to draw up its resolves into some logical form.[64] Although none of the ecclesiological committees can be completely separated from the Independent–Presbyterian controversy, eighteen committees were exclusively dedicated to the Assembly's famous ecclesiological disputations: the work of five committees pertained to the assertion and defence of the *jus divinum* of church government,[65] and thirteen committees focused on the controversy between the Independents and the Presbyterians. Some of these thirteen committees were dedicated to finding some area for accommodation,[66] four committees of Independents were appointed to draft statements of Independent church government,[67] and six committees of the Assembly were appointed to respond to the manuscript and printed pamphlets of the Independents[68] and to announce to Parliament that it had no part in writing the *Apologeticall Narration*.[69]

---

concerning excommunication" (Minutes 2:215r) appears, from the context, to be a reference to the Assembly's second standing committee which was treating the subject of excommunication.

[63] Minutes 2:279r.

[64] Committee to determine what votes have already passed concerning Church Government, Minutes 3:65v; called the committee for methodizing votes, supplemented, Minutes 3:69r; supplemented, Minutes 3:69v; supplemented, Minutes 3:72r.

[65] Committee established, Minutes 3:145r-v; Committee to determine the point in conscience in and at which the Assembly may petition Parliament about the *jus divinum* of Church government, and to prepare a petition, Minutes 3:145v; New Committee to defend the *jus divinum* of Church government, Minutes 3:148v; supplemented, Minutes 3:149r; supplemented, Minutes 3:149v; Committee for the queries, Minutes 3:336v; New committee for queries, Minutes 3:350v; supplemented, Minutes 3:351r.

[66] Committee for accommodation, Minutes 1:240v; re-established, Minutes 1:252v; re-established re: presbytery, Minutes 1:373r; recommissioned, Minutes 1:401v. See Spear, "Covenanted Uniformity," 82-86.

[67] Committee of Independents to consider congregations, with reference to Church Government, Minutes 3:52v; Committee re-established, Minutes 3:56r; Committee re-established, Minutes 3:102r; Committee of Independents to answer Parliament's nine queries, Minutes 3:153v.

Further committees defy tidy classification and include delegations that simply carried documents to the Houses, a panel to specify who could ordain ministers and elders in the London churches, and a commission to refute anti-Presbyterian literature.[70]

Doctrine

Debate over doctrine demanded the highest number of ad hoc committees in the Assembly. Whether the focus was theology proper, the refutation of the many sects in England, or the explication of the one standard of piety required for attendance upon the Lord's Supper, a committee was often required, the grand total reaching sixty-five.[71]

---

[68] Committee to consider the reasons of the dissenting brethren, Minutes 2:293r; to consider the new reasons of the dissenting brethren, Minutes 3:12v; Committee (whole Assembly except Independents) to provide answer to Independents, Minutes 3:8r; Committee to carry up reasons, Minutes 3:14v; Committee to examine reasons and answers once more, Minutes 3:14v; New committee to answer Independents, Minutes 3:33r; new task for the same committee, Minutes 3:102r; supplemented, with duty to attend a committee of Commons, Minutes 3:114.

[69] Minutes 1:362r.

[70] Committee to carry up votes on Church government, Minutes 2:288v; Committee to respond to letter from the classis of Walacria and examine the book, *A Cool Conference*, Minutes 2:24v; and the book *M. S. to A. S.*, Minutes 2:33v; Committee to consider order of the subcommittee of the Grand Committee of the House of Commons about establishing elders in the churches, Minutes 3:70r; supplemented, Minutes 3:72r; Committee to carry up advise to Commons subcommittee re: selection of elders, Minutes 3:71v; supplemented, Minutes 3:74v; New Committee, Minutes 3:75r; New Committee, Minutes 3:77v; Committee to bring in proofs of the 3rd Proposition, Minutes 3:354r; Committee to propose names of ministers to ordain ordinands in London, Minutes 2:195v. For the books to be examined, see Anonymous, *A Coole conference between the cleared Reformation and the Apologeticall narration brought together by a well-willer to both* (London? 1644); Adam Stewart, *An Ansvver to a libell intituled, A coole conference* (London? 1644); Anonymous, *C.C. The Covenanter vindicated from perjurie* (London: printed by T. Paine, 1644); and Anonymous, *M. S. to A. S. with a plea for libertie of conscience* (London: printed by F. N. for H. Overton, 1644).

[71] That figure, like the figures above, does not include the work of standing committees. The standing committee usually prepared reports for debates in the plenary sessions, thus the major work of these committees mirrored the primary focus of the plenary sessions: theology.

The earliest theological ad hoc committees in the Assembly confronted antinomianism. Edmund Calamy makes reference to his attendance on an antinomian committee.[72] Lightfoot provides even more information, including some of the proceedings of the committee, or rather, committees, for the committee was frequently enlarged and, six or seven times, reconstituted.[73] On one occasion, it is not possible to tell whether the committee is supplemented or reconstituted.[74] In addition to the committees established throughout the Assembly to deal with antinomianism, there were also committees dedicated to correcting or refuting or recommending punishments for Anabaptists, anti-Trinitarians, and anti-Sabbatarians, eight in total.[75]

Other doctrinal committees were more predictable, at least after the signing of the Solemn League and Covenant. For example, eighteen committees were used to draft the catechisms and to

---

[72] [Edmund Calamy], *Two solemne Covenants made between God and Man* (London: for Thomas Banks, 1647 [*sic*, i.e. February 1646/7]), 1.

[73] Antinomian committee established, Lightfoot, MS Journal, fo. 15v; New committee, Lightfoot, MS Journal, fo. 40v; the same committee mentioned? Minutes 1:7v; New committee, Minutes 1:54r; new task, Minutes 1:77r; New committee, Minutes 1:95r; supplemented? Minutes 1:162r; supplemented 280v; supplemented, Lightfoot, *Journal*, 107; to meet every Tuesday, Minutes 1:303r; supplemented, Minutes 1:348r; supplemented, Minutes 2:72v; New committee, Minutes 2:138v; supplemented, Minutes 2:147r; New committee, Minutes 3:70r; New committee, Minutes 3:86v. Ann Hughes provides comment on the Assembly's committees in *Gangraena and the Struggle for the English Revolution* (Oxford: Oxford University Press, 2004), 345-46.

[74] Minutes 1:157v. Thus, the committee count for the subject of doctrine could be as high as sixty-six.

[75] Committee to attend the Committee for Plundered Ministers, perhaps about Paul Best, Minutes 3:77r; supplemented, Minutes 3:83v; supplemented, Minutes 3:92v; Committee to refute Anabaptists, Minutes 1:309r; Committee to consider an ordinance for putting laws for the enforcement of the Sabbath into execution, Minutes 2:72v; Committee to present information about Mr. Picot and remedies against Anabaptists and Antinomians to the Honourable Committee for Plundered Ministers (against the Independents wishes), Minutes 2:176v; Minutes 2:205v; Committee to think of a severe law against blasphemy, Minutes 2:265v; Committee to complain of a book by John Archer, Minutes 3:79r; supplemented, Minutes 3:79v; Committee to consider heresy,

discuss related issues such as the Apostles' Creed.[76] Six committees worked on some aspect of the confessions of faith,[77] and three considered the role of the Thirty-Nine Articles after the main *Confession of Faith* was completed.[78] Special committees were formed to deal with specific issues that arose in the revision of the Thirty-Nine Articles and in the drafting of the confessions and catechisms. A committee was sent to find the most authentic copies of the Thirty-Nine Articles.[79] Another drew up a form that was to detail the knowledge necessary for the Lord's Supper, resulting in a document that resembles a small confession.[80] Another committee re-examined the Assembly's decision to ban pictures of

---

blasphemy and dangerous opinion, Minutes 3:116v; supplemented, Minutes 3:123v; Committee to consider a book by Jacob Acontius, Minutes 3:345r; supplemented, Minutes 3:345v.

[76] Catechism committee mentioned, Minutes 3:35v; mentioned, Minutes 3:66v; New committee, Minutes 3:88r; supplemented, Minutes 3:166v, 187v; supplemented, Minutes 3:228r; Committee for the *Shorter Catechism* established, Minutes 3:232r; supplemented, Minutes 3:232v; a catechism committee supplemented, Minutes 3:328r; Committee for review of the catechism mentioned and supplemented, Minutes 3:334r; supplemented by dissenters about the Apostles' Creed, Minutes 3:335r; Committee to draw up a paper since the other paper to accompany the catechism was layed aside, Minutes 3:336r; Committee to review scriptures of catechism, Minutes 3:339r; Committee to discuss scriptures of the catechism? supplemented, Minutes 3:343r; supplemented, Minutes 3:346r. Eleven committees were established for the decalogue: one for each of the ten commandments and one to draft rules for interpreting them, Minutes 3:223r.

[77] Committee established, Minutes 2:158r; supplemented, Minutes 2:171v; two committees to be put into one, Minutes 3:66r; New committee, Minutes 3:66v; New committee to review confession, Minutes 3:113v; supplemented, Minutes 3:160r; supplemented, Minutes 3:173r; New committee to consider order to append Scripture proofs to confession, Minutes 3:183r; Committee for scripture proofs, Minutes 3:192v; supplemented for final review, Minutes 3:200r-v.

[78] Committee to decide what has been done in the Articles of Religion, Minutes 3:189r; supplemented, Minutes 3:191v; Committee to consider something to be presented to the House together with the revised Thirty-nine Articles, Minutes 3:205v; Committee to carry up Scriptures for the *Confession of Faith* and Thirty-nine Articles, Minutes 3:208r.

[79] Lightfoot, MS Journal, fo. 3v.

[80] Committee to answer the House of Commons about knowledge required for the sacraments, resulting in the Assembly's shorter confession, Minutes 3:54v.

God; yet another studied what was meant by the sin against the Holy Ghost.[81] A final eleven committees petitioned Parliament repeatedly concerning the sacrament of the Lord's Supper, first for parliamentary intervention to create an ordinance to keep the sacrament pure, then for Parliament to hurry its ordinance, and finally against Parliament's Erastian solutions.[82] Although set in an ecclesiological context, the work of these eleven committees is almost exclusively theological: evaluating particular sins and their consequences for the unrepentant individual coming to the Lord's Supper.

Fasting

Only four committees treated the matter of fasting in the Assembly, each at the Assembly's initiative. A committee on August 9, 1644

---

[81]　Committee on faith and repentance, to examine Homilies, Minutes 1:66v; Committee to draw up an article on faith and repentance, Minutes 1:69v; perhaps this committee was absorbed into the first Standing Committee of the Assembly, Minutes 1:69v, mentioned again? 1:72r; Committee to consider the Thirty-nine Articles? Minutes 3:60r, 60v; Committee to report about the Law (i.e. law in the scriptures) supplemented, Minutes 3:122r; this committee was supplementing the Third Standing Committee, Minutes 3:177r; Committee to redraft their statement on pictures of God, Minutes 3:123r; Committee to redraft the chapter on "Christian liberty," Minutes 3:125r; Special committee for studying the use of the promises and threatenings of the law, Minutes 3:173v; Special committee for baptism, Minutes 3:177r; Committee to consider the usual ceremonies of oaths, Minutes 3:184v; Committee for the sin against the Holy Ghost, Minutes 3:228v.

[82]　Committee to draw up a petition about keeping the sacraments pure, Minutes 3:48v; supplemented, with intent of answering an order of the Commons, Minutes 3:52v; New committee to prepare list of unquestionably scandalous sins, Minutes 3:74r; New committee, Minutes 3:82r; Committee to prepare a character of scandalous sins, Minutes 3:85v; supplemented, Minutes 3:86v; New committee for a petition, Minutes 3:106v; New committee for enumerating sins, Minutes 3:109r; supplemented, Minutes 3:109r; New committee for enumerating sins, Minutes 3:154r; Committee to compare the reports of the 3 committees re: scandalous sins, Minutes 3:72v; Committee to draw up a preface to the advice and select the portion of the advice to be sent to the Commons, Minutes 3:74v; Committee to carry up petition about hurrying the ordinance for the sacrament, Minutes 3:84v-85r; supplemented, Minutes 3:210v; Committee to attend subcommittee of Commons to debate suspension from the Supper, Minutes 3:85r-v; supplemented 85v.

was to draft a petition for a fast because of parliamentary losses in battle.[83] Exactly one month later, with the war not proceeding well enough for the divines, the Assembly called for a fast and appointed a committee to consider the possible causes of God's wrath, with a special focus on the sins of the army, of Parliament, and of the Assembly.[84] A third committee was called to ask Parliament to keep the fast more solemnly.[85] The final one was called on December 3, 1646 to petition for an additional fast because of bad weather.[86]

Worship

The Assembly appointed a variety of committees relating to the worship of the church. One committee was to consider worship as it was practiced in the universities and elsewhere,[87] and two were called to evaluate and decide whether Francis Rous's or William Barton's metrical versions of the Psalter should replace Sternhold's and Hopkins's Psalter.[88] The remaining five committees

---

[83] Minutes 2:142v.

[84] Established, Minutes 2:187r; supplemented, Minutes 2:190v; fuller details in Lightfoot, *Journal,* 309-10.

[85] Minutes 3:14r.

[86] Minutes 3:188r.

[87] Minutes 3:16r.

[88] Committee to meet with the Scots and Rous about Psalms, Minutes 2:231r; supplemented, Minutes 2:288r; Committee to discuss Barton, supplemented, Minutes 3:101r-v; New committee to answer order of Lords concerning Barton's Psalms, Minutes 3:148r. There was a long running rivalry between parliamentarian Francis Rous and hymn-writer William Barton, both attempting to get Assembly and parliamentary sanction for their own English translation of the Psalter. Barton collected endorsements of many of the Westminster divines for his more poetic version of the Psalter and lobbied for its acceptance through his friends in the House of Lords (Robert Baillie, *Letters and Journals*, 3 vols., ed. D. Laing (Edinburgh: for Robert Ogle, 1841–42), 3:3). Rous also had friends in the Assembly (Baillie, *Letters*, II.120-21). Rous was the first to receive official sanction from the Assembly and the House of Commons, but the Lords made no effort to approve it. As a compromise measure, Rous's more literal Psalter was supposed to have been printed with Barton's hymns, 4 April 1648 (LJ x.178), as *An exact emendation of the whole Booke of Psalmes*, but it does not appear to have been printed.

were associated with the creation of the Directory for Worship and a translation of the Directory into Welsh.[89] While the minutes mention other worship-related committees for the sacraments, preaching, baptism, the Sabbath, singing, and fasting, they appear to be subcommittees of the larger committee for worship, appointed from within that committee and not by the Assembly. The records of the Assembly are unbroken for the period, but the creation of these committees is not recorded; rather, in every case, they are merely mentioned when delivering reports from the committee for the Directory for Public Worship.[90]

The Ad Hoc Committees Compared

With these eight committees for the subject of worship, the ad hoc committees of the Westminster Assembly total 210, with an average of two committees being appointed per month, although most committees were appointed during the first sixty months. As Table 2 indicates, theological issues also required the highest number of ad hoc committees at 31 percent of the total, corresponding with the dominance of doctrinal issues in the plenary sessions of the Assembly. Notably, a full 44 percent of the Assembly's committees were dedicated to tasks not mentioned in the ordinance initially calling the Divines to the Assembly; not

---

[89] Committee for Directory for Public Worship mentioned, Minutes 2:72v; Committee to consider the report, from the existing subcommittee, about fasting, Minutes 3:13r; Committee to translate the Directory for Public Worship into Welsh, Minutes 3:50r; Committee for the Directory for Public Worship title mentioned and supplemented, Minutes 3:50r; New committee to draw up a preface, almost certainly referring to the Directory for Public Worship, Minutes 2:215r; "Former" committee for a preface, Minutes 2:239v; supplemented, Minutes 2:285r, G. Gillespie, "Notes of debates and proceedings of the Assembly of Divines and other commissioners at Westminster," ed. D. Meek, in *Works*, (Edinburgh: Robert Ogle and Oliver and Boyd, 1846), 2:78.

[90] E.g. Subcommittee for sacraments mentioned, Minutes 2:94r, see also 94v; Subcommittee for preaching mentioned, Minutes 2:89r, see also 94v; Subcommittee for baptism, Minutes 2:247r; Subcommittee for the Sabbath day, Minutes 2:247v; Subcommittee for singing, Minutes 3:13r; Subcommittee for fasting, Minutes 3:13r. This is not an exhaustive list of subcommittees.

all of these tasks were theological or pastoral, a fact which may have left some members less than content during their tenure at Westminster, and perhaps less likely to attend.

Table 2

Number of ad hoc committees of the Westminster Assembly
by subject classification

Subject	Number of committees	Percentage of total committees
A	47	22%
B	45	21%
C	41	20%
D	65	31%
F	4	2%
W	8	4%
Total	210	100%

Conclusions

This study has provided an account of the Assembly's work, outlining the primary projects of the Assembly as well as the many ancillary tasks delegated to or assumed by the Assembly. This survey provides a methodical description of the Assembly's major events without imposing order on the kaleidoscopic nature of the Assembly's work schedule and its overlapping activities of document production and debate, both in plenary sessions and in committees. I have tried to do this by creating the first statistical portrait of the Assembly's work, giving a more reliable sense than has previously been available of the relative importance of various subjects of debate, which serves to identify the main areas of debate at the Assembly.

In addition to describing the work of the Assembly, this chapter draws two important conclusions. First, it is obvious that one reason why the Assembly stretched out from year to year had much to do with the fact that Parliament generously loaded the divines with additional tasks not mentioned in the Assembly's summoning ordinance or in the Solemn League and Covenant.[91] As if that were not enough, the Divines, in their reforming zeal, heaped even more work upon themselves. Certainly these tasks were not envisioned by John Selden and William Pierrepont on the Assembly's opening day as they attempted to write the Assembly's history from the outset. But the scope of the Assembly's work has also been lost from sight by most later historians. The importance, number, and variety of these tasks went largely unnoticed because there was no quantified study of the Assembly's committees and no knowledge of the whereabouts of the Assembly's original papers.[92]

Second, and most significantly, this essay demonstrates that a substantial correction is needed to the centuries-old understanding of the Assembly's work. As the comparative Table 3 shows,[93] church government occupied 20 percent of the Assembly's committees and 26 percent of the Assembly's plenary sessions. This is news. So too is the fact that doctrinal matters required 31 percent of the Assembly's committees and 36 percent of its plenary sessions. These statistics probably imply something more than a need to study some neglected areas of the Assembly's history. The case also obtains that at least one neglected topic is probably more important than any other topic at the Assembly: doctrinal debate occupied the most time in the Assembly, and theological subjects

---

[91] Baillie complains of these additional tasks and of Parliament's queries to the Assembly (e.g. *Letters*, II.349, 377).

[92] It must be kept in mind that almost all of the plenary sessions spent examining ministers were held after the ecclesiological and doctrinal work of the Assembly was completed, something which Table 3 does not reflect.

[93] It must be kept in mind that almost all of the plenary sessions spent examining ministers were held after the ecclesiological and doctrinal work of the Assembly was completed, something which Table 3 does not reflect.

occupied far more time and committees per document produced by the Assembly than did ecclesiology or worship.

Table 3

Comparison of the percentage of plenary sessions and committees
by subject categorization

Subject	Percentage of total plenary sessions where subject is known	Percentage of total committees
A	25%	22%
B	6%	22%
C	26%	19%
D	36%	31%
F	1%	2%
W	6%	4%

This analysis of the Westminster Assembly at work is one part of a larger argument moving us toward a different understanding of the Assembly itself. It not only provides the necessary background for future research, it also brings to the foreground certain subjects of debate that require fresh observation and study, thus answering one part of Muller's query, or quest. At the very least, we can conclude from this overview and comparison that there are significant arenas of the Assembly's work which have not been given sufficient prominence in the historiography of the Westminster Assembly. More concretely, this study lays the foundation of a multi storey argument that the history of the Westminster Assembly is no longer an ecclesiastical story but also a liturgical and especially a theological one.

Redemptive-Historical Themes in the Westminster Larger Catechism

Robert J. Cara

Introduction and "Full Disclosure"

The perceptive e-mail from a supporter of my seminary read, "I think that the next systematic theology professor must be able to convincingly wed biblical and systematic theology because of the emotionally charged nature of those currently wishing to pit one against the other."[1] Understanding what is termed either biblical theology, or as I prefer, redemptive-historical theology (R-H[2]), is important.[3] For confessional Presbyterians this is especially important because, as the e-mail indicates, some are pitting R-H

---

[1] This e-mail was sent to the chancellor of Reformed Theological Seminary, Ric Cannada, in the summer of 2003.

[2] I will use "R-H" for "redemptive-historical," "redemptive-history," and "redemptive-historical theology."

[3] In Geerhardus Vos' important book *Biblical Theology: Old and New Testaments,* he complained in the preface that "the term 'Biblical Theology' is really unsatisfactory," but he consented to it due to its past usage by others. Vos noted that if it were possible, "a more suitable name would be 'History of Special Revelation.'" *Biblical Theology: Old and New Testaments* [Grand Rapids: Eerdmans, 1948], v. Herman Ridderbos primarily used "redemptive-historical" and not "biblical theology." This went a long way toward popularizing this term in Reformed circles (see e.g. *Paul: An Outline of His Theology,* trans. John Richard De Witt [Grand Rapids: Eerdmans, 1975], 39).

against the traditional Reformed systematic theology (ST) of the Westminster Standards.

In the 20th century, most conservative Reformed groups have consciously included various R-H themes as part of their overall emphases.[4] For this article, an R-H theme may be either an R-H methodological emphasis (e.g. timeline is important) or an R-H theological emphasis (e.g. creation's relationship to redemption).[5] Some of those who draw a sharp contrast between R-H and traditional Reformed ST tend to talk about R-H as if it is something completely new.[6] However, due to Reformed theology's long emphasis on the Old Testament, and its emphasis on covenant theology (both in the sense of the covenant of grace and covenant of works [i.e. federal theology], and in the sense of the unfolding specific covenants [e.g. Abrahamic, Mosaic]), what are now called R-H themes have always been to varying degrees part of traditional Reformed ST.[7]

In this article I will present a broad-brush description of the biblical themes associated with R-H and a very brief snapshot of the varying degrees to which these themes are emphasized in Reformed circles. Then, for the majority of the article, I will compare two

---

[4]   Many in evangelical scholarship who are not as explicitly Reformed also have a renewed interest in R-H. For example, see *Biblical Theology: Retrospect and Prospect*, ed. Scott J. Hafemann (Downers Grove: InterVarsity, 2002).

[5]   Of course, methodological and theological emphases are interrelated.

[6]   Richard B. Gaffin, Jr., a strong supporter of R-H, notes that "it would be quite misleading, as is often done by its more enthusiastic advocates, to create the impression that biblical theology [R-H] brings something totally new into the life of the church." Gaffin, "Systematic Theology and Biblical Theology," *Westminster Theological Journal* 38 (1975–76): 292. Also see his recent "Biblical Theology and the Westminster Standards," in *The Practical Calvinist: In Honor of D. Clair Davis, Westminster Theological Seminary*, ed. Peter A Lillback (Fearn: Mentor, 2002), 425-42.

[7]   For an interesting creedal example, the Scot's Confession of Faith (1560) Article 4 explicitly connects Gen. 3:15 to Adam, Noah, Abraham, David, and Christ. It should also be noted that the church throughout her entire history has always incorporated aspects of covenant theology, see J. Ligon Duncan, "The Covenant Idea in Ante-Nicene Theology" (PhD diss., University of Edinburgh, 1995).

R-H themes to the WLC and show the strong correlation between the themes and the WLC. My polemic is to emphasize that many of the modern R-H themes *are* in the Westminster Standards. Hence, there should not be a sharp contrast between R-H and ST.

In interests of "full-disclosure," let me briefly state my views. My complaint is that many in Reformed circles (1) *over emphasize* R-H themes and (2) tend not to note that many R-H themes are in traditional Reformed ST. On the other hand, I believe that R-H themes are very important, and I am a big promoter of them. In my New Testament and hermeneutical courses, despite my slight reservations, many of the main textbooks are R-H "classics."[8]

R-H Themes in Modern Reformed Circles

R-H themes have as their core the acknowledgment that God's redemptive actions and Scripture have been progressively revealed through the timeline of biblical history.[9] Given this core starting point, there is variety within modern, conservative Reformed circles as to their methodological and theological emphases under the umbrella term of R-H. I explain R-H themes using three broad, overlapping foci. For convenience, the foci are more oriented toward methodology. I see all three of the foci as biblically important.

The *first* is a focus on the important R-H events of history (i.e. consider what *God* has done through the timeline of biblical

---

[8]   Herman Ridderbos' *Paul: An Outline of His Theology* is the main textbook in my course on Paul. The students also read in my courses: Herman Ridderbos, *When the Time Had Fully Come* (Jordan Station: Paideia, 1982); George Eldon Ladd, *A Theology of the New Testament,* ed. Donald A. Hagner (rev. ed.; Grand Rapids: Eerdmans, 1993); and Sidney Greidanus, *Preaching Christ from the Old Testament: A Contemporary Hermeneutical Method* (Grand Rapids: Eerdmans, 1999).

[9]   Edmund P. Clowney states, "The development of biblical theology is redemptive-historical. The divisions of biblical theology are the historical periods of redemption, marked by creation, the fall, the flood, the call of Abraham, the exodus, and the coming of Christ." *Preaching and Biblical Theology* (Nutley: P&R, 1975), 16.

history). For some, these include the minimum of creation, fall, redemption, and consummation.[10] Others add covenants, exodus, Davidic kingdom, exilic, post-exilic, Christ's states of humiliation and exaltation, etc.[11] In New Testament theology, there is usually a special emphasis on the now/not-yet aspects and our union with Christ in his life/death/resurrection/ascension/second-coming. This focus might be termed *historia salutis*.[12]

The *second* is a focus on any subject coming directly from the biblical text, small or large, viewed through the timeline of biblical history. For example, what does "land"/"rest" mean before the fall, after the fall, in Moses, for the Davidic kingdom, in exile, in Christ's death/resurrection, now, and in the new heavens and earth. Seeing a subject and its possible modifications through time allows us to make appropriate implications about that subject's meaning for today.[13] The Scriptures often use explicit timeline considerations for exegetical conclusions (e.g. Heb. 4:8-10; 7:11-12, 28).

The *third* is a focus on noting that every section of the Bible has a redemptive message for God's people centered on Christ; usually this focus especially affects preaching.[14] Typology of Christ in the

---

[10]   For example, Gordon J. Spykman, *Reformational Theology: A New Paradigm for Doing Dogmatics* (Grand Rapids: Eerdmans, 1992).

[11]   Willem VanGemeren sees "twelve periods of redemptive history." *The Progress of Redemption: The Story of Salvation from Creation to the New Jerusalem* (Grand Rapids: Academie/Zondervan: 1988), 33.

[12]   *Historia salutis* (history of salvation) is usually given the connotation of *God's* major actions in the history of salvation. This is opposed to ordo salutis (plan of salvation), which relates God's forethought and the order of God applying salvation to an individual. The point is usually made in R-H circles that *historia salutis* has logical/causal priority over *ordo salutis* (for example, Ridderbos, *When the Time Had Fully Come*, 47-48). However, I am not sure that all are using the same definition of ordo salutis.

[13]   John Murray does this in *Principles of Conduct: Aspects of Biblical Ethics* (Grand Rapids: Eerdmans, 1957). He looks at a variety of ethical topics (e.g. marriage) and evaluates them through the timeline of R-H.

[14]   For example, *Clowney, Preaching and Biblical Theology*; Sidney Greidanus, *Sola Scriptura: Problems and Principles in Preaching Historical Texts* (Toronto: Wedge, 1970); and Bryan Chapell, *Christ-Centered Preaching: Redeeming the Expository Sermon* (Grand Rapids: Baker, 1994).

Old Testament is an important topic (Luke 24:44). Many times this focus only has concern for Christ's redemptive work.[15] I would rather slightly adjust this focus to: What does every text explicitly and implicitly say about the Triune God – his character (person) and actions (work) – with an emphasis on Christ?

In addition to the variety of foci above, another difficult factor involved in trying to discuss R-H is that there is disagreement within Reformed circles as to the extent to which R-H themes are the *main* themes in the Bible. If I may use my own terms and again paint broadly, I might suggest four positions on a continuum: (1) R-H only, (2) R-H primary, (3) R-H important, and (4) R-H unimportant (ST only).

I define the "R-H only" camp as those who see R-H significantly trumping traditional ST[16] and/or see it as the only way to preach.[17] This usually comes in a package of anti-exemplary exegesis.[18] It is noted that not all in the "R-H only" preaching camp are interested in significantly trumping ST.

The "R-H primary" camp sees R-H as the primary or most important consideration for the correct understanding of Scripture.[19]

---

[15] Christ's work of creation is noted in Heb 1:2, 10-12, which quotes Ps. 102:25-27. His person is also included in the discussion, compare Heb 1:12 and 13:8.

[16] For example, I put into this camp those who are favorable to N. T. Wright's views of justification and the "new perspective." See Wright's *What Saint Paul Really Said: Was Paul of Tarsus the Real Founder of Christianity?* (Grand Rapids: Eerdmans, 1997), 18-20, 113-33.

[17] For an excellent example of "R-H only" preaching, see Sidney Greidanus' *Preaching Christ from the Old Testament: A Contemporary Hermeneutical Method.*

[18] Exemplary exegesis notes a biblical character's actions and traits that are intended to be used as either good or bad examples for readers.

[19] In this category for example, I place two evangelical giants of 20th-century New Testament scholarship: Herman Ridderbos in *Paul: An Outline of His Theology* and *The Coming of the Kingdom*, ed. Raymond O. Zorn, trans. H. de Jongste (Philadelphia: P&R, 1962) and George Eldon Ladd in *A Theology of the New Testament* (Grand Rapids: Eerdmans, 1982). Tremper Longman, III, even while touting the literary aspects of Scripture, concludes that the R-H function of Scripture is most "dominant" in *Literary Approaches to Biblical Interpretation* (FCI 3; Grand Rapids: Academie/Zondervan, 1987), 68-69.

Richard B. Gaffin, Jr. says, "in a word, the concept of theology is redemptive-historically conditioned. The essence of theology is interpretation of the history of redemption."[20]

In the "R-H important" camp I include those, like me, who see R-H themes as important, but not necessarily the primary or only themes in the Bible and not the only method of preaching.[21]

Finally, the "R-H unimportant (ST only)" camp does not exist in *principle* due to traditional Reformed ST always having a level of R-H interest. However in *practice*, many use no other biblical categories except for the main ones used in traditional ST and rarely discuss any topic with timeline sensitivity.[22]

Yes, there are disagreements among the above, but I do not want to overplay this. All would say something to the effect that the person and work of the Triune God with emphasis on Christ is the "center" of the Bible. In practice, "R-H primary" and "R-H important" differ in their methods only by degree. Gaffin might say that R-H is the primary control on a given biblical text, but there are many secondary controls.[23] With a slightly different nuance, I assert that R-H is one of several important controls on a text, but other equally important controls are Trinity, covenants, literary context, ST categories, analogy of Scripture, etc.

---

[20] Gaffin, *Resurrection and Redemption: A Study in Paul's Soteriology* (2nd ed.; Phillipsburg: P&R, 1987), 24.

[21] Reasons for not seeing R-H as primary differ. John M. Frame, who agrees to the importance of R-H, does not see it as primary as per his perspectival system, along with other reasons in *The Doctrine of the Knowledge of God* (Phillipsburg: P&R, 1987), 207-12 and *The Doctrine of God* (Phillipsburg: P&R, 2002), 7-9. Gerhard F. Hassel, who dislikes ST and emphasizes R-H, in the end concludes that no "center can be sufficiently broad" in *New Testament Theology: Basic Issues in the Current Debate* (Grand Rapids: Eerdmans, 1978), 163. Others, like me, see covenant theology (which has many R-H aspects!) as the best organizing principle of Scripture. Still others might find other "centers" to the Bible (e.g. justification by faith).

[22] Some would accuse Louis Berkhof of this, although I would not. See his *Systematic Theology* (4th rev.; Grand Rapids: Eerdmans, 1941).

[23] Gaffin, "Systematic Theology and Biblical Theology," 294. This article is a good starting point for these types of discussions. Also in this article is a brief summary of the relevant views of Gabler, Kuyper, Vos, Warfield, and Murray.

In preaching, the differences between the "R-H only" group and the others do present some tensions.[24] If Christ is the center of Scripture, does that make him equally the "center" of every sermon? Is exemplary exegesis always wrong?[25] What about preaching the third use of the law? Is it proper to use texts of Scripture from different R-H periods and then combine them in a topical sermon?[26] Can grace be assumed in a text simply because the text is part of the Bible, or does grace need to be shown from the specific text? How does a worship service with a confession of sin and assurance of pardon and/or the Lord's Supper affect the sermon? But again, most, but not all, of these tensions are reduced if we agree that the Triune God with emphasis on Christ should be part of every sermon/worship service. Given this, the tensions then relate only to how explicit and to what extent that part is. For example, related to the third use of the law, Chapell states, "'Be' messages are not wrong in themselves; they are wrong messages by themselves."[27] The argument here revolves around what constitutes "by themselves" in a third-use-of-the-law sermon. I sense that in practice Chapell wants a more explicit and extended discussion of Christ than I feel is required. However, we probably are not that far apart in principle.

---

[24] Hendrik Krabbendam notes tensions and complains that R-H preaching is too restrictive. It totally rejects exemplary exegesis and downplays application. Also, it is too Christocentric to the detriment of a full Trinitarian message. See his "Hermeneutics and Preaching," in *The Preacher and Preaching: Reviving the Art in the Twentieth Century* (Phillipsburg: P&R, 1986), 212-45, esp. 233-35.

[25] For a justification of a limited use of exemplary exegesis, see Robert J. Cara, "The Ambiguous Characterization of Barnabas in Acts 15:36-41" (Ph.D. diss., Westminster Theological Seminary, 2001), 154-64 and Richard L. Pratt, *He Gave Us Stories: The Bible Students' Guide to Interpreting Old Testament Narratives* (Brentwood, Tenn.: Wolgemuth & Hyatt, 1990), 91. Clowney does see a use for exemplary or "ethical instruction" (*Preaching and Biblical Theology*, 78-79).

[26] I would argue it is in principle proper because the Bible itself does this with other portions of Scripture (e.g. Rom. 3:9-20). Of course, I am assuming that the Bible's hermeneutic is in principle normative for us.

[27] Chapell, *Christ-Centered Preaching*, 285.

Concerning those in the "R-H only" camp who stress that R-H significantly trumps ST, yes, there are important differences. Once many of the traditional ST categories and conclusions are discounted, the differences are more substantial and could lead to the denial of key Christian doctrines. Of course, those in the "R-H only" camp would simply reply that certain ST doctrines (if not the whole idea of ST) are wrong, and that many other ST doctrines need to be significantly improved by reformulation into R-H categories.[28]

R-H Themes in the WLC

Of the many R-H themes presented above, for convenience I will evaluate the WLC in respect to (1) timeline aspects, which relate more to method, and (2) modern views of union with Christ, which relate more to theology.

Why use only the WLC instead of the complete Westminster Standards? The WLC is the most neglected part of the Westminster Standards.[29] Also, the WLC has a large union with Christ section (WLC 65-90) that needs more highlighting.

---

[28] For example, John Goldingay compares biblical narratives and ST. He complains about ST's use of a Greek-thought framework for the Trinity, and "for all its truth and fruitfulness, the doctrine of the Trinity seriously skews our theological reading of Scripture." ST does not do justice to much of the biblical material because "it presupposes a quest for unity." Greek thinking ST does not match biblical narratives concerning providence. In biblical narratives, "God is committed to the achievement of certain long-term aims, and sometimes acts in history, but does not decide how most events work out in history. If sovereignty means that what happens is what God wants to happen, God is not sovereign." See John Goldingay, "Biblical Narrative and Systematic Theology," in *Between Two Horizons: Spanning New Testament Studies and Systematic Theology,* eds. Joel B. Green and Max Turner (Grand Rapids: Eerdmans, 2000), 123-42, esp. 128-31, 140.

[29] W. Robert Godfrey agrees, "At least in the United States the Larger Catechism is seldom mentioned, much less studied, as a living part of the Presbyterian heritage" in "An Introduction to the Westminster Larger Catechism," in Johannes G. Vos, *The Westminster Larger Catechism: A Commentary,* ed. G. I. Williamson (Phillipsburg: P&R, 2002), ix. The literature specifically on the WLC is limited. Two major works are the just cited Vos work and Thomas

For my purposes, the following is a truncated outline of the WLC. Especially note the union with Christ section.

I. Belief (6-90)
    A.   Trinity: person and work (6-19)
    B.   Covenant of Works/Life (20-30)
    C.   Covenant of Grace (31-35)
    D.   Christ the Mediator of the Covenant of Grace (36-56)
        1.   Person (36-42)
        2.   Work (43-56)
            a)   Prophet, Priest, and King (43-45)
            b)   Humiliation and Exaltation (46-56)
    E.   Application of Christ's Benefits to the Church (57-64)
    F.   Union with Christ (65-90)
        1.   Communion with Christ "in grace" (66-81)
            (Effectual Calling, Justification, Adoption, and Sanctification)
        2.   Communion with Christ "in glory" (82-90)
            ("This life," Intermediate State, and Resurrection)

II. Duty (91-196)
    A.   Law (92-152)
    B.   Means of Grace (153-196)
        1.   Word (155-160)
        2.   Sacraments (161-177)
        3.   Prayer (178-196)

Timeline Aspects in the WLC

Obviously, the Westminster Divines are aware that Scripture presents many subjects with timeline aspects. But how much of

---

Ridgeley, *Commentary on the Larger Catechism* (2 vols.; Edmonton: Still Waters Revival, n.d. [1731-33]). Also see Morton H. Smith, "Theology of the Larger Catechism," in *The Westminster Confession into the 21st Century: Essays in Remembrance of the 350th Anniversary of the Westminster Assembly*, ed. J. Ligon Duncan (3 vols.; Fearn: Mentor, 2003), 1:101-22.

this is included in the WLC? The following is a review of topics from the WLC that are discussed, at least minimally, with timeline aspects. Following the review, I will summarize and then discuss some of the possible weaknesses of the WLC in this regard.

"The scriptures make known . . . his decrees, and the execution of his decrees" (WLC 6). The decrees include "his works of creation and providence" (WLC 14, also 15, 18). Timeline aspects are shown by distinguishing the decrees and the execution of them, and distinguishing between creation and on-going providence.

The federal system (the covenant of works/life and the covenant of grace [WLC 20-22, 30-32]) of the Westminster Standards is well-known. Both of these covenants have timeline aspects. Although the covenant of works was with Adam,[30] the requirement of "perpetual obedience" and the punishments due its violation continue throughout R-H. Mankind is now "liable to all punishments in this world and that which is to come" (WLC 20, 27, 38, 93). Also the "flesh" and "sin" aspects from Adam's fall continue in both believers and unbelievers through R-H (WLC 26, 27, 78, 191, and 193). Finally, the covenant of works is related to the "moral law," which also extends through R-H (WLC 92-94).

Although there is only one covenant of grace, it was "administered" in a different "manner" in the Old Testament than it is in the New Testament epoch (WLC 33-35). In the New Testament, "grace and salvation are held forth in more fulness, evidence, and efficacy, to all nations" (WLC 35). This shows both timeline aspects and, more specifically, a progressive fulfillment through R-H.

---

[30] Bavinck argues that because the covenant of works was conditional for Adam, this implies that at creation Adam did not possess the highest state of blessing. Hence, even the covenant of works itself had a progressive aspect that will not be fully realized until the new heavens and earth. He contrasts this Reformed R-H aspect of the covenant of works against Roman Catholic and Lutheran views. See Herman Bavinck, *In the Beginning: Foundations of Creation Theology*, ed. John Bolt, trans. John Vriend (Grand Rapids: Baker, 1999), 206-12.

In relationship to the covenant of grace, Christ is called the "second Adam" (WLC 31). The relationship between the first and second Adams shows timeline awareness.

Christ's person is described partially in timeline ways. Christ "in the fullness of time became man, and so was and continues to be God and man . . . for ever" (WLC 36, also 47).

The mediator, Jesus, is described using Old Testament categories: Christ, Prophet, Priest, and King. He is "Christ . . . to execute the offices of prophet, priest, and king of his church" (WLC 42, also 43-45). Although not explicitly stated but implied with the use of the footnotes, these Old Testament categories for Jesus give many typological hints for preaching Jesus from Old Testament texts.[31] These categories also imply a progressive fulfillment from the Old Testament to Christ.[32]

The emphasis on the states of Christ in his "humiliation" and "exaltation" shows a timeline movement in Christ's work. The WLC covers Christ's "conception and birth, life, death, and after his death, . . . resurrection, ascension, sitting at the right hand of the Father, and his coming again to judge the world" (WLC 46, 51). As all agree, defining Christ in terms of his humiliation and then his exaltation is one biblical way, among several biblical ways, to summarize Christ's work (e.g. Ps. 118:22; Luke 24:46; Acts 5:30-31; Phil. 2:6-11; 1 Pet. 1:11). The Nicene Creed and the Apostles' Creed do this, along with traditional Reformed ST and modern R-H emphases. Unfortunately, the people in the pews do not generally pick up on this.

The full orbed salvation of believers is shown in timeline terms (*ordo salutis*). This occurs many times in the section on humiliation and exaltation (WLC 46-56). For example, Christ's exalted resurrection is related to believers' "justification, quickening

---

[31] For additional typological hints, see WCF 8.6, 27.5.

[32] Ridgeley, writing in 1721–1723, makes the obvious typological and progressive fulfillment connections. See Ridgeley, *Commentary on the Larger Catechism*, 1:490-98.

in grace, support against enemies, and to assure them of their resurrection from the dead on the last day" (WLC 52). The whole union with Christ section (WLC 65-90) also revolves around the timeline of believers. It is split between our union now ("in grace") and our union in the life to come ("in glory") (WLC 65). More on this later in the union with Christ section of this article.

Upon death, believers are "capable of further communion with Christ in glory" (WLC 85). This shows the progressive nature of salvation. In the discussions of the second coming, it is made especially clear that there is a progressive advancement of believers' salvation. Believers will be "at last perfected at the resurrection and day of judgment" (WLC 82) and "fully and for ever freed from all sin and misery, filled with inconceivable joys, made perfectly holy and happy both in body and soul" (WLC 90).

WLC 79 well shows an example of God's actions through R-H related to the salvation of believers. True believers cannot fall from grace because of the "unchangeable love of God, and his decree and covenant . . . , their inseparable union with Christ, his continual intercession for them, and the Spirit and seed of God abiding in them."

The preface to the Ten Commandments section notes "that he is a God in covenant, as with Israel of old, so with all his people; who, as he brought them out of their bondage in Egypt, so he delivereth us from our spiritual thraldom" (WLC 101). Note the timeline aspects in the typology connecting "bondage in Egypt" to "our spiritual thraldom."

The large Ten Commandments section (WLC 102-48) has modern meanings – that is, "duties required" and "sins forbidden" for today. This indicates some level of timeline sensitivity, if not simply to explicitly show that many Old Testament moral laws have a one-to-one relationship to the New Testament epoch. Also, some of the discussions include slight adjustments from the Old Testament to New Testament (e.g. Saturday to Sunday in the fourth commandment [WLC 116]).[33]

Concerning the Sabbath, a brief timeline is included: "remembrance of the two great benefits of creation and redemption, which contain a short abridgment of religion" (WLC 121). Creation/redemption is a biblical and current R-H emphasis.

WLC 191 speaks of "thy kingdom come." This kingdom has timeline aspects, for example, "the fulness of the Gentiles brought in" and "Christ would rule in our hearts here, and hasten the time of his second coming, and our reigning with him for ever."[34]

Summary and Possible Weaknesses of Timeline Aspects of WLC

As seen from the above review, the WLC exhibits many timeline aspects. As is well-known, traditional Reformed ST's *ordo salutis* has always incorporated timeline aspects that are progressive, and the WLC confirms this. However, the WLC confirms this by discussing the *ordo salutis* as part of the humiliation and exaltation section and also as part of the union with Christ section. This shows a strong correlation between *historia salutis* and *ordo salutis* that most in the modern Reformed circles can wholeheartedly support.

---

[33] Discontinuity of Old Testament laws into the New Testament is explicitly discussed in WCF 19.3-4, 20.1.

[34] A common complaint in some Reformed circles is that the Westminster Standards have a truncated view of the kingdom of God as compared to the view presented by, for example, Geerhardus Vos, *The Teaching of Jesus concerning the Kingdom of God and the Church* (Phillipsburg, P&R, n.d. [1903]). It is usually noted that in WCF 25.2 the kingdom is equivalent to the church. True, in WCF 25.2 the kingdom is equated as far as membership is concerned to the church. Vos also agrees to this in *The Teaching of Jesus concerning the Kingdom of God and the Church*, 86-87. But Vos would go on to argue on p. 87 that "it does not necessarily follow that the visible church is the only outward expression of the invisible kingdom." WLC 191 states, "that he [Christ] would be pleased so to exercise the kingdom of his power in all the world, as best may conduce to these ends." Although this is not clear and does not say as much as I would like, I believe that this implies that kingdom work is broader than the visible church work.

Both the covenant of works and covenant of grace exhibit timeline aspects. They are not only "static" covenants; both have implications throughout R-H. The covenant of grace is portrayed as progressively developing from the Old Testament to the new heavens and new earth.

The person and especially the work of Christ are shown in timeline terms. The humiliation and exaltation scheme has a separate discussion of Christ's conception and birth, life, death, after his death, resurrection, ascension, sitting at the right hand of God, and coming again to judge. Highlighting these *historia salutis* redemptive actions matches many modern R-H emphases.

Given that the WLC did not intend to say everything, are there weaknesses in the WLC pertaining to R-H timeline aspects? In my view there are no explicit R-H errors in the WLC; however, it would have been helpful if the WLC (1) included more on the specifics of the unfolding Old Testament covenants/periods within the covenant of grace (e.g. Abrahamic covenant, Davidic covenant), (2) included more on the typology of Christ in the Old Testament (although Christ as Prophet, Priest, and King gives many hints), and (3) made the *progressive* nature of God's redemptive actions and his Scriptures more explicit.

Union with Christ

The terminology of "union with Christ" is used in both historic Reformed ST and modern R-H emphases. How well does union with Christ in the WLC match to the modern R-H emphasis on it?

Due to Calvin's emphasis and application of union with Christ,[35] this terminology has always been part of historic Reformed ST. However, it has been used in slightly different ways. For example, in the *ordo salutis*, does union with Christ begin with (1) Christ's

---

[35] For example, Calvin connects union with Christ to the sacraments in *Institutes of the Christian Religion*, ed. John T. McNeill, trans. Ford Lewis Battles (Library of Christian Classics, vols. 20-21; Philadelphia: Westminster Press, 1960), 4.15.6, 4.17.2-3.

agreement in eternity past to represent us or (2) our existential union with him as part of our effectual calling?[36] However, much of modern Reformed ST now agrees with Murray that union with Christ is the "central truth of the whole doctrine of salvation" and stretches from eternity past to our glorification.[37]

Union with Christ in Pauline Theology
What concepts are associated with the term "union with Christ" in Reformed circles by those who emphasize R-H? Generally, it matches modern Pauline scholarly usage, which unfortunately is not uniform.

Union with Christ is connected by both modern Pauline critical and conservative scholars to Paul's use of the "in Christ" formula.[38] Also related to this is Paul's use of both "Christ for us"

---

[36] For example, Ames and Witsius connect union with Christ directly to our effectual call in William Ames, *The Marrow of Theology*, ed. and trans. John D. Eusden (Durham, N.C.: Labyrinth, 1983 [1629]), 157; and Herman Witsius, *The Economy of the Covenants between God and Man* (2 vols.; Phillipsburg: P&R, 1990 [1693]), 1:344-45. Louis Berkhof seems to incorporate both (*Systematic Theology*, 418, 449-50). Charles Hodge connects our union to Christ to eternity past, with Christ's work, and our consummation of it by faith. He has a good, but brief, discussion connecting our union with Christ's work to our justification in *Systematic Theology* (3 vols.; Grand Rapids: Baker, 1982 [1871–73]), 3:104, 3:121. For some insightful discussions, see William G. T. Shedd, *Dogmatic Theology*, ed. Alan W. Gomes (3rd ed.; Phillipsburg: P&R, 2003 [1888–94]), 789-90 and Francis Turretin, *Institutes of Elenctic Theology*, ed. James T. Dennison, Jr., trans. George Musgrave Giger (3 vols.; Phillipsburg: P&R, 1992–97 [1679–85]), 2:179-83.

[37] John Murray, *Redemption Accomplished and Applied* (Grand Rapids: Eerdmans, 1955), 161, also 162-73. Sinclair B. Ferguson says, "Every element in the classical ordo salutis is thus a further perspective on the one reality of the believer's union with Christ." Ferguson, *The Holy Spirit* (Contours of Christian Theology; Downers Grove; InterVarsity, 1996), 106. Douglas F. Kelly, my teacher and now colleague, notes in class that "union with Christ is from eternity to eternity" and is the "motor that makes [soteriology] run." Robert L. Reymond acknowledges Murray's view, but insists on the more traditional connecting of union with Christ with effectual calling. Reymond, *A New Systematic Theology of the Christian Faith* (Nashville: Thomas Nelson, 1998), 736.

[38] As to categorizing the "in Christ" statements with different overlapping conclusions, see M. A. Seifrid, "In Christ," in *Dictionary of Paul and His Letters* (eds. Gerald

(e.g. Rom. 5:6, 8; 1 Cor. 15:3; 2 Cor. 5:21) and "we with Christ" (e.g. Rom. 6:8; 2 Cor. 5:14-15; Col. 2:20, 3:1) ideas.[39] (The distinction between "Christ for us" and "we with Christ" has been present in traditional Reformed ST; the 1563 Heidelberg Catechism used it [42-43][40]). Finally for many, these are additionally related to the Adam/Christ parallels ("in Adam"/"in Christ"; "old man"/ "new man"; both Adam and Christ as "image of God").[41]

In scholarly Pauline-studies circles, there is disagreement on exactly what these formulas mean and how they are related. At a minimum, there is agreement that our union with Christ includes our connection to him at his death/resurrection and a related union with Christ when we first believe. Many scholars also see an election aspect to our union with Christ stretching back to the "foundation of the world" (Eph. 1:4). There is also disagreement as to the characterization of the union, with regard to the terminology and the concept itself. Is it federal, forensic, existential, R-H, mystical, spiritual, vital, "a Gnostic conception of the cosmic Anthropos,"[42] etc.?

F. Hawthorne and Ralph P. Martin; Downers Grove: InterVarsity, 1993), 433-36; Donald Guthrie, *New Testament Theology* (Downers Grove: InterVarsity, 1981), 644-56; and I. Howard Marshall, "The Theology of Philippians," in Karl P. Donfried and I. Howard Marshall, *The Theology of the Shorter Pauline Letters* (NTT; Cambridge: Cambridge University Press, 1993), 138-44.

[39] For a critical perspective, see James D. G. Dunn, *The Theology of Paul the Apostle* (Grand Rapids: Eerdmans, 1998), 396-412. For a conservative perspective, see Ridderbos, *An Outline of Paul's Theology*, 57-64, 168-89 and Ridderbos, *When the Time Had Fully Come*, 53-57.

[40] The *Heidelberg Catechism* connects "Christ for us" to justification and "we with Christ" to sanctification. Although Paul often ties "we with Christ" to sanctification (e.g. 2 Cor. 5:14-15), this does not exhaust Paul's meaning as the connection of "we with Christ" to both the Adam/Christ parallel and "in Christ" would indicate (cf. Rom. 5:19; 1 Cor. 1:30, 15:22).

[41] Thomas R. Schreiner has an extended discussion of Paul's "Adam Christology" and how it can be seen in relationship to other Pauline doctrines, including "in Christ." He presents it as one of the main categories to understand Christ in *Paul: Apostle of God's Glory in Christ: A Pauline Theology* (Downers Grove: InterVarsity, 2001), 151-68.

In order to get a starting point to compare against the WLC, allow me to give a very brief overview of my view of the "in Christ" formula in Paul. My view is reasonably common within conservative Pauline scholarship.

Union with Christ ("in Christ") may be defined as *our representation by and our connection with Christ, and all the implications that flow from this.* Union with Christ is multifaceted and covers the whole scope of R-H. It has three key points in R-H. We are (1) united to Christ in eternity past (e.g. Eph. 1; 1 Thess. 5:9-10; Rom. 8:28-29), (2) united to Christ with him in his work of humiliation and exaltation (e.g. Rom. 3:24; Rom. 6; 2 Cor. 5:19; Col. 2:20, 3:1; 1 Thess. 4:14), and (3) united to Christ existentially, which starts when we first believe and continues into the new heavens and earth (e.g. Rom. 8:1; Gal. 2:20; Eph. 6:1; Phil. 4:4; Col. 2:20, 3:1; 1 Cor. 15:58).[43] This is not the place to expand upon the difficult subject of exactly how all three of these points relate to each other.

This union with Christ has federal, forensic, spiritual, and existential aspects, along with a now/not-yet structure,[44] which, I would argue, all match to a full-orbed covenant theology.[45]

---

[42] Rudolf Bultmann, *Theology of the New Testament*, trans. Kendrick Grobel (2 vols.; New York: Charles Scribner's, 1951–55), 2:177.

[43] Gaffin's three terms of "predestinarian," "redemptive-historical," and "experiential" match to my "eternity past," "with his work," and "existential," respectively. See Gaffin, *Resurrection and Redemption: A Study in Paul's Soteriology,* 2nd edition (Phillipsburg: P&R, 1987), 50 & 57. John L. Girardeau, speaking specifically of justification, prefers the term "representative" to refer to our justification in AD 30, and "conscious" to refer to our justification when we first believe. See Girardeau, *The Federal Theology: Its Import and its Regulative Influence,* ed. J. Ligon Duncan (Greenville, S.C.: Reformed Academic, 1994 [1881]), 22.

[44] The now/not-yet structure includes having some of the apparent future-age eschatological benefits brought back into the "now" age. Hence, the two R-H ages overlap. The classic for now/not-yet in Paul is Geerhardus Vos, *The Pauline Eschatology* (Phillipsburg: P&R, 1986 [1930]), esp. 1-41. Compare Luke 18:30, Rom. 8:9, Gal. 1:4, 5:17, and Eph. 1:21. My minor complaint with standard now/not-yet discussions, including Vos's, is that there should be some aspects

Union with Christ in the WLC

WLC 65-90 is an amazingly biblical discussion of many aspects of our union with Christ. Similar to older ST, the terms "union with Christ" (WLC 79) and "union and communion" (WLC 65) relate to our "existential" union with Christ, which begins at believers' effectual calling. This union is defined as a "work of God's grace, whereby they are spiritually and mystically, yet really and inseparably, joined to Christ as their head and husband, which is done in their effectual calling" (WLC 66).

As can be seen from my above truncated outline, the WLC maps out this existential union in two phases: "in grace" (this life, 65, 69-81) and "in glory" (heaven, 65, 82-90).

The "communion in grace" relates to believers' "partaking of the virtue of his mediation, in their justification, adoption, sanctification, and whatever else, in this life, manifests their union with him" (WLC 69).[46] This communion in grace section is typical of traditional ST *ordo salutis* answers, and several R-H emphases do appear.

Concerning the adoption section, a future aspect is included. Those adopted are "fellow-heirs with Christ in glory" (WLC 74).[47] Ridgeley, summarizing the adoption answer, states, "Hence, all the blessings which we have either in hand or in hope, the blessings of both worlds, the blessings which are conferred upon us from our conversion to our glorification, are the privileges which God

---

of eschatological "now" extending from Adam to Christ, albeit reduced aspects compared to the New Testament epoch. Does not Romans 4 imply that David's faith, which is related to "promise," "heir," "grace," and "righteousness," had some aspect of eschatological blessing?

45 For example, the covenantal "I am your God, and you are my people" (e.g. Gen. 17:7-8, Exod. 6:7, Rev. 21:3) shows the existential aspect. Showing now/not-yet aspects, covenants have benefits when they are made, but also look toward future benefits (e.g. "In you [Abraham], all the families of the earth *will* be blessed" [Gen. 12:3]).

46 This answer assumes that one is already effectually called (WLC 66-68).

47 The footnote cites Rom. 8:17: "heirs . . . that we may be glorified with him (συνδοξαζομαι)." Rom. 8:23 even more clearly asserts a future aspect of adoption.

bestows on those who are his adopted children."[48] This shows a now/not-yet structure to adoption.[49]

Sanctification is "through the powerful operation of his Spirit applying the death and resurrection of Christ unto them" (WLC 75). Here is a clear connection between (1) our union with Christ in his work and (2) our existential union with Christ. Also see WLC 52 and 79 in this regard.

In sanctification, Christians are being "renewed in their whole man after the image of God" (WLC 75). This matches the biblical and current R-H emphasis of connecting creation language to redemption language.

The flesh versus Spirit struggle is included in the WLC: "The imperfection of sanctification in believers ariseth from the remnants of sin abiding in every part of them, and the perpetual lustings of the flesh against the spirit" (WLC 78). This shows at least partial awareness of a now/not-yet structure.

WLC 82-90 relates to our "communion in glory" which ostensibly begins "immediately after death." The term "glory" refers to heaven (the heaven now and the future new heavens). However, WLC 82-83 includes a discussion of how our "communion in glory" relates to "this life!" Christians "have communicated to them in this life the first-fruits of glory with Christ, as they are members of him their head, and so in him are interested in that glory which he is fully possessed of." The WLC has an overlap of the "communion in grace" and the "communion in glory." This is a clear example of now/not-yet eschatology, and another connection between our union with Christ in his work and our existential union with Christ.

The WLC well notes the biblical and current R-H emphasis that the body in addition to the soul is to be redeemed. Part of the union with Christ in glory during the intermediate state is the "waiting

---

[48] Ridgeley, *Commentary on the Larger Catechism*, 2:136.

[49] The adoption chapter in the WCF (12) only implies a future aspect of adoption.

for the full redemption of their bodies, which even in death continue united to Christ" (WLC 86). First Thessalonians 4:14 is footnoted for the connection between Christ and believers during the intermediate state that looks forward to believers' bodily resurrection.

WLC 87 is more explicit concerning bodily resurrection. "The bodies of the just, by the Spirit of Christ, and by virtue of his resurrection as their head, shall be raised in power, spiritual, incorruptible, and made like to his glorious body." Again, note the connection between our union with Christ in his work and our existential union with Christ.

The sacraments section (WLC 161-77) also includes union with Christ language. Baptism is "a sign and seal of ingrafting into himself [Christ]" (WLC 165). Our baptism is improved on "by drawing strength from the death and resurrection of Christ, into whom we are baptized, for the mortifying of sin, and the quickening of grace" (WLC 167). In the Lord's Supper, we have our "union and communion with him confirmed" (WLC 168); and "do therein feed upon the body and blood of Christ . . . while by faith [we] receive and apply unto [our]selves Christ crucified, and all the benefits of his death" (WLC 170).

What about our union with Christ in eternity past? It is implicitly included in the "communion of grace" section by the starting point of effectual calling, which has a predestination aspect (WLC 67). This then connects back to the decrees of God (WLC 12-14). God's decrees include "in Christ [God] hath chosen some men to eternal life" (WLC 13). Our union with Christ in eternity past is explicit in that the "covenant of grace was made with Christ as the second Adam, and in him with all the elect as his seed" (WLC 31). Possibly related is WLC 174 where the Lord's Supper is considered a "renewing of their [believers'] covenant with God." Jeremiah 50:5 is footnoted, which refers to an "everlasting covenant." (WCF 11.4 has a threefold discussion of justification, which connects God's decree of justification to Christ's rising for our justification to our actual justification.)

Although a topic for another article, the WLC does make corporate implications (believers' connection to other believers) from our union with Christ (see WLC 64, 168, and 174).

Finally, it should be noted that while WLC 65-90 ostensibly emphasizes what I would call existential union with Christ, one should not assume that the existential aspect alone is the sum total of the Westminster Divines' doctrine of the union with Christ. Given extensive 16th and early 17th-century Reformed discussion of that locus, stretching back to Calvin, Peter Martyr, and Beza, it is likely that the Divines would have acknowledged all the dimensions of union with Christ recognized by modern Reformed theologians.

Summary and Possible Weaknesses of Union with Christ in WLC

The WLC has a large union with Christ section (65-90). Specifically, the term "union with Christ" refers to our union that begins at our effectual calling. How does this compare to current Pauline studies that include our union with Christ in eternity past, our union with him in his work, and our existential union? Given that there is a terminology difference, the WLC *does* match well to union with Christ in Pauline studies. The WLC shows that our threefold union with Christ is (1) connected back to eternity; (2) connected to Christ's life, death, resurrection, ascension, and return; and (3) results in an existential union and benefits for us in this life and the life to come.[50]

Matching to biblical and current R-H emphases, the WLC includes many implicit and explicit now/not-yet statements. Examples include the adoption and resurrection discussions,

---

[50] For purposes of this paper, I did not pursue the discussions concerning the nature of the union (e.g. Does the union have forensic aspects?) and the inter-relationship of the threefold union.

along with the overlapping communion in grace with communion in glory.

Again, given that the WLC did not intend to say everything, a possible weakness in the WLC is that there is no explicit explanation of the overlapping R-H ages. The kernel, however, of the overlapping ages is included. Original and actual sin runs throughout R-H (see WLC 25, 26, 78, 194). Our union with Christ in his work is connected to our union with Christ in grace and in glory (e.g. WLC 87, also see WCF 13.2-3). Our benefits in this life are termed the "first fruits of glory with Christ" (WLC 83). The overlap of the communion in grace and communion in glory, and the covenant of works and covenant of grace also contribute.

Conclusions

First, there are many modern R-H themes in the WLC. Specifically, this article has highlighted timeline aspects and the threefold union with Christ. One may argue, although I would not, that certain aspects of the WLC's presentation of R-H are wrong or many doctrines need to be significantly altered by reformulation along R-H lines. However, to imply that the Westminster Standards' ST does not include many R-H aspects is simply wrong.

Second, the "union with Christ" section (WLC 65-90) is biblical and needs to be better known.

Third, in my opinion, there are no R-H errors in the WLC, although I do think there are some possible weaknesses due to partial omissions. It would have been helpful if the WLC (a) included more on the specifics of the unfolding Old Testament covenants/periods within the covenant of grace (e.g. Abrahamic covenant, Davidic covenant), (b) included more on the typology of Christ in the Old Testament, (c) made the *progressive* nature of God's redemptive actions and his Scriptures more explicit, and (d) gave a more explicit explanation of the overlapping R-H ages.

Subscription to the Confession

Rowland S. Ward

Many chapters in the collection of which this volume forms the third have discussed the content of the Westminster Confession. In practical terms the key question may not be the content but how the church and its office-bearers relate to the content. Is it accepted simply as the church's confession or is it regarded also as a personal confession? Is its teaching accepted in total, or only in the main, or with qualifications? Indeed, does subscription to a confession not call in question the insistence by Protestant Christians on the primacy of Scripture and its place as the sole rule of faith?

The answers to such questions are found (1) in terms of the Act by which a church approves the Confession and (2) in what is commonly called the Formula subscribed by office-bearers as the nexus between the subscriber and the Confession. These two matters are not unrelated since office-bearers will hardly be asked to subscribe the Confession in a form that ignores any qualification the church may have made in adopting it. Before examining these important matters a survey of the development of creeds and their relation to Scripture will be in order.

The Origin and Necessity of Creeds and Confessions

Creed-like formulations are found in the Old Testament. The short creed of Israel, the *Shema* (Hebrew for "Hear") is worth noting.

It reads: "Hear O Israel: The Lord our God, the Lord is one" (Deut. 6:4 NIV).[1] This emphasis on the oneness of God means Israel is to worship him alone. The name Lord speaks of God as living and ever-present to help his people, and its meaning was demonstrated in the events of the Exodus (cf. Exod. 6:3). Another translation is: "Hear O Israel, the Lord our God is the only Lord." On this view the emphasis is that the Lord is the one whose character corresponds with the revelation he has given in mighty deeds for the salvation of his people. He alone is the God who saves. That is the supreme reason why they are to love him in return (v. 5).

The New Testament citation of this passage by Jesus confirms its importance (Mark 12:29). Paul also refers to it: "We know that an idol is nothing at all in the world and that there is no God but one. For even if there are so-called gods, whether in heaven or on earth (as indeed there are many 'gods' and many 'lords'), yet for us there is but one God, the Father, from whom all things came and for whom we live; and there is but one Lord, Jesus Christ, through whom all things came and through whom we live" (1 Cor. 8:4-6). In line with this we can recognize that, while the meaning of the name Lord was disclosed in part in the events of the Exodus from Egypt (cf. Exod. 6:3), full disclosure comes in the saving deeds of God in Christ. Consequently, when Jesus parts from his disciples with the command to baptize "in the name of the Father, and of the Son and of the Holy Spirit" (Matt. 28:19), we have an unpacking of the covenant name, "Lord." We see that redemption was the Father's plan, the Son's purchase, and the Spirit's application. "The one and only Son who is at the Father's side, he has made him known" (John 1:18). Consequently, the distinctive note of New Testament faith is that it is both strictly monotheistic and plainly Trinitarian.

A variety of factors – the interplay of "exegesis, prayer, polemics and politics"[2] – contributed to the elaboration of a

---

[1]   All following Scripture references are taken from the NIV.

[2]   Jaroslav Pelikan, *Credo* (New Haven: Yale University Press, 2003), 125.

brief confession, such as "Jesus is Lord," so as to bring out its implications. As differences arose among those who claimed loyalty to Christ and the Scriptures, it was necessary to set out some of these implications at length. One sees the principle in Scripture itself. For example, the Council at Jerusalem considered afresh the issue of the relationship of justification and works in the light of the controversy over circumcision, and resolved it by application of Scripture to the particular circumstances that had arisen. The results were binding on the churches, and also a blessing to them, since they were guarded from heresy and established in the truth and love of God.[3]

In the early centuries the church found, as is still the case, that it was not enough to cite Scripture against heretics. G. L. Prestige writes:

> Unfortunately, the Bible proved to be common hunting-ground between the follower of the Gospel and the wildest theosophist or the most perverse misbeliever. Heretics showed that they could be as painstaking in their use of Scripture as the saints; their ingenuity sometimes far exceeded the ingenuity of any orthodox teacher in the surprising interpretations which they set upon it. The fact soon became obvious to any intelligent thinker that the principle of "the Bible and the Bible only" provides no automatically secure basis for a religion that is to be genuinely Christian. It is both interesting and important to observe how the difficulty was met. First, the original doctrine of tradition by the Apostles to the Church continued to be the ultimate basis of Christian thought. The Bible was reckoned a part, and the principal part, of the apostolic tradition. Secondly, it was firmly insisted that although the tradition was enshrined in the Bible, a process of interpretation was required in order to extract it. Appeal was made, not to the Bible simply, but to the Bible rightly and rationally interpreted.[4]

---

[3]   Acts 15:1-16:5. Cf. the discussion in James Bannerman, *The Church of Christ* (2 vols.; 1869; repr., Edinburgh: Banner of Truth, 1974), 1:289ff.

[4]   G. L. Prestige, *Fathers and Heretics* (London: SPCK, 1940), 14.

The orthodox Protestant assessment of this development was not to condemn it out of hand. For example, the use of the term "Trinity" immediately reminds us we are not using a word found in Scripture. Yet orthodox Protestants accept the doctrinal conclusions in the Nicene Creed of AD 325, even if they reject some of the speculations held by some of the Nicene Fathers. It is an uninformed, sectarian, or latitudinarian spirit that mouths the cry of William Chillingworth, "The Bible, I say, the Bible only is the religion of Protestants."[5] This sounds pious but is misleading and false. Every group (Protestant or otherwise) claiming "the Bible only" has its interpretation of the Bible, and a creed is simply the expression of these beliefs, either verbally or in writing. Christians should not quibble over mere words, but they do wish to adhere to the true meaning of Scripture, and words are needed to do that. Hence the necessity and honesty of declaring our understanding of controverted teachings of Scripture in a public confession of faith.[6] As Dutch theologian Herman Bavinck (1854–1921) put it: "For the Holy Scripture was not given to the church by God to be thoughtlessly repeated but to be understood in all its fullness and richness. . . ."[7]

The church is bound to be a confessing church, bound to subscribe a statement of what she believes Scripture teaches. Latitudinarians like William Chillingworth in the 17th century, and radical liberals like Bishop Spong in the 21st century, attack orthodox creeds since they do not want to be bound to orthodoxy. Others are influenced by a biblicist approach, perhaps contributed to by a misuse of creeds as the instrument of a narrow sectarianism. In their rejection of creeds in favor of "the Bible only," they seem

---

[5]   William Chillingworth (1602–1644), Anglican latitudinarian scholar, was the popularizer of the phrase in his *The Religion of Protestants a Sure Way to Salvation* (London, 1638), Pt. I, Ch. VI, Sec. 56.

[6]   Cf. John Calvin, *Institutes of the Christian Religion*, ed. John T. McNeill, trans. Ford Lewis Battles (Library of Christian Classics, vols. 20-21; Philadelphia: Westminster Press, 1960), 1.13.3-5.

[7]   H. Bavinck, *Our Reasonable Faith* (Grand Rapids: Eerdmans, 1956), 157.

oblivious to the fact that their distinctive interpretation is a creed and functions as such, as one will find if you advance a different viewpoint.[8]

While the Roman Catholic Church produced its decrees and sought submission to them on the authority of the church, Protestants produced creeds but insisted on the primacy of Scripture, not church or pope. Many confessions were produced in the different lands to which the Reformation spread. The Westminster Confession of 1646/47 comes at the virtual close of the creed-writing age among Protestants. This accounts in part for it being the highwater mark of creedal composition.

The History of Subscription

Subscription to a statement of faith belongs to the nature of Christianity as a revealed religion. God has spoken: we are to hold fast to what he has revealed. The usual subscription has been a verbal or written pledge by the subscriber that the statement of doctrine of the church is his personal belief also, and that he will teach and defend it. This is seen very clearly in the *Profession of Faith* of the Council of Trent (1564) required of all priests and of all converts from Protestantism.[9]

Protestants too set out their position and in a variety of ways pledged adherence to it. Their intention was to maintain the unity of the faith, and the assumption must be that their confessions and catechisms had this aim in view whether or not they were formally subscribed. The notion that only a partial adherence was intended is unhistorical and anachronistic in the 16th and 17th centuries.

---

[8] An anti-creedal, "non-denominational" body such as the Church of Christ is a prime example. Handbooks by members, such as Leroy Brownlow's, *Why I Am a Member of the Church of Christ* (Fort Worth, TX: Brownlow, 1945), form a very definite statement of beliefs.

[9] Text in Peter A. Lillback, "Confessional Subscription Among the Sixteenth Century Reformers," in *The Practice of Confessional Subscription*, ed. David W. Hall (Oak Ridge: Covenant Foundation, 2001), 37.

Luther's two catechisms (1529) were widely used, and the assumption was that they faithfully represented the teaching of Scripture. Lutheran leaders signed the Augsburg Confession (1530), while in 1580 the Formula of Concord, a substantial volume of nearly 500 pages, was widely subscribed as "our teaching, belief and confession." Nevertheless, it was insisted that the "writings of the Old and New Testaments are the only rule and norm according to which all doctrines and teachers alike must be appraised and judged . . . whatever is contrary to them should be opposed and rejected. . . ."[10] In 1552 Andreas Osiander (1498–1552) had objected to the requirement of subscription to the Augsburg Confession by doctoral candidates in Wittenberg on the grounds that it smacked of popery. Subscription was justified by Melanchthon as sanctioned by Luther and necessary because of the heresies of the age. Indeed, Osiander's own presentation of several doctrines might well explain why this disputatious Lutheran chaffed at a definite subscription.[11]

Calvin signed Melanchthon's revision of the Augsburg Confession – the *Variata* (1540) – following change in its teaching about the Lord's Supper. Peter Lillback has argued that Calvin's subscription to this confession can only have been "in-so-far-as" not "because" it agreed with the word of God.[12] But this seems to me a harsh judgment. Conceivably Calvin signed the *Variata,* because it was good as far as it went, and his signature could be helpful in the peculiar political circumstances of the Protestant cause at the time with the division over the Lord's Supper. One need not infer he thought lightly of its content, but rather thought

---

[10] Formula of Concord, Part 1: Epitome as in *The Book of Concord*, ed. T. G. Tappert (Philadelphia: Fortress Press, 1979), 464-65.

[11] Cf. the entry in *The New Schaff-Herzog Encyclopedia of Religious Knowledge* (13 vols.; Grand Rapids: Baker, 1977), 8:280-81.

[12] Peter A. Lillback, "Confessional Subscription," 45-46, 59-60. Whatever the view one takes of Calvin's act, Lillback's conclusion that since fallen people compose confessions we may not dare give more than an "in-so-far-as" subscription (p. 62) seems unguarded.

it inadequate for the steady anchoring of church life in the fullness of the word of God, and hence later opposed its adoption in lieu of a fuller statement.

All of the early Reformed catechisms and confessional statements aim to faithfully represent the teaching of Scripture to which they express their loyalty. Some specifically indicate a readiness to amend anything not in agreement with Scripture. The First Confession of Basel (1534) closes its twelve articles thus: "We submit this our Confession to the judgment of the divine Scriptures, and hold ourselves ready always thankfully to obey God and his Word if we should be corrected out of said Holy Scriptures."[13] In 1536 many of the Reformed cities of Switzerland drew up and presented "a short and common Confession of Faith to all believing and godly men for their consideration and judgment" in twenty-seven articles that we call the First Helvetic Confession, the first five of which relate to Scripture.[14] At the close of the text is added:

> A declaration of witnessing of our mind. It is not our mind for to prescribe by these chapters a certain rule of the faith to all churches and congregations, for we know no other rule of faith but the holy scripture and therefore we are well contented with them that agreeth with these things, howbeit they be in another manner of speaking or confession different apartly to this of ours in words, for rather should the matter be considered than the words. And therefore we make it free for all men to use their own sort of speaking as they shall perceive most profitable for their churches, and we shall use the same liberty. And if any man shall attempt to corrupt the true meaning of this our confession he shall hear both a confession and a defence of the verity and truth. It was

---

[13] Philip Schaff, *The Creeds of Christendom* (3 vols.; New York: Harper & Row, 1931), 1:387.

[14] English text in Jaroslav Pelikan and Valerie R. Hotchkiss, eds., *Creeds and Confessions of Faith in the Christian Tradition* (4 vols.; New Haven: Yale University Press, 2003), 3:280ff.

our pleasure to use these words at this present time that we might declare our opinion in our religion and worshipping of God.[15]

The Scots Confession (1560) states in its Preface:

[I]f any man will note in our Confession any chapter or sentence contrary to God's Holy Word, that it would please him of his gentleness and for Christian charity's sake to inform us of it in writing; and we, upon our honour, do promise him that by God's grace we shall give him satisfaction from the mouth of God, that is, from Holy Scripture, or else we shall alter whatever he can prove to be wrong.[16]

In 1536 Calvin drew up a brief confession which citizens of Geneva were required "to keep and hold." It begins, "First, we declare that we desire to follow Scripture alone as rule of our faith and religion . . ." and it became the basis for the Geneva Catechism of 1541/42. This Catechism was published in its final form in 1545, and was formally subscribed by the Genevan clergy in 1561. The Gallican or French Confession drawn up by Calvin in 1559 was subscribed at La Rochelle in 1571. Other Confessions followed, such as the Belgic Confession (1561), and the Second Helvetic (1566). In these documents there are strong statements concerning the authority of Scripture as the rule of faith, human authority in doctrinal matters is rejected, and Scripture as the judge in religious controversies is insisted upon.[17]

The earliest subscription formula now known from among the Dutch churches dates from 1608 and the rise of Arminian

---

[15] *The confescion of the fayth of the Sweserla[n]des* (London: T.B., 1548) unpaginated; this was the translation by George Wishart (1499–1546) from the Latin. I have modernized the spelling. In Schaff, *Creeds*, 1:389, it is said: "It seems that Bullinger and Leo Judae wished to add a caution against the binding authority of this or any other confession that might interfere with the supreme authority of the Word of God and with Christian liberty." The Swiss-German text of this "caution," which Schaff states is not found in any copy, is given from Hagenbach and Niemeyer in a footnote. It was presumably in the Latin copy from which Wishart translated.

[16] *The Scots Confession of 1560*, trans. James Bullough (Edinburgh: St. Andrew Press, 1991), 4.

[17] See French Confession, Article 5; Belgic Confession, Article 7; Second Helvetic Confession, Chapter 2.

thinking. In regard to the Heidelberg Catechism and the Belgic Confession, subscribers held that the teaching in these "agrees in everything with the Holy Word of God, and consequently with the foundation of the teaching of salvation," so that the teaching was to be maintained and contrary doctrines opposed.[18] The Synod of Dort in 1619 elaborated a subscription form which also provided for the resolution of difficulties arising from a change of view or suspicion of deviation.[19]

The Thirty-Nine Articles of the Church of England (1563–1571) are perhaps not as thorough going on Scripture, yet they sufficiently emphasize that "it is not lawful for the Church to ordain anything that is contrary to God's word written" (Article 20). The Irish Articles (1615) begin by stating: "The ground of our religion and the rule of faith and all saving truth is the Word of God, contained in the Holy Scripture." In the Westminster Confession (1646) the same note is sounded (1.8), and emphasis is placed on decisions of Synods and Councils as helps to faith rather than the rule of faith (31.4).

This brief survey not only shows that a distinction was drawn between Scripture as the rule or norm for faith, and confessions as statements of Scripture's teaching, but that the unity of the church was not regarded as consisting in the identity of documents but in the agreement in doctrine. That may exist though the confession be different in form. Thus, in September 1566, the Scottish Church approved the Second Helvetic Confession, except in regard to Article 24 concerning observing several holy days, and ordered the translation by Robert Pont [1524–1606] to be published.[20] Knox's continuator records:

---

[18] W. Robert Godfrey, "Subscription in the Dutch Reformed Tradition," in *The Practice of Confessional* Subscription, ed. David W. Hall (Oak Ridge: Covenant Foundation, 2001), 68-69.

[19] Ibid., 69-71.

[20] If the work was printed, no copy is now known. An English translation was published in London in 1571 along with the French Confession of 1559 with a preface by Theodore Beza. *A confession of faith, made by divers reformed churches beyond the seas. With an exhortation to the reformation of the church.*

The Churches of Geneva, Berne, and Basle, with other Reformed Churches of Germany and France, sent to the whole Church of Scotland the sum of the Confession of their Faith, desiring to know if they agreed in uniformity of doctrine, alleging that the Church of Scotland was dissonant in some articles from them. Wherefore the Superintendents, with a great part of the other most qualified ministers, convened in September at St Andrews, and reading the said letters, made answer, and sent word again, that they agreed in all points with those Churches, and differed in nothing from them; albeit in the keeping of some festival days our Church assented not, for only the Sabbath day was kept in Scotland.[21]

The Second Helvetic Confession is over four times longer than the Scots Confession but it was readily approved. Five of the six who drew up the Scots Confession of 1560 were among the forty-one signatories to the letter in reply sent to Theodore Beza. The Scots also used Calvin's Catechism from the beginning, while the Genevan Confession (1536) functioned as a summary of doctrine within the Scottish *Book of Common Order* adopted in 1564.[22] Further, the Heidelberg Catechism of 1563 was printed in English in 1615 and used in parts of Scotland. These facts highlight the common factor of commitment to a form of doctrine whether briefly or elaborately expressed. In 1571 the first national synod of the Dutch church adopted the Belgic Confession but also, as a testimony of unity with the French church, the French Confession, in the hope that the French would act similarly and approve the Belgic Confession.[23] This international aspect is also seen in the

---

Perused and allowed according to the Queenes majesties injunctions, trans. John Old (London: Lucas Hanson, 1571).

[21] John Knox, *The History of the Reformation in Scotland*, ed. W. C. Dickinson (2 vols.; Edinburgh: Thomas Nelson, 1949), 2:190. See also David Calderwood, *History of the Kirk of Scotland*, ed. Thomas Thompson (8 vols.; Edinburgh: Woodrow Society, 1845), 2:331-32.

[22] J. Ligon Duncan, "Owning the Confession: Subscription in the Scottish Presbyterian Tradition," in *The Practice of Confessional Subscription*, ed. David W. Hall (Oak Ridge: Covenant Foundation, 2001), 79 and see fn. 8.

[23] W. Robert Godfrey, "Subscription in the Dutch Reformed Tradition," 67.

presence of German, Swiss, and English delegates at the Synod of Dort in 1618/19. The concern for doctrine rather than documents is also seen in 1647 when the General Assembly of the Church of Scotland approved the Westminster Confession judging it "to be most agreeable to the word of God and in nothing contrary to the received doctrine, worship, discipline and government of this Kirk."

The Acceptance of the Westminster Confession

The Solemn League and Covenant was approved by the Assembly of the Church of Scotland in 1643, as also by the Westminster Assembly, and sought

> the preservation of the reformed religion in the Church of Scotland, in doctrine, worship, discipline and government against our common enemies; the reformation of religion in the kingdoms of England and Ireland, in doctrine worship, discipline and government according to the word of God and the example of the best reformed Churches; and shall endeavour to bring the Churches of God in the three kingdoms to the nearest conjunction and uniformity in religion, confession of faith, form of church-government, directory for worship and catechising; that we and our posterity after us, may, as brethren, live in faith and love, and the Lord may delight to dwell in the midst of us.

The Solemn League and Covenant was ratified by Parliament in 1644 and renewed by all ranks in 1648. It was widely signed in Scotland, and there was overwhelming support there for the reforms of the 1640s.

England

In England, during the reign of Edward VI (1547–1553), there was considerable freedom in liturgical practice, but under Elizabeth (1558–1603) this was much curtailed. The requirements of conformity under her and her successors certainly created problems of conscience, and to that extent might have led to scruples as to the propriety of imposing detailed doctrinal tests,[24] certainly on the common people. The mere holding of a heretical opinion ceased to be censurable in 1640, but the distinct issues of toleration and liberty of conscience were not yet worked through.

The intention in the 1640s was to settle the religious issue by thorough reform of the national church. Popery and prelacy were suppressed, but each remaining party was keen for its own form, and Parliament was holding the reins as well. One must fully appreciate that the Westminster Confession is a document intended to safeguard the Calvinistic consensus on the twin-covenant scheme. It would be anachronistic to suggest departure from its teaching was contemplated in the religious uniformity it sought to secure.

In the Form of Presbyterial Church Government of the Westminster Assembly (1644), the form for ordination reads:

---

[24] Anthony Tuckney, a member of the Assembly, did not wish the Confession to be publicly preached or written against, but voted against a proposal to swear to or subscribe the Confession, "our having been burnt in the hand in that kind before" – cited from his letter to Benjamin Witchcote in Thomas McCrie, *Annals of English Presbytery* (London: Nisbet, 1872), 221. Tuckney may have been thinking of the danger of being entangled by words. In a sermon on 2 Tim. 1:13, commended by the Divines who recommended the Rothwel edition of 1658 (currently in print by the FP Church of Scotland), he states: "Though every Title and Iota in it [Scripture] is sacred yet it is the kernel of the doctrine and not so much the shell of the words that we stand upon." *A Good Day Well Improved* (London: S. Gellibrand, 1656), 250. Richard Baxter, not a member of the Assembly, wrote a commendation of the Confession and Catechisms which Thomas Manton incorporated in his recommendatory preface to the Rothwel edition omitting Baxter's words: "I hoped that the Assembly intended not all that long Confession and those Catechisms to be imposed as a Test of Christian Communion; nor to disown all that scrupled any word in it; if I had I could not have commended it for such use, though it be useful for the instruction of families, etc." *Reliquiae Baxterianae, or Mr. Richard Baxter's Narrative of the Most Memorable Passages of his Life and* Times, ed. Matthew Sylvester (London: For T. Parkhurst, J. Robinson, J. Lawrence, and J. Dunton, 1696), 222. This does not touch the Westminster Standards as a test of ministerial communion based on the adherence to their doctrine.

The minister who hath preached shall, in the face of the congregation, demand of him who is now to be ordained concerning his faith in Christ Jesus, and his persuasion of the truth of the reformed religion according to Scripture.[25]

This verbal adherence appears to have been the practice in England[26] since, when Parliament approved the Confession in 1648, minus 20.4, 23.4 (from "much less"), 24.5, 6 and chapters 30 and 31, no formula of subscription was imposed, despite the London ministers voluntarily indicating their assent to it in December 1647 when desiring the Confession be made law. In fact, it only became "the public Confession of the Church of England" in 1660 by action of the "rump" Parliament (minus chapters 30 and 31), but almost at once was put aside with the Restoration of the monarchy.[27]

Ireland

Archbishop Ussher, the Calvinist Anglican much admired by many Scots and Puritans, who had embraced Presbyterians within the Church of Ireland, was in England at the time of the outbreak of the Civil War (1642) and did not return. The structure of the Episcopal Church of Ireland had collapsed, but the invasion by the Parliamentary forces to put down the rebellion of 1641 was also a factor bringing radicals into the picture, as well as enabling the forming of a presbytery in 1642 at Carrickfergus from chaplains and soldier-elders with the army. Presbyterians secured ministers from Scotland from 1645.

---

[25] In the (Westminster) *Form of Church Government* (November 1644) the candidate must have subscribed the Solemn League and Covenant. Note also: "Let none be called, but they that have first subscribed the confession of Doctrine and Discipline" in *A Directory of Church-government. Anciently contended for, and as farre as the Times would suffer, practiced by the first Non-conformists in the daies of Queen Elizabeth* found in Thomas Cartwright's study after his death (1603) and often attributed to Walter Travers (London, February 1644), unpaginated.

[26] McCrie, *Annals*, 223.

[27] The *Savoy Declaration* of the Independents in 1658 was a slight revision of the Parliamentary text.

Political factors were highly relevant with the Scots backing Charles against the English Parliament at the end of 1647 and the resultant Second Civil War. Only six ministers were left in Ulster when the rest were forced out in 1650 for refusing to take an oath abjuring the monarchy. Still, the basics of Presbyterian structure were laid in this period. Of the few records, we have one dated February 22, 1658, which refers to "acknowledging the Scriptures as inspired by God, of infallible authority, the perfect Rule of Faith and Life . . ." retaining the

> Sum of Christian Faith, called the Apostles Creed; as being agreeable to the word of God: which creed they have long since Received . . . And that they receive and hold fast that excellent Confession of Faith, comprised in thirty and three chapters, and compiled by the assembly of Divines for these three nations, as their own Confession of Faith in all the said Congregations (Reserving only to some of us our Liberty of Judgement about a few expressions touching Discipline laid down in that Confession): it being, A Form of Sound Words very consonant to Holy Scripture; and of special use, both for preserving the unity of the Faith amongst us, and for Obviating of Old and Novel errors.[28]

Scotland

In Scotland too, politics from time to time affected attitudes to subscription. For example, there was concern about infiltration of Roman Catholics which led to the Negative Confession subscribed by persons of all classes in 1581, 1590, 1638, and 1639. This Negative Confession rejected current errors and affirmed: "to the which [Scots] Confession and Form of Religion we willingly agree in our conscience in all points, as unto God's undoubted truth and verity, grounded only upon his written word. And therefore we

---

[28] *The Agreement and Resolution of the Ministers of Christ Associated in the City of Dublin, and Province of Leinster; for the furthering of a real and thorough Reformation According to the written Word of God* (Dublin: W. Bladon, 1659), 6-7.

abhor and detest all contrary religion and doctrine. . . ." In 1616 the king imposed a new Confession[29] but this was swept aside by the Presbyterians at the Assembly of 1638 since, although it was Calvinistic, it had not been competently passed into church law and the subscription seemed to endorse the episcopal corruptions the king had introduced.

The Westminster Confession was adopted by the Church of Scotland on August 27, 1647 with certain qualifications (see below). Although it was not formalized by personal addition of actual signatures, it was the avowed confession of the Kirk, and was also approved by the Scottish Parliament on February 7, 1649, and ordained to be "recorded, published and practiced."

In the following outline of the history of subscription, it will be seen that a strict acceptance of the Confession was required by the (Presbyterian) Church of Scotland, and was increasingly formalized, with a gradual breaking down occurring under the onslaught of critical views from about 1870. In other English-speaking lands, where the Presbyterian Church was not the established church, there tended to be a measure of informality in subscription which was tightened when fears of doctrinal error were abroad. In the latter part of the 19th century something of a fall back to an evangelical consensus over against anti-supernaturalism occurred. A further fall back to liberal-evangelicalism was characteristic of the period about 1900: the supernatural facts at the heart of redemption were accepted, but higher critical views of Scripture and an Arminian or even moral influence theory of the atonement became common. In the larger churches subscription was lax from 1880 to 1900. A further fall back to liberal theology from about 1920 was broken by neo-orthodoxy about 1948 with a resurgence

---

[29] Text in Calderwood, *History of the Kirk of Scotland*, 7:233-42. It began, "We believe with our hearts, and confess with our mouths, these articles of religion following . . ." claimed that the Church of Scotland in doctrine and worship was the "one of the most pure kirks under heaven" and concluded with a promise "to continue therein to the end of our life . . . understanding them plainly as they are conceived, without equivocation or mental reservation whatsoever."

of the older Reformed theology of the Confession occurring from the mid 1960s.

Subscription in Scotland[30]

The Assembly of the Church of Scotland in 1647 approved the *Westminster Confession of Faith* as agreeable to the word of God and in nothing contrary to the previously received doctrine of the Church. This approval was as to "the truth of the matter"; that is, it involved acceptance of the doctrines expressed by the language of the Confession. Certain qualifications on matters related to the power of the civil magistrate were also made. It is evident that the Assembly regarded the Confession as binding as regards the entire doctrine, other than as qualified.

Act approving the Confession of Faith [August 27, 1647]

A CONFESSION OF FAITH for the Kirks of God in the three kingdoms, being the chiefest part of that uniformity in religion which, by the Solemn League and Covenant, we are bound to endeavour:

AND there being accordingly a Confession of Faith agreed upon by the Assembly of Divines sitting at Westminster, with the assistance of Commissioners from the Kirk of Scotland; which Confession was sent from our Commissioners at London to the Commissioners of the Kirk met at Edinburgh in January last, and hath been in this Assembly twice publickly read over, examined, and considered; copies thereof being also printed, that it might

---

[30] As well as the Acts of the various Scottish Churches see the listing and commentary in *The Proceedings of the Second General Council of the Presbyterian Alliance* (Philadelphia, 1880), 965-1036; James Cooper, *Confessions of Faith and Formulas of Subscription* (Glasgow: James Maclehose, 1907); A. I. C. Heron, ed., *The Westminster Confession in the Church Today* (Edinburgh: St. Andrews Press, 1982), 17-27, 132-40 and Appendix; K. R. Ross, *Church and Creed in Scotland: The Free Church Case 1900-1904 and Its Origins* (Edinburgh: Rutherford House, 1988); Ian Hamilton, *The Erosion of Calvinist Orthodoxy: Seceders and Subscription in Scottish Presbyterianism* (Edinburgh: Rutherford House, 1990); J. Ligon Duncan, "Owning the Confession," 77-91.

be particularly perused by all the members of this assembly, unto whom frequent intimation was publickly made, to put in their doubts and objections, if they had any:

AND the said Confession being, upon due examination thereof, found by the assembly to be most agreeable to the word of God, and in nothing contrary to the received doctrine, worship, discipline, and government of the Kirk.

AND, lastly, It being so necessary, and so much longed for, that the said Confession be, with all possible diligence and expedition, approved and established in both kingdoms, as a principal part of the intended uniformity in religion, and as a special means for the more effectual suppressing of the many dangerous errors and heresies of these times;

THE GENERAL ASSEMBLY DOTH THEREFORE, after mature deliberation, agree unto, and approve the said Confession, as to the truth of the matter; (judging it to be most orthodox, and grounded upon the word of God); and also, as to the point of uniformity, agreeing for our part, that it be a common Confession of Faith for the three kingdoms.

THE ASSEMBLY DOTH ALSO bless the Lord, and thankfully acknowledge his great mercy, in that so excellent a Confession of Faith is prepared, and thus far agreed upon in both kingdoms; which we look upon as a great strengthening of the true reformed religion against the common enemies thereof.

BUT, lest our intention and meaning be in some particulars misunderstood, it is hereby expressly declared and provided,

THAT the not mentioning in this Confession the several sorts of ecclesiastical officers and assemblies, shall be no prejudice to the truth of Christ in these particulars, to be expressed fully in the Directory of Government.

IT IS FURTHER DECLARED, That the Assembly understandeth some parts of the second article of the thirty-one chapter only of kirks not settled, or constituted in point of government: And that although, in such kirks, a synod of Ministers, and other fit persons, may be called by the Magistrate's authority and nomination, without any other call, to consult and advise with about matters of religion; and although, likewise, the Ministers of Christ, without delegation from their churches, may of themselves, and by virtue of their office, meet together synodically in such kirks not yet constituted, yet neither of these ought to be done in kirks constituted and settled; it being always free to the Magistrate to advise with synods of Ministers and Ruling Elders, meeting upon delegation from their churches, either ordinarily, or, being indicted by his authority, occasionally, and *pro re nata*; it being also free to assemble together synodically, as well *pro re nata* as at the ordinary times, upon delegation from the churches, by the intrinsical power received from Christ, as often as it is necessary for the good of the Church so to assemble, in case the Magistrate, to the detriment of the Church, withhold or deny his consent; the necessity of occasional assemblies being first remonstrate unto him by humble supplication.

The Revolution Settlement of the Scottish Church in 1690 meant that the obligation of the covenants fell away, but the Confession of Faith was again ratified. As part of "securing the true Protestant religion, according to the truth of God's word, as it hath of long time been professed in this land," Parliament resolved to "ratify and establish" the Confession of Faith anew as "the public and avowed Confession of this Church containing the sum and substance of the doctrine of the Reformed Churches."[31] This sum and substance is not an element of the Confession's teaching, but the total of the doctrine expressed by the words of the Confession.

---

[31] Act 7 June 1690, Ratifying the Confession of Faith, and settling Presbyterian Church Government. It should be noted "that 'the sum and substance of the doctrine of the Reformed Churches,' so far as concerns the church of Scotland, is the Confession of Faith as it stands, neither more nor less." William Mair, *A Digest of Laws and Decisions Ecclesiastical and Civil Relating to the Constitution, Practice and Affairs of the Church of Scotland* (Edinburgh: William Blackwood & Sons, 1923), 10. The "sum and substance" means that the Confession contains a summary of the heart of the teaching of the Reformed

Two extremes did not accept the Settlement. Some thousand or so people in the southwest thought the failure to maintain the covenants was wrong, and, with some justification, they regarded the settlement as involving Erastianism.[32] They had a significant influence on many sympathizers in the Established Church. Their protest eventually resulted in the formation of the Reformed Presbyterian Church (1743), and adherence to the Westminster Confession and Catechisms was characteristic of them, along with a testimony to exhibit and apply their understanding of the Confession and the obligations of the Solemn League and Covenant. A very much larger number, particularly in the north-east, were Episcopal in sympathy, and all the bishops and most clergy ("non-jurors") refused to swear an oath of allegiance to William and Mary. William Carstares (1649–1715) was the key leader in steering the church safely through this difficult situation until the Presbyterian Church in Scotland was secure.

The 1690 Assembly included sixty ministers ordained before Presbyterianism was suppressed in 1662, fifty-six ministers ordained by them in the years of trouble, and forty-seven elders, yet there were 926 parishes. The Assembly required that preachers and elders "be obliged to subscribe their approbation of the Confession of Faith." Few of the ministers who had served during Episcopacy retained their parish – 664 parishes were deprived of their ministers between 1688 and 1716,[33] although Episcopal men who would not conform but would take an oath of allegiance by September 1, 1695, were allowed to officiate but not to be

---

churches, and thus it is the doctrine, not the precise forms of expression of the doctrine, that is adhered to. James Cooper, *Confessions of Faith and Formulas of Subscription*, 36, 46-47 wants to go somewhat beyond this without justification in my view.

[32] Note the *Historic Testimony* (1839) of the Reformed Presbyterian Church (Glasgow: George Gallie, 1866), 97-105. The majority of the RP Church joined the Free Church of Scotland in 1876.

[33] A. L. Drummond and James Bulloch, *The Scottish Church 1688-1843* (Edinburgh: St. Andrew Press, 1973), 9.

members of church courts. There were still 154 in this category in 1703.[34]

Initially the religious difference was over church government only; worship practices of the Episcopalians were the same as the Presbyterians. Parliament legislated for subscription by ministers and preachers in 1693, and the Assembly enacted legislation in the following year (text below). In 1696 the Assembly passed an "Act against the Atheistical opinions of the Deists . . .," and forbade ministers and church members from teaching, preaching, printing, or speaking "any doctrine, tenet, or opinion contrary unto, or inconsistent with, the Confession of Faith of this Church, or any article, part, or proposition therein" on pain of censure. In 1697 an Act to restrict sudden lawful changes without due consideration was enacted by the Assembly (commonly called the Barrier Act). Some ministers had still not subscribed the Confession in 1699. From 1700 the formula was to be subscribed by any such and by ruling elders. Teachers and professors were required to subscribe the Confession in 1707. (The office of deacon was in disuse as a consequence of the financial support of the Church by the State.) All this indicates something of the difficulties of the time.

Increasingly, liturgical innovations were introduced by the Episcopalians. In 1707 the *Act Against Innovations* was passed, and in 1711 prescribed questions and a formula rather more explicit of the commitment implied in the 1694 formula were introduced for ministers, and the 1694 formula was retained for elders. These measures all had in view securing Presbyterianism in very unsettled times. In 1712 Queen Anne gave toleration to Episcopalians who pledged allegiance, but they alienated their people by their liturgical practices, and the support of non-jurors for the Jacobite cause proved disastrous for popular episcopacy (cf. The Rising of 1715).

A. C. Cheyne states:

---

[34] A. I. Dunlop, *William Carstares and the Kirk by Law Established* (Edinburgh: St. Andrew Press, 1967), 89, 104.

Not long after the 1707 Union of the Parliaments, resurgent English Toryism – bent upon the destruction, or at the very least the reconstruction, of the Revolution Settlement throughout the United Kingdom – was seeking by every means at its disposal to restore Episcopalian fortunes in Scotland. The Kirk felt understandably imperilled and insecure, and responded with harshly restrictive measures.[35]

The substance of Cheyne's comment is correct, but one doubts that the new subscription terms of 1711 were "harshly restrictive." I find it quite striking that after the 1707 Treaty of Union, which was supposed to leave the Establishment where it was in law, the church took measures bearing on its position which purport to be more stringent. Still, one supposes the church was really only bringing out the implications of where it had always stood against challenges from the kind of conduct that had caused so much strife in the previous century.[36]

In 1694 it was enough to "own" the Confession and declare it the Confession of your faith, to promise to observe uniformity of worship, and "own and acknowledge" the Presbyterian government. In the 1711 version one must "own and believe" the "whole" doctrine of the Confession; "own" the worship "presently authorised and practised, and asserted in the 15th Act"; "own" the Presbyterian government; affirm the scriptural basis of the doctrine, worship, discipline, and government of the church; and specifically renounce whatever is contrary or inconsistent with it.

The church had always expected its ministers to adhere to the doctrine of the Confession and had not allowed exceptions. The new formula was not really novel, although it helpfully emphasized

---

[35] A. C. Cheyne, *Studies in Scottish Church History* (Edinburgh: T&T Clark, 1999), 73.

[36] Note Dunlop's comment, *William Carstares and the Kirk by Law Established*, 131-32: "These questions never had parliamentary sanction, and this fact perhaps gives an indication of how Carstares would have had the Church slowly loosen its Erastian bonds."

the foundation of that doctrine in Scripture. In regard to church government the rejection of divisive courses was an extra, although it hardly added a great deal to what was there already. In regard to worship, the word "own" means "accept" in this context, so the changes on worship aimed to strengthen attachment to it so as to make it more difficult to work for its replacement with something different in kind.

The reference to the Act of Assembly 1707 is important. The third of the prescribed questions reads:

> Do you sincerely own the purity of worship presently authorised and practised in this Church, and asserted in the 15th Act of the General Assembly, 1707, entitled 'Act Against Innovations in the Worship of God'; and do you also own the Presbyterian government and discipline now so happily established in this Church; and are you persuaded that the said doctrine, worship, discipline and government are founded upon the Holy Scriptures and agreeable thereto?

It should be noted that this question does not imply that one accepts a divinely mandated view of the worship or government of the church, beyond the relevant statements on these subjects in the Confession of Faith. Further, in regard to the key expression – "authorised and practised" – the assumption in the questions and formula is that what is practiced is authorized and what is authorized is practiced, and so practiced must mean lawfully practiced. What is lawfully practiced as regards worship is to be found in the word of God. The Confession of Faith highlights the necessity of divine prescription, although recognizing that there are some circumstances "common to human actions and societies, which are to be regulated by the light of nature and Christian prudence, according to the general rules of the word, which are always to be observed" (1.6). The Directory for Public Worship, while it is not directly subscribed, further sets out the aspects of public worship and outlines in a general way how it might be conducted.

Formula of subscription for preachers [April 13, 1694]	**Formula, to be subscribed by all such as shall pass trials, in order to be licensed, and that shall be ordained ministers, or admitted to parishes** [May 22, 1711]
I, , do sincerely own and declare the above Confession of Faith, approven by former General Assemblies of this Church, and ratified by law in the year 1690, to be the Confession of my faith;	I, , do hereby declare, that I do sincerely own and believe the whole doctrine contained in the Confession of Faith, approved by the General Assemblies of this National Church, and ratified by law in the year 1690, and frequently confirmed by divers Acts of Parliament since that time, to be the truths of God; and I do own the same as the confession of my faith: As likewise, I do own the purity of worship presently authorised and practised in this Church and asserted in Act 15th General Assembly 1707, and also the Presbyterian government and discipline now so happily established therein; which doctrine, worship, and Church government, I am persuaded are founded on the Word of God, and agreeable thereto: And I promise, that, through the grace of God, I shall firmly and constantly adhere to the same, and to the utmost of my power, shall, in my station, assert, maintain, and defend the said doctrine, worship, discipline, and government of this Church, by Kirk-sessions, Presbyteries, Provincial Synods and General Assemblies; and that I shall in my practice conform myself to the said worship, and submit to the said discipline and government, and never endeavour, directly nor indirectly, the prejudice or subversion of the same; and I promise, that I shall follow no divisive courses from the present establishment in this Church; renouncing all doctrines, tenets, and opinions whatsoever, contrary to, or inconsistent with, the said doctrine, worship, discipline, or government of this Church.
and that I own the doctrine therein contained to be the true doctrine, which I will constantly adhere to; as likewise, that I own	
and acknowledge Presbyterian Church government of this Church, now settled by law,	
by Kirk-sessions, Presbyteries, Provincial Synods and General Assemblies, to be the only government of this Church, and that I will submit thereto, concur therewith, and never endeavour, directly or indirectly, the prejudice or subversion thereof; and that I shall observe uniformity of worship, and of the administration of all public ordinances within this Church, as the same are at present performed and allowed.	

The *Act Against Innovations* of 1707 further assists in determining what is "authorised and practiced." It notes that the Acts of Parliament in 1690 and 1693 and in 1707[37] provided for the purity and uniformity of worship, but that reports from various presbyteries indicate that innovations in the public worship of God have been promoted "by persons of known disaffection to the present Establishment both of Church and State," that such innovations are both dangerous to the church "and manifestly contrary to our known principle (which is, that nothing is to be admitted in the worship of God but what is prescribed in the Holy Scriptures)" and, accordingly, the practice of them is forbidden, and all proper means to suppress and remove them are to be taken.[38] In 1708 there was a threatened invasion of the French to aid the Jacobite cause, and in 1715 an uprising.

The 1711 Formula has everything to do with resurgent Episcopal practice, including use of the Prayer Book.[39] As it turned out, episcopacy soon lost much of its following and was no longer a serious threat by the 1720s.[40] On the other hand, the Church of

---

[37] The Treaty of Union, by which Scotland became part of the United Kingdom in 1707, provided through the Act of Security that there be no change in the religious settlement: "The true Protestant religion contained in the above mentioned Confession of Faith . . . shall remain and continue unalterable."

[38] This paragraph and the preceding one are largely drawn from and agree with the advice given to the Synod of the Presbyterian Church of Eastern Australia, and recorded on page 20 of the printed minutes of Synod 1969, by F. M. Bradshaw, MA, LLM, the Honorary Procurator of the Synod (1942–92) and also of the General Assembly of the Presbyterian Church of Australia (1959-92).

[39] "After the union the English Book of Common Prayer began to be used extensively in Aberdeen, Elgin, Montrose, and Inverness districts. This led to the passing of the Act against Innovations by the General Assembly of 1707." A. I. Dunlop, *William Carstares and the Kirk by Law Established*, 127fn. Of course few Episcopalians used the prayers for the Queen. The Act has nothing to do with the introduction in a lawful way of a new Psalter, contrary to claims of recent times. Indeed, the Assembly of the Church of Scotland itself envisaged supplementing the materials of public praise. See Rowland S. Ward, *The Psalms in Christian Worship* (Melbourne: Presbyterian Church of Eastern Australia, 1992), 84-86.

[40] "In all the years until 1715 the issue was in doubt as to what the final church government would be; Carstares knew the real possibility of losing the struggle and made it his task to nurse the Revolution Settlement until the Episcopalians,

Scotland was infected with problems arising from the intellectual currents of the age. The gospel was not infrequently seen as a new law (neo-nomianism), the freedom of presentation of Christ to sinners was muted, and discipline was neglected. Two separations resulted: the Secession of 1733, and the deposition of Thomas Gillespie in 1752 which led to the forming of the Presbytery of Relief. Renewal of evangelical life in the Established Church came in the 19th century.

Nevertheless, it is striking that there was no outbreak of Arianism in Scotland in the same way as in England and Ireland (and also in Europe). Robert Wodrow (1679–1734) thought strict subscription had kept Scotland free from the anti-subscription efforts elsewhere in the Calvinist world.[41] William Dunlop's publication of the formularies of the Church of Scotland in 1719 with a lengthy preface vindicating confessions of faith and subscription to them doubtlessly contributed.[42] This is an able piece of work by the young Professor of Ecclesiastical History at Edinburgh, deliberately[43] using arguments from "the common Principles of Reason, and the natural inalienable Rights of Mankind" to rebut arguments emanating from the non-subscribers at Salter's Hall.[44] At the same time there are some passing critical references to the confusing terminology of the Marrow of Modern Divinity[45] which had been

---

who were for the most part Jacobites, would make an unwise move. In 1715 they made one and thereafter the Settlement was secure." A. I. Dunlop, *William Carstares and the Kirk by Law Established*, 80.

[41] Wodrow's *Correspondence*, (3 vols.; Edinburgh, 1843), 237, as cited in Colin Kidd, "Scotland's Invisible Enlightenment: Subscription and Heterodoxy in the Eighteenth Century Kirk" in *Scottish Church History Society Records* 30, (2000): 49.

[42] Dunlop's work was *A Collection of Confessions of Faith, Catechisms, Directories . . .* (Edinburgh: James Watson, 1719). The Preface is paginated v-cxiv plus an index, and is a capable piece of work. The *Preface*, edited by Dr. James Bannerman, was republished in London in 1857.

[43] Ibid., lii.

[44] Ibid., x, civ.

[45] Ibid., cxxxv.

republished in 1718. It is not surprising that it called forth the criticism of James Kid, a strong Marrowman, as well as the non-subscribers,[46] but the validity of the argument was unaffected.

Dunlop states that "All the doctrines then which any Church, and particularly ours, place in their Confessions, are or ought to be the very Doctrines of Christianity, revealed in the Holy Scriptures; and we hope with us that they are the Things themselves, tho' not the precise words whereby they are expressed [in Holy Scripture]."[47] He notes that confessions of faith are not intended to give an account of what God says, but of what a person or church believes, and thus they are an expression of faith as understood by the subscriber. Whereas Scripture is the "perpetual and universal Rule of Faith" and so not confined to the circumstances of a particular time or place, a confession is adapted to the particular state of a nation, the errors of that age, and the ways words are used. "And so according to the Variety of Cases, some phrases may be proper in one case which in another would entirely miss the End, and different Churches may see fit for them to make alteration in their Creeds, and use different Expressions."[48] Thus: "We don't pretend that our Confession is carried to a pitch of unblemished perfection; and that it might not have been amended or adjusted, with greater wisdom and accuracy, to all the designs of such composures."[49]

The Disruption of 1843 and Its Aftermath

After the Ten Years Conflict, in 1843, nearly 40 percent of the ministers of the Established Church of Scotland withdrew [the

---

[46] Colin Kidd, "Scotland's Invisible Enlightenment," 39. After referring to negative reaction from a conservative like Kid to Dunlop's Preface, Dr. Kidd comments, "However, it is a tribute to Dunlop's slipperiness that he should also attract liberal opposition to his defence of human standards." This is both unjust and unscholarly.

[47] *Collection of Confessions*, xxxiv.

[48] Ibid., c.

[49] Ibid., cxxx.

Disruption] and formed the Church of Scotland Free – that is, free from encroachments of the civil authorities on the rights of Christ in his church as hitherto understood. The Free Church of Scotland sought to maintain the original position. As she was not endowed, the office of deacon was revived. The Formula of 1711 was adjusted to the new situation, and subscription was required of all office-bearers:[50]

> ### *Formula of the Free Church of Scotland* [adopted 1846]
> I do hereby declare, that I do sincerely own and believe the whole doctrine contained in the Confession of Faith, approven by the General Assemblies of the Church of Scotland, to be the truths of God; and I do own the same as the confession of my faith; as likewise, I do own the purity of worship presently authorised and practised in the Free Church of Scotland, and also the Presbyterian government and discipline thereof; which doctrine, worship, and church government, I am persuaded, are founded upon the Word of God, and agreeable thereto; I also approve of the general principles respecting the jurisdiction of the Church and her subjection to Christ as her only Head, which are contained in the Claim of Right, and in the Protest, referred to in the questions already put to me; and I promise, that, through the grace of God, I shall firmly and constantly adhere to the same, and to the utmost of my power, shall in my station, assert, maintain, and defend the said doctrine, worship, discipline, and government of this Church, by Kirk-sessions, Presbyteries, Provincial Synods and General Assemblies, together with the liberty and exclusive jurisdiction thereof; and that I shall, in my practice, conform myself to the said worship, and submit to the said discipline and government, and exclusive jurisdiction, and not endeavour, directly nor indirectly, the prejudice or subversion of the same; and I promise, that I shall

---

[50] The *Act Against Innovations* (1707) inherited by the Free Church was not repealed, but is not referred to in the Free Church Questions and Formula of 1846. The Questions for elders and deacons are not quite as detailed as for ministers.

follow no divisive course from the doctrine, worship, discipline, government, and exclusive jurisdiction of this Church, renouncing all doctrines, tenets, and opinions whatsoever, contrary to, or inconsistent with, the said doctrine, worship, discipline, government, or jurisdiction of the same.

The majority of the Free Church together with the United Presbyterian Church, a body formed from 18th-century secessions which had adopted a lax approach to the Confession in the 19th century (particularly in 1879),[51] formed the United Free Church of Scotland in 1900 with a relaxed subscription already anticipated in the Free Church before that date.[52] The 2 percent minority Free Church received recognition from the House of Lords in 1904 as the lawful continuation of the Free Church, and continues to the present on the original basis and the formula of 1846.

Post 1843 Established Church of Scotland

Following the impact of destructive biblical criticism, there was a certain restlessness in the Church of Scotland Assembly, but also constraints on change due to the Parliamentary Acts of 1690/1693/1707. In an expressed desire "to enlarge rather than to curtail any liberty heretofore enjoyed and relieve subscribers from unnecessary burdens as to forms of expression and matters which do not enter into the substance of the faith" the Assembly of 1889 introduced a revised formula and questions for ministers and elders.[53] The formula for ministers was that of 1693 with minor unimportant changes; that for elders was a simple "I hereby declare my approbation of the Confession of Faith as approved by this

---

[51]   For a summary account of this see Ian Hamilton, "The Erosion of Calvinist Orthodoxy" in *The Westminster Confession into the 21ˢᵗ Century*, ed. J. Ligon Duncan (4 vols.; Fearn: Mentor, 2004) 2:171ff.

[52]   For an account of this see J. L. Macleod, "Revision of the Westminster Confession (Declaratory Act of 1892)" in *The Westminster Confession into the 21ˢᵗ Century*, ed. J. Ligon Duncan (4 vols.; Fearn: Mentor, 2003) 1:343-66.

[53]   James Cooper, *Confessions of Faith and Formulas*, 71-75.

Church and ratified by law in 1690. . . ." In regard to the questions, the first was changed from "Do you believe the Scriptures of the Old and New Testaments to be the Word of God, and the only rule of faith and manners?" to "Do you believe the Word of God which is contained in the Scriptures of the Old and New Testaments, to be the supreme rule of faith and morals?"[54] No question required the person to declare explicitly that he believed the doctrines of the Confession. There was no specification of "the substance of the faith," but it was certainly not the whole Confession of Faith. Whatever merits these changes have,[55] they were not evidence of a renewed attachment to Reformed doctrine in the Kirk.

Some ministers were still aggrieved at being committed to the Confession of Faith as the confession of *my faith,* but the Act of Parliament in 1693 required it. The Assembly of 1901 contented itself (178 to 143) with expressing its confidence that office-bearers would not "oppress the consciences of any who, while owning the sum and substance of the doctrine of the Reformed Churches, are not certain as to some less important determinations also contained in it."[56] In 1903 the Assembly declared that "The Confession of Faith is regarded as an infallible rule of faith and worship only insofar as it accords with Holy Scripture interpreted by the Holy Spirit." This is a rather strange wording since no mere human document can be called "an infallible rule of faith." However, the intention was to accept the Confession only insofar as it agreed with Scripture rather than because it agreed with

---

[54] The phrase "the word of God which is contained in the Scriptures" appears in Shorter Catechism 2, but is equivalent to affirming the Scriptures to be the word of God (cf. Larger Catechism 3). The contrast is between the word of God in *oral* form and the word of God in *written* form. The traditional form of words was useful in the later context to allow for the limited inspiration view of the Bible contrary to the teaching of the Bible and Westminster formularies.

[55] The great Scottish historian, A. F. Mitchell, was positive in his *The Scottish Reformation* (Edinburgh: Blackwood, 1900), 122.

[56] James Cooper, *Confessions of Faith and Formulas*, 76ff. Again one notes a new sense being given to an old phrase, "the sum and substance."

Scripture – a very important distinction, but one with ambiguity in this context, despite the appeal to WCF 1.9-10, 20.2, and 31.4. This declaration was from now onwards read to those who were required to subscribe the formula prior to their subscription.

In 1905 the British Parliament passed an Act to adjust property matters in dispute between the Free Church of Scotland and the United Free Church of Scotland. Advantage was taken of the opportunity afforded by the preparation of this legislation to include provisions enabling the Church of Scotland to prescribe the formula of subscription from time to time, subject to the consent of a majority of presbyteries, and to this end to amend civil legislation of 1693. Accordingly, in 1910, the Church of Scotland Assembly adopted a new formula of adherence to unspecified fundamental doctrines rather than to the whole doctrine of the Confession. The Assembly declared that "Subscription of the Confession of Faith, which has been made in terms of the Formula at present in use, or which may be so made prior to the 1st July after the passing of this Act, by ministers, preachers, or other persons above-named, shall be held to be equivalent to Subscription of the Formula herein enacted."

In 1921 Parliament gave civil sanction to certain "Articles declaratory of the Constitution of the Church of Scotland in Matters Spiritual" prepared with the authority of the General Assembly of the Church with a view to facilitate union with other churches. These articles were adopted by the Assembly in 1926 and paved the way for the entry of the majority of the United Free Church into the Church of Scotland in 1929.

Articles Declaratory of the Constitution of the Church of Scotland in Matters Spiritual, 1926.

I. The Church of Scotland is part of the Holy Catholic or Universal Church; worshipping one God, almighty, all-wise, and all-loving, in the Trinity of the Father, the Son, and the Holy Ghost, the same in substance, equal in power and glory; adoring the Father, infinite in Majesty, of whom are all things; confessing our Lord

Jesus Christ, the Eternal Son, made very man for our salvation; glorying in His Cross and Resurrection, and owning obedience to Him as the head over all things to His Church; trusting in the promised renewal and guidance of the Holy Spirit; proclaiming the forgiveness of sins and acceptance with God through faith in Christ, and the gift of Eternal life; and labouring for the advancement of the Kingdom of God throughout the world. The Church of Scotland adheres to the Scottish Reformation; receives the Word of God which is contained in the Scriptures of the Old and New Testaments as its supreme rule of faith and life; and avows the fundamental doctrines of the Catholic faith founded thereupon.

II. The principal subordinate standard of the Church of Scotland is the Westminster Confession of Faith approved by the General Assembly of 1647, containing the sum and substance of the Faith of the Reformed Church. . . .

VIII. The Church has the right to interpret these Articles, and, subject to the safeguards for deliberate action and legislation provided by the Church itself, to modify or add to them; but always consistently with the provisions of the first Article hereof, adherence to which, as interpreted by the Church, is essential to its continuity and corporate life. . . .

Excerpts from the Preamble, Questions, and Formula prescribed in the 1929 Basis and Plan of Union for the Ordination and Induction of Ministers.

The Church of Scotland acknowledges the word of God which is contained in the Scriptures of the Old and New Testaments to be the supreme rule of faith and life. The Church of Scotland holds as its subordinate standard the Westminster Confession of Faith, recognising liberty of opinion on such points of doctrine as do not enter into the substance of the Faith, and claiming the right, in dependence on the promised guidance of the Holy Spirit, to formulate, interpret, or modify its subordinate standards: always in agreement with the fundamental doctrines of the Christian

Faith contained in the said Confession of which agreement the Church itself shall be sole judge.

Formula of Subscription
I believe the fundamental doctrines of the Christian faith contained in the Confession of Faith of this Church.

I acknowledge the Presbyterian government of this Church to be agreeable to the Word of God, and promise that I will submit thereunto and concur therewith. I promise to observe the order of worship and the administration of all public ordinances as the same are or may be allowed in this Church.

(This same Formula is also signed by Elders on their admission to office.)

Despite an appearance of orthodoxy and continuity with the past in the Articles, they and preceding changes show a marked departure from a confessional church as historically understood. Of course one assumes the changes are legally valid notwithstanding the Treaty of Union of 1707,[57] and that the actual practice of the church is indicative of the sense she gives them. One should also note that some matters not in the Confession are nevertheless binding – for instance, of recent years one must consent to women in office; there is no liberty on that.

Subscription in Ireland[58]

Sixty-one of the sixty-eight Presbyterian ministers in Ulster refused to conform to prelacy at the Restoration and were ejected. Although there is no doubt that the Confession was adhered to, and there is evidence of verbal assent being required in the 1670s,

---

[57] It is an assumption open to testing; cf. Francis Lyall, "The Westminster Confession: The Legal Position" in *The Westminster Confession in the Church Today*, ed. A. I. Heron (Edinburgh: St. Andrew Press, 1982), 55-71.

[58] See David Stewart, *The Seceders in Ireland* (Belfast: Presbyterian Historical Society, 1950); J. M. Barkley, *The Westminster Formularies in Irish Presbyterianism* (Belfast, 1956); and A. W. Godfrey-Brown, et al., *Challenge and Conflict: Essays in Irish Presbyterian History and Doctrine* (Antrim: W. & G. Baird, 1981).

it was not until 1698 that the General Synod of Ulster required licentiates "to subscribe the Confession of Faith, in all the Articles thereof, as the Confession of their Faith." In areas outside the jurisdiction of this northern Synod, formal subscription was still not required. The population was greatly increased by migration from Scotland and the numbers of congregations increased from 90 to 130 between 1690 and 1710, although there was much harsh treatment during the reign of Queen Anne.

The intellectual current of the time was influenced by John Locke, and by deistical thought. In 1703 the Rev. Thomas Emlyn was deposed for Arianism (denial of Christ's deity), and in 1705, just before he was released from jail, the 1698 decision was reaffirmed. Any who had been licensed without subscription had to subscribe before ordination. This was also the year the influential "Belfast Society" was formed by the Rev. John Abernethy of Antrim. John Simson, a fellow student of Abernethy, was under suspicion of deism in the Church of Scotland from 1714 to 1717, and he had taught a number of Irish ministers in his capacity as divinity professor in the University of Glasgow.

Legal toleration for Presbyterians in Ireland was granted in 1719 on the basis of the Westminster Confession; but some continued to scruple subscription, and the ordinary people were concerned. The non-subscribers argued that creeds other than the Bible were inconsistent with the final authority of Scripture and with individual freedom. They tended to limit their adherence to the doctrines in the Confession which they judged essential, a subjective and highly unsatisfactory position. In England there were similar issues at this time (see below), and the same was evident in Ireland in 1719 when Abernethy preached a sermon in which he argued that all doctrines were non-essential on which "human reason and Christian sincerity permitted men to differ."

At the following Synod (1720) a Pacific Act was passed which sought to reassure church members that there was no plan to set aside the Confession and Catechisms. The Synod firmly adhered to these, reaffirmed the 1705 decision on subscription, and provided "that if any person called upon to subscribe shall scruple any phrase or phrases in the Confession, he shall have leave to use his own expressions, which the Presbytery shall accept of, providing they judge him sound in the faith." This received unanimous support presumably because those for non-subscription could subscribe but hide behind qualifications. However, the very next month the Rev. Samuel Haliday refused to subscribe the Confession at his induction in Belfast, or renew his subscription made at the time of his licensing in 1706. He offered the following statement:

> I sincerely believe the scriptures of the Old and New Testament to be the only rule of revealed religion, a sufficient test of orthodoxy or soundness in the Faith, and to settle all the terms of ministerial and Christian communion, to which nothing may be added by any synod, assembly or council whatsoever; and I find all the essential articles of the Christian doctrine to be contained in the Westminster Confession of Faith; which articles I receive upon the sole authority of the Holy Scriptures.[59]

So Haliday affirmed the primacy of Scripture, and the utility of the Confession as containing all the essential items of Christian belief, but he did not indicate how much or how little of the Confession he regarded as scriptural. Haliday himself claimed that there were many non-essential items in the Confession. Clearly, his is a basis which does not secure clarity of belief, one of the chief purposes of a Confession. The Synod of 1721 was not happy but counseled forbearance on the assumption of a genuine scruple over the propriety of doctrinal tests rather than the doctrines themselves. The Synod also found it necessary to seek a voluntary declaration of belief in the eternal Deity of Christ, and the upshot of the extensive debate was that twelve ministers in Ulster were found not to hold that doctrine. Problems continuing, the non-subscribers were placed

---

[59] Finlay Holmes, *Our Irish Presbyterian Heritage* (Belfast: Presbyterian Church in Ireland, 1992), 65.

in the Presbytery of Antrim in 1725, and all presbyteries were reminded that the Pacific Act did not allow scruples about doctrine, only about the phrases in which that doctrine had been expressed. The Presbytery of Antrim was excluded from the Synod the following year, but inter-communion continued in the main. In the 1740s the Scottish Seceders began work in Ireland, and prospered considerably because of neglect of discipline in the Synod.

Despite reaffirming subscription in 1784, practice in the Synod of Ulster was lax, and was a factor in the breach in full ministerial communion with the Church of Scotland in 1799. The renewed rise of Arianism in the early 19th century contributed to an effort to enforce subscription. This succeeded in 1829, and the seventeen non-subscribers withdrew and formed the Remonstrant Synod. By 1835/36 the Synod of Ulster had made subscription compulsory for all ministers, licentiates, and elders. Relations were renewed with the Church of Scotland, and the way paved for reunion with the Secession Synod on July 10, 1840, to form the Presbyterian Church in Ireland with the Confession as adopted by the Church of Scotland in 1647 as its basis.

The experience of the Irish Church later in the 19th century was somewhat similar to mainstream Presbyterians elsewhere. The clause in number 14 below was introduced in 1911, and in effect made a majority of the Assembly supreme authority in matters of belief. A division over modernism occurred in 1927, from which the body known as the Evangelical Presbyterian Church of Ireland takes its rise. Today the main Irish body is much more conservative than the Church of Scotland. The Code reads:

12. *The Presbyterian Church in Ireland,* as a witness for Christ, has adopted subordinate standards in which is set forth what she understands the Word of God to teach on several important points of doctrine and worship. These subordinate standards are a testimony for truth and against error, and serve as a bond of union for members of the Church.

13. *The Confession of Faith* (as approved by the Church of Scotland in her Act of 1647) and the Larger and Shorter Catechisms, prepared by the Westminster Assembly of Divines, are the subordinate standards of the Presbyterian Church in Ireland. Accepting these subordinate standards, the Church holds that, although civil rulers are bound to render obedience to Christ in their own province, yet they ought not to attempt in any way to constrain men's religious beliefs, or invade the rights of conscience.

14. *In the Church* resides the right to interpret and explain her standards under the guidance of the Spirit of God.

The subscription is as 1835 but the content of the Code paragraphs interpreting it are changed:

I believe the Westminster Confession of Faith as described in the Code, chapter 1, paragraphs 12-14, to be founded on and agreeable to the Word of God and as such I subscribe it as the Confession of my faith.

The Reformed Presbyterian and Evangelical Presbyterian bodies are quite strict in maintaining adherence to the Confession.

Subscription in England

The Revolution of 1688 brought William and Mary to the throne and the Church of England was recognized as the Established Church. But in reaction, it seems, from the jealousy for the truth in the earlier period that had caused so many divisions, the Dissenters from the Established Church were anxious for a charitable tolerance, and the intellectual currents of the time favored this.[60] Presbyterians and Independents co operated in measure. In 1717 some concerns appeared about the orthodoxy of three of the Presbyterian ministers at Exeter, and in 1719 the Exeter Assembly resolved that no minister would in the future be

---

[60] John Locke's *Essay Concerning Human Understanding* was published in 1689. Locke, who was himself a Dissenter, denied innate ideas, although he emphasized rational demonstration of moral principles and the existence of God. His view of faith was in terms of rational assent rather than a Spirit-wrought trust in Christ.

ordained or recommended to congregations unless he subscribed to the first of the Thirty-Nine Articles (the Trinity), or the fifth and sixth answers of the Shorter Catechism, or assented to the Assembly's own declaration of faith or "sufficiently expressed the same sense in words of his own." This rule continued at Exeter until 1753.[61] Meanwhile, a meeting of most London Dissenting ministers was held at Salter's Hall in February 1719, and by seventy-three to sixty-nine those who considered subscription inappropriate or unnecessary were in the majority. Taking only the Presbyterians, about 60 percent were non-subscribers, 10 percent neutral, and the balance subscribers.[62] The non-subscribers were generally younger and better educated, but had imbibed the spirit of the age. Thus, the drift into definite doctrinal error increasingly became apparent, and Presbyterians in England largely became Unitarian. Revitalization in the 19th century was accompanied by definite subscription along Scottish lines.

Subscription in the United States[63]

The earliest Presbyterian congregations in what is now the United States of America were established by English Puritans in the early decades of the 17th century. Scots-Irish settlers furthered development, and Francis Makemie of Ulster organized the first

---

[61] A. H. Drysdale, *The Presbyterians in England* (London: Presbyterian Church of England, 1889), 502.

[62] Ibid., 505.

[63] See Charles Hodge, *The Constitutional History of the Presbyterian Church in the United States of America* (Philadelphia: Presbyterian Board of Education, 1851), 127-215; also his *The Church and its Polity* (New York: Thomas Nelson and Son, 1879), 317-42; Morton H. Smith, *Studies in Southern Presbyterian Theology* (Phillipsburg: P&R, 1987), 17-44; L. J. Trinterud, *The Forming of an American Tradition: A Re-examination of Colonial Presbyterianism* (1949; repr., Philadelphia: Westminster, 1970); James R. Payton, Jr., "The Background and Significance of the Adopting Act of 1729" in *Pressing Toward the Mark: Essays Commemorating Fifty Years of the Orthodox Presbyterian Church*, ed. C. G. Dennison and R. C. Gamble (Philadelphia: Committee for the Historian of the OPC, 1986), 131-45; David W. Hall, ed., *Practice of Confessional Subscription*, 93-310.

Presbytery in 1706. Formal subscription was not required in the early period, but the effects of erroneous tendencies in Britain and Ireland, outlined above, furthered the desire for strict subscription. A few ministers doubted the propriety of subscription to a man-made document and were not sure orthodoxy could be preserved by such a means. However, on the morning of September 19, 1729, a *Preliminary Act* was passed by the Synod of Philadelphia as follows:

ALTHOUGH THE SYNOD DO NOT CLAIM or pretend to any authority of imposing our faith upon other men's consciences, but do profess our just dissatisfaction with, and abhorrence of such impositions, and do utterly disclaim all legislative power and authority in the Church, being willing to receive one another as Christ has received us to the glory of God, and admit to fellowship in sacred ordinances, all such as we have grounds to believe Christ will at last admit to the kingdom of heaven, yet we are undoubtedly obliged to take care that the faith once delivered to the saints be kept pure and uncorrupt among us, and so handed down to our posterity; AND DO THEREFORE AGREE that all the ministers of this Synod, or that shall hereafter be admitted into this Synod, shall declare their agreement in, and approbation of, the Confession of Faith, with the Larger and Shorter Catechisms of the Assembly of Divines at Westminster, as being in all the essential and necessary articles, good forms of sound words and systems of Christian doctrine, and do also adopt the said Confession and Catechisms as the confession of our faith.

AND WE DO ALSO AGREE, that all the presbyteries within our bounds shall always take care not to admit any candidate of the ministry into the exercise of the sacred function but what declares his agreement in opinion with all the essential and necessary articles of said Confession, either by subscribing the said Confession of Faith and Catechisms, or by a verbal declaration of their assent thereto, as such minister or candidate shall think best. AND IN CASE any minister of this Synod, or any candidate for the ministry, shall have any scruple with respect to any article or articles of said Confession or Catechisms, he shall at the time of his making said declaration declare his sentiments to the Presbytery or synod, who shall, notwithstanding, admit him to the exercise of the ministry within our bounds, and to ministerial communion, if the Synod or Presbytery shall judge his scruple or mistake to be only about articles not essential and necessary in doctrine, worship, or government. BUT if the Synod or Presbytery shall judge such ministers or candidates erroneous in essential and necessary articles of faith, the Synod or Presbytery shall declare them uncapable of communion with them.

AND THE SYNOD DO SOLEMNLY AGREE, that none of us will traduce or use any opprobrious terms of those that differ from us in these extra-essential and not necessary points of doctrine, but treat them with the same friendship, kindness, and brotherly love, as if they had not differed from us in such sentiments.

In the afternoon of the same day this Act was applied by the ministers proposing their scruples. It was then found possible to declare adherence unanimously to the Confession and Catechisms as:

The confession of their faith, excepting some clauses in the twentieth and twenty-third chapters, concerning which clauses the Synod do unanimously declare, that they do not receive those articles in any such sense as to suppose the civil magistrate hath a controlling power over Synods with respect to the exercise of their ministerial authority; or power to persecute any for their religion, or in any sense contrary to the Protestant succession to the throne of Great Britain.

For some years after, there was debate within the church over the intent of what had been done. Some left for smaller Presbyterian bodies who stated that they held to every doctrinal point. A few argued without success that all that was required was belief in the essential doctrines of Christianity rather than the essential and necessary articles of the Confession and Catechisms. The

Synod had not contemplated significant departure from the whole doctrine of the Confession, and all the early ministers are known to have been strict Calvinists. Indeed, in 1730 and 1736 the Synod declared it did not intend such departure.

Perhaps we may understand their intent better if we appreciate that the authors were Christian ministers, not lawyers, and that they had a background in Scots-Irish Presbyterianism. They were now in a situation where the Presbyterian Church was not established by law as in Scotland, and they had some variation in approach to issues of subscription as they sought to organize. These factors account for a lack of full consistency in the cited decisions. Three conclusions may be drawn.

First, the Synod regarded the Confession and two Catechisms as "in all the essential and necessary articles good forms of sound words and systems of Christian doctrine." The implication is that some parts are not essential and necessary, yet later that day the scruples they actually advanced were limited to matters related to church–state issues. This seems to support strict subscriptionists like John Murray and Morton Smith. On the other hand, a distinction between essential and necessary articles and other articles is not a position evidenced in the 17th century and earlier. The older view was that confessions might contain less important things, but not ones that could be regarded as optional for the subscriber.

Second, the Synod also used the plural "systems" to refer to the Confession and Catechisms. This suggests they were thinking of books "containing a comprehensive and regularly arranged exposition of some subject, a systematic treatment,"[64] for that is the usual meaning in the 18th century. As "a group or aggregation of things forming a connected or complex whole," this rules out

---

[64] Oxford English Dictionary (Oxford: Clarendon Press, 1989), Vol. 17, Def. II.8.d (system of doctrine), 497. Compare Anthony Tuckney, *A Good Day Well Improved* (London: J.F. for S. Gellibrand, 1656), 247-48: ". . . their Summes, Institutions, Systems, Syntagmes, Synopses, or by whatever other name you call such Models of Divinity, an orderly lay down together of such divine truths as are scattered up and down the Scripture."

the notion of significant extraneous doctrinal material in these books. Indeed, why would one distinguish "essential and necessary articles" if the term "system" itself carried the notion that the doctrine adhered to is significantly smaller than the doctrine actually expressed. Still, two approaches can be indicated.

The first approach grants that commitment to the "system" as distinct from, say, "all the propositions" allows for different opinions about the way a doctrine is expressed, but does not allow relief from adherence to the doctrine correctly understood. This is really the strict subscription view. It simply clarifies that the adoption of the Confession does not require one to hold that the expression or explanation of the doctrine in it is ideal, or that mere incidental remarks are binding. One can think of the General Synod of Ulster's position in 1725.

The second approach is a bit less strict. As well as the (obvious) points in the first view, it says that the subscriber is only committed to the Calvinistic or Reformed system of doctrine in the Confession as distinct from incidentals and sundry issues – whether the Pope is the Antichrist, whether marriage to a deceased wife's sister is lawful, the grounds of divorce, etc., and on these non-essential-to-the-Calvinistic-system doctrines the Synod or Presbytery can grant relief (so Charles Hodge). However, these are not the kind of issues scrupled by some non-subscribers in the 1720s, although they were a century later. Further, if one were to ask Hodge to spell out other non-essential doctrines than those just noted, I imagine he would be somewhat pressed to find much, since the Confession is such a consistent document. So we should hesitate to suppose "system" subscription was designed to give a meaning to "system" which limits essential doctrines to something less than the doctrine actually set out. Also, perhaps Hodge does not give enough weight to the fact that the subscriber adopts "the Confession as containing the system" and not simply "the system contained in the Confession."

Third, the Synod also envisaged a presbytery judging on what are essential and necessary articles, which assumes that matters scrupled by them as a Synod later that day may not be the only matters legitimately scrupled. This does not support the view that the afternoon resolution in 1729 is the true Adopting Act setting the limits for the future to qualifications of the whole teaching of the Confession (contra Murray). Indeed, it lays the foundation for an ill-defined adherence to the Confession and, by giving presbyteries a role in judging exceptions, leads to division and factions.

It is not easy to reconcile these tensions satisfactorily, and there has been considerable diversity of explanation. Nevertheless, it is obvious that these early Presbyterians themselves held a strict subscription, but were aware of good and godly men who scrupled some matters which they would not wish to be a reason to exclude them. In the Established Church of Scotland and in the Irish Church, there was strict subscription on paper, although failures in practice. In Ireland, the Pacific Act of 1720 allowed scruples over the wording of the Confession but not to the extent of deciding between essential and unessential articles, or even on doctrine; only the wording in which the doctrine was expressed could be scrupled.

Another thing is clear. The Synod of 1729 had undoubtedly given presbyteries the right to judge what was essential and necessary and, as there was no explicit definition of such items, a broadening church could result (so Trinterud, Payton), far beyond any possible intention of the authors, and even to the destruction of any proper understanding of the place and function of a confession. Thus, it has been argued that the move away from strict adherence to the Calvinistic system of doctrine in the Confession which has occurred particularly in the 20th century is in continuity with the 1729 Adopting Act. With even the best wording, defection may occur, but it's a pity that the inadequate drafting in 1729, which doubtless was trying to find a manner of expression suited to all, has provided a handle for the broadening church argument.

In 1758 when a reunion of two synods occurred, the first article read:

> Both Synods having always approved and received the Westminster Confession of Faith, Larger and Shorter Catechisms, as an orthodox and excellent system of doctrine, founded on the word of God; we do still receive the same as the confession of our faith . . . strictly enjoining it on all our ministers and probationers for the ministry, that they preach and teach according to the form of sound words in the said Confession and Catechisms, and avoid and oppose all errors contrary thereto.

One notes in this statement that the Confession and Catechism are regarded as "a system of doctrine" not as containing it, thereby reinforcing the view I have expressed about the intent of earlier uses of this expression.

My own view is that Hodge does not make quite the right distinctions. The notion that strict subscription means one is committed to every proposition is not the old orthodox view but something of a caricature. It is the doctrine not the document that one accepts. I also think William Cunningham (1805–1861), the great Scottish theologian who much admired Hodge, was right (contra W. G. Blaikie) to regard the American formula as so vague as to endanger all discipline.[65] History has certainly shown that 1729 has a case to answer.[66]

---

[65] W. G. Blaikie, "On the Proper Limits of Creeds," in *British and Foreign Evangelical Review*, January 1873, 51-73. Blaikie cites Robert Rainy and James Mackenzie, *Life of William Cunningham* (London: Thomas Nelson, 1871), 463-64.

[66] The main body of American Presbyterians has moved very far from its Confessional moorings. The position of conservative churches such as the Orthodox Presbyterian Church and the Presbyterian Church in America may be seen in David W. Hall, ed., *Practice of Confessional Subscription*.

Subscription in Australia[67]

In concluding this survey some reference to Australia is appropriate as an illustration of how the Scottish experience was exported to British colonies in the 19th century.

The first Presbyterian minister arrived in 1822, and by 1843 there were twenty-two in Eastern Australia, twelve in Tasmania, and two in South Australia. "The Synod of Australia in connection with the Established Church of Scotland" was formed in Sydney on October 5, 1840. There was no avenue of appeal to the parent church. This Synod was divided by the Scottish Disruption controversy when a majority declined to break the legal and moral connection with the Established Church. A minority freed themselves from the compromising name and association by establishing the Synod of Eastern Australia as an independent church court and reaffirming their adherence to the original basis. Although reduced by the withdrawal of 75 percent of its ministers in 1864/65, the Presbyterian Church of Eastern Australia continues on an unchanged basis of subscription to the Confession of Faith with the formula of the Free Church of Scotland in 1846, but is a body of some dozen parishes and a community of fewer than 1,000. Since 1953 it incorporates the parallel body, the Free Presbyterian Church, also formed in 1846, in what is now Victoria.

---

[67] An overall survey is S. D. Gill, "The Battle for the Westminster Confession in Australia" in *The Westminster Confession into the 21st Century*, ed. J. Ligon Duncan (4 vols.; Fearn: Mentor, 2003), 1:247-301. Differences from this in my narrative following are deliberate. Useful references on subscription include: R. S. Ward, *The Bush Still Burns: The Presbyterian and Reformed Faith in Australia 1788-1988* (Melbourne, 1989), 51-52, 79-81, 276-89, 411 and (for 1901) the literature cited on pages 288-89; David Burke, *Introduction to Presbyterian Doctrine* (Burwood, NSW: Presbyterian Church, 1991), 29-36; R. S. Ward, *Divisions and Unions in Australian Presbyterianism 1823-1901 with Special Reference to the Church's Attitude to its Creed* (Th.D. Thesis, Australian College of Theology, Sydney, 1994); Peter Barnes, *Living in A Half-way House: The Rise of Liberal Evangelicalism in the Presbyterian Church of New South Wales 1865-1915* (Th.D. Thesis, Australian College of Theology, 1995).

The other Presbyterian grouping with origins in the early period is the Presbyterian Church of Australia, a federal union of churches in each state which was formed on July 24, 1901. The constituent churches had in most cases been formed from unions between 1859 and 1870 of the several strands of Scottish Presbyterianism which had been planted in each colony. The union Basis drawn up in Victoria in 1855 had been approved by a meeting of Free Church of Scotland leaders in August 1857. This was not surprising since it was not the Basis that was then objected to by anti-unionists in Victoria. Rather, it was the practical application the Established Church sympathizers said they would make of it in receiving Established Church ministers into the Union church without reservation. In Scotland, Established Church ministers were regarded by the Free Church of Scotland as unfaithful to the Confession of Faith, while the United Presbyterian "voluntary" approach, in its more consistent form, was a direct path to the idea of the secular nature of the state anathema to Old School Calvinists. A minority of the Free Presbyterian Church of Victoria opposed the union but was expelled in April 1857 by the Majority. There was also a change of policy in the Free Church Colonial Committee,[68] and the Majority Free Presbyterian body was recognized by the Free Church of Scotland Assembly in May 1858. Scottish leaders like R. S. Candlish favored union in the colonies (and indeed union on a sound basis was very desirable), and the minority was repudiated.

Later in 1858, a new Basis was drawn up in Victoria which gave no clear testimony on church–state relations at all,[69] and union occurred April 7, 1859, leaving some United Presbyterians (opponents of state aid) and a Minority Free Presbyterian Church

---

[68] An illustration is the appointment in 1858 of Rev. J. G. Mackintosh of the Free Church of Scotland to St. Andrews Church of Scotland, Hobart, so undermining the position of the Free Presbytery of Tasmania.

[69] R. S. Ward, *The Bush Still Burns*, gives the text of the union basis in 1855 (pp. 183-84) and 1858 (p. 198).

outside the union. The Minority appealed for recognition to the Free Church of Scotland but was rejected in 1860 and 1861. On the last occasion, Dr. Cunningham made a very effective speech, not on grounds of logical rebuttal but on practical grounds,[70] that ended Free Church relations with the Minority until they were resumed after 1900.

The importance of the 1858 Free Church decision on union was that it set the pattern for general unions in Queensland (1863), New South Wales (1864/65), South Australia (1865), and in Canada. It also anticipated the union between the United Presbyterian Church and the majority of the Free Church of Scotland in 1900.

In the Victorian union, one accepted the Westminster Standards and the Second Book of Discipline (1578) as "the confession of my faith." In New South Wales the basis was more satisfactorily worded, generally in line with the old Scottish position in which one was pledged to "the whole doctrine" of the Confession but did not directly subscribe the other documents. Subsequent developments in Victoria, where 40 percent or more of Australian Presbyterians resided in the 19th century, showed a strong influence from the Free Church tradition, and an endeavor to counter rationalistic thought in the 1870s and 1880s, while not requiring endorsement of everything in the Confession.

The use in Victoria of a Declaratory Act approved but not formally adopted in 1882 is striking.[71] Much was derived from the 1879 Act of the United Presbyterian Church of Scotland. Section 3 stated: "In accordance with practice hitherto observed in this church, liberty of opinion is allowed on such points in the

---

[70] Such was the view of Robert Sutherland, who joined the union, in his *The History of the Presbyterian Church of Victoria* (London: James Nisbet, 1877), 309-10.

[71] Text in Ward, *The Bush Still Burns*, 281. A true Declaratory Act does not need to go through Barrier Act procedure. In this case only five of the eleven presbyteries approved *simpliciter*, and one disapproved. In any case, change to the Act of Parliament under which church property was held would have been desirable or essential to give legal effect to the Act.

Standards as are not essential to the system of doctrine therein taught, as the interpretation of the 'six days' in the Mosaic account of creation, the Church guarding against the abuse of this liberty to the injury of its unity and peace." Section 4 is original to Victoria and reads:

> That the Church does not regard subscription to the Formula as binding the person subscribing to anything more in respect of doctrine than the Formula requires expressly and in terms: To own and believe the whole doctrine contained in the Standards of this Church as an exhibition of the sense in which he understands the Scriptures, and to acknowledge it as the confession of his faith, meaning by the "whole doctrine contained in the Standards" the system of doctrine in its unity, formulated in the Confession of Faith, catechetically exhibited in the Larger and Shorter Catechisms, implied in the statements of the Directory for Public Worship, the Form of Presbyterian Church Government, and the Second Book of Discipline, and historically known as the Calvinistic or Reformed System of Doctrine; but that the Church has always regarded, and continues to regard, those whom it admits to the office of the ministry as pledged to profess, defend, and teach this system in its integrity, and, while giving due prominence in their teaching to all the doctrines it includes, to give a chief place to the central and most vital doctrines thereof, with those objective supernatural facts on which they rest, especially the incarnation, the Perfect Obedience and Expiatory Death, and the resurrection and Ascension of our Lord, avoiding such forms of teaching as might be fitted to weaken or destroy the faith of the people in the same.

The Act is quite interesting, although the initial favorable impression is somewhat modified when one realizes that the church, while committed to supernaturalism, was not committed to a clear penal-substitutionary view of the atonement. In the clauses derived from the United Presbyterian Church of Scotland it involves itself in all the confusion and raising of false issues in regard to the teaching of the Confession in those clauses. Observers from outside the PCV regarded the Declaratory Act as legally incompetent and likely to be pernicious in practice because of its perceived equivocation. Peter MacPherson of the Presbyterian Church of Eastern Australia wrote, and very accurately as history has shown:

> It appears to have been composed with a design to soothe oppo-nents, as well as to satisfy friends. . . . Quite possibly, the Act will be ignorantly applauded by one section of the public, as if it were a solid exposition of the great doctrine, and a vindication of it against the exceptions of sceptical and irreligious critics. Another section will see it as a triumph for these very critics and their criticisms, and will read the Act as a surrender of the Westminster doctrine. Practically, we believe, the latter will prove to be in the right.[72]

Interestingly, MacPherson offered no specific criticism of the liberty of opinion clause, probably because it was so qualified by the adherence to the Reformed system of doctrine, that the liberty granted was theoretically minimal along the line advanced by Charles Hodge.

When the state churches federated in 1901, the Basis of Union set out a Declaratory Statement in the light of which the Confes-sion of Faith is to be read. It owes something both to the 1882 Statement and the Free Church of Scotland Act of 1892, and in-cludes "liberty of opinion on matters not essential to the doctrine therein taught" but with no definition of what is essential to the doctrine.[73] The first section of #4 in 1882 down to the semi-co-lon (see above) is omitted. The formula is: "I own and accept the

---

[72] *The Free Churchman*, June 1882, 46.

[73] The view of the Rev. George Tait (1844–1934), Assembly Clerk, and one of the significant architects of the union, who himself believed in the Virgin Birth, was that belief in the Virgin Birth was not essential nor required by the Presbyterian Church of Victoria or under the Basis of Union of 1901. See George Tait, *The Virgin Birth as a Test of Office in the Christian Church* (Melbourne, 1905) or, conveniently, S. M. Bonnington, "As for Me and My House, We Will Serve the Lord" (Melbourne: South Yarra Presbyterian Church, 2004).

subordinate standard of this church, with the explanations given in the articles contained in the declaratory statement, as an exhibition of the sense in which I understand the Holy Scriptures, and as a confession of my faith. . . . I shall in my station assert, maintain and defend the doctrine. . . ." In 1977 the departure of a majority to the Uniting Church left a more conservative ministry, probably then about 50 percent evangelical. Today the ministry is almost entirely evangelical, although there is something of a range of viewpoint, and the grassroots are not always sympathetic given the long influence of liberal thought.

The Westminster Presbyterian Church, formed in 1970 by people connected with the old Reformed Presbyterian Church Evangelical Synod (USA), draws on the American tradition of subscription to the system of doctrine. The Presbyterian Reformed Church (formed in 1967 by withdrawal of some from the Presbyterian Church of Australia) is a unique case. The Confession is accepted as a faithful interpretation of Scripture, but if the church is convinced of an error from Scripture change may be made. This reminds one of the Preface to the Scots Confession of 1560. To date, the Presbyterian Reformed Church has modified the Confession at 24:4 (1979), 27:4 (1970), 28:2 (1973) (so as in effect to reject the validity of baptism of the Church of Rome and some other groups), 23:3; 31:1-2 (1972) (church and state issues amended generally in line with American practice), and has added new chapter 34 (On the Offer of the Gospel and God's grace therein).

Some Observations from the History of Subscription

A number of matters are clear from the history of subscription. The most obvious is that subscription means little if there is not a clear grasp of both the Presbyterian idea of subscription to a consensus statement of faith, and of the Confession's actual meaning, prior to entrance on the ministry. There must also be a constant maintenance of the standard of doctrine subsequently. Too many divide over particular differences in the statement of a doctrine forgetting that the Confession generally endeavors to highlight the points on which all Calvinists may agree rather than particular schools of thought within the Calvinistic position where people may have their own views. Today the impact of non-Reformed approaches from evangelical Christians is relevant, particularly as out and out liberalism is on the wane. Further, Drysdale notes the impact of academies (training institutions) not under the control of the church in contributing to doctrinal decline in 18th century England, a point not without relevance in the American context today where, even in the best cases, the polarizing of issues of interpretation in the Confession can easily occur.

It needs to be kept in view that the church does not impose the Confession on reluctant office-bearers, but invites those who wish to serve in office to subscribe this form of sound words as a basis for mutual confidence and cooperation: "we believe, we have convictions and *therefore* we speak."[74]

The Confession needs to be studied in its historic context to avoid needless scruples and misunderstandings. The original intent must be understood, as well as the intent of the church which adopted it at some later point, possibly with modifications.[75] The study of the Confession should not be isolated from Scripture, since it aims to be a fitting statement of scriptural teaching and has no authority apart from Scripture. The study of the Confession should not exclude the possibility of clearer insight into the formulation of Scripture's teaching: the Confession is not itself Scripture.[76] The Catholic (Trinitarian), Protestant, and Calvinistic character of the Confession is not subject to change, but the possibility of re-

---

[74] Drysdale, *Presbyterians in England*, 510; the section is worthy of attention.

[75] As far as I know there is no current Presbyterian Church which adopts the Confession in the precise terms in which it left the Assembly and/or was approved by the English Parliament in 1648. As noted already, the Church of Scotland qualified it when giving approval in 1647.

[76] The preceding three sentences draw from Thomas C. Oden, *Doctrinal Standards in the Wesleyan Tradition* (Grand Rapids: Francis Asbury Press, 1988), 108. Note also the Confession's own teaching at 31.4. John Murray states: "To

statement/rearrangement to reflect better the balance of Scripture and deal with particular errors must be kept in view.[77] The Confession must not be allowed to become so sacrosanct that it becomes a museum piece. Its expression in current language is important, particularly for ruling elders, and some careful supplementing at certain points could be helpful in addressing particular needs of the current day.[78] Examination of ministerial candidates must include a quite thorough examination of their understanding of the teaching of the Confession and any areas of real or supposed disagreement.

It is preferable to amend the actual text of the Confession if there are poorly expressed phrases that confuse or which, as sometimes happens, are made into Trojan horses to undermine the binding

---

appraise it [the Confession] as perfect and not susceptible to improvement or correction would be to accord it an estimation and veneration that belong only to the Word of God. This would be idolatry, and would amount to the denial of that progressive understanding that the presence of the Holy Spirit in the church guarantees." *Collected Writings*, (4 vols.; Edinburgh: Banner of Truth, 1982), 4:260.

[77] "But unquestionably, if the standards of a church are subordinate and not supreme, they are not to be reckoned infallible, and not to be accounted unalterably fixed or stereotyped for all generations." James Bannerman, *The Church of Christ* (1869; repr., Edinburgh: Banner of Truth, 1974), 1:308; note the important quotation he gives from George Gillespie, *Miscellany Questions*, X. Similarly, James McGregor: "An unchanged confession, coming down through generations with ever-augmenting *prestige*, is apt to become a rule of men's faith. The result is bondage, a sort of evangelical popery." *British and Foreign Evangelical Review*, 1877, 712 as cited in A. M. Harman, "The Place and Significance of the Reformed Confessions Today" in *Banner of Truth Magazine*, January 1973, 28. J. H. Thornwell's comment is also to the point. In reference to marriage with a deceased wife's sister he writes "If the law of the Church is more stringent, upon this subject, than that of the Bible, it ought to be changed; but as long as we profess to believe that our Standards faithfully exhibit the mind of the Spirit, our practice and our creed ought to be consistent." Thornwell, *Collected Writings* (1875; repr., 4 vols.: Edinburgh: Banner of Truth, 1986), 4:493.

[78] It is of interest to note that although a double covenant scheme (of works and of grace) as in the WCF became the accepted orthodoxy in the Reformed churches in the 17th century, there was no adjustment of the older confessional standards in continental Europe.

character of the Confession in major areas.[79] Thus, the reference to the Pope as "that antichrist" is often misconstrued. Still, it would be a pity to simply strike out the statement in 25.6. The doctrinal point, as evidenced by the illustrative texts, could be expressed by rephrasing such as: "The general spirit and distinctive features of the papal system are opposed to Christ, and represent a serious departure from Christian truth and practice, a departure which was predicted in Scripture itself."[80]

It is desirable to make any textual adjustment to the Confession after inter-church discussion. An organization such as the International Conference of Reformed Churches could be useful in this.

Should exceptions from the doctrines in the Confession be permitted? If the answer is yes, the language of essential/non-essential, necessary/unnecessary is better avoided. Ambiguous or ill-defined "liberty of opinion" or other clauses implying non-essential doctrines are not satisfactory. Many exceptions I have seen are really scruples over the expression of a doctrine that do not affect the doctrine itself and can be removed by tidying up the Confession's text and/or with further instruction. Some small doctrinal points may remain, and the requirement to indicate such exceptions is in fact a good one if it encourages honesty and full disclosure. The Confession itself reminds us that some errors are censurable because of their nature and some only because of the way they are maintained and propagated (cf. WCF 20.4). Some differences, if maintained with appropriate deference for the public confession of the church (surely of more weight than the view of

---

[79] John Murray, *Collected Writings*, 4:260-62 notes a number of "blemishes" in the Confession. Note Thornwell again, writing in 1861: "The Westminster Confession and Catechisms we cordially receive as the mind of the Spirit. We believe them to be faithful expositions of the Word of God. The great system which they teach can never be altered by those who love the Truth; but there are incidental statements, not affecting the plan of salvation and the doctrines of grace, about which our children may not be as well satisfied as ourselves." Thornwell, *Collected Writings*, 4:442.

[80] So the modernized text in R. S. Ward, *The Westminster Confession of Faith and Catechisms in Modern English* (1996; repr., Wantirna: New Melbourne Press, 2001).

an individual), may safely exist, just as do variations in stating doctrines all are agreed on. In some such way one may seek to meet the scruples of tender consciences and minimize the external division of Christ's church.

Still, exceptions to the Confession, if they are to be allowed at all, ought only to be to a list specifically approved by the supreme court of the denomination concerned, so as to prevent mistrust, factions, and arbitrary actions by presbyteries, and to ensure safeguards arising from wrong inferences. In allowing such exceptions one must distinguish the candidate's position from the public and avowed confessional position of the church. Matters that are allowed as exceptions may be expressed publicly – since the WCF (22.7) rightly forbids vows not to teach something one regards as the teaching of the word of God. The proviso must be that the liberty not be abused so as to destroy the unity and peace of the church. If serious division arises, the legitimate method of resolution is not to remove the liberty, but to channel it into appropriate expression. This may mean that those who seek to remove the liberty are liable to censure, as well as any who use the liberty granted inappropriately.

Many endeavors at clarifying or maintaining subscription have been well intended but have not always maintained the right balance between Scripture and Confession, nor appreciated the need to craft legislation unambiguously. Of course, in the end, despite the great importance of clear statements of faith, one must recognize that perfect paper standards do not guarantee a living, orthodox church. The church must be ever-vigilant and ever-dependent on her divine head if she would maintain her life and purity.

The Relationship between Scripture and Confession

Given the recognition that Scripture is the supreme standard, the question arises as to how a confessing church can honor the supreme standard if the condition of office is subscription to a confession of faith. This is not such a severe tension point in cases where one is not required to accept the whole teaching of the confession as one's own confession, but in these cases one is subject to other dangers as we have seen (idiosyncratic interpretation, doctrinal breadth, or heresy under the guise of belief in the Bible). The church is also seen to be failing to bear witness to *all* that Christ has commanded.

The primacy of Scripture *is* to be respected in Christ's church. Elders and ministers are not to be chiefly specialists in canon law, resisting examination of the word of God by a mere citation of the Confession of Faith. They *are* to be capable teachers of the word of God, for it is to such that Christ has committed the affairs of his church. The past cannot be ignored but the gospel must be confessed in the present.

Hence, the FIRST function of a confession of faith is to make sure that Scripture is our primary standard in all matters of faith and conduct.

We make that claim in the very first question addressed to candidates for office. This question is commonly along the lines: *"Do you believe the Scriptures of the Old and New Testaments to be the word of God and the only rule of faith and practice?"* Thus a truly scriptural confession derives its authority from the Scriptures, not the other way around. The placement of the subject of Scripture as Chapter 1 in the Westminster Confession reminds us of this in a striking way. Also important is the way in which the Confession drives us back to the Scriptures in any controversy (1.8-10). We do not honor our Confession if we use it, rather than Scripture, to refute some error that may arise.

A SECOND function of a confession of faith is to provide a rallying point for those of like mind concerning the main teachings of Scripture.

A church with a confession of faith is saying that individualistic interpretation of the Bible is not right. It is within the community of faith that we learn and confess together as Christians. A confession will probably become fuller in the light of fresh disputes or heresies that require a response, although it can never be a kind of definitive commentary on every passage of Scripture. Its explanations, however good and correct, are not inspired as Scripture is. Indeed, it is always open to revision and restatement in the light of Scripture as the primary standard. Given the present fragmented state of the Christian church, it will usually be wise to seek wider counsel from other bodies of Christians with a view to avoiding idiosyncratic change.

A THIRD function of a confession of faith is to serve as a public statement of the faith of the people of God, and to instruct in the faith.

A confession of faith will be carefully expressed, but it should not be written in obscure language lest it fail to be an adequate public statement and means of instruction. It must not become a museum piece. Its coverage is not all the small points of debate in the theological schools, but the grand and clearly revealed truths in the Bible, which it seeks to commend to others. Scriptural confessions and catechisms form excellent devotional manuals and should be used as such.

A FOURTH function of a confession of faith is to be a solemn bond for the office-bearers of the church.

Their subscription to such a form of sound words provides a bond of fellowship and cooperation. The terms of subscription must recognize the primary authority of Scripture as the rule of faith. And the vow must be taken sincerely (WCF 22.4); therefore, the meaning of the Confession must be clear.

A confession produced by a meeting of many minds and/or formally adopted by the church is likely to have greater authority than the opinion of an individual. Office-bearers need to be particularly careful not to elevate personal opinions on subsidiary issues to greater importance than the teachings expressed in a confession. A confession sets out the highway; preoccupation with the side-tracks is not helpful.

A FIFTH function of a confession is to form the basis of the trust on which church property is held.

If these trusts do not give any power of doctrinal change, to that extent they may not conform to the inherent power of the church to formulate her confession, subject to Holy Scripture, as set out above.[81] On the other hand, those who seek change have often done so with a view to modifying adversely the essential doctrine of the Confession, rather than making it an even closer representation of the teaching of Scripture. If there is a genuine unanimity on the scripturalness of proposed changes, there should be no problem.

The Westminster Confession forbids us to make synods or councils the rule of faith (WCF 31.4), and this is a uniform principle of our Reformed tradition (e.g. Belgic Confession, Article 7; Second Helvetic Confession, Chapter 2). Thus, the productions of the Westminster Assembly cannot be regarded as the rule of faith, but they may be and ought to be a help to faith.

The Roman Church made its appeal to Scripture and tradition including decrees of Councils. Canon law was the rule of faith, not the Scriptures. The Confession is not rightly viewed if it is seen as a new canon law.

True, appealing to Scripture against the Confession in any significant way does involve "abandonment of the communion of which the Confession is the bond."[82] Yet even here, any judicial proceeding should emphasize the scriptural grounds for the finding. That will honor the Confession, because that will honor Scripture!

An Example of a Strict Subscription Form

When all is said and done, the preservation of Christian truth is not secured simply by orthodox confessional standards and

---

[81] This point is well made in *Constitutional Catechism of the Free Church of Scotland* (1847), Q.44 and ff.

[82] John Macpherson, *The Westminster Confession of Faith* (Edinburgh: T&T Clark, 1882), 2.

fine formulas of subscription. There must be a well-instructed ministry, godly elders, and men of integrity with a will to maintain the truth in presbyteries and wider assemblies. Only a Christ-focused ministry, thoroughly informed and directed by Scripture, with dependence on the Spirit of truth, will suffice. Nevertheless, the importance of care in subscription forms has been illustrated in this essay. I append an example of a modern subscription in the strict Scottish tradition. I have composed it in the light of the historical experience so as to clarify the nature of subscription and the obligations of the subscriber, and in a manner that can be easily understood by the congregation before whom vows are taken. It would of course be associated with a declaration of just how the church concerned regarded the confession. Such a declaration might read along the following lines:

(1) In consistency with the Act of 1647 of the Assembly of the Church of Scotland approving the Confession of Faith, the Synod declares that the Church adheres to the Confession of Faith as most agreeable to the word of God, and approves it as to the truth of the matter, adhering to all its doctrines both major and minor. In making this declaration the Synod acknowledges that the Confession of Faith is not on a level with the word of God, the Holy Scriptures. The Synod does not claim that the statements of doctrine in the Confession are necessarily formulated in the best manner or with citation of the most suitable illustrative Scripture texts, or that they are exhaustive statements of the doctrines expressed, or that mere allusions or incidental remarks are binding. Still, the Church adheres to all the teachings intentionally conveyed by the Confession of Faith because she believes them to be derived from the Holy Scriptures and agreeable with them.

(2) While the Holy Scriptures are the perpetual and universal rule of faith, a confession is adapted to particular circumstances, such as the condition of society, the errors of the age, and the usage of language. Accordingly, the Church reserves the right to amend the Confession from time to time in an orderly way, not to depart from

Scriptural doctrines but to amend or adjust according to particular circumstances, always in loyalty to Holy Scripture.

(3) Church–State issues:

Synod recognizes that the teaching of the Confession on church and state has been disputed at times and accordingly affirms that the Church understands the Confession consistently with the statements set forth hereunder:

> (i) Ch 23.3. The words "to take order" are understood to be equivalent to "to see to it", and the last sentence is read as limited to circumstances where the church is disorganized or corrupt, with the civil magistrate's power being limited to calling synods, being present at them, and insisting that whatsoever is transacted in them be according to the mind of God' [*vide* Act approving the Confession of Faith, Church of Scotland 27 August 1647].
>
> (ii) Ch. 31.2. "In the case of churches not organised or consti- tuted in government, ministers may meet synodically without commission from their churches, and civil rulers may lawfully call a synod of ministers and other fit persons to consult and advise about matters of religion. In cases where the church is organised, a synod of ministers and elders delegated from their churches may meet as often as is necessary for the good of the church by exercising the inherent right to do so given by Christ, even if the civil authorities withhold or deny their consent" [*vide* Act approving the Confession of Faith, Church of Scotland, 27 August 1647].
>
> (iii) Church and state are distinct and separate institutions; both are accountable to the Lord Jesus Christ who has received all authority in heaven and earth from the Father; the mutually helpful relationship between church and state does not imply subordination of one to the other in its own sphere; and, in particular, the civil authorities have no jurisdiction or authoritative control in the spiritual affairs of Christ's church. In maintaining these scriptural principles, and the ideal of a united Christian church in a Christian nation, the Church does

not regard the involvement of the state in matters concerning religion as *ipso facto* contrary to true liberty of conscience as some Voluntarists and others have held, while yet she firmly rejects intolerance or persecution as methods of advancing the kingdom of God, and recognizes the individual's liberty of conscience and the right of private judgment [cf. Act of the Free Church of Scotland Assembly, 1846].

(4) Other points of clarification:

a. Synod acknowledges a diversity of view point on the precise nature of the creation days in Ch 4.1 has long existed, and the Church has recognized liberty of opinion on the subject provided that this liberty is held in a manner consistent with adherence to the other doctrines of the Confession.

b. Further, while it has been the practice of the Church during most of her history, reflecting her reverence for the word of God and the suitability of the Psalms for the gathered worship of the people of God, to confine the songs used in the praise portion of public worship to the 150 songs of the Psalter, and this practice is anew affirmed, the Church does not regard her office-bearers as bound to regard this scriptural practice as the only proper application of the regulative principle of worship [refer Act of the Church of Scotland Assembly, Session 25, 28 August 1647 as indicating the meaning given to 'psalms' in Ch 21.5 was not restricted to the Psalter].

c. Similarly, the Synod notes that the Church has not enforced the last sentence of Ch 24.4 in a manner so as to exercise church discipline on a person simply because he marries a deceased wife's sister or a deceased husband's brother.

d. The Synod also declares that it does not consider Ch 25.6 of the Confession to expound in a binding way the doctrine of antichrist and the man of sin, as found in Holy Scripture, beyond the affirmation that the Pope is not the church's head, and that the general spirit and distinctive features of the papal system are opposed to Christ, and represent a serious departure from Christian truth and practice, a departure which was predicted in Scripture itself.

(5) The Synod affirms that it requires office-bearers to teach the doctrines of the Confession of Faith with biblical balance. In the words of the Assembly of the Church of Scotland in 1720, emphasis must be given to "The great and fundamental truths, such as the Being and Providence of God, the Divine authority of the Holy Scriptures, the necessary doctrine of the ever-blessed Trinity in the unity of the Godhead; more particularly the eternal deity of our Lord and Saviour Jesus Christ, the satisfaction to divine justice made by him who is our only propitiation, regeneration by efficacious grace, free justification through our blessed surety the Lord Jesus Christ, received by faith alone, and the necessity of a holy life, in order to the obtaining of everlasting happiness." The Synod regards the giving of a central place to the person and work of Christ, and pressing the obligation to repent and believe the Gospel upon all who hear it, as vital to the healthy life and mission of the Church.

(6) Synod expects and requires that, should at any time a question arise as to an office-bearer's understanding of any teachings of the word of God that may seem to conflict with his subscription to the teaching of the Confession, he will not act or teach independently but bring such a matter before the relevant church court for clarification or resolution, including by final appeal to the word of God. Should he have cause in conscience to disagree with a lawful decision of the Church, he may clear his conscience by formal protest but remains obligated to submit to his brothers in Church assembly and to promote the unity of the Church.

The Subscription Form could then read as follows:

1. I …………... .....do hereby declare, that

(1) I believe the Scriptures of the Old and New Testaments to be the word of God, and the only rule of faith and life, and

(2) I sincerely own and believe the whole doctrine contained in the Westminster Confession of Faith of 1647, and explained by the Act of Synod in the year ...., to be the truths of God; and I do sincerely believe and declare the same to be the confession of my faith.

(3) I also sincerely acknowledge the biblical character of the worship authorized by the Confession of Faith, which worship is illustrated in the Directory for Public Worship of 1645 and in Acts of Synod from time to time.

(4) I further sincerely believe and declare that the form of church government warranted in Scripture is Presbyterian, that is, rule by elders, equal in ruling power, and organized in congregational, regional and national assemblies with power to administer the affairs of the church, but always in accordance with the Holy Scriptures and as they shall be accountable to the Lord Jesus Christ, the Church's only king and head.

(5) I also promise, in God's strength, to live a holy and exemplary life; to promote the purity, peace, unity and progress of this Church; and to follow no divisive course from the doctrine, worship, discipline, and government of this Church, but rather to faithfully assert, maintain and defend the same, rejecting whatever is contrary to or inconsistent with it; and to submit myself to the decisions of my brothers in the various courts of this Church.

Deacons

(6) I promise to perform faithfully all the duties of the office to which I have been called, including practicing faithful stewardship myself and encouraging it in others; cultivating the ministry of mercy in the congregation, and generally handling the Lord's money in a manner that is efficient and above reproach, while also paying due regard to my personal devotional life and walk with the Lord, as also the care of my family.

Elders

(6) I promise to perform faithfully all the duties of the office to which I have been called including encouraging the spiritual

growth of the church members, seeking to bring others to know Christ, visiting the sick of mind or body, and attending on the meetings associated with my office, while also paying due regard to my personal devotional life and walk with the Lord, as also the care of my family.

Licentiates or others certified to preach

(6) I promise to seek diligently to become an able expositor of the word of God, an understanding and helpful pastoral visitor, a faithful minister of God, while also paying due regard to my personal devotional life and walk with the Lord, as also the care of my family.

Ministers

(6) I solemnly affirm that I have not used any unlawful or improper means for obtaining this call directly, or indirectly through the hands of others at my request; and that zeal for the honor of God, love to Jesus Christ, and the desire of saving souls, are my great motives and chief inducements to enter upon the work of the holy ministry, and not worldly plans and interests.

(7) I accept the call of this congregation [Or: the appointment to this charge] and promise, by God's grace, to perform faithfully, diligently and cheerfully all the duties of my office, including bringing to my congregation the fruits of careful and earnest study of the word of God as well as understanding and faithful pastoral care; seeking to win the lost to Christ; and taking part in the meetings associated with my office in a positive and constructive way; while also paying due regard to my personal devotional life and walk with the Lord, as also the care of my family.

The Thirty-Nine Articles at the Westminster Assembly

Robert M. Norris

Introduction

The Westminster Assembly of Divines is remembered for the Confession and Catechisms that bear its name. It passes almost without remark that the Assembly was originally called not to author a new confession nor write catechisms, but rather to revise those Articles of Religion that had provided a theological basis for the Church of England. Because this work of revision was never completed, some scholars have assumed that the work was of no consequence. They see the abandonment of the project as a simple prelude to the real work for which the Assembly is remembered. Others have seen the calling of the Assembly to prepare a revision of the Thirty-Nine Articles as a "stalling" measure by a Parliament that was committed to a military alliance with Scotland against the king and knew that any such alliance would require the establishing of a Presbyterian church in England and a thoroughly explicit Reformed confessional basis. Thus the ten weeks of debate devoted to the revision of the articles is seen as irrelevant to the real intent of Parliament in calling the Assembly.

It is my contention that, far from accomplishing nothing, the debates on the Thirty-Nine Articles provided understanding of the central theological tenets of Protestantism and offer a clear understanding of the distinctly Reformed nature of those articles. These debates were conducted with considerable vigor, both intellectually and rhetorically.

The Calling of an Assembly of Divines

On November 8, 1641, the English Parliament expressed its desire that

> there may be a general Synod of the most grave, pious, learned and judicious Divines of this Island; assisted with some from foreign parts professing the same religion with us, who may consider all things necessary for the peace and good government of the church, and represent the results of their consultations to Parliament, to be there allowed of and confirmed, and receive the stamp of authority, thereby to find passage and obedience throughout the kingdom.[1]

This was the culmination of a debate that had taken place within Parliament since its recall in 1640 by the king. After twelve years of personal rule, Charles had been forced to summon Parliament because of the financial burdens that had accumulated as a direct result of his war with Scotland. This war had been provoked by the religious policies of his archbishop, William Laud, who had attempted to impose Episcopal rule, Arminian doctrine, and Prayer Book worship upon Presbyterian and Reformed Scotland. When recalled, the newly formed Parliament gave voice to its criticism of the civil, judicial, and religious life of the nation. In the case of religion, Parliament, which was now composed of a majority of those sympathetic to the Puritan position, was well aware not only of the Scottish issues but also of the hostility that had been engendered by the innovations that Laud had forced upon the established church in England. The House of Commons met on

---

[1] John Rushworth, *Historical Collections of private passages of state, weighty matters in law, remarkable proceedings* . . . (8 vols.; London: D. Browne, 1722), 1:450.

November 3, 1640, to consider both the abuse of the rights and powers of Parliament and the matter of religion.[2]

Parliamentarians of all shades of opinion spoke about the state of religion in the country. The debate moved steadily from seeking to deal with the correction of specific abuses as they were outlined in petitions received from various parts of the country, to a root and branch reformation of the church and the possible abolition of episcopacy. Principled opposition to the Episcopal system of church government was led by Mr. Grimston, a member of the Parliament, who spoke for many when he argued that episcopacy was not the model of church government established by divine appointment, but rather was a human institution. This principled opposition was harnessed to pragmatic political advantage by the leaders of the Puritan Parliament, Rudyard, Seymour, and Pym, who accused the royal favorites of having reintroduced and encouraged "popery" into the English church. Their attack upon the ecclesiastical courts, which they regarded as being corrupt instruments of an absolute monarch, soon broadened into an assault upon the whole structure of episcopacy. The process of denouncing abuses within the national church developed into a movement that called for the reformation of the church "in root and branch."

On November 10, a committee of twenty-four members of Parliament was appointed to examine the religious state of the nation. They received petitions from both individuals and public corporations, calling for the correction of Laudian abuses, including the re-siting of the communion table to distinguish it from an altar. The committee reported to the full Parliament on December 16, 1640. In addition to condemning some specific "Canons" of a royalist Convocation as illegal, Parliament denied to any clergy the right to make any canons for the church without the consent of Parliament. Thus almost unnoticed they gave to Parliament the

---

[2]   Rushworth, *Historical Collections,* 4:34.

legal foundation to initiate the reform of the church, which was to take place with the calling of the Westminster Assembly.

On December 11, the House of Commons received a petition with more than 15,000 signatures from the City of London which listed twenty-eight uncorrected grievances which continued from the administration of the church under Archbishop Laud, and which went on to demand:

> that the government of archbishops, lord bishops, deans, archdeacons, etc., and their courts and administrations in them, with all their dependencies, root and branches may be abolished, as dangerous to the church and commonwealth, and the cause of many foul pressures to the subject in liberties and estates, and the true government according to the word of God established.[3]

Similar petitions were received from other English counties, all of them pressing for the urgent reformation of the church and urging the immediate correction of abuses. On February 8, 1641, Parliament began to debate the question of episcopacy and reform of the church, but the parliamentarians chose to exclude doctrinal matters from their discussion, regarding them as being an area outside of their competence. Over the succeeding months Parliament enacted a series of laws which curtailed the authority of the episcopate and began to move to the complete abolition of the Episcopal system of church government.

An Erastian Body

The various proposed schemes to replace episcopacy reflected the determination of Parliament to control all religious structures in England and place all real power with the nominees of Parliament. This has given credence to the accusation that the Westminster Assembly was a purely Erastian body. The term "Erastian" was commonly used to indicate the doctrine of the supremacy of the state over the church in ecclesiastical affairs. It took its name from

---

[3] Rushworth, *Historical Collections,* 4:93-97.

Thomas Erastus, a Swiss physician and Zwinglian theologian. He raised the question of the power of the state versus that of the church by opposing the church discipline of the Calvinist party in Heidelberg. In his book *"Explicatio gravissimae questionis utram excommunication,"* he contended that the punishment of Christians for their sins is not the function of the church, but rather the state. It was nothing new for England, for after the Reformation the state assumed responsibility for, and control over, church affairs, with both church and state standing under the authority of the monarch. What took place when the Westminster Assembly was called by Parliament was the assumption of the headship of religion by a Parliament which was convinced

> that the freedom of the laity from clerical oppression was bound up with the maintenance of the civil power, no longer represented by the sovereign alone, but by the Houses of Parliament who in a sense claimed to represent unorganised Christian laity of the kingdom.[4]

Erastianism in England in the 1640s stood for the view that disciplinary power, and thus ultimately all ecclesiastical power, rested in the hands of the civil magistrates and also that "no church government be of divine right, but all to be a humane institution depending on the will of the magistrate."[5] Four prominent "Erastians" were part of the Westminster Assembly when it was later called by Parliament. There were two Divines, each of whom was a formidable Hebrew scholar. They were John Lightfoot, who was Master of Catherine Hall Cambridge and Vice Chancellor of the University, and Thomas Coleman, who was given the title "rabbi" in recognition of his Hebrew learning. They were supported by two Parliamentarians who were also members of the Assembly, John Selden and Bulstrode Whitlocke. In their participation in the

---

[4]   A. F. Mitchell, *The Westminster Assembly, Its History and Standards* (Edinburgh, 1883), 27f.

[5]   J. R. De Witt, *Jus Divinum* (Kampen: J. H. Kok, 1969), 27.

debates of the Assembly, the concerns of these men reflect more of an interest in the question of the basis of church government than in its form.

The king repeatedly refused to assent to the calling of any assembly of Divines, and it was not until he had fled from London that the Assembly was actually called by Parliament and the rules were framed that were to govern both its composition and its deliberations. An analysis of the ordinance that called the Westminster Assembly into being immediately reveals the determination on the part of Parliament not to lose any of its control over the religion of the nation:

> this ordinance or anything therein contained shall not give unto any persons aforesaid [the named Divines] or any of them any jurisdiction power or authority ecclesiastical, whatsoever, or any power other then that herein expressed.[6]

The purpose of their calling was limited to "vindicating and clearing of the doctrine of the Church of England from all calamies and aspersions."[7]

The mandate of the Assembly was from the first a doctrinal one. Only when Commissioners from Scotland arrived did the purpose change, and the specific question of an alternative form of government was thrown into relief. Initially they were not involved in any radical reform of church government, though the calling ordinance did expressly mention the fact that the Episcopal system had been abolished and that the Divines were called to advise Parliament on certain ecclesiastical affairs.

Parliament called the Assembly, appointed its members, defined its rights and privileges, determined its areas of debate, delimited its authority, and appointed its prolocutor, Dr. William Twisse,

---

[6]   *Journal of the House of Lords*, 4:84.

[7]   G. Gillespie, "Notes of the Assembly of Divines in The Presbyterian Armoury," *Works of George Gillespie*, ed. W. M. Hetherington (2 vols.; 1846; repr., Edmonton: Still Waters Revival, 1991), 2:vii-ix.

who was a theologian with an international reputation. It also designated the time and place of its first meeting and proposed its expenses. Thus we see that the Westminster Assembly was not a synod of the church. Its members were not chosen to represent the church or empowered to make decisions for the church. It was a parliamentary committee!

Historically it followed the precedents of ancient ecclesiastical councils that had met under the authority of the ruler or magistrates. The Synod of Dort in 1618, which had come together at the command of the Dutch States General, may have offered a practical model for Parliament to deal with theological matters that affected the well-being both of church and state.

In defense of Parliament and the Assembly, there was little else that could be done. Parliament had uprooted episcopacy but had not substituted any alternative form of government. Yet there was still a national church, and that church needed form, order, and discipline. Parliament was preoccupied with its contest with the king and needed an expedient means of regulating and reforming the church. The Assembly was a convenient means of meeting these goals. At the same time it was clear that Parliament wanted the members of the Assembly to maintain a freedom of thought and expression. In the oath that was required of each member such undertakings were mandatory. While Parliament maintained a control over the affairs of the church, they did not desire to subvert the freedom of doctrinal expression within the Assembly.

Regulating the Assembly

Parliament had devised a list of procedural regulations that were to direct the working of the Assembly. John Lightfoot, who was present at the Assembly every day until January 22, 1644, lists eight of them: (1) That two Assessors be joined to the Prolocutor, to supply his place in case of absence or infirmity; (2) Two scribes to be appointed, to set down all proceedings, and these to be Divines who are not to be members of the Assembly (Henry Roborough and Adoniram Byfield); (3) Every member of his first entrance into the Assembly shall make serious and solemn protestation not to maintain anything but that which he believes to be the truth; and to embrace truth in sincerity, when it is presented to him; (4) No resolution is to be given upon any question on the same day as it is first proposed; (5) What any member wishes to establish, must be proved from the Scripture; (6) No man is to continue to speak after the Prolocutor has told him to be quiet, unless the Assembly desires him to go on; (7) No man is to be denied the right to dissent from the Assembly and to state his reasons for it, in any point after it has first been debated by the Assembly; and then, if the dissenting party desire it, to be sent to Parliament by the Assembly (not by any particular man or men, in a private way) when either House shall require it; and (8) All things agreed on and prepared for Parliament are to be debated openly in the Assembly and then offered as the judgment of the Assembly, if the majority agree, providing also that the opinions and reasons of any dissenters are added (if they desire it) as well as any answer made by the Assembly.[8]

To these rules were added others which appear to have been the Assembly's own devising: (1) That every Session begins and ends with prayer, (2) That after the first prayer the names of all members of the Assembly be read and those that are absent be so marked; but if any member comes in afterwards, he shall be allowed to give his name to the scribes, (3) That all Assembly meetings be at ten in the morning, the afternoon to be reserved for committee work, (4) That three of the members be appointed weekly as chaplains, one to the House of Lords, one to the House of Commons, and the third to the committee of both kingdoms.[9]

---

[8] John Lightfoot, *The Whole Works of the Rev. John Lightfoot*, ed. John Rodgers Pittman (13 vols.; London: J. F. Dove, 1822–1825), 13:13

[9] The House of Lords originally proposed yet another rule: "No long speeches to be permitted, that may not be earned by impertinent flourishes, but all debates to be by way of argument, soberly and gravely managed." The House of Commons

From Baillie[10] we learn that every man who wished to speak got up on his own, was not called by the Prolocutor, and could speak as long as he wished without interruption. If more than one rose to speak, then the Assembly called out the name of that man that they wished to hear, and the one who received the loudest support spoke.

Baillie, in the same place, provides us with information on the voting procedure. He wrote that each proposition and text were produced separately and debated. When all debate had ended, it was put before the Assembly by the scribe. Propositions were read, and voting was by acclamation. If, however, there appeared to be a close division, then each Divine was required to stand at his place, voting either for or against, those voting "for" standing first. Once this procedure had been followed, then the matter was ended.

Each member of the Assembly was required to take an oath before they could be seated in the Assembly:

> I, _____, do seriously and solemnly protest in the presence
> of Almighty God, that in this Assembly whereof I am a member
> I will maintain nothing in matters of doctrine but what I think in
> my conscience to be truth; or in point of discipline but what I shall
> conceive to conduce to the glory of God and the good and peace
> of His church.[11]

When this oath had been administered, the Assembly divided into three committees, all committees being open to any of the authorized members of the Assembly who might be interested in their deliberations.

---

objected to this and the Lords agreed to its omission. *Journal of the House of Lords,* 4:114.

[10] Robert Baillie, *Letters and Journals*, ed. David Laing (3 vols.; Edinburgh: Printed for Robert Ogle, 1841), 2:107f.

[11] D. Neal, *History of the Puritans* (5 vols.; :n.p, London, 1822), 3:51; A.F. Mitchell, *The Minutes of the Westminster Assembly* (:n.p, London, 1897), 70.

To accomplish the work prescribed for them by Parliament on July 5 the Assembly was divided into three committees. To the first committee, of which Dr. Burge was appointed chairman, was entrusted the first four articles; to the second, of which Dr. Stanton was chairman, the fifth, sixth, and seventh Articles; and to the third, which had Dr. Gibbon for chairman, the eighth, ninth, and tenth.

Debates on the Thirty-Nine Articles

On Wednesday, July 5, 1643, the Commons and Lords agreed that the Assembly of Divines should consider the first ten of the Thirty-Nine Articles of the Church of England "To free and vindicate the doctrine of these from all aspersions and false interpretations."[12] The Assembly divided the Articles between three committees, and recommendations of alteration to be made, or of Scriptures to be appended, came from these committees to the floor of the Assembly.

The Thirty-Nine Articles that were to be revised formed the confessional basis of the Church of England. Under Queen Elizabeth I, the Forty-Two Articles of Religion that had been drawn up by Archbishop Thomas Cranmer in 1563 had been distilled into Thirty-Nine Articles. They had undergone a final revision in 1571. They were designed as a confessional basis to encompass the beliefs of the national Church of England and to provide a consistent doctrinal foundation for the unity of a Reformed national church. They reflect the diverse influences of Calvin and Luther and seek to provide a middle ground between Roman Catholic thought and Anabaptist thought.

On August 22, 1643, by an order from Parliament, the Assembly was charged with including a further nine Articles within their brief; it was required that these, too, should be cleared and vindicated, "the same from all aspersions and false interpretations."

---

[12]   Lightfoot, *Works*, 13:13.

The "Minutes" of the debates of the Assembly were recorded in unique shorthand by Adoniram Byfield and Henry Roborough who were the scribes of the Assembly and recorded only the debates from Session 45 onwards, though some knowledge of the contents of the first forty-four sessions can be derived from the diaries of some of those present.[13] Also Carruthers[14] considers some of the controversy on the third and eighth Articles.

The debates on the Articles continued until October 12, breaking only for the discussion of the terms and implications of adopting the Solemn League and Covenant. In this time they had revised fifteen of the Articles and were so far engaged upon the sixteenth that they had resolved to change the phrase "may depart from grace given" into "may fail of the grace of God attained." After this date, Parliament ordered that the full attention of the Assembly be directed towards the question of the government and liturgy of the Church. The completed Articles were sent to Parliament as they were, even though the Assembly recorded its unhappiness that the revision should be halted because, as Mitchell says, "they regarded the work as in several ways imperfect and as having relation only to the Church of England, and therefore as superseded by the more recent order sent to them to prepare a Confession of Faith for the Churches of the three kingdoms."[15] Mitchell lists in the same place the various reprintings of the corrected Articles and indicates which forms are the earliest.

The main part of the debates in the "Minutes" deals with the revision of comparatively few of the Articles: Article 11, "Of the Justification of Man before God"; Article 12, "Of Good Works"; Article 13, "Of Works before Justification"; Article 14, "Of Works of Supererogation"; Article 16, "Of Christ Alone without Sin."

---

[13] George Gillespie; Robert Baillie wrote lengthy notes in their papers which are cited here under their names.

[14] S. W. Carruthers, *Everyday Work at the Westminster Assembly* (Lancaster: Presbyterian Historical Society [of America] and the Presbyterian Historical Society of England, 1943), 157.

[15] Mitchell, *Westminster Assembly, Its History and Standards,* 157.

Articles of the Church of England	Revised Articles of the Assembly
Article XI	**Article XI**
Of the Justification of Man	**On the Justification of Man before God**
We are accounted righteous before God, only for the merit of our Lord and Saviour Jesus Christ by faith, and not for our own works or deservings. Wherefore that we are justified by faith only is a most wholesome doctrine, and very full of comfort; as more largely is expressed in the Homily of Justification.	We are justified, that is we are accounted righteous before God, and have remission of sins, not for nor by our own works or deservings, but freely by His grace, only for Our Lord and Saviour Jesus Christ's sake, His whole obedience and satisfaction being by God imputed unto us, and Christ with His righteousness being apprehended rested on by faith only. The doctrine of justification by faith only, is a wholesome doctrine and very full of comfort not withstanding God doth not forgive them that are impenitent, and go on still in their trespasses.
Article XII	**Article XII**
Of Good Works	**Of Good Works**
Albeit that good works, which are the fruits of faith and follow after justification, cannot put away our sins and endure the severity of God's judgement, yet are they pleasing and acceptable to God in Christ, and do spring out necessarily of a true and lively faith, insomuch that by them a lively faith may be as evidently known as a tree discerned by the fruit.	Good works which are the fruits of faith, and follow after justification, cannot put away our sins, and endure the severity of God's judgement, yet are they, notwithstanding their imperfections, in the sight of God pleasing and acceptable unto Him in and for Christ, and do spring out necessarily of a true and lively faith, insomuch that by them a lively faith may be evidently known, as a tree discerned by the fruits.
Article XIII	**Article XIII**
Of Works before Justification	**On Works before Justification**
Works done before the grace of Christ and the inspiration of His Spirit, are not pleasant to God, forasmuch as they spring not of faith in Jesus Christ, neither do they make men meet to receive grace, or (as the School authors say) deserve grace of congruity: yea, rather for that they are not done as God hath willed and commanded them to be done, we doubt not but they have the nature of sin.	Works done before justification by Christ and regeneration by His Spirit, are not pleasing unto God, forasmuch as they spring not of faith in Jesus Christ, neither do they make men meet to receive grace, or [as the school authors say] deserve grace of congruity; yea rather, for that they are not done as God hath willed and commanded them to be done they are sinful.

Article XIV **Of Works of Supererogation** Voluntary works besides, over and above, God's commandments which they call Works of Supererogation, cannot be taught without arrogancy and impiety. For by them men do declare that they do not only render unto God as much as they are bound to do, but that they do more for His sake than of bounden duty is required: Whereas Christ saith plainly, When ye have done all that are commanded to you, say, We be unprofitable servants.	Article XIV **On Works of Supererogation** Voluntary works besides, over and above God's commandments, which they call works of supererogation, cannot be taught without arrogance and impiety. For by them men do declare that they do not only render unto God as much as they are bound to do, but that they do more for His sake than of bounden duty is required, whereas Christ saith plainly, "when ye have done all that are commanded to you say we are yet unprofitable servants."

Article XVI
Of Christ Alone Without Sin
[While this article was debated, no change was made to the article as it stood.]
Christ in the truth of our nature was made like unto us in all things, only except, from which he was clearly void, both in His flesh and in His Spirit. He came to be a lamb without spot, who by sacrifice of Himself once made, should take away the sins of the world; and sin [as St. John saith] was not in Him. But all the rest although baptized and born again in Christ yet offend in many things; and if we say we have no sin we deceive ourselves and the truth is not in us.

The Revision of the Articles betrays little of the intensity and substance of the debates that led to those revisions.

Though the number of Articles dealt with is small, they cover the most distinctive and central doctrines of 17th- century Protestantism, and also embody some of the most controversial issues of Reformed thought.

Imputation

In the Minutes of Sessions 46, 48, 52, and 72 of the debates of the Assembly, the contested issue of the imputation of the active and passive work of Christ absorbs a significant amount of time and space. The issue centered upon the question of whether the obedience of Christ to the law was imputed together with his sacrifice as a means of presenting the elect as "righteous."

The Prolocutor of the Assembly, Dr. Twisse, became the leader of those who most vigorously sought to limit "imputation" to the "passive" work of Christ. In this he reflected the position of the German theologian, Johannes Piscator, who had led the debate in the Reformed churches of the continent.

Piscator had stated that, "Whosoever denies that Christ was subject to the law, denies that he was man." This position had framed much of the debate on justification. Dr. Twisse, Thomas Gataker, Rector of Rotherhithe, and Richard Vines were the principal advocates for restricting the "passive work" of Christ as alone being imputed for forgiveness, maintaining that only the suffering and death of Christ had a satisfactory significance. Dr. Twisse had argued that to impute both the active and the passive work of Christ was to confuse justification with sanctification. Citing Titus 2:14, he wanted to establish that Christ "by his bloud hath redeemed us" as distinct from that "love of Christ that constraines us to every good worke."

Making the point that justification consists not merely of the forgiveness of sins, but requires the imputation of the righteousness of Christ, he argued that while the righteousness of Christ was founded upon the active obedience of law, it was not imputed. He mouthed the arguments of Piscator when he said: "The active obedience of Christ should have a principal part in all the honour and glory wherein to Christ is advanced his sufferings." He went on to argue that unlike mankind, Christ had found obedience natural, as well as required, and therefore had never found it to be burdensome, to bring a perfect obedience both to the ceremonial law and the moral law.

Twisse was attacked on this point by Joshua Hoyle, who was the Regius Professor of Divinity at Oxford. He maintained that it was impossible to maintain any theory that asserted the removal of punishment and yet left the guilt of sin. He was arguing against the possibility of dividing the life and death of Christ. He asserted that it was impossible to restrict the saving worth of the obedience of Christ to his perfect sacrifice when the whole of his life went into producing that perfect obedience. He maintained that Christ could not have given satisfaction simply by his active obedience, because as man, although perfect man, He was still "under the law," which he interpreted to mean "the curse of the law." This was not ultimately seen to have been satisfied until the passion of Christ. Conceding that the obedience of Christ had an effect on the satisfaction that he made, it was nonetheless only an indirect one, in that had he not led a sinless and obedient life, then his death would not have constituted a perfect satisfaction.

This was answered by Dr. Daniel Featley, the Provost of Chelsea College, who was to be the only member of the Assembly ever to be expelled. He was judged to be a supporter of episcopacy and a Royalist, and was suspected of having passed on information from the Assembly to Bishop Ussher, who was with the king at Oxford. He was perhaps the main protagonist on the side of those wanting to see the imputation of the active, as well as the passive work of Christ, and claimed support from Calvin, Peter Martyr, and Augustine. Piscator's use of the Ramist divisions was exactly mirrored in the arguments of Lazarus Seaman, the Master of Peterhouse College, Cambridge. Seaman, however, used the method to controvert the arguments of the Heidelberg theologian by claiming that if the active obedience of Christ was imputed as well as the passive, then man would be freed from obedience as well as the curse. He defined two types of law breaking: by neglect and by defiance. Both, however, were covered by justification. He followed this with an example of the tight argumentation that marked out much of the debate.

The great mystery of the debate is why, when a clear majority of the Divines seemed persuaded by Featley's overwhelming arguments (that both active and passive work were to be imputed), they should, when they wrote the Confession of Faith, restrict the imputation to the "passive work." Perhaps the answer could be found in the addition of the Scots Commissioners.

Clear from these early debates is the fact that the majority came to accept that the person and the work of Christ were indivisible. Great emphasis was placed upon the "one-ness" of the ministry of Christ, and decisive texts such as Galatians 4:4 were used to seek to restrict the imputation to the passive work alone. By the end of the forty-second debate it was determined that sufficient time had been allotted to the discussion and the question was ended. The "Minutes" record interestingly that Thomas Gataker, while taking a leading part in the debate itself, was also the moving advocate to ensure that the exact nature of the obedience of Christ should not be specified!

This became the position of the Assembly established by vote, and their position was made in stated opposition to The Second Helvetic Confession, where the issue was discussed in detail and required affirmation. The Westminster Divines were clear that they did not intend to prevent any men from exercising their ministry because of a disagreement on this particular point. At the same time, they made clear that they were aware of the continental debates and confessional positions and did not regard themselves as being bound by them.

Because it was impossible to reconcile both positions within the article, and because there was no overwhelming certainty about the issue itself, the revised article on justification in the Thirty-Nine Articles was framed to avoid teaching either position as an article of faith, which was to read:

> We are justified, that is we are accounted righteous before God, and have remission of sins, not for nor by our own works or deservings, but freely by His grace, only for Our Lord and Saviour Jesus Christ's sake, His whole obedience and satisfaction being by God imputed unto us.

The resolution of the debate in this way indicates the diversity of opinion on the matter that was present in the Assembly, and also the recognition that the Reformed tradition was broader than any single confession. The Assembly also shows itself independent of the continental Reformed churches, even though they demonstrate an awareness of their actions. We see also a "pastoral" concern within the debates that was not prepared to debar from ministry many who may disagree with a majority. There is here evidence of the acknowledged breadth of the Reformed tradition, which is at odds with many caricatures of the Assembly.

Antinomianism

Antinomianism was one of the most pressing of the issues that the Assembly faced. It was no new debate, but had been given a new form within Lutheran and Reformed Orthodoxy.[16] It existed in the early church, and Paul stringently condemned it; its essential tenets, however, had persisted into the life of the church. In the Middle Ages, various sects had embraced the understanding that Christians were free from the moral constraints of the law. Almaric of Bena (d.1204) had been one of its leading thinkers, and he had maintained that "to those constituted in love, no sin is imputed." While his ideas and his followers had been condemned, the pattern of thought persisted and was resurrected with new forms in the continental Reformation. Indeed, Luther had himself given fresh impetus to antinomianism when he had used strong language to combat the legalism that was inherent in much of medieval Catholic thought. He had maintained that the Mosaic law was an ancient code that had been given for a specific people under unique circumstances and that in the modern states the juridical and ceremonial aspects of the law had been replaced by civil law. He went on to argue that even the Decalogue ought to be carefully employed by Christians. He saw the need to preach the law from a spiritual standpoint only so that the conscience should be humbled to see its need of

---

[16] Particular reference is made to the work of Gomarus, who was the single most cited adversary of Arminius, yet whose own supralapsarian theological positions held problems for the Divines. His written espousal of the place of the law did little to mitigate the fears that in reality the law was being assaulted. Franciscus Gomarus, *Opera Theologica Omnia* (Amsterdam, 1644).

grace. So strong was his disavowal of the Mosaic law as allied with justification that he went so far as to disparage it. He maintained that, "the righteousness of the Gospel be the light and the day, but the righteousness of the law, darkness and night." [17]

While his language had sometimes been extreme and some of his theological speculation had suggested that repentance itself came only from the vision of the work of Christ, Luther more generally maintained that the process of salvation began with the operation of the law upon the soul, which in repentance looks for aid and is met by the promise of forgiveness through Christ.

While clarity was brought to the situation by the work of Melanchthon, who carefully defined Luther's position and placed the preaching of the law at the gateway of Christian instruction, arguing that it led to repentance, which was antecedent to faith; nonetheless Luther's earlier statement caused the issue of Antinomianism to reemerge. The Divines at Westminster frequently cited their opposition to the position of Johann Agricola and the position which he represented. Agricola had been an early supporter of Luther, who was affronted at the position of Melanchthon. He published his own propositions which fuelled the whole of the debate on justification. The Lutheran controversy lasted more than a decade, from 1527 until 1537. Though the Formula of Concord fixed the final terminology of the debate by deciding that the law was a special revelation teaching what is just and pleasing in the sight of God, and refuting whatever is opposed to the divine will, Agricola was never satisfied that Luther or the Lutheran Church ever came to terms with the theological issues that he raised.

Agricola asserted that repentance was not to be taught from the Decalogue nor, indeed, from any part of the Mosaic law, but exclusively from the sight of the suffering and death of Christ, arguing that the Spirit and not the law convicted sinners of their sin. He further maintained that justification was entirely mediated

---

[17] Martin Luther, *Tabletalk*, sec. 289.

by the work of the Spirit alone, and therefore, men are justified without the law through the gospel of Christ alone. Indeed, without the Holy Spirit, the law could only convict men of sin to their damnation. The issues that he raised in the publication of his "Eighteen Theses" formed the theological background against which the Westminster Divines continued their debates. Their frequent references to Agricola demonstrate both the influence that he continued to exert and the power of the issue to frame the doctrinal statements. Nor was the issue restricted to the German Reformation alone.

Calvin had dealt with the antinomian issue when he confronted the "Libertines," who urged a disregard for the law of Moses and indeed for law in general. However, the theological issues arose afresh in the supralapsarian teaching of the Dutch theologians such as Piscator and Gomarus who, though they are not counted as antinomian thinkers, nonetheless asserted that sin takes place in the life of the believer not only as a reality but by the determination and consent of God. While they affirmed that God had given the law and commanded obedience to it, they held that He had made actual obedience impossible. This gave the basis for the development of antinomian thinking.

The development of antinomian thought in England owed much to the influence of Henrik Nikles and his sect of Familists, which was a community devoted to mystical experiences, only loosely connected with historic Christianity. While not denying the teaching of the Bible, the Familists ignored most of its content or else regarded it as a form of preparation for "an age of love." Nikles saw himself as an incarnation of God and Christ; because he was essentially pantheistic, he could also encourage others to share in God in the same way. While these communities did not survive for very long on the Continent, in England they exercised a much greater influence and enjoyed a much longer history, because of their willingness to maintain an outward conformity to established religion while maintaining an inward distance and disdain. Elizabeth and James I had both outlawed their teaching and attempted to eradicate the movement, yet it had survived and continued to grow. Such was its perceived influence that James I attributed the rise of Puritanism to its existence. Indeed, the government created a special form of abjuration to be applied against any members of the sect who could be brought to trial. Some scholars have seen in the history of the Familists the origins of the Society of Friends.

Certainly their existence posed a unique practical challenge to the Westminster Divines. There was combined with this undercover spiritual movement, which held to a practical antinomianism, also a theological Antinomianism present in England. John Eaton had published in 1642, "The Honeycomb of Free Justification by Christ Alone." Here he distinguished three ages of mankind: (1) the age of the law, (2) the age of John the Baptist, and (3) the Christian age. These existed as "glorious, more glorious, and most glorious." He argued that under the Mosaic law "sin was severely taken hold of and punished sharply in God's children. . . . John laid open their sins, and the danger of them, yet we read not of any punishment inflicted on God's children. . . . The third time, the most glorious, is since Christ groaned out his blood and life upon the cross, by which sin itself, and guilt, and punishment are so utterly and infinitely abolished that there is no sin in the church of God, and that now God sees no sin in us. . . ."[18]

The issue of antinomianism was constituted such a significant problem that Parliament specifically requested the Assembly to consider it. On September 12, 1643, they ordered:

> that it be referred to the Assembly of Divines to compare the Opinions of the Antinomians with the Word of God, and with the Articles of the Church of England; and to return their

---

[18] John Eaton, *The Honeycomb of Free Justification by Christ Alone* (London, 1642). Quoted in *The New Schaff-Herzog Encyclopedia of Religious Knowledge*, ed. Samuel Macauley Jackson (13 vols.; New York: Funk & Wagnalls, 1908–1912), 1:198.

opinions and judgments upon them speedily. It is further ordered that the Antinomian books be referred to the Examination and consideration of the Assembly.[19]

In their debates, the Westminster Divines began a vigorous attack upon the whole antinomian position. There were no supporters of this position among the Divines present at Westminster, though Robert Paul, in *The Assembly of the Lord*, has hinted that some of the leading Parliamentarians had these tendencies, and that some of the Independents at the Assembly might have felt pressure to be more tolerant of some of the antinomian positions because of their belief that "the biblical way of dealing with mistaken belief was by spiritual persuasion."[20]

Because of the array of theological issues that were involved in the whole question of antinomianism, the debates were long and intricate. Fiercest in their opposition to the antinomians were Thomas Gataker, the Rector of Rotherhithe, and Thomas Hill, the Master of Trinity College, Cambridge. Debating the phrase "remission of sins" and examining the consequences of this, Gataker undertook a long and detailed examination of the essential theological system of antinomianism to which he stood opposed. He concluded: (1) That the moral law was seen to be of no use to the believer, nor did it provide a guide or rule for Christian life, nor was it designed as a measure against which the Christian could and should examine his own life. Christians instead are freed from the mandatory power of the law. He cites unnamed theologians who "cry away with the Law which cuts off a man's legs and then bids him walk;" (2) That it is as possible for Christ to sin as for a child of God to sin; (3) That no child of God should be encouraged to ask for pardon for their sin, as they have no need of this. Indeed it becomes a blasphemy to ask for such a thing; (4) That God does not punish any of his children for sin, nor is it for sins of his people

---

[19] Lightfoot, *Works*, 13:5.

[20] Robert S. Paul, *Assembly of the Lord* (Edinburgh: T&T Clark, 1985), 177.

that the land is punished; and (5) That if a man knows himself to be in a state of grace, then, regardless of any action, God sees no sin in him.

Each of these positions was ultimately condemned by members of the Assembly, and the condemnations each became enshrined in the later Confession of Faith. In response to the argument that the Law no longer had any place in the Christian life, Thomas Gataker expounded Galatians 3:12 and was supported by each of the subsequent speakers who added more texts. The fruit of this debate was seen in the later work of the Assembly when the Confession of Faith made clear: "The Moral law doth forever bind all, as well justified persons as others, to the obedience thereof." The article was a clear repudiation of antinomian thought and tendencies. As to the second issue, and the suggestion that Christ could sin, the Assembly was clear in its refusal to change the sixteenth Article of the Thirty-Nine. Thus they affirmed:

> Christ in the truth of our nature was made like unto us in all things, only except, from which he was clearly void, both in His flesh and in his Spirit. He came to be a lamb without spot, who by sacrifice of Himself once made, should take away the sins of the world; and sin [as St. John saith] was not in Him. But all the rest, although baptized and born again in Christ, yet offend in many things; and if we say we have no sin we deceive ourselves and the truth is not in us.

This position became the clear background to the confessional statement that Christ "was without sin."

The remaining marks of antinomianism outlined by Thomas Gataker were also dealt with within the Confession of Faith when, in dealing with the nature and practice of repentance, the Divines affirmed: "Men ought not to content themselves with a general repentance, but it is every man's duty to endeavor to repent of his particular sins particularly." Thus, there was a clear repudiation of the essential convictions of antinomian thought, yet there was an awareness of the complexity of the issue and the theological questions raised within Reformed thought. Nowhere is that better demonstrated than in the famous and absolute condemnation of the antinomian sermons of Tobias Crisp by the Prolocutor of the Assembly, Dr. Twisse. He vigorously condemned the sermons and argued for their public destruction, and yet he still recognized and appreciated the clarity of the preaching of the gospel within those sermons!

While there was a determined and clear repudiation of overt antinomianism, the debates demonstrate the reality that the Assembly was aware of the real issues that existed for Reformed thought as it attempted to deal with the balance of Grace and Law.

Arminianism

None of the Divines present at Westminster had attended the Synod of Dort in 1618. Indeed, the only person to have attended that Synod and also to have been invited to the Assembly at Westminster was Samuel Ward, and he never attended! Yet the decisions of the Synod of Dort were of great import to the Assembly. It was the most significant of the recent Reformed synods. It had been both a national and an international meeting, and its decisions had defined what it meant to be Reformed. The "Minutes" of the Assembly contain repeated references to Dort, both to its structure and to its achievements. The Dutch theologian and leader of the strict Calvinist party at Dort, Franciscus Gomarus, is frequently cited in the "Minutes" and his arguments are repeated with approval.[21] The Arminianism that was faced by the Assembly was more than a passing theological aberration; its political effects were real and remembered. In Holland, the result of the Synod of Dort had been to bring about the "fall" of the political champions of the Remonstrants who had advocated the views of Arminius. They had allied the theological movement to a political agenda that involved

---

[21] *Manuscript Minutes of the Assembly*, Sessions 47, 49, 50. The Minutes themselves exist in Dr. Williams' Library, London. Records of Nonconformity. 1-3 Minutes of the Westminster Assembly, August 4, 1643 to March 25, 1652.

them in seeking to limit the power and authority of the Prince of Orange. The result had been a defeat for theological Arminianism and political oligarchy. In England, the influence of Archbishop Laud and his clergy had cast a long shadow upon the memories of the Divines, as was reflected in their constant references to the "errors" of church under his direction. At the same time Arminian views continued to be spread throughout England, and even in London, which was the seat of Parliamentary and Calvinistic influence and power. Thomas Gataker captured the perceived urgency of the situation when he argued before the Assembly, "that worke doth require expedition; when diseases are desperate... noe delay of phisicke, this is as desparate as any sprung up in late days."[22] The Assembly saw Arminianism as the great threat to national unity and also as the greatest barrier to the establishing of a national church. The threat led to some strange action. For instance, Herbert Palmer, a President of Queen's College Cambridge, accused Sidrach Simpson, Master of Pembroke Hall, Cambridge, of holding Arminian views. Indeed he claimed that Simpson had "incouraged the Antinomians, and confessed that we ought not to confesse our sins."[23] These charges were hotly denied and were not accepted. However, they reflect several realities.

First of all, it showed how widespread was the fear that Independents were secretly Arminian in theology. In fact it was known that John Goodwin, Vicar of St. Stephen's Coleman Street, was an open advocate of Arminian views and that he was a supporter of the Independent party and opposed to the Presbyterian form of church government. In itself, this bred a deep suspicion amongst the Presbyterian Divines as they were committed to a single and unified national church with a single and unified Presbyterian form of government, which they understood to be the clear mandate of Scripture. This drove the Independents at the Assembly constantly

---

[22] Ibid., Session 47.

[23] Ibid., Session 48.

to reaffirm their theological orthodoxy on this issue, and perhaps it explains the strength of anti-Arminian statements.

Secondly, the anti-Arminian debate reflects the confusion over the limits of Reformed pluralism. There was no doubt in the minds of the Divines, as can be seen in their debates and their votes. We have seen in their decisions on the question of the imputation of Christ that they understood that there was room for legitimate difference over some doctrinal issues. However, there were difficult questions as to how far such tolerance could be stretched. In the debate on Article 16, "Of Christ Alone without Sin," Thomas Gataker voiced his concern about charging with heresy either of two theologians who were in disagreement. Daniel Tilenus and John Cameron were both theological teachers at Saumur and leaders within the French Reformed Synod. Tilenus had raised questions whether Adam's sin was "imputed or inherited" in his *"Traicte de la cause et de l'origine du peche."*[24] Yet at the same time he had been an opponent of Arminius and his supporters.

John Cameron was the true originator of the distinctive Saumurian theology that was later given the name of "Amyraldianism" or Hypothetical Redemption. His career had led him from Scotland to France and then a brief return to serve James I in England. He succeeded Jean Daille as pastor of the Reformed Church at Saumur in 1626. At the same time his former student and friend, Moses Amyraut, began to lecture at his old college. His lectures demonstrated the influence of his mentor Cameron. Amyraut published his treatise on predestination, *"Brief Traitte de la predestination et de ses principales dependences"*[25] in which he challenged the traditional Calvinist position of "limited

---

[24] Daniel Tilenus taught at Saumur where he was a controversialist. His writings on grace involved him in a debate with John Cameron, also at Saumur and ultimately suppressed by the French National Synod of Tonneia.

[25] Published in 1643, this work was the first revelation of the doctrine of "Hypothetical Universalism" and was the beginning of a fifty year debate on the issue in the French Reformed Church. While censured he was never removed from his teaching position by any Synodical action.

atonement." The debates that followed divided the Reformed Church in France and continued to be a matter of controversy amongst all the continental Reformed churches. The issue was debated from Synod to Synod in the French Church and throughout Reformed Europe, and was well known to the Westminster Divines. Indeed, it has been suggested that because he was an advocate of Amyraut's theology, Richard Baxter was excluded from the Assembly. However, there was no attempt to declare it heresy within the Assembly, for Thomas Gataker cites it as a controversial position but not a heretical one. The "Minutes" do not suggest any discussion on Gataker's judgment, and its silence reinforces the notion that the Assembly both recognized and was sensitive to the unclear lines of demarcation within continental Reformed orthodoxy.

The vigorous anti-Arminianism of the debates of the Assembly also provides the context for the clear development of a strong federal theology that was to be the hallmark of the later Confession of Faith. When the Divines were compelled to produce a confessional statement, their theological articulation had to deal with antinomianism on one hand and Arminianism on the other. Antinomian thinking argued that because the believer was the "elect" of God and, as a consequence, was indwelt by the Holy Spirit, then it was hinted that they were free from the demands of the law. Arminianism, on the other hand, taught that salvation was conditional upon the ethical response of man to God, and made grace a function of human will. The challenge to orthodox Calvinism was to steer a path between both errors and yet still provide a theologically coherent understanding of law and grace. The answer was found in the development of a strong and coherent federal theology. The foundations for "federalism" were developed in the debates on justification as the members of the Assembly provided an exegetical justification for a "covenant of works" and a "covenant of grace." It was made clear that since God had by his free grace entered into covenant with his people, there was place for the ethical response of his people as they tried to fulfill the human side of the covenant. Yet there was no basis to make exaggerated claims for human goodness.

The debates recorded in the "Minutes" of the forty-sixth Session of the Assembly display the "Covenantal" theological structure with its careful delineation of a "covenant of works" and "covenant of grace," while at the same time bridging the ethical gap between law and grace.

The Theological Epistemology of the Assembly

In all the debates there is evidenced the dual purpose of providing: (1) an accurate and exhaustive definition of the dogmas and (2) a determined articulation and refutation of all possible alternatives, departures, and opposites. This aim of affirmation and refutation corresponds to the double design of scholasticism: to establish the truth and at the same time to define and anathematize heresy. In this endeavor the science of dialectic became the most useful of the theological tools. Olivier Fatio has defined it as "the common instrument, of arts and sciences by which one may affirm that which is proper to the material and reject other things."[26] The methodology of dialectic made it the obvious handmaid to "scholasticism." It became characterized by its method of choosing the shortest path in replying to heretics – by attacking fundamental and architectonic principles. It was the Aristotelian methodology of searching out weaknesses in the argument of an opponent, and then exploiting the weaknesses to the fullest measure. In doing this, the use of syllogism became indispensable.

This method involved expressing the argument in the force of two propositions or premises, one of which contained a common term, with a third proposition being the conclusion resulting of the other two. It constrained debaters carefully to define and divide their material, beginning with true arguments and separating and

---

[26] Olivier Fatio, *Methode et Theologie, Lambert Daneau et les debuts de la scolastique reformer* (Geneva: Droz, 1976), 35.

refuting paralogisms. The use of this mode of reasoning demanded a considerable initial application from those debating, but the method itself had the utilitarian virtue of combining brevity with clarity. Fatio sees this as being the "Aristotelian Ciceronian"[27] method, and its value had been recognized by Melanchthon. He and his followers applied this method to dogmatic problems, and it gradually became the tool of choice for most 17th-century theologians.

The method was not without its critics, especially the French logician, Pierre Ramus, whose bitter attack on Aristotle provoked a sharp rejoinder from the scholastic theologians. At Zurich, however, Bullinger also added his influential weight to the attack on Aristotle and Beza. It is to the linking of Protestant theology with the pagan philosophical methodology that he refers when he says, "philosophers are the patriarchs of heretics."[28]

Ramus was a French humanist who was killed in the St. Bartholomew's Massacre in 1572. His work had been the development of a system of pedagogy in which he sought to break the established dependence of theological discussion upon Aristotle. Ramus's master's thesis, presented at Paris when he was twenty-one years old, had consisted of a single proposition; *"Quaecumque ab Aristotele dicta essent, commentitia esse."* His assertion was the fallibility of Aristotle, in defiance of the prevailing notion, championed by Pierre Galland, that all Aristotle had taught was commensurable with Christian truth. Ramus had sought to break the established dependence upon Aristotelian logic as the basis of theological discussion. To facilitate his position and further his cause Ramus had developed his new methodology of dichotomous division. In his book, *Dialecticae partitiones ad Academiam Parisiensem,* Ramus outlined a new methodology of dichotomous division, which involved breaking down large subjects – termed "the general category" – into two parts, and then further dividing the subparts into ever smaller components, and

---

27 Ibid., 36.
28 Ibid., 39.

then arranging them under headings. At the same time he reduced the number of valid syllogisms as he attempted to make logic a more practical discipline. His method was widely adopted by Puritan preachers in the organization of their sermons. Ramus's methodology, while it was introduced as a pedagogical tool, also became a vehicle for the characteristic theological development of the later Assembly, for it made possible the accelerated acceptance of covenant theology – with its full development of a double covenant format, and its insistence upon a pre-fall covenant of works together with a covenant of grace.

A number of the Divines present at the Assembly at Westminster had endured exile on the European Continent and had imbibed the Ramist ideas; others remained firmly under the older scholastic methodology.

The clear division between the two methodologies was outlined in a letter by Theodore Beza, who rejected Ramus's application to be a teacher at Geneva and who gave as one reason for the rejection as ". . . our determination to follow the position of Aristotle, without deviating a line, be it in logic or in the rest of our studies." The two opposing ideas are reflected in the debates at Westminster. A number of the delegates present had spent part of their time in exile at Zurich, and had there encountered the Ramist methodology. The result had been enshrined in the Second Helvetic Confession, which had been recognized as a major Reformed confessional statement. This well-reasoned and articulate compendium of Reformed belief had been adopted as the official Reformed position of the Church in Switzerland, Hungary, Bohemia, and elsewhere. The great majority, however, were more influenced by the scholastic way of thinking. The prevalent idea seems to have been that while dialectic was not capable of giving a definition of faith, the defense and articulation of faith lay within its compass.

It became impossible to escape the division of form and content, and we find a tacit assumption behind all the debates of two cornerstones of the Protestant scholastic method. First was the idea of the absolute authority of Scripture, resting upon its divine and infallible authorship and self-authentication. Out of this comes the construction of an authoritative corpus of systemized truth. This rests upon the assumption that the Holy Spirit uses the rules of dialectic. This was the assurance of faith. Nor did they believe this method to be an innovation. There is little doubt that the Westminster Divines would have sought to trace this approach through Melanchthon, Aquinas, and Augustine back to St. Paul. The first principle – the authority of Scripture – can be shown to underlie the whole of the debates. Most of the debates, as required by Parliament, concern texts of Scripture. The meaning and the implications of the Scripture were the concern both of theologians and politicians. They shared the common assumption that the divine will was revealed through the divine word.

Corroboration for every assertion was sought from scriptural texts. When the same Assembly drafted its Confession of Faith, it formally invested its material principle with that authority which it had accorded to Scripture in its prior debates. The Westminster Confession in Articles 2, 3, and 4 defines the authority of the books of Scripture that are considered as inspired. The Divines rested their case for this authority upon its divine authorship and inspiration. That it was their material principle of theology may be seen from the fact that they placed it first in the Confession of Faith. Indeed, the very act of producing a confession of faith implied a trust in this method. The Divines attempted to provide a definitive exposition of the fundamental system of truth contained in Scripture. In so doing they had to rely upon the given material and the proper use of reason and logic to arrive at a satisfactory result.

Continental Influences upon the Assembly Debates

A letter had been sent from the Divines at the Westminster Assembly to a number of the Reformed churches of Europe.[29] This letter

---

[29] A letter from the Assembly of Divines in England and the Commissioners of the Church of Scotland, to the Belgic, French Helvetian, and other Reformed

had informed the international community of Reformed churches of the meeting and work of the Assembly; however, there were no delegates or observers invited to attend. The reason for this is simply that the Westminster Assembly had been called into being to deal with specific concerns of national interest. This stands in contrast to the Synod of Dort, where the issues dealt with concerned not only the national church but all Reformed churches, and, thus, the debates reflected international interest. This does not mean that other Reformed churches were not interested in the proceedings at Westminster. Nor should it be assumed that the theological formulations were ultimately reflective of only national interests. A. F. Mitchell has argued that the theological formulations of the Assembly reflect a uniquely British theological tradition, which he saw as Augustinian in character, traceable through Cranmer and Tyndall back to Bradwardine.

In fact the structure of the later Confession of Faith produced by the Divines has been shown to derive, in large measure, from the Irish Articles[30] drawn up by James Ussher while he was Professor of Divinity at Dublin in 1615. These articles had been adopted within the Irish Episcopal Church and were distinctly Calvinist in theological articulation. They provide a clear link in the development from the Thirty-Nine Articles to the Westminster Confession of Faith. They show an agreement both in the distinctive order of theological issues dealt with and the headings of chapters (and even some shared language). Both sets of articles begin with "the Scripture" rather than the doctrine of God, which earlier confessions had done. While it is certainly true that the Westminster Divines deliberately blended the "Formal"

---

churches. This letter was ordered November 22, 1643, and was sent March 13, 1644.

30 *The Irish Articles of Religion, 1615.* Composed in large measure by Archbishop Ussher. They were adopted by the archbishops, bishops, and Convocation of the Irish Episcopal Church four years before the Synod of Dort. They display the clear Calvinism of the Episcopal Church.

and "Material" principles of theology in a way that was not found in the continental confessions of the time, an examination of the "Minutes" of the debates that revised the Thirty-Nine Articles shows not only an awareness of continental Reformed debates, but also the influence of those debates.

Many of the Divines present at Westminster had been exiled among the continental church. Others had been present at Dort, and many maintained an extensive correspondence with Reformed pastors and scholars in the continental Reformed churches. The debates of the Assembly reflect an awareness of the continental theological issues. In fact there is no evidence to suggest that the Divines at Westminster saw themselves as doing anything more than providing a reasonable and consistent development of Reformed theology, adapted most assuredly for the specific needs of their national situation, but being only a consistent development of the theology of the European Reformed churches. In the debates there are direct references to continental theologians and their issues. Indeed, there is recognition of the debt that is owed to many of the continental theologians who are frequently quoted and whose positions are summarized. Far from indicating a commitment to a distinctly "British" theological tradition, the "Minutes" reflect a sense of international Reformed theology. Nowhere does this seem clearer than in the debates concerning the central doctrine of justification.

Conclusion

On October 12, 1643, the Assembly received a communication halting their work. Lightfoot records the event:

> We being at that very instant very busy upon the 16th Article of the Thirty Nine Articles of the Church of England, and upon the clause of it that mentions departing from grace, as we have already seen there came an order from both Houses of Parliament enjoining our speedy taking in hand the Discipline and Liturgy of the Church. [31]

---

[31] Lightfoot, *Works,* 13:4.

This is substantiated by the "Minutes" of the Assembly themselves, where in Session 73 the order from Parliament was read aloud. Though the work was interrupted, it was not forgotten; for, the revised articles together with their scriptural proof texts were submitted on demand to Parliament, which caused them to be printed as: "The Proceedings of the Assembly of Divines upon the Thirty Nine Articles of the Church of England."[32] These were then presented to the king in December, 1647 as part of a proposed settlement between king and Parliament. They were to be regarded with the Apostles' Creed as "a sufficient and sure definition of the Protestant Faith," and were to be used as a test of orthodoxy for the ordination of clergy. The king rejected the proposals, and negotiations broke down. Afterwards, no further use was found for the Articles. Was the time and labor invested in the production of the Articles and the work of those who debated in these opening weeks of the Assembly all wasted and energy misplaced?

The argument that the work of revision of the Thirty-Nine Articles may stand only as a prelude to the real work of the Assembly neglects to assess the profound and vigorous debates that allowed the future work of the Assembly to proceed so swiftly. The same Divines who were to later produce the Confession of Faith and the Catechisms produced these revisions.

Clearly some have asserted this, as we have seen. Some have even suggested that these first weeks and the work devoted to a revision of the Thirty-Nine Articles should not be counted as a work of the Westminster Assembly at all. They believe that the greater work upon which the fame of the Assembly rests not only overshadows this original mandate but negates it. Yet there is a real relationship between the debates on the revision of the Thirty-Nine Articles and the production of the Confession of Faith. There is a definite consistency of thought that exists in embryo in the former and that comes to fruition in the latter, with the debates

---

[32] British Museum, Kings Pamphlets, E516.

on the former enabling the debates of the latter. Robert Paul has seen an even more devious plan behind the thwarted effort of the Assembly as it debated the revisions of the Thirty-Nine Articles.[33] He suggests that it was never the intent of Parliament to see the work of the Assembly completed. Rather he posits they wanted to keep an Assembly of Divines in place because they knew all along that the price of Scottish armed aid in their struggle with the king would be the creation and adoption of a new confession of faith. Thus they saw this early work of the Assembly as no more than a means of bringing the Divines together and keeping them employed until their real work could begin.

Parliament did, however, have a real use for the revised Articles. They were submitted to King Charles by the House of Commons in their negotiations with the king. This was a real use, despite the suggestion of a more devious motivation on the part of the Parliamentarians, who, they claim, were never really serious in seeking reconciliation with the king. They were seeking in this document and its anticipated rejection both a final convincing argument for war, and at the same time, a useful delaying tool, until Scottish military allies could be secured and their army prepared for an unavoidable armed conflict.

There has been a conspiracy of silence of the original labors of the Divines to provide a document for the uniting of a national church. The work, though superseded, was not wasted. Indeed, the revisions were published by order of Parliament; and although they have never again been used, they served several important functions.

The procedures and form of debate adopted by the Divines and used in their revision of the Thirty-Nine Articles provided an indispensable structure for the later debates on the Confession of Faith.

The actual revisions of the Articles and the debate around them involved cardinal points of doctrine. The clarity of their thought and the deliberate nature of their discussion served to enable later debates on these central issues to proceed along paths that had already been

---

[33] Paul, *Assembly of the Lord,* 188.

tried, and explains why later "Minutes" of the Assembly devote as little time as they do to major theological issues.

The process of revising the Thirty-Nine Articles made clear the national and international implications of the work. Far from being a local issue of a national church, these debates provided the opportunity to demonstrate their unity with the Reformed theologians of the Continent, to place local theological concerns in the framework of emerging international Calvinism, and to provide the careful consideration of cardinal doctrines. The clear and defined thinking that resulted from these first debates on the revision of the Thirty-Nine Articles reduced the time needed for discussion, and conduced to the clarity and conciseness that are the hallmark of the Westminster Standards.

Karl Barth and the
Westminster Confession of Faith

WILLIAM C. TRAUB

Introduction

How can the Westminster Confession of Faith (WCF), written from 1643 to 1647 be compared with the theology of Karl Barth (1886–1968)? Although both Barth and the WCF stand in the Reformed tradition, it would be inappropriate to measure the theology of the one by the other – specifically, to gauge Barth's theology on the basis of the WCF or *vice versa*. Barth was Swiss and the WCF was never part of their confessional tradition. In fact, by Barth's time, they had essentially abandoned all creedal formulations. Then too for Barth, all written confessions had only a relative authority.[1] So we should not expect that he would view the WCF as a theological "standard." The only practical way to compare the WCF and Barth in such a brief article is to concentrate on statements in Barth's writings where he explicitly mentions the WCF. In this manner, Barth's own view of the WCF may be determined rather than

---

[1]   Cf. Karl Barth, "Das Bekenntnis der Reformation und unser Bekennen," in *Theologische Fragen und Antworten. Gesammelte Vorträge* (Zollikon: Evangelischer Verlag, 1957), 257-81. For an excellent detailed investigation of Barth's view of the authority of confessions, cf. Georg Plasger, *Die relative Autorität des Bekenntnisses bei Karl Barth* (Neukirchen: Neukirchener Verlag, 2000).

speculating as to what he may have thought about the WCF via deduction or extrapolation from the vastness of his theological undertakings. Unfortunately, the scope of this article does not allow for an adequate theological interaction and evaluation of Barth's comments on the WCF. Specifically, this means that there can be no diachronic tracking of theological themes within Barth's development. Neither can there be an in-depth examination of individual doctrines. Nor can there be a detailed critique of what Barth has to say about the WCF. Lack of explicit critique of Barth's views on the WCF in this article should in no way be construed as tacit approval of Barth's comments. There is much that deserves further investigation and criticism, but space limitations simply do not allow it in the context of this brief overview. It is hoped, nonetheless, that English-speaking readers will be provided with a reliable compendium of Barth's comments on the WCF which will serve to provoke further reflection and study.

While Barth did write commentaries on at least two other Reformed confessions, the Scots Confession of 1560[2] and the Heidelberg Catechism of 1563,[3] we have no commentary by him devoted exclusively to the WCF. If we turn to Barth's major work, *Die Kirchliche Dogmatik (KD)* or *Church Dogmatics (CD)*, we find the WCF mentioned only four times.[4] First, in the context of

---

[2] Karl Barth, *Gotteserkenntnis und Gottesdienst nach reformatorischer Lehre. 20 Vorlesungen über das Schottische Bekenntnis von 1560 gehalten an der Universität Aberdeen in Frühjahr 1937 und 1938* (Zollikon: Verlag der Evangelischen Buchhandlung, 1938).

[3] Cf. Karl Barth, *Einführung in dem Heidelberger Katechism* (Zürich: Evangelischer Verlag, 1960). See also Karl Barth, *Die christliche Lehre nach dem Heidelberger Katechismus – Eine Vorlesung gehalten an der Universität Bonn in Sommersemester 1947* (München: Chr. Kaiser Verlag, 1949). An English translation of these two works is available in: Karl Barth, *Learning Jesus Christ through the Heidelberg Catechism*, trans. Shirley C. Guthrie, Jr. (Grand Rapids: Eerdmans, 1981).

[4] It must be noted that, while many in Presbyterian groups would like to reinterpret and/or rewrite the WCF in the light of Barth's theology, Barth himself interacts in the *Die Kirchliche Dogmatik/Church Dogmatics* with the WCF explicitly on only four brief occasions – hardly enough to warrant such an undertaking.

his discussion of the knowledge of God and God's hiddenness, Barth says that it is understandable why the WCF, along with several other Reformed creeds, speak of the incomprehensibility of God.[5] Barth's first real criticism of the WCF in *KD* occurs in the context of his discussion of the grounds for the doctrine of election. In Barth's estimation, things went downhill theologically in the time following Calvin. As part of this negative trend, he charges the WCF with replacing a solid trust in the mercy of God with the assurance of salvation for the elect.[6] Third, Barth faults the WCF for not making election determinative for all other doctrine. The issue for him is not the mere placement of the doctrine of election immediately following the doctrines of Scripture and God and prior to all other doctrines as the WCF does. Rather it is the emphasis of the Westminster Divines that election is the first and most decisive doctrine regarding the will of God in its relation to his creatures, rather than as a revelation of who God is himself.[7] Finally, for Barth, the WCF, along with several other Reformed creeds, maintains the proper Calvinistic emphasis on the doctrine of the perseverance of the saints.[8] Basically, then, Barth sees the WCF as one among various Reformed creeds and its teaching as consistent with that of the Reformed tradition in general. Where he does criticize the WCF, it is because of what he sees as its man-ward focus – away from God's mercy to the assurance of salvation for the elect; away from being a revelation of God's essence to being merely a revelation of his will in terms of his creatures.

---

[5]   Karl Barth, *Die Kirchliche Dogmatik. Die Lehre von Gott*, 3 ed., vol. II.1 (Zürich: Evangelischer Verlag A. G. Zollikon, 1948), 207-08; translated as *Church Dogmatics. The Doctrine of God*, vol. II.1, trans. T. H. L. Parker *et al.* (Edinburgh: T&T Clark, 1957), 185. Henceforth, *Die Kirchliche Dogmatik* will be abbreviated as *KD* and *Church Dogmatics* as *CD*.

[6]   Karl Barth, *Die Kirchliche Dogmatik. Die Lehre von Gott*, 3 ed., vol. II.2 (Zürich: Evangelischer Verlag, 1948), 38-39; Barth, *CD II.2*, 37.

[7]   Barth, *KD II.2*, 83-84; *CD II.2*, 77-78.

[8]   Barth, *KD II.2*, 364; *CD II.2*, 330.

Barth did, however, give a series of lectures during the spring/ summer semester in 1923 at the Georg-August-Universität Göttingen on the theology of the Reformed creeds.[9] Barth's notes for these lectures are available in German[10] and have recently been published in English.[11] These lecture notes on the Reformed confessions will serve as the primary source of this article.[12]

The historical context of these lectures on the Reformed creeds is not only fascinating, but significant as well.[13] Barth had made his break with the older liberal theology in 1916, had already published the first edition of his *Commentary on Romans*[14] in 1919, and had entered his so-called "dialectical" phase with the publication of the famous second edition of his *Commentary on Romans*[15] in 1922.

---

[9] Eberhard Busch, *Karl Barths Lebenslauf. Nach seinen Briefen und autobiographischen Texten*, 4 ed. (München: Chr. Kaiser Verlag, 1986), 162; translated as *Karl Barth. His Life from Letters and Autobiographical Texts*, trans. John Bowden (Grand Rapids: Eerdmans, 1976), 149.

[10] Karl Barth, *Die Theologie der reformierten Bekenntnisschriften. Vorlesung Göttingen Sommersemester 1923*, ed. Hinrich Stoevesandt and Karl Barth-Forschungsstelle an der Universität Göttingen (Leitung Eberhard Busch), Karl Barth Gesamtausgabe II. – Akademische Werke 1923 (Zürich: Theologischer Verlag, 1998). Henceforth: *TRB*.

[11] Karl Barth, *The Theology of the Reformed Confessions 1923*, trans. Darrell L. Guder and Judith J. Guder (Columbia Series in Reformed Theology; Louisville: Westminster John Knox, 2002). Henceforth: *TRC*.

[12] The author would like to express his deepest gratitude to Prof. Dr. Eberhard Busch, Professor of Reformed Theology at the Georg-August-Universität Göttingen and long time assistant of Karl Barth. Prof. Busch allowed the author to study Barth's lecture notes for this article prior to the publication of those notes.

[13] For an interesting look at Barth's time in Göttingen, cf. Wolfgang Trillhaas, "Karl Barth in Göttingen," in *Fides et communicato*, Festschrift for Martin Doerne (Göttingen: Vandenhoeck und Ruprecht, 1970), 362-74.

[14] Karl Barth, *Der Römerbrief* (Bern: G. A. Bäschlin, 1919). Reprinted in, Karl Barth, *Der Römerbrief. Erste Fassung 1919*, ed. Hinrich Stoevesandt, Karl Barth Gesamtausgabe II. – Akademische Werke 1919 (Zürich: Theologischer Verlag, 1985).

[15] Karl Barth, *Der Römerbrief*, 2 ed. (München: Chr. Kaiser Verlag, 1922). Also: Karl Barth, *Der Römerbrief*, 9th. Re-edited version of the 2nd ed. from 1922 ed. (Zürich: Evangelischer Verlag, 1954). For a discussion of the interplay of both the dialectical as well as the analogical methods in the early phases of Barth's

He had been called to be the Honorary Professor for Reformed Theology in Göttingen in 1921, but not without much skepticism on his part.[16] In a letter to his friend, Eduard Thurneysen, Barth voices his misgivings about becoming a professor of "Reformed" theology, a position backed by money from, of all places, America and located in Germany.[17] He even expresses that he would rather go to the moon than Göttingen.[18] However, on October 13, 1921, he did move from his pastorate in Safenwil, Switzerland, to Göttingen, Germany, to begin his teaching responsibilities there.[19] Well after he had arrived in Göttingen and after a walk with Carl Stange (systematic theology professor in Göttingen and source of opposition for Barth during his Göttingen years), Barth wrote to Thurneysen that he thought he had come to some kind of "zoo."[20] In the midst of his own personal reservations about being in

---

theology cf.: Eberhard Jüngel, "Von der Dialektik zur Analogie – Die Schule Kierkegaards und der Einspruch Petersons," in *Barth-Studien*, Ökumenische Theologie (Gütersloh: Gütersloher Verlagshaus Gerd Mohn, 1982); Ingrid Spieckermann, *Gotteserkenntnis: Ein Beitrag zur Grundfrage der neuen Theologie Karl Barths*, ed. Eberhard Jüngel and Rudolf Smend, Beiträge zur evangelischen Theologie, vol. 97 (München: Chr. Kaiser Verlag, 1985); Michael Beintker, *Die Dialektik in der 'dialektischen Theologie' Karl Barths. Studien zur Entwicklung der Barthschen Theologie und zur Vorgeschichte der 'Kirchlichen Dogmatik'*, ed. Eberhard Jüngel and Rudolf Smend, Beiträge zur evangelischen Theologie (München: Chr. Kaiser Verlag, 1987); Bruce L. McCormack, "A Scholastic of a Higher Order: The Development of Karl Barth's theology, 1921-1931" (Dissertation, Princeton University, 1989); McCormack, *Karl Barth's Critically Realistic Dialectical Theology. Its Genesis and Development 1909-1936* (Oxford: Claredon Press, 1995).

[16] Eberhard Busch, *Die Anfänge des Theologen Karl Barth in seinen Göttinger Jahren. Universitätsreden gehalten am 12. Mai 1986 als Gedenkakt zum 100. Geburtstag Karl Barths*, Göttinger Universitätsreden, vol. 83 (Göttingen: Vandenhoeck und Ruprecht, 1987).

[17] Karl Barth, *Karl Barth – Eduard Thurneysen Briefwechsel. 1913–1921*, ed. Hinrich Stoevesandt, Karl Barth Gesamtausgabe V. – Briefe, vol. 1 (Zürich: Theologischer Verlag, 1973), 463. From February 1, 1921.

[18] Ibid., 517. From September 6, 1921.

[19] Busch, *Lebenslauf*, 138; *Life*, 125.

[20] Barth, *Karl Barth – Eduard Thurneysen Briefwechsel. 1913–1921*, 502. From July 14, 1921.

Göttingen and the actual opposition that he faced there, Germany was undergoing hyper-inflation with all of its side effects. In one letter to Thurneysen he mentions the thousands of men and women who were starving and freezing, the strange sicknesses caused by hunger, the increased incidents of tuberculosis, and the students who had to drop out because they did not have enough money to finish their studies.[21] In another letter to Thurneysen he notes that a 100 Mark note was so worthless that even beggars would refuse them and that his salary had reached the level of six million Marks[22] – later it went up into the billions![23] Barth's time in Göttingen was one of intense external economic and political upheaval as well as a time of intense personal and theological struggle for him.

Barth taught at the Georg-August-Universität Göttingen from 1921 until 1925.[24] Hence, right in the middle of his years in Göttingen[25] and less than one year after the publication of the second edition of his *Commentary on Romans*, Barth gave a series of lectures on the Reformed creeds in which he commented extensively on the WCF. The existence of these lectures is somewhat surprising, since Barth himself mentions that at the time of his being called to Göttingen, he did not own nor had he even read the Reformed creeds.[26] In a letter dated May 18, 1923, he does mention not only what he had been able to prepare to that

---

[21] Karl Barth, *Karl Barth – Eduard Thurneysen Briefwechsel. 1921-1930*, ed. Hinrich Stoevesandt, Karl Barth Gesamtausgabe V. – Briefe, vol. 2 (Zürich: Theologischer Verlag, 1974), 122. From December 18, 1922.

[22] Ibid., 160-61. From May 18, 1923.

[23] Ibid., 197. From October 31, 1923.

[24] Busch, *Lebenslauf*, 139-76; *Life*, 126-64.

[25] For a discussion of the debate concerning Barth's movement from dialectics to dogmatics during his time in Göttingen cf. Matthias Freudenberg, *Karl Barth und die reformierte Theologie. Die Auseinandersetzung mit Calvin, Zwingli und den reformierten Bekenntnisschriften während seiner Göttinger Lehrtätigkeit*, Neukirchener Theologische Dissertationen und Habilitationen, vol. 8 (Neukirchen-Vluyn: Neukirchener Verlag, 1997).

[26] Karl Barth, "Autobiographische Skizzen Karl Barths aus den Fakultätsalben der Ev.-Theo. Fakultät in Münster – 26. März 1927," in *Karl Barth – Rudolf Bultmann*

point for the lectures on the Reformed creeds, but also what he intended to include in them.[27] Although the preparation and giving of the lectures involved monumental effort,[28] especially since in the spring/summer semester of 1923 he was also giving lectures on 1 Cor. 15, he indicated to Thurneysen that the preparation of both lecture series had been a joy to him.[29]

Overview of Barth's Lectures on the Reformed Confessions

Barth's lectures on the Reformed confessions are divided into three main sections: *§1. The significance of the Confession in the Reformed churches, §2. The Principle of Scripture and its Basis, §3. Reformed doctrine as a whole.* The last section is broken down into four sub-sections: (a) interaction with the early church, (b) positive teaching of Christianity, (c) interaction with Lutheranism, and (d) relation with current theology. It is in the second sub-section, concerning a positive presentation of Christianity from the Reformed perspective, where Barth discusses the WCF in three four hour lectures held on June 22, 26, and 28, 1923.

The discussion of the WCF in the lecture notes follows the chapter headings of the WCF in a fairly straightforward running commentary. Of the thirty-three chapters of the WCF, Barth did not mention the following fifteen and gave no explanation for their omission: 1. Of Holy Scripture; 2. Of God, and of the Holy Trinity; 4. Of Creation; 6. Of the Fall of Man, of Sin, and of the Punishment thereof; 8. Of Christ the Mediator; 22. Of Lawful Oaths and Vows; 23. Of the Civil Magistrate; 24. Of Marriage and Divorce; 27. Of the Sacraments; 28. Of Baptism; 29. Of the Lord's Supper; 30. Of Church Censures; 31. Of Synods and Councils; 32.

Briefwechsel. 1911-1966, ed. Bernd Jaspert, Karl Barth Gesamtausgabe V. – Briefe (Zürich: Theologischer Verlag, 1994), 298-99.

[27] Barth, *Karl Barth – Eduard Thurneysen Briefwechsel. 1921–1930*, 162-63. From May 18, 1923.

[28] Ibid., 173. From May 29, 1923.

[29] Ibid., 179. From July 15, 1923.

Of the State of Men after Death, and of the Resurrection of the Dead; and 33. Of the Last Judgment. The content of Chapter 3, "Of God's Eternal Decree," while not directly dealt with, is taken up under the heading of the doctrine of predestination. It will be especially disappointing to many that Barth did not comment on the chapter on Scripture in the WCF. However, he had already dealt, at length, with his perspective on the doctrine of Scripture in the Reformed confessions under *§2. The Principle of Scripture and its Basis* of his lectures.[30] He also made a few remarks concerning the Westminster Larger and Shorter Catechisms;[31] however, these lie outside the scope of this article.

Those to whom Barth gave these lectures were, for the most part, completely unfamiliar with the WCF. Hence, Barth quite often simply summarizes in his own words what the WCF says for his students. Interestingly, although Müller provided both an English and a Latin version of the WCF,[32] Barth apparently made use exclusively of the Latin version as is evidenced by the numerous direct Latin quotations and the absence of any quotations in English in his lecture notes. Another factor to take into consideration here at the outset is the fact that Barth does not mention the historical setting of the WCF, nor the theological context in England and Scotland at the time of the writing of the WCF. These are two extremely important factors in the formation of the WCF and its theology.

Barth begins with some positive introductory comments, pointing out that the WCF not only demonstrates the achievement

---

[30] Barth, *TRB*, 63-103; *TRC*, 38-64.

[31] Barth, *TRB*, 228-30; *TRC*, 146-47.

[32] Reference will be made throughout the remainder of this article to two versions of the WCF, each of which has both the English and Latin text of the Confession. The first is the one which, in all likelihood, Barth used for his lectures: "Die Westminster-Confession von 1647" in: E. F. Karl Müller, *Die Bekenntnisschriften der reformierten Kirche* (Leipzig: A. Diechert'sche Verlagsbuchhandlung Nachf., 1903), 542-612. Henceforth: *BSRK*. The second edition is found in Philip Schaff, *The Creeds of Christendom with a History and Critical Notes. The Evangelical Protestant Creeds*, 6 ed., vol. 3 (Grand Rapids: Baker Books, 1996), 600-73. Henceforth, *Creeds vol. 3*.

of Calvinism in England and serves as the confessional standard for the various Presbyterian churches around the world, but it is also the codification of the triumph of Calvinism. He notes the extreme care taken in the formulation of each expression and the selection of every Bible reference of the WCF. He suggests that if one wants to get to know the original intention of the Reformed tradition as well as the Calvinistic form in which it came to dominate the greater part of the Christian world, then one must turn to the WCF.[33] The WCF is, for Barth, without a doubt and in spite of everything in it to which he might want to raise objection, a document rich in knowledge and honor. However, from what is hinted at in the WCF, it is apparent to Barth that what will come after it will be nothing but night and grayness.[34]

Summary of Barth's Comments on the Specific Chapters of the WCF

1. Of the Holy Scripture [not discussed in the lectures]

As indicated earlier, Barth does not deal specifically with chapter 1 of the WCF in his lectures. However, in *§2 The Principle of Scripture and its Basis*, he did discuss his understanding of the view of Scripture set forth in the Reformed confessions in general and mentioned the WCF on numerous occasions. Since these lectures lie between his statements concerning the word of God in the second edition of his *Commentary on Romans*[35] and his later, more detailed teaching in *KD*,[36] it might be interesting to

---

[33] *TRB*, 212-13//*TRC*, 135. Numbers indicate the page references to the published editions of the lecture notes. The page numbers in the German edition (*TRB*) will be followed by // and then the page numbers in the English edition (*TRC*).

[34] *TRB*, 234-35//*TRC*, 151.

[35] Karl Barth, *Der Römerbrief*, 2 ed. (München: Chr. Kaiser Verlag, 1933), 324ff., 347ff.

[36] Karl Barth, *Die Kirchliche Dogmatik. Die Lehre vom Wort Gottes – Prolegomena zur kirchlichen Dogmatik*, 4 ed., vol. I.2 (Zürich: Evangelischer Verlag A. G. Zollikon, 1948), 47-110; *Church Dogmatics. The Doctrine of the Word of God*,

summarize briefly what Barth says here with regard to the doctrine of Scripture at this point in the development of his thought.

For Barth, the Reformed church was characterized by the principle of Scripture whereas the Lutheran church was characterized by the doctrine of justification. The basic notion of the Reformed confession consists, for Barth, in the fact that a confession is merely a form or container. The real contents, he says, are "written by God's finger on the paper of the Bible *and* by God's finger in our hearts, truly and inviolably, completely and sufficiently, neither to be repeated nor to be continued."[37]

According to Barth, in contrast to the Lutherans, who, he maintains, tend to place the Bible, Councils, and the present church situation all on relatively the same plain, for the Reformed, the unique normativity[38] of the Bible is important as the representation – as the only allowed and commanded earthly representation! – of the unique authority of God. The integrating factor in many of the Reformed confessions is, for Barth, a declaration of *where* it is that God's voice is to be heard – namely in Scripture – and *what* is to be affirmed in faith. Hence, he points out, that numerous Reformed confessions, including the WCF, give a formal and complete enumeration of the individual biblical books which are considered as canonical. For Barth, the fundamental act of a Reformed confession is this explicit confirmation of the biblical canon.[39]

Barth highlights the fact that the Reformed church acknowledged the word of God as the sole rule of its proclamation, and it

---

trans. G. T. Thomson and Harold Knight, vol. I.2 (Edinburgh: T&T Clark, 1956), 1-202.

[37] *TRB*, 63-64//*TRC*, 38-39.

[38] Barth uses the expression "isolated normativity of the Bible" (*isolierte Normativität der Bibel*), which, for him, is the only allowable expression of the "isolated authority of God" (*isolierte Autorität Gottes*). "Isolated" in this sense refers to that which is distinct or removed from everything else. In his famous Tambach lecture he expresses a similar notion with the concept of God as the "wholly other" cf. Karl Barth, "Der Christ in der Gesellschaft," in *Das Wort Gottes und die Theologie*, Gesammelte Vorträge (München: Kaiser, 1929), 33-69.

[39] *TRB*, 80-81//*TRC*, 49-50.

found the word of God solely in the Holy Scripture. For him the Reformed principle of Scripture[40] was not merely one proposition among many others, but rather it served as the overriding doctrine permeating the entirety of each confession.[41] According to Barth, one must see the so-called "Biblicism" of the Reformed church fathers as a completely sober and practical rule; in fact, it was their formal principle: the Bible as the only rule of faith and life.[42] In the Reformed tradition, according to Barth, the most frequently used term for the normative character of the biblical word of God is "rule." He mentions that it is no accident that expressions such as "fountain," as the Lutheran *Formula of Concord* applies it to Scripture,[43] or "spring" or "root" or "beginning" or "source" or

---

[40]   For the early development of Barth's view of Scripture cf. especially: Barth, *Römerbrief 1922;* Karl Barth, "Reformierte Lehre, ihr Wesen und ihr Aufgabe – Vortrag gehalten an der Hauptversammlung des 'Reformierten Bundes in Deutschland' Emden 17.09.23," *Zwischen den Zeiten* 2. Jahrgang, Heft 1 = Heft 5 der ganzen Zeitschrift (1924): 8-39; "Das Schriftprinzip der Reformierten Kirche," *Zwischen den Zeiten* 11. Heft, 3. Jahrgang/Heft 3 (1925): 215-45; "Menschenwort und Gotteswort in der Christlichen Predigt," *Zwischen den Zeiten* 10. Heft, 3. Jahrgang/Heft 2 (1925): 119-40; "Die Souveränität des Wortes Gottes und die Entscheidung des Glaubens," *Theologische Studien* Heft 5 (1939): 3-22; "Die Schrift und die Kirche," *Theologische Studien* Heft 22 (1947): 3-44; "Das christliche Verständnis der Offenbarung," *Theologische Existenz Heute* Neue Folge Nr. 12 (1948): 3-35; "Das Wort Gottes als Aufgabe der Theologie," in *Anfänge der dialektischen Theologie*, ed. Jürgen Moltmann, Theologische Bücherei – 17. Band (München: Chr. Kaiser Verlag, 1962), 197-218; *Die Theologie Calvins. 1922 Vorlesung Göttingen Sommersemester*, ed. Hinrich Stoevesandt, Karl Barth Gesamtausgabe II. – Akademische Werke (Zürich: Theologischer Verlag, 1993); *Unterricht in der christlichen Religion. Prolegomena*, ed. Hinrich Stoevesandt, Karl Barth Gesamtausgabe II. – Akademische Werke 1924, vol. 1 (Zürich: Theologischer Verlag, 1985). For a curious and expectedly positive evaluation of Barth's understanding of the authority of Scripture cf. Geoffrey W. Bromiley, "The Authority of Scripture in Karl Barth," in *Hermeneutics, Authority, and Canon*, ed. D. A. Carson and John D. Woodbridge (Grand Rapids: Academie Books, Zondervan, 1986), 271-94.

[41]   *TRB*, 67//*TRC*, 41.

[42]   *TRB*, 71//*TRC*, 43.

[43]   *"Die Konkordienformel"*; in *Die Bekenntnisschriften der evangelisch-lutherischen Kirche*, 10 ed. (Göttingen: Vandenhoeck und Ruprecht, 1986), 834:16-22. For the English text of the *Formula of Concord* referred to here, cf. Robert Kolb and Timothy J. Wengert, *The Book of Concord. The Confessions*

the like do not appear in the Reformed confessions. This suggests, for Barth, that from a Reformed perspective, there is no continuity between the word of God and the faith which is nourished by it. Barth maintains that the word of God breaks into our world in the most visible and audible way, but there is no organic connection between the two. Rather than becoming a part of the world, the word of God is and remains its rule.[44] After indicating that even though Calvin speaks of the "Knowledge of God as Creator" in the first book of the *Institutes*, Barth says that Calvin nowhere develops a natural theology as a preliminary step to revelation. As could be expected, Barth views with disdain the fact that right at the beginning of the WCF, alongside of the works of God, the light of nature (*lumen naturae*) is mentioned. Although the WCF does not define *lumen naturae*, for Barth it refers to that inner light of man consisting of an innate similarity with God, which serves as a source of knowledge, revealing to us the will of God. Needless to say, Barth, with his aversion to anything which is remotely connected to natural theology, especially during his early dialectical phase, finds it inexplicable that the WCF should make use of this concept at all, let alone here at the very beginning of the Confession. Later in his lectures he will again point out what he views as its deleterious effects in association with Chapter 20, "Of Christian Liberty."[45]

According to Barth, the writers of many of the Reformed confessions wrote in a time when the notion of an objective truth was being eroded. Hence, they felt constrained to add supporting grounds to the claim that God speaks in Scripture. As examples of this tendency he cites the various statements in WCF 1.5. Barth points out that the Westminster Larger Catechism requires as a presupposition for useful Bible study the firm persuasion that

---

of the Evangelical Lutheran Church, trans. Charles Arand, *et al.* (Minneapolis: Fortress Press, 2000), 527.

[44] *TRB*, 73-74//*TRC*, 45.

[45] *TRB*, 77-78//*TRC*, 48.

the Scriptures are the very words of God (*ipsissimum verbum Dei*).[46] He does mention, however, that the WCF states clearly and positively that the conviction that Scripture is the word of God is something which only the Holy Spirit can accomplish.[47]

In Barth's estimation, the Reformed confessions brought one relatively simple notion to expression: God speaks! God speaks, according to Barth, specifically in his relationship to the given literal text of the Bible.[48] He claims, however, that this only served to emphasize more sharply the insurmountable and necessary *paradox of revelation*.[49] This paradox arises for Barth, because for him, God is known only directly, via God himself, not indirectly (i.e., not via some element found in history or creation). He understands the Reformed principle of Scripture as giving expression to the directness and paradox of revelation. For Barth, the legitimate witness to the revelation of God can only be the word of Scripture.[50] But it is precisely the fact that the eternal Word of God penetrates our world in the form of prophetic and apostolic writing, which constitutes the paradox for Barth. He maintains that the Reformed fathers were conscious of this paradox when they confessed their view of Scripture.[51] However, for Barth, they moved

---

[46] The Latin text to Question 157 in the WLC includes the following: "cum persuasione firma, esse illas *ipsissimum verbum Dei*, eumque solum efficere posse ut illas intelligamus . . ." (emphasis added). "Der grosse Westminster-Katechismus von 1647" in Müller, *BSRK*, 636.

[47] *TRB*, 93-94//*TRC*, 57-58. Cf. WCF 1.5, in Müller, *BSRK*, 545; Schaff, *Creeds vol. 3*, 602-3.

[48] The German text reads: "Die Bekenntnisschriften haben nun diesen verhältnismäßig einfachen ersten Grundgedanken: Gott spricht! nach einer bestimmten Richtung, nämlich in seinem Verhältnis zu dem gegebenen wörtlichen *Text* der Bibel, spezifiziert und erläutert . . ." (Barth's emphasis) in Barth, *TRB*, 95. The English translation reads: "The confessional documents have specified and explained this relatively simple, first, basic thought – God speaks! – in a certain direction, namely, in his relationship to the given literal *text* of the Bible . . ." (Barth's emphasis) in Barth, *TRC*, 59.

[49] *TRB*, 95//*TRC*, 59.

[50] *TRB*, 79//*TRC*, 48-49.

[51] *TRB*, 75-76//*TRC*, 46.

further and further away from the context of Calvin's thought and were motivated by a scholastic need for completeness and exactness. Barth likens this way of thinking, with regard to the miracle of revelation, to taking an unknown quantity and plugging it into an equation in order to turn it into a known quantity. According to Barth, it is exactly this dubious endeavor of attempting to attain some degree of precision, which produced the doctrine of verbal inspiration.[52]

Barth outlines what the Reformed creeds have to say about the basis of the principle of Scripture in three simple propositions: (1) Holy Scripture is the perfect revelation, (2) it is the work of the Holy Spirit, and (3) this judgment – that it is the work of the Holy Spirit – is itself a work of the Holy Spirit.[53] The repeated reference in Reformed creeds to the perfection of Scripture is the sum of the principle of Scripture for him. He goes on, however, to call this a tautology, since to call the Scripture perfect is nothing else than to say that it is God's word, but that is exactly the point which was to be established. For Barth, this tautology is a demonstration that one has arrived at that which is not capable of being grounded, or, more to the point, at that which is only grounded in God. That there is a Word of God and that this or that word is a Word of God can, according to Barth, only be grounded in God and on no other basis.[54] Seen in this light, it is not surprising that Barth quotes the WCF 1.4 as the classic expression of the principle of Scripture.[55] He maintains that here it is clear that the whole doctrine of the perfection of Scripture is merely another expression of the doctrine of its inspiration. The first proposition (that Scripture is the perfect revelation) means the same thing as the second one

---

[52] *TRB*, 95//*TRC*, 59.

[53] *TRB*, 89//*TRC*, 55.

[54] *TRB*, 91-92//*TRC*, 56-57.

[55] Barth quotes WCF 1.4 in Latin as follows: "Autoritas scripturae sacrae . . . pendet . . . A solo ejus authore Deo, qui est ipsa veritas: eoque est a nobis recipienda, quoniam est verbum Dei" in Müller, *BSRK*, 544; Schaff, *Creeds vol. 3*, 602.

(that it is the work of the Holy Spirit). And the third proposition (the acknowledgment that this is so, is also a work of the Holy Spirit) must be immediately added. For Barth, Spirit can only be acknowledged by Spirit, God by God.[56]

The clearest presentation of the Reformed principle of Scripture for Barth is Calvin's doctrine of inspiration, found in the *Institutes* 1.7.[57] He briefly summarizes Calvin's position by saying that the acknowledgment of the authority of the Bible corresponds with the acknowledgment that God is its author.[58] Some important aspects of Barth's view of Scripture come to light as he contrasts his understanding of Calvin's doctrine of inspiration to the teaching of confessions written after Calvin's time. One such concept is that of the *simultaneity of inspiration*.[59] Barth contends that Calvin thought of revelation as a single timeless or simultaneous act of God with regard to both the biblical authors and to us.[60] Calvin linked then and now, there and here, biblical author and Bible reader,

---

[56] *TRB*, 92//*TRC*, 57.

[57] Institutio Christianae Religionis (1559) I.7 – "Quo testimonio scripturam oporteat sanciri, nempe spiritus: ut certa constet eius autoritas; atque impium esse commentum, fidem eius pendere ab ecclesiae iudicio" in John Calvin, *Ioannis Calvini – Opera Quae Supersunt Omnia. vol. II.* ed. Guilielmus Baum, Eduardus Cunitz, and Eduardus Reuss, Corpus Reformatorum – Vol. XXX (Braunsvigae: Apud C.A. Schwetschke Et Filium, 1864; reprint, 1964), col. 56-61. English: "Scripture must be confirmed by the witness of the Spirit. Thus may its authority be established as certain; and it is a wicked falsehood that its credibility depends on the judgment of the church" in John Calvin, *Institutes of the Christian Religion*, ed. John Baillie, John T. McNeill, and Henry P. van Dusen, trans. Ford Lewis Battles (Library of Christian Classics, vol. 20; Philadelphia: Westminster, 1960), 79ff.

[58] *TRB*, 94-95//*TRC*, 58-59.

[59] Barth's unique view of time and eternity play an important role here. For an excellent critique of Barth's understanding in this area, cf. Cornelius van Til, *Christianity and Barthianism* (Philadelphia: P&R, 1974), 90-113. For an interesting discussion of Barth's view of these concepts, especially as they are developed in *CD*, cf. R. H. Roberts, "Karl Barth's Doctrine of Time: Its Nature and Implications," in *Karl Barth – Studies of his Theological Method*, ed. S. W. Sykes (Oxford: Clarendon Press, 1979), 89-146.

[60] *TRB*, 100//*TRC*, 63.

objective and subjective inextricably together, according to Barth.[61] He points out that for Calvin, the Spirit, who had spoken through the prophets, must gain entrance into our hearts and convince us that they faithfully delivered what God had instructed them.[62] In contrast to this, Barth notes a differentiation made in the *Second Helvetic Confession*.[63] In Bullinger's work, he finds a distinction between God's speaking *then* (i.e., to the prophets and apostles) and *now* (to us through the Scriptures).[64] For Barth, this separates the Bible valued *as something in itself*, from the Bible viewed as the *witness of revelation to us*. This distinction between something *objective* over against something *subjective* threatens, according to Barth, the simultaneity between the biblical authors and us. He maintains that only via this simultaneity can the writing of the apostles and prophets (i.e., that which resulted from the revelation they experienced), become the witness to God's revelation for us (i.e., become God's Word).[65] In the context of his discussion of simultaneity, Barth notes that the WCF neither mentions the recipients of revelation, nor portrays inspiration as being a living relationship between God and them.[66]

Another aspect of Barth's understanding of inspiration concerns the relative disinterest in the text of Scripture over against the overarching emphasis on the work of the Holy Spirit. He points out Calvin's lack of special interest focused on the literal text of the Bible.[67] He

---

[61] *TRB*, 99//*TRC*, 62.

[62] *TRB*, 100//*TRC*, 63.

[63] For the Latin text of the *Second Helvetic Confession* cf. Müller, *BSRK*, 170ff; Schaff, *Creeds vol. 3*, 234ff. For an English translation, cf. Schaff, *Creeds vol. 3*, 831ff.

[64] Barth quotes the Latin text of the *Second Helvetic Confession* 1.1 as follows: "Deus loquutus est . . . et adhuc loquitur . . ." in Barth, *TRB*, 95; *TRC*, 59. For the fuller Latin text cf. Müller, *BSRK*, 170,29-39; Schaff, *Creeds vol. 3*, 237. For an English translation cf. Schaff, *Creeds vol. 3*, 831.

[65] *TRB*, 95-96//*TRC*, 59.

[66] *TRB*, 96//*TRC*, 60.

[67] *TRB*, 99//*TRC*, 62.

also demonstrates the extreme importance Calvin gives to the Holy Spirit in regard to inspiration. Barth argues that, for Calvin, the "proof" of Scripture lies neither with man's reason nor with experience, but with the inner testimony of the Spirit. In other words, the self-authentication of Scripture is a function of the Spirit.[68] For Barth, the formulations found in the *Helvetic Consensus Formula* stand in stark contrast to Calvin's understanding. In Canons I-III of the *Helvetic Consensus*[69] the focus is almost exclusively on the text of Scripture, right down to the insistence that the Hebrew vowel points are inspired.[70] Surprisingly, Barth makes quite clear, that for him, the problem is not the focus on what he calls a "holy text," nor is it the intent motivating that focus – the impedance of biblical criticism, in spite of its lack of success. Rather, what alarms Barth is that the *Helvetic Consensus* omits the third and deciding proposition of his definition of the principle of Scripture, namely that the judgment that this text is a work of the Holy Spirit is itself a work of the Holy Spirit in us.[71] Barth sees an inversion of Calvin's emphasis in the *Helvetic Consensus'* shift of focus toward the text as an objective reality in itself and toward human measures to defend it.

2. Of God, and of the Holy Trinity [not discussed in the lectures]

3. Of God's Eternal Decree

In commenting on this chapter of the WCF, Barth avoids the use of the phrase "decree of God."[72] Instead, he uses the terms "pre-

---

[68] *TRB*, 97-101//*TRC*, 61-63.

[69] For the Latin text cf. Müller, *BSRK*, 862,33-863,17. For an English translation cf. John H. Leith, ed., *Creeds of the Churches. A Reader in Christian Doctrine from the Bible to the Present* (Richmond: John Knox Press, 1973), 309-11.

[70] For the Latin text cf. Müller, *BSRK*, 862. For the English text cf. Leith, ed., *Creeds*, 310.

[71] *TRB*, 98//*TRC*, 61.

[72] Although it had historical precedent among earlier Reformed theologians, Barth demonstrates an aversion here for the term *decretum absolutum*, which

destination" or "election." He claims that the general acceptance of the placement of the doctrine of predestination at the head of the entire system of doctrine in the Reformed tradition comes to full expression in the WCF. This emphasis on predestination does not bother him. In fact he even goes on to call predestination the central doctrine of the Reformed faith.[73] Barth speaks favorably of all that is said in this chapter of the WCF and notes that it raises great expectations for that which will follow. He points out favorably, that the WCF speaks of the election of some men and angels to eternal life and others to eternal death, both in terms of a certain specific number which can neither be increased nor decreased, as well as the fact that the placement in one group or the other does not depend on any cause or condition lying within the creature itself. He further emphasizes that the WCF is not speaking merely about foreknowledge (*praevisio*) but in fact predestination (*praedestinatio*).[74]

Barth asks what purpose this doctrine in the WCF serves and answers from the Confession itself: that those who have become attentive and obedient to God's revelation "may, from the certainty

---

will persist in his theology. See, for instance, his discussion of the *decretum absolutum* in: Barth, *KD II.2*, 107f., 111, 123f., 183, 211; *CD II.2*, 100f., 103f., 115f., 155ff., 166f., 192f.

[73] For a more fully developed statement of Barth's view of election, see: Barth, *KD II.2*, 1-563; *CD II.2*, 1-506. For an interaction with Barth's doctrine of predestination, cf. Gerhard Gloege, "Zur prädestinationslehre Karl Barths [Röm 9-11]," in *Kerygma und Dogma*, ed. Gerhard Gloege, Regin Prenter, and Edmund Schlink (Göttingen: Vandenhoeck und Ruprecht, 1956), 193-217, 223-55. See also: Walter Sparn, "'Extra Internum' – Die christologische Revision der Prädestinationslehre in Karl Barths Erwählungslehre," in *Realisierung der Freiheit*, ed. Trutz Rendtorff, Beiträge zur Kritik der Theologie Karl Barths (Gütersloh: Gütersloher Verlagshaus Gerd Mohn, 1975), 44-75. For a positive comparison of Calvin, Dort, and Westminster on predestination, cf. John Murray, "Calvin, Dort and Westminster on Predestination: a comparative study," in *Crisis in the Reformed Churches. Essays in commemoration of the great Synod of Dort, 1618-1619*, ed. Peter Y. DeJong (Grand Rapids: Reformed Fellowship, 1968), 150-60.

[74] *TRB*, 213-14//*TRC*, 136. Cf. WCF 3.2 and 3.3 in Müller, *BSRK*, 549-50; Schaff, *Creeds vol. 3*, 608-9.

of their effectual vocation, be assured of their eternal Election . . ."[75] What this says for Barth is that the believer drags this highest expression concerning God (i.e., the doctrine of election) down into something to be used for his own benefit. Expressing his understanding of the intention of the WCF here in existentialistic terminology, Barth adds that in order to escape the deepest paradox of his own existence (*der Pradox seines Daseins*), the believer transfers this paradox to God. The problem here for Barth is not the doctrine itself, but rather what he sees as the misuse of it. He calls the striving to gain personal human assurance via this doctrine, the deepest of all pietistic-egocentric purposes.[76]

4. Of Creation [not discussed in the lectures]

5. Of Providence

For Barth, everything said in the WCF about providence would have been well and good – in fact he points out sarcastically that Thomas Aquinas had already said it. However, for Barth the term "cause," in spite of the distinction between "first cause" and "second causes," clearly bears witness to a misconception of the nature of God. He sees in this language an attempt to think of the God of revelation in terms of an analogy to the God of the known world of man and the natural order. Barth maintains that the God of revelation is the Creator, the pure origin (*Ursprung*), not the first cause of the world. He agrees that in the WCF there still are safeguards against the dangerous use of the notion of analogy. Nonetheless, making reference to Schleiermacher,[77]

---

[75] Cf. WCF 3.8, in: Müller, *BSRK*, 552; Schaff, *Creeds vol. 3*, 610-11.

[76] *TRB*, 214//*TRC*, 136. For an excellent discussion of Barth's relation to the Pietists in Germany, cf. Eberhard Busch, *Karl Barth und die Pietisten. Die Pietismuskritik des jungen Karl Barth und ihre Erwiderung*, ed. Eberhard Jüngel and Rudolf Smend, Beiträge zur evangelischen Theologie, vol. 82 (München: Chr. Kaiser Verlag, 1978).

[77] Cf. Friedrich Schleiermacher, *Über die Religion: Reden an die Gebildeten unter ihren Verächtern*, 7 ed. (Göttingen: Vandenhoeck und Ruprecht, 1991); *On*

Barth fears that the time could come when this analogy could receive a sinister independent meaning, where an apologist could attempt to make God into some kind of generic "Universal." He is also concerned that the misuse of the doctrine of predestination suggested by the WCF, namely as a means of personal assurance of salvation, may be tied to that coming development. According to Barth, when the question of man's salvation becomes the focal point for Christianity, it should not come as a surprise when the deciding question becomes that of human truth (*des Menschen Wahrheit*).[78]

6. Of the Fall of Man, of Sin, and of the Punishment thereof [not discussed in the lectures]

7. Of God's Covenant with Man

Barth points out that, in the WCF, the Creator–creature distinction (*distantia inter deum et creatura*) is so great, that even the rational creatures can not have anything in common with the Creator without a special condescending (*condescentio*) of the Creator toward them. For Barth, the law–covenant made with Adam was abrogated by the fall into sin.[79] The attempt of the WCF to then construct a temporal history of salvation (*zeitliche Heilsgeschichte*) runs, in Barth's opinion, into trouble from the very outset. As far as he is concerned, if the starting point is the fall into sin, there is only one possible solution: the reversal of the effects of the fall. However, Barth claims that any historical development based on the fall, no matter how many stages it might have, simply will not achieve that desired goal. For him, the WCF separates law and

---

Religion. Speeches to Its Cultured Despisers (New York: Harper, 1965); *Der christliche Glaube*, 7 ed., vol. 1 & 2 (Berlin/New York: Walter de Gruyter, 1960); *The Christian Faith*, ed. H. R. Mackintosh and J. S. Stewart (Philadelphia: Fortress Press, 1976).

[78]   *TRB*, 215-16//*TRC*, 137.

[79]   *TRB*, 216//*TRC*, 137.

grace temporally, something which he believes Calvin refused to do. It is simply impossible, according to Barth, to maintain the law in this manner as merely one stage of revelation. For him such an ineffective revelation can only be considered not to be revelation at all. On the other hand, Barth rightly points out that any attempt to maintain grace as revelation separate from the law is just as problematic.[80]

Barth says that it is in this context that the WCF posits the second effective condescension of God, the covenant of grace (*foedus gratiae*). For him, it is merely an attempt to ameliorate the situation, when the WCF grants this second covenant retroactive power, claiming that it already existed under the covenant of law in the form of the promises, prophecies, sacrifices, examples, etc., which pointed to the coming of the Messiah and the forgiveness of sins to the elect. He sees this as an attempt to save the unity of revelation – the unity which includes all the various administrations as well as the unity of law and grace. For Barth, the existence of this other, effective covenant (of grace) is a demonstration that the distinction of a special covenant of law (*foedus legis*) is actually superfluous. The WCF lists several things which evidence the advance from the old to the new covenant, namely, preaching, the new sacraments, and the expansion of revelation to all peoples. The English version of the WCF calls these things simply "ordinances." Barth, drawing on the language of the Latin text, calls them a new *ratio*.[81] He maintains that these things cannot be considered sufficient to establish a fundamental difference between the two covenants.[82]

---

[80] *TRB*, 216//*TRC*, 137-38.

[81] The Latin text of WCF 7.6, to which Barth apparently refers, reads "Sub Evangelio autem, exhibito iam Christo, substantia scilicet ac antitypo, *praescriptae rationes* . . ." (emphasis added). The English text says: "Under the gospel, when Christ the substance was exhibited, the *ordinances* in which this covenant is dispensed . . ." (emphasis added), cf. Müller, *BSRK*, 560; Schaff, *Creeds vol. 3*, 618.

[82] *TRB*, 216-17//*TRC*, 138.

Barth points out that with the closing remark of WCF 7.6: "There are not therefore two Covenants of Grace differing in substance, but one and the same under various dispensations";[83] a crossroad is reached. For him, if the "one and the same" had been taken seriously, then the distinction involved in a progression of divine manifestations would have been dropped as an unnecessary word game. On the other hand, if the "under various dispensations" (i.e., the historical development), is taken more seriously than that which itself was made manifest, then revelation is dissolved into a history of religion. Barth concludes his comments on this chapter of the WCF by noting that things are balanced on a razor's edge in the WCF (i.e., the WCF presents a tenuous but balanced formulation). However, Barth states that in the time following the WCF, the second option, stressing the plurality of administrations, was taken and, in his opinion, we continue to suffer from that decision.[84]

8. Of Christ the Mediator [not discussed in the lectures]

9. Of Free Will

Barth summarizes the main elements of this chapter without much comment, giving the impression that he agrees with what the WCF has to say with regard to free will.[85] However, Barth does detect here the onset of what he calls a "historical-psychological" way of looking at things. Barth says that for Luther and Calvin the will of man is either free or not, and, for them, man's will was clearly not free. With Bullinger and Beza, however, according to Barth, we meet the notion that man recovers a free will when he is born

---

[83] The corresponding Latin text of WCF 7.6 upon which Barth draws reads: "Non sunt ergo duo foedera gratiae, re atque natura discrepantia; sed unum idemque, licet non uno modo dispensatum" in Müller, *BSRK*, 560; Schaff, *Creeds vol. 3*, 618.

[84] *TRB*, 217//*TRC*, 138.

[85] *TRB*, 217-18//*TRC*, 138-39.

again. He goes on to point out that even though all experience speaks against this notion, it is indeed possible precisely because it concerns the miracle of God. By way of contrast, in Barth's opinion, grace itself, along with its gifts, is psychologized and drawn into the area of man's experience by the WCF. This grace is, to be sure, capable of giving a certain free will again; yet, according to Barth, it is only an imperfect free will, which must wait until the *status gloriae* for its full perfection. He likens this deficient free will to the ineffective covenant of law proposed by the WCF. Barth maintains that both, while good in themselves, fail to achieve what was intended. He insists that this is the inevitable direction things must take if, in spite of all the energetic assertions to the contrary made by the WCF, Christian doctrine is no longer sure of its object (*Gegenstand*). Once this happens, according to Barth, the divine subject (*Subjekt*) of Christianity begins to sink down to the level of a description of the possible human relationships to this object (*Gegenstand*).[86]

The Ordo Salutis (WCF 10-20): General Comments

Barth acknowledges that, when taken as a unit, what is discussed under the various headings of WCF chapters 10 through 20 is what the systematic theologians of the time of the writing of the WCF and thereafter referred to as the *ordo salutis*. For Barth, the *ordo salutis* refers to the process of acquisition and outworking of revelation as it occurs in time in believing individuals. Barth views this as nothing more than the description of the Christian experience in terms of various stages, as seen from the perspective of a religious psychology with its temporal-biographical sequence.[87]

He notes a parallel here with what was said in WCF chapters 2 through 5. There, the will of the God of creation had its analogy in the regular character of events in the world and nature. Here, according to Barth, the work of the God of salvation has its analogy

---

[86]   *TRB*, 218//*TRC*, 139.

[87]   *TRB*, 218-19//*TRC*, 139.

in the temporal series of religious processes, in the continuity of the reflection of the revelation of grace in the soul of the person. For Barth, although the WCF does not omit or suppress the objective character of what is here being discussed, it makes any implementation of it quite difficult. He oddly criticizes the WCF's presentation of the various stages of the *ordo salutis* as being awkward and implausible, on the basis that the description of the soul and experience developed in the Romantic era had not yet been reached. In spite of all he says with regard to the WCF's discussion of the *ordo salutis*, Barth finds it quite refined in comparison with the naive summary of "Suffering–Salvation–Thankfulness" found in the Heidelberg Catechism or next to the presentation of the Christian struggle with temptation, which served as the pattern for Beza's soteriological development of doctrine.[88] He bemoans the fact that the followers of John Knox were so happy about the Pyrrhic victory of Puritanism expressed in the WCF, that they abandoned their Scottish Confession of 1560 and exchanged the ideal of the *civitas sancta*[89] for the inadequate notion of the *ordo salutis* and the theology of the assurance of salvation.[90] For Barth, the point of this section of the WCF is the description of how someone becomes a Christian and then persists in the faith.

Even though Barth thinks that the details could have been improved, the sense and purpose of this section of the WCF is perfectly clear to him, and he thoroughly disagrees with it! He notes, sarcastically, that for the WCF, the earthly analogy (*die irdische Analogie*) to the divine work (*des göttlichen Tuns*) begins to become important and interesting in and of itself. In bitterly ironic tones Barth continues his criticism. He says that the dark night of objectivism, begun with medieval theology, and in which the Reformers strangely persisted, gives way in this section

---

[88] *TRB*, 219//*TRC*, 139-40.

[89] For the full text of the Scottish Confession, cf. Müller, *BSRK*, 249-65; Schaff, *Creeds vol. 3*, 437-79.

[90] *TRB*, 236//*TRC*, 151-52.

of the WCF to the pleasant dawning of another day. That day, which began, Barth maintains, with Luther, is the one in which Schleiermacher will adduce that the essence of theology is the analysis of the pious self-consciousness.[91]

10. Of Effectual Calling

For Barth, the problem which the Westminster Divines sought to address under the heading of effectual calling corresponds exactly to the relation between the first cause and the second causes discussed in WCF Chapter 2 on the doctrine of God. The difficulty here for Barth is the relation of the grace by which one is called, to the personal experience of grace by the one called (i.e., if God called in the first place, why does there need to be a second, "effective call" here?). According to Barth, the WCF tried to address the situation by saying both that man relates altogether passively,[92] and that he approaches grace freely.[93] In the WCF, the tension is solved by claiming that the passivity turns into willfulness the moment man is brought to life by the Holy Spirit. Barth is unsure what the passiveness and willingness mentioned here really mean. He does not think that the WCF adequately explains how a person is

---

[91] *TRB*, 219-20//*TRC*, 140. It is interesting to note that in the semester following the one in which he gave lectures on the Reformed Creeds, he gave lectures on the theology of Schleiermacher (winter semester of 1923-1924). Perhaps his preparation for those lectures provided the background for his well-founded and growing aversion for Schleiermacher, cf. Karl Barth, *Die Theologie Schleiermachers. Eine Vorlesung, Göttingen, Wintersemester 1923/24*, ed. Hinrich Stoevesandt, Karl Barth Gesamtausgabe II. – Akademische Werke 1923/24, vol. 5 (Zürich: Theologischer Verlag, 1978); *The Theology of Schleiermacher. Lectures at Göttingen, Winter Semester 1923-24*, ed. Dietrich Ritschl, trans. Goffrey W. Bromiley (Grand Rapids: Eerdmans, 1982).

[92] The fuller Latin text quoted from the WCF 10.2 reads: "a nulla autem re in homine praevisa qui in hoc negotio se habet omnio passive . . ." The English text reads: "not from any thing at all forseen in man; who is altogether passive therein . . ." in Müller, *BSRK*, 565; Schaff, *Creeds vol. 3*, 625.

[93] The fuller Latin text quoted from the WCF 10.1 reads: "ita tamen ut illi nihilominus liberrime veniant, volentes nempe; facti per illius gratiam." The English text reads: "yet so as they come most freely, being made willing by his grace" in Müller, *BSRK*, 565; Schaff, *Creeds vol. 3*, 624.

moved from passiveness to willingness by being brought to life and renewed.[94]

11. Of Justification

The WCF's formulation of justification in thoroughly forensic terms finds Barth's hearty agreement. He also approves of the clarification that justification is on the basis of neither the act of faith nor the new obedience, but rather on the merits of Christ alone. He points out that, in the WCF, the transition to sanctification is established with the statement that the faith, which lays hold of justification, cannot remain empty (i.e., cannot be dead faith). Barth does, however, criticize the WCF for viewing justification as a temporal act. In his view, the WCF teaches that, although the justification of the elect is decided by God from eternity, they are not actually justified until, in time, that justification is applied by the Holy Spirit. This interjects, for Barth, the suspicion that that which began in time is liable to come to an end in time. Barth is not surprised, in light of what he views as an anthropocentric focus here, that the WCF adds a statement of assurance that one can never fall from the state of completed justification![95]

12. Of Adoption

The content of this doctrine was well known to the older Reformed confessions; however, for Barth, it is no accident that they omitted adoption in their confessions. According to Barth, they refused to make an article of faith out of religious possessions, as such. Instead, they moved directly from the description of the divine gift, in which everything is contained, on to the description of the tasks required of man. The WCF instead interjects a special grace of adoption between justification and sanctification. Barth claims that, from the perspective of the old Reformed tradition, omitting adoption was the only possibility, because, he maintains,

---

[94] *TRB*, 220//*TRC*, 140.

[95] *TRB* 220-21//*TRC* 140-41.

for them the word grace referred exclusively to God (i.e., not to the benefits accruing from it to man). In Barth's view, once man, who has received grace, begins to become interested in himself as a recipient of that grace, the rapid transition from justification to sanctification found in the old Reformed tradition must seem strange. Barth regrets that adoption is first considered and enjoyed a bit, corresponding to the course of human feelings, instead of moving immediately from justification to sanctification.[96]

13. Of Sanctification

Reiterating the thrust of what he has already said, Barth strongly affirms that sanctification is inseparable from effective calling. While agreeing with the statement in the WCF that sanctification pertains to the totality of human nature, he disagrees with the notion that, in this life, it is imperfect and only leads to the struggle between the flesh and the spirit. Barth notes the assertion of the WCF that in this struggle there yet remains a regenerate part in man which, thanks to the ongoing work of the Spirit, will emerge victorious. However, for him, this does not mitigate the language of the WCF which insists that the corruption, which also remains, can indeed occasionally gain the upper hand. Barth is of the opinion that the WCF confuses sanctification with holiness. For him there is clearly a growth in holiness, but not in sanctification. Barth wants no part of an imperfect sanctification[97] or with whatever is called a partial regeneration.[98] He asks why repentance and obedience are not included in this chapter as well, since what the WCF is actually discussing here is holiness. By way of contrast,

---

[96]   *TRB*, 221//*TRC*, 141.

[97]   The fuller Latin text quoted from the WCF 13.2 reads: "verum in hac vita est imperfecta nonnullis corruptionis reliquiis adhuc in omni parte remanentibus . . . ." The English text reads: "yet imperfect in this life; there abideth still some remnants of corruption in every part . . ." in Müller, *BSRK*, 570; Schaff, *Creeds vol. 3*, 629.

[98]   The fuller Latin text quoted from the WCF 13.3 reads: "pars tamen regenita . . . ." The English text reads: "yet . . . the regenerate part . . ." in Müller, *BSRK*, 570; Schaff, *Creeds vol. 3*, 629.

for him, sanctification is something man experiences passively and which does not enable him to stand on his own two feet or do anything on his own. Yet here, sanctification is discussed as though it were possible for a person to be more or less sanctified. The conclusion Barth comes to is that in this chapter the WCF is teaching a form of hidden naturalism. He sarcastically indicates that the WCF attempts to resolve this tension by starting with those things which man passively experiences, namely calling, justification, adoption, and sanctification, followed by that which is understood as his own spontaneous action.[99]

14. Of Saving Faith

Barth summarizes this chapter of the WCF by saying that faith is the work of the Holy Spirit, accomplished through the working of the Word and the sacraments. Yet he notes that once again a quantitative consideration is introduced into this formulation by the WCF. According to the WCF, faith can be in different degrees, weak or strong, and yet remain victorious; indeed, in many it can become a full assurance.[100] Barth notes that from a purely psychological perspective, what is said is quite correct. However, he insists, the WCF is here speaking about saving faith, not some psychological phenomenon. Barth maintains that faith is equally strong, whether it is psychologically considered as full assurance or only exists in the size of a mustard seed. The grace of faith, for him, can not be larger or smaller. To postulate gradations in the strength of faith is to understand by the term *gratia* a mere human spiritual experience.[101]

---

[99] *TRB*, 222//*TRC*, 141-42.

[100] The Latin text of WCF 14.3, which Barth quotes reads: "Fides haec pro diversis ejus gradibus debilior est aut fortior . . . plenam usque certitudinem . . . ." The English text reads: "This faith is different in degrees, weak or strong . . ." in Barth, *TRB*, 222; *TRC*, 142; Müller, *BSRK*, 571-72; Schaff, *Creeds vol. 3*, 631.

[101] *TRB*, 222-23//*TRC*, 142.

15. Of Repentance unto Life

Barth maintains that the comprehensive manner in which the WCF treats the doctrine of the repentance unto life demonstrates that it is to be understood as a supplement to the doctrine of sanctification. For him, the term grace ill applies to what is here being described. Rather, he believes that just as sanctification had been described in naturalistic terms, so now repentance is described in moralistic-methodistic terms. For Barth, the WCF's treatment of repentance portrays the sinner as repenting and converting, without which he cannot receive any forgiveness. Yet for Barth, it is not clear to what extent repentance and conversion are actually necessary. The only basis for this line of reasoning, according to Barth, is that the Westminster Divines understood repentance as the other side of the coin from sanctification, to correspond equally to human experience. That means for him, however, that the unity in which the original Reformed doctrine had understood repentance and sanctification as a human question and the divine answer is here no longer appreciated. Barth believes that, although this doctrine is restated correctly and comprehensively and even enriched in the WCF, it is in the process of being secretly eroded.[102]

16. Of Good Works

Barth agrees with the WCF's treatment of good works, because it states that good works are good only to the degree that they are done in accordance to God's commandments. He also views positively the statements that good works serve to express the thankfulness of believers, to increase their assurance of salvation, to build up their fellow man, and to glorify God. Naturally, he expresses his agreement with the teaching of the WCF where it says that there is no degree of perfection or merit even in our best works which could attain the forgiveness of sin, but only as we are in Christ can our efforts be pleasing to God. However,

---

[102] *TRB*, 223//*TRC*, 142.

Barth views as totally strange what he sees as numerous additions to the otherwise familiar doctrine that it is the Holy Spirit who works the good works in believers. He specifically takes note of the mention in the Latin text of the WCF of an initial *infusion*[103] of grace. He criticizes the WCF by saying that even this infusion is not enough, since an active influence of the Spirit must be added to it in order to produce the willingness in us and to perfect our works. Further, Barth indicates his disagreement with the statement that one is not to simply sit by and wait for this special awakening through the Holy Spirit, but rather must strive to awaken each grace, which is already present. Barth views this as perhaps not all that badly stated, psychologically speaking. However, he is at a loss to determine the source of this description and its consequences, or how the doctrine of an infused grace came to be included in a Reformed confession. The discussion of the good works of those who are not yet born again, Barth finds completely baffling. First of all, he questions the statement that there can be such good works, which formally conform to the commandments of God and are useful to those performing them as well as to others; yet do not serve to glorify God, are sin, and cannot please God. Further, the assertion of the WCF that, if those who are not born again did not do such good works, they would sin even more grievously and offend God all the more, causes Barth even greater puzzlement. For him, it was bound to come to such casuistic games, the more the religious subject became the focus of attention.[104]

---

[103] The fuller Latin text of WCF 16.3 reads: "Et quo eis praestandis pares fiant, praeter habitus gratiae jam *infusos*, ejusdem Spiritus sancti actualis porro requiritur influentia . . ." (emphasis added). The English text simply has: "besides the graces they have already received . . ." The English text reads: "And that they may be enabled thereunto, besides the graces they have already received, there is required an actual influence of the same Holy Spirit . . ." in Müller, *BSRK*, 575; Schaff, *Creeds vol. 3*, 634.

[104] *TRB*, 223-24//*TRC*, 142-43.

17. Of the Perseverance of the Saints; 18. Of Assurance of Grace and Salvation

For Barth, chapters 17 and 18 on the "Perseverance of the Saints" and the "Assurance of Grace and Salvation" demonstrate why the English took such an interest in the doctrine of predestination and placed it at the beginning of their Confession. Speaking sarcastically, Barth sees in chapters 17 and 18 a veritable fortress of religious security, grounded here for a change, not on the church (in a Roman Catholic manner), nor on faith alone (in a Lutheran manner), but on the consciousness of election. For him, the decree of God is a term with which the Reformed fathers had sought to ensure the knowledge of the freedom and majesty of God. However, he feels that in the WCF it had sunk to the level of being merely a helpful construct intended to grant an unshakable freedom and majesty to Presbyterian Christians. For Barth, this doctrine would enable them to go through the many vicissitudes of sinful life on earth "with the necessary cold-bloodedness" (*mit der notigen Kaltblütigkeit*).[105]

Barth also refers quite negatively to the doctrine of assurance of salvation expressed in the WCF in another context in his lectures. In connection with his summary of the positive teaching of the Reformed confessions in *§3. Reformed Doctrine as a whole*, Barth expresses himself quite strongly against what he calls the totally un-Calvinistic doctrine of the assurance of salvation in the WCF. He views it as an attempt to transform Reformed theology into anthropology.[106]

In spite of this icy evaluation and his aversion to what he views as the preoccupation of the WCF with the notion of assurance, Barth does voice his agreement with several elements of the WCF in these two chapters. He agrees with the WCF that in the life of a believer serious sins are possible as well as the consequent wrath

---

[105] *TRB*, 224//*TRC*, 143.

[106] *TRB*, 234//*TRC*, 150-51.

of God, the grieving of the Spirit, and, to a certain point, even the loss of his grace and comfort. Even the statement of the WCF that each must strive through various means to make his calling and election sure[107] finds Barth's tacit approval. Surprisingly, he further concurs with the WCF that even though there is such a thing as a feigned and imagined assurance, those who believe on the Lord Jesus can indeed gain assurance that they stand in grace. He also appears to agree that even though assurance can be shaken, Christians can neither be robbed of it, nor can they any longer sink into despair. He agrees that those once accepted by God cannot finally and completely fall out of the state of grace, but rather will persevere and attain eternal salvation. The statement in the WCF that assurance is not merely a conjecture, but rather an infallible certainty of faith,[108] finds Barth's complete agreement. He lists the many divine grounds for this assurance given by the WCF: the truth of the divine promises; the grace by which the promises receive an internal evidence; the testimony of the Holy Spirit himself; the unchangeableness of the decision of election; the efficacy of Christ's representation on behalf of his people; and from the very nature of the covenant of grace itself. By way of conclusion to his synopsis of these chapters of the WCF, Barth admits just how well and prudently everything has been formulated, and indeed how true it all is.[109]

Then, however, he points out how strange it is for him that the WCF, a confession of faith in the great deeds of God, has here become almost a technical manual for the assurance of salvation. Barth is of the opinion that the Westminster Divines felt impelled to say so much about assurance apparently because something just

---

[107] The fuller Latin text of WCF 18.3 reads: "quo vocationem suam sibi et electionem certam faciat . . . ." The English text reads: "to make his calling and election sure . . ." in Müller, *BSRK*, 580; Schaff, *Creeds vol. 3*, 639.

[108] The fuller Latin text of WCF 18.2 reads: "verum infallibilis quaedam fidei certitude . . . ." The English text reads: "but an infallible assurance of faith . . ." in Müller, *BSRK*, 579; Schaff, *Creeds vol. 3*, 638.

[109] *TRB*, 224-25//*TRC*, 143-44.

was not right. Barth points out that in the midst of the intended peace of assurance, the Reformed notion of the inseparable unity of faith and obedience comes to expression as a recurring element of concern in the WCF. It does so by insisting that even the infallible certainty of faith mentioned requires the individual to make that faith certain. Yet, voicing his agreement with the WCF, Barth properly reminds us that no amount of "making certain," which an individual attempts, can serve as the basis of the certainty of election. Barth feels that, on the basis of what is said in these chapters of the WCF, it must be acknowledged that the Westminster Divines masterfully and successfully understood the need to struggle with this Reformed difficulty and to come to terms with it.[110]

19. Of the Law of God

In spite of what he had said up to this point concerning the *ordo salutis*, Barth here claims that the WCF's use of it is characteristically Reformed, since it culminates in Chapter 19, "Of the Law," and Chapter 20, "Of Christian Freedom," which are followed by Chapter 21, "Of Religious Worship and the Sabbath Day." He views this as an example of the classic Calvinistic thought pattern: from faith to law to worship. However, Barth believes that whereas Calvin related everything to the knowledge of God – God's giving, demanding, leading, and conducting, the WCF makes man the theme – man's receiving and possessing, achieving and offering. Barth claims that it is impossible in this context for the Reformed transition to ethics to escape receiving a legalistic character. Barth summarizes the chapter as follows. God made the covenant of law with Adam,[111] in which he gave his law to him for personal, complete, and careful observation. And even now, after the fall, it has

---

[110] *TRB*, 225-26//*TRC*, 143-44.

[111] Interestingly, Barth once again avoids using the language of the WCF regarding the covenant of works and prefers instead to speak of the covenant of law made with Adam. It almost seems as if Barth sees what the WCF calls the covenant of works and the covenant of law as interchangeable entities.

not ceased to be the perfect rule for righteousness. Because God is its giver, the Mosaic moral law binds all men, even those who are not justified, to continual obedience. Conversely even those who are justified stand under the covenant of law, i.e., the law is of great use (*vehementer utilis*[112]) to them on several levels. It serves for revelation of the divine will, for the knowledge of sin and self, for the preservation of the fear of God, which seeks for his mercy, and finally for the sake of the promises of the law themselves. For Barth, therefore, no conflict can exist between the gospel and the law, because the gospel causes man to do voluntarily that which the law demands. As good as Barth finds these statements, he points out that Zwingli and Calvin did not find it necessary to base the obedience of believers on the Law, such that it is a *vehementer utilis* to them. Barth asks whether an obedience based in the way the WCF formulates it can ever avoid coming dangerously close to a moralistic externalism.[113]

20. Of Christian Liberty, and Liberty of Conscience

Barth feels that the chapter on "Christian Freedom" speaks beautifully of the fact that God alone is the Lord of the conscience. He also compliments how very well the WCF expresses the point of Christian freedom in 20.3 and merely gives his own translation of it. Barth also speaks well of the statements in WCF 20.4 against the abuse of Christian freedom as a pretense to upset either the state or the church order or even for the spreading of erroneous opinions. However, he does criticize the repeated references in chapters 20 and 21 to the light of nature (*lumen naturae*). He totally disagrees that the *lumen naturae* should serve as the source on whose authority the church order, worship, and the sanctification of the Sabbath rest.[114]

---

[112] The fuller Latin text of WCF 19.6 reads: "Est tamen ea illis non minus quam aliis vehementer utilis . . . ." The English text reads: "yet is it of great use to them, as well as to others . . ." in Müller, *BSRK*, 580; Schaff, *Creeds vol. 3*, 641.

[113] *TRB*, 226//*TRC*, 144-45.

21. Of Religious Worship, and the Sabbath Day

As one might expect, Barth disagrees with the WCF's use of the creation order[115] to establish the requirement of a particular time for worship. On the other hand, he does not seem bothered by the WCF's assertion that the seventh day was set aside via the positive, moral, and perpetual commandment of God.[116] Interestingly, Barth fails to mention the fact that the WCF bases the transition from the Sabbath to Sunday on the resurrection of Christ. He summarizes without comment that the Sabbath is now to be celebrated to the end of the world as the Christian Sabbath,[117] for which one is to prepare himself inwardly and which one is to celebrate by refraining from all activities, even from amusement, and through worship and works of mercy. Barth claims that this expression of the sanctification of the Sabbath, although allegedly Calvinistic, is actually English-Presbyterian in origin.[118] He says that it differs from Calvin's view in two ways. According to Barth, the WCF's view of the Sabbath differs from Calvin *positively* with regard to both the importance placed on explicitly the seventh day (something, Barth maintains, Calvin explicitly refused to do), as well

---

[114] *TRB*, 226-27//*TRC*, 145.

[115] The Latin text of the WCF 21.7 from which Barth apparently draws these remarks reads: "Quemadmodum est de *lege naturae* ut indefinite portio quaedam temporis idonea divino cultui celebrando sejuncta sit ac assignata . . ." (emphasis added). The English text reads: "As it is of the law of nature, in general, a due proportion of time be set apart for the worship of God . . ." in Müller, *BSRK*, 589-90; Schaff, *Creeds vol. 3*, 648.

[116] The fuller Latin text of WCF 21.7 reads: "ita in verbo suo Deus (praecepto morali, positivo ac perpetuo . . . ." The English text reads: "so, in his Word, by a positive, moral, and perpetual commandment . . ." in Müller, *BSRK*, 590; Schaff, *Creeds vol. 3*, 648.

[117] The fuller Latin text of WCF 21.7 reads: "estque perpetuo ad finem mundi tanquam Sabbatum Christianum celebrandus." The English text reads: "and is to be continued to the end of the world, as the Christian Sabbath." in Müller, *BSRK*, 590; Schaff, *Creeds vol. 3*, 649.

[118] For an alternative perspective demonstrating the unity of Calvin and the WCF with regard to the Sabbath, cf. Richard B. Gaffin, Jr., "Westminster and the Sabbath," in *The Westminster Confession into the 21st Century*, ed. J. Ligon Duncan (3 vols.; Fearn: Mentor, 2003), 1:123-44.

as the rigor with which the rest on Sunday is emphasized. And *negatively*, Barth sees the difference between the WCF and Calvin on the Sabbath in the absence of any reference in the WCF to the eternal Sabbath rest from our works. Inexplicably, he also claims that the WCF differs from Calvin in that the WCF does not mention the social foundation of the Sunday rest in view of the working classes![119]

22. Of Lawful Oaths and Vows; 23. Of the Civil Magistrate; 24. Of Marriage and Divorce [not discussed in the lectures]

25. Of the Church

Barth concurs with the strong emphasis in chapters 25 and 26 of the WCF on the catholicity and universality of even the visible church. He makes no comment on the statements in WCF 25.1 concerning the invisible church, but seems almost exclusively interested in the visible church in his summary of these two chapters of the WCF. He mentions the three provisions Christ gave the visible church listed in WCF 25.3: the ministry, oracles, and the ordinances of God. He points out that the church evidences varying degrees of both visibility and purity. For the marks of the visible church, Barth lists: the preaching of the gospel, the administration of the sacraments, and the celebration of public worship. He notes that any mention of church discipline is lacking here, but is taken up in WCF 30. Barth reflects the statements of the WCF that even the purest church can become the synagogue of Satan. He adds that the WCF explains that the Roman Pope is the Antichrist in a separate article (WCF 25.6), so as to avoid any confusion. It is not clear whether Barth intended these last remarks to be taken sarcastically or not.[120]

---

[119] *TRB*, 227//*TRC*, 145. Apparently Barth understands Calvin's oblique mention of "servants" in the *Institutes* 2.8.28, in a somewhat socialist manner. Cf. Calvin, *Institutes*, 395.

[120] *TRB*, 227-28//*TRC*, 145-46.

26. Of the Communion of Saints

Barth is pleased with the emphasis on the social aspect he sees in the WCF's treatment of the doctrine of the communion of the saints. This comes to expression, for Barth, where the church is sketched as an association,[121] whose members are obligated to help each other even in external matters and whose brotherly fellowship extends to all those who call upon the name of Jesus, to the degree that God provides opportunity. For Barth, the conclusion of Chapter 26 presents two important safeguards against misunderstanding what is meant by the communion of the saints. First, it was not intended to be understood in an "enthusiastic"[122] manner. Second, the somewhat idealistic formulation of the communion of the saints was not meant to eliminate the right to private property or ownership.[123]

27. Of the Sacraments; 28. Of Baptism; 29. Of the Lord's Supper; 30. Of Church Censures; 31. Of Synods and Councils; 32. Of the State of Man after Death, and of the Resurrection of the Dead; 33. Of the Last Judgment [not discussed in the lectures]

Concluding Critical Remarks

Barth's comments with regard to what the WCF has to say about Scripture as God's revelation are, for the most part, surprisingly favorable. Although he could have singled out the WCF's doctrine of Scripture as "the" example of a perversion of Calvin's teach-

---

[121] Barth uses the German word *Verein*, which has a wide range of meaning, but is most often used in reference to various clubs or social associations.

[122] Barth uses the German term, "*schwärmerisch*" here to refer to the teaching of the radical or "enthusiast" elements of the Reformation who maintained that believers could mystically partake in the substance of Christ. The text of the WCF (26.3) with which Barth is here stating his agreement reads: "This communion which the saints have with Christ, doth not make them in any wise partakers of the substance of His Godhead, or to be equal with Christ in any respect . . ." in: Müller, *BSRK*, 600; Schaff, *Creeds vol. 3*, 660.

[123] *TRB*, 228//*TRC*, 146.

ing, he chose not to do so. The brunt of his criticism is borne not by the WCF, but rather by the Second Helvetic Confession and the Helvetic Consensus Formula. To be sure, some might want to infer that Barth's criticism of those creeds applies to the WCF as well. However, Barth himself did not set the WCF over against Calvin as some would like us to believe.[124] Barth agrees with the WCF on several important matters: it is in the Scriptures alone that we hear God's voice today; the Scriptures without the illumination of the Holy Spirit are insufficient; and the only source of knowledge of salvation is to be found in Scripture. Nonetheless, there are significant differences as well. Continuing in the vein begun in the second edition of his *Commentary on Romans*, Barth describes Scripture not as revelation itself, but rather as the *witness* to God's revelation. The Bible *becomes* the word of God – both to the biblical authors and to its readers – through the ongoing inspiration of the Holy Spirit (i.e., Scripture is not, in itself, the word of God). Borrowing terminology from Kierkegaard, Barth refers to the *paradox* of revelation. He also speaks of the necessity of a *simultaneity* of revelation to avoid placing what he considers undue stress on the Bible as the word of God, and thus viewing it as an objective reality in itself. By way of contrast, it is interesting to note that Barth omitted reference to several portions of Chapter 1 of the WCF. For instance, it is significant that Chapter 1 of the WCF is entitled: "Of the Holy Scripture," not, "Of the Word of God," emphasizing the written nature of God's revelation. The fact and even necessity of committing God's revelation to writing, discussed in WCF 1.1,[125] is not mentioned by Barth. WCF 1.2

---

[124] For one flagrant example of an attempt to pit Calvin against the WCF, although not primarily with regard to the doctrine of Scripture, cf. Holmes Rolston, *John Calvin versus the Westminster Confession* (Atlanta: John Knox Press, 1972).

[125] "[A]nd afterwards for the better preserving and propagating of the truth, and for the more sure establishment and comfort of the church against the corruption of the flesh, and the malice of Satan and of the world, *to commit the same wholly unto writing*: which maketh the Holy Scripture to be most necessary; those former ways of God's revealing his will unto his people, being now ceased" (emphasis added) in Müller, *BSRK*, 542-43; Schaff, *Creeds vol. 3*, 600-1.

explicitly equates Scripture with the written word of God.[126] God's revelation is to be found in the pages of Scripture, not in some mystical or existential experience or event. Again in WCF 1.4, it is stated that because the authority of Scripture is totally dependent on God, it is to be received precisely because it is the word of God.[127] The WCF affirms that God not only freely chose to reveal Himself, but also that He freely chose to commit that revelation to writing. He did this, according to WCF 1.1, "For the better preserving and propagating of the truth, and for the more sure establishment and comfort of the church against the corruption of the flesh, and the malice of Satan and of the world. . ."[128] Any attempt to move away from the unique objective authority of Scripture, whether by subjecting it to man's reason or placing it outside of human history as an existentialistic event, is to rob the church of its God-given foundation.

Barth seeks neither to eliminate, nor mitigate whatsoever the realities of the doctrine of predestination, but rather gives this doctrine its proper place as stated in the WCF. Interestingly, Barth also refuses to criticize the so-called double predestination of the WCF.[129] By avoiding the terminology of the decrees in his discussion of Chapter 3 of the WCF, Barth does not allow a wedge to be driven between God's decree and the work of Christ, as some do, purportedly following what they perceive to be a Barthian interpretation.[130] Barth agrees with WCF 3.5 where it clearly states that the elect are chosen in Christ (i.e., not separate from him or

---

[126] WCF 1.2: "Under the Name of Holy Scripture, or the Word of God written, are now contained all the books of the Old and New Testament, which are these . . ." in Müller, *BSRK*, 543; Schaff, *Creeds vol. 3*, 601.

[127] WCF 1.4: "The Authority of the Holy Scripture . . . dependeth . . . wholly upon God . . . and therefore it is to be received, because it is the Word of God" in Müller, *BSRK*, 544; Schaff, *Creeds vol. 3*, 602.

[128] WCF 1.1 in Müller, *BSRK*, 542-43; Schaff, *Creeds vol. 3*, 600-1.

[129] Cf. WCF 3.7 in Müller, *BSRK*, 552; Schaff, *Creeds vol. 3*, 610.

[130] As an example of those who set God's decree over against the work of Christ, cf. John Riddell, "God's eternal decrees," *Scottish Journal of Theology* 2 (1949): 352-63 (esp. 359).

his work in any way).[131] Where he does criticize the WCF, it is with regard to what he sees as a twofold misuse or misapplication of the doctrine of election. For Barth, election is an expression of who God is and rightly belongs to the doctrine of God. He claims that the WCF attempts to move election from theology proper to anthropology in two ways: first, by using this doctrine to assure believers of their salvation and second, by using it to enable man to escape the paradox of his being (i.e., the question of his existence). However, this interpretation ascribes intentions to the WCF which simply cannot be substantiated! The WCF 3.3 explicitly states that the purpose of election is to manifest God's glory,[132] and, in keeping with that, to afford the elect occasion for "praise, reverence, and admiration of God, and of humility, diligence and abundant consolation to all that sincerely obey the gospel."[133] Furthermore, subjectivistic and existentialistic questions concerning the "paradox of man's being" were totally foreign to the WCF, and it would be completely inappropriate to read them back into the Confession to be used as a basis of its interpretation.

The WCF's use of the term "first cause" in connection with the doctrine of providence is seen by Barth to be an indication of some kind of casuistic Thomism. However, the WCF introduces the notion of first cause in chapter 5.2, only after, in completely non-causal language, it has expressed the sovereign will of God in 5.1.[134] Barth also seems to view what the WCF has to say about the second causes in a somewhat mechanistic manner. But here again, the WCF clearly distinguishes between God's providence, the second causes, and the means which God uses to accomplish his desired purposes, stressing the fact that God is free to work without, above, or against them at his pleasure.[135] Although Barth will

---

[131] Cf. WCF 3.5 in Müller, *BSRK*, 551; Schaff, *Creeds vol. 3*, 609.

[132] Cf. WCF 3.3 and 3.7 in Müller, *BSRK*, 549-50, 552; Schaff, *Creeds vol. 3*, 608-09, 610.

[133] Cf. WCF 3.8 in Müller, *BSRK*, 552-53; Schaff, *Creeds vol. 3*, 610-11.

[134] Cf. WCF 5.2 in Müller, *BSRK*, 554; Schaff, *Creeds vol. 3*, 612.

later develop a slightly less critical role for analogy,[136] here he sees any trace of analogy as a danger to be avoided. His criticism of the WCF's alleged use of analogy in association with providence flows out of his insistence on the radical disjunction between revelation and nature, as well as between the God of revelation and the so-called God of the known world and natural order. Barth's view raises the question of whether and in what manner the God of revelation can make himself known in a way which human beings can comprehend (i.e., what it means for God to reveal himself or what revelation is). It also appears that Barth missed the point that, for the WCF, providence is first and foremost an expression of the will and wisdom of God, and only secondarily does it come to bear on mankind. Even then, it is not so much in terms of assurance, but "to make them more watchful against all future occasions of sin . . ."[137]

Whereas the WCF speaks of two covenants (a covenant of works and a covenant of grace), Barth quite clearly insists that there is but one covenant, a covenant of grace (*Gnadenbund*). This switch away from his characteristic dialectic to a monistic focus is echoed elsewhere in the priority Barth places on the gospel over the law.[138] It is quite curious that Barth nowhere makes reference to a covenant of works. Rather, he speaks of a "Legal Covenant"

---

[135] Cf. WCF 5.3 in Müller, *BSRK*, 554; Schaff, *Creeds vol. 3*, 612-13.

[136] Cf. Karl Barth, *Die Kirchliche Dogmatik. Die Lehre von der Versöhnung*, vol. IV,1 (Zürich: Evangelischer Verlag, 1953), 709ff., 859ff; *Church Dogmatics. The Doctrine of Reconciliation*, trans. G. W. Bromiley, vol. IV,1 (Edinburgh: T&T Clark, 1956), 635ff., 769ff. See also: Horst Georg Pöhlmann, *Analogia entis oder Analogia fidei?. Die Frage der Analogie bei Karl Barth*, ed. Edmund Schlink, Forschung zur systematischen und ökumenischen Theologie, vol. 16 (Göttingen: Vandenhoeck und Ruprecht, 1965).

[137] Cf. WCF 5.6 in: Müller, *BSRK;* Schaff, *Creeds vol. 3*, 614.

[138] For a pointed presentation of Barth's more developed view of the relationship between the Law and the Gospel, cf. Karl Barth, "Evangelium und Gesetz," in *Gesetz und Evangelium. Beiträge zur gegenwärtigen theologischen Diskussion*, ed. Ernst Kinder and Klaus Hoendler (Darmstadt: Wissenschaftliche Buchgesellschaft, 1968), 1-29.

or "a Covenant of Law." At one point he even sets the law over against grace as though he were discussing the Mosaic Covenant rather than the covenant of works. Barth sees the Covenant and what one might call the history of redemption as two contradictory ways of looking at things. Whereas the covenant, as he understands it, is a reflection of the nature of God and, as such, stands outside of the realm of time, the history of redemption pulls God's activity down into history, distorting it into a process of evolutionary development. However, Barth's rejection of any temporal administration of the covenant places the grace revealed in the covenant beyond the realm of human experience, making it of no value to fallen mankind whatsoever, which is the direct antithesis of the intent of the covenant as taught in Scripture and confessed in the WCF. Barth offers no alternative and no explanation of how a single covenant of grace explains the fall of mankind into sin. He also eschews any attempt to explain the temporal outworking of God's saving grace, be it in redemptive history or the *ordo salutis*. He thus leaves one wondering how or if this covenant of grace has any bearing for man at all. Scripture very clearly reveals God making his covenant with his people in history in order to redemptively restore them into a right relationship with himself. Hence, the covenant includes, among other things, a temporal and anthropocentric aspect; something disallowed by Barth, but accorded proper expression by the WCF. In conclusion, it must be pointed out that, while Barth's view of the covenant differs from that of the WCF at several points, the force of his criticism is directed toward those who came after the Westminster Assembly and, in his opinion, distorted its teaching.[139]

---

[139] Barth does *not* set the WCF's view of the covenant over against Calvin's, *per se*, in his Göttingen lectures. It is with what others did with the notion of the covenant found in the WCF that Barth has his difficulties. Helm rightly demonstrates the unity of Calvin and the WCF on the concept of the covenant: Paul Helm, "Calvin and the Covenant," *Evangelical Quarterly* 55, (April 1983): 65-81. For a positive discussion of some of the more recent debate concerning the WCF's understanding of the covenant, cf. David B. McWilliams, "The

The major focus of Barth's criticism of the various elements comprising the *ordo salutis* centers on their temporal or experiential character. For him, the emphasis which the WCF places on the *ordo salutis* is a psychologizing of God's revelation, shifting the emphasis away from God's revelation to its relevance for believers and a description of Christian experience. Unfortunately, in his proper disdain for the psychologizing and historicizing of theology and revelation, Barth leaves no room for the application of God's grace in the lives of believers. Barth seems unwilling to allow for any purpose of God's grace beyond simply revealing who he is. Grace and salvation remain, at best, tangential to man and one is left not knowing if they have any meaning or have had any effect at all.

The result of Barth's criticism of the WCF is a complete retreat into some kind of timeless or eternal realm outside of human experience, which, among other things, removes any sense from the notion of the effectual calling of the elect in time and space. For Barth, not only election, but even justification takes place outside of the bounds of time and is thus not subject to its vicissitudes. In his view, justification is an eternal event needing neither temporal actualization nor means of assurance. The problem with this

---

Covenant theology of the Westminster Confession of Faith and recent criticism," *Westminster Theological Journal* 53, (Spring 1991): 109-24. For a presentation of those who are critical of the WCF and maintain that Barth's view of the covenant was a "corrective" of the Puritan view expressed in the WCF, returning it to its true Calvinistic roots – a perspective *not* found in Barth's Göttingen lectures, cf. William Klempa, "The Concept of the Covenant in Sixteenth- and Seventeenth-Century Continental and British Reformed Theology," in *Major Themes in the Reformed Tradition*, ed. Donald K. McKim (Grand Rapids: Eerdmans, 1992), 94-107; Arthur C. Cochrane, "Karl Barth's Doctrine of the Covenant," in *Major Themes in the Reformed Tradition*, ed. Donald K. McKim (Grand Rapids: Eerdmans, 1992), 108-16; Francis Lyall, "Of Metaphors and Analogies. Legal Language and Covenant Theology," *Scottish Journal of Theology* 32 (1979): 1-17; Rolston, *John Calvin versus the Westminster Confession;* J. L. Scott, "Covenant in the theology of Karl Barth," *Scottish Journal of Theology* 17, (June 1964): 182-98; James B. Torrance, "Covenant or Contract? A Study of the Theological Background of Worship in Seventeenth Century Scotland," *Scottish Journal of Theology* 23 (1970): 51-76.

perspective, however, is that justification pertains to the elect who live amid the uncertainties of life here and now.

The teaching of the WCF on adoption and assurance of faith seems to have given Barth special difficulty. He viewed both of these as prime examples of an attempt to transform Reformed theology into an anthropology or psychology, since they focused on man, his feelings, his status or needs, rather than on the work of God's grace. However, it must be pointed out that Barth's understanding of the WCF at this point is more than skewed. The WCF expresses these doctrines explicitly in terms of God's grace and ties them inseparably to Christ and His finished work of which believers become the beneficiaries through faith![140] That the God of all grace loves his children and bestows such demonstrations of his love on them in no way detracts from the sovereignty of his grace. Indeed, it is a manifestation of that grace!

Although Barth does not explicitly use the terms forensic and progressive sanctification in his critique of the WCF, he makes it clear that he wants no part of the WCF's view of progressive sanctification. Rather, he views sanctification as a forensic act of God in eternity. Unfortunately, he not only fails to clarify what he sees as a distinction between sanctification and holiness, but he also fails to indicate what bearing such a forensic sanctification would have on the elect (i.e., how it would work itself out in their lives).

To remove saving faith from the realm of human experience, as Barth seems interested in doing, raises the question of what it really means for someone to have faith at all, let alone saving faith. Perhaps that which someone claims to be saving faith is merely self-delusion. The question of the Reformation was: "How can I know that I am righteous before God?" – not merely what saving faith is in the abstract! The practical implications of this question do not seem to interest Barth.

---

[140] Cf. WCF 12 in Müller, *BSRK*, 569; Schaff, *Creeds vol. 3*, 628. cf. the WCF 18.2 in Müller, *BSRK*, 579; Schaff, *Creeds vol. 3*, 638.

The consequence of Barth's extra-temporal and extra-human experience perspective becomes crystal clear in conjunction with his criticism of the WCF's teaching on repentance. For Barth, there is no need for man to repent or be converted, since it is all a matter of God's eternal grace. Barth's comments regarding repentance draw attention to two glaring defects in his position. First is the apparent failure to take seriously the depth and hideousness of sin as an affront and act of rebellion against God. Second is the elision of the clear biblical demand to repent and to evidence such repentance in a changed life.

Good works present a peculiar problem for Barth. On the one hand, he heartily acknowledges that the Reformed tradition has always maintained that good works must flow from the grace of salvation. On the other hand, he realizes that the good works in which the elect must engage take place in time and space, in the context of human experience and are not to be mere existential events, but are to characterize the daily life of the elect. It is precisely at the point of repentance and good works that the eternal salvation of God visibly manifests itself in the concrete terms of a changed human life! It can no longer remain outside of or tangential to human history!

As was the case with the doctrines of repentance and good works, Barth struggles, in conjunction with perseverance and assurance, with the reality of the manifestation of saving grace in the lives of the elect. His disdain for the emphasis placed on assurance in the WCF is evidence of his rejection of any congruity between eternal grace and its application in the realm of time and space in human experience. But it also gives evidence to Barth's failure to take seriously the consequences of sin which give rise to the lack of assurance and the struggle to persevere. It is precisely this reality which the WCF addresses in Chapters 17 and 18.

The WCF formulation with regard to the law does not teach some form of anthropocentric moralism as Barth suggests. Rather, it does do something Barth seems unwilling to do, at least in his

Göttingen lectures. Namely, confront man with the reality of his sin. WCF 19.6 dwells repeatedly on the function of the law to show believers their sin, in order that they might "come to further conviction of, humiliation for, and hatred against sin; together with a clearer sight of the need they have of Christ, and the perfection of His obedience."[141] The use of the law taught here is the conviction of sin in order to drive man to Christ! It is completely Christ and Gospel centered.

WCF 20.1 ties Christian liberty to two important matters, neither of which Barth mentions. First, the liberty believers enjoy was purchased by Christ (i.e., it is a direct result and application of his finished work). Second, that liberty "consists in their freedom from the guilt of sin . . ."[142] Barth once more seems to shy away from the reality of sin. It must be added that, while the WCF does mention the light of nature twice in this context,[143] it nowhere attributes any authority to it with regard to establishing church order, regulating worship, or keeping the Sabbath. It might be debated whether the purported distinction between Calvin and the WCF with regard to the Sabbath is as stark as Barth suggests. However, it is true that the element of promise, so strong in Calvin's understanding of the Sabbath, is missing in the WCF.[144] Interestingly, in his focus on the social aspects of the church, Barth does not mention that the communion of the saints flows from their union to Christ their head and is not merely a matter of social interaction.[145] He also fails to point out that one of the implications and outworkings of the communion of the saints is the maintenance of "an holy

---

[141] Cf. Müller, *BSRK*, 582-83; Schaff, *Creeds vol. 3*, 641-42.

[142] WCF 20.1, cf. Müller, *BSRK*, 584; Schaff, *Creeds vol. 3*, 643-44.

[143] WCF 20.4 and 21.1, cf. Müller, *BSRK*, 576-86; Schaff, *Creeds vol. 3*, 645-46.

[144] Cf. Calvin's treatment in the *Institutes* 2.28-34 in: Calvin, *Institutes*, 394-401. See also the reflection of Calvin's view in Ursinus' exposition of the fourth commandment in his commentary on the Heidelberg Catechism: Zacharias Ursinus, *The Commentary of Dr. Zacharias Ursinus on the Heidelberg Catechism*, trans. G. W. Williard (Grand Rapids: Eerdmans, 1954), 557-71.

[145] Cf. WCF 26.1 in Müller, *BSRK*, 599; Schaff, *Creeds vol. 3*, 659.

fellowship and communion in the worship of God . . . ,"[146] i.e., for the purpose of worship, not merely human fellowship.

By way of summary to this brief look at what Karl Barth had to say about the WCF, three things stand out. First, there are significant differences between the WCF and Barth. Barth's theology, even at the early stage of his theological development evidenced in his Göttingen lectures on the Reformed creeds, cannot be characterized as "Westminsterian" in any way. It was never Barth's intention to replicate the theology of the WCF, and any attempt to either harmonize or synthesize Barth and the WCF must be rejected. Second, those who wish to set the WCF and Barth over against each other as diametric opposites, cannot do so on the basis of Barth's own statements regarding the WCF. In spite of the clear and important differences, on numerous occasions in his Göttingen lectures, Barth expressed the view that the WCF was a balanced formulation of Reformed theology. To be sure, he viewed the teaching of the WCF as balanced on a razor's edge and bemoaned that which came in the time following the Westminster Assembly, but that did not prevent him from often simply summarizing the WCF in a positive manner in his own words. Finally, during the time he gave his lectures on the Reformed creeds, Barth was struggling to formulate a corrective to the abuses of the liberalism and, to a lesser extent, pietism of his day. Rationalism and historicism had reduced theology to a relativized product of human reason. Schleiermacher and others had expressed theology purely in terms of human experience. For him, the WCF expressed some of the same rationalistic and psychologizing tendencies. Hence, the main focus of his criticism of the WCF pertains to what he perceives as its proclivity to make theology into anthropology. For Barth, the only alternative was to put theology and revelation beyond the reach of man, outside of time and space. Unfortunately, his proposal not only makes the notion of revelation meaningless,

---

[146] Cf. WCF 26.2 in Müller, *BSRK*, 600; Schaff, *Creeds vol. 3*, 659-60.

but also minimizes the reality of sin. By removing salvation in all its aspects from the realm of history and human experience, Barth empties it of all significance. With its focus on God's glory, God's written word, man's sin, and the salvation brought to completion by God's grace, the WCF provides a more biblical balance between the teaching regarding God's sovereignty and the outworking of his plan of salvation than does Barth's theology. The WCF is a human testimony to and confession of the wonder of the saving grace of God found in Jesus Christ, breaking into fallen human history to fully redeem an elect covenant people for himself. It is also a call to give that sovereign God of grace all the glory!

Natural Theology and the Westminster Confession of Faith

J. V. FESKO AND GUY M. RICHARD

Introduction

Natural theology is a topic that many might find oddly placed beside the Westminster Confession of Faith. It might elicit a response not unlike Tertullian's (160–220) famous question, "What has Athens to do with Jerusalem?" Within Reformed circles natural theology is typically associated with more philosophically minded theology, which is significantly different than the theology of the Westminster Confession and has therefore largely been rejected. This idea is aptly captured in a letter written by Cornelius Van Til (1895–1987) to Francis Schaeffer (1912–1984) where he stated:

> I think we agree that the biblical gospel of sovereign, saving grace, which modern man needs, is best reproduced in the Reformed Confessions. When the Westminster Confession speaks of God as "alone and unto himself all-sufficient" and as "the alone fountain of being," it is speaking of the triune God, Father, Son and Holy Ghost (Chapter 2) of which the Scripture speaks. It is this triune God of Scripture who is there. . . . I think you will agree, then, that no form of natural theology has ever spoken properly of the God who is there. None of the great Greek philosophers, like Plato and Aristotle, and none of the great modern philosophers,

like Descartes, Kant, Hegel, or Kierkegaard and others, have ever spoken of the God who is there.[1]

Van Til's rejection of natural theology is not unique and goes back even earlier in the 20th century to the famous debate between Karl Barth (1886–1968) and Emil Brunner (1889–1966). Barth responded with a forceful "Nein!" to Brunner's suggestion that the church needed to recover natural theology.[2] Barth writes that "we must learn again to understand revelation as *grace* and grace as *revelation* and therefore turn away all 'true' or 'false' *theologia naturalis* by ever making new decisions and being ever controverted anew." Barth went as far as to say that "if one occupies oneself with real theology one can pass by so-called natural theology only as one would pass by an abyss into which it is inadvisable to step if one does not want to fall."[3] The rejection of natural theology, however, antedates the 20th century and the bounds of the Reformed community. It has roots in Immanuel Kant's (1724–1804) critique of the proofs for the existence of God. If, then, the rejection of natural theology is so strong within Reformed circles, then why need we investigate natural theology and the Westminster Confession? What has natural theology to do with Westminster?

Stated simply, the Westminster Confession and the Divines that composed the document accept natural theology to a greater degree than present-day Reformed theologians. In order to demonstrate this claim, we will trace the trajectory of natural theology through the thought of Aquinas; the Reformation (1517–1564) – Calvin, Musculus, and Vermigli; Early Orthodoxy, or the post-Reformation

---

[1] Cornelius Van Til to Francis Schaeffer, 11 March 1969, in *Ordained Servant* 6, no. 4 (1997): 77.

[2] David F. Wells notes that "Brunner faithfully preserved the Reformers' position on creation and God's revelation through it, while Karl Barth departed from it" in *No Place for Truth: Or Whatever Happened to Evangelical Theology?* (Grand Rapids: Eerdmans, 1993), 144 n. 8.

[3] Emil Brunner and Karl Barth, *Natural Theology*, trans. John Baillie (1946; repr., Eugene: Wipf & Stock, 2002), 71, 75.

(1565–1630/40) – Perkins, Polanus, Du Moulin, and Ussher; and High Orthodoxy (1630/40–1700), during which the Confession was written.[4] We will provide a historical-theological backdrop by which we may better understand the place of natural theology in the Confession. Second, we will then survey the Confession, in particular its use of the phrase, "the light of nature" (1.1, 6; 10.4; 20.4; 21.1), as well as examine a representative cross-section of the works of the Divines. We will see the way in which the Confession and the Divines employ natural revelation and theology. We will demonstrate that they employ natural revelation and theology in a positive manner – to render man inexcusable, to provide man with general principles of conduct, and to serve an instrumental role in apologetics. Before we proceed with our investigation, however, we should briefly define our terms.

Natural theology, or *theologia naturalis*, is "the knowledge of God that is available to reason through the light of nature."[5] Natural theology is not the same thing as natural revelation. Natural or general revelation is based in the created order, and is accessible to all men.[6] We can distinguish natural revelation as the existence of the knowledge of God in the creation and natural theology as the interpretation of that natural revelation. As we will see in our investigation, these two terms are related to the *duplex cognitio Dei*, the twofold knowledge of God, "according to which the general, nonsaving knowledge of God as Creator and as the wrathful Judge of sin, accessible to pagan and Christian alike, is distinguished from special, saving knowledge of God as Redeemer."[7] We may also speak of natural theology and supernatural theology, or special revelation. Keeping these terms

---

[4]   See Otto Weber, *Foundations of Dogmatics*, trans. Darrell L. Guder (2 vols.; Grand Rapids: Eerdmans, 1981), 1:112-27.

[5]   Richard A. Muller, *Dictionary of Latin and Greek Theological Terms: Drawn Principally from Protestant Scholastic Theology* (Grand Rapids: Baker, 1985), 302.

[6]   See Muller, *Dictionary*, 265-66.

[7]   Muller, *Dictionary*, 97.

in mind, we may proceed to investigate the historical-theological background of natural theology with Thomas Aquinas.

Middle Ages: Thomas Aquinas (1225–74)

Thomas Aquinas develops his so-called proofs for the existence of God in both his *Summa Thelogica* and *Summa Contra Gentiles*. We should briefly investigate Thomas' use of his proofs because it will give us a backdrop for the greater picture of the use of natural theology in the Reformation and post-Reformation periods. As stated in the introduction, in post-Kantian theology there is a denigration of the proofs of God's existence as well as the use of natural theology.[8] What many, however, fail to recognize is the specific nature and object of Kant's critique. Kant's critique was primarily leveled against Enlightenment rationalism, specifically that of Christian Wolff (1679–1754) and G. W. Leibniz (1646–1716).[9] This is particularly evident, for example, when Kant writes that "there are only three modes of proving the existence of a Deity on the grounds of speculative reason." Kant believes that whether one approaches the proofs for God's existence by *a posteriori* or *a priori* means that the mind "stretches its wings in vain, to soar beyond the world of sense by the mere might of speculative thought."[10] The specific historical context of Kant's critique is

---

[8] Herman Bavinck, *The Doctrine of God*, trans. William Hendriksen (1951; repr., Edinburgh: Banner of Truth, 1991), 78-79; Karl Barth, *Church Dogmatics*, *The Doctrine of God*, vol. II.1, ed. G. W. Bromiley and T. F. Torrance, trans. T. H. L. Parker, et al. (1957; repr., Edinburgh: T&T Clark, 1997), 135-40; Alvin Plantinga, "The Reformed Objection to Natural Theology," *Proceedings of the American Catholic Philosophical Association* 54 (1980): 49-62.

[9] Richard A. Muller, "The Dogmatic Function of St. Thomas' 'Proofs': A Protestant Appreciation," *Fides et Historia* 24 (1992): 15. See Christian Wolff, *Naturliche Gottesgelahrheit*, (5 vols.; Zürich: Georg Olms Publishers, 1995); G. W. Leibniz, *New Essays on "Human Understanding,"* ed. Jonathan Bennett (Cambridge: Cambridge University Press, 1990); cf. Frederick Copleston, S.J., *A History of Philosophy*, (9 vols.; New Jersey: Paulist Press, 1958), 4:320-32; 6:101-20.

[10] Immanuel Kant, *Critique of Pure Reason* in *Great Books of the Western World*, ed. Robert Maynard Hutchins, et al., trans. J. M. D. Meiklejohn (Chicago: Encyclopaedia Britannica, 1952), 179.

especially evident when he writes that, "The celebrated ontological or Cartesian argument for the existence of a Supreme Being is therefore insufficient."[11] Kant identifies the ontological argument with the position of René Descartes (1596–1650).[12] Additionally, Kant specifically defines the tools of natural theology to be the use of reason, from the analogy of nature, to present a definite conception of God.[13] There are two things that we must note. First, Kant's critique is of the Enlightenment version of the proofs for the existence of God and use of natural theology. Second, Kant does not examine or critique Aquinas' use of natural theology. It is, therefore, important for this study that we examine how Aquinas uses natural theology and the proofs for the existence of God. This will set the stage for the Protestant use of natural theology in the Reformation and post-Reformation periods.

With Aquinas' use of the proofs for the existence of God, we must take careful note of the context in which we find them. A typical assumption is that "Thomas builds a foundation for his system via the proofs by developing a natural or philosophical theology of the existence, essence, and attributes of God and once this rational foundation is laid, proceeds to the discussion of supernatural theology in the doctrine of the Trinity."[14] We find an example of this in Gordon Spykman's (1926–1993) criticism of Thomas when he writes: "Thus philosophy, in the form of natural theology, serves as prolegomena to theology proper, which in turn is viewed as the theoretical contemplation of supernatural truths."[15]

---

[11] Kant, *Critique of Pure Reason*, 182.

[12] See, e.g. René Descartes, *Discourse on Method*, ed. and trans. George Heffernan (Notre Dame: University of Notre Dame Press, 1994).

[13] Kant, *Critique of Pure Reason*, 190.

[14] Muller, "Function of St. Thomas' 'Proofs,'" 18.

[15] Gordon J. Spykman, *Reformational Theology: A New Paradigm for Doing Dogmatics* (Grand Rapids: Eerdmans, 1992), 21. Van Til reads Aquinas through the lens of Enlightenment rationalism and accuses scholasticism and Thomas of building his system upon natural theology rather than the *principium* of Scripture in *The Reformed Pastor and Modern Thought* (Philadelphia: P&R,

This, however, "is a gross misrepresentation of Thomas' *Summa* that entirely misses the point of the proofs."[16] In what context, therefore, do we find Thomas' proofs?

In the *Summa* we do not find the proofs as a philosophical approach or foundation to supernatural truths. It is important that we first recognize that Thomas views the entire contents of his *Summa* as sacred doctrine.[17] Sacred doctrine, according to Aquinas, "is based upon arguments from authority, inasmuch as its principles are obtained by revelation: thus we ought to believe on the authority of those to whom the revelation has been made."[18] We see, then, that Aquinas first roots sacred doctrine in divine revelation, not natural theology. Aquinas writes that "our faith rests upon the revelation made to the apostles and prophets, who wrote the canonical books, and not on the revelations (if any such there are) made to other doctors."[19] What function, then, do the proofs for the existence of God serve? Aquinas explains that, "Although arguments from human reason cannot avail to prove what must be received on faith, nevertheless this doctrine argues from articles of faith to other truths."[20] In other words, Aquinas moves from supernatural revelation to the more general truths of natural theology to demonstrate the reasonable nature of sacred doctrine. This methodology is clearly evident in his *Summa Contra Gentiles*, his major apologetic work, where he consistently brings the testimony of Scripture to bear in his defense of the faith.[21]

1971), 12-13, 24. Greg L. Bahnsen (1948-1995) also interprets Aquinas in this manner in *Van Til's Apologetic* (Phillipsburg: P&R, 1998), 192-93 n. 75.

[16] Muller, "Function of St. Thomas' 'Proofs,'" 18.

[17] Muller, "Function of St. Thomas' 'Proofs,'" 19.

[18] Thomas Aquinas, *Summa Theologica*, trans. Fathers of the English Dominican Province, (5 vols.; 1948; repr., Allen: Christian Classics, 1981), Ia, q. 1, a. 8, ad. 2.

[19] Aquinas, *Summa*, Ia, q. 1, a. 8, ad. 2.

[20] Aquinas, *Summa*, Ia, q. 1, a. 8, ad. 1.

[21] Thomas Aquinas, *Summa Contra Gentiles*, Book 1: God, trans. Anton C. Pegis (1955; repr., Notre Dame: University of Notre Dame Press, 1975), §1.2, p. 60.

Aquinas makes his methodology clear when he explains that

> sacred doctrine makes use even of human reason, not, indeed, to
> prove faith (for thereby the merit of faith would come to an end),
> but to make clear other things that are put forward in this doctrine.
> Since therefore grace does not destroy nature, but perfects it,
> natural reason should minister to faith as the natural bent of the
> will ministers to charity.[22]

He then explains that sacred doctrine makes use of natural
theology and philosophy in the same way that Paul used it with the
philosophers on Mars Hill (Acts 17:28). He goes on to write that
"sacred doctrine makes use of these authorities as extrinsic and
probable arguments; but properly uses the authority of canonical
Scriptures as an incontrovertible proof, and the authority of the
doctors of the Church as one that may properly be used, yet merely
as probable."[23] Richard Muller (1948 –) explains the significance
of Aquinas' use of the proofs in the following manner:

> For the doctrine of God to consist in a series of reasoned
> elucidations of articles of the faith and be truly *doctrina*, teaching,
> and not merely confession, reason must admit what faith believes,
> and then, recognizing its subordinate and instrumental status,
> serve faith by providing not ultimate truths but "extrinsic and
> probable arguments" in support of revelation. Thomas' proofs
> are, even more than being demonstrations of the existence of
> God, demonstrations of the legitimacy of the instrumental use of
> reason in theological system.[24]

It is important, then, that we rightly recognize the place and
function of the proofs, philosophy, and natural theology in the

---

[22] Here we see a clear difference between Aquinas and Reformed theology
regarding the nature of man. Van Til is correct to critique the nature/grace model
of Thomas (*Reformed Pastor*, 24). Cf., e.g. Westminster Confession of Faith,
hereafter, WCF, 9.2.

[23] Aquinas, *Summa*, Ia, q. 1, a. 8, ad. 2.

[24] Muller, "Function of St. Thomas' 'Proofs,'" 24.

thought of Aquinas. Natural theology is merely instrumental in his theological system – it serves to defend the reasonable nature of the claims of divine revelation. Moreover, Aquinas builds his system upon divine revelation, namely Scripture, not natural reason. This is important data to keep in mind, because it serves as a backdrop to the place and function of natural theology in the doctrine of the Reformation and post-Reformation periods. We may turn our attention to the writings of three reformers and trace the trajectory of the use of natural revelation and theology.

Reformation: Calvin, Musculus, and Vermigli

John Calvin (1509–1564)

John Calvin, of course, needs little introduction as most, if not all, historiographers are familiar with his career and writings.[25] Where there is disagreement is over Calvin's use of natural theology. Not all are in agreement, particularly those of the neo-orthodox school of thought, that Calvin taught any form of natural theology.[26] Yet, upon a close examination of Calvin's writings we can see that he does, indeed, make use of natural theology. Calvin writes that "as much in the fashioning of the universe as in the general teaching of Scripture the Lord shows himself to be simply the Creator. Then in the face of Christ he shows himself the Redeemer."[27] This is what Calvin calls the *duplex cognitio Dei*, the twofold knowledge of God.[28] In fact, Calvin identifies the subject matter of the first book of the *Institutes* as the knowledge of God, the Creator. The first

---

[25] For Calvin's early life and general biography see Alexandre Ganoczy, *The Young Calvin*, trans. David Foxgrover and Wade Provo (Philadelphia: Westminster Press, 1987); Alister E. McGrath, *A Life of John Calvin: A Study in the Shaping of Western Culture* (Cambridge: Blackwell, 1990); and W. de Greef, *The Writings of John Calvin*, trans. Lyle D. Bierma (Grand Rapids: Baker, 1993).

[26] See Barth, *Natural Theology*, 94-107; also T. H. L. Parker, *Calvin: An Introduction to His Thought* (Louisville: Westminster John Knox, 1995), 15, 16-18.

[27] John Calvin, *Institutes of the Christian Religion*, ed. John T. McNeill, trans. Ford Lewis Battles (Library of Christian Classics, vols. 20-21; Philadelphia: Westminster Press, 1960), 1.2.1.

means of natural revelation Calvin identifies is the *semen religionis*, seed of religion, or *sensus divinitatis*, an awareness of divinity.[29] What in particular has God placed in this *semen religionis*?

Calvin explains in his commentary on Romans that "God has put into the minds of all men the knowledge of Himself. In other words, He has so demonstrated His existence by His works as to make men see what they do not seek to know of their own accord, viz., that there is a God."[30] This, however, is not the only way that God reveals himself; God also reveals himself in the creation. Calvin, for example, writes that

> you cannot in one glance survey this most vast and beautiful system of the universe, in its wide expanse, without being completely overwhelmed by the boundless force of its brightness. The reason why the author of The Letter to the Hebrews elegantly calls the universe the appearance of things invisible is that this skillful ordering of the universe is for us a sort of mirror in which we can contemplate God, who is otherwise invisible.[31]

Now, what Calvin outlines in his *Institutes* concerning the knowledge of God in the creation, he states in greater detail in his commentary on Romans. Calvin explains that

> no conception of God can be formed without including His eternity, power, wisdom, goodness, truth, righteousness, and mercy. His eternity is evidenced by the fact that He holds all things in His hand and makes all things to consist in Himself. His wisdom is seen, because He has arranged all things in perfect order; His goodness, because there is no other cause for His creation of all

---

[28] Joannis Calvini, *Institutionis Christianae Religionis 1559*, in *Opera Selecta*, ed. Peter Barth and William Niesel, (v. 3; Munich: 1926-52), 1.2.1; hereafter abbreviated as *OS*.

[29] Calvin, *Institutes*, 1.3.1, 1.4.1; *OS*, 37, 40.

[30] John Calvin, *Romans and Thessalonians*, Calvin's New Testament Commentaries, vol. 8, ed. David W. Torrance and Thomas F. Torrance, trans. Ross Mackenzie (Grand Rapids: Eerdmans, 1960), Rom. 1:21, p. 32.

[31] Calvin, *Institutes*, 1.5.1.

things, nor can any other reason than His goodness itself induce Him to preserve them. His justice is evident in His governing of the world, because He punishes the guilty and defends the innocent; His mercy, because He bears the perversity of men with so much patience; and His truth, because He is unchangeable.[32]

So, then, Calvin teaches that knowledge of God as Creator is known both through the *semen religionis* and through the works of creation, namely the order of the cosmos. This argumentation bears great similarities, if not identity, with Thomas' cosmological proof for the existence of God. Though we should note that while the substance of the argument is similar, Calvin presents the cosmological argument in a rhetorical rather than a syllogistic fashion.[33] In what way does Calvin, however, explain the connection between the knowledge of God as Creator and Redeemer?

Calvin believes that there is natural revelation of God, but that because man bears the noetic effects of sin, this knowledge only serves to render him inexcusable. In other words, man's reflection upon natural revelation, that is natural theology, does not lead to salvation. On this point Calvin writes:

> Those, therefore, who have formed a conception of God ought to give Him the praise due to His eternity, wisdom, goodness, and justice. Since men have not recognized these attributes in God, but have conjured up an imaginary picture of Him as though He were an insubstantial phantom, they are justly said to have wickedly robbed Him of His glory.[34]

Man cannot traverse the line between the knowledge of God as Creator and Redeemer, the line between natural and supernatural revelation. We should note, though, that Calvin does not see a defect in the revelation of God but rather in the sinful perception

---

[32] Calvin, *Comm.*, Rom. 1:21, p. 32.

[33] Richard A. Muller, *The Divine Essence and Attributes*, vol. 3 of *Post-Reformation Reformed Dogmatics: The Rise and Development of Reformed Orthodoxy, ca. 1520 to 1725* (Grand Rapids: Baker, 2003), 173. Hereafter cited as *PRRD*.

[34] Calvin, *Comm.*, Rom. 1:21, p. 32.

of man. Calvin does acknowledge that there are some sparks of truth that remain available to fallen man's perception. What sparks of truth remain in man? We see an answer in Calvin's comments on 1 Corinthians 1:20, when he explains that "Paul does not utterly condemn, either the natural insight of men, or wisdom gained by practice and experience, or education of the mind through learning." Nevertheless, "man with all his shrewdness is as stupid about understanding by himself the mysteries of God as an ass is incapable of understanding musical harmony."[35] In the end the sparks of truth are useless to him for his salvation.[36] What does man need to correct his blindness? He needs the "spectacles" of Scripture. It is only through the supernatural revelation of Scripture applied by the work of the Holy Spirit that the people of God can see him clearly in nature. Calvin writes that "not only does he teach the elect to look upon a god, but also shows himself as the God upon whom they are to look."[37] Here we see Calvin develop a natural theology of the regenerate, or what Reformed theologians called a *theologia naturalis regenitorum*.[38]

We can see that Calvin did not believe that natural theology could lead to salvation in his commentary on 1 Corinthians. He argues that no one has ever been able to use nature to come to know God. Calvin writes:

> If anyone puts forward philosophers as exceptions to this, I reply, that in their case especially there is a conspicuous example of our weakness. For you cannot find one of them who has not constantly fallen away from that principle of knowledge which I have already mentioned, to wanderings and misleading speculation. They are mostly sillier than old wives![39]

---

[35] John Calvin, *1 Corinthians*, Calvin's New Testament Commentaries, vol. 9, ed. David W. Torrance and Thomas F. Torrance, trans. John W. Fraser (Grand Rapids: Eerdmans, 1960), 1 Cor. 1:20, p. 38.

[36] Calvin, *Institutes*, 1.5.14.

[37] Calvin, *Institutes*, 1.6.1.

[38] Muller, *Dictionary*, 302-03.

[39] Calvin, *Comm.*, 1 Cor. 1:21, pp. 40-41.

Now it is important that we not misunderstand Calvin on this point. He is not saying that the philosophers have spoken nothing but errors concerning God. Rather, he argues that the philosophers have not come to know God specifically as Redeemer.[40] We can illuminate this point with Calvin's commentary on Acts 17. Commenting on Acts 17:24, Calvin writes that Paul "takes his proof from nature itself, for he would have wasted his time in contending with them by citing scriptural proof-texts."[41] He goes on to explain that the Athenians "were convinced that there was some divinity; their perverted religion was merely requiring to be corrected." We should notice that Calvin sees that there is an apologetic function with natural revelation and theology – taking those points where there is agreement, removing error, and then presenting supernatural theology, or the teaching of Scripture.[42] Calvin sees natural revelation and theology as a point of contact with the unbeliever, just like Aquinas.

We may summarize Calvin's views on natural theology by stating that he holds to a *duplex cognitio Dei*, a knowledge of God as Creator and Redeemer. The knowledge of God as Creator is available through the *semen religionis* and God's works of nature. Man may discern God's eternity, power, wisdom, goodness, truth, righteousness, and mercy through natural revelation and theology, but he nevertheless does not and cannot reason his way to the knowledge of God as Redeemer because of the noetic effects of sin. The only thing that can overcome the noetic effects of sin and enable man to know God as Redeemer is the work of the Holy Spirit in and through Holy Writ. Calvin does allow natural

---

[40] B. B. Warfield, "Calvin's Doctrine of the Knowledge of God" in *The Works of Benjamin B. Warfield*, ed. Ethelbert D. Warfield, et al. (10 vols.; 1931; repr., Grand Rapids: Baker, 1981), 5:41-42 n. 8.

[41] John Calvin, *Acts 14-28*, Calvin's New Testament Commentaries, vol. 7, ed. David W. Torrance and Thomas F. Torrance, trans. John W. Fraser (Grand Rapids: Eerdmans, 1960), *loc. cit.*, 112.

[42] Edward A. Dowey, Jr., *The Knowledge of God in Calvin's Theology* (1952; repr., Grand Rapids: Eerdmans, 1994), 84-85.

theology to serve an apologetic role, as a point of contact in the process of presenting the truth, though natural theology is not a step-ladder to the truth. Regeneration is the only thing that can open a man's eyes to believe in the truth. Let us now turn to the writings of another Reformer.

Wolfgang Musculus (1497–1563)

Wolfgang Musculus studied in the Benedictine monastery near Lixheim and was an advocate of theological reform after reading tracts penned by Martin Luther (1483–1546). He fled the monastery in 1518 and was a preacher in Augsburg from 1531 to 1548, though he was forced out of Germany by the Augsburg Interim in 1548. From there he moved to Switzerland where he was a professor of theology in Bern until his death.[43] The fact that Musculus is a first-generation Reformer makes his views on natural theology relevant for tracing the trajectory of this subject within Reformed dogmatics. Musculus begins his *Common Places* with the question of the existence of God. He writes: "The first question of all that may be moved of God, is whether there be a God: which we should not have cause to speak of, unless the heart of man were sometimes assaulted with this kind of impiety and led to deny God."[44] From this initial question Musculus acknowledges that God's existence may be known from two major sources: "the writings of the Gentiles, as also out of the Holy Scriptures." Musculus, therefore, identifies that man possesses information about God from the writings of the philosophers, such as Cicero (103–43 BC), as well as from Holy Writ. Musculus goes on from this point to explain how these two sources reveal the existence of God.

---

[43] Richard A. Muller, *Prolegomena to Theology*, vol. 1 of *Post-Reformation Reformed Dogmatics* (Grand Rapids: Baker, 1987), 41.

[44] Wolfgang Musculus, *Common Places of Christian Religion*, trans. John Man (London: Henry Bynneman, 1578), § 1. All subsequent quotations are taken from this locus. All archaic spelling in all subsequent old English works have been edited throughout.

Musculus states that there are three specific ways that man can know of God's existence. He writes that "the first way consists in his working, where the majesty of God sets himself to be seen in all his works throughout the compass of all the world, in heaven, as well as in the earth." He continues, "I call this way most general, because it is so set forth to all people of all nations, so no man can excuse himself for not knowing God." Musculus explains the way in which man may know of God's existence through his works of nature. He writes:

It cannot be denied, but there is in us a certain quickness of understanding and strength of reason, as might be the eyes of our minds, whereby we may know in God's works, God himself the maker thereof: but unless the brightness of the works of God were so great, and they did not set forth the majesty of the worker to be seen throughout all the earth, our reason should have had no means to have known that there had been a God. Therefore, the first cause of our knowledge of God is attributed to the light and brightness of the works of God, whereby even the Philosophers did acknowledge the majesty of the invisible God as the Apostle witnesses.

In what ways do the philosophers know of God and his attributes? Musculus continues to write:

For first they did observe in the works of God an exceeding great majesty, an infinite multitude, a wonderful variety, a most constant order, a seemly agreement, an endless continuance, a pleasant vicissitude of intercourse of things coming and going, briefly, such wisdom in creating and bestowing of things and in conserving of them such power and might, that they could ascribe the whole workmanship of all things, heavenly and earthly, to no other nature, but to the nature of God.

Musculus, therefore, sees the knowledge of God's existence in the "brightness of the works of God," or what will also go under the term the "light of nature." He adds that through the works of God "they felt a marvelous terror of lightning, earthquakes, pestilences, gapings of the ground, strange sights from heaven, in the sun, moon, stars, and comets." This, however, is not the only way that man receives knowledge of God's existence. Musculus identifies two other ways. The second way

> consists in the word, for so God has opened himself to our fathers by word and speaking, even from the beginning of the world, until the days of the New Testament, whereof the Apostle speaks saying: Divers and many ways has God spoken to our fathers by the Prophets, but last of all he has spoken to us by his Son. This is a special way, for it happened not to every nation, as it did by a special grace happen to the Israelites.

He writes that this second way by which man knows God is: "the general gift of salvation to all men in the latter times by the means of the mercy of God; [it] came unto the Gentiles that the world might have no cause to complain that they were bereft of this grace." The third way

> by inspiration, is by secret revelation of the Holy Spirit. And this way I called more special, for a difference from the other two that be indifferent to good and evil, and to restrain this way to the elect only, who beside the light of works and the declaration by words, get a most certain knowledge of God, yet rather a feeling and taste of him, by the lively and effectual inspiration and revelation of the Holy Spirit of God.

Now, it is important that we recognize the parameters and limits of natural revelation and theology in Musculus' understanding.

We see, first, that Musculus' three ways that man may know of God are similar to Calvin's *duplex cognitio Dei*.[45] Like Calvin, Musculus makes a clear line of division between natural and supernatural theology. Yes, man may know of God's existence, and several of his attributes, his wisdom, providence, and power, for

---

[45] Muller, *PRRD*, 1:181.

example. Yet, this knowledge is non-saving. The only way that natural revelation can contribute to one's salvation is when it is accompanied by both the preaching of the word and the testimony of the Holy Spirit, what later Reformed theologians called the *vocatio externa et interna*. Lastly, it is also important that we take note of Musculus' methodology in the way he comes to the knowledge of these categories. Musculus does not begin his *Common Places* with bare philosophical conjecture about these categories, but like other theologians of this period, his *principium* is Scripture. This is evident from Musculus' quotation of Scripture throughout this *locus* (Pss. 14:1; 147; Acts 14; Heb. 11:6). We will now turn to another well-known Reformer and examine his statements on natural revelation and theology.

Peter Martyr Vermigli (1500-1562)

Peter Martyr Vermigli studied at Padua and Bolgna while he was the prior of St. Pietro ad Aram near Naples. It was there that he encountered the Reformed ideas of Juan de Valdes (1498–1541). In 1542 Vermigli openly joined the Reformation and left his post in Italy for Basel and Strasbourg. He subsequently succeeded Wolfgang Capito (*c*. 1478–1541) as professor of theology at Strasbourg. From 1547 to 1553, Vermigli taught at Oxford University. When Mary ascended the throne, he returned to teach at Strasbourg (1553–1556) and finished his career at Zurich (1556–1562).[46] Vermigli's views on natural theology can be found in his *Loci Communes*, which were a series of doctrinal excurses that were extracted from his commentaries on Scripture and edited together after his death.[47] In similar

---

[46] Muller, *PRRD*, 1:40. For a biographical account of Vermigli see, Josiah Simler, "Oration on the Life and Death of . . . Peter Martyr Vermigli," in Peter Martyr Vermigli, *Life, Letters, and Sermons*, vol. 5 of *The Peter Martyr Library*, ed. and trans. John Patrick Donnelly; Sixteenth Century Essays & Studies, v. 52 (Kirksville: Jefferson University Press, 1999), 9-62.

[47] John Patrick Donnelly, *Calvinism and Scholasticism in Vermigli's Doctrine of Man and Grace*, vol. 18 of Studies in Medieval and Reformation Thought, ed. Heiko A. Oberman (Leiden: E. J. Brill, 1976), 33, 54-55, 58.

fashion to Calvin and Musculus, Vermigli argues that the knowledge of God comes in two forms: natural and supernatural.

Commenting on Romans 1:19 concerning the natural knowledge of God, Vermigli states that there is a knowledge of God that people attain by natural light. Vermigli explains:

> they knew that God is most mighty by the very fabric of this world. They also knew by the beauty, appearance, and variety of things that such great power was ordered by the highest providence and wisdom. Moreover, the suitability and utility of created things taught them the divine majesty, which consists in acting well towards all. These are the gifts which God bestowed on the heathen; but they abused the gifts of God.[48]

It is important that we recognize a peculiarity in Vermigli's understanding of Romans 1:19. While Calvin, Musculus, and Vermigli understand that natural revelation is manifest to all, we may fairly conclude that Vermigli believes that natural theology is only available to the learned. He argues that when Romans 1:19 states that "'it was manifest in them,' and not 'it was manifest in all,' Scripture distinguishes wise men and philosophers from the crude and ignorant masses."[49] In other words, theological conclusions could not be made by the uneducated masses but only by the educated philosophers such as Plato (427–347 BC), Aristotle (384–22 BC), and Galen (AD 130–203).[50] Now, we should ask, What are the ways by which man obtains this knowledge of God?

As Vermigli stated, the natural knowledge of God is manifest in the creation. On this point he draws attention to both Psalm 19 and the book of Job. He writes that the "speakers he introduces were

---

[48] Peter Martyr Vermigli, *In Epistolam S. Pauli Apostoli ad Romanos* (Basel: P. Perna, 1558), 30; Peter Martyr Vermigli, *Philosophical Works*, vol. 4 of *The Peter Martyr Library*; ed. and trans. Joseph C. McLelland; Sixteenth Century Essays & Studies, v. 39 (Kirksville: Sixteenth Century Journal Publishers, 1996), 18.

[49] Vermigli, *Ad Romanos*, 30; Vermigli, *Philosophical Works*, 19.

[50] Vermigli, *Ad Romanos*, 31; Vermigli, *Philosophical Works*, 21.

heathen, so that the subject is handled by natural reason alone." To what in particular does Vermigli refer? He states that "much is spoken about the revolutions of heaven, about stars, the earth, the sea, light, winds, rain, thunder, lightning, snow, and ice; also of animals such as lions, deer, horses, and Behemoth which many think to be the elephant, and finally of Leviathan the greatest beast of the sea." To what end does Vermigli believe these natural phenomenon point? They "proclaim to us the eternal power and divinity of God."[51] Vermigli argues that "knowing the series of causes and their relation to effects, and clearly understanding that it is not proper to posit an infinite progression," the great philosophers "reasoned that they must arrive at some highest being, and so concluded that there is a God."[52] The astute reader will notice that this argument is essentially Aquinas' cosmological argument. Now, if man, or at least the philosophers, can reason their way to God's existence, does this mean that Vermigli believes that natural revelation and theology lead to a saving knowledge of God?

Quite simply, no. Vermigli does not believe that natural theology can save an individual. Vermigli argues that "there are many divine mysteries that we cannot reach naturally, such as that God would justify us freely, forgive our sins through Christ crucified, and restore these very bodies of ours to eternal happiness. These and the like are not taught us by nature."[53] Vermigli, then, draws a clear line of demarcation between those things that belong to natural and supernatural revelation. Vermigli not only includes God's eternal power, divinity, and existence in the sphere of natural theology, but he also includes things such as the final judgment and general ethics.[54] Vermigli is careful to note that there are two types of natural knowledge of God: "One is effectual, by which we are so changed that we try to express what we know in works;

---

[51] Vermigli, *Ad Romanos*, 31; Vermigli, *Philosophical Works*, 21-22.

[52] Vermigli, *Ad Romanos*, 31; Vermigli, *Philosophical Works*, 21.

[53] Vermigli, *Ad Romanos*, 30; Vermigli, *Philosophical Works*, 18.

[54] Vermigli, *Ad Romanos*, 31-32; Vermigli, *Philosophical Works*, 22.

Scripture ascribes this knowledge of God to the faithful alone. The other is frigid, by which we do not become better people."[55] Therefore, because of the noetic effects of sin, man cannot take advantage of natural revelation or theology for the purpose of salvation. In the end, natural revelation only serves to render man inexcusable, though Vermigli comments that God does not reveal himself in nature strictly to render man inexcusable. Rather, man is inexcusable because of his own sinfulness, not because there is a defect in God's natural revelation.[56] Vermigli is careful to delineate the reason for the ineffectiveness of natural revelation in salvation:

> Truth has the same nature on both sides; the difference arises from the ways and means by which it is perceived. Natural strength is corrupt, weakened and defiled through sin, so that the truth which it grasps has no effect. But faith has joined with it the divine inspiration and power of the Holy Spirit so that it apprehends truth effectively. Hence, the difference is not in truth itself but in the means.[57]

What we see, then, is a division between natural theology and supernatural revelation; by natural theology man can know of God's eternal power, divinity, existence, the final judgment, and general ethics. On the other hand, justification, the person and work of Christ, the resurrection of the body, and the proper use of natural revelation belong to the realm of supernatural revelation and saving grace.

Summary and Analysis

In the explanations of all three Reformers, we find the *duplex cognitio Dei*. There are slight differences in the degree of accuracy

---

[55]   Vermigli, *Ad Romanos*, 32; Vermigli, *Philosophical Works*, 23.

[56]   Vermigli, *Ad Romanos*, 32-33; Vermigli, *Philosophical Works*, 24.

[57]   Peter Martyr Vermigli, *Common Places*, ed. and trans. Anthony Marten (London, 1583), § 11; Vermigli, *Philosophical Works*, 27.

that fallen man can achieve with natural theology among Calvin and Musculus and Vermigli. Calvin attributes less accuracy in natural theology to the philosophers than did Musculus, and especially Vermigli.[58] We do not, however, want to posit such a large chasm between Calvin and Musculus and Vermigli and say that their views are antithetical. We can see a great degree of agreement between Vermigli's statements and Calvin's comments, for example, on Acts 17. Regardless of the differences between the three theologians on the accuracy of the natural theology of the philosophers, all three agree that man knows of God's existence, that his existence can be proved from the creation, and that he should be worshiped. All three also agree that natural theology cannot lead to supernatural theology. Natural theology serves only to render man inexcusable or in an apologetic function in relation to the unbeliever. These conclusions lead us to some important points regarding the use of natural theology in the Reformation.

It is important that we see the connection between the methodology of Calvin, Musculus, Vermigli, and Aquinas. Aquinas uses natural theology, not as an independent means of knowing God, but hand in hand with supernatural revelation. This twofold approach is evident not only in Aquinas' approach but also in the three Reformers' uses of various passages of Scripture in conjunction with their explanations of natural revelation and in the apologetic value assigned to natural theology. The positive use of natural revelation and theology is not something that is unique to these three Reformers, but is instead quite common to both wings of the Reformation, Lutheran and Reformed. One can find the use and appropriation of natural theology, for example, in the writings of Philip Melanchthon (1497–1560) and Zacharias Ursinus (1534–1583), two key representatives for each confessional tradition.[59]

---

[58] David C. Steinmetz, *Calvin in Context* (Oxford: Oxford University Press, 1995), 31; Steinmetz, "Calvin and the Natural Knowledge of God," in *Via Augustini: Augustine in the Later Middle Ages, Renaissance and Reformation*, ed. Heiko A. Oberman, et al. (Leiden: E. J. Brill, 1991), 142-56.

We will now proceed to the theology of the post-Reformation and continue to trace the trajectory of the use of natural revelation and theology.

Post-Reformation: Perkins, Polanus, Du Moulin, and Ussher
William Perkins (1558–1602)

William Perkins is perhaps the most significant English Reformed theologian of the early post-Reformation period and, as such, is important for our discussion of natural theology leading up to the Westminster Assembly.[60] His work is vital for any study of the post-Reformation era, not only because of his prominence, but also because of the claims of those like R. T. Kendall (1935 –), who see Perkins as one of the primary architects of English Calvinism's initial divergence from the theology of Calvin.[61] This divergence is understood by Kendall and others as being responsible for producing the theology of the Westminster Confession of Faith. As we will see, however, such claims cannot be sustained in regard to natural theology.

Perkins' views on natural theology are in clear continuity with the views of Calvin and the reformers in regard to the *duplex cognitio*

---

[59] Philip Melanchthon, *Loci Communes 1543*, trans. J. A. O. Preus (St. Louis: Concordia, 1992), § 2:34-35; cf. John Platt, *Reformed Thought and Scholasticism: The Arguments for the Existence of God in Dutch Theology, 1575-1650* (Leiden: E. J. Brill, 1982), 10-33; Zacharias Ursinus, *The Commentary on the Heidelberg Catechism* (1852; repr., Philipsburg: P&R, n. d.), pp. 3-6; q. 26, pp. 139-46.

[60] Richard A. Muller, "Perkins' *A Golden Chaine*: Predestinarian System or Schematized Ordo Salutis?" *Sixteenth Century Journal* 9, no. 1 (1978): 69. Gisbertus Voetius in the seventeenth century called Perkins "the Homer of practical Englishmen" and said that "to this day, stands above all" in *Concerning Practical Theology* in *Reformed Dogmatics*, ed. John Beardslee (New York: Oxford University Press, 1965), 274.

[61] R. T. Kendall, *Calvin and English Calvinism to 1649* (Oxford: Oxford University Press, 1979). One of the biggest problems within the Calvin vs. Calvinist debate is that it borders on reductionism, finding the *locus* of Reformed orthodoxy in the theology of one man rather than in that of a group of like-minded reformers. Few, if any, of the men who followed Calvin ever called themselves "Calvinists."

Dei. In his commentary on Galatians, Perkins says that the "knowledge of God is twofold, *Natural*, or *revealed knowledge*."[62] Natural knowledge, which he also calls "literal knowledge," is "that which all men have in their minds by the light of nature, which also they may gather by the view and observation of the creatures."[63] This knowledge, for Perkins, is gained both internally and externally. Internally, it has been "engrafted in man's nature" and written upon his conscience – Calvin's *semen religionis* – and functions as God's judge within him. Externally, it is perceived in the works of creation and providence.[64] The result is that all people naturally know God both as Creator and as Judge. This knowledge, however, is imperfect and "weak: because it serves only to cut off excuse, and it is not sufficient to direct us in the worship of God."[65]

The problem is that all of man's faculties and inclinations are tainted with sin because of the fall. The result, for Perkins, is not that the natural person does not know God, but that he suppresses that knowledge by idolatry.[66] Thus, the natural person will think both that God exists and that He does not exist.

> We must know that these two thoughts, *There is a God, and there is no God*, may be, and are both in one and the same heart: the same man, that by the light of nature think there is a God, may by that corruption and darkness of mind that came by *Adam's* fall, think there is no God: for two contraries being not in the highest degree, may be in one and the same subject: as light and darkness in the same house: heat and cold in the same body.[67]

---

[62] William Perkins, *The Workes of that Famous and Worthy Minister of Christ, in the Universitie of Cambridge, Mr. William Perkins* (3 vols.; London, 1616–18), 2:280. Muller claims that the *duplex cognitio Dei* underlies all of "Perkins' schematization of the causes of salvation and damnation" in his *A Golden Chaine*; see Muller, "Perkins' *A Golden Chaine*," 79.

[63] Perkins, *Workes*, 2:280, 282.

[64] Ibid., 1:517; 2:459. See also Perkins, *An Exposition of the Symbole, or Creede of the Apostles* (London, 1616), 55-56, 80, 91.

[65] Perkins, *Workes*, 2:280, 282.

[66] Perkins, *Creede*, 98.

[67] Perkins, *Workes*, 2:459.

It is important for our discussion that we note here that the suppression of the natural knowledge of God by idolatry does not eliminate the reality of this knowledge but simply renders it insufficient in itself to lead the natural person to salvation. He must be "enlightened by the spirit of God, with the knowledge of God, by the word, and according to the word" in order to attain to a saving knowledge of God.[68] Only a "revealed" or "Spiritual" knowledge, "which is set down in the written word, whereby we may know what God is in himself, and what he is to us: namely, a father in Christ, giving pardon of sin and life everlasting," can lead to salvation.[69]

More than simply emphasizing the existence of natural theology, however, Perkins also identifies several positive uses for it. First, natural theology functions to confirm our faith by offering proofs of God's existence. These proofs are taken from the works of creation and providence and the universal *semen religionis*, and are to be used primarily for "our better knowledge and assurance," rather than as a foundation for supernatural truth.[70] This is like Calvin's natural theology of the regenerate. Second, the light of nature and the works of creation should motivate the Christian to praise God more fully, because they show him "God's power, wisdom, love, mercy, and providence, and all his attributes, and in all things his glory."[71] Third, Perkins, like Aquinas and the reformers, ascribes an apologetic role to natural theology in much the same way that the Apostle Paul does in Acts 14 and 17: "By the work of creation we may discern the true *Jehovah* from all false gods and idols in the world. . . . If a man asks you how you know the true God from all false gods: you must answer, by the work of creation:

---

[68] *Ibid.*, 2:282.

[69] *Ibid.*, 2:280. Elsewhere Perkins says that "if we would know the true God, and know him to our salvation, we must know him only in Christ crucified" (Ibid., 1:630).

[70] *Ibid.*, 2:49-52.

[71] *Ibid.*, 1:144.

for he alone is the maker of heaven and earth, and all things in them."[72] Furthermore, natural theology for Perkins also prepares and induces people unto salvation by their "considering that the same God which once created them, is also as able to save them: and will show himself as mighty in their redemption, as he was in their creation of nothing."[73] Natural theology, though it can never lead one to the supernatural knowledge of God as Redeemer, can prepare the natural person to embrace God when he is revealed in his word.

Amandus Polanus (1561–1610) and Pierre Du Moulin (1568–1658)

To provide a more complete picture of post-Reformation thinking in regard to natural theology, we will shift our focus away from the British context temporarily and look briefly at two continental theologians, Amandus Polanus and Pierre Du Moulin. Polanus was professor of Old Testament at Basel from 1596, and was highly regarded in the late 16th and early 17th centuries as an exegete and theologian. Besides translating the New Testament into German, Polanus devoted his lifetime labors to winning Basel over to the ideas of Reformed theology. His *Syntagma Theologiae Christianae*, published posthumously in Geneva in 1617, clearly exhibits the Reformed notion of the *duplex cognitio Dei*, even down to the very phrase: "The knowledge of God is twofold, truly, of God the Creator and of God the Redeemer."[74] The former, the *cognitio Dei Creatoris*, Polanus says, is innate to natural man and is gained from Scripture and from nature.[75] The latter, the *cognitio Dei Redemptoris*, however, is wholly supernatural and is received only by the Holy Spirit working through God's special revelation

---

[72] *Ibid.*, 1:144.

[73] *Ibid.*, 1:144-45.

[74] Amandus Polanus, *Syntagma Theologiae Christianae* (Geneva, 1617), 9.7, p. 594: "Cognitio Dei est duplex, nimirum, Dei *Creatoris*, & Dei *Redemtoris*."

[75] *Ibid.*, 1.10, p. 12; 9.7, p. 594.

in Scripture.[76] Thus, natural theology for Polanus, because it is gleaned from Scripture as well as from nature, is not always or altogether idolatrous. It can be a true and Christian theology, though it will always fall short of supernatural theology, which is only available through the work of the Spirit in and through the word.[77] This has definite implications for apologetics. Because natural theology is not always or altogether idolatrous, it simply needs to be corrected – again, like Calvin, taking those points where there is agreement, removing the error, and then presenting the teaching of supernatural theology.

Pierre Du Moulin the Elder was the son of a Huguenot minister who, because of rising tensions in France, traveled to England to study under William Whitaker (1548–1595) at Cambridge. Upon leaving Cambridge, Du Moulin began teaching ancient languages and philosophy in the University of Leiden and later moved to Sedan in 1625, where he spent the remainder of his life. Brian Armstrong claims that Du Moulin was "unquestionably the prophet and the principal spokesperson for French Calvinism" in the late 16th and early 17th centuries.[78] Du Moulin's literary output alone gives credence to this claim, as Armstrong's work further demonstrates. For the purposes of this essay, however, we will concentrate on one of Du Moulin's works in particular, *De Cognitione Dei Tractatus*, first published in 1624.

In this work, Du Moulin demonstrates that he too sees a distinction between the knowledge of God as Creator and Judge and the knowledge of God as Redeemer. He asserts that "we have

---

[76] *Ibid.*, 9.7, p. 594. Polanus says: "*Cognitio Dei Redemtoris . . . naturalis non est, sed tantum patefacta.*" And he later defines "*Patefacta cognitio Dei*" as "quae ex doctrina Prophetarum & Apostolorum hausta est."

[77] Muller, *PRRD*, 1:182; Muller, "'*Duplex cognitio Dei*' in the Theology of Early Reformed Orthodoxy," *Sixteenth Century Journal* 10, no. 2 (1979): 58.

[78] Brian G. Armstrong, ed., *Bibliographia Molinæi: An Alphabetical, Chronological and Descriptive Bibliography of the Works of Pierre Du Moulin (1558–1658)* (Geneva: Librairie Droz, 1997), ix.

three ways of knowing God, one by the works of God, second by the Law, and third by the Gospel." The first "two knowledges propose God to our minds, as the creator, the Lord, and the Master of our life" and are derived from both nature and Scripture, but the last presents him "as father and redeemer" and is gained only from the gospel.[79] Du Moulin believes that the creation and "the seeds of honesty and equity, and the stings of the conscience" are the ways that God affects all men, even the most "untamed" or "barbaric," with a *sensus divinitatis* and a "form of religion" such that they know God as Creator and Judge and are without excuse before his tribunal.[80] But he insists that this knowledge is insufficient for salvation. The Bible is necessary, and so God "has unfastened his sacred mouth, that by his word he might imbue us with the knowledge of himself." It is the Holy Spirit working in and through the word that alone brings a saving knowledge of God as Redeemer.[81]

Du Moulin, like Polanus, admits that natural theology, although it is insufficient for salvation, is not altogether idolatrous; it can and does provide some true knowledge of God to man. The natural theology of the philosophers, for instance, has revealed that God is "the most perfect Being, from whom flows and on whom depends all entity and perfection."[82] Thus, we should not be surprised to find that Du Moulin also ascribes an apologetic role to natural theology. The "natural sparks of the knowledge of God . . . [are] to be awakened and exposed" and then corrected and inflamed by supernatural theology.[83] Thus far we have seen a continuity between the teaching of Aquinas, the Reformation, and post-Reformation in both English and Continental theologians in their use of natural theology. As we approach the period of High

---

[79] Pierre Du Moulin, *De Cognitione Dei Tractatus* (Hagae-Comitis, 1631), 126.

[80] *Ibid.*, 25-26, 36-37.

[81] *Ibid.*, 128, 161-67.

[82] Muller, "*Duplex cognitio Dei*," 58.

[83] Du Moulin, *De Cognitione Dei*, 95, 25-53, 160-61.

Orthodoxy, we should first survey the views of James Ussher due to his influence upon the Westminster Assembly.

James Ussher (1581–1656)

We now return to the British scene in order to examine the natural theology of one of the most important figures in the development of the theology of the Westminster Confession of Faith, Ireland's Archbishop of Armagh, James Ussher. Although Ussher was summoned to be a member of the Westminster Assembly, he never participated in its proceedings. Mitchell, however, in his work on the Assembly, confidently claims that the Assembly "gave unmistakable proof of its high regard for him" by relying heavily upon the Irish Articles, which are believed to have been prepared by Ussher, and upon his *Body of Divinity*, in its formulation of the Confession and catechisms.[84] In order to obtain a right understanding of the Confession's teaching in regard to natural theology, then, we must first examine Ussher's own beliefs.

In his *Body of Divinity*, Ussher states that before any person can know God, God must reveal himself to his creatures. This revelation of God to his creatures takes two forms: "his divine works" or "the creation and Preservation of the World and all things therein" and "his holy Word."[85] The result of God's revelation of himself in and through the works of creation and providence is that all people know God (Rom. 1:19-20; Acts 14:17; 17:27-28). This knowledge of God, which is held forth by his divine works, according to Ussher, serves to render man without excuse before God. Thus it is "sufficient unto condemnation" but insufficient unto salvation, because the noetic effects of sin and the works of creation and providence do not teach "the distinction of the Persons in the Godhead, the fall of man from God, and the way to

---

[84] Alexander F. Mitchell, *The Westminster Assembly: Its History and Standards* (London: James Nisbet, 1883), xvi, 98, 117, 372-73, 422-23.

[85] James Ussher, *A Body of Divinity, or the Summe and Substance of Christian Religion* (London, 1645), 5.

repair the same."[86] The saving knowledge of God, therefore, can only be found in his holy word.

Ussher too, like Perkins, goes a step further, though, in ascribing two additional positive uses for natural theology. Not only does natural theology serve to render the individual inexcusable before God, but it also plays a role in encouraging the Christian to praise God more fully and serves an apologetic function as well. First, Ussher asserts that natural theology should be used by Christians to "stir them up continually to reverence his majesty, to honor and obey him, to repose their trust in him."[87] Second, Ussher clearly attaches apologetic significance to natural theology, in that it works to assist men "further to salvation: and that by preparing and inducing men to seek God, if happily by groping they may find him (as the Apostle shows, Acts. 17:27). Whereby they are made more apt to acknowledge him when he is perfectly revealed in his word."[88] We may now draw some conclusions regarding our survey thus far.

Summary and Analysis

In the writings of all four post-Reformation theologians, we see a continuation of the idea of the *duplex cognitio Dei*. To be sure, there are slight differences between the Reformers and these four theologians in the accuracy ascribed to natural theology. Polanus and Du Moulin, for example, attribute more accuracy to natural theology than did Calvin, especially concerning the natural theology of the philosophers. There is, however, clear continuity here. All four men agree with the reformers not just in believing that natural revelation exists but in recognizing that natural theology exists as well. They agree that all people know that God exists, that the creation and the light of nature show this, and that God should be worshiped. They also agree that natural theology can be

---

[86] *Ibid.*, 5-6, 136, 143-44.

[87] *Ibid.*, 6.

[88] *Ibid.*, 5-6.

used positively – to render man inexcusable, to provide him with general morality, to serve as an instrument in apologetics, and to stir the Christian to worship God more fully – but that it cannot lead in itself to supernatural theology. At no point then is there a progression in the post-Reformation era toward rationalism or toward the view that natural theology provides a foundation on which supernatural theology could build. Rather, as Muller states regarding the theology of the post-Reformation period, "The issue for Reformed orthodox theology was . . . the defense of a view of natural theology that taught the existence of such knowledge but insisted not only on its inefficacy in salvation but also in its disjunction from the special or supernatural revelation of God."[89] Having thus surveyed natural theology through the Reformation and post-Reformation periods, we will now turn our attention to the teaching of the Westminster Confession.

The Westminster Confession of Faith

In order to discern the teaching of the Westminster Confession on natural theology and determine whether it is in continuity with Reformation and post-Reformation thinking, we will examine the Confession (WCF), the Larger Catechism (WLC), the Scripture proof texts, and the writings of select prominent Divines. In so doing, we will see that the *duplex cognitio Dei* and the positive treatment of natural theology, both of which we saw in Calvin and in the Reformers and which continued to find expression throughout the early post-Reformation period, also lie behind the language of the Confession.

The Text of the Confession

One does not have to search far to encounter the Confession's teaching on natural revelation and natural theology; it can be found in the opening section of the first chapter.

---

[89] Muller, *PRRD*, 1:173, 190.

Although the light of nature and the works of creation and providence do so far manifest the goodness, wisdom, and power of God, as to leave men inexcusable; yet are they not sufficient to give that knowledge of God and of His will, which is necessary unto salvation. Therefore it pleased the Lord, at sundry times, and in divers manners, to reveal Himself, and to declare that His will unto His Church; and afterwards . . . to commit the same wholly unto writing: which makes the Holy Scripture to be most necessary; those former ways of God's revealing His will unto His people being now ceased (WCF 1.1).[90]

It is important to note in this section that the Confession is not merely teaching the existence of a natural revelation of God that is by "the light of nature and the works of creation and providence," but that men receive this revelation to such a degree as to render them "inexcusable" before God. In other words, the Confession is teaching the existence of a natural theology, an idea we will explore more fully by examining the Confession's use of the phrase "the light of nature."

The phrase "the light of nature" occurs five times in the Confession (1.1; 1.6; 10.4; 20.4; and 21.1) and three times in the Larger Catechism (qq. 2, 60, and 151) and refers primarily to an internal and natural or inborn testimony concerning God, a *sensus divinitatis*. In WLC q. 2, the "light of nature" is depicted as being "in man" and, in both WLC 2 and WCF 1.1, it is clearly distinguished from the external works of creation.[91] The Scripture proof texts, in particular Romans 1:19-20 and 2:14, along with the proof texts for 1.6, further demonstrate that the light of nature resides within the individual and includes the conscience, among other faculties, as a judge within us and a means for distinguishing right from wrong.

In addition to alerting us as to the presence of the light of nature within us, however, the Divines also instruct us as to the knowledge that it conveys to us: "The light of nature shows that there is a God,

---

Quotations from the WCF and WLC are taken from *Westminster Confession of Faith* (1646; repr., Glasgow: Free Presbyterian Publications, 1995).

who hath lordship and sovereignty over all, is good, and doth good unto all, and is therefore to be feared, loved, praised, called upon, trusted in, and served, with all the heart, and with all the soul, and with all the might" (WCF 21.1). The thought in 21.1 should not be limited to merely the idea that the light of nature only "shows" these things (i.e., natural revelation), but it should clearly also include that these things are perceived and received by the individual (i.e., natural theology) to such an extent that he knows them and is thus rendered inexcusable for not worshiping God. We know from WLC q. 2 and the stated Scripture proof texts, that though the light of nature does not "sufficiently and effectually" reveal God unto men for their salvation, it does declare God's eternal power, divinity, and judgment "plainly" and "clearly," such that they are "known," "clearly seen," and "understood" by all.[92] The logic of the Confession at this point is plain: all people have a natural knowledge of God and are thus inexcusable. Yet this knowledge is insufficient to reach a supernatural knowledge of God. "Therefore," God was pleased to reveal himself supernaturally, by way of his word, in order that people might attain a supernatural knowledge of him and his will, by which they can be saved.

It is in this way that we find the Confession making use of the *duplex cognitio Dei*, a notion that emerges more clearly when we observe that in each of the eight occurrences of the phrase "the light of nature," it is contrasted with the light of the word. For example, in 1.1, the light of nature and the works of creation provide a knowledge of God that is contrasted with "that

---

[91] The original manuscript and first published versions of the Confession contained a comma following the phrase "light of nature," thereby further distinguishing it from the "works of creation and providence"; see S. W. Carruthers, ed., *The Confession of Faith of the Assembly of Divines at Westminster from the Original Manuscript Written by Cornelius Burgess in 1646* (Glasgow: Free Presbyterian Publications, 1978), 4; Carruthers, *The Westminster Confession of Faith* (Manchester: Aikman, 1937), 2.

[92] The Divines repeatedly appeal to Romans 1:19-20, 32; 2:1, 14-15; and Psalm 19:1-3, in delineating their views of natural theology and the natural knowledge of God.

knowledge of God" contained in his word, which alone can lead to salvation;[93] in 1.6, the light of nature is again contrasted with the light of the word in regard to ordering circumstances connected to worship and governing the church that are beyond the scope of Scripture; and in 21.1, the light of nature is set beside the light of the word in establishing and limiting the proper worship of God. Thus, for the Divines, the light of nature and the light of the word clearly comprise two contrasting lights offering two contrasting "knowledges" of God, so to speak. The light of nature and the works of creation and providence provide a knowledge of God as Creator or as Judge, but the light of the word is required for the saving knowledge of God as Redeemer.[94]

The Writings of Prominent Divines

The Confession in no way attempts to present a systematic and comprehensive treatment of natural theology. This should not surprise us, however. In minimally treating natural theology, the Confession is following the tendency within the Reformed orthodox

---

[93]   In respect to the phrase, "that knowledge of God," it is important to emphasize that the Confession does not say that "the light of nature and the works of creation and providence" are not sufficient to give *a* knowledge of God, or even *the* knowledge of God, but *that* knowledge of God, "which is necessary unto salvation." By selecting this phrase, the Divines were clearly indicating their belief in a twofold knowledge of God: one that is received by the individual primarily through "the light of nature and the works of creation and providence," or general revelation, and another that is received only through supernatural or special revelation. As a result of the testimony of the internal light of nature and the works of creation and providence, every individual has a "natural" knowledge of God, whereby he or she can and does know God as Creator or Judge but not as Redeemer. Knowing God as Redeemer requires more than the light of nature and the works of creation; it requires God's "word and Spirit" which alone "do sufficiently and effectually reveal him unto men for their salvation" (WCF 1.1; WLC q. 2).

[94]   The Confession obviously echoes the teaching of Calvin at this point. Ford Lewis Battles, translator of the most popular English edition of Calvin's *Institutes*, however, has claimed that because the Westminster Assembly never quoted Calvin, this is clear evidence of their shift away from his theology in their developing of the teaching of the Confession; see Wayne Spear, "The Westminster Confession of Faith & Holy Scripture," in *To Glorify and Enjoy*

tradition, which did not seek to construct and develop a separate *locus* for natural theology so much as defend its existence, declare its insufficiency in salvation, and preserve the necessity of Scripture.[95] In order to understand better the thinking that lies behind the Confession's teaching on natural theology, therefore, we will briefly examine the writings of several key Westminster Divines on this issue. We have selected several of the more prominent Divines, believing that their thinking exerted more influence upon the Assembly and its work. In particular, we will examine the natural theology of William Twisse (1578–1646), Samuel Rutherford (1600–1661), Anthony Tuckney (1599–1670), and Thomas Goodwin (1600–1680).

William Twisse was the Prolocutor of the Assembly until his death in July 1646. He was a staunch scholastic and was called by a contemporary "the most able disputer in England" at that time.[96] Samuel Rutherford, also highly scholastic, was one of four ministers that came to the Assembly representing the Church of Scotland.[97] His importance in the work of drafting the Confession and catechisms is demonstrated by the fact that, among the four Scottish advisors, Rutherford alone was commended for his great assistance and constant attendance at the debates of the Assembly.[98]

God: A Commemoration of the 350*th* Anniversary of the Westminster Assembly*, ed. John Carson and David Hall (Edinburgh: Banner of Truth, 1994), 98. B.B. Warfield has asserted the contrary, stating that there is nothing in the WCF "which is not to be found expressly set forth in the writings" of Calvin in *Studies in Theology* (New York: Oxford University Press, 1932), 148. Clearly in this case, Warfield's evaluation strikes closer to the mark.

[95] See Muller, *PRRD*, 1:173.

[96] Robert Baillie, *The Letters and Journals of Robert Baillie*, ed. David Laing (3 vols.; Edinburgh: Bannatyne Club, 1841–42), 1:303.

[97] Rutherford was accompanied by George Gillespie (1613–1648), Robert Baillie (1602–1662), and Alexander Henderson (1583–1646) at the Assembly; see Alexander Mitchell and John Struthers, *Minutes of the Sessions of the Westminster Assembly of Divines* (Edinburgh and London: Blackwood and Sons, 1874), lxxxiv; William Barker, *Puritan Profiles: 54 Contemporaries of the Westminster Assembly* (Fearn: Christian Focus, 1999), 96-119.

[98] Mitchell and Struthers, *Minutes*, 488.

Anthony Tuckney, an English Divine who was also commended by the Assembly for his constant attendance, was a member of the committee that prepared material for the Confession and was convener of the committee that prepared the Shorter Catechism.[99] James Reid claims that "many of the answers in the Larger Catechism . . . were his, and were continued for the most part in the very words which he brought in."[100] Thomas Goodwin was among the most prolific of the English Divines at the Assembly. Although he was in the minority as a defender of Independency, Goodwin was outspoken in the debates of the Assembly and was viewed by his contemporaries as a very considerable scholar, writer, and preacher, among the "most eminent English Divines for sermons and practical divinity."[101]

Each of these Divines clearly embraces the notion of the *duplex cognitio Dei,* and thus is in continuity with Reformation and post-Reformation theologians. For example, Twisse states concerning God that "all men have power to . . . know him as the Author of Nature, but we must take forth, and know him as a Redeemer, and author of grace."[102] Although it is natural for man to know God, it is not natural for him to love God. This, Twisse says, is wholly supernatural.[103] Rutherford too claims that man by nature "knows there is a God, and that sin is forbidden, but this knowledge is weak and insufficient to bring us" to eternal life, which can only be gained by knowing "God and him whom he has sent, Jesus

---

[99] James Reid, *Memoirs of the Westminster Divines* (1811; repr., Edinburgh: Banner of Truth, 1982), 187.

[100] Ibid., 187.

[101] Edmund Calamy, *An Account of the Ministers, Lecturers, Masters and Fellows of Colleges and Schoolmasters, who were Ejected or Silenced after the Restoration of 1660* (London, 1713), 60; John Wilkins, *Ecclesiastes: or, A Discourse Concerning the Gift of Preaching* (London, 1669), 82; Reid, *Memoirs*, 340-41.

[102] William Twisse, *A Treatise of Mr. Cottons, Clearing certain Doubts Concerning Predestination. Together with an Examination Thereof* (London, 1646), 213.

[103] Twisse, *A Discovery of D. Jacksons Vanitie* (n.p., 1631), 654.

Christ."[104] Rutherford elsewhere insists that even profane men are able to "explain and understand" the literal sense of Scripture, and thus come to a natural but true knowledge of God, but "this knowledge is not enough for salvation." A "spiritual opening and declaration of the literal sense" of Scripture, which flows from the Holy Spirit is required to give them that knowledge of God which is unto salvation.[105] Tuckney asserts that whereas the "justice and righteousness of God is *theologiae naturalis*," faith in Jesus Christ is wholly of "supernatural and evangelical" theology.[106] For Goodwin, God has "afforded corrupt nature a little light of truth" and has left "prints" of the first table of the law by creating the world and by teaching people "to read . . . and learning them to spell his eternal power and Godhead out of that."[107] It is important to note that, according to Goodwin, God not only has "afforded" natural people knowledge about himself (i.e., revealed it to them), but he has assured that they will perceive it "by 'teaching' them to read it and 'learning' them to spell it." This natural theology, however, will never lead the unregenerate to "the right way of salvation," because "natural light is utterly ignorant" of that knowledge. The Holy Spirit working in and through Scripture is necessary in order for man to attain the saving knowledge of God.[108]

---

[104] Samuel Rutherford, *Ane Catachisme conteining the Soume of Christian Religion*, in *Catechisms of the Second Reformation*, ed. Alexander Mitchell (London: James Nisbet, 1886), 161, 174.

[105] Rutherford, *Examen Arminianismi* (Utrecht, 1668), 84. Rutherford here uses language that is strikingly Perkinsian when he speaks of a "literal" versus a "spiritual" knowledge.

[106] Tuckney, *Eight Letters of Dr. Anthony Tuckney, and Dr. Benjamin Whichcote*, in *Moral and Religious Aphorisms, Collected from the Manuscript Papers of the Reverend and Learned Doctor Whichcote*, ed. Samuel Salter (London: Pater-Noster-Row, 1753), 20, 69.

[107] Thomas Goodwin, *The Works of Thomas Goodwin, D.D.* (12 vols.; Edinburgh: James Nichol, 1861), 1:388; 10:144.

[108] Goodwin, *Works*, 6:375. In this discussion, Goodwin also mentions the necessity of preaching to bring men to the saving knowledge of God.

What is most interesting for our discussion here, however, is not the Divines' definitions of natural theology but the positive uses they make of it, in particular the role they ascribe to natural theology in apologetics. Twisse, though he is quick to affirm that no one can come to Christ unless God the Father draws him through the work of the Holy Spirit through Scripture, does clearly establish an apologetic role for natural theology:

> I no where say, nor ever thought that all men had a sufficiency of power to believe or come to Christ. Far be it from me to avouch such ungracious Pelagianism; But this I say, God gives to the men of this world, this world, I say, as opposed to the elect, such means and helps of seeking after the Lord, and finding mercy from him. . . . Else how shall we understand these and sundry such like places of Scripture, *Act.* 17.25, 26, 27. *Rom.* 1.19 to 25. *Rom.* 2.4, 5. 14, 15.[109]

These "means and helps" include both the "knowledge of God in Nature," or the light of nature, generally speaking, and the knowledge "of grace in Christ," or the light of the word, and are designed by God to lead all people to a saving knowledge of God. According to Twisse, because God has established these means and helps for a specific purpose, viz., to lead all men to salvation, they are sufficient to some degree in accomplishing this purpose:

> The means that God uses for these good ends, are in some measure sufficient. . . . to bring them to the attainment of these ends: for when God says himself, he uses these means for these ends; for us to say, these means are not sufficient for these ends, seems to me to derogate from the wisdom and sufficiency of God, whose works are all of them perfect, *Deut.* 32.4, and so sufficient for the ends for which he wrought them.[110]

Because God uses these means and helps for the purpose of leading men to salvation, Twisse believes that we should too.

---

[109] Twisse, *A Treatise of Mr. Cottons*, 207.

[110] Ibid., 208.

Rutherford, though he does not speak as explicitly as Twisse, also ascribes an apologetic role to natural theology. This is because the image of God has not been wholly effaced in man after the fall. The same "natural Theology, that we had in our first creation" essentially remains in all men and is "written in the soul, in deep letters, yet the Ink is dim and old, and therefore this light is like the Moon swimming through watery clouds, often under a shadow, and yet still in the firmament."[111] In other words, for Rutherford as for Polanus and Du Moulin, natural theology is not altogether or always idolatrous. It can and does provide some true knowledge of God to man, albeit "literal" and non-saving. Rutherford is clear that natural theology cannot lead one to salvation and that one cannot reason his way to a saving knowledge of Christ. Only the Holy Spirit working in and through Scripture can do that. He does, however, see natural theology and the *imago Dei* in man as carrying apologetic significance – again, like Calvin, the idea is taking those areas where there is agreement, correcting the error, and then presenting the teaching of Scripture. Rutherford is not alone in this.

For Goodwin too there is an apologetic use for natural theology. Like Twisse, Goodwin clearly refers to natural theology as a guide that is designed to lead people to a saving knowledge of God – but not without the Holy Spirit, because no one can come to the Father to be saved except the Father draw him. He alludes to its use in this regard in preparing the heart of the jailor for salvation in Acts 16.[112] Furthermore, Goodwin believes there are certain "principles – whether left in corrupt nature as relics of the image of God, as men call them, or whether put in [by God]" – which are inherent to all people.[113] These principles include five

---

[111] Samuel Rutherford, *The Divine Right of Church-Government and Excommuni-cation* (London, 1646), 66; Rutherford, *A Free Disputation against Pretended Liberty of Conscience* (London, 1649), 7.

[112] Goodwin, *Works*, 4:194.

[113] *Ibid.*, 1:403.

things in particular and clearly provide the basis for his ascribing an apologetic role to natural theology. First, Goodwin says that there are "seeds of truth" in the understanding, which enable all people to understand not only the truth of this world but also of the Godhead. Second, there is a "natural devotion to a deity" within all people, which leads them to worship "some god or other." Third, there is a "seed of light in the heart of every sinner, that he deserves eternal death for his sin, and that this God will punish him." Fourth, Goodwin claims that "it is natural" for the sinner "to think of a mediator; to use somebody to intercede for him to God."[114] And fifth, he asserts that all people have a "natural desire of happiness, of a greater good than what this world hath," which cannot rest on or be satisfied with anything in this world.[115] We may now draw some conclusions regarding our survey of natural theology in the Westminster Confession and the writings of these four prominent Divines.

Summary and Analysis

In our survey of the Westminster Confession and the writings of four prominent Divines we have seen that there is continuity between the natural theology of Aquinas, the Reformation, and post-Reformation periods. All of the surveyed theologians acknowledge the *duplex cognitio Dei* and beside it both natural and supernatural theology. Without question, all of the theologians drew a firm line of division between natural and supernatural theology that could not be traversed by man unless he was regenerated by the work of the Holy Spirit. Natural theology can not lead to salvation. Man can know God through natural revelation and theology and this knowledge ultimately renders him inexcusable in the Day of Judgment. Nevertheless, natural theology provides unregenerate man with general principles of ethics and conduct. Various theologians

---

[114] To support his argument here Goodwin cites 1 Corinthians 8:5 and the example of Simon Magus wanting Peter to pray for him (see *Ibid.*, 1:403-05).

[115] *Ibid.*, 1:403-5.

recognized a natural theology of the regenerate – the Christian's reflection upon general or natural revelation. There is also, however, a tendency to employ natural theology in apologetics. It is the last two observations that deserve some further analysis.

Many contemporary Reformed theologians acknowledge the existence of natural revelation and argue that it renders the unconverted man inexcusable on the Day of Judgment. We must be careful to note that they acknowledge the propriety of natural *revelation*, not natural *theology*.[116] The general argument is that the regenerate and unregenerate have everything ontologically and metaphysically in common, but do not have any epistemic common ground. For example, Van Til writes,

> Calvinism cannot find a direct point of contact in any of the accepted concepts of the natural man. He disagrees with every individual doctrine of the natural man because he disagrees with the outlook of the natural man as a whole. He disagrees with the basic assumption of the natural man. For it is this basic assumption that colors all his statements about individual teachings. . . . The Reformed apologist . . . does not first travel in the same direction and in the same automobile with the natural man for some distance in order then mildly to suggest to the driver that they ought perhaps to change their course somewhat and follow a road that goes at a different slant from the one they are on.[117]

In other words, there is no epistemic point of contact. Yet, one thing is clear; the Confession, evidenced by the Scripture proof texts, and in the writings of the theologians we have surveyed, especially Calvin, Perkins, Ussher, Twisse, Rutherford, and Goodwin, allow for an epistemic point of contact between the believer and non-believer.

The most common form of the argument is well stated by Calvin when he writes that in Acts 17:24 Paul "takes his proof from

---

[116] Bahnsen, *Van Til's Apologetic*, 192-94.

[117] Cornelius Van Til, *The Defense of the Faith* (1955; repr., Phillipsburg: P&R, 1967), 112-13.

nature itself, for he would have wasted his time in contending with them by citing scriptural proof-texts."[118] Like Aquinas who argued from the vantage point of supernatural theology and demonstrated its reasonable nature with natural theology, so too Calvin, et al., follow the same methodology. This is not to say that Aquinas and these Reformed theologians agreed on issues of nature and grace and the noetic effects of sin. Nevertheless, they, unlike many contemporary Reformed theologians, saw a point of contact with the unregenerate through natural theology. The question we must ask is, What has caused this shift in Reformed theology?

There is likely a twofold answer to this question. The probable causes of this shift away from natural theology lie in: (1) the devolution of Reformed theology after the period of High Orthodoxy and (2) the influence of Kant. First, we must note that after the period of High Orthodoxy (1630/40–1700) the careful line of division between natural and supernatural theology was abandoned. The seeds for this departure, however, were sown during High Orthodoxy. All of the surveyed theologians gave natural man access only to a general knowledge of God through natural theology. It was in the theology of Richard Baxter (1615–1691), however, where this carefully guarded line began to be blurred.

Baxter is known for his many practical works, but few are aware of his technical theological works. Baxter was quite a proficient scholastic theologian, familiar with the writings of Aquinas, John Duns Scotus (*c.* 1266–1308), and Francisco Suarez (1546–1617). In fact, Baxter's work in his *Catholick Theologie* clearly reflects a positive appropriation of medieval nominalist thought.[119] Where Baxter clearly departed from the norm in regard to natural theology is in connection with the limits of natural reason and the

---

[118] Calvin, *Comm.*, Acts 17:24, p. 112.

[119] Carl R. Trueman, "A Small Step Towards Rationalism: The Impact of the Metaphysics of Tommaso Campanella on the Theology of Richard Baxter," in *Protestant Scholasticism: Essays in Reassessment*, ed. Carl R. Trueman and R. S. Clark (London: Paternoster, 1999), 184-85.

doctrine of the Trinity. In defending the rationality of the Trinity, Baxter writes that the "essential immanent acts of God are three: 1. *Sibi vivere*, or to be essential active life in Himself; 2. *Se intelligere*, to know Himself; 3. *Se Amare*, or to be *amor sui*."[120] Baxter goes on to write that, "Seeing the Trinity of divine principles (or formal essentialities) and the threefold act, are so certainly evident to natural reason itself, that no understanding person can deny them."[121] What had influenced Baxter to the position that the Trinity could be demonstrated by natural reason when Reformed theology had previously assigned the knowledge of the Trinity to supernatural revelation? It was the impact of the philosophy of Tomasso Campanella (1568–1639). Trueman notes that Baxter's theology was influenced by reading, not Scripture, but Campanella's work and coming to the conclusion that God had impressed his Trinitarian nature on all of his higher works.[122] What did this mean for Reformed theology? Trueman writes that "we see hints of that truly rationalistic tendency within theology which was ultimately to bring about the collapse of Reformed orthodoxy in the following century."[123] Indeed, Reformed theology on the continent suffered a serious blow and moved into rationalism.

The most decisive step towards rationalism came from the theology of J. A. Turretin (1671–1737), the son of Francis Turretin (1623–1687). J. A. Turretin did not have a zeal for the theology of the post-Reformation and High Orthodoxy periods, particularly that of his father. He also had forged strong relationships with the faculty of the Remonstrant seminary in Amsterdam. In fact, Turretin used the same apologetic method of the Remonstrants, who emphasized external proofs to establish the authority of Scripture, a departure from the traditional Reformed method.[124] Moreover, in

---

[120] Richard Baxter, *Catholick Theologie* (London, 1675), 1.3.25, p. 4.

[121] Ibid., 1.3.27, p. 5.

[122] Trueman, "Towards Rationalism," 187.

[123] Ibid., 195.

[124] Cf. Platt, *Reformed Thought and Scholasticism*, 179-201.

his theology he accorded rational argumentation an equal footing with biblical revelation, claiming that both are in complete harmony.[125] Whatever line of demarcation that had existed between natural and supernatural theology no longer existed. By the mid-eighteenth century the faculty at Calvin's Academy denied the doctrine of the Trinity and the incarnation because they did not square with reason.[126] It is important that we note that natural theology was not the cause of these heretical results but that it was the abandonment of the line of separation between natural and supernatural theology; the creeping advance of rationalism eventually caused the collapse of Reformed theology in Europe, not natural theology.

Second, it is the influence of Kant upon contemporary thought that has caused many theologians to look upon natural theology with a degree of suspicion. The rejection of natural theology is certainly evident in the thought of Barth who writes that, "If God's revelation is alongside a knowledge of God proper to man as such, even though it may never be advanced except as a prolegomenon, it is obviously no longer the revelation of God, but a new expression (borrowed or even stolen) for the revelation which encounters man in his own reflection." Barth goes on to write that even a natural theology of the regenerate "very respectfully and in all humility recasts revelation into a new form of its own devising. But for all that its behavior is so respectful and forbearing, for all that it subordinates itself so consciously and consistently, natural theology has already conquered it at the very outset, making revelation into non-revelation."[127]

As is especially the case with Barth, many theologians fail to read aright the trajectory of the positive appropriation of natural theology

---

[125] Martin I. Klauber, *Between Reformed Scholasticism and Pan-Protestantism: Jean-Alphonse Turretin (1671–1737) and Enlightened Orthodoxy at the Academy of Geneva* (Selinsgrove: Susquehenna University Press, 1994), 10, also 140-42.

[126] Ibid., 191-92.

[127] Barth, *Dogmatics*, II.1, 139-40.

from Aquinas through the Reformation and post-Reformation periods. Theologians read the errors of the Enlightenment back into the theology of Aquinas, dismiss it, and then recast the theology of the Reformation in Kantian terms. Or, in the case of those such as Kendall, some try to pit the Reformation against the post-Reformation, i.e., Calvin vs. the Calvinists. The evidence that we have presented, however, adequately demonstrates the positive use of natural theology in the sixteenth and seventeenth centuries and is reflected in the Westminster Confession, especially by those phrases that speak of the "light of nature."

Conclusion

In recent years there has been a greater effort to reevaluate the relationship between the Middle Ages and the Reformation and post-Reformation periods. Previous studies have often argued for total discontinuity between the three periods. Yet, in recent years the work of many scholars, such as Heiko Oberman, David Steinmetz, and Richard Muller, has demonstrated that there are no clear lines of separation between these three periods. This is certainly evident in our study of natural theology. There is a trajectory of common methodology in the use of natural theology in the thought of Aquinas, Calvin, Musculus, Vermigli, Perkins, Polanus, Du Moulin, Ussher, the Westminster Confession, Twisse, Rutherford, Tuckney, and Goodwin. Though there are variations among them all, especially on the matter of accuracy, there is a clear acceptance among them all of natural theology.

In light of this primary source evidence, Reformed theologians should reopen the study of natural theology and reengage what our theological forefathers saw as an important subject. Theologians, however, must be careful to guard the line of demarcation between natural and supernatural theology that was so diligently maintained in the theology of the aforementioned theologians. Ultimately, the church should reopen this area of theology, not simply because there is historical precedent, but because our Reformed patriarchs saw natural theology in the pages of Scripture. This is especially evident in the repeated references and citations of Psalm 19, Acts 17, and Romans 1. The church should not fear the use of natural theology; rather she should fear its abuse. What has natural theology to do with Westminster? Ultimately, very much, because the two are related to the *duplex cognitio Dei*, the knowledge of God as Creator and Redeemer. Should we not know God as both? Should we not study the revelation of God in both Word and nature? For indeed, God is the author of both.

The Westminster Consensus on the Decree:
The Infra/Supra Lapsarian Debate[*]

Derek Thomas

As one who teaches systematic theology at a seminary, I find that my students fall into one of four categories when it comes to the lapsarian debate. First, there are those who are keen to identify their Reformed credentials as the "non-wimpy" variety. None of that "soft Calvinism" that deems it unfair of God to seemingly elect some to salvation "out of mere sovereignty," irrespective of any consideration of any assumed sinfulness – a consideration which at the very least "softens" the decree. For this group, adoption of supralapsarianism[1] is the way to go, and it brings added comfort to be associated with the likes of Theodore Beza (1519–1605),[2] William Perkins (1558–1602), William Twisse (1578?–1646) and in our era, A. W. Pink (1886–1952).[3]

---

[*] The following address was given at "The Westminster Confession into the 21st Century" conference hosted by the Reformed Presbyterian Theological Seminary, Pittsburgh in June 2004.

[1] For a summary of this position, see Karl Barth, *Church Dogmatics*, ed. G. W. Bromiley and T. F. Torrance (1957; repr., Edinburgh: T&T Clark, 1994), II.2:127-45. Barthianism aside, this is a splendid summary of the doctrine from a (granted) distorted perspective and devotee of supralapsarianism. Barth's adoption of supralapsarianism has to be understood, of course, within his Christomonistic perspective.

[2] See, Joel Beeke, "The Order of the Divine Decrees at the Genevan Academy: From Bezan Supralapsarianism to Turretinian Infralapsarianism," in *The Identity of Geneva: The Christian Commonwealth, 1564–1864*, ed. John B. Roney and Martin I. Klauber (Westport, Conn.: Greenwood Press, 1998), 57-76.

A second category comprises those who balk at any consideration of "mere sovereignty" in the decree, finding it outrageously
insensitive, fundamentally unjust, or evangelistically offensive.
Gospel formulations are expressed along lines such as: "God,
knowing that no one deserves forgiveness, chose some to eternal
life and salvation." The assumption of guilt before any consideration of election places these squarely in the infralapsarian camp
(though many election-affirming "biblical theologians," who
deem the lapsarian debate as the prime example of how systematic
theology is riddled with philosophical presuppositions which have
no place in the hermeneutics of a theology of the Bible, assume
this very mode of gospel presentation!). Students in this category read chapter three of the Westminster Confession, "Of God's
Eternal Decree," as most definitely infralapsarianism. The Divines

---

[3] Others in the supralapsarian category would include Francis Gomarus (1563–
1641), William Ames (1576–1633), Samuel Rutherford (1600–1661), Thomas
Goodwin (1600–1680), John Gill (1697–1771), Alexander Comrie (1707–
1774), Augustus Toplady (1740–1778), Abraham Kuyper (1837–1920), Herman
Hoeksema (1886–1965), and (for different reasons) Cornelius Van Til (1895–
1987) and Gordon Clark (1902–1985). Some have argued a strong case for
including John Calvin (1509–1564) in this category – and others have equally
been insistent on Calvin's infralapsarianism. See Theodore Beza's famous
ocular catechism, *Ordo Rerum Decretarum*, in *Summa totius Christianismi .
. . in Tractationum Theologicarum* (Geneva: Eusthathius Vignon, 1582). Beza
also provided a summary of supralapsarianism in *A Briefe and Pithie Summe of
the Christian Faith* (London, 1572), 4, first published as *Confessio Christianae
Fidei* (Geneva, 1560). Fred Klooster, *Calvin's Doctrine of Predestination*
(Grand Rapids: Baker, 1977), 55-58; Joel Beeke, "Order of Divine Decrees,"
74 n. 82. For Calvin as a supralapsarian, see, J. V. Fesko, "The Westminster
Confession and Lapsarianism: Calvin and the Divines" in *The Westminster
Confession into the 21ˢᵗ Century*, ed. J. Ligon Duncan (4 vols.; Fearn: Mentor,
2004), 2:477-525. See also, Fesko's published dissertation, *Diversity Within
the Reformed Tradition: Supra- and Infralapsarianism in Calvin, Dort, and
Westminster* (Greenville: Reformed Academic Press, 2001). For a counter view,
see Francis Turretin, *Institutes of Elenctic Theology*, ed. James T. Dennison, Jr.,
trans. George Musgrave Giger (3 vols.; Phillipsburg: P&R, 1992), 1:349-50;
W. G. T. Shedd, *Dogmatic Theology*, ed. Alan W. Gomes (Phillipsburg: P&R,
2003), 361-63. (For Shedd's defense of his own infralapsarian position, see
pages 340-44); and especially, Richard A. Muller, *After Calvin: Studies in the
Development of a Theological Tradition* (Oxford: Oxford University Press,
2003), 11-12.

– at least the ones that matter, so they surmise, were infralapsarians – just like J. I. Packer! Any other view makes evangelism impossible and Calvinism harsh and uncaring. For this group, infralapsarianism is the way to go, and in affirming it they join such stalwart theologians as Francis Turretin (1623–1687),[4] John Owen (1616–1683), Jonathan Edwards (1703–1758) and in our era, John Murray (1898–1975).[5]

There is also a sizable group of students who belong to a third grouping. They are skeptical at best, and hostile at worst of the

---

[4] See, note 3.

[5] Others in the infralapsarian category would include Thomas Watson (1620–1686), Matthew Henry (1662–1714), Thomas Boston (1676–1732), George Whitefield (1714–1770), Charles Hodge (1797–1878), J. H. Thornwell (1812–1862), R. L. Dabney (1820–1898), W. G. T. Shedd (1829–1894), C. H. Spurgeon (1834–1892), William Cunningham (1805–1861), B. B. Warfield (1851–1921), J. Gresham Machen (1881–1936), Martyn Lloyd-Jones (1898–1981), Loraine Boettner (1901–1990) and J. I. Packer (1926–).

Louis Berkhof seems sympathetic to both infralapsarianism and supralapsarianism. Louis Berkhof, *Systematic Theology* (Grand Rapids: Eerdmans, 1996), 118-25. See especially page 124 where Berkhof discusses the merits and demerits of both views. Boettner's trenchant critique of supralapsarianism can be found in *The Reformed Doctrine of Predestination* (Philadelphia: P&R, 1966), 126-30.

We have included Dabney here, even though he categorizes himself as "sublapsarian," and this after making the comment that the lapsarian issue "ought never to have been raised"! R. L. Dabney, *Systematic Theology* (Edinburgh: Banner of Truth, 1985), 233. Dabney was capable of some speculative theology of his own, as a reading of his review of Charles Hodge's *Systematic Theology* and the issue of intellectualism/voluntarism will show. See Robert L. Dabney, "Hodge's Systematic Theology" in *Discussions: Evangelical and Theological* (Edinburgh: Banner of Truth, 1982), 1:229-81. Some members of the Assembly itself expressed similar concerns over the inclusion of "scholastical things": thus, Edward Reynolds urged, "Let not us put in disputes and scholastical things into a Confession of Faith." However, his concern was *not* due to any doubt as to its inherent merit or validity, but rather that the scope of the Confession was for (in B. B. Warfield's terms) "generic Calvinism" rather than "any particular variety of it." See, B. B. Warfield, "The Making of the Westminster Confession, and Especially of its Chapter on the Decree of God," in *The Works of Benjamin B. Warfield* (10 vols.; Grand Rapids: Baker, 2000), 6:136. J. H. Thornwell had no difficulties in a robust defense of infralapsarianism or as he terms it, "sublapsarianism," "Outline of the Covenant of Grace and Testimony to Sublapsarianism" in *The Collected Writings of James Henley Thornwell*, (4 vols.; Edinburgh: Banner of Truth, 1986), 2:17-27.

entire lapsarian debate. They avow "symphonic theology" as the queen of theological disciplines. Systematic theology, and the lapsarian debate in particular, is wedded to Aristotelian (or, as in the lapsarian controversy, Ramist) philosophy.[6] The result is something which is loosely (and decidedly derogatively) termed "scholastic."[7] Theology must navigate between the Scylla of Scholasticism and the Charybdis of what is perceived to be an exegetically-deficient theology. Hodge and Dabney must be replaced by Vos and Ridderbos (though neither of these thought the issue entirely irrelevant!). Their exegetical skills are far too nuanced to allow themselves to be sullied by this 17th-century debate that cheapens theology and results in the kind of arid speculation that gives reformed theology a bad name![8]

And, to be fair, there are a loyal group of students who think the issue a valid one, but one that is beyond any reasonable hope of resolution – at least whilst employing traditional modes of thought. They appeal to Herman Bavinck's conclusion on the issue:

---

6   Petrus Ramus (1515–1572) wrote several influential texts, including *Dialectica Institutiones* (1543, 1547), and *De Religiona Christiana* (1576). His influence on Protestant theology (particularly on William Perkins [1558–1602] and William Ames [1576–1633]) is evidenced in the work *The Logike of the Moste Excellent Philosopher P. Ramus, Martyr*, trans. Ronald MacIlmaine (1574), edited with an introduction by Catherine M. Dunn (Northridge, Calif., San Fernando Valley State College, 1969), introduction, xi-xxii; Keith L. Sprunger, "Ames, Ramus, and the Method of Puritan Theology," in *Harvard Theological Review* 59 (1966): 133-51; and Keith L. Sprunger, "Technometria: A Prologue to Puritan Theology" in *Journal of the History of Ideas* 29 (1968): 115-22. On the charge of Ramist influence, see, Lynne Courter Boughton, "Supralapsarianism and the Role of Metaphysics in Sixteenth-Century Reformed Theology" in *Westminster Theological Journal* 48 (1986): 63-96; Water J. Ong, *Ramus, Method and the Decay of Dialogue* (Cambridge: Harvard University Press, 1958), 295-318; Richard Muller, *Post-Reformation Reformed Dogmatics: The Rise and Development of Reformed Orthodoxy, ca. 1520 to ca. 1725* (4 vols.; Grand Rapids: Baker, 2003), 1:112-13, 181-84; Richard Muller, *Christ and Decree* (Grand Rapids: Baker, 1986), 140-47.

7   On the seventeenth century use of the term, see Carl Trueman, *The Claims of Truth: John Owen's Trinitarian Theology* (Carlisle: Paternoster, 1998), 31-32.

8   In categorizing in this way, we do not intend to imply that students do not adopt any one of these positions out of a firmly held conviction as to its merit.

"neither supra- nor infralapsarianism has succeeded in its attempt to solve this problem and to do justice to the many-sidedness of Scripture."[9]

"A Solemn and Carefully Framed Expression"

The lapsarian issue is one that, strictly speaking, only surfaces at the Synod of Dort (1618–1619), though some theologians have suggested a pre-Reformation origin.[10] Martin Luther, John Calvin, and Huldrych Zwingli did discuss the issue of whether the fall was *actively* willed or *passively* foreseen, all three concluding the former. But discussions of the logical priority of the decrees of election and the fall did not surface, despite anachronistic attempts to read them back into their writings.[11]

The lapsarian issue does find expression in the Westminster Confession in its third chapter, "Of God's Eternal Decree" at sections 6 and 7:

6. As God hath appointed the elect unto glory, so has He, by the eternal and most free purpose of His will, foreordained all the means thereunto.[xii] Wherefore, they who are elected, being fallen in Adam, are redeemed by Christ,[xiii] are effectually called unto faith in Christ by His Spirit working in due season, are justified, adopted, sanctified,[xiv] and kept by His power, through faith, unto salvation.[xv] Neither are any other redeemed by Christ, effectually called, justified, adopted, sanctified, and saved, but the elect only[xvi]

7. The rest of mankind God was pleased, according to the unsearchable counsel of His own will, whereby He extendeth or withholdeth mercy, as He pleaseth, for the glory of His sovereign

---

9   Herman Bavinck, *The Doctrine of God*, trans. William Hendriksen (Grand Rapids: Baker, 1977), 389.

10   E.g. Charles Hodge speaks of Augustine's infralapsarianism. See *Systematic Theology* (New York: Scribner, Armstrong, & Co., 1877), 2:318-19.

11   On the development of the issue, especially the conclusion drawn by the early Reformers that the issue of the fall cannot be divorced from the divine decree, see G. C. Berkouwer, *Divine Election* (Grand Rapids: Eerdmans, 1960), 254-77.

power over His creatures, to pass by; and to ordain them to dishonor and wrath for their sin, to the praise of His glorious justice. xvii

---

xii 1 Pet. 1:2; Eph. 2:4-5, 10; 2 Thess. 2:13. xiii 1 Thess. 5:9-10; Tit. 2:14. xiv Rom. 8:30; Eph. 1:5; 2 Thess. 2:13. xv 1 Pet. 1:5. xvi John 17:9; Rom. 8:28; John 6:64-65; 10:26; 8:47; 1 John 2:19. xvii Matt. 11:25-26; Rom. 9:17-22; 2 Tim. 2:19-20; Jude 4; 1 Pet. 2:8.

Commenting on section 7, John Murray made the observation:

No paragraph in the whole compass of confessional literature excels for precision of thought, compactness of formulation, and jealousy of the various elements of truth in the doctrine concerned in Section VII of the Confession.[12]

B. B. Warfield has also noted the care taken in the formation of the third chapter of the Westminster Confession; the choice of words and phrases are deliberate:

The third chapter of the Confession is distinctly the work of the Assembly itself, and comes to us as the well-pondered and

---

[12] John Murray, "Calvin, Dordt and Westminster on Predestination – A Comparative Study," in *Collected Writings of John Murray*, (4 vols.; Edinburgh: Banner of Truth, 1982), 4:209-10. See also, "The Theology of the Westminster Confession of Faith," 2:241-63; "The Importance and Relevance of the Westminster Confession," 1:316-22. This, of course, is in marked contrast to the vehement criticism leveled at the Westminster Confession for its doctrine of predestination. Brian Armstrong, Basil Hall, and J. B. Torrance, among others, have criticized the displacement of predestination from the doctrine of soteriology (as in Calvin's 1559 edition of the *Institutes*) and into the doctrine of God (as in Calvin's "first thoughts" on the issue in the 1536 edition of the *Institutes*). See, Brian Armstrong, *Calvinism and the Amyraut Heresy: Protestant Scholasticism and Humanism in Seventeenth Century France* (Madison: University of Wisconsin Press, 1969), 41-42; Basil Hall, "Calvin Against the Calvinists," in *John Calvin*, Courtenay Studies in Reformation Theology, vol. 1, ed. G. E. Duffield (Appleford: Sutton Courtenay Press, 1966), 27; J. B. Torrance, "Strength and Weaknesses of the Westminster Theology," in *Westminster Confession in the Church Today*, ed. Alasdair I. C. Heron (Edinburgh: Saint Andrew Press, 1982), 46-47; cf. Alasdair I. C. Heron, "The Concept of Federal Theology – Was Calvin a Federal Theologian?" in *Calvinus Sacrae Scripturae Professor: Calvin as Confessor of Holy Scripture*, ed. Wilhelm H. Neuser (Grand Rapids: Eerdmans, 1994), 18-20.

thoroughly adjusted expression of the living belief of that whole body. The differences that existed between the members were not smoothed over in ambiguous language. They were fully ventilated. Room was made for them when they were considered unimportant and mere *apices logici*: but when they concerned matters of moment, after full discussion, the doctrine of the Assembly – well-reasoned and fully thought out – as distinguished from that of individuals, was embodied clearly and firmly in the document. The document as it stands is thus emphatically the Confession of Faith of the Westminster Assembly. We cannot say that this or that clause represents this or that part in the Assembly. There were parties in the Assembly, and they were all fully heard and what they said was carefully weighed. But no merely party opinion was allowed a place in the document. When it came to voting the statements there to be set down, the Assembly as such spoke; and in speaking it showed itself capable of speaking its own mind. It is doing only mere justice to it, therefore, to read the document as the solemn and carefully framed expression of its reasoned faith.[13]

Warfield is conscious of the comments of one of the Scottish delegates to the Assembly, Robert Baillie, who wrote in a letter, "We had long and tough debates about the decree of election."[14]

---

[13] Warfield, "Making of the Westminster Confession," 6:146-47.

[14] Robert Baillie, *The Letters and Journals of Robert Baillie: Principal of the University of Glasgow 1637-1652*, ed. David Laing (3 vols.; Edinburgh: Robert Ogle, 1841), 2:325. Fesko observes that the change of title for the third chapter from the original title of James Ussher's *Irish Articles*, "Of God's Eternal Decree and Predestination" to simply "Of God's Eternal Decree" implies that the Assembly may well have had some who objected to the very word predestination. However, Warfield's more nuanced explanation – that there was an element of tautology in Ussher's title – seems a better explanation, particularly since the language of predestination occurs four times in the text of the chapter (in addition to a threefold use of the language of foreordination). See Fesko, *Diversity*, 260-61; Warfield, "Making of the Westminster Confession," 6:124-26.

"Being Fallen in Adam"

The key sentence is the one that is found in section 6: "Wherefore, they who are elected, being fallen in Adam, are redeemed by Christ." The issue concerns the interpretation of the words, "being fallen in Adam" (*homo creatus et lapsus*): Should this clause be viewed *sub specie aeternitatis* – viewing it as suggesting a logical priority in the mind of God (and therefore *infra*lapsarian), or *sub specie temporis* – viewing it as addressing the temporal chronology/sequence of the application of redemption (and therefore *supra*lapsarian)? The fact that many read the statement as suggesting the former (infralapsarian) point of view[15] should not cloud the fact that certain influential members of the Assembly and architects of this chapter most certainly did not![16] Alexander Mitchell makes the interesting, if debatable observation:

> Some of them [Covenanting ministers of Scotland] even favoured the supralapsarian view, and resolutely defended it, though granted that the questions in which they differed from their brethren were questions to be discussed in the schools rather than to be determined in a Confession of Faith.[17]

The issue becomes acute whenever we recall that the original draft of this statement evidently bore a decidedly supralapsarian twist. Warfield, who confesses that it is not possible to "reconstruct in its entirety the original form of the section," suggests from the material available to him that the original draft proposal must have

---

[15] As an example of an infralapsarian reading of the text, Roland S. Ward comments: "Those who are saved are reckoned as 'fallen in Adam' that is, the decree of election is reckoned in order of logic as contemplating men as already fallen." *The Westminster Confession for the Church Today* (Melbourne: Presbyterian Church of Eastern Australia, 1992), 39.

[16] Despite the comment of John MacPherson: "[of supralapsarianism] this notion is contrary to the whole tenor of Scripture" in *The Confession of Faith* (Edinburgh: T&T Clark, 1977), 50.

[17] Alexander F. Mitchell, *The Westminster Assembly: Its History and Standards* (Edmonton: Still Water Revival Books, [1883] 1992), 352-53. Mitchell cites Baillie's *Letters*, 3:6.

read along these lines: "As God hath appointed the elect unto glory, so hath He, to bring this to pass, ordained by the same decree to permit man to fall."[18] This formulation makes the fall *the means* of accomplishing God's decree of salvation (*medium executionis decreti*) particularly since it insists that *"the same decree"* is in view. Thus the fall is viewed as a "happy occurrence" (*felix culpa*). The formulation was *specifically* nuanced *sub specie aeternitatis* and was, therefore, supralapsarian.

According to the supralapsarian view the logical order of the decrees (*sub specie aeternitatis*) is,

- To elect some men to life and to condemn others to destruction
- To create
- To permit the fall
- To send Christ to redeem the elect
- To send the Holy Spirit to apply redemption to the elect[19]

---

[18] Warfield, "Making of the Westminster Confession," 6:134-35. It is hoped that Chad van Dixhoorn's studies may uncover the original draft of this formulation.

On the first day of scheduled debate (October 20, 1645), George Gillespie (1613–1648) suggested that the wording be altered to read thus: "As God hath appointed to elect unto glory, so hath He for the same end ordained to permit the fall," but this, too, was viewed (rightly, since Gillespie was supralapsarian!) as saying the same thing in different words. The next day, it fell to Edward Reynolds (1599–1667) to make a more favorable suggestion, along these lines:

As God hath appointed the elect unto glory, so hath He by the same eternal and most free purpose of His will fore-ordained all the means thereunto, which He in His counsel is pleased to appoint for executing of that decree; wherefore who are endowed with so excellent a benefit, being fallen in Adam, are called in according to God's grace.

[19] Robert Reymond argues for a more nuanced (!) ordering of the supralapsarian position on the basis that the traditional order fails to maintain the logic of its own standard of "retrograde movement." He argues for the following order:

- Decree to elect some *sinful* men to salvation in Christ; the reprobation of the rest of *sinful* mankind in order to make known the riches of God's gracious mercy to the elect
- Decree to apply Christ's redemptive benefits to elect sinners
- Decree to redeem elect sinners by the cross work of Christ
- Decree that men should fall
- Decree to create the world and men

The corresponding infralapsarian scheme is usually represented thus:

- To create
- To permit the fall
- To elect to eternal life and blessedness a great multitude out of this mass of fallen men, and to leave others to suffer the just punishment of their sins
- To give his Son, Jesus Christ, for the redemption of the elect
- To send the Holy Spirit to apply to the elect the redemption which was purchased by Christ[20]

The principal issue of concern within this logical progression is the relative location of the decree to allow the fall to the decree of election and reprobation. In the supralapsarian scheme, the decree of election comes "above (*supra*)" the decree to permit the fall.

Infralapsarianism reverses this, insisting that the decree of election and reprobation only follows an already perceived context of *fallen*-ness. In particular, the reprobates, who in the language of the Westminster Confession, are "passed by" for election and rather consigned to perdition. The point being that in the foreordination to perdition there is a sense that they are receiving the just consequence of their own sinfulness. Justice is perceived to overshadow any sense of unfairness in the selection. "None deserve to be elected," folk will sometimes say, without regard to the lapsarian position thereby being presupposed.[21]

---

[20]   See, B. B. Warfield, *The Plan of Salvation* (Grand Rapids: Eerdmans, 1966), 92-93. Amyraldianism reverses the decree of election/reprobation and the decree to send Christ to provide atonement thereby rendering what is in effect a hypothetical atonement for all, even though they maintain a rigorous doctrine of election (and are not universalists). Interestingly, the Baptist systematician, A. H. Strong, argues for this order: "The true order of the decrees is therefore as follows: 1. the decree to create; 2. the decree to permit the fall; 3. the decree to provide a salvation on the part of some, – or, in other words, the decree of Election." *Systematic Theology* (Philadelphia: Judson Press, 1943), 778.

[21]   It is interesting to note that those who insist that the lapsarian issue is an illegitimate one, derived from an unwarranted use of Aristotelian/Ramist logic

A Consensus Document?

The strength and vigor of this debate must be weighed against the commitment of some of the Assembly's most able members to a lapsarian position. For the purposes of this lecture, we will consider just two of them: William Twisse and Samuel Rutherford.

William Twisse, the prolocutor of the Assembly, published one of the definitive accounts of the supralapsarian way shortly before his death in 1646, *A Treatise of Mr. Cottons Clearing Certaine Doubts Concerning Predestination together with An Examination Thereof.*[22] Twisse's supralapsarian position is evident almost immediately as he postulates what is *primary* in God's electing and reprobating decree: is it "to glorify rather his grace and justice, then his power and sovereignty"? Twisse holds that the question is essentially ill-defined because, he argues, God seeks *equally to display all his attributes* not just his grace and justice.[23] The infralapsarian concern to insist on justice *before* sovereignty (God

---

or a complete lack of exegetical (textual) warrant will nevertheless present the gospel along these lines thereby signaling their infralapsarian presuppositions!

[22] *A Treatise of Mr. Cottons Clearing Certaine Doubts Concerning Predestination Together with An Examination Thereof* (London, 1646). In 1640, Richard Baxter of Kidderminster, is said to have "plunged himself into the study of Dr. Twisse" and considered him "a man very famous for his Scholastical Wit and Writings in a very smooth triumphant Stile." Twisse became the author Baxter "most esteemed" adding in *Plain Scripture Proof* (1650) that he had read "six of Dr. Twisse's books again and again (which I think are all)." See, J. I. Packer, *The Redemption and Restoration of Man in the Thought of Richard Baxter* (1954; repr., Vancouver: Regent College Publications, 2003), 194. Twisse died before the Assembly had completed its work, but more importantly for our consideration here, before the Assembly had completed its work on the lapsarian issue. Its first draft was in the hands of the Great Committee by July 16, 1645. Debate ensued from August 29 until November 11 on some twenty different days, portions of the chapter being sent to special committees. Further days of debate followed in June of the following year, 1646, before it was finally ordered. There appears to have been an attempted alteration in December 1646 by Jeremiah Whitaker, and further debate ensued. The proof texts were added over the course of four days in January 1647. The entire third chapter was passed on April 6, 1647. The entire Assembly attended Twisse's burial on July 29, 1646. Fifteen years later, at the restoration of Charles II, his bones were exhumed and thrown into an unmarked common grave.

[23] *Treatise of Mr. Cottons*, 37-38.

chooses from that which is already fallen) is *prima facie* ill-judged. According to Twisse, there are three basic views concerning "the object of predestination":

1. *massa nondum condita* (mass not yet made)
2. *massa pura: condita nondum corrupta* (mass pure, that is made but not yet corrupt)
3. *massa corrupta* (mass corrupt)[24]

Twisse's argument here is convoluted:

> Concerning the order here mentioned, though my opinion be, that the object of predestination is *massa nondum condita*, yet in no moment of nature, or reason, was the decree of God concerning Christ's incarnation, and our salvation by him, before the decree of creation, and of permission of Adam's fall, and consequently Election unto Salvation had the consideration of *massa corrupta* concomitant with it, though not precedent; only the consideration of *massa nondum condita* being antecedental to all these decrees.[25]

---

[24] For an example of this position, see B. B. Warfield's statement: "The mere putting of the question seems to carry its answer with it. For the actual dealing with men which is in question, is, with respect to both classes alike, those who are elected and those who are passed by, conditioned on sin: we cannot speak of salvation any more than of reprobation without positing sin. Sin is necessarily precedent in thought, not indeed to the abstract idea of discrimination, but to the concrete instance of discrimination which is in question, a discrimination with regard to a destiny which involves either salvation or punishment. There must be sin in contemplation to ground a decree of salvation, as truly as a decree of punishment. We cannot speak of a decree discriminating between men with reference to salvation and punishment, therefore, without positing the contemplation of men as sinners as its logical prius." *Plan of Salvation*, 15-29.

[25] Twisse continues in this extract to add the interesting historical observation regarding the Synod of Dort and the views of Calvin: "Likewise, in my opinion, they do mistake, who take the Synod of Dort to maintain the consideration of *massa corrupta*, as precedent to Election, though they begin with signifying what God purposed to bring to pass, upon the fall of mankind, in Adam. And Calvin in his answer to Pighius confesseth, that the safest course is to treat of predestination, upon the consideration of the corrupt mass in Adam." *Treatise of Mr. Cottons*, 38. For a treatment that takes note of these issues, see Patrick Gillespie's *The Ark of the Covenant Opened: Or, A Treatise of the Covenant*

This statement, and others like it, is interesting, not least because of Twisse's espousal of supralapsarianism on the one hand, but also, on the other hand, his insistence that considerations of sin, *and therefore of human culpability*, are not exclusive of each other. In a statement which affirms the *equal ultimacy* of election and reprobation, Twisse at the same time seeks to maintain that considerations of faith (in the case of election) and sin (in the case of reprobation) are not illegitimate issues of consideration in the decree.

> For, let us first make the decrees of salvation and condemnation matches: As for example, Reprobation, as it is accounted the decree of condemnation, is a decree of punishing with everlasting death. Now, if you will match election unto this, as it is the decree of salvation, it must be conceived as a decree of rewarding with everlasting life. Now let any man judge, whether this decree must not as necessarily be conjoined with the consideration of faith, repentance, and good works, in men of ripe years; as the decree of condemnation, or of punishing with everlasting death, must be conjoined with the consideration of those sins for which God purposeth to punish them. And I will further demonstrate it thus: Like as the decree of permitting some men to sin, and to continue therein to the end, and God's decree of condemning for sin, are joint decrees, neither afore nor after the other; and consequently, the decree of condemning for sin must necessarily be conjoined with the consideration of sin: In like sort, God's decree of giving some faith, repentance, and good works, and his decree of rewarding them with everlasting life, are joint decrees, neither of them afore or after the other; and consequently, God's decree of saving them, and rewarding them with everlasting life, is joined with the consideration of faith, repentance, and good works.[26]

Twisse seems to be saying in these passages something which others (e.g. Van Til) have also suggested: that the *logical* order

---

of Redemption between God and Christ, as the Foundation of the Covenant of Grace (London, 1677), especially chapter 3.

[26] *Treatise of Mr. Cottons*, 112.

of the decrees takes place in non-temporal categories and that strictly speaking, there is no "moment" when these issues exist independently of the other (which leads Cornelius Van Til and John Frame to regard the entire debate as irrelevant!).[27] However, the use of "moment" is misleading. It is not a temporal priority that is in view but a logical one and Twisse's attempt to soften his espousal of supralapsarianism is ultimately unconvincing.

"Strict Federal and Predestinationist Principles": Samuel Rutherford

Another important figure of the Assembly was undoubtedly the pastor of Anwoth, the exile in Aberdeen, the professor of St. Mary's College in St. Andrews, and Westminster Divine, Samuel Rutherford (1660–1661).[28] Accurately, if with some disdain, T. F. Torrance describes Rutherford's theology as being

> cast within a framework of strict federal and predestinationist principles, which meant that his formulation and presentation of doctrine was governed throughout by forensic and logically necessary relations, and was characterized by a concentration on individual election and particular redemption.[29]

---

[27] Frame gives ten (perspectival!) reasons as to why he does not take a position regarding this debate. Of interest here is his fifth reason: "In God's mind, where the decrees take all others into account, all may be considered ends, and all may be considered means." *The Doctrine of God* (Phillipsburg: P&R, 2002), 334-39. Wayne Grudem also has little time for the debate, consigning the entire issue to a footnote in his *Systematic Theology*! He comments, "The discussion is complex and highly speculative because there is very little direct biblical data to help us with it. Good arguments have been advanced in support of each view, and there is probably some element of truth in each one. But in the last analysis it seems wiser to say that Scripture does not give us enough data to probe into this mystery, and, moreover, it does not seem very edifying to do so." *Systematic Theology* (Grand Rapids: Zondervan, 2000), 679 n. 12.

[28] For brief summaries of Rutherford's theological contributions, see John MacLeod, *Scottish Theology* (1943; repr., Edinburgh: Banner of Truth, 1974), 68-78; James Walker, *The Theology and Theologians of Scotland 1560–1750* (1872, 1888; repr., Edinburgh: Knox Press, 1982), 8-13; Sherman Isbell, "Samuel Rutherford," *Dictionary of Scottish Church History & Theology*, ed. Nigel M. de S. Cameron (Downers Grove: InterVarsity, 1993).

Rutherford's supralapsarianism is evident in his adoption of the view that the atonement was not a *necessary* element in the salvation of fallen men. God, so Rutherford reasoned, *could have if he had so willed it*, saved fallen men without a decree of atonement.[30] Peculiar as this may be, this view was also held by John Owen until he later changed his mind.[31] Rutherford's supralapsarianism can also be seen in his *The Covenant of Life Opened: or a Treatise of the Covenant of Grace*.[32] True, as Fesko points out with respect to another of Rutherford's works, *Ane Catechisme conteining the Soume of Christian Religion*,[33] his supralapsarianism is not apparent. In answer to the question, *What is the decree of predestination?*, the answer is given: *It is God's free appointment whereby*

---

[29]   Thomas F. Torrance, *Scottish Theology from John Knox to John McLeod Campbell* (Edinburgh: T&T Clark, 1996), 93. Alexander Whyte famously referred to Rutherford's "sad extremes" in *Samuel Rutherford and Some of his Correspondents* (Edinburgh & London: Oliphant Andersen and Ferrier, 1894), 17.

[30]   See Rutherford's *Disputatio Scholastica de Providentia* (1640); and *Christ Dying and Drawing Sinners to Himselfe* (1647). See also, James Walker, *Theology and Theologians of Scotland*, 68; John MacLeod, *Scottish Theology*, 70-71. Note that Rutherford's second work is published in 1647 and therefore lends proof of his (supralapsarian) view *during* the Assembly's debates on the decree.

[31]   See Carl Trueman, *Claims of Truth*, 105-11. The view was also held by William Twisse. See, *Vindiciae Gratiae* (Amsterdam, 1632). Owen's "early" view is seen in his volume on limited atonement (1647), and the later view in his work on divine justice (1653). Both are published in the *same* volume of his complete works (volume 10). See, *The Works of John Owen* (24 vols.; London: Johnstone and Hunter, 1850–1855).

[32]   (Edinburgh: Andro Anderson, 1655). See, T. F. Torrance's criticism of its doctrine of the decrees as "rigidly logical and determinist" in *Scottish Theology*, 105. Rutherford's federalism can also be seen in *Christ Dying and Drawing Sinners to Himselfe. Or A Survey of our Saviour in all his soule suffering, his loveliness in his death, and the efficacie thereof* (London, 1647). See especially the reference to "the two absolute decrees of Election and Reprobation, from eternity," 311 and the discussions on pp. 401f.

[33]   The Catechism was first published from manuscript form by A. F. Mitchell in 1886 in a collection of Catechisms, including one by Herbert Palmer [also a member of the Assembly]. Mitchell debates as to whether it was Palmer's or Rutherford's Catechism that lies principally behind the form and structure of the Shorter Catechism. See, A. F. Mitchell, *Catechisms of the Second Reformation* (London: James Nisbet, 1886).

he decrees to pass by some and to leave them to the hardness of their heart – a decidedly *infra*lapsarian answer![34] What are we to make of this? Either Rutherford regarded the issue as wholly unimportant such that his conscience wasn't the least bit troubled by a statement which clearly went contrary to his views, or what *seems to be infralapsarian* (the language of preterition – that reprobation takes account of existing sinfulness, and therefore is an act of justice rather than mere sovereignty) turns out on further inspection to be more nuanced than at first appears.

Explanations for the Consensus

Many have pointed out that the majority of the Westminster Divines were infralapsarians.[35] Others have equally been insistent (as we have seen) of the Confession's infralapsarianism.[36] If this is indeed the case, it means that the supralapsarians were willing to concede something which they felt important enough to argue strongly, both at the Assembly itself *and* in published volumes on predestination. True, Twisse died before the final outcome of the chapter was agreed upon, and one can but conjecture what he would have made of it; but, others (including Rutherford) could subscribe to it without controversy.

One explanation (Fesko) is to suggest that the supralapsarians did not hold to their view with any great enthusiasm. Another is to suggest that the Divines were possessed of such irenic zeal for unity that such divisions on "subtle questions" belonged to professional theologians rather than confessions.[37]

---

[34] The question and answer comes early in the Catechism on the section (4), "Of Predestination." See, Mitchell, *Catechisms of the Second Reformation*, 163. See, Fesko, "The Westminster Confession and Lapsarianism," 2:498.

[35] Mitchell, *Westminster Assembly*, 338; Mitchell, *Minutes*, 150-51; Warfield, "Westminster Assembly," 374; Hodge, *Systematic Theology*, 2:317; Fesko, "Westminster Confession and Lapsarianism," 2:497.

[36] MacPherson, *Confession of Faith*, 50.

[37] Mitchell, *Minutes*, 150. Fesko notes a similar comment of Rutherford's Scottish colleague, Robert Baillie, *Letters and Journals*, 3:6. See Fesko, "Westminster Confession and Lapsarianism," 2:498.

But this explanation is unconvincing, not least because interpreters of the Confession continue to insist that it adopts an infralapsarian position, rather than a neutral one. There may not have been much zeal to adopt a specific *ordo decretorum* within the Confession, *but adopt one they did* – one to which both supralapsarians and infralapsarians could subscribe without caveat.

Perhaps another explanation is in order, one that raises significant hermeneutical issues: that the Confession *deliberately* chose a wording to which both supralapsarians and infralapsarians could equally subscribe.

The point must be made again, that the lapsarian issue was one dear to the hearts of many at the Assembly, and strongly held views were maintained on both sides. These were Calvinists of the strongest kind.

There is no suggestion that they were producing something which merely required general, unspecified assent. How, then, could both supralapsarians and infralapsarians adopt the wording: "they who are elected, *being fallen in Adam*, are redeemed by Christ" (3.6) and "The rest [the non-elect] of mankind God was pleased . . . to pass by; and to ordain them to dishonor and wrath *for their sin*" (3.7) – both statements viewed by many as infralapsarian? Only, it would seem, if both groups read these statements differently – the supralapsarians *sub specie temporis*, the infralapsarians *sub specie aeternitatis*. Far from refusing to adopt a position on the *ordo decretorum*, the Divines produced a formulation that was agreeable to two diverse parties! John Murray is therefore correct (and almost singularly so) when he suggests that the chapter "is non-committal on the supralapsarian and infralapsarian debate."[38] To assume that the expression "being fallen in Adam" assumes that the decree of election and reprobation contemplates (logically)

---

[38] John Murray, "Theology of the Westminster Confession," 4:249.

their fallen condition is unwarranted.[39] The supralapsarians would never agree to that!

Much is made of the distinction in the language of Chapter 3 of the Confession between "predestination" and "foreordination." The elect are said to be "predestinated," and the reprobate are said to be "foreordained." It is sometimes argued in the interest of avoiding the doctrine of "equal ultimacy" that the Divines deliberately chose to signal their distaste for the view that election to everlasting life and election to everlasting death were mirror images: both sovereignly determined in the same manner and to the same degree.[40]

It is doubtful that this is what the chapter means. As John Murray has so eloquently expressed, no ground or reason is given for the passing by of the non-elect except the sovereign will of God – "God was pleased, according to the unsearchable counsel of His own will, whereby He extendeth or withholdeth mercy, as He pleaseth, . . . to pass by."

> If sin were introduced as the reason for passing by, then all would be passed by in this category. But it is otherwise when the thought of ordination to dishonour and wrath is introduced. The only ground upon which dishonour and wrath may be inflicted is sin. These are the judgment of God upon sin; therefore, sin must be posited wherever they are in exercise. The distinction is thus obvious, and if we once accede to the pure sovereignty of God in the differentiation between elect and non-elect, the distinction will be seen to be necessary.[41]

True, the Assembly did not see the lapsarian issue as one worth separating over; it did not belong to primary doctrine, but neither

---

[39] It is equally possible to apply the same interpretation to Rutherford's Catechism, *The Sum of Saving Knowledge*. God's decree "to pass by" is a sovereign determination made without any consideration of sin. If sin were to be introduced at this point as a consideration, all would be passed by!

[40] E.g. Berkouwer, *Divine Election*, 172-217.

[41] John Murray, "Theology of the Westminster Confession," 4:250.

was a formulation on predestination possible without some regard to the issue. The assumption that the Divines did so by using an infralapsarian formulation is too simplistic.

The third chapter of the Confession, then, provides evidence of the sheer brilliance of the Divines: men whose concern for unity did not outweigh their concern for doctrine that many have considered scholastic and austere.

The Amyraldians

A. F. Mitchell argued that the Confession's formulation on the decree in chapter 3 made it possible not only for the infra- and supralapsarians to agree to it, it also made it possible for the Amyraldians to do so.[42] Both William Cunningham and B. B. Warfield disagreed.[43] Whatever the conclusion may be in regard to Chapter 3 (and it is difficult to be certain), it is made abundantly clear in Chapter 8: "Of Christ the Mediator." Section 5 makes the statement

---

[42] Mitchell, *Minutes*, xx, 152. I employ the generic term, "Amyraldianism" in this paper, though recent research tends to employ the term "hypothetical universalism" when referring to the likes of Edmund Calamy because his position isn't strictly derived from Continental Amyraldianism. See, A. Craig Troxel, "Amyraut 'at' the Assembly: The Westminster Confession of Faith and the Extent of the Atonement" in *Presbyterion* 22, no. 1 (1996): 43-55. The principal Amyraldian at the Assembly was the Cambridge Calvinist, Edmund Calamy (1600–1666). Although not a member of the Assembly (he died before its inception), John Davenant (1576–1641), a strong Amyraldian and a member of the Synod of Dort, was known to have heavily influenced certain members of the Assembly. Calamy argued that all men should be *salvabiles, non obstante lapsu Adam* . . . [salvable, notwithstanding Adam's fall]. Exchanges between Calamy, Gillespie, and Rutherford make it clear that the debate over Amyraldian principles was intense. See, David Blunt, "Debate of Redemption at the Westminster Assembly," *British Reformed Journal*, January-March 1996.

[43] See William Cunningham, *Historical Theology*, (2 vols.; London: Banner of Truth, 1969), 2:327-28; B. B. Warfield, "Westminster Assembly and Its Work," 6:56; John Murray, "The Theology of the Westminster Confession of Faith," 4:255-56. Murray comments on page 256: "It has been maintained that the Assembly formulated at least one section so as to allow for an Amyraldian doctrine of the atonement. The Minutes of the Assembly give no support to this contention. There are three principles enunciated in the Confession that exclude the Amyraldian view. The first is that redemption has been purchased

that Christ "purchased, not only reconciliation, but an everlasting inheritance in the kingdom of heaven, for those whom the Father has given unto Him." Whilst this does not refer to the decree, nor in itself rule out the possibility of a hypothetical atonement in addition to this effectual one, what is said in section 8 is interpretively significant: the atonement is made existentially effective in *all those for whom Christ has purchased salvation.* The only option is universalism (and the Amyraldians were *not* universalists) or a declaration of limited atonement making it impossible for the Amyraldians to subscribe. J. V. Fesko makes a valiant attempt to adopt Mitchell's thesis: that the welcome of Edmund Calamy at the Assembly implies "explicit disapprobation of Amyraldianism is not present in the Confession."[44] Only by ignoring the explicit connection in WCF 8.8, of the *intent* of the atonement ("all those for whom Christ has purchased salvation") and the *application* of redemption ("He does certainly and effectually apply and communicate the same") can this be achieved. Amyraldian, this is not!

The Confession into the 21ˢᵗ Century

What lessons can we draw in the 21st century from this 17th century debate? Three seem to be apparent:

First, the Divines saw no contradiction in espousing a doctrine of predestination that included a statement that appears to some to be an infralapsarian rendition of the relationship between the fall and election, and to others a supralapsarian one. Whatever our interpretation of Chapter 3, it is evident that, in some form or another, the Divines tackled one of the most prickly issues of all

---

for the elect. . . (Chapter VIII, Section V). The second is that impetration and application are coextensive . . . (Chapter VIII, Section VIII). The redemption purchased includes . . . the purchase of an everlasting inheritance, and this is therefore said to be communicated to all for whom redemption was purchased. . . . The third principle is the exclusiveness of redemption . . . (Chapter III, Section VI)."

44   "Westminster Confession and Lapsarianism," 2:508-13.

theology, then as now. Charges that the Divines were influenced by the scholastic trend of late 16th and early 17th-century theology – predestinarian theology as formulated by Theodore Beza on the continent and William Perkins in England to be precise – are often made with more hysteria than precision.[45] Recent scholarship in this area has been much more accommodating to the positive contributions of scholastic scholarship employed by the Assembly rather than seeing purely detrimental implications.[46] These men loved truth so much that they dared to express it in ways so "precise" (the original charge made against the Puritans is they were "too precise" and therefore, "precisionists") that we still find ourselves endeavoring to interpret it today. Truth mattered to them. The doctrine of predestination, as expressed by Calvin, Beza, Perkins, and others found its way into everyday religious language. Far from shunning the truth, they embraced it. They were passionate about the expression of it. We need a recovery

---

[45] The charge has been made in various forms, the more important of them being, Brian G. Armstrong, *Calvinism and the Amyraut Controversy*, 38-42, 128-33, 158ff; R. T. Kendall *Calvin and English Calvinism to 1649* (Oxford: Oxford University Press, 1979), 1-41 and 209ff; and "The Puritan Modification of Calvin's Theology," in *John Calvin: His Influence in the Western World*, ed. W. Stanford Reid (Grand Rapids: Zondervan, 1982), 199-216; Phillip Holtrop, *The Bolsec Controversy on Predestination, from 1551-1555* (Lampeter: Mellen, 1993). Responses have also come in a variety of forms, some of the most important of which are Richard Muller, *Christ and the Decrees: Christology and Predestination in Reformed Theology from Calvin to Perkins* (Grand Rapids: Baker, 1988); Paul Helm, *Calvin and the Calvinists* (Edinburgh: Banner of Truth, 1982); Richard Gamble, "Switzerland: Triumph and Decline" in *John Calvin: His Influence in the Western World*, 55-73; Joel Beeke *Assurance of Faith: Calvin, English Puritanism, and the Dutch Second Reformation* (New York: Peter Lang, 1991), 78-104; and before these, William Cunningham, *The Reformers and the Theology of the Reformation* (1862; repr., London: Banner of Truth, 1967), 345-512.

[46] For "positive" evaluations of scholastic influence on the sixteenth century, see Richard A. Muller, *Post-Reformation Reformed* Dogmatics, (4 vols.; Grand Rapids: Baker, 2004); Willem van Asselt, Eef Decker, and Richard A Muller, eds., *Reformation and Scholasticism: An Ecumenical Enterprise* (Grand Rapids: Baker, 2001); Carl Trueman, and R. Scott Clark , eds. *Protestant Scholasticism* (Carlisle: Paternoster, 1999).

of that infectious theological debate. Ignorance and distaste for theological precision infects our age and our church. Chapter 3 of the Westminster Confession is a humbling indictment of our theological ignorance. Can we return to these heady days when the language of the intricacies of the decree produced passionate responses? At the very least, the seventeenth century was passionate about theology in a way that ours seemingly is not.

Second, the Divines were men of irenic temperament. It wasn't truth *or* unity. It was both. One gets the impression that Christ's prayer for the church's unity mattered deeply to them: "Holy Father, keep them in your name, which you have given me, that they may be one, even as we are one" (John 17:11 ESV). Unity comes by embracing the truth, not by discarding it. Of interest here is that the Divines made it possible for the infra- and supralapsarians to agree on a joint consensus wording, but one which equally made it impossible for Amyraldians to subscribe. It is an interesting commentary upon the Assembly ecclesiology when accommodation was made possible for supralapsarians but not for "four-pointers." In refusing to formulate detailed formulations on the order of the decrees, as well as the millennium, mediate or immediate imputation of Adam's sin, or a definitive explanation of what constitutes Presbyterian polity, the Westminster Divines were giving credence to a Pauline concept of "first things" (1 Cor. 15:3). No confession should contain judgments on what is speculative, private, or cultural. As such, the Confession continues to be a template for both orthodoxy and consensus.

Third, it is crucial to see the placing of the doctrine of decrees in the Confession. Some might argue (drawing from Calvin) that it should be placed later, possibly after Chapter 8. That would establish the Christological (and infralapsarian!) focus of the Confession. As such, it would reflect the order of Romans – post *ordo salutis* (chapters 9–11). But too much is made of this Calvinian *Retractiones*. Biblical warrant for the placing of the discussion of the decrees within a doctrine of God is also Pauline, as Ephesians 1 testifies.[47] The Confession places a robust chapter on the doctrine of God *before* its chapter on the decrees. The sovereignty thus espoused in Chapter 3 is the sovereignty of the Trinitarian God of Chapter 2. And any suggestion that this is an employment of "scholastic logic" (even of the kind Samuel Rutherford termed "needle-headed schoolmen")[48] needs to be carefully weighed by the Assembly's regard to the fundamental nature of the doctrine of Scripture in Chapter 1. Indifference over the lapsarian debate is impossible! The key issue is *not* the logical sequence in the decree; rather; it is in the condition of humanity as considered by the decree. Evangelism will employ a position one way or another and the Confession's magisterial pronouncement would be difficult to improve upon.

---

[47] For a robust and careful treatment of this entire issue, see Muller, *After Calvin*, 63-72, 95-98.

[48] *Christ Dying and Drawing Sinners to Himselfe* (London, 1647), page 2 of the introductory epistle (no page numbers in the original), cited by Trueman, *Claims of Truth*, 31.

The New Perspective:
Paul, Luther, and Judaism

Donald Macleod

The phrase, "The New Perspective on Paul," was first used by Professor James D. G. Dunn, who chose it as the title of his 1982 Manson Memorial Lecture.[1] Ever since, he has been one of its foremost proponents, but, as he himself was quick to acknowledge, its real architect was E. P. Sanders, whose *Paul and Palestinian Judaism* (published in 1977)[2] had broken the mold into which descriptions of Paul's life and theology had been poured for centuries. Krister Stendhal, however, had already given Pauline studies a severe jolt with his seminal article, "The Apostle Paul and the Introspective Conscience of the West."[3] Other scholars quickly adopted the New Perspective, most notable among them being N. T. Wright, who gave it a qualified endorsement as early as 1978[4] and continued to use it as the foundation of a series of major Pauline studies.[5] Soon, the New Perspective had

[1] Subsequently reprinted in the *Bulletin of the John Rylands Library* 65 (1983): 95-122.

[2] E. P. Sanders, *Paul and Palestinian Judaism* (London: SCM Press, 1977).

[3] Reprinted in *Paul among Jews and Gentiles* (Philadelphia: Fortress, 1976), 78-96. First published in *Harvard Theological Review* 56 (1963): 78-96.

[4] See Wright's article, "The Paul of History and the Apostle of Faith" in the *Tyndale Bulletin* 29:61-88.

[5] Most notably, *The Climax of the Covenant* (Edinburgh: T&T Clark, 1991); "Romans and the Theology of Paul" in D. M. Hay and E. E. Johnson, eds.,

precipitated what Douglas Moo called "an avalanche of print."[6] Much of this "avalanche" is safe only for experts in Second Temple and Tannaitic Judaism, but the New Perspective also has clear implications for historical and systematic theology. It has particularly serious implications for the confessional theology (and hence the preaching) of Protestantism. If Stendahl, Sanders, Dunn, and Wright are correct, Luther and Calvin were profoundly wrong, Protestant theologians have seriously miscued the whole doctrine of salvation, and Protestant creeds and pulpits have been preaching a flawed message.

Judaism: A Religion of Grace

In the first instance the New Perspective is not so much a new perspective on Paul as a new perspective on Judaism. Here, the lines of battle are clearly drawn. The Old Perspective is that of Martin Luther, who, driven by his "introspective conscience" drew a sharp contrast between Judaism and Christianity, attributing to the former the worst features of medieval Catholicism. Christianity was a religion of grace; Judaism was a religion of law, proclaiming salvation by works and urging men and women to build up a balance of merit by performing "works of torah," thus ensuring that their good deeds outweighed their bad deeds.

Sanders rejects this as a travesty of Judaism and argues the opposite: far from being a legalistic religion of "works righteousness," Judaism was a religion of grace. Israel's faith was rooted in divine election, and this was a matter of mercy, not of human achievement. You did not earn membership of the covenant people by keeping the Torah. The Torah was for those who were already *in*, by grace. The Law was about "staying in," not about

---

Pauline Theology: Volume III, Romans (Minneapolis: Fortress, 1995), 30-67; and "The Letter to the Romans: Introduction, Commentary and Reflections" in *The New Interpreter's Bible* (Nashville: Abingdon, 2002), 10:393-770.

[6] Douglas Moo, "Paul and the Law in the Last Ten Years," *Scottish Journal of Theology* 40 (1987): 287-307. The words quoted occur on p. 288.

"getting in"; and even staying in did not require perfect compliance with the law. It required, instead, what Sanders called "covenantal nomism," and one key element of this was that it actually provided for infringements of the Torah. There was a covenant way of dealing with breaches of the law. You made atonement (through the cultic sacrifices) and you repented.

Sanders was not the first to question Luther's portrayal of Judaism. Thirty years earlier, W. D. Davies had warned against the tendency to contrast Pauline Christianity as a religion of faith and the Spirit with rabbinic Judaism as "a religion of obedience and the Torah."[7] Davies himself was following in the footsteps of G. F. Moore who, as early as 1927, spoke of the prejudice with which many scholars referred to Judaism and described that prejudice as a Protestant inheritance from Luther's controversy with Catholicism. Moore went on to assert that "a lot in the world to come" (the closest approximation in Judaism to the Christian idea of salvation) "is ultimately assured to every Israelite on the ground of the original election of the people by the free grace of God, prompted not by its merits, collective or individual, but solely by God's love. . . . These facts are ignored when Judaism is set in antithesis to Christianity. . . . If the one is grace, so is the other."[8]

We should note, however, that if Luther was driven by an introspective conscience, the modern Christian West has its own problem of conscience: the Jewish Holocaust. There is little doubt that one force driving the New Perspective is real sensitivity to the possibility that Nazi anti-Semitism grew on the root of Lutheran anti-Judaism. This is reflected in, for example, N. T. Wright's approach to Romans 9–11: "If this section is ignored or downplayed, there is an open and often-travelled road towards anti-Semitism. A case can be made out, in fact, for saying that the standard

---

[7] W. D. Davies, *Paul and Rabbinic Judaism* (3rd ed.; London: SPCK, 1970), 221.

[8] G. F. Moore, *Judaism in the First Centuries of the Christian Era* (3 vols.; Cambridge: Harvard, 1927–30), 2:93-95.

Protestant exegesis of Romans, in which Romans 9–11 was marginalized, robbed the church of the best weapon it could have had for identifying and combating some of the worst evils of the Third Reich. . . . No one who has followed the main movements of modern theology will need reminding how important these issues have been in the post-holocaust re-evaluation of the church's relationship to Judaism."[9]

Jürgen Moltmann shows a similar sensitivity, although from a different perspective. He is anxious lest his emphasis on the uniqueness of Christ be seen as anti-Judaism: "Christian-Jewish dialogue today must be a tentative dialogue – especially in Germany – for it is a dialogue between the sufferers and the guilty."[10] Yet contrition for the Holocaust cannot by itself offer a total explanation for either the emergence of the New Perspective or the welcome accorded to it. As P. S. Alexander points out, "It is surely significant that most of these scholars have either been Christians of liberal Protestant background or Jews arguably influenced by liberal Protestant ideas."[11] Such a background would provide little sympathy with classical Lutheranism. Instead, it would predispose them to see their own liberalism reflected from the bottom of the rabbinic well. It would then be tempting to minimize the differences between Judaism and Christianity and

---

[9]   *The Climax of the Covenant*, 233. Cf. Wright's later comment: "It was not merely neo-paganism, but Christian complicity with neo-paganism, that sent millions of Jews to their deaths in our own century" (p. 253).

[10] J. Moltmann, *The Way of Jesus Christ* (London: SCM, 1990), xvii. Cf. Stuhl-macher's comment on the background to the New Perspective: "We must also keep in mind the apparent goal of these authors to make a new beginning in Pauline interpretation, so as to free Jewish-Christian dialogue from improper accusations against the Jewish conversation partners" in *Revisiting Paul's Doctrine of Justification* (Downers Grove: InterVarsity, 2001), 34.

[11] From an essay, "Torah and Salvation in Tanaitic Literature" in Carson, O'Brien, and Seifrid, eds., *Justification and Variegated Nomism, Volume I: The Complexities of Second Temple Judaism* (Grand Rapids: Baker, 2001), 271. Besides Sanders, Alexander has in mind such scholars as G. F. Moore, S. Schechter, and C. G. Montefiore.

in particular to play down any suggestion that the one faith is superior to the other.

This meshes well with the post-Holocaust theme. The psychology of modern European theology sees it as part of our collective repentance to mute our criticism of Jewish theology and to replace "mission" to the Jews with dialogue; and at the same time liberal Protestantism is happy to see Christianity as no more than a new phase or dispensation of Judaism. Krister Stendahl clearly reflects this when he speaks of Paul's Damascus Road experience as not a "conversion" but a "calling." Saul of Tarsus did not give up his ancestral faith. He remained a Jew, but one called to engage in mission to the Gentiles; and by the same token his converts, the Gentile Christians, were in reality "honorary Jews."[12]

But not all those who sympathise with the New Perspective share this assessment of the relation between Judaism and Christianity. N. T. Wright, for example is fully aware that since the Holocaust, "Shrill voices from all sides" denounce Christian missions to Jews on the ground that "to say that Jesus is the true Messiah for Jews as well as Gentiles is to be implicitly anti-Semitic or at least anti-Judaic, hinting that Judaism is somehow incomplete."[13] Wright sees this as running exactly counter to Paul's argument in Romans 9–11, where the apostle's whole concern is to demonstrate that Gentile Christians have not "replaced" Jews as the true people of God and that the church has not become "an exclusively Gentile possession." In fact, Wright sees the anti-missions position as profoundly ironic: "Precisely because the gospel stands athwart all ethnic claims, the church cannot erect a new racial boundary. The irony of this is that the late twentieth century, in order to avoid anti-Semitism, has advocated a position (the non-evangelisation of the Jews) *which Paul regards precisely as anti-Semitic.*"[14]

---

[12] K. Stendahl, *Paul among Jews and Gentiles* (Philadelphia: Fortress, 1976), 9, 37.

[13] *The Climax of the Covenant*, 253.

[14] Ibid., 253. The italics are Wright's.

There is also another balancing factor. As G. F. Moore points out, Judaism itself was a missionary religion and as such extremely successful in securing proselytes. This itself rested on the principle of exclusiveness: if Yahweh was the one true God then Judaism was the one true religion and all others were false. This is the main reason that Judaism posed such a problem to the legislators of the Roman Empire. In that world all sorts of religions existed amicably and respectfully beside each other. The Jews didn't fit into this. They saw Judaism as destined to become the one universal faith and regularly commented scathingly on the idolatry, folly, and viciousness of other religions.[15] Nothing can detract from the horror of the Holocaust, and the church cannot lightly absolve itself of responsibility. But we must avoid the opposite error of portraying Judaism as all sweetness and light, free from the stigma of intolerance. Judaism itself could be a persecuting religion: indeed, under such leaders as Saul of Tarsus it came within an ace of destroying Christianity in its cradle. Admittedly, Jews alone were excluded from the universal toleration practiced by Rome, but this "was chiefly because they alone were intolerant."[16] When it became clear that Christians saw themselves as the true heirs to the covenant, Jesus as the only Lord, and faith in Christ as the only way to salvation, they quickly fell victims to this very intolerance.

Luther

There can be no denying that Martin Luther saw Judaism as a legalistic religion which encouraged its adherents to believe in salvation by works. In Luther's later years this degenerated into fierce anti-Semitism.[17] Yet there is no reason to think that he ever

---

[15] See, for example, N. T. Wright's observation that in his indictment of paganism in Romans 1:18-32 Paul "draws extensively on traditional Jewish critiques of the pagan world" in "The Letter to the Romans," in *The New Interpreter's Bible*, vol. 10 (Nashville: Abingdon, 2002), 428.428.

[16] G. F. Moore, *Judaism*, 1:323.

abandoned his belief (expressed particularly in his commentary on Romans 11:28), that "the Jews at the end of the world will return to the faith."[18] It is notable, too, that his negative comments in the great soteriological commentaries (*Romans* and *Galatians*) are seldom directed at Judaism as such and certainly not at Judaism exclusively. The real target is the medieval religion of merit, identified with "the sophists and the scholastics." Judaism is targeted only by analogy. For example, commenting on Galatians 3:13 he writes, "No sophist or legalist or Jew or fanatic or anyone else speaks this way."

In the "Argument" to the same commentary he writes:

> So it is that the Turks perform different works from the papists, and the papists perform different works from the Jews. And so forth. But although some do works that are more splendid, great and difficult than others, the content remains the same and only the quality is different. That is, the works vary only in appearance and in name. For they are still works. And those who do them are not Christians; they are hirelings, whether they are called Jews, Mohammedans, papists or sectarians.[19]

This same pattern appears in Melanchthon's *Loci Communes*, where the real target is not Judaism specifically but "the godless

---

[17] On Luther's anti-Semitism see G. Keith, *Hated Without a Cause?* (Carlisle: Paternoster, 1997), 149-74. Keith warns against equating Luther's attitude with that of the Third Reich, arguing that the Reformer "never envisaged attacks on the persons of the Jews." Nevertheless, Luther did allow himself to write, "Dear Christian, be on your guard against the Jews, who . . . are consigned by the wrath of God to the devil, who has not only robbed them of a proper understanding of Scripture, but also of ordinary human reason, shame, and sense, and only works mischief with Holy Scripture through them. Therefore, they cannot be trusted and believed in any other matter either" (cited by Keith, 159).

[18] Luther's *Works* (Saint Louis: Concordia, 1972), 25:429.

[19] *Works*, 26:10. Cf. Luther's comments in *The Freedom of a Christian*, referring to those who, "having no faith, boast of, prescribe, and insist upon their ceremonies as means of justification": "Such were the Jews of old, who were unwilling to learn how to do good. These [the Christian] must resist, do the very opposite, and offend them boldly lest by their impious view they drag many with them into error. In the presence of such men it is good to eat meat, break the fasts, and

sophist professors of theology" or "the common run of sophists."[20] Neither Luther nor Melanchthon had any pretensions to being experts on Tannaitic Judaism: they drew with a broad brush. More recent Lutherans have been both better informed and more specific. Bultmann, for example, remarking that the fundamental idea of the Jewish ethic is blind obedience, writes:

> Along with this view, belief in the *meritoriousness* of conduct according to the Law easily established itself. In fact the dependence on good works, the pride in good works, evidently played a fatal part in late Judaism. The religious man expects to be able to call God's attention to his merits, he believes that he has a claim on God.[21]

Calvin and Calvinism fully endorsed Luther's doctrine of justification, including its critique of Judaism. For example, commenting on Romans 2:25 Calvin wrote: "The Jews thought that circumcision was of itself sufficient for the purpose of obtaining righteousness. . . . With regard to the Pharisees, who are content with making an external pretence of holiness, we need not wonder that they so easily delude themselves."[22]

For the most part, Calvin's dialogue, like Melanchthon's, is with "our opponents," under such soubriquets as "the schools of

---

for the sake of liberty of faith do other things which they regard as the greatest of sins" in *Works*, 31:373.

[20] W. Pauck, ed., *Melanchthon and Bucer* (Library of Christian Classics, Vol. 19; Philadelphia: Westminster, 1969), 74, 89.

[21] R. Bultmann, *Jesus and the Word*, trans. Louise Pettibone Smith and Erminie Huntress Lantero (London: Collins, 1958), 56. A similar modern Lutheran perspective appears in Ernst Käsemann's essay, "Paul and Israel": "Religion always provides man with his most thorough-going possibility of confusing an illusion with God. Paul sees this possibility realised in the devout Jew: inasmuch as the announcement of God's will in the law is here misunderstood as a summons to human achievement and therefore as a means to a righteousness of one's own" in *New Testament Questions of Today*, (New Testament Library 41; London: SCM, 1969), 184.

[22] John Calvin, *The Epistles of Paul the Apostle to the Romans and to the Thessalonians* (Grand Rapids: Eerdmans, 1995), 55.

Sorbonne."[23] Yet there were significant differences between Lutheranism and Calvinism. It would be foolhardy to claim that the Reformed churches have never been tainted by anti-Semitism, but they have certainly produced a fair number of Judeo-philes. Some of these Judeo-philes have been premillennialists such as Andrew Bonar and Robert McCheyne.[24] Others, such as the English Presbyterian, Adolph Saphir, have themselves been of Jewish background. Saphir, who along with Dr. Alfred Edersheim was profoundly influenced by Dr. John Duncan's mission to Jews in Budapest (1841–1843), was particularly careful not to exaggerate the legalism of the Pharisees: "Do not think that the Pharisees were all hypocrites. They were all in danger of becoming hypocrites, and some of them were hypocrites, but many of them were godly, religious, earnest men, and they truly reverenced the Scriptures, and had a zeal for God."[25] On the other side of the Atlantic, Dr. J. Gresham Machen was uttering a similar caution: "Exaggerations certainly should be avoided; there are certainly many noble utterances to be found among the sayings of the Jewish teachers; it is not to be supposed that formalism was unrelieved by any manifestations of goodness of the heart."[26]

Such Judeo-philia has not led to any let-up in anti-pharisaic polemic, but it has certainly limited anti-Semitism in countries such as Scotland where the Reformed influence was strong. This has been openly acknowledged by Jews themselves. For example, David Daiches, the son of an Edinburgh rabbi, records his father's warm feelings for Scotland as "one of the few countries in Europe . . . where the Jews had never been persecuted," and his constant

---

[23] John Calvin, *Institutes of the Christian Religion*, ed. John T. McNeill, trans. Ford Lewis Battles (Library of Christian Classics, vols. 20-21; Philadelphia: Westminster Press, 1960), 3.15.7.

[24] See A. A. Bonar and R. M. McCheyne, *Narrative of a Mission of Inquiry to the Jews* (Edinburgh, 1842).

[25] Adolph Saphir, *The Divine Unity of Scripture* (London: Hodder and Stoughton, 1892), 98.

[26] J. G. Machen, *The Origin of Paul's Religion* (Grand Rapids: Eerdmans, 1947), 178.

assumption "of the closest natural sympathy between Scottish Presbyterians and Jews."[27] But this was not due merely to natural Scottish tolerance. It rested on the deeply held belief that the Jews were still central to God's purpose. They were not his "ancient people," but, quite simply, his people. This was the impetus behind Presbyterian missions to the Jews. They were not a gesture of hostility towards Judaism, but a commitment to working in harmony with God's plan to save "all Israel."[28] Whether such a missiology is biblically justified may, of course, be debated, but it is at least a far cry from anti-Semitism.

Of far greater theological significance, however, was Calvinism's radically different attitude to the law. For Lutheranism, the law had two functions: one civil, the other theological.

> The first understanding and use of the law is to restrain the wicked. . . . The other use of the law is the theological or spiritual one, which serves to increase transgressions. This is the primary purpose of the Law of Moses, that through it sin might grow and be multiplied, especially in the conscience. Paul discusses this magnificently in Rom. 7. Therefore the true function and the chief and proper use of the Law is to reveal to man his sin, blindness, misery, wickedness, ignorance, hate and contempt of God, death, judgement, and the well-deserved wrath of God. Yet this use of the Law is completely unknown to the hypocrites, the sophists in the universities, and to all men who go long in the presumption of the righteousness of the Law or of their own righteousness.[29]

---

[27] D. Daiches, *Two Worlds* (ed.2; Edinburgh: Canongate, 1997), 97.

[28] See, for example, the remark of Bonar and McCheyne (*Narrative*, 322): "There is no country under heaven to which Christians turn with such a lively interest as Immanuel's land . . . those who love Israel bear it upon their hearts, because its name is inwoven with the coming conversion of Israel."

[29] Luther, *Works*, 26:308ff. (commenting on Galatians 3:19). Cf. Melanchthon (*Melanchthon and Bucer*, 79): "The work of the law is to kill and to damn, to reveal the root of our sin, and to perplex us. It mortifies not only avarice and desire, but the root of all evils, our love of self, the judgement of reason, and whatever good our nature seems to possess."

This is the classic Lutheran understanding of the law as "the schoolmaster" who leads us to Christ. The law reveals sin, convicts of sin, and thus drives us away from all self-righteousness into the arms of the Savior.[30]

Calvin fully endorsed these two uses of the law, but he would not have endorsed Luther's protests that the law has nothing to do with Christians.[31] On the contrary, his doctrine of the "third use" of the law insists strenuously on its applicability to believers: "The third and principal use, which pertains more closely to the proper purpose of the law, finds its place among believers in whose hearts the Spirit of God already lives and reigns."[32] This is a conscious rejection of the views of those who argue that in respect of believers the law is completely abrogated. Instead, says Calvin, it is the law which shows us on a daily basis what the will of God is; and it is the law which incites us to obedience: "The law is to the flesh like a whip to an idle and balky ass, to arouse it to work. Even for a spiritual man not yet free of the weight of the flesh the law remains a constant sting that will not let him stand still."[33]

This immediately alerts us to the fact that the Torah may play a far more significant role in Calvinism than it does in Lutheranism. It also creates an instant possibility that Calvinism can assimilate the notion of "covenantal nomism" in a way that Lutheranism never could: a possibility which requires further exploration.

---

[30] See Luther on Galatians 3:24: "With its whippings it drives us to Christ, just as a good teacher whips, trains and disciplines his pupils in reading and writing with the purpose of bringing them to a knowledge of the liberal arts and of other good things, so that eventually they may do with pleasure what initially, when they were forced to do it by the teacher, they did involuntarily" in *Works*, 26:346.

[31] "The righteousness of the heart ignores all laws, not only those of the pope but also those of Moses." (*Works*, 26:226).

[32] Calvin, *Institutes*, 2.7.12. This is reflected in the Westminster Confession: cf. *The Marrow of Modern Divinity*, ed. Thomas Boston (1726; repr., Edinburgh, 1818).

[33] *Institutes*, 2.7.12.

E. P. Sanders

But despite these qualifications, historic Lutheranism and historic Calvinism stand shoulder to shoulder on the core issue: the Judaism confronted by the Apostle Paul was a form of legalism. Has the work of Sanders rendered this view untenable?

We must note, first of all, that Sanders' portrayal of Judaism would serve as an entirely accurate description of Old Testament religion. This was no legalism. It was a faith rooted firmly in election, mercy, and grace. This is clearly emphasized in the giving of the Decalogue itself. Israel was not redeemed from Egypt because it had kept the Torah. It would keep the Torah because it had been redeemed: "I am the Lord your God, who brought you out of the land of Egypt, out of the house of bondage. You shall have no other gods before me" (Exod. 20:2 RSV[34]). Here, the indicatives of salvation take clear precedence over the imperatives of the law. Salvation comes before works.

The same note is sounded in the affirmation of Israel's election in Deuteronomy 7:7: "It was not because you were more in number than any other people that the Lord set his love upon you and chose you, for you were the fewest of all peoples; but it is because the Lord loves you, and is keeping the oath which he swore to your fathers."

The piety of Israel clearly grasped this principle. In Psalm 51, for example, the covenant-breaker, David, knows with absolute certainty that there can be no legalistic or cultic atonement for his sin: "For thou hast no delight in sacrifice; were I to give a burnt offering, thou wouldst not be pleased" (Ps. 51:16). Instead, his whole trust is in the mercy of God: "Have mercy on me, O God, according to thy steadfast love; according to thy abundant mercy blot out my transgressions" (Ps. 51:1). This explains why Calvin can speak of the Old Testament as established by the free mercy of God and of the Jews as "those to whom the doctrine

---

[34] All following Scripture references are taken from the RSV.

of the righteousness of faith was imparted."[35] These sentiments are echoed in the Westminster Confession: "The justification of believers under the Old Testament was . . . one and the same with the justification of believers under the New Testament" (WCF 11.6). This, of course, is the precise argument which Paul *appears* to be using in Romans 4:1-12 and Galatians 3:6-18. Abraham and David were both justified by faith, apart from works of law.[36]

The second point to be made is that Sanders has no difficulty finding rabbinic sources from which he can quote statements to the effect, for example, that some rabbis kept the indicatives and the imperatives well balanced and in the right order; that entrance into the covenant was prior to keeping the commandments; that God first chose Israel and only then required her obedience; that disobedience as such did not remove one from the covenant; and that God's justice always gives way to his mercy whenever the two conflict. He can even argue that rabbinic thought is dominated by the idea of God's love rather than by the idea of his justice.

This does not prove, however, that there was no legalism in Jewish thought. Even less does it prove that the Judaizers with whom Paul was in conflict were not legalists. Judaism, like Christianity, embraces a wide range of opinions, and even if the evangelical note was dominant there may well have been other voices much more legalistic in tone. These voices may have been very influential in the circles in which Paul (and Jesus) moved. To some extent, Sanders himself concedes this: "The possibility cannot be completely excluded that there were Jews accurately hit by the polemic of Matt. 23, who attended only to trivia and neglected the weightier matters. Human nature being what it is, one supposes that there were some such. One must

---

[35] *Institutes*, 2.10.4.

[36] This exegesis has been challenged by, for example, N. T. Wright, who categorically dismisses the idea that Romans 4 is "an Old Testament proof" of justification by faith. See Wright's essay, "Romans and the Theology of Paul" in D. M. Hay and E. E. Johnson, eds., *Pauline Theology*, 39.

say, however, that the surviving Jewish literature does not reveal them."[37]

This last sentence cleverly excludes the Gospels (and possibly Paul) from the body of relevant evidence. Leaving that aside, however, the force of the whole argument is considerably weakened by Sanders' own admission (on the very same page) with regard to the paucity of sources for Judaism prior to AD 70:

> We have not discussed the Pharisees and Sadducees as such, for example, but only the surviving literature. It seems to me quite possible that we not only have no Sadducean literature, but also virtually no Pharisaic literature, apart from fragments embedded in the rabbinic material. Thus I know a good deal less about Pharisaism than has been "known" by many investigators.[38]

Because of these gaps in the literature, our knowledge of Judaism in the time of Paul is, according to Sanders, almost entirely inferential. We have to "hypothesize" that covenantal nomism was the basic *type* of religion known to Paul and Jesus because it is maintained so consistently in the sources available from 200 BC to AD 200. For the same reason we have to say that "the Judaism of before 70 kept grace and works in the right perspective, did not trivialise the commandments of God and was not especially marked by hypocrisy."[39]

At this point, however, Sanders' argument faces two difficulties, not necessarily fatal, but nevertheless significant.

First: is it safe to assume such consistency within Judaism between, for example, the time of Paul and the era of the Tannaim? Certainly, rabbinic Judaism has remained remarkably consistent since the end of the second century AD. But it may not always have been so. There is some evidence that the "Common Judaism" of the post-Tannaitic period was preceded by a period when there was "a

---

[37]   Sanders, *Paul and Palestinian Judaism*, 426.

[38]   Ibid.

[39]   Ibid., 427.

conglomeration of many competing Judaisms."[40] Besides, even if there was uniformity in the pre-Tannaite period, we cannot simply assume that the Rabbis reproduced it. Moore asserts, for example, that the task of the Tannaites was "one of conservation, not of reformation."[41] But what impact did the destruction of the Temple have on Judaism? We know that it rendered for ever impossible the offering of piacular sacrifice and thus made imperative the formulation of a doctrine of atonement by repentance alone. This was a paradigm shift, by any standard. What other adjustments followed in its wake?

Then there is the question of the impact which Christianity itself had on Judaism. We know, for example, that in the light of Christian use of the Septuagint the Jews commissioned and adopted the version of Aquila. Were there other changes? In particular, did the Tannaim, in response to the criticisms of Paul, modify their soteriology to give more emphasis to grace and less to the merit of obeying the Torah?

The second difficulty is that it is by no means clear that the post-70 Jewish sources are as uniform as Sanders assumes. To some extent this is a question of methodology. Following G. F. Moore, advocates of the New Perspective wish to give primacy to the official Tannaitic literature. Moore insists that, "Judaism may properly claim to be represented by the teachers and the writings which it has always regarded as in the line of its catholic tradition."[42] One problem with this is that this "catholic tradition" was launched only after AD 70. A second, and more important, problem is that it re-

---

[40] The phrase is from R. Deines in Carson, et al. eds., *Justification and Variegated Nomism*, 444. Commenting on the Tannaitic literature, P. S. Alexander makes a similar point: "It is important to realize at the very outset of our enquiry that these texts do not represent the sum-total of Judaism in the first few centuries of the current era, or even, necessarily, Jewish 'orthodoxy' at this time. This literature is the product of one particular party or movement within Judaism" ("Torah and Salvation," 262).

[41] G. F. Moore, *Judaism*, 1:131.

[42] Ibid., 1:127.

quires us to discount the numerous other Jewish writings which have come down to us from the very same period, on the ground that they are ignored in the Tannaitic literature and in the Talmud.

This is very convenient for the New Perspective, since some of this literature reflects points of view much closer to Luther's impression of Judaism. This is particularly true of the literature which has survived from the period immediately following AD 70: most notably, 4 Ezra, the *Apocalypse of Baruch*, and Josephus.[43] Sanders is aware that these embarrass his central thesis. He virtually ignores the *Apocalypse of Baruch*, and he dismisses 4 Ezra with the words, "in IV Ezra one sees how Judaism works when it actually does become a religion of individual self-righteousness. In IV Ezra, in short, we see an instance in which covenantal nomism has collapsed. All that is left is legalistic perfectionism."[44]

Sanders' solution is to note that this "legalistic perfectionism" is "contrary to the generally prevailing view." Moore takes a similar line: "inasmuch as these writings have never been recognised by Judaism, it is a fallacy of method for the historian to make them a primary source for the eschatology of Judaism, much more to contaminate its theology with them."[45] But although the Pseudepigrapha were never incorporated into canonical Judaism as defined by the Tannaim after AD 70, they may nevertheless have had considerable popular influence. Indeed, Moore himself concedes that, "From such books the historian gets glimpses of the religion of the times outside the schools."[46] It may have been in precisely such quarters that the opposition to Paul arose, and we have no right to conclude that, prior to AD 70, it represented only an insignificant minority of Jews.

---

[43] For an informed discussion of the significance of these documents see Simon Gathercole, *Where Is Boasting? Early Jewish Soteriology and Paul's Response in Romans 1–5* (Grand Rapids: Eerdmans, 2002), 136-60

[44] Sanders, *Palestinian Judaism*, 409.

[45] Moore, *Judaism*, 1:127.

[46] Ibid., 127.

A moment's reflection on the history of Christian theology should be sufficient to warn us of the risk involved in arguing that a religious community could not have held certain beliefs or observed certain practices because they are out of keeping with its creed (in the case of Paul and Judaism, a creed a hundred years later than the period under review). Christianity prides itself on being a religion of grace and has enshrined that in centuries of hymnody. Yet a recent televised rendering of the great Christmas hymn, *The First Noel*, dared to insert the following:

> If we in this life do well
> We shall be free from death and hell.

Reformed theology has sometimes suffered similar infiltrations. All its great creeds and all its representative theologians clearly set forth a religion of grace: eternal, unconditional love; justification by faith alone; preservation ("staying in") by divine power. Yet it would be perilous to argue from the mere existence and unanimity of such authorities that legalism never infiltrated the Reformed community; even more perilous to argue that no one could ever have accused it of harboring legalism because its creeds explicitly disavow it. Nor has that legalism been confined to the usual suspects, such as the Sabbatarians of the Western Isles. Take, for example, *The Marrow of Modern Divinity*. This is a full-blooded statement of Protestant theology, contemporaneous with the Westminster Confession of Faith. Yet already there is a clear awareness that legalism has reared its head within the Reformed community. One of Evangelista's dialogue partners is Nomista. His very name and presence are testimony that even as early as 1646, Calvin's doctrine of the third use of the law was being perverted in a way that threatened the evangelical heritage of the Reformation. Nomista speaks as follows:

> God requires that every Christian should frame and lead his life according to the rule of the Ten Commandments; the which if he do, then may he expect the blessing of God both upon his own

soul and body; and if he do not, then can he expect nothing else but his wrath and course upon both.[47]

The later discussion in the *Marrow* shows that Nomista saw himself as depending for salvation on a covenant of works, seeking to please God by "strict walking according to the law." It would be vain to argue that Nomista is an impossible caricature on the ground that Reformed theology has been consistently anti-legalistic.[48] It would also be risky to suppose that the legalistic Calvinist is a rarity or that the Protestant pulpit has always been faithful to Luther's doctrine of justification. Whatever the clarity of the official Protestant doctrine, there can be little doubt that the piety of many Protestants was heavily tainted with a doctrine of justification by works. This is one reason why so many (unlike Luther and Calvin) had problems with assurance. Whatever their creeds might say, "grace" suffered from fatal admixtures of self-righteousness. In all probability there was a similar disconformity between Tannaitic teaching and other streams within Judaism.

Sanders might reply, however, that Nomista is a documented figure and that there is no such documented figure within Palestinian Judaism.

Part of the answer to this is that it begs the question. The non-Tannaitic literature of Judaism may provide precisely such documentation. The Gospels and the Pauline epistles may do the same. But there is a more fundamental issue. Can we simply take Sanders' case as proved and henceforth regard it as axiomatic that the religion of the Mishnah, the Midrashim, the Targums, and the

---

[47] *The Marrow of Modern Divinity*, ed. Thomas Boston (1726; repr., Edinburgh, 1818), 27f. Boston's Preface includes a comment from Thomas Halyburton: "I dread mightily that a rational sort of religion is coming in among us; I mean by it, *a religion that consists in a bare attendance on outward duties and ordinances*" (italics mine).

[48] For the opposite point of view (that Reformed theology is inherently antinomian) consider James Hogg's *Confessions of a Justified Sinner* available in numerous editions. Luther's Jew is no more impossible (and perhaps no more typical) than Hogg's Calvinist.

Talmud was one of grace: that is, one in which eternal life was entirely a matter of divine mercy to the exclusion of works?

That question can be answered only by experts in Tannaitic and later Jewish literature. There can be no denying that the New Perspective currently holds the field, but, as Douglas Moo points out, "further critical assessment of Sanders' covenantal nomism proposal is required. Many of us *Neutestamentler* feel that Sanders' proposal fails to do justice to some important elements in both Paul and Judaism, yet feel incompetent to explore the mass of Jewish material. We eagerly await the work of the next generation of scholarship in Judaism."[49] One of that new generation is Simon Gathercole, who has subjected Sanders' thesis to detailed scrutiny in *Where Is Boasting?: Early Jewish Soteriology and Paul's Response in Romans 1–5*. Gathercole, following F. Avemarie,[50] is particularly critical of Sanders' use of rabbinic sources, arguing that far from unambiguously supporting Sanders' key concept, covenantal nomism, they actually create serious difficulties for it. Covenant language is rare in Tannaitic literature and never associated with the hope of life to come. This makes it difficult to use the covenant as an architectonic principle around which one can organize the rest of the Jewish material. But this is what Sanders does, and in the process he falls victim to his own "systematising tendency."[51] The paradigm of covenantal nomism excludes the idea of salvation or damnation by works, and this tempts Sanders into mishandling key elements in the rabbinic material: "Texts that are problematic for the main thesis are *underinterpreted*, and texts that might just support it are stretched beyond their limits."[52]

---

[49] *Scottish Journal of Theology* 40 (1987): 306 (*op. cit.*).

[50] F. Avemarie, *Tora und Leben* (Tubingen: JCB Mohr, 1996). Unfortunately, Avemarie's work has not yet been translated into English. Gathercole's high opinion of it is shared by P. S. Alexander, Professor of Post-Biblical Jewish Literature at the University of Manchester, who speaks of it as "a highly competent and subtle analysis of the rabbinic texts" in Carson, et al., eds., *Justification and Variegated Nomism*, 273.

[51] Gathercole, *Where Is Boasting?*, 155.

[52] Ibid., 155.

Gathercole, following Avemarie, cites as examples Sanders' use of three texts from Rabbi Akiba.[53] The first asserts that the world is judged by grace, but everything is according to the majority of works. The second declares that God will incline the scale in favour of anyone who has performed just one *mitsvah*. The third lays down that anyone who does *one* of the things specified in Ezekiel 18:5-9 will live.

Sanders' response is to assert that these texts provide no ground for the view that "weighing fulfilments against transgressions constitutes rabbinic soteriology."[54] Neither Gathercole nor Avemarie would dispute this. They point out, however, that Sanders completely ignores the fact that each of these texts underlines the importance of *deeds* and presupposes that obedience to the commandments is the way to salvation.[55] Indeed, the doctrine of final salvation according to works was "an integral part of the theology of Palestinian Judaism"[56] and Sanders' refusal to face this (since there is no place for it in his system) means that his model of rabbinic soteriology is inadequate, particularly in its assessment of the link between obedience to the Torah and life in the age to come.

Wider Theological Issues

When we move from the rarefied atmosphere of rabbinical studies to address wider biblical and theological issues, the New Perspective faces further serious difficulties.

What, for example, does Sanders mean by "legalism"? Moises Silva appreciates the force of some of Sanders' criticism of the Old Perspective, but nevertheless regards Sanders as operating with a definition of legalism which is fuzzy and misleading.[57] Sanders'

---

[53] Ibid., 151-52.

[54] Sanders, *Paul and Palestinian Judaism*, 138.

[55] Gathercole, *Where Is Boasting?*, 152.

[56] Ibid., 160.

[57] Moises Silva, "The Law and Christianity: Dunn's New Synthesis" in *Westminster Theological Journal* 53 (1991): 349.

touchstone is the so-called medieval merit-system according to which one's sins and one's good deeds were weighed in the divine balance and judgment passed according to which preponderated. This was certainly a caricature of Judaism (and probably also of the medieval theologians). It also misconceived the point at issue at the Reformation. The target of the Protestant polemic was not "balance," but self-salvation. Legalism is the idea that we win acceptance with God on the basis of something that is true about ourselves. That may be something we have done, something we have experienced, something infused into us, or some privilege which distinguishes us from other people. Whatever it is, if it allows us to boast about ourselves before God, it is legalism. If we deemed ourselves justified on the basis of national privilege, that would be legalism. If we deemed ourselves justified on the basis of our own covenant-keeping, that would be legalism.

Sanders operates with a much narrower definition unrelated to historical Christian theology. Indeed, according to Silva[58] he actually quotes in support of his thesis passages from (for example) Ecclesiasticus, which, to Lutheran or Protestant ears, are clearly legalistic. He prefaces these with the remark that, "Ben Sirach shared the general belief that atonement is possible. Among good deeds, two are singled out which atone for transgression. They are honouring one's father and giving alms."[59] He then quotes as follows:

Whoever honours his father atones for sins. (Eccles. 3:3)

For kindness to a father will not be forgotten,
    and as a substitute for sins it shall be firmly planted;
in the day of your affliction it will be remembered in your favour;
    as frost in fair weather, your sins will melt away. (3:14-16)

---

[58] Silva, "Law and Christianity," 348.

[59] *Paul and Palestinian Judaism*, 338.

Water extinguishes a blazing fire:
>   so almsgiving atones for sin. (3:30)

Store up almsgiving in your treasury,
>   and it will rescue you from all affliction.

This, surely, brings us within a hairsbreadth of the medieval notion of penance, with its three elements: confession, contrition, and satisfaction. To Ben Sirach, almsgiving and honoring one's father are clearly potent satisfactions.

When, later, Sanders came to focus more specifically on Paul, his fuzzy understanding of legalism betrayed him yet again, although the aberration was more pardonable. One of the subtler elements in the Protestant doctrine of justification was the insistence that faith is not the *ground* of our acceptance with God. We are justified *through* faith, not *on account of* it. The latter point of view (known as neonomianism) is represented by Nomista in the *Marrow of Modern Divinity* and, more formally, by Richard Baxter.[60] It is firmly repudiated in the Westminster Confession (11.1): "Those whom God effectually calleth he also freely justifieth . . . not by imputing faith itself, the act of believing, or any other evangelical obedience to them as their righteousness." This refinement is not known to Sanders, who writes, for example: "God righteouses the uncircumcised and the circumcised on the same basis, faith. . . . Abraham was not in fact righteoused by works . . . works would not count towards righteousness, since God counts only faith."[61] Here is the very point Protestant orthodoxy sought to avoid: the portrayal of faith itself as a meritorious work. Were Baxter's position correct, it would land us in the absurd position of putting our faith in faith itself.[62]

---

[60] See Baxter's *Imputative Righteousness Truly Stated* (London, 1679); *contra*, R. Traill, *A Vindication of the Protestant Doctrine of Justification* in Traill, *Works* (repr., Edinburgh: Banner of Truth, 1975), 1:252-96.

[61] *Paul, the Law and the Jewish People*, 33.

[62] Cf. Traill: "This faith, in the office of justification, is neither condition, nor qualification, nor our gospel-righteousness, but in it's very act a renouncing of all such pretences."

The Prophets' Critique of Old Testament Religion

But there is another infinitely more serious problem facing the New Perspective: the Old Testament prophets often spoke of the religion of their contemporaries in terms that fully match Luther's strictures on Judaism. The prophets focus on the nation's self-satisfaction, its sense of special privilege, and its reliance on formal, routine performance of the less exacting demands of the law.

Take, for example, the expression of Yahweh's displeasure in Isaiah 1:10-20, reminiscent in many ways of Paul's indictment of the Gentiles in Romans 1:18-32. The people have been indulging in useless religion: sacrifices, incense, festivals, and solemn assemblies. "'I have had enough of burnt-offerings of rams and the fat of fed beasts,' cries the Lord. 'I do not delight in the blood of bulls, or of rams, or of he-goats. Bring no more vain offerings; incense is an abomination to me. New moon and Sabbath and the calling of assemblies – I cannot endure iniquity and solemn assembly'" (Isa. 1:11-13). Instead, he says, "cease to do evil, learn to do good; seek justice, correct oppression; defend the fatherless, plead for the widow" (Isa. 1:17).

Amos sounded a similar note: "I hate, I despise, your feasts, and take no delight in your solemn assemblies" (Amos 5:21). These so-called worshipers are the very people who are "at ease in Sion" (Amos 6:1), enjoying the luxury of their ill-gotten gain while at the same time paying mere lip-service to the law:

> Hear this, you who trample upon the needy, and bring the poor of the land to an end, saying, "When will the new moon be over, that we may sell grain? And the Sabbath, that we may offer wheat for sale, that we may make the ephah small and the shekel great, and deal deceitfully with false balances, that we may buy the poor for silver and the needy for a pair of sandals, and sell the refuse of the wheat?" (Amos 8:4-6).

In Jeremiah the point of attack is Israel's sense of her own special status: she was secure because she had the Temple (Jer. 7:4). The prophet warns: "Will you steal, murder, commit adultery, swear falsely, burn incense to Baal, and go after other gods that you have not known, and then come and stand before me in this house, which is called by my name, and say, 'We are delivered!'?" (Jer. 7:9f.). Yahweh will have none of it: "Therefore will I do to the house which is called by my name, and in which you trust, and to the place which I gave to you and to your fathers, as I did to Shiloh" (Jer. 7:14).

Such passages surely raise the interesting possibility that Luther drew the inspiration for his portrayal of Judaism not from his own introspective conscience, but from the Old Testament prophets. We have to bear in mind, too, that these prophetic criticisms were not aimed at peripheral minorities in Israel and Judah. On the contrary, it was those who loved Yahweh and obeyed the voice of his servants (Isa. 50:10) who were the minority. This is Paul's "remnant according to the election of grace," described so movingly by Zephaniah: "I will leave in the midst of you a people humble and lowly. They shall seek refuge in the name of the Lord . . . they shall pasture and lie down, and none shall make them afraid" (Zeph. 3:12).

The question is: Did post-exilic Judaism undergo such a revolution that those proportions were reversed, the minority becoming the majority and securing such influence that it was the theology of the Remnant that ultimately came to be encapsulated in the so-called Common Judaism of the Tannaitic literature? That is what the New Perspective requires us to believe.

The Baptist's "Warning-Oracles"

When we turn to the New Testament the first voice we hear is that of resumed prophecy in the person of John the Baptist. The critique has lost none of its edge:

> But when he saw many of the Pharisees and Sadducees coming for baptism, he said to them, "You brood of vipers! Who warned you

to flee from the wrath to come? Bear fruit that befits repentance, and do not presume to say to yourselves, 'We have Abraham as our father'; for I tell you, God is able from these stones to raise up children to Abraham. Even now the axe is laid to the root of the trees; every tree therefore that does not bear good fruit is cut down and thrown into the fire" (Matt. 3:7-10).

N. T. Wright asserts (twice) that such a critique is no sign that one is being "anti-Jewish,"[63] and this is, of course, true, as his further comment that John's "warning-oracles" were "a sign of deep loyalty to Israel's true God and true vocation."[64] But although John was not anti-Jewish, he was certainly anti-Pharisaic, and this is of real significance for the New Perspective. After the fall of Jerusalem, the Sadducees became irrelevant to Judaism. The Pharisees, on the other hand, were the custodians of the oral tradition and it was that tradition which, under the Tannaim, became the core of Common Judaism. We have no reason to believe that the Gospels misrepresent them. Indeed, quite the opposite, according to G. F. Moore: "The gospels themselves are the best witness to the religious and moral teaching of the synagogue in the middle forty years of the first century, and the not infrequent references, with approval or dissent, to the current Halakah are evidence of the rules approved in the schools of the Law and taught to the people."[65]

We are entitled, then, to take John's warnings as directed not against the Pharisees personally, but against the "type" of religion they represented. They are the people who "made the mistake of thinking that physical descent from Abraham granted them an automatic immunity from God's eschatological wrath."[66] It would be hard to exaggerate the severity of John's warning. These men, the custodians and champions of what was later enshrined in the Mishnah, the Midrashim, and the Talmud, were "a brood of

---

[63] *Jesus and the Victory of God* (London: SPCK, 1996), 323n, 324.

[64] Ibid., 324.

[65] Moore, *Judaism*, 1:137.

[66] D. Hagner, *Word Biblical Commentary: Matthew 1-13* (Dallas: Word, 1993), 50.

vipers"; and because of them, the axe is laid to the root of the trees. The axe, of course, is the axe of divine judgment, to be expressed historically in the fall of Jerusalem and the destruction of the Temple. The trees, however, are not merely the Pharisees, but the whole Jewish people. To return to Wright: what drove John's ministry was "deep distress at the corruption which seemed endemic in the national life."[67] To John, that corruption was encapsulated in Pharisaism; and it was that corruption, linked to reliance on descent from Abraham and focused on the oral tradition rather than on the written Torah, which would bring the whole nation under the judgment of God: "Jerusalem, under its present regime, had become Babylon."[68] If, as Sanders argues, the theology of the Pharisees was homogeneous with the "covenantal nomism" codified by the Tannaim, then we have to reckon seriously with the possibility that it was the religion bred by that very theology which, in the Baptist's judgement, exposed the nation to retribution and ruin.

Jesus and the Pharisees

The tradition of prophetic critique continues unabated in the ministry of Jesus. One of his most dramatic portrayals of the Pharisees is in the parable of the Pharisee and the Publican (Luke 18:9-14). We must be cautious, of course, in using the parables to construct a portrait of Judaism: Jesus may have drawn eccentric rather than typical figures. However, as Gathercole points out, "the parables can embody in a *character* what theological discourse can only do with difficulty: that is, to capture the spirit of what Jesus perceived himself to be 'up against.'"[69] The Pharisee in Luke 18:9-14 is one such character. In all probability Jesus had in mind a real person and, although he may not necessarily have been a typical Pharisee, he is at least a reminder that such Pharisees existed; and a reminder,

---

[67] *Jesus and the Victory of God*, 324.

[68] Ibid., 32.

[69] Gathercole, *Where Is Boasting?*, 120.

too, that Jesus regarded them as so dangerous that he felt justified in making them the subject of a solemn warning. They were a group of religionists who trusted in their own righteousness and regarded others with contempt.

Both points are clearly emphasized in the story. The Pharisee looks God in the eye and appeals with total confidence to his own record, betraying no sense of the need for mercy and grace. On the contrary, he has complete confidence in his own righteousness. Indeed, he is a living commentary on Paul's description of his own Pharisaic days (Phil. 3:5f.): as to righteousness in terms of the law, he is blameless. He fasts twice a week and he tithes everything he buys. In both of these claims, of course, the Pharisee was going beyond the requirements of the Old Testament (the written Torah), performing what were almost exact counterparts of medieval works of supererogation. The Torah required only one annual fast (*yom kippur*): he fasted twice a week. It required tithing, but not of all purchases (such commodities as corn, wine, and oil had already been tithed by the producer). The Pharisee tithed everything.

The other plank in the Pharisee's platform was his superiority to his fellow human beings and even to his fellow Jews: "God, I thank thee that I am not like other men, extortioners, unjust, adulterers or even like this tax-collector." It would be hazardous to assume that this is an isolated instance of Pharisaic self-righteousness. Jeremias cites a similar prayer from the Talmud:

> I thank thee, O Lord, my God, that thou has given me my lot with those who sit in the house of learning, and not with those who sit at the street-corners; for I am early to work, and they are early to work; I am early to work on the words of the Torah, and they are early to work on things of no moment. I weary myself, and they weary themselves; I weary myself and profit thereby, and they weary themselves to no profit. I run, and they run; I run towards the life of the age to come, and they run towards the pit of destruction.[70]

---

[70] J. Jeremias, *The Parables of Jesus* (London: SCM Press, 1963), 142.

We have to remember, of course, that such humbug is not confined to Pharisaic Judaism. It is endemic to all human religion. Who can forget "Holy Willie's Prayer":

> I bless and praise thy matchless might,
> When thousands thou has left in night
> That I am here before thy sight
>   For gifts and grace
> A burning and a shining light
>   To a' this place
> O Lord, thou kens what zeal I bear,
> When drinkers drink, and swearers swear,
> And singin' there, and dancin' here,
>   Wi' great an' sma';
> For I am keep it by thy fear,
>   Free from them a'.

If Burns spoke a grain of truth, so, too, did Jesus (and Luther).

It is sometimes said that the point of the parable of the Pharisee and the Publican is that even tax-collectors are accepted by God.[71] That is, of course, a valid inference from the story. But the real focus of the parable, as Luke's editorial link makes clear, is the Pharisee as the representative of self-righteousness. The tax-collector is a foil. Yet, as Moses Silva points out, his prayer poses a real challenge to the New Perspective. The sentiment, "God, have mercy on me, a sinner!" is *not* a recurring theme in the very literature that Sanders so extensively surveyed.[72]

In Matthew 15:1-20 (and its parallel, Mark 7:1-23), we have an account of a direct confrontation between the Pharisees and Jesus on the precise question of his relation to the oral tradition. It is noteworthy that it was they who took the initiative: "Pharisees and scribes came to Jesus from Jerusalem." The religious authorities

---

[71] See, for example, I. H. Marshall, *The Gospel of Luke: A Commentary on the Greek Text* (Exeter: Paternoster, 1978), 677.

[72] *Westminster Theological Journal* 53 (1991): 350.

were clearly conscious of a tension between Jesus' teaching and their own. The account turns on a sharp antithesis between "the tradition of the elders" and "the word of God." Jesus' disciples ate their meals without first attending to the prescribed ceremonial washing of the hands. This was not a requirement laid down anywhere in the Old Testament, but it was clearly laid down in the oral tradition, apparently because the Pharisees sought to apply to the ordinary domestic situation the levels of ritualistic purity required of the priests when attending to their temple duties.[73] Since the priests were required to wash their hands (and their feet), the Pharisees wanted all Jews to do the same before eating a meal (another instance of supererogation?).

Jesus' disciples did not, and as their rabbi he was responsible. He says nothing to rebut the charge. Instead, he makes a counter-charge: the Pharisees transgress the commandment of God for the sake of their tradition (Matt. 18:3). He cites as a specific example the Fifth Commandment, "Honour your father and your mother." Part of this honoring was that children had financial responsibilities towards their parents. It was possible to evade these, however, by declaring your property to be *korban* (Mark 7:11), that is, dedicated to God. According to the scribes, such a vow was absolutely binding, taking precedence over even obligations to parents. But it had one striking advantage: "This convenient declaration apparently left the property actually still at the disposal of the one who made the vow, but deprived his parents of any right to it."[74]

Jesus' indictment of this "tradition" could not have been more severe: it was nothing less than a violation of the Torah itself.

---

[73] See Hagner, *Matthew 1–13*, 430.

[74] R. T. France, *The Gospel according to Matthew* (Leicester: InterVarsity, 1985), 243. France concedes that "later rabbinic legislation allowed for such an oath to be waived in favour of obedience to the fifth commandment," but "clearly it was not always waived in Jesus' day" (243).

C. E. B. Cranfield, in *The Gospel according to Saint Mark* (Cambridge: Cambridge University Press, 1959), 238, offers an alternative view of the way that scribal interpretation of the law of *korban* affected compliance with the

They were setting tradition above the word of God and rendering the latter utterly void (Mark 7:13).

In Matthew 23:23, the charge is not that the scribes and Pharisees evaded the law, but that they trivialized it. They tithed mint, dill, and cummin, but neglected justice, mercy, and faithfulness. Here again, the Pharisees seemed to be more rigorous than the Torah itself, which had required (Deut. 14:22f.) the tithing of grain, wine, and oil, but had said nothing about tithing garden herbs. Jesus did not condemn such scrupulosity in itself. He says, instead, "Tithe these if you wish, but don't neglect the weightier matters of the law." This, in his judgment, is exactly what the Pharisees were doing. Scrupulous in minor ritualistic and ceremonial detail, they were neglecting justice, mercy, and faithfulness (a summary of the Law reminiscent of Micah 6:8, which defines the "good" as acting justly, loving mercy, and walking humbly with God). These, and not the tithing of parsley, were the things that really mattered, and in view of their cavalier attitude towards them the Pharisees, in Jesus' view, were no more than blind guides. He drives the point home with biting irony in verse 24. They were so punctilious in their attention to minor details that they would strain the tiniest gnat out of their drinks and yet they would swallow a camel (an animal not only large, but unclean). In other words, they would lose sleep over the slightest ritualistic irregularity, but none at all over serious acts of injustice or cruelty. Luther never said anything more scathing than that.

This has an important bearing on the question of legalism. As J. G. Machen pointed out, "A low view of law leads to legalism in religion; a high view of law makes a man a seeker after grace."[75] The easier we make it to keep the law the easier it becomes to delude ourselves that we have complied with it and therefore have

---

Fifth Commandment. Someone who had rashly vowed away his property, later regretted it and now wanted to use it for the benefit of his parents was prevented from doing so by the scribes' rigid interpretation of the binding nature of oaths.

[75] J. G. Machen, *The Origin of Paul's Religion*, 179.

no need of divine grace. This is what provides the impetus towards relaxing the divine standard. If we judge ourselves by whether we have acted justly, loved mercy, and walked humbly before God, we shall find little ground for satisfaction. But if the criterion is whether we have tithed our mint, it is easy to produce a warm glow. The problem is by no means confined to the Pharisees. Many a Protestant reduces righteousness to wearing a hat, not using Sunday transport, being punctilious about "quiet times," or going mechanically through prayer notes.

If there is a Christian "covenantal nomism," then its terms are spelt out by Jesus in the Sermon on the Mount, negatively in Matthew 5:20 and positively in Matthew 7:21. According to the former passage, our righteousness must exceed that of the scribes and Pharisees. According to the latter, we must do the will of our Father who is in heaven.

Jesus leaves us in no doubt as to his attitude to the Torah. It will last as long as the universe itself; and his personal mission is not to destroy it, but to fulfill it. Matthew's account makes this point so emphatically that we can scarcely avoid the impression that rumours were current that Jesus was disrespectful to the law. He rebuts these rumours vigorously, but even from his rebuttal it is easy to see how they could arise. The six antitheses (Matt. 5:14-48) make plain that at the very least Jesus and the Pharisees disagreed about the *interpretation* of the Torah. But at no point does he suggest either the abrogation or the relaxation of the law. From this point of view, as Davies emphasizes, the teaching of Jesus was no revolutionary or radically new phenomenon:

> The Law remains in force. . . . To interpret on the side of stringency is not to annul the Law, but to change it in accordance with its own intention. From this point of view, we cannot speak of the Law being annulled in the antitheses, but only of its being intensified in its demand, or interpreted in a higher key.[76]

---

[76] W. D. Davies, *The Setting of The Sermon on the Mount* (Cambridge: Cambridge University Press, 1966), 29.

Yet even in the antitheses there is a strong under current of anti-Pharisaism. They condemned murder, but not hate; adultery, but not lust. They loved their neighbor, but hated their enemy. It is hard to stand before such facts and draw the conclusion that the Pharisees were crypto-Christians or that Christians were honorary Pharisees. Whether Christians lived up to their Lord's expectations is, of course, another matter. But his expectations were clear enough: a righteousness which exceeded that of scribes and Pharisees.

Finally, there is the case of Nicodemus, central to the whole argument yet curiously neglected. It throws into sharp and dramatic focus Jesus' view of the relationship between the Pharisees and the kingdom of God.

The story derives its force from Nicodemus' impeccable credentials. He was a Jew, of course, a member of God's elect people, chosen by divine grace and mercy. That itself would have been enough in the eyes of many to secure his participation in the kingdom. As Carson points out (citing the Mishnah), "Predominant religious thought in Jesus' day affirmed that all Jews would be admitted to that kingdom apart from those guilty of deliberate apostasy and extraordinary wickedness."[77] This probably explains why "we find virtually no individual quest for salvation in Jewish literature. The question is whether or not one is an Israelite in good standing."[78]

But Nicodemus was not merely an Israelite. He was a Pharisee, "the strictest party of our religion" (Acts 26:5); he was a member of the Sanhedrin, the supreme ruling council of Judaism; and he was a teacher of Israel. Indeed, if we give the definite article its full force, he was *the* teacher of Israel: its most highly regarded

---

[77] D. Carson, *The Gospel according to John* (Leicester: InterVarsity, 1991), 189.

[78] Sanders, *Paul and Palestinian Judaism*, 237. Sanders does add, however, that "simple heredity did not ensure salvation. That came to all those Israelites who were faithful." But this does not detract from the fact that they were born "in." The "faithfulness" related to "staying in." Even here there is an implicit legalism. Salvation was the reward of faithfulness, but faithfulness to what? To the Torah?

theologian. As such, he was the expert when it came to defining the entry requirements for the kingdom of God.

And yet he himself does not belong to the kingdom. Jesus is almost brutally blunt. Here is someone who by all the received standards of the day had complied fully with the stipulations of covenantal nomism. To "get in," he had to do nothing: he was born "in." To "stay in," he had to accept the yoke of the Torah, repent when he failed, and make appropriate cultic atonement. He had met these conditions and, by the time he went to see Jesus, no doubt about his own spiritual security had ever troubled his mind. But that night he had doubts, not about himself, but about Jesus: for all that men were saying about him, perhaps he was, after all, "from God." The signs certainly pointed that way. No man could do the things that Jesus did unless God were with him.

He went, therefore, to give Jesus his endorsement. It was the beginning of a spiritual pilgrimage which would eventually lead to fully committed, risk-taking discipleship. But Jesus ignored his endorsement. Instead, he immediately changed the subject: "Let's talk about you!" He told the great man that being a fully paid-up member of the covenant community (an Israelite, a Pharisee, a Ruler, and a Teacher) was no guarantee of membership in the kingdom of God. He had to be born again, be re-created, regenerated, receive a new heart, and become a new man. You entered the kingdom not as a Great One (a *rabbi*), but as a little child. "You've never entered the kingdom!" Jesus said. "You can't even see the kingdom! You are the Teacher of Israel ("the Reverend Professor Doctor,"[79]) and yet you don't know the most basic truths about entry into the kingdom." These truths had been clearly taught by the Old Testament, particularly in such passages as Ezekiel 36:26, "A new heart I will give you, and a new spirit I will put within you; and I will take out of your flesh the heart of stone and give you a heart of flesh." Even the *Pseudepigrapha* had

---

[79] Carson, *The Gospel according to John*, 198.

sounded a similar note: "I shall create for them a holy spirit, and I shall purify them so that they will not turn away from following me from that day and forever" (*Jubilees* 1:23).[80] Yet here was a teacher of outstanding reputation, an expert in "heavenly things," who was completely nonplussed by the notion of the new birth and sincerely believed that if you were a Jew you were "in" (and, presumably, that if you were a Gentile you were "out").

In effect, Jesus put Nicodemus and his fellow rabbis in the same class as the Gentiles later described by Paul: the natural (*psychikos*) man does not receive the things of the Spirit of God. Instead, they are folly to him (1 Cor. 2:14). Nicodemus, great rabbi and great teacher though he was, was still a "natural" man, afflicted with fatal spiritual blindness. His only hope was that the Spirit who gave the universe its beginning (Ps. 33:6) would infuse his soul with the life of God. Little did Nicodemus suspect, then, that participation in the kingdom would mean Jesus living for ever in his heart.

Conclusion

Sanders was right to place question-marks against Luther's account of Judaism. It could not be equated simplistically with legalism or dismissed as proto-Scholasticism. But neither was Judaism the crypto-Lutheranism or implicit Christianity that the New Perspective suggests. The tendency to self-righteousness is endemic to human nature and this makes it easy for the doctrine of self-salvation to suck all religions into its vortex. Medieval Christianity disappeared into it and so, later, did dysfunctional Protestantism. In Luther's perception the religion of the Jews had suffered the same fate, and, being who he was, he had to tell it as he saw it. In his telling, he drew his inspiration from the Old Testament prophets, John the Baptist, and Jesus. Modern academic discourse has higher standards of courtesy and accuracy than prevailed in Luther's day, and our greater knowledge of Tannaitic literature

---

[80] J. H. Charlesworth, ed., *The Old Testament Pseudepigrapha* (2 vols.; New York: Doubleday, 1983-85), 2:54.

demands considerable fine-tuning of Luther's perspective. But this does not detract from the fact that anyone who comes from the New Testament to the Mishnah or the Talmud finds herself in a foreign world. The one is a world of *halakhah,* laying down meticulous instructions and promising life on the basis of obedience. Compared with the Old Testament, it leaves the theology untouched, but vastly expands the ethics. The other is a world of *kerygma* and *didache*, leaving the ethics untouched, but vastly expanding the theology. Above all else, the New Testament expanded the doctrine of justification, placing it in the brilliant light of incarnation and vicarious atonement. The only alternative to self-righteousness is *imputed* righteousness; and where could that be found except in a Last Adam? Judaism has none such. Every man must be his own savior. That has bred its own moments of towering heroism and overflowing humanity. It has not brought hope to the ungodly.

A Missiological Analysis of the Westminster Confession of Faith – Chapter 14

Valdeci S. Santos

Introduction

The quest for a missiological approach to the Westminster Confession of Faith (WCF) is of continuing relevance among Protestants. As a classical example in the ecclesiastical realm, we have the revision of the Confession in 1903 by the Presbyterian Church in the USA. That endeavor resulted in the addition of two chapters in the Confession, of which one focused on missions.[1] Turning to the academic realm, we have Donald McGavran's proposal that every creed should be missiologically reformulated. According to McGavran, "all creeds and confessions, if they would be fully Christian, should express the overriding intention of God that men, in answer to God's choice of them, believe on Christ, repent, and live in him."[2] Finally, it is even possible to say that the quest for a missiological approach to the WCF is the unpaid debt of Reformed scholars, since they usually approach it theologically,[3] apologetically,[4] or historically,[5] rather than missiologically.

---

[1] Benjamin B. Warfield, *The Confession of Faith as Revised in 1903* (Richmond: Whittet & Shepperson, 1904), 14.

[2] Donald A. McGavran, "A Missionary Confession of Faith," *Calvin Theological Journal* 7 (November 1972): 133.

The relevance of a missiological approach to the WCF can be amplified by analyzing four other factors. First, we have the missiological and evangelistic concern of some of the Westminster Divines. For instance, Thomas Goodwin, one of the leading members of the Assembly, used the Great Commission to emphasize the minister's duty "to teach all nations," and he accentuated the importance of the general call of the gospel for both elect and non-elect.[6] Second, though scarce, it is possible to find significant literature on the missiology of some of the Puritan Divines during the time of the Assembly.[7] J. I. Packer, for example, reminds us that the Puritans were the ones that invented the genre of evangelistic literature.[8] Third, we can observe the missiological concern of other Puritans in the historical context of the Westminster Assembly. For instance, Richard Baxter, the apostle of Kidderminster, giving some directions about professing our religion to others insists that "our profession is a means of saving others," and "God hath required our open and bold profession of him, with the strictest commands, and upon the greatest penalties."[9] Also, we

---

3   Cf. Archibald A. Hodge, *A Commentary on the Confession of Faith* (Philadelphia: Presbyterian Board of Publication and Sabbath-School Work, 1901); Robert Shaw, *An Exposition of the Confession of Faith* (Fearn: Christian Focus Publications, 1980); and R. L. Dabney, *The Westminster Confession and Creeds* (Dallas: Presbyterian Heritage Publications, 1983).

4   Gordon H. Clark, *What do Presbyterians Believe?*, (Phillipsburg: P&R, 1965).

5   Benjamin B. Warfield, *The Westminster Assembly and Its Works* (Edmonton: Still Waters Revival Books, 1991); and William M. Hetherington, *History of the Westminster Assembly of Divines* (Edmonton: Still Waters Revival Books, 1993).

6   Thomas Goodwin, *The Works of Thomas Goodwin* (12 vols.; New York: Harper San Francisco, 1996), 11:346-47; 9:185.

7   Harry Lee Poe, "Evangelistic Fervency among the Puritans in Stuart England, 1603–1688" (Ph.D. diss., Southern Baptist Theological Seminary, 1982); J. I. Packer, "Puritan Evangelism," *The Banner of Truth* (February 1967): 4-13; and Joel Beeke, *Puritan Evangelism: A Biblical Approach* (Grand Rapids: Reformation Heritage Books, 1999).

8   Packer, "Puritan Evangelism," 4.

9   Richard Baxter, *A Christian Directory* (Morgan, Pa.: Soli Deo Gloria Publications, 1996), 563.

have the missionary activity of Jim Eliot among the American Indians,[10] and the foundation of the Society for Propagation of the Gospel in New England in 1649.[11] In this regard, attention must also be given to the missiological *endeavor* of those who carried the Puritan tradition and firmly held to the Westminster Standards. Jonathan Edwards is a solid representative in this regard, but many others could also be cited.[12] Fourth, attention should be given to B. B. Warfield's claim that the added chapter, "Of the Love of God, and Missions," by the revision of the Confessions in 1903, was only a reaffirmation of the doctrines already cited in the original Confession.[13] Warfield virtually admitted that the Confession, as it was originally written, disclosed a missiological concern.

The purpose of this essay is to set forth a missiological analysis of WCF 14. Although it is possible and even academically sound to undertake a cross-reference between the teachings of this chapter with the rest of the Confession, this exercise will not occupy our major focus. Our central attention will be driven to the teaching of Chapter 14 – the doctrine of saving faith. This choice relies upon the fact that the doctrine of saving faith is a topic of paramount importance in Christian tradition. The writers of the New Testament unanimously maintained that faith is the indispensable channel of salvation (Heb. 11:6; Eph. 2:8-9). Faith is so fundamental in Christianity that the church is described as the "household of faith" (Gal. 6:10 ESV), Christians are the sons of God by faith (Gal. 3:26), and Christ dwells in their hearts through

---

[10] Sidney Rooy, *The Theology of Missions in the Puritan Tradition* (Grand Rapids: Eerdmans, 1965).

[11] R. E. Davies, "The Great Commission from Calvin to Carey," *Evangel* (Summer 1996): 45.

[12] Cf. Ernst Benz, "Pietist and Puritan Sources of Early Protestant World Missions," *Church History* 20, ed. J. H. Nichols and Wilhelm Pauck (New York: The American Society of Church History, 1951), 28-51.

[13] Warfield, *The Confession of Faith as Revised in 1903*, 14.

faith (Eph. 3:17). Rediscovering the biblical truth of *sola fide* for justification, Martin Luther stated that it is *articulus standis et cadentis ecclesiae*.[14] Also, the Puritan Thomas Goodwin observed, "faith in its first act discovers at once with one eye a man to be poor and ungodly, and with the other looks up to Christ's riches, and to him that justifies the ungodly."[15] It seems fair to say, therefore, that it is difficult to overemphasize the importance of the doctrine of saving faith in Christianity, especially for the mission of the Church.

Before considering the missiological focus of WCF 14 directly, we will consider two preliminary issues: (1) the doctrine of faith in the context of the English Reformation, and (2) the general theology of the chapter.

The Doctrine of Faith in the Context of the English Reformation

The historical context of English Puritanism was highly productive in terms of theological discussion. According to Packer, "It is not too much to say that theology became the national hobby."[16] In that context, the Westminster Divines were active in theological research and debates.[17] But the Puritans' interest in theology sprang from their devotion and zeal for God's glory and pastoral concern for God's flock. Packer understands that the Puritans' aim "was to turn the Reformers' legacy, a national profession of the gospel, into a living experience of its power."[18] Consequently, the

---

[14] "The article with and by which the Church stands, without which it falls." Cf. Martin Luther, *What Luther Says: An Anthology*, ed. Ewald M. Plass (3 vols.; St. Louis: Concordia, 1959), 2:704.

[15] Goodwin, *The Works of Thomas Goodwin*, 8:339.

[16] J. I. Packer, "The Puritan Treatment of Justification by Faith," *Evangelical Quarterly* 24 (July 1952): 131.

[17] R. A. Finlayson, *Reformed Theological Writings* (Fearn: Christian Focus Publications, 1996), 232.

[18] Packer, "The Puritan Treatment of Justification by Faith", 132.

doctrine of saving faith occupied a place of prominent importance in their theology.

Initial consideration must be given to the fact that "the Assembly was the beneficiary of almost 125 years of Protestant theology."[19] The theology expressed in the WCF is said to be "the ripest fruit of Reformed creed-making."[20] Warfield explains this claim further by saying that "the Divines had acquired an intimate acquaintance with the prevailing errors and remarkable facility in the formulation of the Reformed doctrine in opposition to them, which bore rich fruit in their Confessional labors."[21] Packer states that "the Confession represents Puritan orthodoxy in its mature form, and is the best starting-point for the study of their treatment of any doctrine."[22] Puritan theology, however, needs to be assessed in relation to the theology of: (1) the Church of Rome, (2) the Reformers, and (3) the Arminians.

The Roman Catholic Understanding of Saving Faith

The dominant concept of faith in the theology of the Roman Catholic Church during the 16th and 17th centuries was influenced by Scholasticism and expressed officially by the Council of Trent (1546–1563). Scholasticism was a "derogatory term meant to indicate a tradition-bound, logic-chopping mentality, involving a slavish adherence to Aristotle."[23] But historically it was the Scholastics that considered most carefully the relation between faith and reason and, therefore, continue to be a source of inspiration to both philosophers and theologians in the Catholic tradition. Influenced by Aristotle, the Scholastics speculated on

---

[19]   John H. Leith, *Assembly at Westminster* (Richmond: John Knox Press, 1973), 37.

[20]   Warfield, *The Westminster Assembly and Its Works*, 58.

[21]   Ibid., 57-58.

[22]   Packer, "The Puritan Treatment of the Justification by Faith", 139.

[23]   A. Vos, "Scholasticism," in *New Dictionary of Theology*, ed. Sinclair B. Ferguson, David F. Wright, and J. I. Packer (Downers Grove: InterVarsity, 1988), 621.

the relationship between nature and grace, understanding this last as "an infused quality or virtue empowering nature to rise above itself."[24] In this scheme, the three theological virtues (faith, hope, and love) were studied in relation to the spiritual faculties of intellect and will, and faith was initially "conceived as an intellectual assent to the truths pronounced authoritatively by the ecclesial magisterium."[25] As a logical development:

> The Scholastics distinguished between a *fides informis*, that is, a mere intellectual assent to the truth taught by the Church, and a *fides formata (charitate)*, that is, a faith informed (given a characteristic form) by love, and regarded the later as the only faith that justifies, since it involves an infusion of grace.[26]

Though Scholastics developed other concepts of faith,[27] these two (*fides informis* and *fides formata*) were of central importance in the period of the Reformation. According to Calvin, it was a labyrinth – a rejection of the ministry of the Spirit.[28]

The Roman Catholic distinction between *fides informis* and *fides formata* was attached to several other concepts. First, Catholicism asserted that though it is possible to assent to the divine and revealed truth by the use of natural faculties, saving faith is "always infused, supernatural, and essentially a mysterious gift."[29] This concept of faith supports the view of justification as a process

---

[24] James Michael Lee, *Handbook of Faith* (Birmingham: Religious Education Press, 1990), 142.

[25] Wolfgang Beinert and Francis Schüssler Fiorenza, eds., *Handbook of Catholic Theology* (New York: Crossroad Publishing Company, 1995), 251.

[26] Louis Berkhof, *Systematic Theology* (Grand Rapids: Eerdmans, 1949), 796.

[27] E.g. Scholastic theologians distinguished *fides implicita* (the habitual belief in what the church taught) and *fides explicita* (explicit assent of the mind to Catholic truth), *fides acquisita* (acquired through natural mean), *fides infusa* (supernaturally infused into the soul), and *fides demonum* (the historical objective faith held even by demons). Cf. Susan E. Schreiner, "Faith," in *The Oxford Encyclopedia of Reformation*, ed. Hans J. Hillerbrand (New York: Oxford University Press, 1996), 90.

[28] John Calvin, *Institutes of Christian Religion*, ed. John T. McNeill, trans. Ford Lewis Battles (Philadelphia: Westminster, 1960), 545, 552.

rather than an act, and the disposition to grace becomes *meritum de congruo*.[30] Second, it carries the presupposition that the infallible rule of faith is the truth revealed through the ordinary and solemn *magisterium* of the church.[31] Hence, the distinction between *fides informis* and *fides formata* directs man's attention away from the Word and toward the church. R. L. Dabney points out that it makes faith an "implicit exercise of the mind, in which the believer accepts the doctrines, not because of his own clear understanding of their evidence, but because of the pious and submissive temper of mind towards the Church."[32] Moreover, it reduces faith to mere intuition, which may never achieve certainty in this life.[33] Also, it weakens and discourages holiness since a person cannot observe nor practice a doctrine unless he comprehends it.[34] And finally, Louis Berkhof reasons that through this concept of faith "a foundation was laid for human merit."[35]

With the rise of the Protestant Reformation, Roman Catholicism restated its beliefs at the Council of Trent (1546–1563). However, the Catholic reformulation of the doctrine of faith in Trent was somewhat paradoxical. On one hand, it stated that "faith is the beginning of human salvation, the foundation and root of all justification."[36] Thus, it acknowledged faith to be an integrating component of justification.[37] On the other hand, the Council

---

[29] P. K. Meagher, "Theology of Faith," in *New Catholic Encyclopedia*, ed. Patrick A. O'Boyle (Washington, D.C.: Catholic University of America, 1967), 798.

[30] "Congruous or quasi-merit"; Martin Chemnitz, *Examination of the Council of Trent* (4 vols.; St. Louis: Concordia Publishing House, 1971), 1:558.

[31] Meagher, "Theology of Faith", 799.

[32] R. L. Dabney, *Systematic Theology* (Carlisle: Banner of Truth, 1996), 601-02.

[33] Anthony A. Hoekema, *Saved by Grace* (Grand Rapids: Eerdmans, 1989), 146.

[34] Gordon H. Clark, *Faith and Saving Faith* (Jefferson, Md.: The Trinity Foundation, 1983), 21.

[35] Berkhof, *Systematic Theology*, 496.

[36] H. J. Schroeder, trans., *Canons and Decrees of the Council of Trent.* (Rockford, Ill.: Tan Books and Publishers, 1978), 35.

[37] Bienert, *Handbook of Catholic Theology*, 251.

declared baptism as the instrumental cause of justification since it "is the sacrament of faith."[38] The Council even warned against an individual flattering "himself with faith alone, thinking that by faith alone he is made an heir and will obtain the inheritance."[39] Furthermore, according to Trent, "unless hope and charity be added to it [faith], neither unites man perfectly with Christ nor makes him a living member of His body."[40] It also insisted that "no one can know with the certainty of faith, which cannot be subject to error, that he has obtained the grace of God."[41]

It seems fair to say that a new Scholastic view of faith prevailed in Trent, and the Roman Catholic Church was lifted up as the guarantor of the believer's faith. As Martin Chemnitz rightly indicates, the Catholic theologians at Trent understood that "divine grace only moves and excites free will, which therefore is able, from its own natural powers, to begin and render" the preparations for justification.[42] Human merit thus lay at the heart of Trent's understanding of faith.[43]

Neither the Reformers nor the English Puritans accepted the Roman Catholic teaching on the doctrine of faith as it was restated in the Council of Trent. As has been pointed out, "missing from the Roman Catholic formula is the word *alone*."[44] Against these factors, the Divines raised their theological objections in the formulation of WCF 14.

The Reformers' Understanding of Faith

The Reformation has been properly defined as a rediscovery of grace, that is, "a deeper plunge into the meaning of the gospel

---

[38] Schroeder, *Canons and Decrees of the Council of Trent*, 33.

[39] Ibid., 37.

[40] Ibid., 34.

[41] Ibid., 35.

[42] Chemnitz, *Examination of the Council of Trent*, 1:563.

[43] Ibid., 551-611.

[44] R. C. Sproul, *Grace Unknown* (Grand Rapids: Baker, 1997), 66.

than even Augustine had made."[45] Alister McGrath identifies it as a "movement which sought to return the Western church to a more biblical foundation in relation to its belief system, morality and structures."[46] In that context, the most easily identified theological controversy was the doctrine of justification by faith. At the heart of that controversy, however, was the underlying debate about the true nature of faith.[47]

The Reformers' view of faith is the *conditio sine qua non* for the understanding of their soteriology. The Reformers unanimously maintained that "saving grace becomes ours by faith, which, because it is a 'gift of God,' is not a product of our decision or action, but which, on the other hand, is always accompanied by our trusting in the action of Christ on our behalf."[48] In this dialectical relation between divine act and human responsibility, faith encompasses the whole event of salvation. So, in one of Luther's classical definitions of faith we read:

> Faith is a living and unshakable confidence, a belief in the grace of God so assured that a man would die a thousand deaths for its sake . . . That is what the Holy Spirit effects through faith . . . It is impossible, indeed, to separate works from faith . . . just as it is impossible to separate heat and light from fire.[49]

In the same vein, Calvin spoke of faith as "a firm and certain knowledge of God's benevolence toward us, founded upon the truth of the freely given promise in Christ, both revealed to our minds and sealed upon our hearts through the Holy Spirit."[50] Thus, it is clear

---

[45] William Childs Robinson, *The Reformation: A Rediscovery of Grace* (Grand Rapids: Eerdmans, 1962), 59.

[46] Alister E. McGrath, *Christian Theology: An Introduction* (Cambridge, Mass.: Blackwell, 1977), 60.

[47] Schreiner, "Faith", 89.

[48] Lee, *Handbook of Faith*, 165.

[49] Cf. John Dillenberger, *Martin Luther: Selections from His Writings* (Garden City, N.Y.: Doubleday, 1961), 24.

[50] Calvin, *Institutes*, 551.

that the Reformers never identified the freedom of faith as freedom from the responsibility for good works.[51] Another element of faith in the theology of the Reformers was its Christocentric nature.[52] Also, there is a clear emphasis on the activity of the Holy Spirit as the author of faith in the human heart.[53] And finally, the theology of the Reformers highlighted the importance of *sola fide*, which avoids any merit and may bring assurance to the Christian soul.[54]

The Reformers' teaching on faith was directly opposed to the Scholastic concept of *fides informis* and *fides formata*. According to Susan Schreiner, "the concepts of formed and unformed faith came under the most direct attack in the Reformation."[55] The strength of the Scholastic distinction relies upon a medieval distinction between the justice of Christ, which was granted in baptism and renewed in the sacrament of penance, and the justice of God, which is the final judgment of the believer. In this scheme, only by cooperating with grace could the Christian do the meritorious works that enabled him to stand before God. In Luther's exegetical discovery of Romans 1:17, however, the justice of Christ and the justice of God are granted simultaneously in the act of justification by faith alone.[56] Along with Luther, Calvin rejected the Scholastic distinction on faith and considered it as mere ignorance.[57] Contrary to the Scholastics, the Reformers understood faith as neither mere intellectual assent nor as grace infused, but as a trust which has its seat in the will and affects the whole person. According to Berkhof, "the Reformers . . . were unanimous and explicit in teaching that justifying faith does not

---

[51] Schreiner, "Faith", 91.

[52] Cf. Lee, *Handbook of Faith*, 184-85; and Chemnitz, *Examination of the Council of Trent*, 1:573.

[53] Robinson, *The Reformation*, 23-24.

[54] Cf. Chemnitz, *Examination of the Council of Trent*, 1:585; and Sproul, *Grace Unknown*, 66.

[55] Schreiner, "Faith", 90.

[56] Dillenberger, *Martin Luther: Selections from His Writings*, 11.

[57] Calvin, *Institutes*, 545.

justify by any meritorious or inherent efficacy of its own, but only as the instrument for receiving or laying hold on what God has provided in the merits of Christ."[58]

The Westminster Divines followed the Reformers' teaching on faith. Packer even suggests that they "completed the work the Reformers had begun" on this issue.[59]

Faith in the Rising Influence of Arminianism

The official confrontation with Arminianism was won in the courts of the Synod of Dort in 1618–1619.[60] Among the English Puritans, Arminian theology influenced John Goodwin,[61] and temporarily held other Puritans in its ranks. Even the renowned Thomas Goodwin had early interests in Arminian doctrine. However, Thomas Goodwin later abandoned Arminianism and expressed his firm conviction that "the doctrine of Arminianism was not true."[62] Arminianism in England also aroused the theological anger of John Owen, who skillfully exposed the weakness of its theological propositions.[63] The influence of Arminianism in the context of the Westminster Assembly forces us to examine its understanding of the doctrine of faith.

The Arminians' understanding of faith springs from the teaching that "God bestows a universal grace on man, which is sufficient to enable the sinner to believe and obey the gospel."[64] According to this, man is justified *on account* of his faith, and not *by* faith. Hence,

---

[58] Berkhof, *Systematic Theology,* 497.

[59] Packer, "The Puritan Treatment of Justification by Faith", 138.

[60] McGrath, *Christian Theology*, 453-54.

[61] There is no family connection whatsoever between John Goodwin and Thomas Goodwin. Cf. J. I. Packer, *A Quest for Godliness: The Puritan Vision of the Christian Life* (Wheaton: Crossway Books, 1990), 184.

[62] Goodwin, *The Works of Thomas Goodwin*, 2:53.

[63] John Owen, *The Works of John Owen*, William H. Goold (16 vols.; Carlisle: Banner of Truth, 1993), 10:2-137.

[64] Louis Berkhof, *The History of Christian Doctrines* (Grand Rapids: Baker, 1975), 221.

"Arminianism made man's salvation dependent ultimately on man himself, saving faith being viewed throughout as man's own work and, because his own, not God's in him."[65] In defense of Jacobus Arminius, John M. Hicks raises the possibility of a distortion of his teaching by his disciples.[66] Despite his efforts, Hicks cannot erase either the Arminian synergistic approach to faith or its emphasis upon the ability of human nature toward salvation.[67] The Arminian concept of faith falls short of the theology of the Reformers and comes close to semi-Pelagianism.

In the Westminster Assembly, the Puritans rejected Roman Catholicism's view on faith, supported the Dutch opposition to Arminianism, and remained faithful to the Reformers' tradition.[68] In their pastoral care, the Puritans proved to be well versed on the subject of faith,[69] and their findings on this subject were well summarized in WCF 14. This chapter bears an important role in the understanding of the missiological perspective of the Divines.

The Theological Exposition of WCF 14

In the theological framework of the WCF, the fourteenth chapter is part of the section that deals with the application of redemption. By emphasizing the federal nature of the Confession, R. A. Finlayson classifies this chapter as part of the benefits of the covenant upon the elect.[70] In this theological system, John Murray distinguishes two orders: (1) the actions in which God is the agent, and (2) the

---

[65] Packer, *A Quest for Godliness*, 128.

[66] John M. Hicks, "The Theology of Grace in the Thought of Jacobus Arminius and Philip van Limborch: A study in the Development of Seventeenth Century Dutch Arminianism" (Ph.D. diss., Westminster Theological Seminary, 1985), 1-3.

[67] Ibid., 66-67.

[68] Finlayson, *Reformed Theological Writings*, 233.

[69] Joel Beeke asserts that "at least twenty seven members of the Assembly wrote treatises pertinent to the doctrine of faith and assurance." Cf. Joel R. Beeke, *Assurance of Faith* (New York: Peter Lang, 1994), 141.

[70] Finlayson, *Reformed Theological Writings*, 253-57.

responses on the "part of the persons savingly acted upon by God."[71] The elaboration of this chapter, according to Warfield occurred as follows:

> From August 21 to August 31 inclusive the Assembly sat only as a Grand Committee, lacking a quorum for a formal meeting: During this time the report on Saving Faith was reviewed. This report was formally called up in the Assembly, September 4. It was debated September 9, and reviewed and ordered September 16. The Scriptural proofs were reported February 12, 1647: they were reviewed April 8.[72]

The final result was a chapter rich in biblical and relevant teachings, both pastorally and missiologically. Let us then approach chapter 14 of the WCF using a twofold division: its presuppositions and its propositions.

Presuppositions

From the outset, this chapter displays three major presuppositions: (1) saving faith is only one type of faith, (2) saving faith is a grace of God, and (3) saving faith belongs to the elect. Each of these assumptions reveals the Calvinistic theology of the Divines.

It has been a common practice among Protestant theologians to talk about four kinds of faith: (1) historical, (2) miraculous, (3) temporary, and (4) saving faith.[73] In this scheme, historical faith "is a bare assent to revealed and known truth, possessed even by devils . . . which is referred to in James 2:19."[74] The miraculous faith is "a persuasion wrought in the mind of a person that a miracle will be performed by him or in his behalf . . . It is not necessarily,

---

[71] John Murray, *Collected Writings of John Murray* (4 vols.; Carlisle: Banner of Truth, 1982), 4:258.

[72] Warfield, *The Westminster Assembly and Its Works*, 110-11.

[73] Francis Turretin, *Institutes of Elenctic Theology*, ed. James T. Dannison, Jr. (3 vols.; Phillipsburg: Reformed Publishing Company, 1994), 3:559-60; Dabney, *Systematic Theology*, 600; Berkhof, *Systematic Theology*, 501-02.

[74] Turretin, *Institutes of Elenctic Theology*, 3:559.

but may be accompanied with saving faith."[75] Regarding temporary faith, it is a persuasion of the religious truths, which is not rooted in a regenerate heart and, therefore, is evanescent and which is referred to in such passages as Matt. 13:20 and Heb. 6:4-7. And saving faith can be defined as "a response to God's call by the acceptance of Christ with the total person – that is, with assured conviction of the truth of the gospel, and with trustful reliance on God in Christ for salvation, together with genuine commitment to Christ and to his service."[76] Although not presenting the same development, the teaching of Chapter 14 of the WCF recognizes the existence of different kinds of faith.

The Divines' specific focus on saving faith virtually admits the identification of other kinds of personal beliefs. As A. A. Hodge says, "this difference arises partly from the nature of its objects, and partly from the nature or form of the testimony on which it is founded."[77] Furthermore, the conviction that the Bible does not always speak of religious faith in the same sense may have guided the Divines' minds in their stress upon *this faith* – saving faith.[78]

A second presupposition in this chapter is that faith is a grace of God, which must be responded to by man. Once more, the Divines closely followed the biblical emphasis that God bestows faith upon his elect (Phil. 1:29; Eph. 2:8), that faith is a result of regeneration (1 John 5:11), that it is a result of the Spirit's operation (1 Cor. 12:3), and that Jesus is the author of faith (Heb. 12:2). However, it does not overlook the human responsibility of believing in the gospel, but assumes that even the elect must be brought to saving faith.[79]

By emphasizing the grace of God and human responsibility in answering God's call, the Divines avoided any possibility of misunderstanding faith as meritorious in the salvation process.

---

[75] Berkhof, *Systematic Theology*, 502.

[76] Hoekema, *Saved by Grace*, 140.

[77] Hodge, *A Commentary on the Confession of Faith*, 67.

[78] WCF, 14.2.

[79] WCF, 14.1.

As Anthony Hoekema highlights, "though it is our responsibility to believe the gospel, our faith is not in any way meritorious."[80] Moreover, it must be emphasized that "it is not, strictly speaking, even faith in Christ that saves, but Christ that saves through faith. The saving power resides exclusively, not in the act of faith or the attitude of faith or the nature of faith, but in the object of faith."[81] And, since saving faith is a gift of God, "this faith is not first of all an activity of man, but a potentiality wrought by God in the heart of the sinner."[82]

The final presupposition of WCF 14 is that saving faith belongs to God's elect. By referring to the faith "whereby the elect are enabled to believe,"[83] the Divines display their covenantal hermeneutic. They also emphasize saving faith as fruit of God's election. In support of this emphasis are biblical passages such as John 6:44-45; 1 Peter 1:2; and 2 Peter 1:1. Another portion of Scripture that certainly supports this truth is Acts 13:48, which says that "all who were appointed for eternal life believed" (NIV[84]). Commenting on this passage, F. F. Bruce says, "We cannot agree with those who attempt to tone down the predestinarian note of this phrase by rendering 'as many as were disposed to eternal life.' The Greek participle is *tetagmenoi* from *tasso*, and there is papyrus evidence for this verb in the sense of 'inscribe' or 'enroll.'"[85] Heinrich Heppe sees this connection between saving faith and election as a principle of comfort, since "we are not to fear that the elect who have not yet attained to conversion may never appropriate the call of grace."[86]

---

[80] Hoekema, *Saved by Grace*, 145.

[81] Benjamin B. Warfield, *Biblical and Theological Studies*, ed. Samuel G. Craig (Philadelphia: P&R, 1968), 425.

[82] Berkhof, *Systematic Theology*, 503.

[83] WCF, 14.1.

[84] All following Scripture references are taken from the NIV.

[85] F. F. Bruce, *Commentary on the Book of Acts* (Grand Rapids: Eerdmans, 1955), 72.

[86] Cf. Heinrich Heppe, *Reformed Dogmatics* (London: George Allen & Unwin, 1950), 516.

The presupposition that saving faith belongs to the elect bears two other implications. First, the one who determined the end of salvation also determined the means and conditions for the fulfillment of his decree. Robert Shaw explains it by affirming, "All whom God from eternity elected to everlasting life are in time brought to believe to the saving of their souls."[87] A second implication of this connection is that even the elect must exercise faith for salvation. In other words, the elect are neither automatically nor instantaneously saved, but God will certainly bring them to saving faith. R. C. Sproul elucidates this point by stating, "Since justification is by faith, we understand that only the predestined will ever have faith. . . . The Reformed view holds that we are elect unto faith and justification. Faith is a necessary condition for salvation, but not for election."[88]

These presuppositions lay the foundation for our understanding of this chapter. Either neglecting or overlooking them may create difficulties for our next step. Also, they can be used as strong motivations to the missionary work. This truth can be well illustrated by an event in the life of the Apostle Paul: "One night the Lord spoke to Paul in a vision: 'Do not be afraid; keep on speaking, do not be silent. For I am with you, and no one is going to attack and harm you, because I have many people in this city'" (Acts 18:9-10).

Propositions

The propositions of the three paragraphs in WCF 14 can be classified into three subtopics: (1) the nature of saving faith, (2) the objects of saving faith, and (3) the acts of saving faith. Each topic is closely connected to the others.

Regarding the nature of saving faith, the Divines make a clear point that it is the work of the Holy Spirit, who ordinarily works it by the ministry of the word. Also, saving faith is dynamic. So,

---

[87] Shaw, *An Exposition of the Confession of Faith*, 146.

[88] Sproul, *Grace Unknown*, 145.

the Divines promptly rejected the concept of faith as a theoretical assent only, a grace infused, or a work of inherent human ability.[89] In an attempt to explain the process by which the Spirit works faith in the human mind, Gordon Clark says:

> Faith is produced in the souls of the elect by the Holy Spirit. Faith is indeed something that we do; it is our own mental activity; but it is an activity that could not have been initiated by any decision of a free will, nor produced by ordinary human striving. . . . If therefore the Spirit works faith in us, we have faith; if he does not, we don't.[90]

Also, "It is only after God has implanted the seed in the heart that man can exercise faith."[91] So, Scripture calls the Holy Spirit "the Spirit of faith" (2 Cor 4:13), and it mentions faith among the fruits of the Spirit (Gal. 5:22). This same truth is expressed elsewhere in the WCF when it insists that faith is an act of the regenerated soul.[92]

The ordinary process by which the Spirit works faith in the elect's heart is by the ministry of the word. By this, the Divines did not overlook special cases, such as those who die in infancy or the mentally insane, nor deny the freedom of the Spirit.[93] They only underscored that "the Spirit usually works by means, and the Word read or preached is the divinely appointed means by which he usually communicates his influence."[94] Clark understands it to be one of the reasons why "historic Protestantism has always made preaching the central part of the worship service because it is by preaching that faith is produced and propagated."[95] Thus, we see that, ordinarily, the elect must believe the message of the

---

[89] Cf. Hodge, *A Commentary on the Confession of Faith*, 280-81.

[90] Clark, *What do Presbyterians Believe?*, 143.

[91] Berkhof, *Systematic Theology*, 503.

[92] WCF, 11.1-2.

[93] WCF, 10.3.

[94] Shaw, *An Exposition of the Confession of Faith*, 148.

[95] Clark, *What do Presbyterians Believe?*, 146.

gospel, and this fundamentally affects the missionary work of the church.

Finally, the Divines stressed the dynamic nature of saving faith, which is "different in degrees"[96] and can be "increased and strengthened."[97] And this dynamic element of saving faith should motivate a continuing participation in the means of grace.[98] So, the preaching of the word, prayers, and the administration of the sacraments are the means by which the Holy Spirit works and confirms faith in the hearts of men. Also, the dynamic nature of saving faith should motivate believers to pursue the assurance of faith, which, though not being the *esse*, is the *bene esse* of salvation.[99] But the dynamic element of saving faith should also develop a pastoral attitude in the minister toward those who are weak in their faith.[100] Hence, "whatever tends to promote sanctification must promote the strength of faith, which is its main root. Therefore, faith must be nourished by truth, prayer, the sacraments and every means of grace."[101]

The teaching of the Confession on saving faith also stresses the objects of such a faith. In this point, the Divines underscored two principles: The general object of faith is the word of God, and the special object of faith is the work and person of Jesus Christ.[102] Clark sees it as a point of essential importance and highlights the point that "saving faith is faith in Christ, but we must not empty the name of Christ from its biblical meaning."[103] The general object of saving faith includes "an assent of the heart to all the

---

[96] WCF, 14.3.

[97] WCF, 14.1.

[98] WCF, 14.1

[99] Thomas Brooks, *The Works of Thomas Brooks*, ed. Alexander B. Grosart (Carlisle: Banner of Truth, 1980), 317.

[100] Goodwin, *The Works of Thomas Goodwin*, 8:339.

[101] Hodge, *A Commentary on the Confession of Faith*, 278.

[102] WCF, 14.2.

[103] Clark, *What do Presbyterians Believe?*, 147.

truths revealed in the Word of God, whether they relate to the law or to the gospel; and that, not upon the testimony of any man or Church, nor because they appear agreeable to the dictates of natural reason."[104] Confirming this point, Hodge declares, "the whole word of God, therefore, as far as known to be individual, to the exclusion of all traditions, doctrines of men or pretended private revelations, is the object of saving faith."[105] This is the reason why some representatives of the Reformed tradition insist that faith in the Scriptures also includes "everything that is explicitly taught in Scripture or can be deduced from it."[106]

Specifically speaking, saving faith is *solo Christo*. Shaw asserts that "to know Christ, and God as manifested in him, is comprehensive of all saving knowledge – a term by which faith is sometimes expressed."[107] And referring to faith in Christ alone, Hodge explains it to be "an act of the whole man – intellect, affection, and will – embracing the truth."[108] This act also includes a belief in whatever the Scriptures reveal to us as to the person, offices, and work of Christ. Hence, this principle clearly points toward the exclusiveness of Christ for salvation.

In Scripture, faith is always active (cf. James 2:22; Heb. 6:18), and the Divines rightly emphasized this point when they spoke of the "acts of saving faith."[109] It is because faith is active that Scripture considers unbelief as a sin (John 14:9; 1 John 3:23), not as a mere intellectual ignorance.[110] Furthermore, the acts of saving faith involve knowledge, assent, and trust, which appeal to the commitment of the whole person. Since this emphasis triggers the question of how much knowledge one must have to be save, Hoekema answers,

---

[104] Shaw, *An Exposition of the Confession of Faith*, 148.

[105] Hodge, *A Commentary on the Confession of Faith*, 280.

[106] Berkhof, *Systematic Theology*, 506.

[107] Shaw, *An Exposition of the Confession of Faith*, 148.

[108] Hodge, *A Commentary on the Confession of Faith*, 281.

[109] WCF, 14.2.

[110] Dabney, *Systematic Theology*, 606.

"Our knowledge may be as slender as that of the thief on the cross (Luke 23:42); yet, he had enough faith to be saved."[111]

The Divines' stress on the acts of saving faith displays their rejection of any attempt to make faith a mere intellectual assent. The acts of faith are described to be "accepting, receiving and resting upon Christ alone for justification."[112] Hodge explains these acts as presupposing "that faith is not a bare intellectual conviction of the truth of truths revealed in the Scriptures, but that it includes a hearty embrace of and a confident reliance upon Christ, his meritorious work and his gracious promises."[113] Furthermore, Shaw comments that these acts distinguish "the true believer from such as rest their hope of salvation on the general mercy of God, without any respect to the mediation of Christ, or upon their own works of righteousness, or upon the righteousness of Christ and their own works conjoined."[114] And the Divines' emphasis upon faith – resting upon Christ for justification, sanctification, and eternal life – should be understood as an emphasis on complete salvation.

Finally, it must be observed that the Confession includes obedience to God's commands as another act of saving faith.[115] Developing this point, Hoekema reminds us that "though it is often said that faith is passive, there is also a sense in which faith is active. Faith is active in obedience."[116] Thus, it seems that the Divines would agree that nothing is more determinative of the quality of our Christian lives than our faith.

After paying close attention to the presuppositions and propositions of this chapter, it seems accurate to say that the Divines did not qualitatively contradict the Reformers, but gave a quantitative

---

[111] Hoekema, *Saved by Grace*, 142.

[112] WCF, 14.2.

[113] Hodge, *A Commentary on the Confession of Faith*, 282.

[114] Shaw, *An Exposition of the Confession of Faith*, 150.

[115] WCF, 14.2.

[116] Hoekema, *Saved by Grace*, 143.

continuity to their understanding of faith. This concept has strong missiological principles that need to be explored.

The Missiological Focus of WCF 14

Some scholars have suggested that the missiology of the Puritans was essentially anchored to their theology, and especially their soteriology.[117] Consequently, it seems right to suppose that the majority of the Puritans would agree with McGavran that every Christian doctrine should be colored with the dimension of God's concern for the lost. Three issues receive special focus: (1) its missiological motivations, (2) its missiological implications, and (3) its missiological application.

Missiological Motivations

The missiological strength of the doctrine of saving faith in the WCF is displayed not only in its missiological applications or implications, but also in its element of missiological motivation. In this regard, attention must be directed to the Divines' conviction that saving faith "gets the victory."[118] This victory is only possible because "salvation [from beginning to end] comes from the Lord" (Jonah 2:9). The Divines' emphasis on the sovereignty of God in salvation motivates missionary endeavor.

The certainty that saving faith attains final victory is not only a comfort to the striving Christian; it is also a motivation to missionary endeavor. David Brigham emphasizes two important principles on this issue. First, he asserts that "moved by faith, the church will persevere in her efforts for the conversion of the world to Christ."[119] This element of perseverance sustains the church even when she faces persecutions in a pagan society

---

[117] Rooy, *The Theology of Missions in the Puritan Tradition*, 310-36; Packer, "Puritan Evangelism", 6-7.

[118] WCF, 14.3.

[119] David Brigham, *Faith: The Grand Motive Power in the World's Conversion* (Boston: Press of T. R. Marvin, 1854), 11.

(cf. Acts 14:22; Eph. 6:18-20; and Rev. 3:10). The second principle asserted by Brigham is that "faith will constrain to 'fervent,
effectual prayer.'"[120] Faith can lead a church to develop a stronger
prayer life for missions. But the conviction that faith gets final
victory can also motivate a missionary in his work in the field.
Though conscious of his weakness, the success of the missionary
enterprise does not rely upon his human ability, but upon God who
meets all our needs "according to his glorious riches in Christ"
(Phil. 4:19). And the conviction that faith will finally attain victory
may sustain a missionary even in moments of disappointment (cf.
Phil. 1:6).

Missiological Implications
The exposition of the doctrine of saving faith in chapter 14 of the
WCF carries some missiological implications that must not be
overlooked, including: (1) the ministry of the word as a means
for generating saving faith, (2) the uniqueness of Christ for salvation, and (3) the indispensable work of the Spirit in generating
saving faith.

The first missiological implication found in this chapter is the
emphasis on the ministry of the word as the ordinary means by
which faith is wrought in the elect.[121] The missiological strength
of this emphasis springs from the fact that "since saving faith
comes only through the Word of God, one can easily understand
why we place such a great emphasis on the Word and on its being
preached."[122] Hoekema elaborates: "the preaching and teaching
of the gospel are divinely ordained means whereby people are
brought to faith."[123] Also, T. L. Wilkinson insists that "to bring
people to a living faith, the Word of God has to be diligently
taught and expounded, and there is absolutely no substitute for

---

[120] Ibid., 16.

[121] WCF, 14.1.

[122] Clark, *What do Presbyterians Believe?*, 144.

[123] Hoekema, *Saved by Grace*, 88.

this medium."[124] This emphasis on the preaching of the gospel led the Puritans to strive for a comprehensive presentation of the gospel.[125] The importance of the ministry of the word points toward a centrality of evangelism in the mission of the Christian church. As J. H. Bavinck insists, "any method which forgets to preach Christ is improper and wrong, and any method which permits Christ to be preached is both proper and good."[126]

Another clear missiological implication in this chapter is the uniqueness of Christ for salvation, which is expressed in the second paragraph. Sproul suggests that the eye of the storm in the Reformation was the word *alone* as it was applied to God's grace, faith, Scriptures, and Christ.[127] Consequently, the Divines reproduced the Reformers' concern regarding the uniqueness of Christ, and it is a sound implication for missionary activity of the church. Furthermore, some of Thomas Goodwin's works such as: *Christ Set Forth*, *Of Christ the Mediator*, and *A Discourse of the Supereminence of Christ above Moses*, provide an example of the relevance of this topic in the Puritan context.[128]

The uniqueness of Christ has become an important and much debated issue in recent years. The issue arises within Scripture itself (cf. Acts 15). In missiological circles, the debate around this topic became prominently popular "during the last five centuries of missionary expansion – both Roman Catholic and Protestant."[129] Most recently, through the influence of some pluralistic theologians such as John Hick, relativism has become a key to understanding religious truth. In this scheme, non-Christian religions are understood to be an 'ordinary way' to salvation,

---

[124] T. L. Wilkinson, *The Westminster Confession* (Melbourne: National Library of Australia, 1992), 100.

[125] Packer, *A Quest for Godliness*, 167-69.

[126] J. H. Bavinck, *Introduction to the Science of Missions*, trans. David H. Freeman (Phillipsburg: P&R, 1960), 132.

[127] Sproul, *Grace Unknown*, 66.

[128] Cf. Goodwin, *The Works of Thomas Goodwin*, 4:1-92; 5:3-436; 5:439-62.

[129] Charles Van Engen, *Mission on the Way* (Grand Rapids: Baker, 1996), 170.

whereas Christianity is a very special and extraordinary way.[130] In this theological/missiological context, a return to the Divines' emphasis on the uniqueness of Christ is not only relevant but also extremely necessary for the upholding of true Christianity. As John McIntosh asserts, "the uniqueness of Christ as Saviour is bound up with the uniqueness of the Christian faith as a whole, indeed with the uniqueness of the true and living God himself."[131]

A final missiological implication of the Divines' understanding of saving faith comes from their teaching on the indispensable work of the Spirit generating saving faith in the elect.[132] This teaching not only points to human inability in conversion, but also to the Puritan conviction that "the conversion of a sinner is a gracious sovereign work of Divine power."[133] Commenting on this paragraph of the Confession, Wilkinson argues, "Although faith is something that we consciously exercise, back and behind that activity is the mysterious work of the Holy Spirit awakening our hearts and minds to believe the Gospel."[134]

In the Divines' teaching on the work of the Holy Spirit in generating faith, the accent is on the mission of God, the *missio Dei*.[135] This emphasis reflects the Divines' understanding that saving faith is a work of the divine grace, a work of divine power, and a work of divine sovereignty.[136] In this context, grace is irresistible not because it drags men to Christ, but because the Spirit changes men's hearts so "they come most freely, being made willing by

---

[130] Cf. Ajith Fernando, *The Supremacy of Christ* (Wheaton: Crossway Books, 1995), 17-25.

[131] John McIntosh, "Biblical Exclusivism: Toward a Reformed Approach to the Uniqueness of Christ," *The Reformed Theological Review* (January/April 1994): 27.

[132] WCF, 14.1.

[133] Packer, "Puritan Evangelism", 6.

[134] Wilkinson, *The Westminster Confession*, 99.

[135] Fred Klooster, "Missions – The Heidelberg Catechism and Calvin," *Calvin Theological Journal* (November 1972): 200.

[136] Packer, "Puritan Evangelism", 7-8.

his grace."[137] It is never man, but always the sovereign God, who determines when an elect sinner shall believe. The rediscovery of this principle is ultimately relevant for a correct way of engaging in missions.

Missiological Application

The doctrine of saving faith in the WCF contains elements of special application to the missionary work. A missiological analysis of saving faith must include the place of faith in the application of redemption. The Divines referred to saving faith as the instrument "whereby the elect are enabled to believe to the saving of their souls."[138] It is by this faith that a person is enabled to accept, receive, and rest upon Christ alone for complete salvation.[139] In this vein, Shaw correctly declares, "If a Saviour was necessary to the recovery of lost sinners, faith in that Saviour is no less necessary to the actual enjoyment of salvation."[140] And Murray, writing about the relation between faith and regeneration asserts, "there is no such state or condition of regeneration without faith always coincident."[141]

Another important element of missiological application in the teaching of this chapter comes from the identification of obedience as an act arising from saving faith.[142] The missiological significance of this factor relies upon the fact that genuine missionary enterprise is rooted in obedience to God's commands, so that "fulfilling the missionary task is nothing more than obedience to the command of the Lord."[143] In this sense, John Stott argues

---

[137] WCF, 10.1.

[138] WCF, 14.1.

[139] WCF, 14.2.

[140] Shaw, *An Exposition of the Confession of Faith*, 146.

[141] Murray, *Collected Writings of John Murray*, 2:262.

[142] WCF, 14.2.

[143] Johannes Verkuyl, *Contemporary Missiology: An Introduction* (Grand Rapids: Eerdmans, 1987), 164.

that "individual Christians and local churches not committed to world evangelization are contradicting (either through blindness or through disobedience) an essential part of their God-given identity."[144] The Puritan emphasis on obedience as an act of saving faith can be directly applied to the missionary practice of the church.

Conclusion

The initial purpose of this essay was to analyze the fourteenth chapter of the WCF from a missiological perspective. This analysis has provided us with two major findings regarding the mission-mindedness of the Puritan Divines. First, it seems accurate to say that the denial of the Puritan mission-mindedness bears either an academic ignorance of the Puritans' works and writings, or a practical divorce from the Puritan tradition. Furthermore, any approach to the Puritan form of evangelism and missions must not overlook the fact that Puritan missiology does not fit in the pattern of the modern evangelism rooted in the practice of Charles Finney. Puritan theology of evangelism and mission is essentially God-centered rather than man-centered.

Regarding the missiological focus on the doctrine of saving faith in the WCF, it is clear that it contains several applications, implications, and motivations for the missionary enterprise. Further studies could be done by attempting a comparison between this chapter and the rest of the Confession, or between this chapter and the rest of the Westminster Standards. Another area recommended for future research is a comparison between this chapter and the writings of the Divines (e.g. sermons, letters, theological treatises, etc.). And finally, it seems right to summarize the missiological focus of the fourteenth chapter of the WCF by saying that

---

[144] John R. W. Stott, "The Bible in World Evangelization," in *Perspectives on the World Christian Movement: A Reader*, ed. Ralph D. Winter and Steve C. Hawthorne (Pasadena: William Carey Library, 1992), A – 4 and 5.

the Puritan approach to the task of winning souls was controlled by the knowledge that fallen men cannot turn to God by their own strength, nor is it in the power of evangelists to make them do so. The Puritan position was that only God, by His Spirit, through His word, can bring sinners to faith.[145]

Thus, the Puritan missiology in this chapter also reveals the God-centered character of their theology of mission.

---

[145] Packer, *A Quest for Godliness*, 163.

The Nature of the Lord's Supper According to Calvin and the Westminster Assembly

Wayne R. Spear

Introduction

This study had its origin in a seminar on Calvin's *Institutes* which has been offered at the Reformed Presbyterian Theological Seminary in recent years. In that seminar, both instructor and students read through the *Institutes* in a period of ten weeks. That concentrated reading led to some new insights into the thought of the great Genevan Reformer. One part of Calvin's thought which struck members of the seminar was the way Calvin spoke of the Lord's Supper, particularly his insistence that communicants partake of the very *substance* of Christ's body and blood. As the instructor, I looked for an opportunity to explore this aspect of Calvin's thought more deeply.

There seems to be a growing interest in Reformed circles to follow Calvin's doctrine of the Lord's Supper more closely, especially with regard to weekly observance. Robert Godfrey called for such a return to Calvin in an address at the Philadelphia Conference on Reformed Theology in 1981.[1] Calvin's desire for

---

[1]   W. Robert Godfrey, "This Is My Body," *Tenth: An Evangelical Quarterly* 11, no. 3 (July, 1981).

frequent observance needs to be seen against the background of his understanding of the nature of the Supper.

Calvin's view of the Lord's Supper has been a controversial issue in Presbyterian circles for a long time. As a part of that debate, scholars have argued whether or not the *Westminster Confession* followed Calvin, and, if so, how closely.[2] At the heart of the disagreement is the summary of Calvin's view given by Charles Hodge:

> So the body of Christ is in heaven, but from that glorified body there radiates an influence, other than the influence of the Spirit (although through his agency), of which believers in the Lord's Supper are the recipients. In this way they receive the body and blood of Christ, or, their substance, or life-giving power. [Calvin] held, therefore, that there was something not only supernatural, but truly miraculous, in this divine ordinance.[3]

In what follows, we take a fresh look at that discussion, seeking a clearer understanding of the language of the Westminster documents on the Lord's Supper.

John Calvin's View of the Lord's Supper

Some of the most intense debates of the Reformation era were about the Lord's Supper. Not only was there sharp disagreement between Catholics and Protestants, but the Protestant movement itself splintered because its leaders, despite strenuous efforts, could not achieve a genuine consensus. Calvin was abreast of all of those discussions, and was indeed an active participant in them. In his many writings on the Supper, he mentions and interacts with such writers as Luther, Zwingli, Oecolampadius, Peter Martyr, Bucer, and Jan a Lasco, as well as his chief opponents, the Lutherans

---

[2] John Adger, "Calvin Defended Against Drs. Cunningham and Hodge," *Southern Presbyterian Review* 27 (1876): 133-66. This article is carried on the PCA website: pcanet.org/history/periodicals.

[3] Charles Hodge, *Systematic Theology*, Vol. 3 (1872; repr., Grand Rapids: Eerdmans, 1952), 628.

Westphal and Heshusius. He had some points of agreement with all of them.

Not only that, but Calvin consciously sought to hold on to all that was sound and biblical in the long history of the church's discussion of, and teaching about, the Lord's Supper. The Jesuit writer Kilian McDonnell, in a surprisingly sympathetic study of Calvin's eucharistic teaching, concludes that ". . . almost all of Calvin's eucharistic concerns were part of the earlier eucharistic tradition." He mentions, among others, Isidore of Seville, Radbertus, Ratramnus, Berengarius, Wyclif, the followers of John Hus, and, most of all, Augustine, as writers who had some views similar to those of Calvin.[4]

Most of all, Calvin sought to be a biblical theologian, going to the Scripture as the ultimate source and final judge of doctrine. As he described what was objectionable in the Mass of the Roman Catholic Church, he wrote,

> But let us, on the other hand, to avoid falling into the same pit, fix our ears, eyes, hearts, minds, and tongues completely upon God's sacred teaching. For that is the school of the best schoolmaster, the Holy Spirit, in which we so advance that nothing need be acquired from elsewhere, but that we ought willingly to be ignorant of what is not taught in it.[5]

Calvin was sincere in his commitment to the principle of *sola scriptura*. However, in his interpretation of the word regarding the Supper, he was without question influenced by the whole history of discussion.

Calvin's writing on the subject of the Supper is extensive, and so is the secondary literature which seeks to interpret Calvin.[6] In

---

[4] Kilian McDonnell, *John Calvin, the Church, and the Eucharist* (Princeton: Princeton University Press, 1967), 58-59.

[5] John Calvin, *Institutes of the Christian Religion*, ed. John T. McNeill, trans. Ford Lewis Battles (Library of Christian Classics, vols. 20-21; Philadelphia: Westminster, 1960), 4.17.36.

[6] See the footnotes and Bibliography for the works consulted for this paper.

this part of the paper, we seek to give a clear summary of Calvin's view as a basis for the later comparison with the language of the documents of the Westminster Assembly. Calvin's doctrine regarding the Eucharist may be expressed in a series of propositions, which we now present and discuss.

The Supper is a memorial of the saving work of Christ (in particular, his sacrificial death), and is not itself a propitiatory sacrifice.

In the history of debate, the word "memorial" is usually identified with the Zwinglian view, often with the pejorative qualification: "*only* a memorial." Calvin rejected the "only," but did not hesitate to speak of the Supper as an occasion for remembering what the incarnate Christ has done for our salvation. In his *Short Treatise on the Holy Supper*, he movingly portrayed the distress of one who is conscious of personal sin and guilt, and then described how the Lord's Supper alleviates that distress:

> Now our heavenly Father, to succour us from [such misery], gives us the Supper as a mirror in which we contemplate our Lord Jesus Christ crucified to abolish our faults and offences, and raised to deliver us from corruption and death, and restoring us to a heavenly immortality. Here, then, is the peculiar consolation we receive from the Supper, that it directs and conducts us to the cross of Jesus Christ and to his resurrection, in order to assure us that, whatever iniquity there may be in us, the Lord does not cease to regard and accept us as righteous; whatever material of death may be in us, he does not cease to vivify us; whatever wretchedness we may have, yet he does not cease to fill us with all felicity.[7]

Calvin frequently used the metaphor of the Lord's Supper being a *mirror* in which the believer beholds Christ and his saving work.

---

[7] John Calvin, *Short Treatise of the Holy Supper of Our Lord and only Saviour Jesus Christ*, trans. J. K. S. Reid (Library of Christian Classics, vol. 22; Philadelphia: Westminster, 1954), 145.

In his exposition of the words of institution in 1 Corinthians 11, he used the "Zwinglian" term:

> Hence the Supper is a memorial . . . appointed as a help to our weakness; . . . The Supper then is (so to speak) a kind of memorial, . . . and it has been appointed for this purpose, that Christ may put us in mind of the benefit of his death, and that we may recognize it before men.[8]

In this context Calvin even spoke of Christ as in some sense absent from the Supper, a concept for which the Zwinglians were often criticized.

Since the Supper was a memorial of the one true sacrifice which Christ offered for the sins of his people, Calvin rejected the Catholic teaching, soon to be reiterated by the Council of Trent, that the Supper itself was a propitiatory sacrifice.[9] In the *Institutes*, he gave a lengthy exposition of the argument of the Epistle to the Hebrews, and concluded:

> Christ himself, when he seals the assurance of pardon in the Supper . . . sends [his disciples] to the sacrifice of his death, signifying that the Supper is a remembrancer, or memorial . . . from which men may learn that an expiatory victim, by which God was to be appeased, ought to have been offered but once. For it is not enough to understand that Christ is the sole victim, unless we add that there is only one sacrifice, so that our faith may be made fast to his cross.[10]

It follows that the Supper is in no sense a renewed offering for sin. However, it may be properly regarded as the offering of the sacrifice of praise.

---

[8] John Calvin, *Commentary of the Epistles of Paul the Apostle to the Corinthians*, trans. John Pringle (Grand Rapids: Baker, 1979), 381, 384.

[9] *Decrees of the Ecumenical Councils*, vol. 2, ed. Norman P. Tanner (Washington, D.C.: Georgetown University Press, 1990), Session 22, 733ff.

[10] Calvin, *Institutes*, 4.18.6.

As a memorial of Christ's sacrifice, the Supper strengthens faith, and thus enhances the enjoyment of the benefits of his saving work. On one hand, Calvin taught that faith was necessary for properly receiving the Lord's Supper. Those who come to the Table must examine themselves as to whether they have faith (with its invariable accompaniment, repentance). The faith that is required is no merely "historical" faith, a mental assent to the truth of Christianity, but "a lively feeling of faith and repentance."[11] Because this is so, clear teaching is needed in conjunction with the celebration of the Supper, in order that communicants may understand what is presented to them in it.[12] Word and sacrament must always go together.

On the other hand, faith always needs to be strengthened, and the sacraments are given to be "another aid to our faith related to the preaching of the Gospel." A sacrament is ". . . an outward sign by which the Lord seals on our consciences the promises of his good will toward us in order to sustain the weakness of our faith . . ."[13] Reflection on the sacrifice of Christ strengthens the assurance of salvation in the believer's experience. So, in a pastoral way, Calvin encouraged those who struggle with doubt and imperfect faith to come to the Lord's Supper, in order that their weak faith might become stronger.[14]

The Supper is a means by which the believer's union with Christ is strengthened; that union involves a "substantial participation" in the flesh and blood of Christ.

With this proposition we come to the heart of Calvin's understanding of the Lord's Supper. Up till now, what has been explained is quite compatible with the Zwinglian view, as usually understood.

---

[11] Calvin, *Corinthians*, 386, 388.

[12] Calvin, *Short Treatise*, 161.

[13] Calvin, *Institutes*, 4.14.1.

[14] Calvin, *Corinthians*, 388. "For faith, when it is but begun, makes those *worthy* who were *unworthy*."

Calvin was sympathetic with the desire to exclude any notion of a "carnal" or "local" presence of Christ in the elements, but felt that Zwingli had gone too far, and had robbed the Supper of its deepest significance.[15] Scattered through Calvin's writings are a series of significant statements about the Supper which take the form "not only . . . but":

> Christ . . . unites us into the same life with himself, and not only applies the fruit of his passion to us, but becomes truly ours . . . and accordingly joins himself to us, as head and members form one body.[16]

> Our communion, as stated by me, is not only in the fruit of Christ's death, but also in his body offered for our salvation.[17]

> For certainly the truth and reality of the sacrament is not only the application of the benefits of Christ, but Christ himself with his death and resurrection.[18]

> . . . the Lord intended, by calling himself the bread of life [John 6:51], to teach not only that salvation for us rests on faith in his death and resurrection, but also that, by true partaking of him, his life passes into us and is made ours – just as bread when taken as food imparts vigor to the body.[19]

For Calvin, union with Christ is at the heart of the meaning of the Lord's Supper. That union, as he describes it, is more than a relationship; it is a *substantial* communion and participation, not just with the Person of Christ, but in his flesh and blood.[20] In many

---

[15] Calvin, *Short Treatise*, 165-66.

[16] John Calvin, *A clear explanation . . . concerning the true partaking of the flesh and blood of Christ in the Holy Supper*, trans. J. K. S. Reid (Library of Christian Classics, vol. 22; Philadelphia: Westminster, 1954), 268.

[17] Ibid., 276.

[18] John Calvin, *The best method of obtaining concord . . .*, trans. J. K. S. Reid (Library of Christian Classics, vol. 22; Philadelphia: Westminster, 1954), 329.

[19] Calvin, *Institutes*, 4.17.5.

[20] Calvin, *Explanation*, 278, 287.

places, Calvin speaks of believers receiving the *substance* of the body and blood of Christ as they partake of the Lord's Supper. For example:

> We must then really receive in the Supper the body and blood of Jesus Christ, since the Lord there represents to us the communion of both . . . Jesus Christ gives us in the Supper the real substance of his body and blood, so that we may possess him fully . . .[21]

> Hence when we speak of the communion which we have in Christ, we understand the faithful to communicate not less in his body and blood than in his Spirit, so that they possess the whole Christ . . . [the Spirit] really feeds us with the substance of the body and blood of the Lord to everlasting life, and vivifies us by participation in them.[22]

> I say . . . that in the mystery of the Supper, Christ is truly shown to us through the symbols of bread and wine, his own body and blood . . . First, that we may grow into one body with him; secondly, having been made partakers of his substance, that we may also feel his power in partaking of all his benefits.[23]

Many other examples of such language might be given.

This is the most difficult and the most controversial part of Calvin's eucharistic doctrine. In order to understand it properly, we need to consider a number of subordinate points.

"This is my body" is to be understood *figuratively, not literally.* Because of his repeated use of the word *substance*, it might be thought that Calvin is approaching the Catholic and Lutheran view that the physical substance of the body and blood of Christ are literally and locally present in the Lord's Supper. Such is not the case. He plainly rejects the Catholic doctrine of transubstantiation,

---

[21]   Calvin, *Short Treatise*, 148.

[22]   G. Farel, John Calvin, and P. Viret, *Confession of Faith concerning the Eucharist*, trans. J. K. S. Reid (Library of Christian Classics, vol. 22; Philadelphia: Westminster, 1954), 168. [It is a question whether "Spirit" refers to the Holy Spirit or to Christ's spirit; probably the latter.]

[23]   Calvin, *Institutes*, 4.17.11.

and also the Lutheran view called consubstantiation. With Zwingli, he argues at length that the words of Jesus, "This is my body," cannot be interpreted literally. In harmony with many similar expressions in Scripture, Jesus' words are to be taken as a case of metonymy, a figure of speech in which there is substituted for the name of something, the name of a thing closely related to it. Calvin wrote, "There is here [an] instance of metonymy, and . . . the term *body* is applied to the bread, as being the sign and symbol of it."[24] The bread does not change, therefore, to become the flesh of Christ, nor is the flesh of Christ "in, with, and under" the bread. Calvin firmly rejects a local presence of the body and blood of Christ in the sacrament.

The rejection of the local presence is not based only on exegetical grounds; it also has a Christological foundation. The Scripture testifies to the fact that in the incarnation the Son of God took to himself a true human nature; in the language of the Creed of Chalcedon, he was "consubstantial with us as regards his humanity." Calvin argued that it is one of the unalterable characteristics of a human body that it cannot be in many places at the same time. Since Christ has ascended into heaven, and will remain there until the consummation, his body cannot be locally present wherever the Lord's Supper is celebrated.[25]

The virtue [life-giving power] of Christ's glorified body is communicated to the souls of believers in the Supper, but its substance is not mixed with their own, nor infused into them. Interpreters of Calvin have debated at length his use of the term *substance* when he discussed the Lord's Supper.[26] It is possible to identify at least three senses in which he used the term. First, Calvin used it when he was criticizing the Catholic doctrine of transubstantiation; *substance* in this context is used to speak of the basic physical reality of the bread and the wine. He held that

---

[24] Calvin, *Corinthians*, 377.

[25] Calvin, *Institutes*, 4.17.12.

[26] McDonnell, *John Calvin, the Church, and the Eucharist*, 232.

the physical substance of the elements is not changed in the action of the Supper.[27] Secondly, he often used *substance* to speak of the essence, or the central reality of the Supper, which is Jesus Christ. The Supper points to union with Christ, the whole Christ, and then to his body and blood, and then to the blessing and benefits which believers have from him. Calvin wrote:

> But because the blessings of Jesus Christ do not at all belong to us, unless he first be ours, it is necessary . . . that he be given us in the Supper, so that the things which we have mentioned be really accomplished in us. For this reason, I am accustomed to say that the matter and substance of the sacraments is the Lord Jesus Christ . . . all benefit which we ought to seek from the Supper is annulled unless Jesus Christ be there given to us as substance and foundation of all.[28]

In these statements, Calvin used the terms *matter* and *foundation* as synonyms for *substance*. Third, Calvin used *substance* specifically in reference to the body and blood of Christ, in which believers participate by faith, and in the Supper. It is this specific use of the word which we are seeking to understand more clearly.

Calvin was zealous to have the Lord's Supper understood as truly a means of grace, which affected believers in their experience. He saw the sacrament as involving union with Christ in the most intimate way, a union which engaged believers with the full humanity of Christ as well as his divinity. As he wrote his convictions, in the context of discussions about the "real presence" of the Savior in the Supper, his use of the term *substance* was liable to misunderstanding. When he responded to his critics, he clarified what he meant by *substantial participation* in the flesh and blood of Christ. He did not mean that in some way the physical "stuff" of his human body entered into the souls [much less the bodies] of communicants, but rather that his glorified body was the source of

---

27 Calvin, *Short Treatise*, 163.
28 Ibid., 146.

life-giving energy which was conveyed to them by the agency of the Holy Spirit.[29] As he wrote in his *Clear Explanation*:

> ... I am so far from rejecting the term substance, that I simply and readily declare, that spiritual life, by the incomprehensible agency of the Spirit, is infused into us from the substance of the flesh of Christ ... we are substantially fed on the flesh and blood of Christ, though I discard the gross fiction of a local compounding ... When I say that the flesh and blood of Christ are substantially offered and exhibited to us in the Supper, I at the same time explain the mode, namely, that the flesh of Christ becomes vivifying to us, inasmuch as Christ, by the incomprehensible virtue of his Spirit, transfuses his own proper life into us from the substance of his flesh, so that he himself lives in us, and his life is common to us.[30]

Calvin uses a number of analogies to make his meaning clear. The spiritual vitality which has its source in the body and blood of Christ is like the sap in a tree which flows into the branches to make them fruitful, or like the life-force conveyed to the body from the head.[31] Another analogy is taken from the sun:

> For if we see that the sun, shedding its beams upon the earth, casts its substance in some measure upon it in order to beget, nourish, and give growth to its offspring – why should the radiance of Christ's Spirit be less in order to impart to us the communion of his flesh and blood?[32]

A fourth analogy is introduced when Calvin is teaching that his flesh and blood are the proximate source of spiritual life, while the ultimate source is in the Father. With Cyril of Alexandria, Calvin understood John 5:26 to indicate that the Father bestowed upon the Son in his Incarnation the power to give life to those united to him:

---

[29] This view has been called "virtualism" by some (e.g. McDonnell, *John Calvin, the Church, and the Eucharist*, 232).

[30] Calvin, *Clear Explanation*, 264, 267.

[31] Calvin, *Best Method*, 326.

[32] Calvin, *Institutes*, 4.17.12.

> Water is sometimes drunk from a spring . . . yet it does not flow forth from itself . . . but from the very source, which by unceasing flow supplies and serves it. In like manner, the flesh of Christ is like a rich and inexhaustible fountain that pours into us the life springing forth from the Godhead into itself.[33]

In spite of some statements which seem to say otherwise – sometimes in the same context – Calvin asserted that what is conveyed to believers is not actually the substance of his flesh and blood, but this life-giving energy: "For it is enough for us that, from the substance of his flesh Christ breathes life into our souls – indeed pours forth his very life into us – even though Christ's flesh itself does not enter into us."[34]

The virtue of Christ's flesh and blood is conveyed to believers by the Holy Spirit; it is in this sense that there is a "spiritual presence" of Christ in the Supper. It is fairly common in Reformed circles to describe Calvin's view as asserting the spiritual presence of Christ in the Supper.[35] This language is not often found in Calvin. He clearly denied the local presence of Christ, and spoke more often of spiritual eating than of spiritual presence.[36] Primarily, he used the adjective spiritual to designate the work of the Holy Spirit which makes the sacraments effective in the lives of believers. The sacraments do not work by themselves, *ex opere operato*:

> [they] fulfill their office only when the Spirit, that inward teacher, comes to them, by whose power alone hearts are penetrated and affections moved and our souls opened for the sacraments to enter in. If the Spirit be lacking, the sacraments can accomplish nothing more in our minds than the splendor of the sun shining upon blind eyes, or a voice sounding on deaf ears.[37]

---

[33] Ibid., 4.17.9. See also Calvin's comment on John 6:57.

[34] Ibid., 4.17.32.

[35] E.g. Louis Berkhof, *Systematic Theology* (Grand Rapids: Eerdmans, 1959), 646.

[36] Calvin, *Clear Explanation*, 279; Calvin, *Institutes*, 4.17.33.

[37] Calvin, *Institutes*, 4.14.9.

The body of Christ is not physically present in the Supper; as a component of a true human nature it cannot be present in many places at once. How, then, can believers truly feed on the body and blood? Calvin's answer was that the Holy Spirit, by his incomparable work, brings together things that are separated in space. To correct a misunderstanding of his use of the term *spiritual*, he wrote:

> Another disputed point concerns the term *spiritually*. To this many are averse because they think that something vain or imaginary is denoted . . . Spiritual then is opposed to carnal eating. By carnal is meant that by which some suppose the very substance of Christ to be transfused into us just as the bread is eaten. In opposition to this it is said that the body of Christ is given to us in the Supper spiritually, because the secret virtue of the Spirit makes things separated in space to be united with each other, and accordingly enables life from the flesh of Christ to reach us from heaven.[38]

Calvin described this mysterious work of the Spirit in two different ways. In the passage just cited, the movement is from the body of Christ which is in heaven downward to believers on earth. In other contexts, Calvin spoke of believers being in some fashion lifted up to heaven by way of the Supper. In Calvin's communion service, the pastor was to say to the people,

> . . . let us raise our hearts and minds on high, where Jesus Christ is . . . Then only will our souls be disposed to be nourished and vivified with his substance, when they are thus raised above all terrestrial objects, and carried as high as heaven, to enter the kingdom of heaven where he dwells.[39]

Because unbelievers do not experience this hidden operation of the Holy Spirit, they cannot benefit from the Lord's Supper. While

---

[38] Calvin, *Best Method*, 329.

[39] *Form of Administering the Sacraments*, in Calvin's Selected Works, vol. 2, ed. and trans. Henry Beveridge (1849; repr., Grand Rapids: Baker, 1983), 120-21. (This language is a modification of the *sursum corda* of the traditional liturgy.)

the body and blood of Christ are truly offered to them, they reject the gift, and eat and drink to their own condemnation.[40]

The mode of this communication is beyond the power of mere human reason to grasp; it is a mystery. His opponent Heshusius charged Calvin with being a rationalist in rejecting the local presence of Christ, because the denial was based on reasoning from the nature of a human body. Calvin responded that he was following Scripture, and further, he denied that his views were governed by an unbiblical philosophy. He distinguished between three kinds of reason: (1) natural reason, implanted in human nature, and limited by the word of God; (2) fallen, vitiated reason, which subjects divine things to its own judgment; and (3) right reason, which finds its basis in the Scripture. Calvin, following (as he believed) Scripture and right reason, affirms as reasonable what is rejected by the wisdom of this world:

> For what is more repugnant to human reason, than that souls, immortal by creation, should derive life from mortal flesh? This we assert. What is less in accordance with earthly wisdom, than that the flesh of Christ should infuse its vivifying virtue into us from heaven?[41]

It is because his teaching about the nature of the Supper is above human reason, that Calvin constantly uses the adjectives *secret, mysterious,* and *incomprehensible* when referring to the operation of the Holy Spirit in it. In a famous passage, he acknowledged that the reality of which he wrote was beyond his own capacity to understand: "Now if anyone should ask me how this takes place, I shall not be ashamed to confess that it is a secret too lofty for either my mind to comprehend or my word declare. And, to speak more plainly, I rather experience than understand it."[42]

---

[40] Calvin, *Institutes*, 4.17.33.

[41] Calvin, *Clear Explanation*, 272-73.

[42] Calvin, *Institutes*, 4.17.32.

The Lord's Supper in the Documents of the Westminster Assembly

We now consider the extent to which Calvin's view of the Lord's Supper is reflected in the documents of the Westminster Assembly. In this examination, we look not only at the Confession of Faith, but also at the Larger and Shorter Catechisms, and at the Directory for Worship.

The Westminster documents clearly view the Supper as a memorial of the saving work of Christ, and reject the view that it is a propitiatory sacrifice.

In agreement with Calvin, the Confession of Faith states that Christ instituted the "sacrament of His body and blood...for the perpetual remembrance of the sacrifice of Himself in His death . . ."[43] Communicants are to "take and eat the bread, and to drink the wine, in thankful remembrance that the body of Christ was broken and given, and his blood shed, for them."[44] In the administration of the Lord's Supper, The Directory for Worship advocates the use of the words "This do in remembrance of me," from 1 Corinthians 11:24.[45]

The Confession also follows Calvin in its strong disagreement with the teaching of the Roman Catholic Church that the Lord's Supper itself has a propitiatory character:

> In this sacrament Christ is not offered up to His Father; nor any real sacrifice made at all for remission of sins of the quick and dead; but only a commemoration of that one offering up of Himself, by Himself, upon the cross, once for all; and a spiritual oblation of all possible praise unto God for the same . . .[46]

---

[43] *The Westminster Confession of Faith*, ed. S. W. Carruthers (Manchester: R. Aikman & Son, n.d.), 29.1.

[44] *The Larger Catechism*, in *The Confession of Faith; The Larger and Shorter Catechisms, etc.* (Inverness: Free Presbyterian Publications, [1983]), Q. 169.

[45] *The Directory for the Publick Worship of God*, in *The Confession of Faith; The Larger and Shorter Catechisms, etc.* (Inverness: Free Presbyterian Publications, [1983]).

[46] WCF, 29.2. The words "by Himself" indicate that only Christ, and not any priest, can make the offering.

The remembering of Christ and his work which takes place in the Lord's Supper calls for the exercise of faith on the part of worthy communicants. With Calvin, and perhaps more strongly, Westminster emphasizes the instrumentality of faith for profitable participation. It is "inwardly by faith" that believers "receive and feed upon Christ crucified." The body and blood of Christ are "spiritually . . . present to the faith of believers in that ordinance."[47] The Larger Catechism gives a more experiential description of how that faith is exercised. Worthy communicants are not passive, but ". . . by faith . . . receive and apply unto themselves Christ crucified, and all the benefits of his death." During the time of communing they are to ". . . affectionately meditate on his death and sufferings, and thereby stir themselves to a vigorous exercise of their graces . . . in earnest hungering and thirsting after Christ, feeding on him by faith, receiving of his fulness, trusting in his merits, rejoicing in his love, giving thanks for his grace...."[48] Faith, for Westminster, is not only a precondition for blessing in the Communion, but the very instrument through which that blessing comes.

The Westminster Documents view the Supper as a means by which the believer's union with Christ is strengthened; but Calvin's notion that that union involves a "substantial participation" in the flesh and blood of Christ is absent.

According to the Westminster Confession, for true believers, the Supper is "a bond and pledge of their communion with Him, and with each other, as members of his mystical body." In it they ". . . have their union and communion with Him confirmed."[49] According to the Directory for Worship, in the suggested prayer in which the elements are blessed, the pastor asks that ". . . we may receive by faith the body and blood of Christ, crucified for us, and so feed

---

[47] WCF, 29.7.

[48] WLC, Q. 170, 174.

[49] WCF 29.1; WLC, Q. 168.

upon him, that he may be one with us and we one with him . . ."[50] For Calvin, union with Christ was at the center of the meaning of the Lord's Supper. While, as indicated, it is not absent from Westminster's view, it needs to be said that it is not so prominent in their documents as it is in Calvin. For Westminster, *confirmation* of union with Christ, i.e., the strengthening of assurance of it, has greater prominence.

In even more striking contrast to Calvin, the Assembly does not include any treatment of the questions of the location of Christ's body in heaven, or of the life-giving virtue of his body and blood, and certainly nothing about "substantial participation."[51] Echoing Scripture, the Catechisms do speak of feeding on (or partaking in) the body and blood of Christ.[52] More often, the documents speak of feeding on Christ, or on Christ crucified, which places the emphasis on the whole person of Christ, and his saving work, instead of his body.[53] It appears that in Larger Catechism, Q. 170, the figurative language of feeding on Christ's body and blood is explained by the more literal succeeding clause:

> . . . they that worthily communicate in the sacrament of the Lord's supper do therein feed upon the body and blood of Christ, not after a corporal and carnal, but in a spiritual manner; yet truly and really, while by faith they receive and apply unto themselves Christ crucified, and all the benefits of his death.

The Westminster documents do not emphasize the work of the Holy Spirit in the Lord's Supper in the way that Calvin did.
Calvin recognized the problems connected with his view that believers, in a realistic way, partake of the substance, or better, the virtue of the actual body and blood of the Lord when they

---

[50] *Directory*, 385.

[51] The term *substance* occurs only in rejection of the Catholic position. WCF, 17.5, 7.

[52] WLC, Q. 170; WSC, Q. 96.

[53] WCF, 29.7; WLC, Q. 170, 174, 177; WSC, Q. 97.

participate in the Communion. One of his responses was to stress the secret work of the Holy Spirit, who puts believers in touch with the absent body of Christ. He explained that this is what is meant by the expression *spiritual eating*.

The term "spiritual" is often used in the statements of the Assembly with regard to feeding on Christ. For example,

> Worthy receivers outwardly partaking of the visible elements in this sacrament, do then also, inwardly by faith, really and indeed, yet not carnally and corporally, but spiritually, receive and feed upon Christ crucified, and all the benefits of his death . . .[54]

"*Spiritually*" is contrasted with *carnally and corporally*; the truth and reality of the action is stated, but there is no explicit reference to the Holy Spirit. The emphasis seems to be on the faith of the recipients. Only in the Directory for Worship, in the prayer of blessing, is the Spirit mentioned. There, thanks is given that God's people ". . . are permitted to eat and drink at his own table, and are sealed up by his Spirit to an assurance of happiness and everlasting life." The Lord is asked ". . . to vouchsafe his gracious presence with us [note: not specifically the presence of *Christ*], and the effectual working of his Spirit in us."[55] The work of the Spirit is seen here as making the observance of the sacrament as a whole to be effective in the lives of believers; not particularly to make the life-giving virtue of the body and blood to be present to them. Calvin's distinctive perspective on the action of the Spirit in the Supper is absent.

The Westminster statements do not speak of the mysterious character of the presence of Christ's body in the Supper.
It is not that the Westminster Divines had lost all sense of mystery. In speaking of God's eternal decree, the Westminster Confession did not hesitate to speak of *mystery*: "The doctrine of this high

---

[54] WCF, 29.7.

[55] *Directory*, 385.

mystery of predestination is to be handled with special prudence and care . . ."[56] As we have seen, Calvin regarded the mode of Christ's presence in the Supper to be beyond human understanding, and to be the effect of the secret, incomprehensible, mysterious work of the Holy Spirit. When the Confession describes the nature and operation of the Supper, the concept of mystery is not used.[57]

The rejection of the Catholic doctrine of transubstantiation was based on the fact that it is ". . . repugnant, not to Scripture alone, but even to common sense and reason . . ." The implication is that Westminster's doctrine of the Supper is in accordance with sanctified common sense and right reason.

This does not mean that the Westminster Assembly was more rationalistic than Calvin. However, it is evidence that they did not follow Calvin in his notion of *substantial participation* in the body and blood of Christ.

The Westminster Doctrine in the Light of Earlier Documents

The language of the Westminster documents should be understood in the context of the development of the theology of the Lord's Supper, particularly in the British Isles. We will look now at three of the most significant preceding confessional statements produced in those lands.

---

[56] WCF, 3.8.

[57] When this paper was first presented, I erroneously stated that the concept of mystery was not used in this chapter of the Confession. In fact it does appear, in passing, in Section 8; the Lord's Supper is called "these holy mysteries." This language reflects that of the Book of Common Prayer. However, the concept of mystery, as stated above, is not part of the *explanation* of the sacrament. The Minutes of the Assembly have the following entry for December 12, 1645: "Report of Sacrament in general debated. Debate about the word 'mystery.'" No action is recorded. *Minutes of the Sessions of the Westminster Assembly of Divines*, ed. Alex. F. Mitchell and John Struthers (Edinburgh and London: William Blackwood and Sons, 1874), 169.

Thirty-Nine Articles (1571), Article 28:

> The Supper of the Lord, is not only a signe of the loue that Christians ought to haue among them selues one to another: but rather it is a Sacrament of our redemption by Christes death. Insomuch that to suche as ryghtlie, worthily, and with fayth receaue the same the bread whiche we break is a parttakyng of the body of Christe, and likewyse the cuppe of blessing, is a parttakyng of the blood of Christe . . . The body of Christe is geuen, taken, and eaten in the Supper only after an heauenly and spirituall maner: And the meane whereby the body of Christe is receaued and eaten in the Supper is fayth.[58]

The Scots Confession (1560), Article 21:

> . . . in the Supper rightlie used, *Christ Jesus* is so joined with us, that hee becummis very nurishment and fude of our saules . . . bot this unioun and conjunction, quhilk we have with the body and blude of *Christ Jesus* in the right use of the Sacraments, wrocht be operatioun of the haly Ghaist, who by trew faith carryis us above al things that are visible, carnal, and earthy, and makes us to feede upon the body and blude of *Christ Jesus,* quhilk now is in heaven, and appearis in the presence of his Father for us . . . So that we confesse, and undoubtedlie beleeve, that the faithfull . . . do so eat the bodie and drinke the blude of the Lord *Jesus,* that he remaines in them, and they in him: Zea, they are so maid flesh of his flesh, and bone of his bones; that as the eternall God-head has given to the flesh of *Christ Jesus* . . . life and immortalitie; so dois *Christ Jesus* his flesh and blude eattin and drunkin be us, give unto us the same prerogatives . . .[59]

---

[58] The Thirty-Nine Articles of the Church of England (1571), in Philip Schaff, ed., *The Creeds of Christendom*, Vol. 3 (1877; repr., Grand Rapids: Baker, 1993), 505-06.

[59] Ibid., 468-69.

The Irish Articles of Religion (1615), Articles 92, 94, 95:

> The Lord's Supper . . .[seals] unto us our spiritual nourishment
> and continual growth in Christ . . . In the outward part of the
> holy Communion, the body and blood of Christ is in a most lively
> manner *represented*; . . . But in the inward and spiritual part the
> same body and blood is really and substantially *presented* unto
> all those who have grace to receive the Son of God, even to all
> those that believe in his name. And unto such as in this manner do
> worthily and with faith repair unto the Lord's table, the body and
> blood is not only signified and offered, but also truly exhibited
> and communicated.[60]

When these three confessional statements are compared with the
Westminster documents, it appears that the language of Westminster
most closely approaches that of The Thirty-Nine Articles. The Irish
Articles are closer to the language of Calvin, when the body and
blood or Christ are said to be "really and substantially *presented*"
in the Supper. The Scots Confession is closest of all to Calvin,
agreeing with him in virtually every detail. (This is not surprising,
since in 1560 John Knox had just come from what he regarded as
"the most perfect school of Christ" in Calvin's Geneva.)

This evidence could be read in two ways. Some would interpret
Westminster in the light of these earlier confessions as embodying
Calvin's view in full. That interpretation is certainly possible. On
the other hand, one might be struck with the fact that the Assembly
chose not to use language similar to that of the Scots Confession
and the Irish Articles, because they wished to allow for some
latitude among different convictions regarding the Lord's Supper.
This was a strategy not uncommonly followed by the Assembly.[61]

Robert Paul has shown that in some practical details in the
observance of the Supper, such compromise language was in

---

[60] Ibid., 542-43.

[61] See Wayne R. Spear, "Covenanted Uniformity in Religion." (Ph.D. diss., University of Pittsburgh, 1976), 82-86.

fact adopted.[62] Since the Minutes of the Assembly give almost no details of the discussions which took place, further investigation is needed into the writings of the various members of the Assembly in order to make a better-founded judgment on this matter.[63] For the present writer, the view that the Assembly deliberately chose not to repeat the language of Calvin's distinctive doctrine is the more attractive option.

Later Reflections on the Presence of Christ in the Supper

As we seek to assess the validity of the views of Calvin and the Westminster Assembly, it will be helpful to ponder the comments of Francis Turretin on the question of the presence of Christ in the Lord's Supper. [64] Turretin wrote more than a century after the time of Calvin, but in his discussion he was clearly interacting with and responding to Calvin's views (though he only mentioned him once by name). It may be that he expressed what was Calvin's intention more clearly than Calvin himself did.

In the section on the sacraments, Question 28, Turretin discussed the presence of Christ in the Lord's Supper, primarily to reject the Catholic and Lutheran doctrine of the corporal and local presence. Instead of their view, he affirmed a *spiritual* presence, which he explained in such statements as these:

> . . . in spiritual things, things are said to be present when they are offered to the intellect in such a way that it can apprehend and enjoy them with its own power. Christ is said to be present to the mind of the believer in the celebration of this mystery . . .we do

---

[62] Robert S. Paul, *The Assembly of the Lord* (Edinburgh, T&T Clark, 1985), 367-73.

[63] To this point, I have identified only one substantial treatment of the doctrine of the Lord's Supper by a member of the Assembly. That is Edward Reynolds, *Meditations on the Holy Sacrament of the Lord's Last Supper*, in *The Works of Edward Reynolds*, vol. 3 (1826; repr., Morgan, Pa.: Soli Deo Gloria Publications, 1999).

[64] Francis Turretin, *Institutes of Elenctic Theology*, ed. James T. Dennison, Jr., trans. George Musgrave Giger, vol. 3 (Phillipsburg: P&R, [1997]), 505-19.

not deny that Christ's body is present in the sacrament, inasmuch as in the lawful use it exerts its power in the communicants according to God's ordination.[65]

Turretin understood that the presence of Christ, with his body and blood, is in the *consciousness* of the believer. The power and efficacy of Christ are not absent, but they become effective as the truth and promise embodied in the Supper is understood and embraced by one who has been enlightened by the Holy Spirit. According to the words of institution in Luke 22:19:

> . . . Christ's body is proposed in the Supper to us and represented by the sacramental signs as dead and his blood as poured out of his veins (in which manner it is impossible for Christ's body to be made present to us at this day corporeally and indistantly . . ., since he can die no more) . . .[66]

The only way in which the dying of Christ (his broken body and shed blood) can be present to us is by our remembering.

The Lord's Supper, then, is entirely spiritual. The *food* is spiritual: ". . . both because it ought to be the nourishment of the mind not of the body, and because the life which is to be sustained is spiritual and heavenly (consisting in the remission of sins and the practice of sanctification) . . ." The *eating* is spiritual, by the mouth of faith, by which ". . . we apply to ourselves his flesh given for the life of the world by a living apprehension of his merit . . ." The *effects* are spiritual: ". . . our mystical union with Christ (John 6:27), a glorious resurrection (v. 54), and the fruition of eternal life (vv. 47-49)."[67]

Like Calvin, Turretin sees union with Christ as central to the meaning of the Lord's Supper (and to the reality of the Christian life). That union, real and intimate, is to be understood in terms of relationship, not in sharing of substance. He argues that in the

---

[65] Turretin, *Institutes*, 28.3, pp. 506-07.

[66] Ibid., 28.5, p. 508.

[67] Ibid., 28.9, p. 510.

light of the context of 1 Corinthians 10:16, the "communion of the body and blood of Christ" means a communion of "fellowship and society." This is so because the passage also speaks of the communion which exists between believers, even those who are distant from one another, including those who are in heaven; and that union does not involve any sharing of substance: ". . . we are one with Christ in the same manner as also we being many are one body in Christ (to wit, by one Spirit, not by a transition of substance into substance)."[68] With an allusion perhaps to Calvin's use of the term *substantial*, Turretin says that union with Christ is substantial or essential only in terms of its *reality*.[69]

By way of contrast with Turretin's concept of the nature of union with Christ, we should note that Calvin frequently cited the words of Ephesians 5:30 as he spoke of union with Christ and of the Supper: "We are members of His body, of His flesh and of His bones."[70] But when one considers the analogy which is being used by Paul, it is clear that the union thus described is *relational*, not *substantial*. In marriage, there is no passing of life-giving virtue from one partner to another, no sharing of substance. The relationship is covenantal, not ontological. Eating the flesh and drinking the blood, then, is symbolic language for remembering and applying to one's self the precious truth that in his true humanity, in his flesh and blood, he suffered death for his people.[71]

R. L. Dabney was deeply influenced by Calvin and Turretin as he developed his doctrine of the presence of Christ in the Lord's Supper. He agreed with both that union with Christ is central in the meaning of the Supper. He asserted that one's view of the nature of that union with Christ is crucial for how one understands the nature and efficacy of the sacrament. He then contrasted two views of union with Christ, the latter being Calvin's:

---

[68] Ibid., 28.31, pp. 518-19.

[69] Ibid., 28.23, p. 217.

[70] Ibid., 4.17.9.

[71] In 2 Sam. 5:1; 19:12-13, "flesh and bones" indicates a relationship of kinship or loyalty, not *substantial participation*.

Is the vital union, then, only a secret relationship between Christ, and the soul, instituted when faith is first exercised, and constituted by the indwelling and operation of the Holy Ghost: or, is it a mysterious, yet substantial conjunction, of the spiritual substance, the soul, to the whole substance of the mediatorial Person, including especially the humanity?[72]

Following in essence the argumentation of Turretin, Dabney chose the first description as that which is true, rejecting Calvin's view as "untenable and unscriptural."[73]

Dabney's assessment of the view of the Lord's Supper in the Westminster Confession was the same as that offered earlier in this paper: that the Assembly avoided language which would definitely express concurrence with the distinctive features of Calvin's doctrine. In contrast to the notion of *substantial participation*, the Assembly's view as summarized by Dabney is as follows:

Hence we construe the Confession . . . to mean by the receiving and feeding, precisely the spiritual actings of faith in Christ as our Redeemer, and on His body slain, and blood poured out, as the steps of His atoning work; so that the thing which the soul actually embraces, is not the corporal substance of His slain body and blood, but their redeeming virtue. . . . In this sense only, the sacrament brings Christ before us; that it places Him, in faith, before the cognizance of the sanctified understanding and heart.[74]

This view involves a figurative interpretation of what is meant by eating the flesh and drinking the blood of Christ in the Supper. The body and blood are not considered in themselves, but as the vehicle in which Christ fulfilled all righteousness, atoned for the sins of his people, and purchased their salvation (see Heb. 2:14). In Dabney's words, "The sixth chapter of John contains many internal marks,

---

[72] R. L. Dabney, *Systematic and Polemic Theology* ed. 5; Richmond: Presbyterian Committee of Publication [1871]), 810.

[73] Ibid., 811.

[74] Ibid.

by which the feeding on Christ is identified with faith, and his flesh is shown to be only a figure for the benefits of his redemption." He points to John 6:63: "It is the Spirit who gives life; the flesh profits nothing. The words that I speak to you are spirit, and they are life," and paraphrases their meaning in this way:

> [Redemption] is a spiritual work; no material flesh can have any profitable agency to promote it, as it is a propagation of life in the soul; the agency must be spiritual, not physical. And the vehicle of that agency is the gospel word, not any material flesh, however connected with the redeeming Person. The thing you lack is not any such literal eating, . . . but true, living faith on Christ.[75]

Conclusion

While following Calvin for the most part in developing the doctrine of the Lord's Supper, many later Reformed theologians have taken exception to his distinctive doctrine of a substantial participation in the body and blood of Christ.[76] It is the conclusion of this study that they were correct in doing so. Scripture does not teach that there is a virtue or life-giving power which resides in the glorified flesh of the Savior, and that comes to us through the Lord's Supper. By the power of the Holy Spirit, we are intimately and vitally united to his *Person*. By that same Spirit, the whole Person of Christ acts through the means of grace to apply the benefits of his saving work. He acts through the word, so that when people hear the word truly preached, they hear Christ, and are taught by him.[77] And he acts by his Spirit in the observance of the Lord's Supper, so that, by remembering him and his atoning death and triumphant resurrection, believers grow in grace. Their faith is strengthened, and their assurance of salvation is deepened.

---

[75] Ibid.

[76] In addition to Turretin and Dabney, the following may be mentioned: Charles Hodge, William Cunningham, Louis Berkhof, and Robert Reymond.

[77] Rom. 10:14; Eph. 4:20, 21.

Is there a connection between Calvin's notion of *substantial participation* in Christ's flesh and blood, and his advocacy of frequent observance of the Supper? Calvin affirmed that there is no benefit in the Lord's Supper which is not also found in the word.[78] The sacrament serves as " . . . another aid to our faith related to the preaching of the gospel."[79] However, in the preaching of the word, generally speaking, there is not a constant reference to the life-giving virtue of the body and blood of Christ. The tendency of Calvin's doctrine, intended or not, is to find a benefit which is specially to be found in the Supper in distinction from the word. If so, God's people would be missing that benefit without frequent observance.

The French Reformed pastor Adolphe Monod conducted worship in his home every week, while he was dying, including the celebration of the Lord's Supper. In one of those services, he preached on "Frequent Communion." He quoted from the French Confession of Faith:

> We confess that the Lord's Supper is a testimony to us of the union which we have with Jesus Christ, inasmuch as He was not only once dead and raised from the dead for us, but also feeds and nourishes us truly with His flesh and blood, so that we are one with Him, and His life is communicated to us . . . This we hold indeed to take place spiritually, not to substitute in place of fact and truth what is merely imagined or thought, but inasmuch as this mystery surpasses in its loftiness the measure of our senses and all the order of nature.[80]

These words of the French Confession express clearly and fully Calvin's position; he was indeed their principal author. Monod explicitly links frequent communion to Calvin's distinctive view.

---

[78] Calvin, *Clear Explanation*, 291.

[79] Calvin, *Institutes*, 4.14.1.

[80] Adolphe Monod, *Adolphe Monod's Farewell to his friends and to his church*, trans. Owen Thomas (London: Banner of Truth, 1962), 15.

The discussions about frequency of communion, then, ought to include also discussion of Calvin's position about *substantial participation* in the body and blood of Christ.

The Westminster Confession is not explicitly Calvinian in its doctrine of the Lord's Supper in the way that the French Confession is. It does not exclude the distinctive view of Calvin, but does not bind its adherents to that view. The discussion of the nature of the Lord's Supper should proceed with an awareness of the diversity within the Reformed churches on the subject, and with a final appeal to the exegesis of the relevant Scriptures. With that procedure, both Calvin and the Westminster Divines would be in agreement.

Works Cited

Adger, John. "Calvin Defended Against Drs. Cunningham and Hodge." *Southern Presbyterian Review* 27 (1876). [This article is carried on the PCA website: pcanet.org/history/periodicals.]

Berkhof, Louis. *Systematic Theology.* Grand Rapids: Wm. B. Eerdmans, 1959.

Calvin, John. *The best method of obtaining concord . . .* In *Library of Christian Classics,* Vol. XXII. Translated by J. K. S. Reid. Philadelphia: Westminster Press, 1954.

_____. *A clear explanation . . . concerning the true partaking of the flesh and blood of Christ in the Holy Supper.* In *Library of Christian Classics,* Vol. XXII. Translated by J. K. S. Reid. Philadelphia: Westminster Press, 1954.

_____. *Commentary of the Epistles of Paul the Apostle to the Corinthians.* Translated by John Pringle. Grand Rapids: Baker Book House, 1979.

_____. *Form of Administering the Sacraments,* in *Calvin's Selected Works, Vol. 2.* Edited and translated by Henry Beveridge. Grand Rapids: Baker Book House, 1983.

_____. *Institutes of the Christian Religion.* In *The Library of Christian Classics,* Vol. XX & XXI. Edited by John T. McNeill. Translated by Ford Lewis Battles. Philadelphia: Westminster Press, [1960].

_____. *Short Treatise of the Holy Supper of Our Lord and only Saviour Jesus Christ*. In *Library of Christian Classics*, Vol. XXII. Translated by J. K. S. Reid. Philadelphia: Westminster Press, 1954.

Dabney, R. L. *Systematic and Polemic Theology*. ed. 5 Richmond, Va.: Presbyterian Committee of Publication, [1871].

Decrees of the Ecumenical Councils, Vol. II. Edited by Norman P. Tanner. London: Sheed & Ward; Washington, D.C.: Georgetown University Press, 1990.

The Directory for the Publick Worship of God. In *The Confession of Faith; The Larger and Shorter Catechisms, etc.* Inverness: Free Presbyterian Publications, 1983.

Farel, G., John Calvin, and P. Viret. *Confession of Faith concerning the Eucharist*. In *Library of Christian Classics,* Vol. XXII. Translated by J. K. S. Reid. Philadelphia: Westminster Press, 1954.

W. Robert Godfrey. "This Is My Body." *Tenth: An Evangelical Quarterly* 11, no. 3 (July 1981).

Charles Hodge. *Systematic Theology*, Vol. III. Grand Rapids: Wm. B. Eerdmans, 1952.

The Irish Articles of Religion (1615). In *The Creeds of Christendom*, Vol. III. Edited by Philip Schaff. Harper & Row, 1877. Reprint, Grand Rapids: Baker Book House, 1983.

The Larger Catechism. In *The Confession of Faith; The Larger and Shorter Catechisms, etc*. Inverness: Free Presbyterian Publications, 1983.

McDonnell, Kilian. *John Calvin, the Church, and the Eucharist*. Princeton, N.J: Princeton University Press, 1967.

Monod, Adolphe. *Adolphe Monod's Farewell to his friends and to his church*. Translated by Owen Thomas. London: The Banner of Truth Trust, 1962.

Paul, Robert S. *The Assembly of the Lord*. Edinburgh, T.&T. Clark, 1985.

Reynolds, Edward. *Meditations on the Holy Sacrament of the Lord's Last Supper*. In *The Works of Edward Reynolds*, Vol. III. B. Holdsworth, 1826. Reprint, Morgan, Pa.: Soli Deo Gloria Publications, 1999.

The Scots Confession (1560*)*. In *The Creeds of Christendom*, Vol. III. Edited by Philip Schaff. Harper & Row, 1877. Reprint, Grand Rapids, Michigan: Baker Book House, 1983.

The Shorter Catechism. In *The Confession of Faith; The Larger and Shorter Catechisms, etc.* Inverness: Free Presbyterian Publications, 1983.

Spear, Wayne R. "Covenanted Uniformity in Religion." PhD diss., University of Pittsburgh, 1976.

The Thirty-Nine Articles of the Church of England (1571). In *The Creeds of Christendom*, Vol. III. Edited by Philip Schaff. Harper & Row, 1877. Reprint, Grand Rapids: Baker Book House, 1983.

Turretin, Francis. *Institutes of Elenctic Theology*, Vol. 3. Translated by George Musgrave Giger. Edited by James T. Dennison, Jr. Phillipsburg, N.J.: Presbyterian & Reformed Publishing, [1997].

The Westminster Confession of Faith. Edited by S. W. Carruthers. Manchester: R. Aikman & Son, n.d.

Calvin and Westminster on the Lord's Supper: Exegetical and Theological Considerations

Wayne R. Spear

The Lord's Supper has become a subject of controversy in Reformed circles in our time. The disagreements are largely about practical questions: Should the Supper be celebrated weekly? Should fermented wine be used, as a matter of principle? Should covenant children, not yet professing, be admitted to the Table?

The reasons for these questions being raised are not entirely clear. One significant factor may be a recent book by Keith Mathison, *Given for You,* which advocates weekly Communion, the use of fermented wine, and (with some hesitation) paedocommunion.[1] The book is well-written, and reflects serious research into the whole history of views of the Lord's Supper, with a focus on Calvin's view. Its influence is enhanced by Dr. Mathison's affiliation with Ligonier Ministries and R. C. Sproul, who has written a very favorable Foreword for the book. There is a natural appeal to Reformed people of a book which purports to "reclaim" a neglected teaching of John Calvin.

Mathison's thesis is as follows: "By the beginning of the nineteenth century, the Calvinistic doctrine of the Lord's Supper had been largely abandoned in many segments of the Reformed

---

[1] Mathison, Keith A., *Given for You: Reclaiming Calvin's Doctrine of the Lord's Supper* (Phillipsburg: P&R, 2002).

church." The abandonment was found in such writers as Turretin, á Brakel, and Jonathan Edwards. By the late nineteenth century, "Calvin's doctrine was not merely quietly rejected, but was explicitly condemned" by influential theologians such as Charles Hodge, Robert Dabney, and William Cunningham. In Mathison's view, their harmful influence was effectively countered by John W. Nevin's Mercersburg theology.[2] In his historical survey, Mathison characterizes the Westminster Confession as " . . . ambiguous in its sacramental theology but tending toward a Calvinistic view."[3] The purpose of the book is to call the Reformed churches back to the high sacramental theology of Calvin.

Using Mathison as a starting-point, then, this paper begins with a cautionary examination of John W. Nevin's contribution to the debate. (The reason for the examination and caution will be explained later.) Then we will do an exploration of the biblical basis which Calvin used for his distinctive view of the nature of the Lord's Supper, subjecting his exegesis to respectful criticism. This will lead to a description of the sacramental theology of several Westminster Divines. Finally, we will undertake an interpretation of the language of the Westminster documents in the light of their historical and theological context.

John W. Nevin on the Presence of Christ in the Lord's Supper

Nevin's understanding of the Lord's Supper is considered here because he was an influential interpreter of Calvin and of the Reformed Confessions in the 19th century.[4] Keith Mathison's perspective on the historical development of Reformed sacramental theol-

---

2   Ibid., 126, 128, 129, 176.

3   Ibid., 111.

4   John W. Nevin, *The Mystical Presence and Other Writings on the Eucharist*, in Bard Thompson and George H. Bricker, eds. *Lancaster Series on the Mercersburg Theology*, vol. 4 (Philadelphia and Boston: United Church Press, 1966). Nevin taught at the Theological Seminary of the German Reformed Church at Mercersburg, Pennsylvania from 1840 to 1851.

ogy is closely parallel to Nevin's. As he summarizes the literary debate between Charles Hodge and John Nevin, it is clear that Mathison's sympathies lie with Nevin; he offers no substantial criticism of his theology.[5] However, Nevin's defense of the Calvinian doctrine of the Supper is set in a radically different theological framework than Calvin's, a framework which is clearly heterodox. Mathison fails to give a needed warning about the dangerous unsoundness of the Mercersburg theology.

With regard to the Lord's Supper, Nevin held that there is a sharp contrast between the "old Reformed view" [Calvin's] and the "modern Puritan view."[6] For brevity, the contrast may be displayed in a table (see following page).

When the contrast is set up in this way (involving some overstatement of the "Puritan" position), the Calvinian view is intriguing. However, it is necessary to understand carefully what Nevin meant by the terms and expressions he used.

Nevin held that the doctrine of the Lord's Supper is not just one aspect of the Christian faith. He wrote, "The doctrine of the Eucharist is intimately connected with all that is most deep and central in the Christian system as a whole, and it is not possible for it to undergo any material modification . . . without a corresponding modification at the same time of the theory and life of religion at other points."[7] One's doctrine of the Lord's Supper will determine also one's view of the Person of Christ, of the Church, and of salvation. For Nevin, the nature of the Lord's Supper is the key to his whole theological system.

Starting from the Lord's Supper, Nevin and his "Mercersburg Theology" operated with a realistic view of original sin and the saving work of Christ. The "realistic" theory of original sin is that all of mankind is held guilty of Adam's trespass because the

---

5   Mathison, *Given for You*, 136-56.

6   Nevin, *The Mystical Presence*, 104-16.

7   *Ibid.*, 29.

Calvinian	Modern Puritan
1. Communion with Christ in the Supper is *specific* in its nature, different from what takes place in other parts of worship.	1. Christ is present in the same manner in all ordinances; by his Spirit, he makes them effectual means of salvation.
2. The sacramental transaction is a *mystery*; even, a *miracle*, transcending human understanding.	2. The Supper is *comprehensible*, appealing to the senses, imagination, heart, and understanding.
3. There is an *objective force* in the Sacrament; it confers what it represents to believers.	3. The Supper is entirely *subjective*; it ratifies the covenant, instructs and affects the believer.
4. The Sacrament includes a real participation in the *person* of Christ. ("Christ first, and then his benefits.")	4. Communicant participates in the *benefits* of Christ's work, and the influence of his Spirit, but not in his *substantial life*.
5. Communion with Christ is with the life which flows from his *flesh* [humanity]. We "take into us the substance of what he was as man."	5. We have no communion with Christ's incarnate life, except by way of remembering what he endured in it for our salvation.
6. Union with Christ is the power of one and the same life.	6. Union with Christ is a correspondence of thought and feeling.
7. The Supper is a pledge of a special invisible grace present in the transaction itself.	7. The Supper is a sign and seal only of God's grace in general.
8. We are united to the person of Christ.	8. We are united to the merits of Christ only.
9. In the Supper we communicate in a real way with the whole person of Christ.	9. We communicate only with Christ's divinity.

whole of humanity was in Adam when he sinned. He rejected the alternative doctrine of the federal headship of Adam."[8]

One of the standard objections to the realistic theory is that it does not fit the parallelism between Adam and Christ in Romans 5:12-21. Reformation theology holds that our justification does not lie in our actual participation in the righteousness of Christ, but in the gracious imputation of that righteousness to sinners.

---

[8] "The Bible knows nothing of a simply outward imputation, by which something is reckoned to a man that does not belong to him in fact. The fall of Adam is adjudged to be the fall of his posterity, *because it was so actually* [emphasis added] . . . Our participation in the actual unrighteousness of his life, forms the ground of our participation in his guilt and liability to punishment." Ibid., 191.

Nevin, however, maintains that the parallelism is explained by the application of the realistic theory to the work of Christ.

The meaning of John 1:14, "The Word became flesh," according to Nevin, is that in the incarnation, the whole of humanity was united with the Logos. It is not that the Logos took a distinct *human nature* into union with his divine Person; he became *humanity*. In his suffering, ". . . he acted for himself and yet for the race he represented at the same time. For it was no external relation simply, that he sustained to this last. He was himself the race. Humanity dwelt in his person as the second Adam . . ."[9] Jesus was not simply a man; he was mankind.

Nevin's realistic view of the Person of Christ carries over into his doctrine of salvation. The atonement was not a propitiatory sacrifice, offered by Christ to satisfy divine justice. It was rather the victory of the new humanity in Christ over sin and death.[10] The atonement was not something that happened outside of us, and was then imputed to us: "When Christ died and rose, humanity died and rose at the same time in his person; not figuratively but truly; just as it had fallen before in the person of Adam."[11]

It might seem that this view involves the conclusion that salvation is universal. However, Nevin goes on to speak of the way in which individual believers participate in this salvation. By faith, and especially by the Lord's Supper, they are joined to Christ in the "mystical union." Only so are they justified. Just as he denied imputation of Adam's guilt apart from participation in his sin, so now he denies the possibility of being reckoned righteous as something distinct from participation in Christ's life.

> The imagination that the *merits* of Christ's life may be sundered from his life itself, and conveyed over to his people under this abstract

---

9 Ibid., 162.

10 "The assumption of humanity on the part of the Logos involved the necessity of suffering, as the only way in which the new life with which it was joined could triumph over the law of sin and death it was called to surmount." Ibid., 162.

11 Ibid., 163.

form, on the ground of a merely legal constitution, is unscriptural and contrary to all reason . . . In the very act of our justification, by which the righteousness of Christ is accounted to be ours, it becomes ours in fact by our actual insertion into Christ himself.[12]

It is clear that Nevin rejects Calvin's soteriology, and that of the Westminster Confession. Reformed orthodoxy teaches that justification is a forensic act of God, declaring a sinner to be judicially righteous by the imputation of the righteousness of Christ. The righteousness by which we are made just is an *alien* righteousness, not something infused into us. Union with Christ and justification cannot be separated, but they must be distinguished from one another.

In a time when the nature of justification is under discussion among Reformed people, there is a need to be on guard against a theology like that of Nevin's. Since Keith Mathison's book fails to note the heterodoxy of John Nevin, his own work must be approached with caution.

The Distinctive Feature of Calvin's Doctrine of the Lord's Supper

We now turn to a consideration of Calvin's own writings on the Lord's Supper. We seek to understand more clearly that aspect of his thought which later came under criticism by Hodge, Dabney, and others: namely, that the Lord's Supper involves "substantial participation" in the flesh and blood of Christ by communicants.

In his response to Nevin, Charles Hodge gave a clear summary of explanations given by Calvin and other Reformed writers of the 16th century of what is meant by receiving the flesh and blood of Christ in the sacrament: "There is one thing in which all parties agreed, viz., that our union with Christ was a real union, that we receive him and not his benefits merely; that he dwells in his people by his Spirit, whose presence is the presence of Christ." All were

---

12 Ibid., 192.

agreed that receiving Christ's flesh and blood meant receiving the "virtue, efficacy, life-giving power of his body." This latter expression, however, was understood in two ways:

> Some intended by [this affirmation], not the virtue of Christ's body and blood as flesh and blood, but their virtue as a body broken and of blood as shed, that is, their sacrificial, atoning efficacy. Others, however, insisted that beside this there was a vivifying efficacy imparted to the body of Christ by its union with the divine nature, and that by the power of the Holy Ghost, the believer in the Lord's Supper and elsewhere, received into his soul and by faith this mysterious and supernatural influence. This was clearly Calvin's idea, though he often contented himself with the expression of the former of these views.[13]

For clarity, we may designate the first of the views described by Hodge as that of "faith-efficacy." In this view, the Lord's Supper is a means of grace because it confirms and enhances the communicant's faith in the sacrificial, atoning work of Christ. The Supper presents the body of Christ *as broken*, and the blood *as shed*, for our salvation. This understanding of the Lord's Supper emphasizes the need for instruction in the symbolic meaning of the elements and actions in the Supper. It calls for preparation on the part of the communicant. It is particularly a *covenantal* perspective, in which the relationship of the believer to Christ is renewed and strengthened as he reviews the promises of the covenant of grace, and renews his commitment to the stipulations of the covenant.

The second view, which believes that a life-giving power or virtue resides in the very essence of Christ's flesh and blood, we may call that of "substance-efficacy." This explanation of the efficacy of the Lord's Supper is found in Calvin's *Clear Explanation*:

---

[13]   Charles Hodge, "Doctrine of the Reformed Church on the Lord's Supper," in *Essays and Reviews, selected from the Princeton Review* (New York, Robert Carter and Brothers, 1857), 363.

... I am so far from rejecting the term substance, that I simply and readily declare, that spiritual life, by the incomprehensible agency of the Spirit, is infused into us from the substance of the flesh of Christ ... we are substantially fed on the flesh and blood of Christ ... When I say that the flesh and blood of Christ are substantially offered and exhibited to us in the Supper, I at the same time explain the mode, namely, that the flesh of Christ becomes vivifying to us, inasmuch as Christ, by the incomprehensible virtue of his Spirit, transfuses his own proper life into us from the substance of his flesh, so that he himself lives in us, and his life is common to us.[14]

Calvin always turned to the Scriptures as the final authority, and the final judge of the validity of all church teaching and practice. In seeking to evaluate his teaching about substance-efficacy (not the whole of his teaching on the Lord's Supper), we now turn to his commentaries on the Scriptures which give instruction about the Lord's Supper.

Calvin's Exposition of Scripture on the Lord's Supper

John 6:26-63

We begin with this passage because it comes earlier in time than the others, and provides a background for them. As Calvin acknowledges, this passage as such is not about the Lord's Supper. He adds, "At the same time, I confess that nothing is said here that is not figured and actually presented to believers in the Lord's Supper."[15]

There are two of Calvin's comments on John 6 which appear to express the idea of substance-efficacy. The first is on John 6:51:

---

[14] John Calvin, *A clear explanation ... concerning the true partaking of the flesh and blood of Christ in the Holy Supper*, trans. J. K. S. Reid (Library of Christian Classics, vol. 22; Philadelphia: Westminster, 1954), 264, 267.

[15] *Calvin's Commentaries: The Gospel according to St John 1-10*, ed. David W. Torrance and Thomas F. Torrance, trans. T.H.L. Parker (1961; repr. Grand Rapids: Eerdmans, 1979), 170.

". . . the bread which I shall give is my flesh, which I shall give for the life of the world." On this verse Calvin says:

> But it is objected that the flesh of Christ cannot give life, since it was liable to death and even now is not in itself immortal; and again, that it is not the property of flesh to give life to souls. I reply, although this power comes from another source than the flesh, this is no reason why this office [of giving life] may not accord with it. For as the eternal Word of God is the fountain of life, so His flesh is a channel to pour out to us the life which resides intrinsically, as they say, in His divinity. In this sense it is called life-giving, because it communicates to us a life that it borrows from elsewhere.[16]

He speaks of "life-giving flesh," which is able to give life to souls. While this may seem to express the notion of substance-efficacy, Calvin immediately explains that the flesh of Christ is life-giving precisely because of the work of atonement accomplished in that flesh:

> This will not be at all obscure if we consider what is the reason for life, namely, righteousness. Although righteousness flows from God alone, we shall not have the full manifestation of it anywhere else than in Christ's flesh. For in His flesh was accomplished man's redemption; in it a sacrifice was offered to atone for sins, and an obedience yielded to God to reconcile Him to us; it was also filled with the sanctification of the Spirit; finally, having overcome death, it was received into the heavenly glory. Therefore it follows that in it are placed all the parts of life . . . He delivered up Himself for the life of men; and now He invites us to receive the fruit of His death.[17]

This statement of Calvin's does not set forth the substance-efficacy of Christ's flesh as distinct from and in addition to its faith-efficacy. A second comment is on John 6:55. Calvin remarks,

---

[16] Ibid., 167.

[17] Ibid., 167-68.

"For when He states that His flesh is meat indeed, He means that souls are starved if they lack that food. You will only find life in Christ when you seek the substance of life in His flesh." Then he goes on to speak of the saving work of Christ:

> Thus we should glory with Paul in I Cor. 2.2 that we regard nothing as excellent but Christ crucified; for as soon as we depart from the sacrifice of His death, we encounter nothing but death . . . For by His emptying Himself, we were enriched with the abundance of all blessings; His humiliation and descent raised us up to heaven; by bearing the curse of the cross He set up a noble banner of righteousness.[18]

Again, the life-giving virtue of Christ's flesh does not lie in its inherent power, but in the saving work accomplished by the Word made flesh. Calvin here expresses the sacrificial significance, the faith-efficacy of Christ's body and blood.

Matthew 26:26-30; Mark 14:22-25; Luke 22:17-20

In his exposition of the Gospel accounts of the Last Supper, Calvin argues convincingly that Jesus' words "This is my body . . . This is my blood" are to be understood symbolically: Jesus meant, "These elements *represent* my body and blood." For Calvin, this does not at all take away the reality of what happens in the Lord's Supper. What is represented by the sign is actually given to communicants. He writes:

> In vain would the Lord be telling His people to eat bread affirming it to be His body unless the effect truly matched the representation . . . Even though we see nothing there but bread, He does not leave us with nothing or mock us when He takes our souls to feed them with His flesh. The true eating of the flesh of Christ is not only displayed in sign but demonstrated in real effect.[19]

---

[18] Ibid., 170.

[19] *Calvin's Commentaries: A Harmony of the Gospels Matthew, Mark, and Luke*, Vol. III, *and of the Epistles of James and Jude*, ed. David W. Torrance and

In stressing the reality of the Lord's Supper as a means of grace, Calvin uses the language, apparently, of substance-efficacy: ". . . souls are fed with the very flesh of Christ just as bread imparts vigour to our bodies. The flesh of Christ is spiritual food, because it is life-giving to us. It is life-giving because the Holy Spirit pours into us the life that rests in it."[20]

But Calvin moves without a clear break to speak of the sacrificial efficacy of the flesh and blood of Christ. Commenting on Matthew 26:29, he writes:

> Again, as He meant in the holy Supper to set His death before their eyes as in a mirror, He deliberately testified again that He was now leaving the world . . . He leads the disciples by the hand to the cross, and thence raises them to the hope of resurrection. They had to be guided by Christ's death that they might use it as a ladder to ascend into heaven . . .[21]

And a little later, on Luke 22:19,

> [T]he reason that the bread is Christ's flesh for us is that in it, salvation once for all is gained for us....the eating would be lifeless and of virtually no importance unless in respect of the offering of the sacrifice, once for all. Any who desire the nourishment of Christ's flesh should see it as offered on the cross, to be the price of our reconciliation with God.[22]

On Matthew 26:28, "This is my blood of the covenant, which is shed for many unto remission of sins," Calvin's comment is, "[I]n these words we are directed to the sacrifice of Christ's death, and to neglect this thought makes any due celebration of the Supper impossible."[23] The Supper is efficacious, because it points the faith of the communicant to the atoning death of Christ.

Thomas F. Torrance, trans. A. W. Morrison (Grand Rapids: Eerdmans, 1972), 135-40.

[20] Ibid., 136.

[21] Ibid., 137.

[22] Ibid., 137-38.

1 Corinthians 10:1-18

Paul wrote in 1 Corinthians 10:4 of the rock from which water flowed for the Israelites: "That rock was Christ." Calvin concludes from these words that the rock had sacramental significance, as did the manna, essentially the same as the Lord's Supper has for us. This leads to a question, which Calvin answers in terms of faith-efficacy:

> Since we now eat the body and drink the blood of Christ, how were the Jews partakers of the same spiritual meat and drink, when the flesh of Christ was not yet in existence for them to eat? To this I reply that although the flesh did not yet exist [in Moses' day], it was food for them all the same . . . for their salvation depended on the benefit of the death and resurrection, and *for that reason* [emphasis added] on the flesh and blood, of Christ.[24]

This important passage indicates that Calvin frequently uses language which might be understood as expressing substance-efficacy when he means faith-efficacy. Indeed, substance-efficacy is impossible here: the flesh and blood of Christ did not exist when the Israelites partook of it, except in the redemptive purpose of God. The benefits of the saving work of Christ were applied to them, although his death was still future.

Calvin seems to have the faith-efficacy of the Supper in mind when he explains 1 Corinthians 10:16. The wine becomes a sign of the blood of Christ when it is set apart for that purpose "by the Word of promise, when, in accordance with Christ's direction, believers meet together to keep the memorial of his death in the sacrament."[25]

One might expect to find Calvin speaking of substance-efficacy when he deals with Paul's expressions, "communion of the blood.

---

[23] Ibid., 138.

[24] *Calvin's Commentaries: The First Epistle of Paul the Apostle to the Corinthians*, ed. David W. Torrance and Thomas F. Torrance, trans. John W. Fraser (Grand Rapids: Eerdmans, 1960), 205.

[25] Ibid., 215.

. . .[and] of the body of Christ" in this text. He interprets this language as referring to union with Christ: ". . . what is the source of that . . . communion which exists among us, but the fact that we are united to Christ so that we are 'flesh of His flesh and bone of His bones'"? Beyond citing the words from Ephesians 5:30 (which we will discuss later), Calvin does not describe the nature of our union with Christ. There is no definite assertion that we draw life and vitality from the flesh and blood of Christ as such, which is the defining feature of the doctrine of substance-efficacy.

1 Corinthians 11:23-29

This passage, which gives apostolic instruction regarding the Lord's Supper, is crucial to any right understanding of the Supper.[26] It is in his commentary on these words of institution that Calvin's use of the concept of substance-efficacy is most clearly stated:

> But I myself maintain that it is only after we obtain Christ Himself, that we come to share in the benefits of Christ. And I further maintain that He is obtained, not just when we believe that He was sacrificed for us, but when He dwells in us, when He is one with us, when we are members of His flesh, when, in short, we become united in one life and substance (if I may say so) with Him . . . Christ does not offer us only the benefit of His death and resurrection, but the self-same body in which He suffered and rose again . . . the body of Christ is really (*realiter*), to use the usual word, i.e. truly (*vere*) given to us in the Supper, so that it may be health-giving food for our souls . . . our souls are fed by the substance of His body, so that we are truly (*vere*) made one with Him . . . a life-giving power from the flesh of Christ . . . is poured into us through the medium of the Spirit, even though it is at a great distance from us, and is not mixed with us . . .[27]

---

[26] Although Nevin wrote, "The idea of settling the sense of the Eucharist by the Words of Institution separately taken, is perfectly quixotic." *The Mystical Presence*, 253.

[27] John Calvin, *The First Epistle of Paul the Apostle to the Corinthians*, 246.

He regards as inadequate the view of those who think that receiving the body of Christ means only embracing Christ as crucified and raised, and thereby receiving the benefits which he purchased by that saving work (i.e. the view we call faith-efficacy).

Calvin does not give adequate exegetical reasons for this strong assertion that in the Supper we first receive the flesh and blood of Christ, and then the benefits of his life, death, and resurrection. He had argued earlier that the words "This is my body" are an instance of metonymy, in which the sign is given the name of the thing signified.[28] Now he seems to become more literal, and to insist that "body" cannot stand for his Person, or the work accomplished in the body, or for the benefits purchased by that work. "I am paying attention to the implication of the words, for Christ does not offer us only the benefit of His death and resurrection, but *the self-same body* in which He suffered and rose again."[29] He breaks up what is one continuous sentence: "This is my body, which is broken for you," in order to make a sharp distinction between being fed with the substance of his body, and receiving the benefits of his death and resurrection. This division of the sentence has no adequate justification.

In what follows, and in line with the actual content of the text, Calvin goes on to speak of the faith-efficacy of the Supper. In a summary statement, he seems to bring together what he had previously separated, with a focus on the death of Christ:

> That is why the Supper is a mirror which represents Christ crucified to us, so that a man cannot receive the Supper and enjoy its benefits, unless he embraces Christ crucified . . . The Supper is therefore a memorial . . . provided to assist our weakness; for if we were otherwise sufficiently mindful of the death of Christ, this help would be superfluous.[30]

---

[28] Ibid., 245.

[29] Ibid., 246.

[30] Ibid., 248.

Ephesians 5:30-32

This passage presents Paul's teaching on marriage, and does not deal directly with the Lord's Supper. Calvin makes the connection by seeing in marriage a metaphor for union with Christ, "a symbol and pledge of which is given to us in the holy Supper." In response to those who hold to the faith-efficacy of the Supper, Calvin appeals to the language of this passage, that we are "members of his body, of his flesh and of his bones." "Do we wonder, then, if in the Supper He offers His body to be enjoyed by us, to nourish us unto eternal life?"[31]

Calvin uses the reference to marriage in two ways to give support to the notion of the substance-efficacy of the Supper. First, in marriage, the husband and wife come together in such a way as to become one person: "The relationship goes beyond what is found in human society in general. Between a man and his wife there is a far closer relation; for they not only are united by a resemblance of nature, but by the bond of marriage are unified into one man." Secondly, with particular reference to Adam and Eve, the woman was derived from Adam's rib. "As Eve was formed out of the substance of her husband Adam, and thus was part of him, so, if we are to be true members of Christ, we grow into one body by the communication of His substance."[32]

With respect, I make two observations. (1) In marriage, husband and wife do not literally become one person. They are (or ought to be) united in the closest possible intimacy, committed to one another by covenant. But they remain distinct persons genetically, and in terms of personality and responsibility. (2) In the extraordinary case of Adam and Eve, after the initial formation of Eve, she also was a distinct person, and did not continue to derive her existence from Adam. She sinned first, and Adam later. So the

---

[31] *Calvin's Commentaries: The Epistles of Paul the Apostle to the Galatians, Ephesians, Philippians and Colossians*, ed. David W. Torrance and Thomas F. Torrance, trans. T. H. L. Parker (Grand Rapids: Eerdmans, 1965), 209.

[32] Ibid., 208.

example of marriage does not really make Calvin's point; it supports a covenantal rather than a substantial understanding of union with Christ.

In summary, a survey of Calvin's exposition of Scripture passages pertaining to the Lord's Supper does not make a convincing argument for his distinctive doctrine that in the Supper we derive life from the actual body and blood of Christ. This lack of a substantial exegetical basis lends weight to Hodge's observation that the notion of substance-efficacy

> was an uncongenial foreign element derived partly from the influence of previous modes of thought, partly from the dominant influence of the Lutherans and the desire of getting as near to them as possible, and partly, no doubt, from a too literal interpretation of certain passages of Scripture, especially John vi. 54-58, and Eph. v. 30.[33]

The Views of Some Members of the Westminster Assembly on the Lord's Supper

At the beginning of this study, I had hoped to find extensive exegetical work by Westminster Divines on the passages which have been discussed above. In works to which I have access, there is not much by way of biblical commentary. However, there are a number of available treatises by the Westminster Divines on the subject of the Supper, as well as published sermons. For this study, the writings of four members of the Assembly have been examined: those of Jeremiah Burroughs, Richard Vines, Edward Reynolds, and Thomas Goodwin.[34] We now consider these, with the question in mind, "Did members of the Westminster Assembly

---

[33] Hodge, "Doctrine of the Reformed Church on the Lord's Supper," 365.

[34] I have read two treatises on the Lord's Supper attributed to Edmund Calamy. Since there were six men who bore that name, and insufficient publication data is given in the reprint available to me, I have placed a description of his view in an appendix. If this is the Calamy who was a member of the Assembly, it is evidence of a covenantal view of the Supper held by a prominent member.

follow Calvin's doctrine of the substance-efficacy of the Lord's Supper?" The purpose of this inquiry is to better understand the theological context which influenced the language of the Westminster Confession in Chapter 29.

Jeremiah Burroughs

Burroughs, one of the "Independents" in the Assembly,[35] presented his doctrine of the Lord's Supper in three of the sermons published under the title *Gospel Worship*. The title indicates that he places the Supper in the broader context of worship, or drawing near to God. His aim is to assist worshippers to participate in Communion with reverence and spiritual benefit.

In these three sermons there are a few expressions which approach the idea of substance-efficacy. For example:

> We must sanctify God's name in this because it is the Sacrament of our communion with Christ wherein we come to have such a near union and communion with Him so as to eat His flesh, drink His blood, and to sit at his table. We come to have communion with Christ even in all our senses.[36]

Later, among the meditations which are recommended to those who are at the Lord's Table is the following:

> Though a believer is never so weak, yet seeing that God has appointed the body and blood of His Son for him to feed upon and to drink in a spiritual way, then surely the weakest in all the world will be strengthened . . . It's this which preserves the weakest grace in a believer, namely the spiritual nourishment that God the Father has appointed to them, even the feeding upon the body and drinking the very blood of His Son.[37]

---

[35]   William Barker, *Puritan Profiles* (Fearn: Christian Focus, 1996), 80ff.

[36]   Jeremiah Burroughs, *Gospel Worship: or, The Right Manner of Sanctifying the Name of God in General* (1648; text modernized, Morgan, Pa.: Soli Deo Gloria Publications, 1990), 288.

[37]   Ibid., 354.

This language clearly repeats the biblical terminology found in John 6, but does not go on to explain the meaning of the words in the way that Calvin does, i.e. as though some virtue resided in Christ's flesh and blood as such.

In contrast, the burden of Burrough's exposition is that the Lord's Supper is a renewal of the covenant of grace, and a believing remembrance of the sacrificial death of Christ.

> Now every time you come to receive this sacrament, you come to renew this covenant. It is as if you should say . . ., 'Lord, here I renew it and set my seal to it, to promise and covenant with You . . . I will give up myself forever to you as you have given the body and blood of Christ for my salvation.'[38]

One of the meditations suggested for those communing is this:

> Here is presented to us what this Mediator has done to reconcile us to God. His body was broken. He subjected Himself to the breaking of His body and to the pouring forth of His blood for our reconciling. It is not merely . . . that God has said, 'I'll pardon them,' but it cost Christ, undertaking to make peace between His Father and us, the breaking of His body and the pouring forth of His blood.[39]

In fact, eight of the ten meditations recommended by Burroughs deal with the atonement, the suffering of Christ for our salvation. The language of substance-efficacy is almost incidental; the bulk of his exposition presents the view of faith-efficacy. "The truth is, when we come to this holy communion, we are to look upon Christ as if we saw Him hanging upon the cross."[40]

Richard Vines

Vines was a famous and powerful preacher, and the member of the Assembly who made the motion that resulted in *two* Catechisms

---

38 Ibid., 334.

39 Ibid., 350.

40 Ibid., 317.

from the Assembly, the Larger and the Shorter.[41] In his work entitled "The Passover: Its Significance, and the analogy between It and Christ our Passover," Vines describes in detail the analogy which exists between the Old Testament Passover and the Lord's Supper. The following passage fairly represents his understanding:

> The Passover or Paschal lamb, as killed and roasted and the blood sprinkled, was a sacrifice; as eaten by the Israelites and feasted upon, it was a sacrament . . . So in our Supper, there is a sacrifice slain and offered up for atonement, and that is Christ's body and blood. And then there is an eating and drinking of this sacrifice in the sacrament of bread and wine . . . We have a true sacrifice, Christ, offered up to God for us. We have a true sacrament, as that sacrifice is eaten and drunk by us. The oblation belongs to God to propitiate and redeem; the communication belongs to us to be refreshed and nourished . . . Had He not been a sacrifice offered up for us, what profit would there have been in eating and drinking sacramentally and spiritually that body and blood?[42]

The effect of the Sacrament, for Vines, is predominantly upon the mind and the faith of the communicant. "The mouth eats the sacrament; the eye of faith discerns the sacrifice . . . God would have the sacrifice of Christ for our sin . . . to be observed and kept in mind by a lasting trophy and monument, our Supper."[43] His view is that of the faith-efficacy of the Lord's Supper; it confirms and refreshes the faith of the believer.

In another treatise by Richard Vines, there is a passage in which he closely follows Calvin's peculiar view; indeed, he cites Calvin by name.[44] Among the benefits which the believer receives in the Lord's Supper is intimate union with Christ's body and blood, for

---

41 Barker, *Puritan Profiles*, 132ff.

42 Richard Vines, "The Passover," in *The Puritans on the Lord's Supper*, ed. Don Kistler (Morgan, Pa.: Soli Deo Gloria Publications, 1997).

43 Ibid., 15-16.

44 Richard Vines, "The Fruit and Benefit of Worthy Receiving," in *The Puritans on the Lord's Supper*, 121ff.

spiritual nourishment. Vines follows Calvin in asking how the body and blood of Christ, which are in heaven, can reach believers who are on the earth? His answer is that the union is "mystical," beyond human understanding. The best he can say is that ". . . the human nature of Christ is the root of this union, but this union must not be distorted by too subtle curiosity because it is mystical."[45]

Before and after this passage, which expresses the substance-efficacy of the Lord's Supper, there are sections which focus on faith-efficacy. In a prior discussion, Vines sets forth the covenantal nature of the Lord's Supper: it is a seal confirming God's Covenant of Grace.

> As a seal refers to some covenant, so the sacrament refers to God's covenant with man, which is this: God promises to accept into favor and into His propriety all who believe in and receive Christ, and to bestow upon them all the blessings and benefits thereof. God gives Christ by way of covenant.[46]

The subsequent discussion focuses on assurance of forgiveness: in Communion, believers ". . . touch the hem of Christ, receive here the pardon of sin, and question not the seal of it."[47]

Edward Reynolds

The Westminster Confession was developed by several different committees of the Assembly. A man who served on three of the most important of those committees, including the committee of seven which made the original draft, was Edward Reynolds.[48]

In his *Meditations on the Holy Sacraments*, Reynolds discusses at length six "ends or effects" of the sacraments. We give a summary of his discussion of four of them.

---

[45] Ibid., 122-23.

[46] Ibid., 119.

[47] Ibid., 124.

[48] Barker, *Puritan Profiles*, 179-85.

(1) The Lord's Supper (along with Old Testament sacraments) is a means ". . . for the exhibition and conveyance of Christ, with the benefits of his passion unto the faithful soul."[49] He makes clear what he means by "exhibition": ". . . to exhibit a thing, is nothing else but to present it, or to make it present unto the party to whom it is exhibited . . ."[50] This leads to an illuminating discussion of the "spiritual presence" of Christ in the Supper. Reynolds rejects the Lutheran doctrine of the ubiquity of Christ's human nature, and the Roman Catholic teaching of a local, substantial presence of Christ's body and blood through transubstantiation. His own view is that Christ is present through the powerful agency of the Holy Spirit:

> That presence then of Christ in the sacrament . . . is a spiritual presence, of energy, power, and concomitancy with the element, by which Christ doth appoint, that *by* and *with* these mysteries, though not *in* and *from* them, his sacred body should be conveyed into the faithful soul.[51]

In language which closely approaches that of the Westminster Confession, he states:

> Christ is locally in heaven . . . yet having instituted these elements for the supply, as it were, of his absence, he is accounted present with them; . . . they which receive them with that reverend and faithful affection, as they would Christ himself, receive him too, really and truly, though not carnally or physically, but after a mystical and spiritual manner.[52]

(2) Another effect of the Lord's Supper is to confirm and increase the believer's union with Christ. Earlier, he had explained his understanding of this doctrine in a way that in some respects

---

[49] Edward Reynolds, *Meditations on the Holy Sacrament of the Lord's Supper*, in *The Whole Works of the Right Rev. Edward Reynolds, D.D.*, Vol. 3 (1826; repr., Soli Deo Gloria Publications, 1999), 67.

[50] Ibid., 69.

[51] Ibid., 73.

[52] Ibid., 72.

anticipates Nevin. Our connection with Adam is conceived as a realistic one:

> Now as, from Adam, there is a perpetual transfusion of original sin on all his posterity, because we were all then not only represented by his person, but contained in his loins; so from Christ, who on the cross did represent the church of God, and in whom we are – is there by a most special influence transfused on the church some measure of those graces…which were given to him without measure; . . . – because Christ and we do both partake of the same Spirit . . .[53]

This perspective embodies Calvin's teaching about the substance-efficacy of the Supper: it is a means whereby the vital power of Christ's own human nature is conveyed to us.

(3) "Another principle end or effect of this holy supper, is to signify and obsignate ['confirm or ratify by sealing'], unto the soul of every believer, his personal claim and title unto the new covenant of grace."[54] Here Reynolds, like Calvin, is asserting the faith-efficacy of the sacrament. In the believer's state of corruption, he is subject to temptation and doubt. The Supper serves to strengthen his hope, on the basis of the sacrifice of Christ. God has given it as a pledge and seal of our salvation, ". . . that we might, at this spiritual altar, see Christ (as it were) crucified before our eyes, cling unto his cross, and grasp it in our arms . . ."[55] The covenantal significance of the sacrament is found here, which is closely connected with the perspective of faith-efficacy.

(4) Closely connected to the previous point, the Lord's Supper has as its "most express end" the memorializing of Christ's death,

---

[53] Ibid., 46-47. Reynolds differs from Nevin in his strong advocacy of the substitutionary atonement, and in teaching that believers only, and not the whole of humanity, have this kind of union with Christ.

[54] Ibid., 83.

[55] Ibid., 83.

". . . that invaluable price of our double redemption; redemption from hell, and redemption unto glory."[56] Being a remembrance of the suffering and death of Christ, the Lord's Supper helps the believer call to mind the benefits which come to us from his passion: deliverance from the guilt of sin, a just claim to the righteousness of Christ, a new relationship to the law, hope for final freedom from the corruption of sin. This is the efficacy of faith: the sacrament confirms and enhances the believer's grasp on the truths of the gospel.[57]

In Reynolds, then, we find both the perspective of substance-efficacy and that of faith-efficacy. Of the Westminster divines whose writings have been examined for this paper, Reynolds comes closest to the full view of Calvin.

Thomas Goodwin

Goodwin was the leader of the Independents in the Assembly, and the most frequent speaker in the debates on church government.[58] He included a discussion of the Lord's Supper in his work, "Of Gospel Holiness in the Heart and Life."[59]

Goodwin's view of the Lord's Supper is strongly covenantal, and he sees it as a means of grace which works through the faith of the believer. Two citations will give the essence of his teaching:

> . . . the nature and intent of this ordinance . . . 1st, On God's part, it is to represent and exhibit the whole of Christ as crucified for us, in the most direct, immediate, adequate, and expressive manner. 2dly, On our parts it is publicly to solemnize and shew forth his death, and erect a fresh memorial of it, with profession of our interest in his person, his death, and all the benefits thereof.[60]

---

[56] Ibid., 87.

[57] Ibid., 92-104.

[58] Barker, *Puritan Profiles*, 70-77.

[59] Thomas Goodwin, "Of Gospel Holiness in the Heart and Life," in *The Whole Works of Thomas Goodwin, D.D.*, vol. 7 (Edinburgh: James Nichol, 1863).

[60] Ibid., 311.

> [The Lord's Supper] represents Christ in the most immediate and
> expressive manner . . . in this ordinance of the Lord's supper we
> have to do with Christ himself, his person, &c. We are put upon
> him, let into him immediately and directly, and are to converse
> with him, as a spouse with her husband, in the nearest intimacies
> . . . the bread is Christ, of which he says 'This is my body,' and
> of the wine, 'This is my blood;' yea, and it is Christ entire, whole
> Christ . . . the whole of his person, the whole of his death, the
> whole of his benefits, promises; yea, all that was purchased and
> procured by him . . . Whilst one eye of faith is called to look up
> to his person [note: not just his body and blood] as now in heaven
> glorious . . . with another eye we look back upon him as formerly
> hanging on a tree, bearing our sins in his body . . .

Goodwin's understanding of the efficacy of the Lord's Supper is
that it impacts the faith of the communicant, to confirm and re-
fresh that faith, and so strengthen his covenant relationship with
God through Christ.

In these four prominent members of the Westminster Assembly,
there is a strong consensus that an essential part of the meaning of
the Lord's Supper is that it is a God-given means of remembering
the sacrificial death of Christ. The Supper is a means of grace as
it confirms the covenant of grace, and strengthens the faith of the
communicant. Jeremiah Burroughs and Thomas Goodwin limit
their exposition to this view. If they speak of eating the flesh and
drinking the blood of Christ, they speak metaphorically, using the
very language of Scripture, without drawing the conclusion that
there is substance-efficacy in the Supper. Richard Vines and Edward Reynolds follow Calvin in attributing to the sacrament both
substance-efficacy and faith-efficacy.[61]

---

[61] Reynolds later became a bishop in the Church of England under Charles II.
Barker, *Puritan Profiles*, 183.

The Westminster Documents on the Sacraments

In conclusion, we examine some expressions in Chapters 27 and 29 of the Confession, and in the Larger Catechism, relating to the Lord's Supper.

WCF 27.1

"Sacraments are holy signs and seals of the covenant of grace . . . to represent Christ and his benefits, and to confirm our interest in him . . ."[62]

This basic definition of sacraments stresses their covenantal significance, which correlates with faith-efficacy. They represent Christ (not just his body and blood) and his benefits, that is, the fruit of his atoning work. When they confirm our interest in him, our faith is strengthened.

WCF 29.1

> Our Lord Jesus . . . instituted the sacrament of his body and blood . . . for the perpetual remembrance of the sacrifice of himself in his death, the sealing all benefits thereof unto true believers, their spiritual nourishment and growth in him, their further engagement in and to all duties which they owe unto him, and to be a bond and pledge of their communion with him, and with each other, as members of his mystical body.

This statement of the ends for which Christ gave the Supper continues the covenantal perspective of the Confession. Only the words "their spiritual nourishment and growth in him" suggest the idea of substance-efficacy. However, the expression is very general, and accords well with faith-efficacy, which explains that communicants are nourished by their believing remembrance of the death of Christ, and of the benefits procured by it.

---

[62] See WLC, Q. 162.

WCF 29.2

> In this sacrament . . . [is, not any real sacrifice, but] only a commemoration of that one offering up of himself, by himself, upon the cross, once for all . . . the alone propitiation for all the sins of the elect.

In rejecting the Roman doctrine of the sacrificial character of the Mass, the Confession stresses the memorial function of the Supper.

WCF 29.7

> Worthy receivers, outwardly partaking of the visible elements in this sacrament, do then also inwardly by faith, really and indeed, yet not carnally and corporally, but spiritually, receive and feed upon Christ crucified, and all the benefits of his death . . . the body and blood of Christ being then . . . as really, but spiritually present to the faith of believers in that ordinance, as the elements themselves are to their outward senses.

While stressing the reality of that which is done in the Supper, these words deny the local, corporal presence of Christ's body. The body and blood are present to the *faith* of the communicant, and *by faith* they receive and feed upon Christ. That on which they feed is not the body and blood as such, but *Christ crucified*, and the benefits of his death. The view presented here is entirely compatible with a faith-efficacy perspective.

WLC Q. 170

> Q. How do they that worthily communicate in the Lord's supper feed upon the body and blood of Christ therein?

> A. As the body and blood of Christ are . . . spiritually present to the faith of the receiver, no less truly and really than the elements themselves are to their outward senses; so they that worthily communicate in the sacrament of the Lord's supper, do therein

feed upon the body and blood of Christ, not after a corporal and carnal, but in a spiritual manner; yet truly and really, while by faith they receive and apply unto themselves Christ crucified, and all the benefits of his death.

This answer is based on Chapter 29.7 of the Confession, though the language is slightly different. The Confession speaks of "feeding on Christ crucified, and his benefits." The Catechism uses the words, "feeding on the body and blood of Christ." Keith Mathison concludes that the Catechism more closely approaches the view of Calvin.[63]

However, there is really no significant difference between the Confession and the Catechism. Taking the meaning of the conjunction "while" to be "throughout the time that; as long as," the two parts of the description of feeding on the body and blood should be understood as standing in apposition to one another; the latter explaining the former. Thus the sense is thus:

Worthy communicants feed on the body and blood of Christ, not after a corporal and carnal, but in a spiritual manner, yet truly and really, while by faith they receive and apply unto themselves Christ crucified, and all the benefits of his death.

This is the view of the working of the Lord's Supper which we are calling faith-efficacy.

Conclusion

Reformed believers have agreed that the Lord's Supper is not *merely* a memorial, nor *only* a profession of faith. They have believed and taught that Christ is really at work, by the Holy Spirit, in the Supper which he gave to his church. But they have not agreed as to the way in which the Supper is efficacious. All have stressed the importance of faith, and have seen the sacrament as working to confirm and strengthen faith in Christ, whose death

---

[63] Mathison, *Given for You*, 110

is vividly set before us in it. This is the view which we have labeled faith-efficacy. But Calvin and many of the Reformed confessions of the sixteenth century, also taught that in a mysterious way the Supper actually brings an influence or power from the glorified body of Christ to the communicant's soul. Because Calvin often speaks of our sharing in Christ's substance, we have called this view substance-efficacy.

Our study of Calvin's commentaries on the relevant passages has shown that his biblical basis for the view of substance-efficacy is highly questionable. It comes down to two brief expressions, in 1 Corinthians 11:24 and Ephesians 5:30. In relation to neither of these verses has Calvin given convincing evidence to support his particular view that we participate substantially in his flesh and blood.

The published views on the Lord's Supper by members of the Westminster Assembly give mixed evidence. All express the faith-efficacy of the Supper; in addition, two prominent members also put forth the substance-efficacy view.

When the language of the Westminster Confession and Larger Catechism is interpreted against this background, the conclusion of my earlier paper on this subject is reinforced, namely: "The Westminster Confession is not explicitly Calvinian in its doctrine of the Lord's Supper . . . It does not exclude the distinctive view of Calvin, but it does not bind its adherents to that view."[64]

If the Supper brings us some benefit which we do not receive through the preaching of the gospel (i.e. substantial participation in Christ's flesh and blood), then there is a strong reason for very frequent communion. If the Lord's Supper operates primarily to confirm the faith which is engendered by the word, and requires intelligent preparation and participation, then elders may arrange the frequency of observance to meet the needs of their particular flocks. When understanding the significance of the Lord's Supper

---

[64] Wayne Spear, "The Nature of the Lord's Supper according to Calvin and the Westminster Assembly," *The Westminster Assembly into the 21st Century*, ed. J. Ligon Duncan (3 vols.; Fearn: Mentor, 2004), 355-384.

is regarded as needed in order for people to partake of its blessing, then the case for paedocommunion loses much of its appeal.

The practical discussion about frequency of observance of the Lord's Supper, and whether children should commune, needs to be carried on in close connection with a clear understanding of the sacrament, and of the way in which it is effective as the means of grace. As Calvin so strongly taught, that understanding must be arrived at by careful study of the Scripture.

In my judgment, the Scripture does not teach the doctrine of substantial participation in the body and blood of Christ in the Lord's Supper, i.e. "substance-efficacy." The Supper is effective as a means of grace as the Holy Spirit enables us to remember with thankfulness that Christ died for us. Our covenant with him is renewed, and we are moved to greater thankfulness and commitment to his service.

Appendix I

Edmund Calamy

Calamy [if this is indeed he] was one of the "divine right Presbyterians" in the Westminster Assembly, and one of the most active in its debates.[65] He wrote two sermons on the Lord's Supper, in which he presents it primarily as a renewal of the covenant of grace.[66]

There is no reference in these sermons to partaking of the substance or the virtue of the actual body and blood of Christ. As the titles indicate, Calamy thought of the sacrament primarily as a "sign and seal of the Covenant of Grace." We give two passages which fairly summarize Calamy's conception of the nature of the Lord's Supper:

---

[65] Barker, *Puritan Profiles*, 208 ff.

[66] Edmund Calamy, "The Lord's Supper is a Federal Ordinance . . . ," and "The Express Renewal of Our Christian Vows Every Time We Come to the Holy Communion . . . ," in *The Puritans on the Lord's Supper*, ed. Don Kistler (Morgan, Pa.: Soli Deo Gloria Publications, 1997).

[A]s the Jewish feasts were upon the flesh of the sacrifices they offered to God, so is our holy Supper a feast upon the sacrifice which Christ once offered for us . . . whereby, eating and drinking at His own table and partaking of His meat, we are taken into a sacred covenant and inviolable league of friendship with Him . . . He confirms His covenant with us by the sacred symbols at His table of which He allows us to partake. And as the people [of Israel], by feasting on those sacrifices with God, ratified and confirmed the covenant on their part, so we, by feasting on this sacrifice, ratify and confirm the covenant between God and us.[67]

Another passage concentrates on the sacrificial significance of the Supper:

Our Lord, is, at His table, represented in our view as a sacrifice for sin, enduring the utmost torments, miseries and sorrows for our sake, all which have a loud voice to us. He seems, as it were, at His table to adjure every one by His agonies and conflicts, by His blood and wounds, by His cross and passion, by all that He underwent for their sakes, to love Him and be faithful to Him; to hate and fly from sin and renounce the devil and all his works . . . Those therefore who, after this, lay their hands on the memorials of the broken, bleeding body of Christ do, as it were, call heaven and earth to witness that they will ever live to Him who died for them, and rather die than renounce His service.[68]

The evidence from Edmund Calamy, then is entirely on the side of a faith-efficacy view of the Lord's Supper. The Supper brings blessing by reminding us of what Christ suffered for us as the surety of the covenant of grace, and by stimulating us to renew our trust in and commitment to him.

---

[67] Ibid., 33.

[68] Ibid., 34.

Improving the Means of Grace:
The Larger Catechism on Spiritual Growth

MARK E. ROSS

The Larger Catechism of the Westminster Assembly is largely a forgotten document, and a neglected treasure, among Presbyterians today. In an age that cries out for relevant preaching and practical application, the Larger Catechism stands as a goldmine of resources for the preacher of God's word and the suppliant in search of spiritual help. Its teaching on the effective use of the means of grace is particularly helpful in guarding us against mere ritualism in public worship, and guiding us toward a faithful and fruitful participation in the divine ordinances appointed for our spiritual nourishment and growth. It instructs the preacher in the preparation and delivery of sermons that can feed the people of God on the finest of the wheat, and it exhorts the people of God to active engagement with the preaching of the word and the administration of the sacraments. This paper will explore what the Larger Catechism has to say to us on "improving" (or making the best use of) the means of grace which God has appointed for us.

Introduction

The Larger Catechism (WLC) of the Westminster Assembly is clearly the most neglected and least quoted of the three great confessional documents of the Westminster Assembly. Robert

Godfrey maintains that "B. B. Warfield showed himself to be a master of understatement when he observed: 'In the later history of the Westminster formularies, the Larger Catechism has taken a somewhat secondary place.'" Godfrey himself describes the WLC as "a very distant second indeed . . . seldom mentioned, much less studied."[1] Similarly, Chad Van Dixhoorn remarks that the WLC is "neither loved, often used, or influential."[2]

Of the WLC, none of its phrases have entered into common parlance the way in which the answer to the first question of the Shorter Catechism has. The WLC's great length and detailed answers do not make it attractive for memorization. Even teaching from it can be tedious, given the long, complicated sentences that make up the answers to the questions. Still, for all its difficulties, I join my voice to others like Robert Godfrey, G. I. Williamson, Morton Smith, and Chad Van Dixhoorn who lament the neglect of the WLC by the Reformed churches today.[3] It has virtues of its own that simply are not duplicated elsewhere. Philip Schaff, for instance, gives the WLC high praise when he writes: "It is a masterpiece of catechetical skill, superior to any similar work, and exhibits in popular form a complete system of divinity . . . "[4] Godfrey likewise praises the WLC as a "full, balanced, edifying summary of the Christian faith."[5] On specific topics, John

---

[1] W. Robert Godfrey, "An Introduction to the Westminster Larger Catechism," in Johannes G. Vos, *The Westminster Larger Catechism: A Commentary*, ed. G. I. Williamson (Phillipsburg: P&R, 2002), ix. Morton Smith also complains of a neglect of the WLC, "even by Presbyterians," in his "Theology of the Larger Catechism," *The Westminster Confession into the 21st Century*, ed. J. Ligon Duncan (4 vols.; Fearn: Mentor, 2003), 1:121f.

[2] Chad B. Van Dixhoorn, "The Making of the Westminster Larger Catechism," *Reformation and Revival* 10, no. 2 (Spring 2001): 97-113.

[3] For Williamson's comments, see Vos, *The Westminster Larger Catechism*, vii. For Godfrey's, see ibid., xi-xviii. For Morton Smith, see "Theology of the Larger Catechism," 121.

[4] Philip Schaff, *The Creeds of Christendom* (New York: Harper & Brothers, 1877), 1:786.

[5] Godfrey, "An Introduction to the Westminster Larger Catechism," xvii.

Murray commends its statement of the covenant of grace over the Westminster Confession's own treatment of the subject, as well as its treatment of the imputation of Adam's sin in relation to the covenant of works.[6] Godfrey puts special emphasis on the WLC's treatment of the doctrine of the church, a topic he describes as "almost entirely absent" from the Shorter Catechism (WSC).[7] Morton Smith regards the WLC's commentary on the law and the Lord's prayer as the "most complete," and praises its insight into the person and work of Christ and the sacraments.[8] Testimonies like these should strongly encourage us to explore more deeply the resources provided to us in the WLC.

My own enthusiasm for this project is in part based on personal experience. For nearly fifteen years now I have taught courses on Christian ethics at both Reformed Theological Seminary in Charlotte and Jackson, and at Erskine Theological Seminary in Due West, SC. The courses have been structured by the Ten Commandments, and I have used the Bible and WLC's exposition of the Ten Commandments as the basic texts for the course, supplemented by various other readings like John Murray's *Principles of Conduct*, J. Douma's *The Ten Commandments*, John Gerstner's *Reasons for Duty*, and Michael Horton's *The Law of Perfect Freedom*. I have found nothing quite so helpful in teaching students the depth and breadth of the law of God as the WLC. From the WLC's pattern of breaking down the commandments into the things required and the things forbidden by each of the commandments, and the abundant proof texts which are supplied in justifying and illustrating the specific applications and implications of the commandments, students are encouraged to compare Scripture with Scripture. They are helped to see that the commandments of the Decalogue

---

6   John Murray, "The Catechisms of the Westminster Assembly," *Presbyterian Guardian* (December 25, 1943): 363. This work has been cited from Godfrey, "An Introduction to the Westminster Larger Catechism," xii.

7   Godfrey, "An Introduction to the Westminster Larger Catechism," xiii.

8   Smith, "Theology of the Larger Catechism," 122.

are indeed *summary* obligations which are then broken out in detailed applications in the remainder of the law. When even these ten comprehensive commandments are further summarized by our Lord (Matt. 22:34-40) in the two great commandments of love toward God and one's neighbor as oneself, then a unity in Scripture appears that before was unperceived by the students, and a much more developed sense of appreciation and importance for the law ensues. There is already within the students an appreciation for *love* as an important, guiding ethical principle. To see the way in which the detailed laws of the Bible derive from love through the Ten Commandments is to have their "spiritual immune system" strengthened against the infection of antinomianism and indifference to the law of God.

Moreover, when students begin with the commandments themselves, as the WLC does, and then move out to specific issues and applications – rather than starting with issues and working back to principles – I have found that students begin to think more principially. More than once I have heard testimonies from students about how their eyes have been opened to the law of God through the WLC, and how much help they have received from this type of study in the commandments. When from time to time I run into former students, I again hear testimonies of how the study of the commandments has helped them in their ministries and how they still use the WLC in preparation for teaching and preaching.

In grading papers, teachers can easily fall into despair over how much they have failed to communicate to students; and teachers may even admit to praying – as I have been told John Dewey used to pray – "Lord, deliver me from my disciples." But teachers will be more than amply compensated for these failures if they discover that students have found a new tool to help them in their study and understanding of the Scriptures by having made friends with the Larger Catechism.

In this paper, I want to show the helpfulness of the WLC for participation in the means of grace, beginning with what might seem to be the hardest test case: the once-administered sacrament of baptism. Since in this volume, as in its predecessors, we are looking at *The Westminster Confession into the 21st Century*, I believe that a renewed emphasis on the study and the teaching of the Larger Catechism, particularly by ministers of the word, could help us toward a more knowledgeable and more effective use of the means of grace.

Furthermore, I believe that despite the imposing format of the Larger Catechism, the time is ripe for a renewed use of it in our churches. We live in a time where there is much impatience toward "doctrinal" preaching. People, so we are told, long for practical preaching, for easy to understand applications on how they ought to live. Of course, there are those who are impatient even with practical preaching, longing only to be entertained and not challenged either intellectually or morally. Here, I am not concerned with treating that malady. I am concerned with feeding the flock of God, particularly with those who hunger and thirst after righteousness and long to grow in the grace and knowledge of our Lord and Savior Jesus Christ. For people who stand in need of instruction in the ways of God, and how to grow and mature to be more like Christ in every way, the WLC can be of great help. For preachers who must labor in preparing sermons and lessons to feed the flock of God, the WLC is a rich source of practical help and instruction. It gives guidance in equipping God's people for a more active and profitable participation in the means of grace, without loss of any of the doctrinal content.

The Practical Nature of the Larger Catechism

Consider, for a moment, just how practical the WLC really is on the means of grace. Merely reading the questions can make the point:

- Q. 155, "How is the word made effectual to salvation?"
- Q. 157, "How is the word to be read?"

- Q. 159, "How is the word to be preached by those that are called thereunto?"
- Q. 160, "What is required of those that hear the word preached?"
- Q. 171, "How are they that receive the sacrament of the Lord's supper to prepare themselves before they come unto it?"
- Q. 174, "What is required of them that receive the sacrament of the Lord's supper in the time of the administration of it?"
- Q. 175, "What is the duty of Christians, after they have received the sacrament of the Lord's supper?"

The answers to these and similar questions provide excellent guidance for participating in the means of grace. Admittedly, taken by themselves apart from the general context of the Confession and the WLC, and their teaching on the atoning work of Christ the Mediator, of the forgiveness of sins and the grace of God in Christ, of the perseverance of the saints, and the assurance of grace and salvation, one could easily understand these instructions in a legalistic way. The detailed, what Philip Schaff calls the "over-minute,"[9] applications made of the Ten Commandments, for instance, give some measure of pause even to the hardiest lovers of Puritan casuistry. But the Confession and the Catechisms are steadfastly opposed to legalism in all its forms.[10] The Westminster Divines had a full appreciation for the danger and the evil of lording it over the consciences of men.[11] So, the detailed plumbing of the depths of Scripture for every application that can be made of divine truth is not done because the Divines delight in laying heavy burdens upon the shoulders of God's people while they themselves will not lift a finger to help (Matt. 23:4). They are especially not the kind that delights in tithing mint, dill, and cummin, while neglecting the weightier matters of the law – justice, mercy, and faithfulness (Matt. 23:23). No, their animating spirit is the same

---

[9] Schaff, *The Creeds of Christendom*, 786.

[10] For a brief but effective defense of the WLC against the charge of legalism, see Godfrey, "An Introduction to the Westminster Larger Catechism," xii-xiii.

[11] See WCF, 20.

as that found in Psalm 119, which extols the beauty and goodness of the law of God in all its breadth and depth, and which diligently and persistently seeks for a knowledge of that law which is equal to the law itself.

> Teach me, O LORD, the way of your statutes;
>> and I will keep it to the end.
> Give me understanding, that I may keep your law
>> and observe it with my whole heart.
> Lead me in the path of your commandments,
>> for I delight in it.
>
> (Ps. 119:33-35 ESV)

"Improving" the Means of Grace?

Turning now to the WLC's teaching on the means of grace, we need to speak a word about the title to this paper. It echoes the language of WLC Q. 167 which asks, "How is our baptism to be improved by us?" Today many people will perhaps suppose that what is in view here are innovations in worship practice; that is, new ways of administering the sacrament of baptism so as to make it better in some sense. Improving our baptism, or improving the means of grace generally, has nothing to do with innovations in worship.

For the Westminster Divines, when they speak of "improving" the sacrament of baptism, they are using the word in a sense very common to their own day, though much less common in our own. For them, "improving" our baptism means, as Johannes Vos clearly puts it,[12] "using it to good purpose in our daily life."[13] The

---

[12] Vos, *The Westminster Larger Catechism*, 480.

[13] There is now a modern English version of the Larger Catechism which has been produced by the Evangelical Presbyterian Church and adopted as one of their confessional statements. See *The Westminster Confession of Faith and Catechisms in Modern English* (Signal Mountain, Tenn.: Summertown Texts, 2004). The wording of Q. 167 in that version is, "How do we continue to use our baptism?" While this is not subject to the misunderstanding that "improve"

Oxford English Dictionary, for instance, cites a use of the term from 1632 concerning property deeded to a Mr. John Winthrop to the effect that the deed shall become void "if the said . . . John Winthrop shall . . . suffer the ileland to lye wast, and not improve the same."[14] I believe this precisely captures the idea that the divines had in mind when they spoke of "improving" one's baptism: it is not to lie waste, but must be put to good use, and turned to one's advantage.[15]

What is in view here is just one example of making what the divines call "diligent use" of all the means whereby Christ communicates to us the benefits of his mediation. Question. 153 asks, "What does God require of us that we may escape his wrath and curse due to us by reason of the transgression of the law?" To this the answer is, "That we may escape the wrath and curse of God due to us by reason of the transgression of the law, he requireth of us repentance toward God, and faith toward our Lord Jesus Christ, *and the diligent use of the outward means whereby Christ communicates to us the benefits of his mediation.*" In the next question (Q. 154), the sacraments are identified as among those outward means whereby Christ communicates to us the benefits of his mediation. In Q. 57, the benefits of Christ's mediation which have been procured for us are specified as "redemption, with all other benefits of the covenant of grace." In Q. 65, the special benefits enjoyed by members of the invisible church are identified as union and communion with Christ. Question. 66 explains union with Christ as that union which by the work of God's grace the elect

---

might carry in this day, it seems to miss the idea of profitable and effective use which, along with continued use, is inherent in the notion of "improving" one's baptism.

14   *The Compact Edition of the Oxford English Dictionary*, vol. 1 (Oxford: Oxford University Press, 1971), 1393.

15   Parts of this article here and following are based upon an article I previously published in a now defunct journal. See "Improving Your Baptism," *Faith and Practice: A Journal of the Associate Reformed Presbyterian Church* 1, no. 1 (Spring 1995): 21-25. Copyright is the author's.

have with Christ "whereby they are spiritually and mystically, yet really and inseparably, joined to Christ as their head and husband; which is done in their effectual calling." Question. 69 explains the communion in grace as "partaking of the virtue of his mediation, in their justification, adoption, sanctification, and whatever else, in this life, manifests their union with him."

Putting all this together we may say that by his mediation Christ has purchased and procured for his elect many benefits, among which are union with Christ, redemption, effectual calling, justification, adoption, and sanctification; all which are either acts or works of God's free grace in which God accomplishes the salvation of his people (where "salvation" is to be understood in the broadest sense). Sometimes, perhaps most times in this confused age, salvation is used as if it were equivalent to justification. In that limited and specific sense, faith is the "alone instrument of justification" or salvation in this narrow sense (WCF, Ch. 11.2). But for salvation in the broad sense – wherein we are not only set right with God and delivered from the guilt and punishment of sin, but are also delivered increasingly, finally, and completely from the presence and power of sin, being perfectly conformed to the image of Christ – faith is not the alone instrument for our salvation. Again, Q. 153 asks, "What does God require of us, that we may escape his wrath and curse due to us by reason of the transgression of the law?" The answer is, "repentance toward God, and faith toward our Lord Jesus Christ, *and the diligent use of the outward means whereby Christ communicates to us the benefits of his mediation.*" For justification, then, faith is the "alone" or sole instrument whereby Christ communicates to us the benefits of his mediation; but for sanctification and salvation broadly considered, there are several means whereby Christ communicates to us the benefits of his mediation. Those means are all the ordinances of Christ, but "especially the word, sacraments, and prayer; all of which are made effectual to the elect for their salvation" (Q. 154), in the fullest sense.

To "improve" our baptism, therefore, is to make diligent use of it, to put it to good use and to gain benefit from it. This kind of "diligent use" is required of us for all the means of grace, especially the word, prayer, and the sacraments. Now one can easily understand how to make diligent use of the word, prayer, and the Lord's Supper. But how does one make diligent use of the one-time administration of baptism? I believe that in understanding this, we will come to a deeper understanding of how we "improve" the means of grace generally.

Improving Our Baptism

Q. 167 of the WLC asks, "How is our baptism to be improved by us?" The answer given is quite full. It begins in this way:

> The needful but much neglected duty of improving our baptism, is to be performed by us all our life long, especially in the time of temptation, and when we are present at the administration of it to others . . .

Here the WLC indicates that those who are baptized have a duty to "improve" or make diligent use of their baptism throughout their whole life. The one time administration of baptism is simply a beginning, providing a person with something – a sensible sign and seal of God's covenant of grace – which is to be used repeatedly and steadily throughout one's life. Two times are especially singled out for making diligent use of baptism: times of temptation, and when present at the administration of baptism to another. Thus, our baptism is intended to be for us "an effectual means of salvation," in which Christ repeatedly communicates to us the benefits of his mediation. The communication of these benefits to us is not tied to the moment when baptism is administered, but may and should occur throughout our whole life. How does this occur?

Consider the following: among the benefits of Christ's mediation is sanctification, in which we are "through the powerful operation of his Spirit applying the death and resurrection of Christ unto

[us], renewed in [the] whole man after the image of God; having the seeds of repentance unto life, and all other saving graces, put into (our) hearts, and those graces so stirred up, increased, and strengthened, as that (we) more and more die unto sin, and rise unto newness of life" (Q. 75).

The WLC is teaching us – yea, reminding us that the Scriptures teach us – that baptism stands among those means by which, through which, in which this "powerful operation" of God's Spirit communicates to us the grace we need to die more and more unto sin, and rise unto newness of life. Thus, baptism is especially to be improved by us (i.e. put to diligent use) in the time of temptation precisely so that we might overcome the temptation, dying to our sin, and rising unto newness of life.

What are we to do in making such diligent use of our baptism? The answer to Q. 167 continues by saying:

> The needful but much neglected duty of improving our baptism, is to be performed by us all our life long, especially in the time of temptation, and when we are present at the administration of it to others; by serious and thankful consideration of the nature of it, and of the ends for which Christ instituted it, the privileges and benefits conferred and sealed thereby, and our solemn vow made therein . . .

The first step in improving our baptism is to make serious and thankful consideration of the nature of baptism, and the ends for which Christ instituted it, the privileges and benefits conferred and sealed thereby, and our solemn vow made therein. Such "serious and thankful consideration" ought to begin with WLC Q. 165, which says that baptism is

> a sign and seal of ingrafting into [Christ], of remission of sins by his blood, and regeneration by his Spirit; of adoption, and resurrection unto everlasting life; and whereby the parties baptized are solemnly admitted into the visible church, and enter into an open and professed engagement to be wholly and only the Lord's.

Some care must be taken in interpreting these words, for the compressed nature of the catechism's teaching can easily give rise to a misunderstanding. For instance, how are we to understand the WLC's statement that baptism is "a sign and seal of our ingrafting into Christ, of remission of sins by his blood, and regeneration by his Spirit; of adoption and resurrection unto everlasting life . . . " A theology of the first glance might suggest that baptism signifies that those who have been baptized have been ingrafted into Christ, have received remission of sins, regeneration by his Spirit, etc. However, it is not the case, as the Confession of Faith certainly makes clear, that all who are baptized are automatically ingrafted into Christ, or that they will be eventually (WCF, 27.5).

> Although it be a great sin to contemn or neglect this ordinance, yet grace and salvation are not so inseparably annexed unto it, as that no person can be regenerated or saved without it, or that all that are baptized are undoubtedly regenerated.

Thus, according to the Confession, persons can be saved without being baptized, and they can be baptized without being saved. For proof of the latter, the WCF footnotes the example of Simon Magus from Acts 8. Simon was baptized under the preaching of Philip in Samaria, but when he tried to buy the power of the Holy Spirit from Peter and John, Peter perceived that his heart was not right before God and that he was still in the bondage of iniquity (Acts 8:20-23).

So if those who are baptized are not necessarily saved and ingrafted into Christ, in what sense can we say that baptism is a sign and seal of ingrafting into Christ? In this sense, I would argue: *baptism signifies and seals* (not that all who are baptized are ingrafted into Christ but) *that all who believe are ingrafted into Christ*. Baptism assures us that those who believe are ingrafted into Christ, because it confirms the promise of God that he will and does ingraft into Christ all those who believe. Baptism is thus a sign and seal to us of the truthfulness of the promise of God.[16]

It is not a mark of validation upon something that has already occurred in the life of the one who is baptized.[17]

Of course, it is sometimes true that those who are baptized have already been ingrafted into Christ. This is in fact true in every case where one's baptism follows one's regeneration and coming to faith and repentance, just as Abraham's circumcision followed his regeneration and faith. But the temporal order in which baptism and regeneration occur does not determine the meaning of baptism; so whether baptism precedes or follows one's regeneration, the meaning of one's baptism is the same. Hence the meaning of a professing adult's baptism is the same as the meaning of an infant's baptism who makes no profession of faith. The sign and seal of baptism point first and foremost to the promise of God, confirming its truth. Thus it provides us with additional assurance concerning the truth of God's promise. The truth of God's promise is not in any way affected by whether we are regenerate or not when we receive the sign of baptism which signifies and seals that promise to us.

Perhaps we should mention at this point that the addition of the sign to the word of promise is not done because God's promise needs additional strengthening. Adding the sign does not make the promise more trustworthy. The sign is added not because the promise is weak, but because our faith is weak and needs continually to be strengthened and confirmed. For this, God has given us sensible signs in the sacraments by which we are to remember his promises

---

[16] On this, see Calvin's discussion of sacraments in the *Institutes*, Chapter 14. Note especially his definition of a sacrament: ". . . it is an outward sign by which the Lord seals on our consciences the promises of his good will toward us in order to sustain the weakness of our faith . . ." See *Calvin: Institutes of the Christian Religion*, ed. John T. McNeill, trans. Ford Lewis Battles (Library of Christian Classics, vols. 20-21; Philadelphia: Westminster, 1960), 1277.

[17] Reformed theologians have sometimes been guilty of obscuring this point. See, for instance, my discussion of how both John Murray and James M. Boice have done this in their commentaries on Romans. See my "Baptism and Circumcision as Signs and Seals" in *The Case for Covenantal Infant Baptism,* ed. Gregg Strawbridge (Phillipsburg: P&R, 2003), 89ff.

and be assured of their truth.[18] Furthermore, the help we receive from baptism to strengthen our faith is not due to the baptism itself, but to the *sacramental union*[19] between baptism and the promise of God. Our faith thus rests not in the fact of our baptism (as if God had promised to save all who are baptized), but in the promise of God to save those who believe. Baptism, then, cannot save us; only faith can do that. But baptism can assure us that faith is enough.

Sacraments thus function in part in the same way as the oath which God swore to Abraham in Genesis 22:16 – *to confirm the promise previously made to Abraham*. The author of Hebrews explains this swearing of an oath as God *"desiring even more to show to the heirs of the promise the unchangeableness of His purpose . . . in order that by two unchangeable things, in which it is impossible for God to lie, we may have strong encouragement, we who have fled for refuge in laying hold of the hope set before us"* (Heb. 6:17f. NASB, *italics* added). The sacrament of baptism thus provides a vivid reminder – visible and tangible – of the truth that those who believe are ingrafted into Christ.

From this union with Christ we may derive additional truth. Romans 6 assures us that if we have been united with Christ, then we have been united with him in his death and resurrection. Our old self was crucified with Christ so that we would no longer be enslaved to sin. Hence sin is no longer master over us. Recalling this in the time of temptation, and trusting in these truths, a believer can be strengthened for overcoming the temptation. This is one way in which we "improve" our baptism.

In addition, baptism speaks to us of our engagement to be the Lord's (WLC Q. 165); that is, it signifies that we belong to the Lord and are obligated to live as his children, faithfully keeping

---

[18] The issue of how to understand the language of *sign* and *seal*, I have more fully discussed in "Baptism and Circumcision as Signs and Seals."

[19] WCF, 27.2: "There is in every sacrament a spiritual relation, or sacramental union, between the sign and the thing signified; whence it comes to pass that the names and effects of the one are attributed to the other." This notion is crucial to the understanding of Romans 6.

his covenant. Recalling our baptism at the time of temptation reminds us of the privilege we have in being God's children and bearing his name. In this our baptism also speaks of the duty and obligation which we owe to God, because of his covenant with us and especially in the light of the grace shown to us in bringing us into that covenant. The word of institution for baptism speaks loudly concerning the duty and obligation of those who are baptized to live as disciples faithfully performing their master's will: ". . . make disciples of all nations, baptizing them in the name of the Father and of the Son and of the Holy Spirit, teaching them to observe all that I have commanded you" (Matt. 28:19f. ESV). Here the commandment to baptize is framed by the instructions to make disciples and to teach them to observe all that Christ has commanded. Our baptism thus signifies and seals to us that we have been engaged "to be wholly and only the Lord's" (WLC Q. 165).

On this part of baptism's meaning, we must especially note that what baptism signifies about discipleship is that we are *duty-bound* or *obligated* to be such disciples, not that we have agreed to be such disciples or that we have promised to be such disciples. This point is easily missed. The examples of New Testament baptism given to us are often cited by anti-paedobaptists to show that all those baptized in the New Testament were baptized following repentance and profession of faith. Some of these examples do follow repentance and faith, though not all. But, again, this fact should not be allowed to obscure the meaning of the baptism. As we have observed, Abraham's circumcision likewise post-dated his coming to faith and post-dated many of the steps of faith he had already taken in response to the call of God. But his circumcision was not meant to signify that Abraham had faith or that he had promised to live in obedience to God. If we suppose that his circumcision did signify these things, then we are at a loss to explain what Ishmael's circumcision meant on that same day, and what Isaac's circumcision meant some years later. Abraham's circumcision indicated his covenant relationship with God and, along with the promises God had made to him, signified and sealed his obligation to live faithfully according to the demands of that covenant. The circumcision of Ishmael on that very day signified the same for him: the covenant relationship established, the promises made, and the obligations imposed. The circumcision of Isaac some years later, and later still the circumcisions of Jacob and Esau, signified their obligation to live in covenant faithfulness; not that they had already begun to do so, or that they were promising to do so. So it is with baptism: it signifies that we are called or obligated to live as disciples, not that we have already begun to do so, or that we have or are now committing ourselves to do so. While someone's baptism may be accompanied with repentance, profession of faith, and a promise to live as a disciple, the meaning of baptism does not signify any of these. Baptism points to God's promise and to our obligations.

Jesus' word of institution says that we are baptized *into* the name of the Father, the Son, and the Holy Spirit.[20] God's name is thus put upon us in baptism, and while that means many things and not just one, one thing it does mean is that we are now marked as belonging to God. As those who belong to God, then, baptism marks us as obligated to live as his disciples. So whether one is baptized before or after coming to faith, the meaning of one's baptism is not changed; just as Abraham's circumcision and Jacob's circumcision meant the same, though the temporal order of their regeneration and circumcision differed. If we do not understand

---

[20] English versions usually translate this verse as "in the name . . ." The Greek preposition in this phrase is *eis*, and "into" is perhaps the better translation here. The idea is not simply that the baptism is done with a mention of the name of the Father, the Son, and the Holy Spirit, but that the name of the Father, the Son, and the Holy Spirit is put upon the one who is baptized so that subsequently the person bears that name as God's covenant child. The idea of incorporation into the name of God and into covenant relationship with God is perhaps not understood by many today upon hearing the baptism formula. Similarly, the idea that by the baptism God has made public his claim over the one baptized, demanding of him covenant fidelity, is not understood.

the meaning of baptism in this way, then the meaning of baptism is evacuated by everyone who, like Simon Magus, manifests that he is still in the bonds of iniquity subsequent to his baptism.

Anti-paedobaptists are, therefore, right to connect the sacrament of baptism with a commitment to Christ and to discipleship, but the connection is not that baptism is given to signify that we have made such a commitment, nor that we are promising to live as disciples of Christ. Baptism signifies that such a commitment has been laid upon us, and is demanded from us; not that we have made such a commitment, or that we have agreed or promised to be Christ's disciples. Furthermore – and this point needs to be stressed in the contemporary church where child dedications are regarded as equivalent to baptism – the commitment which has been laid upon us in baptism is laid upon us by God himself, not by believing parents. Parents may indeed prayerfully dedicate their children to God, but baptism is not given to us as a means for performing such a pious act. Baptism is God's act toward us, not ours toward him, and in it he speaks to us about his promises and lays upon us solemn obligations.

Now, according to WLC Q. 167, in times of temptation, we are to make "serious and thankful consideration of the nature of [baptism] . . . *and our solemn vow made therein.*" Q. 165 says that in baptism we "enter into an open and professed engagement to be wholly and only the Lord's." The "vow" and "*professed engagement*" in view here must be understood in the light of the previous discussion, for infants do not make a vow when they are baptized. But the effect is the same. The life of obedience which one might "vow" to the Lord upon being baptized, when this is done following one's regeneration, repentance, and profession of faith, is what God demands of every infant or adult when they are baptized. It is the demand of God that is primary, not the vow or profession one might make in connection with it. The profession is God's, claiming the baptized for himself, and marking him as a farmer brands his cattle. Graciously, the "brand" speaks of the grace of God to those who trust in him. So, in times of temptation, recalling one's baptism can help to strengthen one to resist the temptation, by giving a vivid representation of the ownership which God has over one's life, and the duties and obligations which accompany that status. When we consider that the mark of ownership in view speaks loudly of the grace of God in that covenant to wash away one's sins, then the reminder of grace on top of the reminder of duty does much to strengthen one's sense of obligation to resist the temptation and to yield to God that covenant faithfulness which is owed. "Love so amazing, so divine, demands my soul, my life, my all."[21]

In brief, then, summarizing what we have proposed concerning the meaning of baptism, we may say that baptism is the sign and seal of God's promise to us, not our promise to God; and it is the sign of what God has commanded us, not how we have responded to God's commands. Making serious and thankful consideration of these things in times of temptation can do much to strengthen us to stand firm in our faith and obedience.

Word and Sacrament

Now there is much, much more in the answer to WLC Q. 167 about how to improve one's baptism, but I leave that to your own development. I move now to consider how the sacrament of baptism relates to the ministry of the word, another means of grace of which we are to make "diligent use" and "improve." Paul's dealing with the Corinthians who patronized prostitutes can help to illustrate this.

Given the rampant sexual immorality and promiscuity of Corinthian society, Paul observed that some in the church at Corinth had not fully separated themselves from their former lives and yielded to temptations. He appealed to them from two directions. First, he argues that the bodies of Christians are members of Christ,

---

[21] From Isaac Watts' hymn "When I Survey the Wondrous Cross."

so if a Christian person is joined to a prostitute, he thus joins Christ to a prostitute (1 Cor. 6:15). "May it never be!" Second, he argues that Christians have been bought with a price – the precious blood of Jesus Christ. Hence, we are not our own. We belong to God, so we must glorify God in our body (1 Cor. 6:20).

Notice that the appeal made by Paul is first to our ingrafting into Christ or our union with him (from which it follows that Christ dwells in us by His Spirit), and then to the duty and obligation which we owe to God because of that union. These two appeals are based on truths that are at the heart of the meaning of baptism: our ingrafting into Christ, and our belonging to Christ. Paul could therefore have appealed to the Corinthians through their baptism, in addition to the appeal he made directly through the truths of the word. These same truths are signified and sealed in their baptism. The word of truth, and the sacrament which testifies to that truth, are one. So in the same way that Paul hopes to stir up the Corinthians to renewed obedience by his appeal to them through the word of Scripture, the same appeal could be made by the sacrament of baptism. What Q. 167 of the WLC is telling us is that we should make this appeal to ourselves in the moment of temptation, "by serious and thankful consideration of the nature of (baptism), and of the ends for which Christ instituted it, the privileges and benefits conferred and sealed thereby, and our solemn vow made therein . . ." The sacrament is not so much a separate means of grace, but an additional way in which the word of God is given to us. Word and sacrament work in combination toward one end.

Engagement and wedding rings, which are signs and seals of earthly covenants, function in much the same way. They signify and seal promises made and obligations owed. When a man gives an engagement ring to a woman, it signifies and seals his promise to take her as his wife, and to bestow upon her all that he is and has. (At least that is how marriage was traditionally understood in our culture.) The woman who has an engagement ring on her hand is the recipient of a marriage promise, and thus is obligated to live as one promised in marriage. In our society, this example does involve the woman's agreement to this relation, but that agreement is not essential to the example and one can easily point to societies where a woman's agreement is not part of the engagement. The point I want to make is simply that the ring testifies to the promise made by the giver of the ring to take the woman as a wife. As the woman wears the ring, she is thus more conscious of the promises which have been made to her. At the same time, she is also reminded of the obligations upon her to live as one who is promised in marriage. So there are promises to be remembered and there are duties to be kept, both belonging to the covenant which has been made.

This is a very close parallel to the way in which baptism functions in relation to God's covenant of grace. Baptism speaks of the ingrafting into Christ – if you will, the marriage with Christ – which is promised to those who believe in Christ (and which is accomplished in those who have believed). It also speaks of the duty to live as one belonging to Christ. This tangible sign and seal of the promises made to us, and of the duties imposed upon us, can help us in the time of temptation. These promises and duties are given to us in God's word. The sacrament of baptism points to these promises and duties; it signifies and seals them to us. The Scriptures provide us with their full content. So improving our baptism is really the same thing as making diligent use of the Scriptures as a means of grace. Notice the similarity in how a Christian is to approach the ministry of the word with how we are to improve our baptisms. Question. 155 asks, "How is the word made effectual to salvation?" The answer given is:

> The Spirit of God maketh the reading, but especially the preaching of the word, an effectual means of enlightening, convincing, and humbling sinners; of driving them out of themselves, and drawing them unto Christ; and of conforming them to this image, and subduing them to his will; of strengthening them against temptations and corruptions; of building them up in grace and

establishing their hearts in holiness and comfort through faith unto salvation.

Comparing this answer with the answer to Q. 167 on how we are to improve our baptism will reveal many similarities. This is to be expected, since baptism is pointing to the word of God, both in what has been promised and what has been commanded.

When we ask how we are to make "diligent use" of the word as a means of grace, the WLC provides us with practical help in both reading and preaching:

Q. 157, "How is the word to be read?"

A. "The holy scriptures are to be read with an high and reverent esteem of them; with a firm persuasion that they are the very word of God, and that he only can enable us to understand them; with desire to know, believe, and obey the will of God revealed in them; with diligence, and attention to the matter and scope of them; with meditation, application, self-denial, and prayer."

If one looks closely here, an outline for a short course on how to read and study the Bible emerges. Pastors can use this answer as a guide for assisting their people for personal study of the Scriptures, and once instructed, the people can go back to this question and recall what they have been taught.

For preparation in hearing the word of God preached, the WLC offers this:

Q. 160, "What is required of those that hear the word preached?"

A. "It is required of those that hear the word preached, that they attend upon it with diligence, preparation, and prayer; examine what they hear by the scriptures; receive the truth with faith, love, meekness, and readiness of mind, as the word of God; meditate, and confer of it; hide it in their hearts, and bring forth the fruit of it in their lives."

Here too there is a well-organized set of instructions aimed at helping people get the most out of the preaching of the word.

Notice that *preparation* for hearing the word of God preached is required, as is *examination of it after it is heard*. Here are two very practical duties that are probably ignored by many who hear the word preached. How many church attendees would there be in our day who make preparation for hearing the word of God preached? How many would make a conscious effort afterward to examine what they heard by the Scriptures? Probably there are few. Yet it is in precisely these ways that the word of God becomes to us an effectual means of salvation,

> through the powerful operation of his Spirit, applying the death and resurrection of Christ unto [us, renewing us in the] whole man after the image of God; having the seeds of repentance unto life, and all other saving graces, put into [our] hearts, and those graces so stirred up, increased, and strengthened, as that [we] more and more die unto sin, and rise unto newness of life (WLC Q. 75).

Only by improving the means of grace do they become for us effectual means of salvation. If we would do so, the WLC provides us with most helpful guidance.

Prayer, Word, and Sacrament

Notice that in each of the answers to how the word is to be read and what is required of us for hearing the word preached, there is an emphasis upon prayer, which is another of the means of grace. The WLC gives a full exposition of the Lord's Prayer, and it is one of the best to be found. Here, however, I would emphasize that prayer must accompany our diligent use of the word and our improvement of the sacraments. We are to read the word of God "with meditation, application, self-denial, and prayer" (Q. 157). We attend upon the preaching of the word "with diligence, preparation, and prayer" (Q. 160). Considering prayer in this context indicates that the kind of praying in view is specific praying: not just a general "Lord, bless me and help me," but many specific prayers of praise, thanksgiving, and petition which arise out of the specific verses of Scripture in view, or specific aspects of the word which are signified by the sacraments. People who learn to pray, or are taught to pray, in the context of making diligent use of the means of grace are praying in much more specific ways, and are therefore much more intentionally focused in their prayers. People who pray this way, in connection with their diligent meditations and applications of the word, and in connection with improving the sacraments, are much less likely to look into the mirror of Scripture and go away forgetting what kind of people they are (James 1:22ff.). "But the one who looks into the perfect law, the law of liberty, and *perseveres*, being no hearer who forgets but *a doer who acts*, he will be blessed in his doing" (James 1:25 ESV, *italics* added).

It is such people that the Father seeks to worship him. It is the combination of prayer, word, and sacrament that makes each an effectual means of grace. The WLC helps us to see this more clearly, and instructs us in how it is to be done.

"Improving" the Larger Catechism

Let me conclude with a few comments about "improving" the WLC, that is, putting it to good use within our churches today, as we look toward *The Westminster Confession into the 21ˢᵗ Century*. As noted at the outset, there are certain hindrances that stand in the way of a popular use of the WLC in today's churches. Older language, lengthy answers with complicated sentence structures, and even just the observation that 196 questions make up the WLC can be off-putting in this day of lax spirituality and passivity. Pastors might do well, therefore, not to put the whole wagon-load of teaching from the WLC in front of their people at one time, unless the congregation is better prepared than most and familiar with such language and teaching. There is perhaps room for the publication of many booklets, based upon the WLC and breaking apart its long, complicated sentences into bullet points and shorter sentences, much more easily digested by the small mouths and stomachs of many of today's Christians. A modern English version of the Larger Catechism has now been completed by the Evangelical Presbyterian Church, and some will perhaps find this much easier going for reading the WLC. This can certainly help, though, for myself, I far prefer using the original and believe that there is much to be gained in teaching our people to use it.

For personal and classroom study, today's church has been enormously helped by P & R Publishing's commentary on the WLC done by Johannes G. Vos and edited by G. I. Williamson. Vos wrote these articles many years ago in the *Blue Banner Faith and Life* magazine, and his style is clear and concise. The publication format by P & R Publishing is attractive, eminently suited for study classes and personal study. I have received very positive comments on it from students in my classes. It contains the whole text of the WLC, organized into seventeen general topics. Many of the proof texts (though not all) given by the Westminster divines to support the doctrinal claims of the WLC are listed, though the verses are not printed out. But the citation of the references does contain brief comments by Vos to help the reader understand the way in which the prooftexts support the doctrine. As an introduction the volume also contains the article on the Larger Catechism written by Robert Godfrey for the commemoration of the 350th anniversary of the Westminster Assembly, held back in 1993.[22]

Perhaps the most significant step forward, however, would be a wider and more intensive use of the WLC in connection with the Confession of Faith for the preparation of ministerial candidates. Seminaries and presbyteries need to look more closely at this matter. I believe it would pay rich dividends for the life of the whole church, sending better-equipped ministers of the word out among the flock of God.

---

[22] Robert Godfrey, "The Westminster Larger Catechism," *To Glorify and Enjoy God*, ed. John L. Carson and David W. Hall (Edinburgh: Banner of Truth, 1994), 127-41.

Given that the use of the Shorter Catechism was so severely eroded during the twentieth century, advocating a greater use of the Larger Catechism for the 21st century might seem to be a wasted effort in the extreme. Still, I cling to the conviction that the effort will prove worthwhile. The reformation begun in ancient Israel under the young king Josiah took on renewed zeal and greater depth after the discovery of the lost "book of the law of the LORD" (2 Kings 22, 2 Chron. 34). While the loss of the WLC to our churches is not at the same level as the loss of Scripture itself, it should not be underestimated and dismissed lightly. Our doctrinal understanding and integrity leave much to be desired. Reintroducing the WLC to a more significant place in the church's pedagogy could well help us toward a more mature understanding and commitment to the truth of God given to us in the Holy Scriptures. It could also aid us in appropriating that truth into our lives. The means of grace given to us by God are the same today as they have always been. "Improving" them is still essential to our spiritual growth and salvation. The WLC can certainly aid us in making that diligent use of the means of grace so necessary for us to be more conformed to the image of Christ, to whom belongs honor and glory forever and ever. Amen.

The Westminster Standards and the Structure of Christian Ethics*

David Clyde Jones

The Questions of Ethics

C. S. Lewis, in his wartime broadcasts on the Christian faith, sub-sequently published as *Mere Christianity* (still a best-seller among religious publications), used the figure of a fleet of ships sailing in formation to illustrate "the three parts of morality." A successful convoy would require not only rules to keep them from bumping into each other (interpersonal and social ethics), but also rules for keeping each ship seaworthy (personal ethics). These two compo-nents exist for the sake of a third: to arrive at the right destination (the purpose of human life as a whole; what human beings were made for).

Whatever we may think of the illustration – it would surely have resonated with the British listening audience in the early 1940s – the threefold analysis of the principles of moral conduct is illuminating and shows up in a variety of authors on ethics. Menachem Marc Kellner takes this approach. He writes: "Ethics . . . deals with (1) the ends which truly fulfill human personality, (2) the character of moral agents, (3) the nature of moral

---

* In preparing this address I have drawn freely at times on my treatment of some of the same themes in *Biblical Christian Ethics* (Grand Rapids: Baker, 1994) where the material is presented in more detail.

obligation."[1] The late John Murray, lecturing on the doctrine of original sin, expressed the following criteria of divine judgment: "Love to God must be the impelling motive, the will of God the directing principle, and the glory of God the controlling purpose."[2] Similarly, the Confession of Faith places the works of unregenerate men under divine judgment "because they proceed not from an heart purified by faith; nor are done in a right manner, according to the Word; nor to a right end, the glory of God."[3]

Disposition, norms, and goal thus have a prominent, if not indispensable, role in critical reflection on human conduct, the branch of philosophy the Greeks called *ta ethika*. In our day, the norms of right and wrong are the part of ethics that grab the headlines on a daily basis: human cloning, embryonic stem cell research, same-sex marriage – the list goes on. But ethics is not just about issues of right and wrong; it's also about the kind of persons we ought to be – people who think issues of right and wrong really matter, who love the right and hate the wrong, who can be counted on to do the right thing even under stress. It's about the content of our character as well as rules of conduct. The kind of persons we ought to be is inevitably linked to some broader vision of the way things ought to be, which in turn depends on certain worldview issues: explanation of the origin of the universe and man; diagnosis of the human condition; articulation of the means to human fulfillment.

A recent report from Mozambique on the AIDS crisis by New York Times columnist David Brooks illustrates the point. "The problem," Brooks notes, "is that while treatment is a technical problem, prevention is not. Prevention is about changing behavior. It is getting into the hearts of people in their vulnerable moments

---

[1] Menachem Marc Kellner, *Contemporary Jewish Ethics* (New York: Sanhedrin Press, 1978), 3.

[2] John Murray, classnotes taken by the author, 1960-61.

[3] WCF, 16.7. Cf. *Heidelberg Catechism*, q. 91. Good is "only that which arises out of true faith, conforms to God's law, and is done for his glory."

– when they are drinking, when they are in the throes of passion – and influencing them to change the behavior that they have not so far changed under the threat of death."[4] The AIDS crisis is about evil in the form of predatory males who knowingly infect women without the least regard for their suffering. It is also about the loss of the sanctity of life as people have come to regard their lives of so little worth that ruinous behavior goes unresisted. AIDS is about things, Brooks concludes, that "can be addressed only by the language of ought, by fixing behavior into some relevant set of transcendent ideals and faiths."[5] He found that language spoken in Mozambique in a church with a tin roof and walls of sticks.

It is characteristic of the New Testament to use the term *anastrophe* (way of life) for what we call morality or ethical practice. Following this linguistic lead, and bearing in mind the classic *paraklesis* of Romans 12:1-2, Christian ethics (as a discipline) may be defined *as the study of the way of life that conforms to the will of God as revealed in Christ and the Holy Scriptures*. It seeks to answer the question: What is God calling (summoning and enabling) us (his redeemed people, individually and corporately) to be and to do for his glory? The contribution of the Westminster Standards may perhaps be more fully appreciated by relating the threefold structure of goal, disposition, and norms to the thematic unity of covenant theology. I propose looking at these respectively as covenant purpose, covenant virtue, and covenant practice.

Covenant Purpose

It would be easy to suppose that the subject of ethics is not broached until Question 39 of the Shorter Catechism, "What is the duty which God requires of man?" Actually, the Catechism

---

4   David Brooks, "The Wisdom We Need to Fight AIDS." *New York Times*, June 12, 2005, Late Edition-Final, sec. 4.

5   Ibid.

opens with the classic prime ethical question: "What is the chief end of man?" The Catechism understands that to be human is to be a teleological being. It wants to know what we should aim for in life as a whole. Rules are necessary, but they are subordinate and instrumental (as indicated by the second question). The Catechism presupposes that there is some supreme purpose for human beings, some ultimate goal that fulfills human nature, some absolute value that gives meaning to the whole, some "highest good" that is intrinsically worthy and totally satisfying.

With this beginning, the Catechism identifies with the Augustinian tradition in Christian ethics. Augustine observed: "There is no doubt about it. We all want to be happy. Everyone will agree with me, before the words are even out of my mouth. . . .So let us see if we can find the best way to achieve it."[6] For Augustine, the desire for happiness (*eudaemonia* in Greek, now generally rendered as "flourishing") is a human given – everybody has a hungry heart. This natural inclination of human beings for fulfillment and satisfaction is something implanted by God by virtue of our creation in his image. In the memorable words from the opening chapter of Augustine's *Confessions*, "You have made us for yourself, and our heart is restless until it comes to rest in you."[7]

The Catechism's answer to its first question is equally memorable: "Man's chief end is to glorify God, and to enjoy him forever." (The Larger Catechism has '. . .and fully to enjoy him forever." The divines may occasionally split theological hairs, but never an infinitive.) The answer harks back to the Confession; "fruition of [God] as blessedness and reward" is made possible only by the "voluntary condescension on God's part, which he has been pleased to express by way of covenant."[8] This perspective is fairly represented by Psalm 25:14, "The friendship of the Lord is for those who fear him, and he makes known to them his

---

6   Augustine, *The Standards of the Catholic Church*, 3.4.

7   Augustine, *Confessions*, 1.1.

8   WCF, 7.1.

covenant" (ESV[9]). Psalm 25 happens to be the first Psalm to make *explicit* reference to God's covenant (10, 14). It opens in faith: "To you, O Lord, I lift up my soul, O my God, in you I trust" (vv. 1-2), which is followed by a passionate prayer for divine instruction: "Make me to know your ways, O Lord; teach me your paths. Lead me in your truth and teach me, for you are the God of my salvation, for you I wait all the day long" (4-5; cf. 8-9, 12-13).

The heart of the Psalm is verse 14. The word translated "friendship" may also be rendered "secret counsel." Here it connotes the intimacy of relationship in which God reveals his covenant, his gracious purpose, to his friends. It is ultimately fulfilled in Jesus' words to his disciples: "No longer do I call you servants, for the servant does not know what his master is doing; but I have called you my friends, for all that I have heard from my Father I have made known to you" (John 15:14 ; cf. 1 Cor. 2:9-10). Abraham, who through faith in God's covenant promises is "the father of us all" (Rom. 4:16) is also called in Scripture "God's friend" (Isa. 41:8, 2 Chron. 20:7, James 2:23).

Yet friendship with God does not exhaust God's covenant purpose. Abraham "was looking forward to the city that has foundations, whose designer and builder is God" (Heb. 11:10). As Cornelius Plantinga has effectively pointed out, the Hebrew word *shalom* is biblical shorthand for God's design for his creation. "In the Bible, shalom means universal flourishing, wholeness, and delight – a rich state of affairs in which natural needs are satisfied and natural gifts fruitfully employed, a state of affairs that inspires joyful wonder as its Creator and Savior opens doors and welcomes the creatures in whom he delights."[10] See, for example, Isaiah 2:2-4, 11:1-9, 32:14-20, 42:1-12, 60:1-22, 65:17-25. This goal – the will of God in the broadest sense – defines for us the good and shapes the sort of persons we aspire to be. "To be a responsible person

---

[9] All following Scripture references are taken from the ESV.

[10] Cornelius Plantinga, Jr., *Not the Way It's Supposed to Be: A Breviary of Sin* (Grand Rapids: Eerdmans, 1995), 10.

is to find one's role in the building of shalom, the re-webbing of God, humanity, and all creation in justice, harmony, fulfillment, and delight . . . and then, funded by the grace of God, to fill this role and delight in it."[11] God's ultimate goal is to bring all things under the rule of Christ (Eph. 1:9-10). The goal of human life, accordingly, is to share in the glory and joy of Christ, and live in his kingdom of peace forever.

The Abrahamic covenant, stripped to its bare bones, looks like this: The Lord promises blessing, Abraham believes the Lord, a way of life ensues (Gen. 18:19, 26:5). God's glory is revealed in all his works, but especially in the salvation of his people (Eph. 1:3-14). "To glorify God" is to reflect his glory, preeminently by being conformed to the image of his Son. True fulfillment consists in being conformed to the image of Christ so as to be pleasing to God and to be happy in him. Beatitude is objective fulfillment of our human nature as well as subjective satisfaction. The precepts are pro-human, the way things ought to be, authentic human existence, not burdensome, but deep-down, rock-bottom fulfilling and satisfying. Plantinga explains:

> The point of our lives is not to get smart or to get rich or even to get happy. The point is to discover God's purposes for us and to make them our own. The point is to learn ways of loving God above all and our neighbor as ourselves . . . To glorify God is to do these things and, by doing them, to make God's intentions in the world more luminous and God's reputation more lustrous. To enjoy God forever is to cultivate a taste for this project, to become more and more the sort of person for whom eternal life with God would be sheer heaven.[12]

Plantinga goes so far as to say, "According to all traditional Christian wisdom, human flourishing is the same thing as glorifying God and enjoying him forever."[13] Both evangelical Protestant and

---

[11]   Ibid., 197.

[12]   Ibid., 37.

Roman Catholic authors have recently tapped into this tradition, some with phenomenal popular success.

John Piper's *Desiring God* (1986) launched a movement he himself labeled "Christian Hedonism." More traditionally the Augustinian tradition had been perceived as a form of eudaemonism – that is, pursuit of happiness – as flourishing rather than, or even contrasted with, the pursuit of pleasure as the goal of life. Piper overcomes this by expanding the meaning of pleasure using biblical categories. I personally think it would be better to substitute *joy* for *pleasure*. The Bible affirms joy copiously, but pleasure only marginally in a positive sense. Piper's suggestion that the Catechism should read: "Man's chief end is to glorify God *by* enjoying him forever" struck a responsive chord as this aspect had been neglected. His exposition recovered an important and neglected truth. But it is not the whole truth; glorifying God is objective reflection of the divine holiness as well as enjoyment of the divine happiness. This later statement is more balanced: "The single, all-embracing, all-transforming reason for being [is] a passion to enjoy *and display* God's supremacy in all things for the joy of all peoples."[14]

Rick Warren, having asked for a forty day commitment to "discovering God's purpose for my life," opens his exposition of *The Purpose Driven Life* with this one-sentence paragraph: "It's not about you. The purpose of your life is far greater than your own personal fulfillment, your peace of mind, or even your happiness."[15] The main point: "You were made *by* God and *for* God – and until you understand that, life will never make sense."[16] Glorifying God centers around five purposes: worshiping him, loving other believers, becoming like Christ, serving others with

---

[13] Plantiga, 38.

[14] John Piper, *Don't Waste Your Life* (Wheaton: Crossway, 2003), 37, emphasis added.

[15] Rick Warren, *The Purpose Driven Life: What on Earth Am I Here for?* (Grand Rapids: Zondervan, 2002), 17.

[16] Warren, 18.

our gifts, telling others about him.[17] Piper's emphasis on glorifying God by enjoying him has apparently slipped from view.[18]

The Dominican Servais Pinckaers, responding to the Second Vatican Council's call for renewal in moral theology, leads with recovery of the treatise on happiness in Thomas Aquinas' *Summa Theologicae*.[19] His popular treatise on the Beatitudes appeals to the Augustinian thesis: "God has placed the desire for happiness in the heart of every man as a fundamental thrust, and He wants to respond to it by sharing His own happiness with us."[20] "The Beatitudes take up the promises made to the Chosen People since the time of Abraham."[21] Since the promises come first in God's design, only a morality rooted in grace and embraced by faith does justice to the biblical revelation. The following statement is typical:

> Salvation, freedom, justice, and happiness come to us from our faith in the divine promises and our hope in mercy and grace, rather than from the merits we may acquire by our own strength in adhering to the observances of the Law. Faith, which engenders hope, will therefore come first in biblical and Christian morality, and will become the source of good works.[22]

The apologetic significance of the purpose-oriented approach to ethics may be observed from Paul's Areopagus address (Acts 17:22-31). The Athenians were very religious, but Paul seiz-

---

17   Ibid., 56-57.

18   Chuck Colson, *The Good Life: Seeking Purpose, Meaning, and Truth in your Life* (Carol Stream:Tyndale 2005).

19   Relying on Augustine and Thomas, Pinckaers made this the burden of his scholarly *Les sources de la morale chrétienne* (Fribourg: Éditions Universitaires, 1985); *The Sources of Christian Ethics*, trans. Mary Thomas Noble (Washington: Catholic University of America Press, 1995). His contribution there is made available to the general reader in *Morality: The Catholic View* (South Bend: St. Augustine Press, 2001).

20   Servais Pinckaers, *The Pursuit of Happiness – God's Way* (Staten Island: Alba House, 1998), 28.

21   Ibid, 9.

22   Ibid, 27.

es on their self-confessed ignorance in the altar dedicated "to the unknown God." The God they did not know was the infinite-personal God, the creator of everything, the ruler of earth and heaven, the giver of life to human beings. "He made from one man every nation of mankind to live on the face of the earth . . . *that they should seek God, in the hope that they might feel their way toward him and find him.*" There is nothing in the world more important than knowing God. "Yet he is actually not far from each one of us," Paul continues, citing their own poet-philosophers on God's immanence and the source of what is distinctive in human nature: "In him we live and move and have our being" and "For we are indeed his offspring." Whatever inclinations human beings have toward truth and goodness, they have by virtue of their creation in the image of God and preservation after the fall by God's common grace. These propensities or aspirations, which may be summed up as the yearning for shalom, are reflections of something instilled in human nature from the beginning, for which the gospel is the perfect fit.

Covenant Virtue

The famous first question-and-answer of the Westminster Shorter Catechism does not resonate with everyone, and it is sometimes met with outright hostility. The response of humanist author Paul Kurtz is particularly revealing. Citing the Catechism, Kurtz asks, "What kind of life can be said to be significant," he asks, "if we are totally dependent upon this God for our existence and sustenance? Is not the life of an independent free man to be preferred to one of eternal bondage?"[23] He goes on to quote Bertrand Russell to the effect that "to sing hymns in praise of Him and hold hands throughout all eternity would be sheer boredom," as though heaven were some sort of celestial kumbayah instead of the biblical vision of shalom. I think it is fair to say that heaven is an acquired

---

[23] Paul Kurtz, *The Fullness of Life* (New York: Horizon Press, 1974), 86.

taste. Fallen humanity is alienated from its true end. Sinners do not naturally pursue friendship with a holy God; blessedness entails holiness, and "the natural mind is hostile to God and will not submit to his law; those under its control cannot please God (Rom. 8:7-8). In Kurtz's view, which seems to be a hardened position: "The traditional supernaturalistic moral commandments are especially repressive of our human needs. They are immoral insofar as they foster illusions about human destiny and suppress vital inclinations."[24] It is hard to imagine a sharper conflict in worldviews and the implications for ethics. Something radical has to happen for sinful human beings to delight in God and his will for human flourishing. The Bible calls it being born again, being raised from death to life.

How can a person become willing at heart to seek God as his or her goal? The clear biblical answer is *sola gratia*: by grace alone. The good news is that God's grace in salvation uproots the hostility of the heart towards God and implants a new disposition of affection for him. The gospel transforms moral conduct from within. Moral goodness is produced, not by external amendment of life, but by union with Christ through faith. True virtue is covenant virtue, because God, in the covenant of grace,

> freely offers unto sinners life and salvation by Jesus Christ; requiring of them faith in him, that they may be saved, and promising to give unto all those that are ordained to eternal life his Holy Spirit, to make them willing, and able to believe.[25]

Everything turns on faith, the pivotal or cardinal virtue.

The key text on having one's heart purified or cleansed by faith is Acts 15:9. In the immediate context Peter is recalling how in the early days of the great commission, God had chosen him "that by my mouth the Gentiles should hear the word of the gospel and believe." Only God can know the heart, and so he bore the

---

[24] Paul Kurtz, *The Humanist Alternative* (Buffalo: Prometheus Books, 1973).
[25] WCF, 7.3.

Gentiles witness "by giving them the Holy Spirit just as he did to us." Peter draws the inevitable conclusion: "he made no distinction between us and them, *having cleansed their hearts by faith*" and "we believe that we will be saved through the grace of the Lord Jesus, just as they will." Believers are described as "those who call on the Lord from a pure heart" (2 Tim. 2:22).

The Lord in his covenant grace gives to his chosen ones a new disposition or heart (Ezek. 36:26). *Disposition* refers to the prevailing aspect of one's nature (the technical theological term is *habitus*). What we call a "virtuous disposition" is more precisely the *habitus* of grace. In contrast to the classical understanding of virtue as self-developed, acquired by habitual acts (as one might iron pleats in an article of clothing), covenant virtue is not a human achievement in which one takes pride, but a divine gift for which one is thankful. New Testament virtues are consistently described as *fruit*: of faith, of righteousness, of the gospel, of the Vine, of the Holy Spirit. A good person is thus more accurately a gracious person through union with Christ: "from his fullness we have all received, grace upon grace" (John 1:16).

Faith, hope, and love are regularly mentioned together as components of the dispositional change brought about by the gospel (e.g. 1 Thess. 1:3, 5:8; 1 Cor. 13:13; Rom. 5:1-5; Col. 1:4-5; Gal. 5:5-6; Heb. 6:10-12; 1 Pet. 1:21-22). They form the great trio of graces bestowed by the Holy Spirit in the application of redemption. Faith is primary as the Holy Spirit applies the redemption purchased by Christ by working faith in us and so uniting us to Christ. Along with faith we are given hope, being "born again to a living hope though the resurrection of Christ from the dead" (1 Pet. 1:3-4), "and hope does not put us to shame, because God's love has been poured into our hearts through the Holy Spirit who has been given to us" (Rom. 5:5). Peter Kreeft suggests an analogy: the Christian life is a plant with faith as the root, hope the stem, and love the blossom.

In the Old Testament the great commandment to "love the Lord your God with all your heart" (Deut. 6:4) immediately follows the *shema* and is repeated in the book of Deuteronomy eight times (Deut. 11:1, 13, 22, 13:3, 19:9, 30:6, 16, 20). The New Testament builds on this foundation; presupposing that God gives what he commands, it addresses believers in the indicative as those who love God (Rom. 8:28; 1 Cor. 2:9, 8:3; Eph. 6:24; James 1:12, 2:5; 1 Pet. 1:8). Clearly this love is a *responsive* love (1 John 4:19). In response to God's gracious initiative, God's people begin to love. Redeemed by his grace and enabled by his Spirit, they become loving persons, joined to Christ and to one another in a community love (1 Cor. 13:13). Without question, the impelling motive of the Christian life is love for God, especially Christ our Savior (2 Cor. 5:14-15).

In the end, we become like what we love. Union with Christ is the basic fact of salvation; conformity to Christ is the progressively realized goal of salvation (cf. Col. 1:27, "Christ in you the hope of glory"). Glorification consists in being made like Christ, the perfect image of God in human nature. The goal is finally attained in the age to come, but even now those whom God calls are being transformed into the Lord's likeness with ever-increasing glory (2 Cor. 3:18; cf. Eph. 4:24, Col. 3:10). To be renewed in the image of God is to be made like Christ, who not only is God but who also as a human being functioned in perfect harmony with the will of God. Christian character formation is having Christ formed in us (Gal. 4:19, "my little children . . . I am again in the anguish of childbirth until Christ is formed in you!"). The fruit of the Spirit, who not only regenerates but indwells to further his renewing work in the believer, produces the "habitudes" of love, joy, peace, patience, goodness, kindness, faithfulness, gentleness, self-control (Gal. 5:22). The excellencies of Christ are produced in his people by his Holy Spirit (WLC 32, "all other saving graces" is tied in the proof text to the fruit of the spirit). In sanctification the Holy Spirit "infuses grace, and enables to the exercise thereof . . . growing up to perfection" (WLC 77). The glory of the new covenant is the ministry of the Spirit, poured out on God's people in the fullness of saving blessing in union with Christ. The indwelling Spirit of Christ "enlightens us concerning the Word we have heard and moves us to live it with sincerity."[26]

Covenant Practice

Salvation is by grace through faith unto good works: "For we are his workmanship (*poiēma*), created in Christ Jesus for good works, which God prepared beforehand, that we should walk in them" (Eph. 2:10). The handiwork of God's new creation is exhibited in discipleship. Love for God, besides taking holy delight in the being of God, includes the disposition to walk in his ways, to follow him out of reverence for who he is and gratitude for what he has done, to be obedient to what he is calling his people to be and to do. Love gladly submits to God's authority, sincerely desires to be guided by his instructions, and is devoted to carrying out his gracious will. Love for God is both affectional and volitional. The covenant way of life may be summed up as *obedient love*.[27] The controlling purpose is the glory of God, the impelling motive is the love of God, and the directing principle is the law of God (following the Hebrew use of Torah for the inscripturated word of God, meaning "divinely revealed instruction in the way of life").

Christian love, so far from being without shape or structure, is embodied in certain characteristic practices for the glory of God. The primary forms of love are what Jesus calls the weightier matters of the law: justice, mercy, and faithfulness (Matt. 23:23). The Old Testament equivalents in Hebrew are *mishpat, chesed, amunah*; taken together they constitute covenant righteousness (*tzedaqah*). Jesus restores the proper perspective on love's obedience by marking out those practices that God wants us to follow above all

---

[26] Pinckaers, *Morality: The Catholic View*, 85.

[27] John 14:15, "If you love me you will keep my commandments."

as they mirror his moral attributes. It is a ringing reaffirmation of the great summary of the revealed will of God in Micah 6:8: "He has told you, O man, what is good; and what does the Lord require of you but to do justice (*mishpat*), and to love kindness (*chesed*), and to walk humbly with your God?" The connection with the Ten Commandments is explicit in Hosea 4:1-2:

> Hear the word of the LORD, O children of Israel,
> for the LORD has a controversy with the inhabitants of the land.
> There is no faithfulness (*amunah*) or steadfast love (*chesed*),
> and no knowledge of God (frequently coordinated with *mishpat*)
> in the land;
> there is swearing, lying, murder, stealing, and committing adultery . . .

God's revealed will for human beings, the moral law, is summarily comprehended in the Ten Commandments, the essence of which is love (WSC, 40-42). There is only one moral law, and all human beings are subject to it.[28] The universal norms of love are instilled in human nature from the beginning (*lex indita*) and subsequently promulgated (made known by open declaration, clearly, forcefully, and authoritatively) at Sinai, first orally (Exod. 20:1, "And God spoke all these words saying . . .") then in writing (*lex scripta*) by the Lord himself (Exod. 31:18, "And he gave to Moses . . . the two tablets of the testimony, tablets of stone, written with the finger of God").[29] The substance of the moral law is the same whether revealed constitutionally in human nature or propositionally in Scripture.[30]

---

[28] Although the Ten Commandments were promulgated at Sinai, their moral content is obviously assumed in the biblical narrative leading up to it. See Gen. 4:10; 6:5; 6:11; 8:21; 18:17-19; 18:20; 18:23; 20:11; 26:5; 39:9; Exod. 1:17; 1:21; 18:21.

[29] Cf. Deut 5:22, "These words the Lord spoke to all your assembly at the mountain out of the midst of the fire, the cloud, and the thick darkness, with a loud voice; and he added no more. And he wrote them on two tablets of stone and gave them to me."

The first edition of the written law is in the form of a covenant (Exod. 34:28, "And he wrote on the tablets the words of the covenant, the ten words"). The Decalogue is the "seed" from which the whole canon of Scripture as covenantal revelation developed.[31] The Book of the Covenant immediately follows (Exod. 24:1-8), providing an interpretive context. The Mosaic revelation culminates in the inscripturated word (Acts 7:38, "[Moses] received living oracles to give to us"). Moses communicated orally to the people all the words of the Lord. Then, at the Lord's command, he wrote all the words and read them in the hearing of all the people. Whether the Lord himself speaks from the top of the mountain, Moses delivers the word of the Lord orally, or Moses reads from the Book of the Covenant, there is only one correct response: "All that the Lord has spoken we will do."

The "Holiness Code" provides further context. Leviticus 19 opens with "You shall be holy as the Lord your God is holy." What follows is an exposition of the Decalogue – the prologue and all ten stipulations – that twice summons the law of neighbor-love, sojourner as well as fellow-Israelite (Lev. 19:18, 34).

	Prologue	Lev. 19:36
1.	Other gods	Lev. 19:4
2.	Images	Lev. 19:4
3.	Name	Lev. 19:12
4.	Sabbath	Lev. 19:3, 30
5.	Parents	Lev. 19:3

---

[30] Turretin enumerates five reasons for promulgation of the moral law: (1) that the natural law might be confirmed, (2) that it might be corrected, (3) that it might be supplemented, (4) that the necessity of a Mediator might be understood and a desire for him be enkindled, and (5) that the people of Israel might be joined by this law into one Republic, and be separated from all other nations. *Institutes of Elenctic Theology,* ed. James T. Dennison, Jr., trans. George Musgrave Giger (3 vols.; Phillipsburg: P&R, 1992-97 [1679-85]), 2.7.

[31] Cf. Meredith Kline, *The Structure of Biblical Authority* (Grand Rapids: Eerdmans, 1972), 43.

6.	Murder	Lev. 19:16
7.	Adultery	Lev. 19:29
8.	Theft	Lev. 19:11, 13
9.	False witness	Lev. 19:11, 16
10.	Covetousness	Lev. 19:17-18

The setting of the promulgation of the law – the awesome physical phenomena that manifest the immediate presence of God – serves to highlight God's majestic holiness. In the prologue God asserts his sovereignty ("I am the Lord") and grace ("who delivered you from bondage"). The covenant relationship is established by this word. Though not an imperative, as the first word it is highly significant for all that follows. Theologically it forever establishes the proper connection between prevenient grace and obedient love.[32] Israel needed deliverance not only from the hostile power of the evil empire (Exod. 12:12) but from inward degradation and sin (Josh. 24:14; Exod. 14:11-12, 31). Israel's deliverance is by divine omnipotence, sovereign grace, and substitutionary atonement, represented by the Passover, a prophetic symbol of the work of Christ.

By the inscripturation of the covenantal revelation, the word of God is given a permanent form for the instruction of his people. The written form of the word of God functions as a norm over the redeemed community, guiding their faith and practice. Scripture is the word of God in its abiding, covenantal form. The self-revelation of God culminates in Christ (Heb. 1:1-2). The ultimate interpretive context is the person and obedience of Christ. As the purpose of Scripture is to make us wise for salvation through faith in Christ Jesus, the law is promulgated for the sake of the gospel. Commenting on Romans 10:4 ("Christ is the end (*telos*) of the law"), C. E. B. Cranfield writes, "Christ is the goal, the aim, the

---

[32] Cf. Deut 4:37, "And because he loved your fathers and chose their offspring after them and brought you out of Egypt with his own presence, by his great power."

intention, the real meaning and substance of the law – apart from him it cannot be properly understood at all."[33]

The use of the Ten Commandments for the systematic exposition of biblical ethics was pioneered by Philo of Alexandria (*c*.20 BC – AD 50), the most outstanding representative of Hellenistic Judaism at the time of Christ. Philo provided for his Greek-speaking audience a commentary on the Pentateuch that included a treatise on the Decalogue, followed by four books on the "special laws" arranged under the Ten Commandments as summary heads. Philo is notable also for his division of the Decalogue into two groups dealing respectively with the service of God and human justice.

> The superior set of five . . . enactments begins with God the Father and Maker of all, and ends with parents who copy His nature by begetting particular persons. The other set of five contains all the prohibitions, namely adultery, murder, theft, false witness, covetousness or lust.[34]

Only those who practice both tables are whole in virtue, being both lovers of God (*philotheoi*) and lovers of humankind (*philanthrôpoi*).[35]

Not until the second century did the Christian church follow Philo's lead in earnest, being much more inclined toward exposition of the Sermon on the Mount than the Ten Commandments. The latter were typically regarded as existing for an early stage of instruction in Christian practice. Irenaeus (*c*.130 – *c*.200) is representative. He defends the permanence of the Ten Commandments as "natural precepts" which God gave humanity from the beginning. The patriarchs had the virtue of the Decalogue written in their hearts

---

[33] C. E. B. Cranfield, *A Critical and Exegetical Commentary on the Epistle to the Romans* (The International Critical Commentary; 2 vols.; Edinburgh: T&T Clark, 1979), 2:519.

[34] Philo, *Decalogue*, 51.

[35] Both Philo and Josephus take Exod. 20:2-3 together as the first commandment (as does also Calvin); the standard Jewish enumeration takes v. 2 as the first and vv. 3-6 as the second commandment.

before Sinai.[36] In his *Demonstration of the Apostolic Preaching* (Ch. 86–96), Irenaeus proposed the Decalogue for the early stage of Christian instruction, followed by the Sermon on the Mount for Christians maturing in their faith and obedience.

The *Didache*, also known as "The Teaching of the Apostles" or "The Teaching of the Twelve Apostles," cannot be dated with certainty but is thought to be from around AD 100. It is referred to by patristic authors but was lost until the discovery in 1875 of a manuscript dated 1056. The opening paragraph uses the Sermon on the Mount to expound the summary of the law presented as follows: "The way of life is this. First of all, thou shalt love the God that made thee; secondly, thy neighbor as thyself. And all things whatsoever thou wouldest not have befall thyself, neither do thou unto another."[37] The second paragraph quotes and expands on the Decalogue:

> And this is the second commandment of the teaching. Thou shalt do no murder, thou shalt not commit adultery, thou shall not corrupt boys, thou shalt not commit fornication, thou shalt not steal, thou shalt not deal in magic, thou shalt do no sorcery, thou shalt not murder a child by abortion nor kill them when born, thou shall not covet thy neighbour's goods, thou shalt not perjure thyself, thou shall not bear false witness, thou shalt not speak evil, thou shalt not cherish a grudge, thou shalt not be double-minded nor double-tongued; for the double tongue is a snare of death. Thy word shall not be false or empty, but fulfilled by action. Thou shalt not be avaricious nor a plunderer nor a hypocrite nor ill-tempered nor proud. Thou shalt not entertain an evil design against thy neighbour.[38]

The paragraph concludes with an eloquent analysis of neighbor-love: "Thou shalt not hate any man, but some thou shalt reprove,

---

[36] Irenaeus, *Against Heresies*, 4.15.1.

[37] *Didache*. cf. WLC, 102, 122.

[38] *Didache*.

and for others thou shalt pray, and others thou shalt love more than thy life."[39]

Augustine (354–430) provided an exposition of the Sermon on the Mount but did not expound the Decalogue as such. As the catechumenate developed in the early church, those undergoing progressive instruction in the Christian faith were divided into four groups: (1) *accedentes* (candidates for instruction in the faith), (2) *catechumeni* (candidates for baptism), (3) *competentes* (those approved for baptism), and (4) *neophyti* (the newly baptized). Augustine's *First Catechetical Instruction* (*c.*405) is the only surviving work dealing with the *accedentes*, consisting of pagans and heretics (covenant children received instruction in the home). The instruction is in the form of narrative (creation–fall–redemption). It was given in a single lesson, after which the candidate is asked whether he believes these things and desires to observe them. In paragraph 41 Augustine provides this summary of Christian practice.

> [Jesus] sent to [his disciples] the Holy Spirit (for so He had promised), that through the love poured forth in their hearts by Him, they might be able to fulfill the law not only without its being a burden but even with delight. Now this law was given to the Jews in ten commandments, which they call the Decalogue.[40] And these again are reduced to two, namely, that we should love God with our whole heart, and with our whole soul, and with our whole mind; and that we should love our neighbor as ourselves. For that on these two commandments depend the whole law and the Prophets the Lord Himself has both said in the Gospel and made manifest by his own example.[41]

As Augustine entered the last decade of his life, he wrote a small treatise in response to the request of a certain lay Christian, Lau-

---

[39] *Didache.*

[40] Augustine divided the "tables" of the law 1-3 (the third being the Sabbath) and 4-10 (the ninth and tenth being covetousness). *Confessions*, 8.16; cf. *Sermon* 9.

[41] Augustine, *First Catechetical Instruction*, paragraph 2.

rentius, who wanted a portable handbook containing the answers to some key questions of apologetics. Augustine interprets the request as a desire for a summary of the true wisdom which consists in the service of God. Because to say, "God is to be served in faith, hope, and love," would be too brief an answer even for Laurentius, Augustine wrote an exposition of faith, hope, and love. He gave it the Greek title *Enchiridion* (handbook), intending it to function as a comprehensive summary of the Christian way of life. Having spent 113 sections expounding the Creed, Augustine wraps it up with three on hope, the substance of which is contained in the Lord's Prayer, and five on love, which fulfills the law by grace and the power of the Holy Spirit.

Following the division of the church into East and West in 1054, there was a revival of interest in the Decalogue among Western theologians. The *Institutiones* of Hugh of St. Victor (1096–1141) gave a brief exposition of each commandment and love as the fulfillment of the law. Hugh directly influenced Peter Lombard (1100–1160), whose inclusion of a section on the Decalogue in the *Sentences*, the prime textbook of systematic theology in the Middle Ages, was a first. The Franciscan, Alexander of Hales (*c.*1170–1245), professor at the University of Paris, introduced commentary on Lombard's *Sentences*, replacing traditional commentary on the Scriptures. Thomas Aquinas (*c.*1225–1274) provides a complete account of Christian ethics, including a detailed exposition of the Decalogue, in his *Summa Theologicae*. Both Aquinas and Bonaventure produced model sermons on the Decalogue. The pre-reformer Jan Hus (*c.*1372–1415†) produced an *Exposition of the Decalogue* that begins with a rehearsal of Exodus 19 and proceeds with a well-organized plan through the two tables, freely citing Augustine and other church fathers, cross-referencing many Scriptures, and addressing contemporary issues such as usury and false indulgences.

The Ten Commandments entered the catechetical tradition due in part to a far-reaching legislative act of the Fourth Lateran

Council (1215), canon 21, known by its incipit *Omnis utriusque sexus [fidelis]*.

> All the faithful of both sexes, after they have reached the age of discretion, must confess all their sins at least once a year, to their own parish priest, and perform to the best of their abilities the penance imposed, reverently receiving the sacrament of the Eucharist at least on Easter Sunday. . . . Otherwise they shall be cut off from the Church during their lifetime and shall be without a Christian burial in death.[42]

Archbishop John Peckham of Canterbury in 1281 bound the English clergy to teach four times a year the articles of faith, the commandments of the Decalogue, the two precepts of the gospel, the seven works of mercy, the seven capital sins, the seven principal virtues, and the seven sacraments of grace. John Thoresby, Archbishop of York, issued his "Lay Folks' Catechism" in both Latin and English in 1357, consisting of the Lord's Prayer, Ave Maria, Creed, Ten Commandments, the two precepts of the gospel, the seven sacraments, the seven works of corporeal mercy (feed the hungry, give drink to the thirsty, clothe the naked, shelter the homeless, help those in prison, visit the sick, bury the dead), the seven works of spiritual mercy (teaching, counsel, reproof, consolation, forgiveness, patience, prayer for enemies), the seven virtues, and the seven deadly sins. John Wycliffe (*c.*1330–1384) issued an adaptation with an expanded exposition of the Ten Commandments, providing rhymed couplets for each commandment to assist the memory.

> Thou schalt haue o[ne] god and no mo.
> Ouyr al thynge loue hym al-so.
> And thy neghebore bothe frend and fo . . .
> These ar the commaundementys ten

---

[42] Mary Flowers Braswell, *The Medieval Sinner: Characterization and Confession in the Literature of the English Middle Ages* (London: Associated University Presses, 1983), 26.

that god ghaf to alle men.

Mekyl ioy schal be to [t]hem.

that kepe wel and trewly [t]hem.

All presentations of the Decalogue were not as edifying as Wycliffe's engaging catechesis. The combination of sacerdotalism and meritorious works resulted more often in a highly legalistic understanding of the commandments. On the eve of the Reformation, the Franciscan Dietrich Kolde (1435–1515) published the first printed catechism in German, *A Fruitful Mirror or Small Handbook for Christians* (1470). Receiving the imprimatur of the theological faculties of Cologne and Louvain, it was reprinted nineteen times before 1500 and at least twenty-eight times afterward.[43] The preface recommended it to be carried by Christians at all times "since it contains everything that is necessary for the well-being and salvation of the soul." It takes up in order: the creed; the Decalogue; the five commandments of the church; the seven deadly sins; the nine alien sins; the openly discussed sins and the mute sins against nature; the six sins against the Holy Spirit; the great sins of the tongue; six conditions of forgiveness; seven signs of the state of grace; repentance, confession, and satisfaction; various devotional instructions and prayers, including the Paternoster and Ave Maria; and how to die. The sacrament of penance is of central importance.

> You should know that according to canon law the penance we receive from the priest is not sufficient even for the least mortal sin that we have committed. Therefore it is necessary for us to do even more penance, for example by groaning, crying out, begging help, giving alms, private mortification of the flesh, sharp clothes or belts around the body, or by disciplines, or vigils, or humbly going on pilgrimages.[44]

---

[43] Denis Janz, ed., *Three Reformation Catechisms: Catholic, Anabaptist, Lutheran* [Kolde's "Mirror for Christians" (1480); Hubmaier's "Christian catechism" (1527); Luther's "Small catechism" (1529)], (New York: Edwin Mellen Press, 1982), 8.

[44] *A Fruitful Mirror or Small Handbook for Christians* (1470), Ch. 22.

Little wonder that the first thesis Martin Luther (1483–1546) posted for debate in 1517 concerned the sacrament of penance. It also helps explain why Luther's Small Catechism – the famous *Der Kleine Katechismus* – was such a raging success when it was published a dozen years later. It was first issued in the form of placards or posters for display in churches, schools, and homes. That press run immediately sold out. The catechism was then printed in more conventional form with equal and lasting success.[45] The parts of Luther's Small Catechism are: Ten Commandments, Apostles' Creed, Lord's Prayer, Baptism, Communion, and the Office of the Keys, including Confession. The logic of Luther's order was: conviction of need, where to find aid, and how to ask for it. In 1516–1517 Luther preached a series of sermons on the Ten Commandments in Wittenberg. These were published the following year, as was also his *Short Explanation of the Ten Commandments*, written as a preparative for confession. In 1520 he published his three main pastoral works: *A Short Form of the Ten Commandments, of the Creed, and of the Lord's Prayer*.

The contribution of John Calvin (1509–1564) to the evangelical catechetical tradition begins with the first edition of his *Institutes of the Christian Religion* (1536). The first five chapters follow the standard catechetical format: Decalogue, Creed, Lord's Prayer, Sacraments (with a fifth chapter on False Sacraments). The sixth chapter is an *apologia* in three parts: Christian Freedom, Ecclesiastical Power, Civil Government. This was followed by a catechism in French, *Instruction et Confession de Foy* (1537) and Latin, *Catechismus, sive Christianae Religionis Institutio* (1538). This was followed by the *Catechism of the Church of Geneva* (1541 French, 1545, Latin). The order is: Concerning the Faith (creed), the Law (Decalogue), Prayer (paternoster), and the Sacraments (baptism and the Lord's Supper). The catechism asks a total of 373

---

[45] The larger *Deutsch Catechismus* was published later the same year (1529). In 1580 both were made official doctrine by inclusion in the Book of Concord.

questions, beginning with "What is the chief end of human life?" Answer: "To know God."

In 1555 Calvin preached sixteen sermons on the Ten Commandments as part of a nearly year-and-a-half series on the book of Deuteronomy. On the relation between love and law, Calvin says:

> [T]he beginning of obedience, as well as its source, foundation, and root, is [the] love of God . . . this love cannot exist until we have tasted the goodness of our God. For as long as we conceive of God as being opposed to us, of necessity we will flee from him. Therefore do we wish to love him? Do we wish to be reformed by being obedient to him that we might receive all of our pleasure in his service? Then we must realize that he is our Father and Savior, that he only wants to be favorable to us. Thus once we have tasted his mutual love which he reserves for us, then we will be motivated to love him as our Father. For if this love is in us, then there will be no doubt that we will obey him and that his law will rule in our thoughts, our affections, and in all our members.[46]

There were two prominent contrasting mid 16th-century productions. The first was the thoroughly evangelical Heidelberg Catechism (1563). We learn our misery from the law of God, which requires us to love God and our neighbor, neither of which we are able to live up to perfectly because of our natural tendency to the opposite; as a result, we are liable to eternal punishment (Questions 3–11). Deliverance comes through faith in Christ, the mediator, expressed in the articles of the Creed (Questions 12–64) and confirmed and maintained through the sacraments (baptism and the Lord's Supper) and the keys (preaching and discipline). Gratitude is expressed in good works (Questions 32–115) and prayer (Questions 116–119). The sacerdotal position is represented by the *Catechism of the Council of Trent for Parish Priests* (1566), divided into four parts: Creed, Sacraments, Ten Commandments, Lord's Prayer. It provided a compendium of church teaching for

---

[46] *John Calvin's Sermons on the Ten Commandments*, ed. and trans. Benjamin W. Farley (Grand Rapids: Baker, 1980), 76.

priests to use in instructing the faithful. It remained the official catechism of the Roman Catholic Church until publication of the *Catechism of the Catholic Church* in 1994.

The Westminster Standards (1647) represent the culmination of the evangelical catechetical tradition. The New Testament warrant for using the Ten Commandments for a systematic exposition of Christian ethics is found in such texts as Matthew 5:17-48, 15:19, 19:16-22 (cf. Luke 18:18-27); Eph. 6:1-4 (cf. Col. 3:5-6, 20); and 1 Timothy 1:8-11. Especially relevant is the coordination of the Ten Commandments and the "law of love" in Romans 13:8-10; Galatians 5:13-14; and James 2:8-11. The principles of Jesus' exposition of the moral law in the Sermon on the Mount, taken as precepts for all rather than counsels for a spiritual elite, are incorporated in the "rules for right understanding of the ten commandments" (WLC, 99). The full import (perfection) and reach to the thoughts and intents of the heart (spirituality) are applied to each commandment in turn, habitudes and actions inseparably joined in covenant practice.

The Larger Catechism helpfully brings out the evangelical understanding of the moral law by a series of questions on its use. In brief, it is of use to all human beings to inform them of the holy nature and will of God, and thus to humble them and show them their need of Christ. For the unregenerate, its threats are useful in driving them to Christ, leaving them inexcusable if they continue as they are. For the regenerate, it continues to inform and to humble, but its special use is

> to show them how much they are bound to Christ for his fulfilling
> it, and enduring the curse thereof in their stead, and for their good;
> and thereby to provoke them to more thankfulness, and to express
> the same in their greater care to conform themselves thereunto as
> the rule of their obedience (WLC, 97).

Such use of the law is not contrary to the grace of the gospel: "the Spirit of Christ subduing and enabling the will of man to do that freely, and cheerfully, which the will of God, revealed in the law, requires to be done" (WCF, 19.7). With that clarification, the Confession segues into the chapter on Christian liberty, which consists preeminently in "freedom from the guilt of sin, the condemning wrath of God, the curse of the moral law," and freedom to yield obedience, "not out of a slavish fear, but a childlike love and willing mind." As the psalmist says, "I will run in the way of your commandments, for you set my heart free" (Ps. 119:32).

Conclusion

The prayer of the Apostle Paul in Philippians 1:9-11 provides a fitting conclusion:

> And it is my prayer that your love may abound more and more, with knowledge and all discernment, so that you may approve what is excellent, and so be pure and blameless for the day of Christ, filled with the fruit of righteousness that comes through Jesus Christ, to the glory of God.

Paul begins with the *impelling motive* (love), which in symbiotic relationship with the *directing principle* ("what is excellent" translates *ta diapheronta*, the expression Paul uses in Romans 2:18 with reference to the will of God as revealed in the law) leads to fulfillment of the *controlling purpose* (the glory of God). All this in the confidence "that he who began a good work in you will bring it to completion at the day of Jesus Christ" (Phil. 1:6). God has granted his elect "his precious and very great promises" (1 Pet. 1:4 ; cf. the Beatitudes), and what God has promised he is able to perform.

Recent Objections to Covenant Theology: A Description, Evaluation and Response

LIGON DUNCAN

Introduction

Covenant theology is the Gospel set in the context of God's eternal plan of communion with his people, and its historical outworking in the covenants of works and grace (as well as in the various progressive stages of the covenant of grace). Covenant theology explains the meaning of the death of Christ in light of the fullness of the biblical teaching on the divine covenants, undergirds our understanding of the nature and use of the sacraments, and provides the fullest possible explanation of the grounds of our assurance.

Although not everyone shares a positive assessment of covenant theology, there are many interested in analyzing and evaluating it. As a matter of fact, in the last fifty years, particularly in Reformation and Puritan studies, the amount of research devoted to covenant or federal theology has been formidable.[1]

---

[1] Of course, the historiography of the covenant idea in the nineteenth and early twentieth centuries was considerable, see for instance, A. B. van Zandt, "The Doctrine of the Covenants Considered as the Central Principle of Theology," *Presbyterian Review* 3 (1882): 28-39; T. M. Lindsay, "The Covenant Theology," *British and Foreign Evangelical Review* 28 (1879): 521-38; J. L. Girardeau, "The Federal Theology" in *Memorial Volume for Columbia Seminary*, ed. B. M. Palmer (Columbia: Presbyterian Publishing House, 1884); R. Rainy, "Federal Theology," *CP* 5 (1881): 341-49,427-34; and G. Vos, "The Doctrine

We may point to two historiographical landmarks which have, to a certain extent, fostered the current historical interest in the covenant idea in general and covenant theology in particular. The first is the work of Perry Miller on Puritanism.[2] Writing in a day which had little time for Calvin or Calvinists, Miller managed to rehabilitate the Puritans by depicting them as the authors of a "revision of Calvinism."[3] The Puritans, according to Miller, mollified the harsher characteristics of Calvinism by the "invention" of covenant or federal theology. This covenant theology supposedly had the effect of creating a space for human responsibility in an oppressive predestinarian system. Hence, in Miller's presentation, the covenant idea was a theological tool used by the Puritans to change Calvinism for the better. Miller's work has exerted a tremendous influence on subsequent writing on the idea of covenant in the Reformed tradition.[4]

---

of the Covenant in Reformed Theology," in *Redemptive History and Biblical Interpretation* [*De verbondsleer in de Gereformeerde theologie*] (Grand Rapids: Drupkers, 1891); for an extensive bibliography of nineteenth century treatments of the development of the covenant theology see, A. A. Woolsey, "Unity and Continuity in Covenant Thought: A Study in the Reformed Tradition to the Westminster Assembly" (Ph.D. Thesis, University of Glasgow, 1988), 101-28.

2   P. Miller, *The New England Mind: The Seventeenth Century* (Boston: Beacon Press, 1939).

3   See G. M. Marsden's classic analysis of Miller's work on the Puritans, "Perry Miller's Rehabilitation of the Puritans: A Critique," *CH* 39 (1970): 91-105.

4   Marsden put it well when he said, "As for the thesis that the covenant of grace represented a revision of Calvinism, Miller has created a myth that has been so elegantly presented and widely repeated that it will be difficult to destroy," "Perry Miller: A Critique," 105; Miller's influence can be seen in the work of L. J. Trinterud whose "two-tradition" theory of the development of covenant theology was a modification of the Miller thesis, see "The Origins of Puritanism," *CH* 20 (1951): 37-57; see also M. McGiffert, "Grace and Works: The Rise and Division of Covenant Divinity in Elizabethan Puritanism," *HTR* 75 (1982): 463-502; and McGiffert, "William Tyndale's Conception of the Covenant," *JEH* 32 (1981): 167-84; J. W. Baker's *Heinrich Bullinger and the Covenant: The Other Reformed Tradition* (Athens: Ohio University Press, 1980) is an expansion of the Trinterud thesis; for similar approaches see, G. D. Henderson, "The Idea

A second catalyst for modern historical consideration of the covenant idea may be found in Karl Barth's criticism of the older covenant theology.[5] Whereas other modern theologians tended to ignore the Reformed theology of the seventeenth century, Barth both appreciated and interacted with the covenant theologians of that period. He also recognized that the covenant idea which had attained to such a prominent place in their system was not absent from the earlier reformers.[6] But Barth was very critical of these federal theologians at certain points.[7] He was particularly displeased with the concept of a pre-fall covenant of works and the use of covenant theology to maintain a doctrine of limited atonement.[8] These "later developments" in covenant theology, Barth suggested, were given confessional status for the first time in the Westminster Confession.[9] Since Barth made these observations, a plethora of writing has sought to substantiate historically his theological criticism of the covenant theology.[10] According to writers

---

of the Covenant in Scotland," *EQ* 27 (1955): 2-14; and J. G. Møller, "The Beginnings of Puritan Covenant Theology," *JEH* 14 (1963): 46-67; for helpful correctives to this sort of interpretation see, J. von Rohr, *The Covenant of Grace in Puritan Thought* (Atlanta: Scholars Press, 1986); D. A. Stoute, "The Origins and Early Development of the Reformed Idea of the Covenant," (Ph.D. Thesis, Cambridge University, 1979); and D. B. Calhoun, "The Covenant in Bullinger and Calvin" (Th.M. paper, Princeton Theological Seminary, 1976).

[5]   For a distillation of Barth's views on covenant see, *Church Dogmatics*, 4.1, trans. G. W. Bromiley (Edinburgh: T&T Clark, 1956), 1-78; see esp. 54-66, where he discusses federal theology.

[6]   Barth, *Church Dogmatics*, 4.1, 54-55.

[7]   For an elaboration of Barth's own covenant theology and his criticism of the Cocceian school see, J. L. Scott, "The Covenant in the Theology of Karl Barth," *SJT* 17 (1964): 182-98, and B. L. McCormack, "A Scholastic of a Higher Order: The Development of Karl Barth's Theology, 1921-1931" (Ph. D. Thesis, Princeton Theological Seminary, 1989), 2:626-63.

[8]   Barth, *Church Dogmatics*, 4.1, 57-63.

[9]   Barth, *Church Dogmatics*, 4.1, 59.

[10]   See for example, J. C. McClelland, "Covenant Theology – A Re-evaluation," *CJT* 3 (1957): 182-88; C. S. McCoy, "Johannes Cocceius: Federal

in this school, the systematization of an "unbiblical" conception of covenant led to a revision of Calvinism (similar to Miller's thesis), but for the worse (*contra* Miller). There are a few recurring issues in these historical examinations of covenant theology: the conditionality or unconditionality of the covenant,[11] the role of the law and its relation to covenant,[12] the question of single versus multiple traditions of covenant thought in Reformed theology,[13] and the role of covenant in the structure of redemptive history.[14]

Theologian," *SJT* 16 (1963): 352-70; H. Rolston, "Responsible Man in Reformed Theology: Calvin versus the Westminster Confession," *SJT* 23 (1970): 129-56; Rolston, *John Calvin versus the Westminster Confession* (Richmond: John Knox, 1972); J. B. Torrance, "The Contribution of McLeod Campbell to Scottish Theology," *SJT* 26 (1973): 295-311; J. B. Torrance, "The Covenant Concept in Scottish Theology and Politics and its Legacy," *SJT* 34 (1981): 225-43; J. B. Torrance, "Covenant or Contract? A Study of the Theological Background of Worship in Seventeenth Century Scotland," *SJT* 23 (1970): 51-76; M. C. Bell, *Calvin and Scottish Theology* (Edinburgh: Handsel Press, 1985); D. Weir also tends to follow this line in *The Origins of Federal Theology in Sixteenth-Century Reformation Thought* (Oxford: Clarendon, 1990), see my review of Weir in the *Scottish Bulletin of Evangelical Theology* 12.1 (Spring 1994): 55-57; for cogent criticism of this sort of historical approach see M. W. Karlberg, "The Original State of Adam: Tensions within Reformed Theology," *EQ* 59 (1987): 291-309; P. A. Lillback, "The Binding of God: Calvin's Role in the Development of Covenant Theology," (Ph.D. Thesis, Westminster Theological Seminary, 1985); Lillback, "The Continuing Conundrum: Calvin and the Conditionality of the Covenant," *CTJ* 29 (1994): 42-74; Richard A. Muller, "The Covenant of Works and the Stability of Divine Law in Seventeenth-Century Reformed Orthodoxy: A Study in the Theology of Herman Witsius and Wilhelmus À Brakel," *CTJ* 29 (1994): 75-101; and A. A. Woolsey, "Unity and Continuity in Covenantal Thought," esp. 129-98.

[11] See for instance, C. S. McCoy, "Johannes Cocceius," 362-64; J. B. Torrance, "Covenant or Contract?," esp. 54-57; the same preoccupation with conditionality/unconditionality may be noted in the latter's "The Covenant Concept in Scottish Theology," 228-31.

[12] See for example, H. Rolston, "Responsible Man in Reformed Theology"; F. Lyall, "Of Metaphors and Analogies: Legal Language and Covenant Theology," *SJT* 32 (1979): 1-17; and J. D. Eusden, "Natural Law and Covenant Theology in New England 1620-1670," *NLF* 5 (1960): 1-30.

[13] See L. J. Trinterud, "The Origins of Puritanism"; M. McGiffert, "Grace and Works"; and J. W. Baker, *Heinrich Bullinger and the Covenant*, for

These two sources have informed over a generation of contemporary criticism of classical covenant or federal theology, and
even some with sympathies for the federal theology have felt the
force of their historical and theological strictures. What then can
be said to these things? Well, for starters, it would be useful to
catalogue some of these objections, classify them, and assemble
them in one place. This article begins that project. Furthermore,
though countless articles have been written and even books have
been produced in an attempt to reply to the various arguments set
forth today against the older Reformed presentation of covenant
theology, it would be useful to provide a brief consolidated response to the most significant objections to federal theology. This
essay aims to begin that also. As such, it is offered as a preliminary
polemical and didactic piece of exegetical, historical, and systematic theology.

The Current Neglect of Covenant Theology

One hundred and seventeen years ago John L. Girardeau, in an
address delivered to the Columbia Theological Seminary Alumni
Association, said with a note of alarm that "it is to be feared that
indications are beginning to manifest themselves of a growing
tendency towards a departure from [covenant or federal theol-
ogy]."[15] His sentiments would be echoed a few years later by the

---

presentations of the "two-tradition" hypothesis, and A. A. Woolsey, "Unity
and Continuity in Covenantal Thought"; P. A. Lillback, "The Binding of
God"; and J. von Rohr, *Covenant of Grace in Puritan Thought*, for alternative
evaluations of the development of covenant theology.

[14] See C. F. Lincoln, "The Development of the Covenant Theory," *BS* 100
(1943): 134-63; W. C. Kaiser, "The Old Promise and the New Covenant,"
JETS 15 (1972): 11-23; and J. Feinberg ed., *Continuity and Discontinuity*
(Westchester: Crossway, 1988), 37-62.

[15] *Memorial Volume of the Semi-Centennial of the Theological Seminary at Columbia, South Carolina* (Columbia: Presbyterian Publishing House, 1884),
97. This volume informs us that after a morning meeting in the "Lecture
Room" of the Presbyterian Church on Monday November 7, 1881, "[t]he

great Scottish theologian Hugh Martin in his lectures on the atonement (1887). Martin solemnly remarked, "It has come to pass, we fear, that the federal theology is at present suffering a measure of neglect which does not bode well for the immediate future of the Church amongst us."[16]

Sadly, the concerns of both these stalwarts were confirmed. Under the incessant pounding of theological rationalism, popular evangelical Arminianism, advancing Dispensationalism, and the general reductionistic doctrinal trends of the age, the federal theology – as part of core teaching on the doctrines of salvation – fell into oblivion in the early part of the twentieth century (save as a prop for sacramental theology in Presbyterian circles). American Reformed Christianity virtually abandoned this perennial emphasis of its theological heritage. And, now, even after more than 30 years of renaissance in the various Reformed churches, it has yet to reappear with the same force, or command an equal breadth of consensus in our communions as it once did.[17] This is a curious fact in light of developments outside of Reformed circles.

An Intriguing Irony

Just as Reformed Christianity was beginning to lose its allegiance to covenant theology, mainstream Biblical scholarship began to

---

Association then took recess to meet again this evening at 7½ o'clock in this room, and repaired informally to the church, to hear the last of discourses upon the programme of the Semi-Centennial celebration. This discourse was delivered to an earnestly attentive and deeply interested audience, by the Rev. Professor John L. Girardeau, D.D., LL.D., upon 'The Federal Theology: Its Import and Its Regulative Influence'"; xvii.

[16] Hugh Martin, *The Atonement: In Its Relations to The Covenant, The Priesthood, The Intercession of Our Lord* (Edinburgh: Knox Press, 1976), 25.

[17] James Walker could call covenant theology "emphatically" "*the* old theology of Scotland," *The Theology and Theologians of Scotland, 1560-1750* (Edinburgh: Knox Press, 1982), 73; but J. I. Packer recently observed, in his introduction to Herman Witsius' *Economy of the Covenants* (Escondido: den Dulk Foundation, 1990), that "in modern Christendom covenant theology has been unjustly forgotten."

take notice of it. Advances in our knowledge of OT treaty forms, and the theology of early Judaism and nascent Christianity, in combination with the meteoric popularity of the biblical theology movement[18] have led non-Reformed Christianity to pay new attention to the covenants. Diverse theological traditions are now recognizing the consequence of the covenants (e.g., Dispensationalism [particularly in its "progressive" form], Liberation Theology, Roman Catholicism, Barthianism, etc.), however different their "covenant theology" is from the standard Reformed view. O. Palmer Robertson once observed, "Virtually every school of biblical interpretation today has come to appreciate the significance of the covenants for the understanding of the distinctive message of the Scriptures."[19]

Furthermore, the history of federal theology has become linked to several significant debates in current historical theological studies of the development of Protestant doctrine. For instance, it has been drawn into the discussion of the relation of the theology of the Reformers to that of Protestant Orthodoxy ("Scholasticism") and, more specifically, to the relation of Calvin to Westminster. It is also connected to the formulation of the doctrine of limited atonement and the development of the doctrine of assurance in Calvin and the Puritans.

A Brief Review of Covenant Studies

Few subjects have received more sustained attention in biblical and historical studies in recent years than the covenant idea and covenant theology, but for the sake of brevity, we will only survey covenant studies up until about 1985, with the hopes of updating this survey elsewhere and more extensively in the near

---

18   I mean to imply the ephemeral nature of the biblical theology movement here; James Barr's post-mortem may be found in his article on the subject in *Interpreter's Dictionary of the Bible*, Supplementary Volume (Nashville: Abingdon, 1976), 104-11.

19   Robertson, *Christ of the Covenants*, vii.

future. In the realm of OT studies, since Wellhausen appealed to the development of the covenant concept in the OT as supporting evidence for the evolutionary development of Israel's religion, countless pages have been devoted by OT scholars to scrutinizing the covenant idea.[20] There have been philological investigations of *berith*,[21] studies of the role of the covenant idea in Israel's *cultus*,[22] comparisons of OT covenant forms with Ancient Near Eastern treaty forms,[23] considerations of the prophets' use of the covenant idea,[24] examinations of covenant and kingship,[25] and attempts

---

[20] For good, brief accounts of the development of the covenant idea in the OT, see G. E. Mendenhall, "Covenant," in *IDB* 1:714-23; G. E. Mendenhall and G. A. Herion, "Covenant," in *ABD* 1:1179-1202; and L. Köhler, *OT Theology*, trans. A. S. Todd (London: Lutterworth, 1957), 59-75; D. R. Hillers gives a popular but useful account, dependent on Mendenhall, in *Covenant: History of a Biblical Idea* (Baltimore: Johns Hopkins, 1969), 1-168; R. Kraetzschmar provides a revision and expansion of the Wellhausen thesis concerning covenant in *Die Bundesvorstellung im AT* (Marburg: Elvert, 1896); E. W. Nicholson attempts a resurrection of this view in *God and His People: Covenant and Theology in the OT* (New York: Oxford University Press, 1986); see also G. Quell, s.v., "diatheke," in *TDNT* 2:109-24.

[21] For example, see J. Begrich, "Berit. Ein Beitrag zur Erfassung einer alttestamentlichen Denkform," *ZAW* 60 (1944): 1-11; L. Kohler, "Problems in the Study of the Language of the OT," *JSS* 1 (1956): 4-7; W. Schottroff, "'Gedanken' im Alten Orient und im AT," *WMANT* 15 (1964): 202-24; J. Barr, "Some semantic notes on the Covenant," in *Beitrage zur Alttestamentlichen Theologie*, ed. H. Donner, et al (Gottingen: Vanderhoeck and Ruprecht, 1977), 23-38; and G. Quell, who provides additional bibliography for philological studies of covenant, in *TDNT* 2:106-9.

[22] For example, see S. Mowinckel, *The Psalms in Israel's Worship*, trans. D. R. Ap-Thomas (2 vols.; Oxford: Blackwell, 1962); and M. G. Kline, *By Oath Consigned* (Grand Rapids: Eerdmans, 1968), 13-49.

[23] For example, see G. E. Mendenhall, *Law and Covenant in Israel and the Ancient Near East* (Pittsburgh: Biblical Colloquium, 1955); D. J. McCarthy, *Treaty and Covenant*, (2nd ed.; Rome: Pontifical Biblical Institute, 1978); M. G. Kline, *Treaty of the Great King* (Grand Rapids: Eerdmans, 1963); K. Baltzer, *The Covenant Formulary in Old Testament, Jewish, and early Christian Writings*, trans. D. E. Green (Oxford: Blackwell, 1971); E. Gerstenberger, "Covenant and Commandment," *JBL* 84 (1965): 38-51; G. M. Tucker, "Covenant Forms and Contract Forms," *VT* 15 (1965): 487-

to construct a unified OT theology around the central theme of covenant.[26] Though these studies manifest a variety of concerns with and approaches to the covenant idea, there are a few recurring issues in debate. First, there is the question of definition. Is a covenant a divine disposition or a compact? If it is an agreement, is it unilateral or bilateral, unconditional or conditional.[27] Second,

---

503; and M. J. Buss, "The Covenant Theme in Historical Perspective," *VT* 16 (1966): 502-4.

[24] For example, see R. E. Clements, *Prophecy and Covenant* (London: SCM, 1965); J. Bright, *Covenant and Promise* (London: SCM, 1977); W. Zimmerli, *The Law and the Prophets*, trans. R. E. Clements (Oxford: Blackwell, 1965); H. B. Huffmon, "The Covenant Lawsuit and the Prophets," *JBL* 78 (1959): 286-95; J. Harvey, "Le '*rîb*-Pattern,' réquisitoire prophétique sur la rupture de l'alliance," *B* 43 (1962): 172-96; F. C. Fensham, "Common Trends in the Curses of the Near Eastern Treaties and Kudurru-inscriptions Compared with the Maledictions of Amos and Isaiah," *ZAW* 75 (1963): 155-75; J. R. Boston, "Les attachés litteraires, l'origine et la signification de l'expression biblique 'Prendre à témoin le ciel et la terre,'" *VT* 16 (1966): 8-25; and W. Brueggemann, *Tradition for Crisis: A Study in Hosea* (Richmond: John Knox Press, 1968).

[25] For example, see J. Bright, *A History of Israel* (London: SCM, 1960); A. Alt, "Das Königtum in den Reichen Israel und Juda," *VT* 1 (1951): 2-22; G. Widengren, "King and Covenant," *JSS* 2 (1957): 1-32; and J. R. Porter, *Moses and Monarchy* (Oxford: Blackwell, 1963). The first two authors argue that the monarchy represented a defection from an earlier, purer covenant idea. The latter two, on the other hand, argue for the priority of the Davidic covenant.

[26] For example, see W. Eichrodt, *Theology of the Old Testament*, trans. J. A. Baker (2 vols.; London: SCM, 1961); W. J. Dumbrell, *Covenant and Creation: An Old Testament Covenantal Theology* (Exeter: Paternoster, 1984); T. E. McComiskey, *The Covenants of Promise: A Theology of the Old Testament Covenants* (Nottingham: InterVarsity, 1985); F. C. Fensham, "Covenant, Promise and Expectation in the Bible," *TZ* 23 (1967): 305-22.

[27] Some writers tend to stress the unconditionality of the covenant, such as J. Begrich, "Berit," *ZAW* 60 (1944): 1-11; the general consensus, however, is to recognize the mutuality of the covenant without denying the divine initiative or graciousness in the covenant relationship, for example, see D. J. McCarthy, *Old Testament Covenant: A Survey of Current Opinions* (Oxford: Blackwell, 1973), 2-4; A. Jepsen, "Berith. Ein Beitrag zur Theologie der Exilzeit," in *Verbannung und Heimkehr: Beitrage zur Geschichte und Theologie Israels im 6 und 5 Jahrhundert v Chr*, ed. A. Kuschke (Tubingen:

and along with this, is the question of the relation of law and covenant, and their respective roles in Israel's relationship with God.[28] Third, scholars attempting to detail the development of the covenant idea in the OT inevitably must address (or assume an answer to) the question whether there is a univocal concept of covenant in the OT.[29] This is obviously a critical issue for those who are endeavoring to construct an OT theology around covenant. These common issues in OT covenant studies are of interest because they tend to recur in NT and historical studies of the covenant idea.

When compared to the volume of writing on covenant in the OT, research on the covenant idea in the intertestamental era may seem sparse. Nevertheless, a good number of significant studies have been devoted to analysis of the covenant concept in the Apocrypha, Pseudepigrapha, Qumran texts, and the Cairo Damascus fragments.[30] These studies have been important in identifying

---

J. C. B. Mohr, 1961), 161-80; O. Loretz, "Berith—'Band, Bund,'" *VT* 16 (1966): 239-41; E. Kutsch goes so far as to deny that berith means covenant or relationship, and asserts that it means obligation in "Gesetz und Gnade. Probleme des alttestamentlichen Bundesbegriff," *ZAW* 79 (1967): 18-35.

[28] Numerous studies on law and covenant argue for close relationship of the two (i.e., covenant is not set over against commandment as grace often is over against law), see W. Eichrodt, "Covenant and Law: Thoughts on Recent Discussion," *Int* 20 (1966): 302-21; G. E. Mendenhall, *Law and Covenant in Israel and the Ancient Near East*; M. G. Kline, *The Structure of Biblical Authority* (Grand Rapids: Eerdmans, 1972).

[29] D. J. McCarthy is critical of scholars who begin their surveys of covenant in the OT with the assumption that all covenant in the OT is of one kind, see *Old Testament Covenant*, 4-6, 31-32, 86-89; D. R. Hillers, while observing that covenant in the OT may not be simply one idea, describes recent attempts to detail the OT conception of covenant: "It is not a case of six blind men and the elephant, but of a group of learned paleontologists creating different monsters from the fossils of six separate species," in *Covenant: The History of a Biblical Idea*, 7.

[30] For instance, see D. J. McCarthy, "Covenant in Narratives from Late OT Times," in *The Quest for the Kingdom of God: Studies in Honor of G. E. Mendenhall*, ed. H. B. Huffmon, et al. (Winona Lake: Eisenbrauns, 1983), 77-94; R. F. Collins, "The Berith-Notion in the Cairo Damascus Covenant

the role played by covenant in early Judaism and providing background for the study of covenant in the NT.

Though literature on covenant in the NT is less abundant than in the OT, the subject is at least equally controversial. One of the major issues in NT covenant studies is the meaning(s) of *diatheke* in the NT writings. Indeed, there has been a continuing debate on the translation of *diatheke* in the NT since Deissmann said that ". . . no one in the Mediterranean world in the first century A.D. would have thought of finding in the word διαθήκη the idea of 'covenant.'"[31] Deissmann's assertion was not received without dissent, however, and recent scholarship tends to prefer covenant as the usual translation of *diatheke* in the NT.[32] Another concern in NT

___

and its Comparison with the NT," *ETL* 39 (1963): 555-94; J. G. Harris, "The Covenant Concept Among the Qumran Sectaries," *EQ* 39 (1967): 86-92; E. P. Sanders, "The Covenant as a Soteriological Category and the Nature of Salvation in Palestinian and Hellenistic Judaism," in *Jews, Greeks and Christians*, ed. R. Hamerton-Kelly (Leiden: E. J. Brill, 1976), 11-44; A. Jaubert, *La Notion D'Alliance Dans Le Judaisme aux abords de l'ere chretienne* (Paris: Editions du Seuil, 1963); for additional bibliography see E. Kutsch, s.v., "Bund" [II. Frühes Judentum] in *TRE* 7: 405.

[31] Of course, there had been considerable discussion of the translation of διαθήκη before Deissmann [e.g., *DIATHEEKEE, Covenant, Not Testament*, (London: Trubner, 1856), an anonymous but learned tract]. At the time of the issue of the Revised Version, for instance, scholarship was favoring covenant over testament. The AV had translated διαθήκη as covenant twenty-one times, testament twelve times. The RV changed ten of these twelve and so covenant appeared in thirty-one of thirty-three occurrences of διαθήκη in the NT. By Deissmann's time this trend was reversing and his remarks provided impetus for renewed discussion of the issue. For Deissmann, the question of translating διαθήκη as testament (which he understood to imply a unilateral enactment) or covenant (which indicated a bilateral agreement) was ultimately whether Christianity was a religion of grace or works; see A. Deissmann, *Light from the Ancient East*, trans. L. R. M. Strachan (London: Hodder and Stoughton, 1910), 337-38.

[32] Two early studies of διαθήκη which supported Deissmann's position (i.e., διαθήκη = testament) are J. Behm, *Der Begriff DIATHEKE im NT* (Erlangen: Lippert, 1912); and E. Lohmeyer, *Diatheke: Ein Beit. zur Erläuterung des neutestamentliches Begriffs* (Leipzig: Hinrich'sche Buchhandlung, 1913); however their conclusions were contradicted by the Roman Catholic scholar L. G. Fonseca who argued that διαθήκη = compact (except in two places)

covenant studies, in view of the occurrence of covenant theology in the Eucharistic narratives of the Synoptics and 1 Corinthians, has been to determine the significance of covenant in the sacramental theology of the NT theologians.[33] There has been further interest in investigating the covenant theology of Hebrews,[34] and comparing it to the Pauline conception of the covenant.[35] Some of these

---

in the NT, "Diatheke—Foedus an Testamentum?" *B* 8 (1927): 31-50, 161-81, 290-319, 418-41; and 9 (1928): 26-40, 143-60; G. Vos took a position between the extremes in "Covenant or Testament?" *Bible Magazine* 2 (1914): 205-25; H. A. A. Kennedy calls Deissmann's assertion "absurd" in "The Significance and Range of the Covenant Conception in the New Testament," *E*, 8th ser. 10 (1915): 385-410; E. D. Burton provides a brief but superb survey of διαθήκη in classical, LXX, later Greek and NT usage, then argues that διαθήκη = covenant everywhere in the NT (except in Hebrews 9:16-17), in *Epistle to the Galatians* (*ICC*) (New York: Scribners, 1920); see also G. E. Mendenhall, "Testament," in *IDB* 4:575; D. F. Estes, "Covenant (NT)," in *ISBE* 1:793; and W. Selb, "Diatheke im NT," *JSS* 25 (1974): 183-96.

[33] F. Lang, "Abendmahl und Bundesgedanke im NT," *EvTh* 35 (1975): 524-48; A. R. Millard, "Covenant and Communion in First Corinthians," in *Apostolic History and the Gospel*, ed. W. Gasque and R. P. Martin (Exeter: Paternoster, 1970), 242-48; A. R. Eagar, "St. Luke's Account of the Last Supper: A Critical Note on the Second Sacrament," *E*, 7th ser. 5 (1908): 252-62, 343-61; T. H. Robinson, "My Blood of the Covenant," *BZAW* 41 (1925): 232-37; H. S. Gehman, "The Covenant: Old Testament Foundation of the Church," *TT* 7 (1950): 40, 41; W. Most, "A Biblical Theology of Redemption in a Covenant Framework," *CBQ* 29 (1967): 17-19; Mendenhall, "Covenant," in *IDB* 1:722-23; N. Clark, *An Approach to the Theology of the Sacraments* (London: SCM, 1956); see also J. Jeremias, *The Eucharistic Words of Jesus*, trans. N. Perrin (London: SCM, 1966); M. G. Kline presents an intriguing argument for a covenantal understanding of the sacrament of baptism in *By Oath Consigned*, see esp. 50-102.

[34] For instance, G. Vos, "Hebrews, the Epistle of the Diatheke," in *Redemptive History and Biblical Interpretation*, ed. R. B. Gaffin (Phillipsburg: P&R, 1980), 161-233; C. Spicq, "La théologie des deux Alliances dans l'Epître aux Hébreux," *RSPT* 33 (1949): 15-30; A. Carr, "Covenant or Testament? A Note on Hebrews 9:16, 17," *E*, 7th ser. 7 (1909): 347-52; and G. D. Kilpatrick, "Diatheke in Hebrews," *ZNW* 68 (1977): 263-65; see also O. P. Robertson, *The Christ of the Covenants* (Phillipsburg: P&R, 1980), 138-46.

[35] For studies of the covenant concept in Paul see, W. C. van Unnik, "La conception paulinienne de la Nouvelle Alliance," in *Sparsa Collecta*, (3 vols.;

studies have also given attention to the matter of relating the new covenant to the OT law.[36] These particular inquiries are indicative of a more general concern to evaluate the role of covenant in the NT theologians' presentations of salvation history.[37] Hence, we may note a number of similar discussions in NT and OT covenant studies.

So, despite the overwhelming evidence of the fundamental importance of the covenant concept to OT, Inter-testamental, and NT religion, and the established significance of the covenant in church doctrine in general and in the Reformed tradition in particular; and perhaps because of the sustained assault on federal divinity from ostensibly Reformed quarters, the older Reformed theology of the covenants is still widely ignored in our pulpits and in disrepute in our theological halls.

This essay is an attempt to sound a call for the revival of classical federal theology in our gospel preaching and theological reflection. We will give some explanations for the current antipathy to classical covenant theology, give some responses to this aver-

---

Leiden: E. J. Brill, 1973), 1:174-93; W. Wallis, "The Pauline Conception of the Old Covenant," *P* 4 (1978): 71-83; C. Roetzel, "Diatheke in Romans 9:4," *B* 51 (1970): 377-90; H. Ridderbos, *Paul: An Outline of His Theology*, trans. J. R. DeWitt (London: SPCK, 1977), 333-41; Y. K. Yu, "The New Covenant: The Promise and its Fulfillment" (Ph.D. dissertation, Durham University, 1989); for comparisons of Paul and Hebrews see, U. Luz, "Der alte und der neue Bund bei Paulus und im Hebraerbrief," *EvTh* 27 (1967): 318-36; H. A. A. Kennedy, "The Significance and Range of the Covenant Conception in the NT," esp. 395-410; and R. V. Moss, "The Covenant Conception in Early Christian Thought" (Ph.D. Thesis, University of Chicago, 1954), 140-53.

[36] In addition to works mentioned below 6, n.16, see E. P. Sanders, *Paul, The Law, and the Jewish People* (Philadelphia: Fortress, 1983), esp. 137-41; Sanders, *Jesus and Judaism* (London: SCM, 1985), esp. 245-69; Sanders, *Paul and Palestinian Judaism* (London: SCM, 1977), esp. 511-15; and H. Hubner, *Law in Paul's Thought*, ed. J. Riches, trans. J. C. G. Greig (Edinburgh: T&T Clark, 1984), esp. 67-100.

[37] For discussions of the role of covenant in NT *heilsgeschichte* see, Moss, "The Covenant Conception," 140-53; Most, "A Biblical Theology," 10-19; Hillers, *Covenant*, 169-88; and Robertson, *Christ of the Covenants*, 271-300.

sion, and then suggest the importance of covenant divinity for our preaching of Christ.

Contemporary Criticisms of Classic Covenant Theology

Some suggested causes of neglect or abandonment

What are the causes of this neglect or abandonment of covenant theology? That is too complex a question to answer adequately here, but we offer the following five-point surmise.

First, there is a general impatience amongst us with historical theology. We prefer to write our theology in the first person, thereby confirming many students' ignorance of their theological heritage. We critique the movements of the past without our students even being superficially acquainted with those movements. This, in combination with general historical and theological illiteracy; the trend of theological reductionism; and denominational flux, may be one important factor in the eclipse of covenant theology in the Reformed and evangelical tradition.

Second, for some time now the function of covenant theology (even in Reformed circles) has either been limited to sacramental discussions, or has been deployed in an eccentric form as a justification for some specialized view of children in the household of faith, or in the service of a worldview program, or as part of a platform for expounding the Christian's role in society. Without denying the importance of sphragistics, or engaging right now with the modern hyper-Calvinist spin on covenant theology, we should see emphatically, that the older covenant theology claimed a fundamental place in the Christian message. It asserted an explanation of the imputation of Adam's sin that has been widely influential in evangelical Protestantism, as well as suggested a consistent scheme of understanding the NT language of economic trinitarianism in such a way as to avoid crude subordinationism and to highlight the distinctive contributions of the persons of the Trinity in the *ordo salutis*.

Third, it may be that the widespread influence of Dispensationalism in evangelical and Reformed circles, specifically in conservative Presbyterianism in the middle fifty years of this last century, has had an eroding effect on the grasp and appreciation of covenant theology in our community.

Fourth, the current objections to systematic theology come to bear on covenant theology as well. For covenant theology, rightly understood, is not merely biblical theology; more than that, it is systematic theology. However, we live in a day and age in which many have a distaste for system (or at least claim so), and are, therefore, suspicious of anything in our heritage which displays too much organization and synthesis. We live in the day of thematic theology, not systematic theology, and so, often, even those who think of themselves as covenant theologians are merely carrying out biblical covenant themes without the hard work of coordination and correlation. Our fear of inferences and distinctions leaves us cold toward the older Reformed covenant theology.

Fifth, the direct assault on federal theology from within the Reformed community has, no doubt, had its effect. Yes, Dorner and Lindsay popularized this mud-slinging a century ago, but it has certainly intensified. Indeed, as the corpse of federalism has grown colder, the attacks upon it have grown more ferocious, so that, now, often the only thing that people know about federal theology, they know from its opponents second-hand. Scotland's Torrance clan and their adherents lead the way in this fight. J. B. Torrance's almost pathological obsession with the extermination of covenant theology (as if it were being heralded from every pulpit in the land) is evident in everything that he has ever written. Holmes Rolston, R. T. Kendall, M. Charles Bell, Alisdair Heron, and others have followed in the Torrances' wake. Many far sounder theologians have been unfortunately impacted by the Barthian critique of federal divinity, and even John Murray did some semantic back-peddling on the covenant of works which has proved unhelpful to his theological descendants.

A. Some recent objections to covenant/federal theology

J. B. Torrance, arch-enemy of federalism, puts forward at least five (he has more!) great weaknesses of federal theology. For him, these are matters of dire concern because they involve "an impoverishment and restriction of the concept of grace."[38]

[1] Federal theology treats a covenant as a contract.

Torrance urges that "the whole federal scheme is built upon the deep-seated confusion between a covenant and a contract."[39] How does a covenant theologian respond? First, by noting that behind this charge is Torrance's view that covenants, as opposed to contracts, are unconditional. Such a view will not stand biblical scrutiny, for most OT covenants are explicitly conditional. Indeed, there is no such thing as an unconditional covenant. Biblical covenants (even divine ones) have contractual elements. Torrance's charge is actually reflective of his denial of mutuality and obligation in the covenant relationship, which is biblically unsustainable and resultant from his hyper-objectivistic soteriology (Christomonism).

[2] Federal theology creates nature/grace dichotomy.

Thomas Aquinas is most closely associated with this idea: Nature can take you so far in understanding God (natural law), but grace takes you the rest of the way. Torrance further asserts that "the federal scheme made a radical dichotomy between the sphere of Nature and the sphere of Grace, of natural law and the Gospel, so that the Mediatorial Work of Christ is limited to the covenant of grace and the Church, the sphere marked out by the covenant of grace."[40] Torrance goes on to charge that this is a reversion to the medieval view that nature is prior to grace. Donald Macleod demolishes this argument:

---

[38]   J. B. Torrance, "Covenant or Contract?" *SJT* 23 (1970): 70.

[39]   Ibid., 66.

[40]   Ibid., 67.

The obvious response to this is that there is always something (sin) which is prior to grace; and always something (law) which is prior to sin. To make grace prior to sin is to end up in the most unacceptable kind of supralapsarianism. Men and women must be related to God as sinners before they can be reconciled to him through a gracious adoption.[41]

By distinguishing the covenants of works and grace, the federal theology is simply articulating the undeniably Scriptural facts that Adam was in a relationship with God that did not entail sin-necessitated mediation, which required obedience, held out promise of further blessing, and made no provision for blessing despite demerit. This relationship was marked by condescending love and justice.

[3] Federal theology moves the emphasis from Christ to ourselves.
Torrance again warns: "The whole focus of attention moves away from what Christ has done for us and for all men, to what we have to do IF we would be (or know that we are) in covenant with God."[42] Again, Macleod dismantles this objection with understatement:

It would, however, be very difficult to document this. In covenant theology faith itself is the gift of God, granted to the people of Christ in accordance with the covenant of redemption: and the object of faith was emphatically not anything we do for ourselves, but Christ crucified.[43]

I think, historically and theologically, Macleod is irrefutably correct. Historic covenant theology championed the objective work of God in the atonement, justification, the means of grace and more. So, *contra* Torrance, covenant theology exalts Christ and

---

[41] Donald Macleod, "Covenant Theology" in *Dictionary of Scottish Church History &Theology*, ed. Nigel M. de S. Cameron (Downers Grove: InterVarsity Press, 1993), 217.

[42] J. B. Torrance, "Covenant or Contract?" 69.

[43] D. Macleod, "Covenant Theology," 217.

expects our proper response to him as the only mediator of the covenant.

[4] Federal theology makes justice God's central attribute (and mercy optional).

Torrance regularly charges federalism with making holiness and justice central in God's attributes and love and mercy peripheral. However, (1) This charge rests on a false antithesis between justice and mercy. Mercy is not the opposite of justice, injustice is. (2) Federal theology does not make justice more central than love or mercy, but recognizes that God can never be unjust (that is the whole ground of our security) and that the exercise of mercy is, by definition, optional—or it would not be mercy.

And, if we want to get technical, mercy is not an attribute of God. It is the expression of an attribute of God. It is always responsive. Love is an attribute, but mercy, by definition, is optional. Otherwise, we must be universalists, believing that everyone, including Satan, will be saved.

[5] Federal Theology makes atonement prior to God's love.

Whenever Torrance roams back to thoughts of the trial of Macleod Campbell, he trots out the old heretic's idea that forgiveness is prior to atonement. He thus charges federalists with teaching that the atonement was designed to condition God's love. His whole discussion is characterized by confusion between God's love and God's forgiveness.[44] Once again, federal theology has always emphasized that the atonement is the provision of the Father's love. The Son does not make the Father love at the cross. The Son is on the cross because of the Father's love. Nevertheless, the cross is certainly the ground of our reconciliation, as Paul makes clear in Romans 5:10.

William Klempa has also offered some strong criticism of classical covenant theology, though with much more subtlety than

---

[44] Ibid., "Covenant Theology," 217-8.

Professor Torrance. We turn now our attention to some of the objections that he has raised.

[6] Federal theology's double-covenant scheme lacks biblical basis.
On the contrary, federal theology has more solid, explicit, exegetical footing than any of its rivals, and its central themes have been shown to be correct in broad, modern scholarly research. The bi-covenantal (as opposed to mono-covenantal) approach to covenant theology is based not only upon the Adam-Christ parallels of the NT, but also on a distinction drawn from the radical implications of the fall for man's relationship with God. Covenant theology realizes the legitimate distinction that theologians make when they speak of both the majestic and moral holiness of God. But covenant theologians also recognize (as the Barthians do not) that biblical reconciliation has in view man in his moral estrangement from the holy God. The alienation remedied in redemption is moral not metaphysical.

[7] Federalism teaches that God deals with man two different ways.
The charge here is that covenant theology has God relating to man originally on condition of obedience and subsequently by grace only because of failure. Again, Klempa's view of grace does not have in clear view grace's biblical antecedent: sin. Federal theology teaches without apology that man's fall into sin has necessitated God to provide for another way of communion (consequent absolute necessity) if God desires further relationship with man, because there can be no fellowship with God without perfect holiness. A low view of sin and the fall lurks behind this objection.

[8] Federalism's inter-trinitarian covenant opens up dualism in God.
Klempa's objection here comes directly from Barth. He writes,

> When the covenant was based on a pact between two divine persons, a wider dualism was introduced into the Godhead—again in defiance of the Gospel as the revelation of the Father by the Son and of the Son by the Father, which took place in

Jesus Christ. The result was an uncertainty which necessarily relativised the unconditional validity of the covenant of grace, making it doubtful whether in the revelation of this covenant we really had to do with the one will of the one God.[45]

Now, to be fair, we need to note that many thoroughly orthodox covenant theologians have struggled with the idea of the covenant of redemption. Girardeau, Murray, Robertson, and Gaffin, to name a few, have problems with the Scriptural basis of the concept. Nevertheless, in historic, mainstream, covenant theology the covenant of redemption functions to help us take seriously what Jesus says about his own mission and the trinitarian nature of the plan of redemption. Herman Bavinck, after acknowledging some of the inadequate formulations of and for the covenant of redemption (*Pactum Salutis*, or council of peace), affirms that it is a Scriptural doctrine and goes on to say, "The pact of salvation makes known to us the relationships and life of the three persons in the Divine Being as a covenantal life, a life of consummate self-consciousness and freedom."[46]

Scripture clearly stresses that the work of salvation is a work of the Trinity, and yet it also clearly attributes differing roles to the persons within the Godhead. For instance, it is the Father who sends the Son (John 5:37; 6:44, 57; 8:16, 18; 12:49; 14:24). The Son was sent and serves as the only Mediator. The Father did not die for the sins of his people, nor did the Spirit; it was the Son alone who performed this task (John 14:6; Acts 4:12; 1 Tim. 2:5). Further, it is the Spirit who is the comforter of the people of God. These tasks were not assigned at the incarnation, but were embraced before time in the eternal purposes of God, in which the three persons of the Godhead, in one common purpose, chose to save sinners (1 Pet. 1:20). Thus, the covenant of redemption does not open

---

[45]   *Church Dogmatics*, 4.1, 65.

[46]   Herman Bavinck, *Reformed Dogmatics: Sin and Salvation in Christ*, ed. John Bolt, trans. John Vriend (Grand Rapids: Baker Academic, 2006), 214.

up God to dualism, since it is one common purpose within the Godhead to save sinners, despite the diversity of function within the outworking of this plan of redemption.

Objections to covenant theology, however, do not just come from the Barthian wing of the Reformed community. John Murray, in particular, has raised some major objections to the idea of the covenant of works, and its biblical basis.

[9] The Covenant of Works does not account for the elements of grace in the Adamic Administration.

John Murray writes, "The term [covenant of works] is not felicitous, for the reason that the elements of grace entering into the administration are not properly provided for by the term 'works'."[47] The rejoinder of classical covenant theology to this objection is that grace, in its fullest sense, does not and cannot exist before the fall, because sin did not exist in humanity before the fall, and grace, in its fullest sense, entails the overcoming of sin or demerit. In denying that God showed "grace" to Adam prior to the fall, or in refraining from speaking of God's relation to Adam as "gracious" we do not intend to diminish in any way the extravagant love and goodness of God in creating and entering into relationship with Adam. We are not saying that Adam in any way deserved the relationship that he possessed with God, but we are saying that his continuation in that state of blessing was based upon his obedience to God's stipulations ("In the day that you eat of it you shall surely die"). So in the absence of sin, and in the absence of demerit, there cannot be sin-overcoming and demerit-overcoming favor—or grace.

Thus, the assumption that Adam's relationship to God is one of grace prior to the fall fails to do justice to the meaning of grace, in its fullest redemptive sense. The Hebrew word for grace and favor (*chen*) does not occur until Genesis 6:8. The context of this

---

47 Murray, *Collected Writings of John Murray*, vol. 2 (Edinburgh: Banner of Truth Trust, 1977), 49.

initial use, with regard to the relationship between Noah and God, is one of gross immorality and the wickedness of man's heart. The word "grace," thus, appears nowhere in Genesis 1-2. If we are to speak of Adam's relationship to God prior to the fall as gracious, we must be able to prove that elements of grace are present, since the vocabulary is not. To be sure, this can be done in Genesis 3 after the fall, even though the vocabulary is not present. But to say that God's relationship prior to the fall is gracious leaves us with discussing man's *pre-lapsarian* and *post-lapsarian* relationship with God in the same terms. To do that would greatly diminish or at least blur the consequences of the fall. Prior to the fall, Adam was not in a position of demerit, but after the fall he was. Without sin, grace cannot be said to be present in its fullest sense, which makes the covenant of works and covenant of grace distinction helpful.

From a definitional standpoint, *chen* and *charis*, can mean either grace (Noah who received undeserved mercy despite his demerit) or favor (Jesus was sinless and was said to grow in favor). In the English language, it would be quite odd to refer to God's relationship with Christ as one of "grace," "favor" to be sure, but not "grace." If one were to do so, explanation would certainly be in order. Terminology can be employed in different ways, so we must try to use terminology that is most clear and helpful. Speaking of Adam's pre-fall relationship to God as one of "grace" is confusing, to say the least.

R. J. Rushdoony similarly denies that there can ever be a covenant with God that is not of grace. In support of this assertion, Rushdoony points out the vast difference between the parties in the covenant, and that God initiates the covenant.[48] While these things are true, they are irrelevant to the issue of the presence of grace in God's original covenantal relationship with Adam. God, rather, chose that this original act of condescension would be a covenant

---

[48] Rousas John Rushdoony, *Systematic Theology: In Two Volumes* (Vallecito, California: Ross House Books, 1994), 376.

of works, whereby man, upon the fulfillment of the stipulations as set forth according to God's sovereign will, would receive life.

[10] Scripture does not refer to God's relationship to Adam prior to the fall as a covenant.

Murray, in the second place objects:

> It is not designated a covenant in Scripture. Hosea 6:7 may be interpreted otherwise and does not provide the basis for such a construction of the Adamic economy. Besides, Scripture always uses the term covenant, when applied to God's administration to men, in reference to a provision that is redemptive or closely related to redemptive design.[49]

It is interesting to note that Murray is ready to find "grace" in the Adamic Administration even though the term is not there, and yet deny that it is a covenant because the term is not there. But, by way of response, we ought to note that in 2 Samuel 7 God establishes a covenant with David, yet the word *berith* is nowhere to be found. Is 2 Samuel 7, then, to be seen as something other than a covenant? Psalm 89 says otherwise. "You have said, 'I have made a covenant (*carithi berith*) with my chosen one; I have sworn to David my servant'" (Ps. 89:3, ESV; Ps. 89:4, Hebrew). Scripture, then, does not have to employ specifically the word *berith* in the initial context for a covenantal relationship to be present.

Although quickly dismissed by Murray, we should give some attention to Hosea 6:7, a verse that can be interpreted in four major ways,[50] one of which would be referring to a covenant with Adam. The possibilities are as follows: (1) An emendation can be made

---

[49]   Murray, *Collected Writings of John Murray*, vol. 2 (Edinburgh: Banner of Truth Trust, 1977), 49.

[50]   More recently, with the discovery of a refined form of Hebrew parallelism, Janus Parallelism or Pivotal Polysemous Parallelism, which acts like a *double-entendre*, there is a new interpretation of this passage. This interpretation states that both the translations "as Adam" (as the first man, Adam) and "as Adam" (the inhabitants of Adam), a view that is similar to the Wellhausen interpretation of "at Adam" without textual emendation, are correct at the same time. This

to the Masoretic Text, thereby choosing an alternate reading of "in" or "at Adam" rather than "as Adam."[51] This interpretation, based largely on the word "there," proposes that there was some sin committed at a place called Adam that was notorious in Hosea's day but of which there is now no extant record. Thus, it is presumed that the city identified in Joshua 3:16 was the locale of some national sin.[52] This interpretation, although possible, is not probable. There is no indication in the Bible that there was some violation of covenant at Adam. Further, there does not appear to be legitimate grounds for textual emendation, when the text makes perfect sense as it stands.

It should be noted that this view has been altered a little to carry the same meaning without textual emendation. In the Elberfelder Bibel, 1985, revision, "as Adam" refers to the inhabitants of Adam collectively. Still, this does not provide a definitive solution, since the violation of this covenant in Adam is simply unverifiable.

(2) The word "adam" is one of four words that have different meanings than usual in this passage. In this instance, it is proposed, "adam" can also mean dirt. Thus, the meaning of the passage would be that Israel transgressed God's covenant "underfoot" or "treated it like it was dirt."[53] D. Stuart, following M. Dahood and W. Kuhnigk,[54] offers this translation: "But look—they have walked on my covenant

---

view is advanced by Byron G. Curtis in "Hosea 6:7 and Covenant-Breaking like/at Adam" in *The Law is Not of Faith: Essays on Grace and Works in the Mosaic Covenant*, eds. Bryan D. Estelle, J. V. Fesko, and David VanDrunen, (Phillipsburg: P&R Publishing, 2008), 230-280.

[51] This emendation, proposed by Wellhausen, has found considerable traction among most recent commentators. See G. I. Davies, *New Century Bible Commentary: Hosea* (Grand Rapids: Eerdmans, 1992), 171.

[52] See James Luther Mays, *Hosea: A Commentary* (Philadelphia: The Westminster Press, 1969), 99-101. Graham I. Davies, *New Century Bible Commentary: Hosea* (Grand Rapids: Eerdmans, 1992), 171-173. A. A. Macintosh, *A Critical and Exegetical Commentary on Hosea* (Edinburgh: T&T Clark, 1997), 236.

[53] See Douglas Stuart, *Word Biblical Commentary*, vol. 31: *Hosea-Jonah* (Waco, TX: Word Books, 1987), 99, 111.

like it was dirt, see, they have betrayed me!"[55] This view, however, is difficult to support. G. I. Davies observes, "This makes emendation unnecessary, but it attributes new and controversial meanings to several of the Hebrew words (like the older suggestion based on Arabic that *sam* here means not **there** but 'then')."[56]

(3) The third view, following the LXX, is that "as adam" refers to "as men." That is, "But they like men have transgressed the covenant."[57] Between this rendering of the text and the following option it is difficult to decide.

(4) The fourth view, following the Vulgate, holds that Hosea 6:7 refers to the covenant that Adam broke in Eden.[58] C. F. Keil says, "The local expression 'there,' refers to the place where the faithless apostasy occurred, as in Ps. xiv. 5."[59] Robertson concludes, "It is difficult to settle on one of these last two interpretations. But in either case, something would be implied about the relation of the non-Israelite man to his Creator-God."[60]

Without opting to emend the Masoretic Text, postulating an historical situation based on the word "there," or choosing questionable lexical definitions for the Hebrew words, we are left with two viable options, both of which speak of God's covenantal relationship with man, and thereby "apply covenantal terminology to the relation of God to man established by creation."[61]

---

[54] M. Dahood, "Hebrew-Ugaritic Lexicography VI," *Biblica* 49 (1968) 362. W. Kuhnigk, *Nordwestsemitische Studien zum Hoseabuch* (Rome: Biblical Institute Press, 1974), 81.

[55] Douglas Stuart, *Word Biblical Commentary*, vol. 31: *Hosea-Jonah* (Waco, TX: Word Books, 1987), 98-99.

[56] Graham I. Davies, *New Century Bible Commentary: Hosea* (Grand Rapids: Eerdmans, 1992), 171.

[57] William Rainey Harper, *A Critical and Exegetical Commentary on Amos and Hosea* (Edinburgh: T&T Clark, 1905, 1960 reprint), 288.

[58] See C. F. Keil, *The Twelve Minor Prophets* (Grand Rapids, Eerdmans, 1949), 99-100.

[59] Ibid., 100.

[60] O. Palmer Robertson, *The Christ of the Covenants*, 23.

[61] Ibid., 4.

Without wanting to assert too much, it is safe to say that Hosea 6:7 cannot be simply dismissed as illegitimate proof of a covenant of works. Furthermore, as illustrated above using 2 Samuel 7, the word "covenant" is not necessary for a covenantal relationship to be present. Should one choose, however, to dismiss Hosea 6:7 as proof for the covenant between Adam and God; it must be observed, as Berkhof points out, that all the elements of a covenant are present in Genesis 1-3.[62] Similarly, Macleod writes:

> But all the elements of a covenant were there, [Federal theologians] argued. There were two partners: God and Adam (as representative of all mankind). There was a clear stipulation: perfect obedience, focused in the prohibition of one fruit. And there was a clear promise of threat. Obedience would mean life, disobedience would mean death.[63]

Macleod goes on to conclude that although Murray rejected the covenant of works, "Murray agreed, however, that the divine arrangements with Adam involved both conditions and promises, and traditional federal theologians would probably not have asked for more."[64] Thus, the elements of a covenant are present even though the specific vocabulary is not.

[11] In the Bible, the term covenant is limited to a redemptive provision.
We meet Murray's objection here with a flat denial. Was the covenant between David and Jonathan redemptive in design (1 Sam. 18:3)? No. Was the covenant between Jacob and Laban redemptive in design (Gen. 31:44)? No. It is crucial that we understand that covenants are not in-and-of-themselves gracious or redemptive. Rather, God pours his grace into his redemptive covenants. Murray's thought was insufficiently clear on this point.

---

[62] Louis Berkhof, *Systematic Theology* (Grand Rapids: Eerdmans, 1996), 213.

[63] D. Macleod, "Covenant Theology," 215.

[64] Ibid., 217.

Secular near-eastern covenants were asymmetrically mutually beneficial social contracts. The biblical text witnesses to this definition, and though God's gracious, redemptive covenants in Scripture far transcend this understanding, they do not negate the basic fact of what a covenant was in secular contexts.

[12] Covenant entails a security that does not exist in the Adamic Administration, because Adam fails and falls.
This fourth objection by Murray does not account for the fact that if Adam had obeyed, his relationship would have been secured. The problem is not with the covenant; the problem, rather, is with Adam. Furthermore, it should be noted that even God's redemptive covenants are broken in the Bible by God's people. If they are not, why, then, is there a "new" covenant in Jeremiah 31:32? If you answer that this is because the Mosaic covenant was a "republication" of the covenant of works, you still have to reckon with the breaking of the new covenant itself (Heb. 10:29).

Now, we turn to three more objections that have been raised against different aspects of covenant theology.

[13] Man can merit nothing before God.
This objection to the covenant of works is voiced by various individuals, including R. Rushdoony, H. Hoeksema, and D. Fuller. The objection, however, misses the entire point that is being made in the covenant of works, which simply states that God gave a command to Adam with the promise of curse upon infraction and the implied promise of blessing upon obedience. If man is obedient, as a matter of justice, God will uphold his end of the covenant. Thus, it is not a matter of meriting something before God; the blessing finds its source and root in God's unmerited decision to offer the promise of continued life upon Adam meeting the condition that was laid down. Calvin made a similar argument with respect to objections made concerning the merit of Jesus Christ.

In discussing Christ's merit, we do not consider the beginning of merit to be in him, but we go back to God's ordinance, the first cause. For God solely of his own good pleasure appointed him the Mediator to obtain salvation for us. Hence it is absurd to set Christ's merit against God's mercy. For it is a common rule that a thing subordinate to another is not in conflict with it. For this reason nothing hinders us from asserting that men are freely justified by God's mercy alone, and at the same time that Christ's merit, subordinate to God's mercy, also intervenes on our behalf.[65]

[14] Covenant is not an agreement; it is a relationship or friendship. This objection, asserted by Hoeksema[66] and many within the Federal Vision camp,[67] fails to grasp the precise nature of a covenant, and the way that Scripture uses the term and concept. Referring to a covenant as a relationship may be good, true and helpful in some contexts, but when false dichotomies are posed (e.g. "a covenant is relational not legal," or "marriage is a covenant, which shows that a covenant is a relationship not a contract") then the appeal to covenant as "relationship" actually serves to obscure the Bible's usage of the word and idea of covenant. First it ought

---

[65] John Calvin, *Institutes*, xvii, 1. See also Robert A. Peterson, Sr., *Calvin on the Atonement: What the renowned pastor and teacher said about the cross of Christ* (Fearn Ross-shire: Christian Focus, 1999), 101-106.

[66] Herman Hoeksema, *Reformed Dogmatics* (Grand Rapids: Reformed Free Publishing Association, 1966), 222.

[67] John Barach, "Covenant History" (2002 Auburn Avenue Presbyterian Church Pastor's Conference sermon). Steve Wilkins, "Covenant, Baptism, and Salvation," in *The Auburn Avenue Theology, Pros and Cons: Debating the Federal Vision*, ed. E. Calvin Beisner (Fort Lauderdale, Fla.: Knox Theological Seminary, 2004), 254. Douglas Wilson, "The Objectivity of the Covenant," *Credenda/Agenda* 15/1:4. Ralph Smith, *The Eternal Covenant: How the Trinity Reshapes Covenant Theology* (Moscow, Ida.: Canon, 2003), 51. For helpful interaction with these authors and their ideas, cf. Guy Prentiss Waters, *The Federal Vision and Covenant Theology: A Comparative Analysis* (Phillipsburg, N.J. P&R Publishing, 2006), 10-14.

to be noted that marriage is a legal relationship or a relationship with legal dimensions (it carries with it, inextricably, social and moral required obligations and prohibitions). So, setting "legal" over against "relational" in one's definition of marriage, actually diminishes clarity and promotes error in our conception of the meaning and significance of the term and condition of marriage. Indeed, the legal or forensic stipulations of marriage are precisely designed to protect and strengthen the relationship between husband and wife. Second, as with marriage, it is impossible to do justice to the biblical idea and terminology of covenant and underplay the legal or forensic elements of it.[68] Third, we ought

---

[68] J. V. Fesko, dealing with proponents of the Federal Vision, writes, "The first issue with which we must begin is the very definition of the term *covenant*. As we saw, Jordan defines a covenant as "a personal-structural bond which joins the three persons of God in a community of life, and in which man was created to participate." We must ask, however, where in the Scriptures do we see a covenant defined only as a relationship? While relationships certainly take place within the context of a covenant, we must recognize that Scripture sees a covenant primarily as an agreement. Defining a covenant as an agreement, pact, or treaty, for example, is evident in the use of the term *berith* in the OT. We see covenants as treaties or agreements in Abraham's covenant with Abimelech (Gen. 21.27), Isaac and Abimelech (Gen. 26.28), Jacob and Laban (Gen. 31.44), Israel and the Gibeonites (Josh. 9.15), to name just a few. In fact, anywhere one finds stipulations or conditions, such as blessing for compliance with the terms of the covenant and death for violation, we must conclude that the covenant is based upon an agreement. Reformed theologians have noted the OT's use of the term and have therefore defined a covenant in terms of an agreement. Zacharias Ursinus (1534-83), for example, in his exposition of the Heidelberg Catechism defines a covenant as "a mutual contract, or agreement between two parties, in which the one party binds itself to the other to accomplish something upon certain conditions." Similar definitions of the term persist to this day. Even among those reformed theologians who prominently feature the idea of covenant defined as a relationship still see that it is a relationship based upon an agreement. That a covenant by definition is an agreement, means that a covenant creates a relationship but that it is one that has a legal element. The legal element, for example, is clearly evident in the stipulated conditions of the covenant. If one fails to meet the terms of the covenant, or agreement, then there are consequences for such failure. The legal element in the covenant is not a problem unless one argues, as does the federal

---

to note that the Bible deploys the terminology of "covenant" in at least four ways (and theologians often add a fifth, by deduction). 1. Covenant, most precisely and specifically, refers to the way by which a promissory and obligatory relationship is secured (see Gen. 15:18). 2. Covenant, by synecdoche, thus refers to a special kind of secured relationship (see Josh. 9-10, esp. 9:11). This is the way we most often think about the term, but in doing so, we must never forget the originating and specific meaning. 3. Covenant may also refer to the sign or rite which represents and confirms the secured relationship (Gen. 17:10). 4. Covenant can refer to the written revelation that derives from a period of redemptive history, because the revelation is associated with a particular administration of the God's covenant (see 2 Cor. 3:14). 5. Covenant may thus, by extension, refer to an era characterized by or associated with a particular covenant administration. Hence, sometimes when theologians speak of the old covenant and new covenant, they are referring to the particular *arrangements* or *characteristics* of the redemptive *administrations* associated with Moses and Christ, respectively, and sometimes they are talking about the *era* in which those administrations obtained.

Now, more, much more could be said about this, but this (at least) is clear. Calling a covenant "a relationship" does not sufficiently address the essence of what a covenant is. A covenant is not just a relationship in general but a very specific type of relationship which always entails promises and obligations. And even when we use the term in this way (entirely justified in doing so by the example of Scripture), we must never forget that most specifically a covenant is the way that an already-existing binding relationship is secured.

The covenant-making ceremony of Genesis 15 did not create or inaugurate a special relationship between God and Abraham, it represented and secured it. The relationship came into being by

---

vision, that covenant is part of the *opera ad intra* of the trinity." J.V. Fesko, "The Federal Vision and the Covenant of Works," 9-10. This article can be found at the website www.genevaopc.org.

grace and election (way back in Gen. 12). It was secured by means of a covenant (years later in Gen. 15). This is the way covenants always function in the Scripture. And this is one of the very areas in which Hoeksema and many proponents of the Federal Vision miss the mark in their attempts to improve classic formulations of covenant theology.

[15] The theory that Adam would inherit eternal life had he obeyed the probationary command does not fit with the rest of Scripture. Hoeksema makes this objection in various forms in his *Reformed Dogmatics.*[69] Essentially, Hoeksema finds it unfounded to say that Adam would have received eternal life upon obedience. By way of response, we will quote Macleod at length.

> The fact that "God has foreordained whatsoever comes to pass" should make us careful in speaking of God's purpose for man *if* he had never fallen. Two points may be made, however, because they relieve certain difficulties which may be pressed on the supposition that man had not fallen. First, it is altogether likely that at some point in his probation man would have been confirmed in holiness. The only alternative is that the race should have had to live on an everlasting probation, which is scarcely conceivable and is in contradiction of God's procedure elsewhere, as in the case of the angels who kept their first estate. Secondly, it is also probable that Adam would have been exalted to a higher kind of life, although the precise nature of the exaltation needs to be carefully defined. We can only argue in terms of the analogy between Adam and the redeemed. The redeemed, like Adam, will know perfect holiness and perfect blessedness. But they will also experience a transformation of their bodies that will bring them into conformity to the body of the glory of Christ. It is unlikely that this privilege granted to man the sinner would have been denied to man the keeper of the covenant.[70]

---

[69] Hoeksema, *Reformed Dogmatics.*

[70] Macleod, "Covenant 2," 23.

It becomes clear, then, that although there have been a number of objections raised against classic covenant theology, there are relatively simple answers to these criticisms, and classic covenant or federal theology (as articulated in the Westminster Confession of Faith) holds up well under this scrutiny.

Commending Covenant Theology

Covenant theology is the Bible's way of explaining and deepening our understanding of: (1) the atonement (the meaning of the death of Christ); (2) assurance (the basis of our confidence of communion with God and enjoyment of his promises); (3) the sacraments (signs and seals of God's covenant promises — what they are and how they work); and (4) the continuity of redemptive history (the unified plan of God's salvation). Covenant theology is also an hermeneutic, an approach to understanding the Scriptures—an approach that attempts to biblically explain the unity of biblical revelation.

Covenant theology is a blending of both biblical and systematic theology. If biblical theology is the thematic survey of redemptive history, with an emphasis on the theological development – era to era – of whatever loci is being studied, then covenant theology could rightly be called "biblical, biblical theology." That is, covenant theology recognizes that the Bible itself structures the progress of redemptive history through the succession of covenants.

Covenant theology is systematic theology in that it recognizes the covenants as a fundamental architectonic or organizing principle for the Bible's theology. Thus it proceeds to integrate the biblical teaching about the federal headships of Adam and Christ, the covenantal nature of the incarnation and atonement, the continuities and discontinuities in the progress of redemptive history, the relation of the Jewish and Christian scriptures, law and gospel, into a coherent theological system.

Covenant theology is central, not peripheral, to the biblical story. When Jesus wanted to explain the significance of his death to his disciples, he went to the doctrine of the covenants (see

Matt. 26; Mark 1; Luke 22; 1 Cor. 11). When God wanted to assure Abraham of the certainty of his word of promise, he went to the covenant (Gen. 12, 15, and 17). When God wanted to set apart his people; ingrain his work in their minds; tangibly reveal himself in love and mercy; and confirm their future inheritance, he gave the covenant signs (Gen. 17; Exod. 12, 17, 31; Matt. 28; Acts 2; Luke 22). When Luke wanted to show early Christians that Jesus' life and ministry were the fulfillment of God's ancient purposes for his chosen people, he went to the covenant of grace and quoted Zacharias' prophecy, which proves that believers in the very earliest days of "the Jesus movement" understood Jesus and his messianic work as a fulfillment (not a "Plan B") of God's covenant with Abraham (Luke 1:72-73). When the Psalmist and the author of Hebrews wanted to show how God's redemptive plan is ordered and on what basis it unfolds in history, they went to the covenants (see Pss. 78, 89; Heb 6-10).

Covenant theology is not a response to Dispensationalism. It existed long before the rudiments of classical Dispensationalism were brought together in the nineteenth century. Covenant theology is not an excuse for baptizing children, nor merely a convention to justify a particular approach to the sacraments (modern paedocommunionism and baptismal regenerationism). Covenant theology is not sectarian. It is an ecumenical, Reformed approach to understanding the Bible, developed in the wake of the magisterial Reformation, but with roots stretching back to the earliest days of catholic Christianity and historically appreciated in all the various branches of the Reformed community (Baptist, Congregationalist, Independent, Presbyterian, Anglican, and Reformed). Covenant theology cannot be reduced to serving merely as the justification for some particular view of children in the covenant (covenant successionism), or for a certain kind of eschatology, or for a specific philosophy of education (whether it be homeschooling, Christian schools, or classical schools). Covenant theology is bigger and more important than that.

The doctrine of the covenant lies at the root of all true theology. It has been said that he who well understands the distinction between the covenant of works and the covenant of grace, is a master of divinity. I am persuaded that most of the mistakes which men make concerning the doctrines of Scripture are based upon fundamental errors with regard to the covenants of law and of grace. May God grant us now the power to instruct, and you the grace to receive instruction on this vital subject.[71]

C.H. Spurgeon said that. As the great English Baptist preacher, Spurgeon is beyond our suspicion of secretly purveying a Presbyterian view of the sacraments to the unsuspecting evangelical masses.

Covenant theology flows from the trinitarian life and work of God. God's covenant communion with us is modeled on and a reflection of the intra-trinitarian relationships. The shared life, the fellowship of the persons of the Holy Trinity, what theologians call *perichoresis* or *circumincessio*, is the archetype of the relationship, the gracious covenant God shares with his elect and redeemed people. God's commitments in the eternal covenant of redemption find space-time realization in the covenant of grace.

---

[71] *The Sermons of Rev. C. H. Spurgeon of London*, 8th Series ed. (New York: Robert Carter and Brothers, 1893), 172.

Appendix: An Analysis of the Plenary Sessions of the Westminster Assembly[1]

CHAD B. VAN DIXHOORN

Introduction

This analysis of the plenary sessions of the Westminster Assembly contains each numbered and unnumbered plenary session of the Assembly. Date, day of the week, and volume and folio information are provided, as well as an index to other supporting or supplementing sources and a brief description and classification of the subject of debate for each plenary session. This sessional analysis constitutes the first attempt to provide a complete profile of the work of the gathering. Those who are more intimately acquainted with the goings on at the Assembly will know already that it is almost impossible to keep a view of the whole with the sometimes erratic method of the Synod and of its scribes. For this reason I only summarize the main event or events of each plenary session. Some of these summary descriptions may warrant adjustment or even reclassification at a later date but, as each of these sessions was classified with care, I think the center of my argument which builds on this analysis will hold.

---

[1]   I am grateful to Dr. Jason Rampelt and Dr. Jonathan Moore for their comments on an early draft of this table.

This table not only provides an analysis of the Assembly's plenary sessions. It also helps persons studying the Assembly to locate individual sessions or topics of debate in the Assembly. And it allows the reader to identify session numbers and dates using volume and folio numbers from the minutes and Lightfoot's manuscript and published journals and to locate the available sources for any day in the Assembly.

The format of the table is simple. The minutes for each session, where extant, are indicated in the minutes folios column. Other extant sources of information are listed in the column to the right. The table includes all recorded plenary sessions and all sessions where the entire Assembly sat as a "grand committee." Save for the one routine committee session recorded by Adoniram Byfield in the minutes, this table does not include information about the standing and ad hoc committees of the Assembly. However, because they explain irregularities in the plenary sessions, this table does include fast days, although most of them were not numbered as sessions.[2] This table also supplies missing dates and session numbers and silently corrects them when necessary.[3] It does not attempt to correct sequences of errors in the numbered sessions or folios, where a number is missing or repeated.

Abbreviations

An abbreviated classification of subjects for each plenary session of the minutes is necessary for the analysis provided in my essay, "The Westminster Assembly at Work." The subject classifications in the table of contents are repeated here for the reader's convenience.[4] I also supply a key for the source codes used in the "Analysis."

---

[2] For the dates of Parliamentary fasts, funerals, and thanksgivings, I rely on J. F. Wilson, *Pulpit in Parliament: Puritanism During the English Civil Wars, 1640-1648* (Princeton: Princeton Univ. Press, 1969), 237-54.

[3] Where I have reconstructed the session numbers, such as in the opening months of the Assembly, the session numbers are provided in brackets.

[4] For discussion of these classifications, see "The Westminster Assembly at Work," pages 19-54.

Subject classification

A: Approving candidates: All matters pertaining to the examination of men for chaplaincies, churches, and university appointments.

B: Business: Business relating to the Assembly, its ordering, regulating and procedures, its payment or its members; welcoming visitors; correspondence with foreign churches (including the Scots); works of charity or dealings with politicians.

C: Church Government: Ordination, Rights of church government, structure of the national church, Presbyterianism and the establishment of Presbyteries.

D: Doctrine: The 39 Articles, Confession and Catechisms, the doctrinal and moral standard for admission to the Lord's Supper and confuting heretics.

F: Fast: Fast day or discussion about fasting.

W: Worship: All matters having to do with the directory for worship, Sabbath observance and the Psalter.

?:   No information or insufficient information about the session.

Source Codes

G: George Gillespie, "Notes of debates and proceedings of the Assembly of Divines and other commissioners at Westminster," ed. D. Meek, in *Works*, (Edinburgh: Robert Ogle and Oliver and Boyd, 1846), 2:9-100.

L: Lightfoot's published journal of the Assembly's debates in J. Lightfoot, *Works*, ed. J. R. Pitman London: J. F. Dove, 1824), vol. 13.[5]

L: Where Lightfoot's indicator is in bold and italics, Lightfoot's unpublished journals are referred to, with foliation provided (Cambridge University Library Dd.xiv.28.4, fos. 1r-62v). A transcription of this journal is provided in C. B. Van Dixhoorn, "Reforming the Reformation: theological debate at the Westminster

---

[5]   I do not distinguish between Lightfoot's full, daily reports and his second hand retrospective reports for days where he is absent.

Assembly, 1643-1652," (unpublished Ph.D. diss., University of Cambridge, 2004), 2:1-116.

R: Recorded votes from a second set of minutes;[6] some are found in the Bodleian Library, Nalson MS 22, fos. 118r-119v; most are recorded in George Gillespie, 'Votes passed in the Assembly of divines in Westminster,' ed. D. Meek, in *Works*, (Edinburgh: Robert Ogle and Oliver and Boyd, 1846), 2:1-8.

Other codes

?: No information or insufficient information

[ ] Editorial insertion or conjecture.

bold Manuscript material not previously published.[7] A transcription of this material can be found in Van Dixhoorn, 'Reforming the Reformation,' vols. 3-7.

bold Manuscript material not previously known to or used by historians. A transcription of most of this material can be found in Van Dixhoorn, "Reforming the Reformation," vol. 2.

---

[6] For information on the second set of minutes see the introduction to C. B. Van Dixhoorn and D. F. Wright, eds., *The Minutes and Papers of the Westminster Assembly*, Oxford University Press, in preparation.

[7] Although never published, sessions 45-74 are not marked in bold face because Robert M. Norris provides a transcription of them in his 1977 doctoral thesis, R. M. Norris, "The Thirty-nine Articles at the Westminster Assembly" (unpublished Ph.D. diss., University of St. Andrews, 1977). For my concerns about Norris's transcription, see Van Dixhoorn, "Reforming the Reformation," 2:xliv-xlvi.

An analysis of the plenary sessions of the Westminster Assembly
Minutes: Volume I

Sess.	Date	Day	Min. folios	Other sources	Main subject(s) of discussion	Subj. class.
	1643					
	1 July	Sat		L 1r	Opening Day	
[1]	6 July	Th		L 1v	Business	B
	7 July	F			Fast	
[2]	8 July	Sat		L 3r	Business	B
	10 July	M		L 3v	Committee meetings	
	11 July	Tu		L 3v	Committee meetings	
[3]	12 July	W		L 3v	39 Arts.	D
[4]	14 July	F		L 4r	Business	B
[5]	15 July	Sat		L 4v	Business; 39 Arts.	B, D
[6]	17 July	M		L 4v	39 Arts.	D
[7]	18 July	Tu		L 5r	39 Arts.	D
[8]	19 July	W		*L 6r*	39 Arts.	D
	21 July	F			Fast	
[9]	22 July	Sat		*L 7r*	39 Arts.	D
[10]	24 July	M		*L 7r*	39 Arts.	D
[11]	25 July	Tu		*L 7v*	39 Arts.	D
	26 July	W			Fast	
[12]	27 July	Th		*L 8r*	39 Arts.	D
[13]	28 July	F		*L 8v*	39 Arts.	D
[14]	31 July	M		*L 10v*	39 Arts.	D
[15]	1 Aug	Tu		*L 10v*	39 Arts.	D
[16]	1 Aug pm	Tu		*L 11r*	39 Arts.	D
[17]	2 Aug	W		*L 11v*	39 Arts.	D
[18]	3 Aug	Th		*L 12r*	39 Arts.	D
[19]	4 Aug	F		*L 12r*	39 Arts.	D
[20]	7 Aug	M		*L 13r*	39 Arts.	D
[21]	8 Aug	Tu		*L 13r*	39 Arts.	D
[22]	9 Aug	W		*L 13v*	39 Arts.	D
[23]	10 Aug	Th		*L 13v*	39 Arts.	D
[24]	10 Aug pm	Th		*L 15r*	39 Arts.	D
[25]	11 Aug	F		*L 15v*	39 Arts.	D
[26]	14 Aug	M		*L 15v*	39 Arts.	D
[27]	15 Aug	Tu		*L 16v*	39 Arts.	D
[28]	16 Aug	W		*L 17r*	39 Arts.	D
[29]	17 Aug	Th		*L 19r*	39 Arts.	D
[30]	18 Aug	F		*L 19v*	39 Arts.	D
[31]	21 Aug	M		*L 20r*	Sects	D
[32]	22 Aug	Tu		*L 20v*	Sects; 39 Arts.	D
[33]	23 Aug	W		*L 20v*	39 Arts.	D
[34]	24 Aug	Th		*L 20v*	39 Arts.	D
[35]	25 Aug	F		*L 21r*	39 Arts.	D
[36]	28 Aug	M		*L 22r*	SLC	B
[37]	28 Aug pm	M		*L 22r*	SLC	B

Sess.	Date	Day	Min. folios	Other sources	Main subject(s) of discussion	Subj. class.
[38]	29 Aug	Tu		*L 22v*	SLC	B
[39]	29 Aug pm	Tu		*L 22v*	SLC	B
[40]	30 Aug	W			Fast	F
[41]	31 Aug	Th		*L 23r*	SLC	B
[42]	1 Sept	F		*L 23v*	39 Arts.	D
[43]	1 Sept	F		*L 23v*	SLC	B
[44]	2 Sept	Sat		*L 24r*	SLC	B
45	4 Sept	M	1:2r	*L 24r*	39 Arts. (14th) supererogation and *consilia evangelica*	D
46	5 Sept	Tu	1:5v	*L 25r*	39 Arts. (11th, 15th)	D
47	6 Sept	W	1:10r	*L 25v*	39 Arts. (11th)	D
48	7 Sept	Th	1:15v	*L 27r*	39 Arts. (11th)	D
49	8 Sept	F	1:24r	*L 29v*	39 Arts. (11th)	D
50	11 Sept	M	1:29r	*L 31v*	39 Arts. (11th); SLC	D, B
51	11 Sept pm	M	1:40r		39 Arts. (11th); SLC	D, B
52	12 Sept	Tu	1:41r	*L34r*	39 Arts. (11th); SLC	D, B
53	12 Sept pm	Tu	1:45r	*L35r*	39 Arts. (11th)	D
54	13 Sept	W	1:49r	*L 37r*	39 Arts. (11th)	D
55	14 Sept	Th	1:53v	*L 40v*	39 Arts. (11th)	D
56	15 Sept	F	1:56r	*L 43r*	39 Arts. (11th); SLC	D, B
57	18 Sept	M	1:61v	*L 44v*	39 Arts. (11th)	D
58	19 Sept	Tu	1:65v	*L 46r*	39 Arts. (11th, 12th, 13th)	D
59	20 Sept	W	1:69v	*L 47r*	39 Arts. (12th, 16th)	D
60	21 Sept	Th	1:72r	*L 50r*	Sects	D
61	21 Sept pm	Th	1:72r	?	?	
62	22 Sept	F	1:74r	*L 51r*	sects	B
63	25 Sept	M	1:77r	*L 52r*	Fast – signing of the SLC	F
	27 Sept	W			Fast	
64	28 Sept	Th	1:77v	*L 52v*	Business; SLC	B
65	29 Sept	F	1:79r	*L 52v*	Business; SLC (SLC ceremony)	B
66	2 Oct	M	1:79rb	*L 53r*	39 Arts. (12th)	D
67	3 Oct	Tu	1:83r	*L 55r*	SLC	B
68	4 Oct	W	1:84r	*L 55r*	39 Arts. (12th, 19th)	D
69	5 Oct	Th	1:87r	*L 56v*	Business; SLC	B
	6 Oct	F			Fast (SLC ceremony)	
70	9 Oct	M	1:90r	*L 57r*	39 Arts. (13th)	D
71	10 Oct	Tu	1:95r	*L 57v*	39 Arts. (13th); sects	D
72	11 Oct	W	1:97v	*L 59r*	39 Arts. (13th)	D
73	12 Oct	Th	1:102r	*L 60r*	39 Arts. (13th, 15th, 16th)	D
74	13 Oct	F	1:106v	L	Fast Business	F
[75]	16 Oct	M		L	Fast	F
76	17 Oct	Tu	**1:107v**	R, L	Church gov. (Procedures)	C
77	18 Oct	W	**1:114r**	L	SLC	B
78	19 Oct	Th	**1:116r**	L	Church gov. (officers)	C
79	20 Oct	F	**1:120v**	R, L	Church gov. (Christ the head)	C
80	20 Oct pm	F	**1:122v**	L	Church gov. (officers)	C
81	23 Oct	M	**1:122v**	R, L	Church gov. (preface; officers); Scots Commis.	C, B
	25 Oct	W			Fast	
82	26 Oct	Th	**1:124r**	R, L	Church gov. (preface; officers); Business	C, B

Sess.	Date	Day	Min. folios	Other sources	Main subject(s) of discussion	Subj. class.
83	27 Oct	F	**1:126v**	L	Church gov. (officers)	C
84	30 Oct	M	**1:129v**	R, L	Church gov. (officers)	C
85	31 Oct	Tu	**1:137v**	R, L	Church gov. (officers)	C
86	1 Nov	W	**1:145r**	R, L	Church gov. (officers)	C
87	2 Nov	Th	**1:152r**	R, L	Church gov. (officers)	C
88	3 Nov	F	**1:157v**	R, L	Church gov. (officers)	C
89	6 Nov	M	**1:162r**	R, L	Church gov. (officers)	C
90	7 Nov	Tu	**1:164v**	R, L	Church gov. (officers)	C
91	8 Nov	W	**1:167r**	R, L	Church gov. (officers); sects	C, D
92	9 Nov	Th	**1:170v**	R, L	Church gov. (officers), sects	C, D
93	10 Nov	F	**1:176r**	L	Church gov. (officers)	C
94	13 Nov	M	**1:179v**	L	Church gov. (officers)	C
95	14 Nov	Tu	**1:185r**	R, L	Church gov. (officers)	C
96	15 Nov	W	**1:190v**	R, L	Church gov. (officers)	C
97	16 Nov	Th	**1:195v**	R, L	Church gov. (officers)	C
98	17 Nov	F	**1:198v**	L	Church gov. (officers)	C
99	20 Nov	M	**1:204v**	L	Church gov. (officers)	C
100	21 Nov	Tu	**1:210r**	R, L	Church gov. (officers)	C
101	22 Nov	W	**1:211v**	L	Church gov. (officers)	C
102	23 Nov	Th	**1:216r**	L	Church gov. (officers)	C
103	24 Nov	F	**1:220v**	L	Church gov. (officers)	C
104	27 Nov	M	**1:224r**	L	Church gov. (officers)	C
	29 Nov	W			Fast	
105	30 Nov	Th	**1:229r**	L	Church gov. (officers)	C
106	1 Dec	F	**1:234r**	L	Church gov. (officers)	C
107	4 Dec	M	**1:241r**	L	Church gov. (officers)	C
108	5 Dec	Tu	**1:241v**	R, L	Church gov. (officers)	C
	5 Dec pm	Tu	**1:242v**	L	(recorded committee meeting)	
109	6 Dec	W	**1:245r**	L	Church gov. (officers)	C
110	7 Dec	Th	**1:249r**	L	Church gov. (officers)	C
111	8 Dec	F	**1:252v**	R, L	Church gov. (officers)	C
112	11 Dec	M	**1:256r**	R, L	Church gov. (officers)	C
113	12 Dec	Tu	**1:261v**	R, L	Church gov. (officers)	C
114	13 Dec	W	**1:265r**	L	Church gov. (officers)	C
115	14 Dec	Th	**1:269r**	L	Church gov. (officers)	C
116	15 Dec	F	**1:275r**	R, L	Church gov. (officers); Funeral of Pym	C
117	18 Dec	M	**1:280r**	L	Business	B
118	19 Dec	Tu	**1:280v**	L	Church gov. (officers)	C
119	20 Dec	W	**1:283r**	L	Church gov. (officers)	C
120	21 Dec	Th		R, L	Church gov. (officers)	C
121	22 Dec	F		R, L	Church gov. (officers)	C
	27 Dec	W			Fast	
122	28 Dec	Th		R, L	Church gov. (officers)	C
123	29 Dec	F		R, L	Church gov. (officers)	C
	1644					
124	1 Jan	M		L	Church gov. (officers)	C
125	2 Jan	Tu		R, L	Church gov. (officers; ordination)	C
126	3 Jan	W		R, L	Church gov. (officers; ordination)	C
127	4 Jan	Th		R, L	Church gov. (officers; ordination)	C

Sess.	Date	Day	Min. folios	Other sources	Main subject(s) of discussion	Subj. class.
128	5 Jan	F		L	Church gov. (ordination)	C
129	8 Jan	M		R, L	Church gov. (officers; ordination)	C
130	9 Jan	Tu		L	Church gov. (ordination)	C
131	10 Jan	W		R, L	Church gov. (ordination)	C
132	11 Jan	Th		R, L	Church gov. (ordination)	C
133	12 Jan	F		R, L	Church gov. (ordination)	C
134	15 Jan	M		R, L	Church gov. (ordination)	C
135	16 Jan	Tu		R, L	Church gov. (ordination)	C
136	17 Jan	W		L	Church gov. (ordination); Fast business	C, F
	18 Jan	Th		L	Thanksgiving	
137	19 Jan	F		L	Church gov. (ordination)	C
138	22 Jan	M		L	Church gov. (ordination *pro tempore* by presby.)	C
139	23 Jan	Tu		R, L	Church gov. (ordination *pro tempore* by presby.)	C
140	24 Jan	W		R, L	Church gov. (ordination *pro tempore* by presby.)	C
141	25 Jan	Th		R, L	Church gov. (ordination *pro tempore* by presby.)	C
142	26 Jan	F		R, L	Church gov. (ordination *pro tempore* by presby.)	C
143	27 Jan	Sat		L	Church gov. (ordination *pro tempore* by presby.)	C
144	29 Jan	M		L	Church gov. (ordination *pro tempore* by presby.)	C
	31 Jan	W			Fast	
145	1 Feb	Th		R, L	Church gov. (presbytery)	C
146	2 Feb	F		L, G	Church gov. (presbytery or ordination *pro tempore* by presby.)	C
147	5 Feb	M		L, G	Church gov. (presbytery); sects	C, D
148	6 Feb	Tu		L, G	Church gov. (presbytery)	C
149	7 Feb	W		L, G	Church gov. (presbytery)	C
150	8 Feb	Th		L, G	Church gov. (presbytery)	C
151	9 Feb	F		L, G	Church gov. (presbytery)	C
152	12 Feb	M		L, G	Church gov. (presbytery)	C
153	13 Feb	Tu		L, G	Church gov. (presbytery)	C
154	14 Feb	W		L, G	Church gov. (presbytery)	C
155	15 Feb	Th	**1:300r**	L, G	Church gov. (presbytery)	C
156	16 Feb	F	**1:303r**	L, G	Church gov. (presbytery)	C
157	19 Feb	M	**1:308v**	L, G	Church gov. (presbytery)	C
158	20 Feb	Tu	**1:316r**	L, G	Church gov. (presbytery)	C
159	21 Feb	W	**1:320v**	L, G	Church gov. (presbytery)	C
160	22 Feb	Th	**1:327r**	R, L, G	Church gov. (presbytery)	C
161	23 Feb	F	**1:334r**	R, L, G	Church gov. (presbytery)	C
162	23 Feb pm	F	**1:336v**	L,	Church gov. (presbytery)	C
163	26 Feb	M	**1:339v**	R, L, G	Church gov. (presbytery)	C
	28 Feb	W			Fast	
164	29 Feb	Th	**1:342v**	R, L, G	Church gov. (presbytery)	C
165	1 Mar	F	**1:348r**	R, L, G	Church gov. (presbytery)	C
166	1 Mar pm	F	**1:352r**	R, L, G	Church gov. (presbytery)	C
167	4 Mar	M	**1:356r**	R, L, G	Church gov. (presbytery)	C
168	5 Mar	Tu	**1:357v**	R, L, G	Church gov. (presbytery)	C
169	6 Mar	W	**1:360r**	L, G	Church gov. (presbytery)	C
170	6 Mar pm	W	**1:362r**	L	Church gov. (presbytery)	C
171	7 Mar	Th	**1:364v**	R, L, G	Church gov. (presbytery)	C
172	8 Mar	F	**1:369r**	L, G	Church gov. (presbytery)	C
173	8 Mar pm	F	**1:372v**	L, G	Church gov. (presbytery)	C

Sess.	Date	Day	Min. folios	Other sources	Main subject(s) of discussion	Subj. class.
174	11 Mar	M	**1:373v**	R, L	Church gov. (presbytery)	C
175	12 Mar	Tu	**1:378v**	R, L, G	Church gov. (presbytery)	C
176	13 Mar	W	**1:382v**	L, G	Church gov. (presbytery)	C
177	14 Mar	Th	**1:386v**	L, G	Church gov. (presbytery)	C
178	15 Mar	F	**1:389r**	L	Approving and licensing	A
179	18 Mar	M	**1:391r**	R, L	Church gov. (ordination)	C
180	19 Mar	Tu	**1:394v**	L, G	Church gov. (ordination)	C
181	20 Mar	W	**1:398r**	R, L, G	Church gov. (ordination)	C
182	20 Mar pm	W	**1:399v**	R, L	Church gov. (ordination)	C
183	21 Mar	Th	**1:401v**	R, L, G	Church gov. (ordination)	C
184	22 Mar	F	**1:402r**	R, L, G	Church gov. (presbytery; ordination)	C
185	22 Mar pm	F	**1:402v**	L	Church gov. (presbytery)	C
186	25 Mar	M	**1:405v**	L	Church gov. (presbytery; ordination)	C
	27 Mar	W			Fast	
187	28 Mar	Th	**1:407r**	L, G	Church gov. (ordination)	C
188	29 Mar	F	**1:411v**	L	Church gov. (ordination)	C
189	1 Apr	M	**1:416r**	L	Approving and licensing	A
190	2 Apr	Tu	**1:416v**	L, G	Church gov. (presbytery)	C
191	3 Apr	W	**1:419r**	L, G	Church gov. (ordination)	C
192	3 Apr pm	W	**1:419v**	L	Church gov. (ordination)	C
193	4 Apr	Th	**1:420v**	L, G	Church gov. (presbytery)	C
194	5 Apr	F	**1:422v**	L, G	Church gov. (ordination)	C
195	5 Apr pm	F	**1:427r**	L	Church gov. (ordination)	C
	9 Apr	T			Thanksgiving	
196	10 Apr	W	**1:427v**	L, G	Church gov. (ordination)	C
197	10 Apr pm	W	**1:429v**	L	Church gov. (presbytery)	C
198	11 Apr	Th	**1:431v**	L, G	Church gov. (ordination, presbytery)	C

Minutes: Volume II

Sess.	Date	Day	Min. folios	Other sources	Main subject(s) of discussion	Subj. class.
	1644 Cont.					
199	12 Apr	F	**2:4r**	L, G	Church gov. (presbytery)	C
200	15 Apr	M	**2:9r**	L, G	Church gov. (presbytery)	C
201	16 Apr	Tu	**2:14r**	L, G	Church gov. (presbytery)	C
202	17 Apr	W	**2:16r**	L, G	Church gov. (ordination, presbytery)	C
203	18 Apr	Th	**2:17v**	L, G	Church gov. (ordination)	C
204	19 Apr	F	**2:19v**	L	Church gov. (ordination)	C
	23 Apr	T			Thanksgiving	
	24 Apr	W			Fast	
205	25 Apr	Th	**2:20r**	L, G	Church gov. (presbytery)	C
206	26 Apr	F	**2:32**	L, G	Church gov. (presbytery)	C
207	29 Apr	M	**2:23v**	L, G	Church gov. (presbytery)	C
208	30 Apr	Tu	**2:25v**	L	Church gov. (presbytery)	C
209	1 May	W	**2:27v**	L, G	Church gov. (presbytery)	C
210	2 May	Th	**2:29v**	L, G	Church gov. (presbytery)	C
211	3 May	F	**2:30v**	L, G	Church gov. (presbytery)	C

Sess.	Date	Day	Min. folios	Other sources	Main subject(s) of discussion	Subj. class.
212	6 May	M	2:32v	L, G	Church gov. (presbytery)	C
213	7 May	Tu	2:34r	L	Church gov. (ordination)	C
214	8 May	W	2:40v	L, G	Church gov. (ordination)	C
215	9 May	Th	2:45r	L, G	Church gov. (ordination)	C
216	10 May	F	2:49r	L, G	Church gov. (ordination)	C
217	13 May	M	2:52v	G	Church gov. (ordination)	C
218	14 May	Tu	2:54r	L, G	Church gov. (presbytery)	C
219	15 May	W	2:55v	L	Church gov. (ordination)	C
220	16 May	Th	2:60r	L	Church gov. (ordination)	C
221	17 May	F	2:60v	L	Fast in Assembly	F
222	20 May	M	2:69v	L	Church gov. (censures)	C
223	21 May	Tu	2:72v	L	Church gov. (censures)	C
224	22 May	W	2:77v	L	Church gov. (censures)	C
225	23 May	Th	2:80v	L	Church gov. (censures)	C
226	24 May	F	2:84v	L	Church gov. (censures); Worship	C
227	27 May	M	2:86v	L	Worship	W
228	28 May	Tu	2:87v	L	Worship	W
	29 May	W			Fast	
229	31 May	F	2:87v	L	Business; Worship	B, W
230	3 June	M	2:88v	L	Worship	W
231	4 June	Tu	2:89r	L	Worship	W
232	5 June	W	2:90r	L	Worship	W
233	6 June	Th	2:90v	L	Worship	W
234	7 June	F	2:91r	L	Worship	W
235	10 June	M	2:94r	L	Worship	W
236	11 June	Tu	2:94v	L	Worship	W
237	12 June	W	2:94v	L	Worship	W
238	13 June	Th	2:95r	L	Worship	W
239	14 June	F	2:96v	L	Worship	W
240	17 June	M	2:97r	L	Worship	W
241	18 June	Tu	2:99r	L	Worship	W
242	19 June	W	2:100r	L	Worship	W
243	20 June	Th	2:100r	L	Worship	W
244	21 June	F	2:101r	L	Worship	W
245	24 June	M	2:102r	L	Worship	W
	26 June	W			Fast	
246	27 June	Th	2:102v	L	Approving and licensing; Worship	A, W
247	28 June	F	2:105r	L	Worship	W
248	1 July	M	2:108r	L	Worship	W
249	2 July	Tu	2:110r	L	Worship	W
250	3 July	W	2:112r	L	Worship	W
251	4 July	Th	2:114v	L	Worship	W
252	5 July	F	2:117v	L	Worship	W
253	8 July	M	2:121r	L	Worship	W
254	9 July	Tu	2:124r	L	Worship	W
255	10 July	W	2:125r	L	Business	B
256	11 July	Th	2:126r	L	Worship	W
257	12 July	F	2:129r	L	Worship	W
258	15 July	M	2:129v	L	Worship	W

Sess.	Date	Day	Min. folios	Other sources	Main subject(s) of discussion	Subj. class.
259	16 July	Tu	**2:131v**	L	Worship	W
	18 July	Th			Thanksgiving	
260	19 July	F	**2:134v**	L	Worship	W
261	22 July	M	**2:136r**	L	Worship	W
	31 July	W			Fast	
262	7 Aug	W	**2:138v**	L	Worship	W
263	8 Aug	Th	**2:141r**	L	Worship	W
264	9 Aug	F	**2:142v**	L	Worship; Fast Business	W, F
	13 Aug	Tu			Fast	
265	14 Aug	W	**2:152r**	L	Approving and licensing; Worship	A, W
266	15 Aug	Th	**2:153v**	L	Worship	W
267	16 Aug	F	**2:155v**	L	Worship	W
268	19 Aug	M	**2:157r**	L	Church gov. (ordination)	C
269	20 Aug	Tu	**2:158r**	L	Church gov. (ordination)	C
270	21 Aug	W	**2:159v**	L	Church gov. (ordination)	C
271	22 Aug	Th	**2:160r**	L	Church gov. (ordination)	C
272	23 Aug	F	**2:161v**		Church gov. (ordination)	C
273	26 Aug	M	**2:162v**		Church gov. (ordination)	C
	28 Aug	W			Fast	
274	29 Aug	Th	**2:163r**		Sects; Church gov. (ordination)	D, C
275	30 Aug	F	**2:165v**		Church gov. (ordination)	C
276	2 Sept	M	**2:167r**		Sects	D
277	3 Sept	Tu	**2:169r**		Church gov. (ordination)	C
278	4 Sept	W	**2:171v**	L, G	Church gov. (censures)	C
279	5 Sept	Th	**2:176r**	L, G	Sects	D
280	6 Sept	F	**2:177r**	L, G	Church gov. (presbytery)	C
281	9 Sept	M	**2:180r**	L, G	Fast business	F
282	10 Sept	Tu	**2:187r**	L, G	Fast business	F
283	10 Sept pm	Tu	**2:189r**	L, G	Fast Business	F
	12 Sept	Th			Fast	
284	13 Sept	F	**2:190r**	G	Church gov. (presbytery)	C
285	16 Sept	M	**2:195**	L, G	Church gov. (presbytery)	C
286	17 Sept	Tu	**2:201v**	L, G	Church gov. (presbytery)	C
287	18 Sept	W	**2:204v**	L, G	Church gov. (presbytery)	C
288	19 Sept	Th	**2:205r**	L, G	Church gov. (presbytery)	C
289	20 Sept	F	**2:210r**	G	Church gov. (presbytery)	C
290	23 Sept	M	**2:213v**	G	Church gov. (presbytery)	C
	25 Sept	W			Fast	
291	26 Sept	Th	**2:215v**	G	Church gov. (presbytery)	C
292	27 Sept	F	**2:219r**	G	Church gov. (presbytery)	C
293	30 Sept	M	**2:225r**	G	Church gov. (presbytery)	C
294	1 Oct	Tu	**2:229v**	G	Church gov. (presbytery)	C
295	2 Oct	W	**2:234v**	L, G	Church gov. (presbytery)	C
296	3 Oct	Th	**2:239v**	L, G	Church gov. (ordination)	C
297	4 Oct	F	**2:240r**	L, G	Church gov. (presbytery)	C
298	7 Oct	M	**2:242r**		Church gov. (presbytery)	C
299	8 Oct	Tu	**2:244r**	G	Church gov. (censures)	C
300	9 Oct	W	**2:247r**	L, G	Worship	W
301	10 Oct	Th	**2:249r**	L, G	Worship	W

Sess.	Date	Day	Min. folios	Other sources	Main subject(s) of discussion	Subj. class.
302	11 Oct	F	2:253r	L, G	Worship	W
303	14 Oct	M	2:254v	G	Church gov. (censures)	C
304	15 Oct	Tu	2:260r	G	Business	B
305	16 Oct	W	2:262v	L, G	Church gov. (censures)	C
306	17 Oct	Th	2:265v	L, G	Church gov. (censures)	C
307	18 Oct	F	2:269r	L, G	Church gov. (censures)	C
	22 Oct	Tu			Fast	
308	23 Oct	W	2:273rL		Fast	F
309	23 Oct pm	W	2:273r	L	Church gov. (censures)	C
310	24 Oct	Th	2:275r	L, G	Church gov. (censures)	C
311	25 Oct	F	2:278r	L, G	Church gov. (censures)	C
312	28 Oct	M	2:279v		Business (Prince Elector entertained)	B
313	28 Oct pm	M	2:281v		Worship	W
	30 Oct	W			Fast	
314	31 Oct	Th	2:282r		Worship	W
315	1 Nov	F	2:285r		Worship	W
	5 Nov	Tu			Powder plot anniversary	
316	6 Nov	W	2:286r		Worship	W
317	7 Nov	Th	2:287v	L	Church gov. (presbytery); Worship	C, W
318	8 Nov	F	2:288r	L	Church gov. (presbytery); Worship	C, W
319	11 Nov	M	2:289r	L	Worship	W
320	12 Nov	Tu	2:289v	L	Worship	W
321	13 Nov	W	2:290v	L	Worship	W
322	14 Nov	Th	2:291r	L	Church gov. (presbytery); Worship	C, W
323	15 Nov	F	2:291v	L, G	Church gov. (presbytery)	C

Minutes: Volume III

Sess.	Date	Day	Min. folios	Other sources	Main subject(s) of discussion	Subj. class.
	1644 Cont.					
324	18 Nov	M	3:1r	L	Church gov. (ordination)	C
325	19 Nov	Tu	3:2r	L	Worship	W
326	20 Nov	W	3:2v	L	Worship	W
327	21 Nov	Th	3:4v	L	Worship	W
328	22 Nov	F	3:6rb	L	Worship	W
329	25 Nov	M	3:6vb		Worship	W
	27 Nov	W			Fast	
330	28 Nov	Th	3:6vb		Worship	W
331	29 Nov	F	3:7r	L	Worship	W
332	2 Dec	M	3:7v	L	Church gov. (presbytery)	C
333	3 Dec	Tu	3:8r	R, L	Worship	W
334	4 Dec	W	3:9r	L	Worship	W
335	5 Dec	Th	3:10r	L, G	Church gov. (presbytery)	C
336	6 Dec	F	3:10v	L	Church gov. (presbytery)	C
337	9 Dec	M	3:10v	L, G	Worship	W
338	10 Dec	Tu	3:11r	L, G	Worship	W
339	11 Dec	W	3:12v	L	Worship	W
340	12 Dec	Th	3:12v	L	Worship	W

Sess.	Date	Day	Min. folios	Other sources	Main subject(s) of discussion	Subj. class.
341	13 Dec	F	3:13r	L	Worship	W
342	16 Dec	M	3:13r		Worship	W
343	17 Dec	Tu	3:13v	L	Church gov. (presbytery)	C
	18 Dec	W			Fast	
344	19 Dec	Th	3:14r	L	Worship	W
345	20 Dec	F	3:14r		Worship	W
346	23 Dec	M	3:14v		Worship	W
	25 Dec	W			Fast	
347	24/26 Dec	Tu/Th	3:15r		Business	B
348	27 Dec	F	3:15v		Worship	W
349	30 Dec	M	3:15v	G	Worship	W
350	31 Dec	Tu	3:16r	G	Church gov. (censures)	C
	1645					
351	1 Jan	W	3:18r		Church gov. (censures)	C
352	2 Jan	Th	3:18r	G	Scots	B
353	3 Jan	F	3:18v	G	Business	B
354	6 Jan	M	3:20r		Church gov. (censures)	C
355	7 Jan	Tu	3:20r		Church gov. (censures)	C
356	8 Jan	W	3:22v		Business; Church gov. (censures)	B, C
357	9 Jan	Th	3:23r		Church gov. (censures)	C
358	10 Jan	F	3:24v		Church gov. (censures)	C
359	13 Jan	M	3:26r		Church gov. (censures)	C
360	14 Jan	Tu	3:26r		Church gov. (censures)	C
361	15 Jan	W	3:26v		Church gov. (censures)	C
362	16 Jan	Th	3:27v		Church gov. (censures)	C
363	17 Jan	F	3:27v		Church gov. (censures)	C
364	20 Jan	M	3:28r		Church gov. (presbytery)	C
365	21 Jan	Tu	3:29r		Church gov. (censures)	C
366	22 Jan	W	3:29r		Church gov. (censures)	C
367	23 Jan	Th	3:29v		Church gov. (censures)	C
368	24 Jan	F	3:29v		Church gov. (censures)	C
369	27 Jan	M	3:30r		Church gov. (censures)	C
	29 Jan	W			Fast	
370	30 Jan	Th	3:31v		Church gov. (censures)	C
371	31 Jan	F	3:32r		Church gov. (censures)	C
372	3 Feb	M	3:33r		Church gov. (censures)	C
373	4 Feb	Tu	3:33r		Church gov. (censures)	C
374	5 Feb	W	3:34r		Church gov. (censures)	C
375	6 Feb	Th	3:34v		Church gov. (censures)	C
376	7 Feb	F	3:35r		Church gov. (presbytery; censures)	C
377	10 Feb	M	3:35v		Church gov. (appeals)	C
378	11 Feb	Tu	3:37r		Church gov. (appeals)	C
379	12 Feb	W	3:38v		Church gov. (appeals)	C
380	13 Feb	Th	3:41r		Church gov. (appeals)	C
381	14 Feb	F	3:43r		Church gov. (appeals)	C
382	17 Feb	M	3:43r		Church gov. (appeals)	C
383	18 Feb	Tu	3:44r		Church gov. (appeals)	C
384	19 Feb	W	3:46r		Church gov. (synods)	C
385	20 Feb	Th	3:46r		Approving and licensing	A

Sess.	Date	Day	Min. folios	Other sources	Main subject(s) of discussion	Subj. class.
386	21 Feb	F	3:46r		Church gov. (synods)	C
387	24 Feb	M	3:48r		Church gov. (synods)	C
	26 Feb	W			Fast	
388	27 Feb	Th	3:48v		Church gov. (synods)	C
389	1 Mar	Sat	3:48v		Worship; Business	W, B
390	3 Mar	M	3:49r		Church gov. (synods)	C
391	4 Mar	Tu	3:50r		Worship; Church gov. (synods)	W, C
392	5 Mar	W	3:50v		Sacrament	D
393	6 Mar	Th	3:50v		Worship	W
394	7 Mar	F	3:50v		Church gov. (synods)	C
395	10 Mar	M	3:51r		Church gov. (synods)	C
	12 Mar	W			Thanksgiving	
396	13 Mar	Th	3:51v		Church gov. (synods)	C
397	14 Mar	F	3:51v		Church gov. (synods)	C
398	17 Mar	M	3:51v		Church gov. (synods)	C
399	18 Mar	Tu	3:52r		Church gov. (classis)	C
400	19 Mar	W	3:52r		Church gov. (classis)	C
401	20 Mar	Th	3:52r		Approving and licensing	A
402	21 Mar	F	3:52v		Church gov. (presbytery); Business; sacrament	C, B, D
403	24 Mar	M	3:53r		Sacrament	D
	26 Mar	W			Fast	
404	27 Mar	Th	3:53r		Church gov. (congregations)	C
405	28 Mar	F	3:54v		Sacrament; Church gov. (congregations)	D, C
406	31 Mar	M	3:55r		Church gov. (congregations)	C
407	1 Apr	T	3:55r		Church gov. (congregations)	C
408	2 Apr	W	3:55v		Church gov. (congregations)	C
409	3 Apr	Th	3:56r		Church gov. (congregations)	C
410	4 Apr	F	3:56r		Business	B
411	7 Apr	M	3:56r		Business	B
412	8 Apr	Tu	3:56v		?	?
413	9 Apr	W	3:57r		Scots; Business	B
414	10 Apr	Th	3:58r		Business; Church gov. (congregational)	B, C
415	11 Apr	F	3:58v		Church gov. (congregational); Approving and Licensing	C, A
416	14 Apr	M	3:59r		Church gov. (congregational)	C
417	15 Apr	Tu	3:59r		Church gov. (congregational)	C
418	16 Apr	W	3:59r		Church gov. (congregational)	C
419	17 Apr	Th	3:59v		Church gov. (congregational)	C
420	19 Apr	F	3:60r		Church gov. (gathering churches)	C
421	21 Apr	M	3:60v		Church gov. (gathering churches)	C
422	22 Apr	Tu	3:61r		Church gov. (gathering churches)	C
423	23 Apr	W	3:62r		Church gov. (gathering churches)	C
424	24 Apr	Th	3:62v		Church gov. (gathering churches)	C
425	25 Apr	F	3:63r		Church gov. (gathering churches)	C
426	28 Apr	M	3:63r		Church gov. (gathering churches)	C
	30 Apr	F			Fast	
427	1 May	Th	3:64r		Church gov. (gathering churches)	C
428	2 May	F	3:64r		Church gov. (gathering churches)	C
429	5 May	M	3:65r		Business	B
430	6 May	Tu	3:65r		Church gov. (civil magistrate)	C

Sess.	Date	Day	Min. folios	Other sources	Main subject(s) of discussion	Subj. class.
431	7 May	W	3:65v		Church gov. (presbytery)	C
432	8 May	Th	3:66r		Church gov. (presbytery)	C
433	9 May	F	3:66r		Church gov. (congregational)	C
434	12 May	M	3:66v		Approving and licensing; Confession	A, D
435	13 May	Tu	3:67r		Catechism	D
436	14 May	W	3:69r		Church gov. (deacons and Church wardens)	C
437	15 May	Th	3:69r		Church gov. (deacons and Church wardens)	C
438	16 May	F	3:69r		Church gov. (deacons and Church wardens)	C
439	19 May	M	3:69v		Church gov. (presbytery)	C
440	20 May	Tu	3:70r		Sacrament	D
441	23 May	F	3:70r		Sacrament	D
442	26 May	M	3:70v		Church gov. (presbytery)	C
	28 May	W			Fast	
443	29 May	Th	3:71r		Church gov. (presbytery; ordination)	C
444	30 May	F	3:71r		Church gov. (ordination)	C
445	2 June	M	3:71v		Sacrament; Church gov. (ordination)	D, C
446	3 June	Tu	3:72r		Church gov. (presbytery)	C
447	4 June	W	3:72r		Sacrament	D
448	5 June	Th	3:72v		Sacrament	D
449	6 June	F	3:72v		Sacrament	D
450	9 June	M	3:73r		Sacrament	D
451	10 June	Tu	3:73r		Sects; Fast Business	D, F
452	12 June	Th	3:74r		Sacrament	D
453	13 June	F	3:74v		Sacrament	D
454	16 June	M	3:74v		Sacrament	D
455	17 June	Tu	3:75r		Sacrament	D
	19 June	Th			Thanksgiving	
456	20 June	F	3:76r		Church gov.	C
457	23 June	M	3:76v		Business; Church gov.	B, C
	25 June	W			Fast	
458	26 June	Th	3:76v		Church gov.	C
459	30 June	M	3:77r		Church gov.; Fast Business	C, F
460	2 July	W	3:77r		Church gov.	C
461	3 July	Th	3:77v		Church gov.	C
462	4 July	F	3:77v		Church gov.; Confession	C, D
463	7 July	M	3:78r		Confession	D
464	8 July	Tu	3:78r		Confession; Business	D, B
465	9 July	W	3:78v		Confession	D
466	10 July	Th	3:79r		Business	B
467	11 July	F	3:79r		Confession	D
468	14 July	M	3:79v		Sects; Confession	D
469	15 July	Tu	3:80r		Confession	D
470	16 July	W	3:80r		Confession; Sects	D
471	17 July	Th	3:80v		Confession; Sects	D
472	18 July	F	3:81r		Confession	D
	22 July	Tu			Thanksgiving	
473	23 July	W	3:81r		Confession	D
474	24 July	Th	3:81r		?	?
475	25 July	F	3:81v		Sects	D

Sess.	Date	Day	Min. folios	Other sources	Main subject(s) of discussion	Subj. class.
476	28 July	M	3:82v		Church gov. (discipline)	C
	30 July	W			Fast	
477	31 July	Th	3:82v		Church gov. (discipline)	C
478	1 Aug	F	3:83r		Church gov. (discipline); Catechism	C, D
479	4 Aug	M	3:83v		Catechism	D
480	5 Aug	Tu	3:83v		Catechism	D
481	6 Aug	W	3:84r		Approving and licensing; Sacrament	A, D
482	7 Aug	Th	3:84v		Approving and licensing; Sacrament	A, D
483	8 Aug	F	3:84v		Approving and licensing; Sacrament	A, D
484	11 Aug	M	3:84v		Sacrament	D
485	12 Aug	Tu	3:86r		Approving and licensing; Sacrament	A, D
486	13 Aug	W	3:86r		Business; Sacrament	B, D
487	14 Aug	Th	3:86v		Approving and licensing; Sacrament	A, D
488	15 Aug	F	3:87r		Business	B
489	18 Aug	M	3:87v		Sacrament	D
490	19 Aug	Tu	3:87v		Approving and licensing; Catechism	A, D
491	20 Aug	W	3:87v		Approving and licensing; Catechism	A, D
	22 Aug	F			Thanksgiving	
492	25 Aug	M	3:88r		Church gov. (Presbytery)	C
	27 Aug	W			Fast	
493	28 Aug	Th	3:88v		Approving and licensing; Committees	A
494	29 Aug	F	3:88v		Approving and licensing; Confession	A, D
495	2 Sept	M	3:89r		Confession	D
496	3 Sept	Tu	3:89v		Confession	D
497	4 Sept	W	3:90r		Confession	D
	5 Sept	Th			Fast	
498	8 Sept	M	3:90v		Business; Confession	B, D
499	9 Sept	Tu	3:91r		Confession	D
[500]	10 Sept	W			?	?
501	11 Sept	Th	3:91v		Confession	D
502	12 Sept	F	3:92r		Confession; Psalter	D, W
503	15 Sept	M	3:92v		Confession	D
504	16 Sept	Tu	3:92v		Confession	D
505	17 Sept	W	3:93r		Confession	D
506	22 Sept	M	3:93r		Business; Church gov. (presbytery); funeral for William Strode	B, C
	24 Sept	W			Fast	
507	25 Sept	Th	3:93v		Confession	D
508	26 Sept	F	3:93v		Fast Business	F
509	29 Sept	M	3:94r		Confession	D
510	30 Sept	Tu	3:94r		Confession	D
	2 Oct	Th			Thanksgiving	
511	3 Oct	F	3:94r		Confession	D
512	6 Oct	M	3:94v		Fast Business	F
513	7 Oct	Tu	3:95r		Grand committee for Psalms	W
514	8 Oct	W	3:95r		Fast	F
515	9 Oct	Th	3:101r		Business	B
516	10 Oct	F	3:101v		Catechism	D
517	13 Oct	M	3:101v		Church gov. (presbytery)	C
518	14 Oct	Tu	3:102r		Business	B

Sess.	Date	Day	Min. folios	Other sources	Main subject(s) of discussion	Subj. class.
519	17 Oct	F	3:102v		Confession	D
520	20 Oct	M	3:102v		Confession	D
521	21 Oct	Tu	3:103v		Confession	D
522	22 Oct	W	3:103v		Confession	D
523	23 Oct	Th	3:106v		Sacrament; Confession	D
524	24 Oct	F	3:108r		Confession	D
525	27 Oct	M	3:108v		Sacrament	D
	29 Oct	W			Fast	
526	30 Oct	Th	3:109r		Confession	D
527	31 Oct	F	3:109r		Confession	D
528	3 Nov	M	3:109r		Confession	D
	5 Nov	W			Powder plot anniversary	
529	6 Nov	Th	3:109r		Confession	D
530	7 Nov	F	3:109v		Sacrament	D
531	10 Nov	M	3:109v		Sacrament	D
532	11 Nov	Tu	3:110r		Confession	D
533	12 Nov	W	3:110r		Confession	D
534	13 Nov	Th	3:110v		Confession	D
535	14 Nov	F	3:110v		Psalms; Confession	W, D
536	17 Nov	M	3:111r		Confession	D
537	18 Nov	Tu	3:111r		Confession	D
538	19 Nov	W	3:111v		Confession	D
539	20 Nov	Th	3:111v		Confession	D
540	21 Nov	F	3:111v		Confession	D
541	24 Nov	M	3:112r		Confession	D
	26 Nov	W			Fast	
542	27 Nov	Th	3:112v		Church gov. (presbytery)	C
543	28 Nov	F	3:112v		Confession	D
544	1 Dec	M	3:112v		Confession	D
545	2 Dec	Tu	3:113r		Confession	D
546	3 Dec	W	3:113r		Confession	D
547	4 Dec	Th	3:113r		Confession	D
548	5 Dec	F	3:113v		Confession	D
549	8 Dec	M	3:113v		Confession	D
550	9 Dec	Tu	3:114r		Confession	D
551	10 Dec	W	3:114r		Church gov. (presbytery); Confession	C, D
552	11 Dec	Th	3:114r		Confession	D
553	12 Dec	F	3:114v		Business; Confession	B, D
554	15 Dec	M	3:115r		Confession	D
555	16 Dec	Tu	3:115r		Confession	D
556	17 Dec	W	3:115r		Confession	D
557	19 Dec	F	3:115v		Church gov. (presbytery)	C
558	22 Dec	M	3:115v		Sacrament; Approving and licensing; Adjourned for lack of quorum	D, A
559	23 Dec	Tu	3:116r		Approving and licensing; Business	A, B
560	24 Dec	W	3:116r		Confession	D
561	25 Dec	Th	3:116v		Confession	D
562	26 Dec	F	3:116v		Confession	D
563	29 Dec	M	3:116v		Confession	D
	31 Dec	W			Fast	

Sess.	Date	Day	Min. folios	Other sources	Main subject(s) of discussion	Subj. class.
	1646					
564	1 Jan	Th	3:117r		Confession	D
565	2 Jan	F	3:117v		Confession	D
566	5 Jan	M	3:117v		Confession	D
567	6 Jan	Tu	3:119r		Confession	D
568	7 Jan	W	3:119r		Confession	D
569	8 Jan	Th	3:119r		Confession	D
570	9 Jan	F	3:119v		Confession	D
571	12 Jan	M	3:119v		Confession	D
572	13 Jan	Tu	3:119v		Confession	D
	14 Jan	W			Fast	
573	15 Jan	Th	3:120r		Confession	D
574	16 Jan	F	3:120r		Confession	D
575	19 Jan	M	3:120v		Confession	D
576	20 Jan	Tu	3:121r		Approving and licensing; Confession	A, D
577	21 Jan	W	3:121r		Confession	D
578	22 Jan	Th	3:121v		Business	B
579	23 Jan	F	3:121v		Business; Confession?	B, ?
580	26 Jan	M	3:122r		Confession	D
	28 Jan	W			Fast	
581	29 Jan	Th	3:122r		Confession	D
	30 Jan	F	3:122v		?	?
582	2 Feb	M	3:122v		Confession; Sacrament	D
583	3 Feb	Tu	3:123r		Sacrament	D
	5 Feb	Th			Thanksgiving	
584	6 Feb	F	3:123r		Business	B
585	9 Feb	M	3:123v		Confession	D
586	10 Feb	Tu	3:123v		Confession	D
587	11 Feb	W	3:124r		Confession	D
588	12 Feb	Th	3:124r		Church gov. (ordination); Confession	C, D
589	13 Feb	F	3:124v		Business	B
590	16 Feb	M	3:125r		Confession	D
591	17 Feb	Tu	3:125r		Business; Confession	B, D
	19 Feb	Th			Thanksgiving	
592	20 Feb	F	3:125v		Approving and licensing	A
593	23 Feb	M	3:126r		Approving and licensing; Confession	A, C
	25 Feb	W			Fast	
594	26 Feb	Th	3:127r		Confession (Church gov.)	D
595	27 Feb	F	3:127r		Confession (Church gov.)	D
596	2 Mar	M	3:127r		Confession (Church gov.)	D
597	3 Mar	Tu	3:127v		Confession (Church gov.)	D
598	4 Mar	W	3:127v		Confession	D
599	5 Mar	Th	3:127v		Confession	D
600	6 Mar	F	3:128r		Confession (Church gov.)	D

Minutes: Volume III (Unrevised and revised sessions, 601-900)

Sess.	Date	Day	Min. folios	Other sources	Main subject(s) of discussion	Subj. class.
	1646 Cont.					
601	9 Mar	M	3:128r	3:144r	Church gov. *(jure divino)*; Confession (Church gov.)	C, D
602	10 Mar	Tu	3:129v	3:144r	Confession	D
	12 Mar	Th			Thanksgiving	
603	13 Mar	F	3:130r	3:144v	Church gov. *(jure divino)*	C
604	16 Mar	M	3:134r 241r;	3:144v	Church gov. *(jure divino)*	C
605	17 Mar	Tu	3:244v	3:144v	Church gov. *(jure divino)*	C
606	18 Mar	W	3:244v	3:145r	Church gov. *(jure divino)*	C
607	19 Mar	Th	3:246r	3:145r	Church gov. *(jure divino)*	C
608	20 Mar	F	3:246v	3:145v	Confession	D
609	23 Mar	M	3:247r	3:146r	Sacrament	D
	25 Mar	W			Fast	
610	26 Mar	Th	3:247v	3:146r	Confession	D
611	27 Mar	F	3:247v	3:146v	Confession	D
612	30 Mar	M	**3:249v**	3:147r	Confession	D
613	31 Mar	Tu	3:249v	3:147v	Confession	D
	2 Apr	Th			Thanksgiving	
614	3 Apr	F	3:249v	3:147v	Church gov. *(jure divino)*	C
615	6 Apr	M	**3:252r**	3:147v	Confession	D
616	7 Apr	Tu	3:252r	3:148r	Church gov. *(jure divino)*	C
617	8 Apr	W	3:252v	3:148r	Church gov. *(jure divino)*	C
618	9 Apr	Th	3:253r	3:148r	Church gov. *(jure divino)*	C
619	10 Apr	F	**3:253v**	3:148v	Church gov. *(jure divino)*	C
620	13 Apr	M	**3:253v**	3:148v	Church gov. *(jure divino)*	C
621	14 Apr	Tu	3:253v	3:149r	Church gov. *(jure divino)*	C
622	15 Apr	W	3:254r	3:149r	Church gov. *(jure divino)*	C
623	16 Apr	Th	3:255r	3:149r	Church gov. *(jure divino)*	C
624	17 Apr	F	**3:256r**	3:149v	Church gov. *(jure divino)*	C
625	20 Apr	M	**3:256r**	3:149v	Church gov. *(jure divino)*	C
626	21 Apr	Tu	**3:256v**	3:150r	Church gov. *(jure divino)*	C
627	22 Apr	W	**3:256v**	3:150r	Church gov. *(jure divino)*	C
628	23 Apr	Th	**3:256v**	3:150r	Church gov. *(jure divino)*	C
629	24 Apr	F	**3:257r**	3:150v	Church gov. *(jure divino)*	C
630	27 Apr	M	**3:257r**	3:151r	Church gov. *(jure divino)*	C
	29 Apr	W			Fast	
631	30 Apr	Th	3:257r	3:151r	Church gov. *(jure divino)*	C
632	1 May	F	3:262r	3:151v	Fast Business	F
633	4 May	M	3:263v	3:152r	Church gov. *(jure divino)*	C
634	5 May	Tu	3:264r	3:152r	Church gov. *(jure divino)*	C
635	6 May	W	3:264v	3:152r	Fast	F
636	7 May	Th	3:268v	3:152v	Church gov. *(jure divino)*	C
637	8 May	F	3:269r	3:152v	Church gov. *(jure divino)*	C
	12 May	Tu			Thanksgiving	
638	13 May	W	**3:269r**	3:153r	Church gov. *(jure divino)*	C
639	14 May	Th	3:269v	3:153r	Church gov. *(jure divino)*	C

Sess.	Date	Day	Min. folios	Other sources	Main subject(s) of discussion	Subj. class.
640	15 May	F	**3:270r**	3:153v	Church gov. *(jure divino)*	C
641	18 May	M	3:270r	3:154r	Church gov. *(jure divino)*	C
642	19 May	Tu	**3:270r**	3:154r	Church gov. *(jure divino)*	C
643	20 May	W	**3:270v**	3:154v	Sacrament	D
644	21 May	Th	**3:270v**	3:155r	Sacrament	D
645	22 May	F	**3:271r**	3:155r	Approving and licensing	A
646	25 May	M	3:271r	3:155v	Church gov. *(jure divino)*	C
	27 May	W			Fast	
647	28 May	Th	3:271r	3:156r	Church gov. *(jure divino)*	C
648	29 May	F	**3:271v**	3:156r	Approving and licensing	A
649	1 June	M	**3:271v**	3:156v	Church gov. *(jure divino)*	C
650	2 June	Tu	**3:272r**	3:157r	Church gov. *(jure divino)*	C
651	3 June	W	**3:272r**	3:157r	Approving and licensing	A
652	4 June	Th	**3:272v**	3:157v	Approving and licensing	A
653	5 June	F	**3:272v**	3:157v	Church gov. *(jure divino)*	C
654	8 June	M	**3:273r**	3:158r	Church gov. *(jure divino)*	C
655	9 June	T	**3:273r**	3:158r	Church gov. *(jure divino)*	C
656	10 June	W	**3:273r**	3:158v	Church gov. *(jure divino)*	C
657	11 June	Th	**3:273v**	3:159r	Church gov. *(jure divino)*	C
658	12 June	F	**3:273v**	3:159r	Church gov. *(jure divino)*	C
659	15 June	M	**3:273r**	3:159v	Church gov. *(jure divino)*	C
660	17 June	W	**3:274r**	3:160r	Confession	D
661	18 June	Th	**3:274v**	3:160r	Confession	D
662	19 June	F	**3:274v**	3:160v	Confession	D
663	22 June	M	**3:274v**	3:160v	Confession	D
	24 June	W			Fast	
664	25 June	Th	**3:275r**	3:161r	Confession	D
665	26 June	F	**3:275r**	3:161r	Business	B
666	29 June	M	**3:275v**	3:161r	Confession	D
667	30 June	Tu	**3:275v**	3:161v	Confession	D
668	1 July	W	**3:275v**	3:161v	Church gov. *(jus divinum)*	C
669	2 July	Th	**3:276r**	3:162r	Church gov. *(jus divinum)*	C
670	3 July	F	**3:276v**	3:162v	Church gov. *(jus divinum)*	C
671	6 July	M	**3:276v**	3:163r	Church gov. *(jus divinum)*	C
672	7 July	Tu	**3:277r**	3:163r	Church gov. *(jus divinum)*	C
673	8 July	W	3:278r	3:164r	Approving and licensing; Church gov. *(jus divinum)*	A, C
674	9 July	Th	**3:279v**	3:164v	Church gov. *(jus divinum)*	C
675	10 July	F	**3:280r**	3:165v	Church gov. *(jus divinum)*	C
676	17 July	F	**3:280v**	3:165v	Church gov. *(jus divinum)*	C
	21 July	Tu			Thanksgiving	
677	22 July	W	3:281r	3:166r	Business	B
678	23 July	Th	**3:281v**	3:166v	Confession	D
679	24 July	F	**3:281v**	3:166v	Confession	D
	27 July	M	**3:281v**	3:167r	Grand committee	?
	29 July	W			Fast; Burial of William Twisse	
680	30 July	Th	**3:281v**	3:167r	Confession	D
681	31 July	F	**3:281v**	3:168r	Confession	D
682	3 Aug	M	**3:282r**	3:168r	Confession	D
683	4 Aug	Tu	**3:282r**	3:169r	Confession	D

Sess.	Date	Day	Min. folios	Other sources	Main subject(s) of discussion	Subj. class.
684	5 Aug	W	**3:282r**	3:169r	Confession (synods)	D
685	6 Aug	Th	**3:282r**	3:169v	Confession (synods)	D
686	7 Aug	F	**3:282v**	3:170r	Confession (synods)	D
687	10 Aug	M	**3:282v**	3:170r	Confession (synods)	D
688	11 Aug	Tu	**3:283r**	3:170v	Business	B
689	12 Aug	W	**3:283r**	3:170v	Approving and licensing	A
690	13 Aug	Th	**3:283v**	3:171r	Confession (synods)	D
691	14 Aug	F	**3:283v**	3:171r	Confession (synods)	D
692	17 Aug	M	**3:284r**	3:171v	Confession (synods)	D
693	18 Aug	Tu	**3:284r**	3:171v	Church gov.	C
694	19 Aug	W	**3:284r**	3:172r	Church gov.	C
695	20 Aug	Th	**3:284v**	3:172v	Church gov.; Confession	D
	21 Aug	F	**3:284v**		Approving and licensing	A
	24 Aug	M	**3:284v**		?	?
	26 Aug	W			Fast	
	27 Aug	Th	**3:284v**		?	?
	28 Aug	F	**3:284v**		Confession	D
	31 Aug	M	**3:284v**		?	?
696	1 Sept	Tu	**3:284v**	3:173r	Confession	D
697	2 Sept	W	**3:285r**	3:173v	Confession	D
698	3 Sept	Th	**3:285r**	3:174r	Confession	D
699	4 Sept	F	**3:285r**	3:174r	Confession	D
	8 Sept	Tu			Fast	
700	9 Sept	W	**3:285v**	3:175r	Confession	D
701	9 Sept pm	W	**3:285v**	3:175v	Confession	D
702	10 Sept	Th	**3:285v**	3:176v	Confession	D
703	10 Sept pm	Th	**3:286r**	3:177r	Confession	D
704	11 Sept	F	**3:286r**	3:177r	Confession	D
705	14 Sept	M	**3:286r**	3:177v	Confession	D
706	14 Sept pm	M	**3:286v**	3:177v	Catechism	D
707	15 Sept	Tu	**3:286v**	3:177v	Confession	D
708	15 Sept pm	Tu	**3:286v**	3:178r	Catechism	D
709	16 Sept	W	**3:287r**	3:179r	Confession	D
710	17 Sept	Th	**3:287r**	3:179r	Confession	D
711	17 Sept pm	Th	**3:287r**	3:179r	Catechism	D
712	18 Sept	F	**3:287r**	3:179v	Confession	D
713	21 Sept	M	**3:287v**	3:180r	Confession	D
714	22 Sept	Tu	**3:287v**	3:180r	Catechism	D
715	23 Sept	W	**3:287v**	3:180v	Confession; Catechism	D
716	23 Sept pm	W	**3:288r**	3:181r	Confession	D
717	24 Sept	Th	**3:288r**	3:181r	Catechism	D
718	24 Sept pm	Th	**3:288r**	3:181v	Confession	D
719	25 Sept	F	**3:288v**	3:181v	Confession; Catechism	D
	28 Sept	M	**3:288v**	3:182r	Lack of quorum	
	30 Sept	W			Fast	
720	1 Oct	Th	**3:288v**	3:182r	Confession	D
	2 Oct	F	**3:289r**	3:182r	Grand committee; Catechism	D
721	6 Oct	Tu	**3:289r**	3:182r	Approving and licensing	A
722	7 Oct	W	**3:289v**	3:182v	Confession	D

Sess.	Date	Day	Min. folios	Other sources	Main subject(s) of discussion	Subj. class.
723	8 Oct	Th	**3:289v**	3:182v	Confession	D
724	9 Oct	F	**3:289v**	3:182v	Confession	D
725	12 Oct	M	**3:289v**	3:183r	Confession	D
726	13 Oct	Tu	**3:290r**	3:183r	Confession	D
727	14 Oct	W	**3:290r**	3:183r	Confession	D
728	15 Oct	Th	**3:290v**	3:183v	Confession	D
729	16 Oct	F	**3:290v**	3:183v	Confession	D
	19 Oct	M	**3:290v**	3:183v	Approving and licensing	A
730	20 Oct	Tu	**3:290v**	3:184r	Confession	D
731	21 Oct	W	**3:291r**	3:184r	Confession	D
	22 Oct	Th			Funeral for Earl of Essex	
	23 Oct	F	**3:291r**	3:184r	Approving and licensing	A
	28 Oct	W			Fast	
732	29 Oct	Th	**3:291r**	3:184r	Approving and licensing	A
733	30 Oct	F	**3:291r**	3:184v	Confession	D
	2 Nov	M	**3:291v**	3:184v	Approving and licensing	A
734	3 Nov	Tu	**3:291v**	3:184v	Confession	D
	5 Nov	Th			Powder plot anniversary	
735	6 Nov	F	**3:291v**	3:184v	Confession	D
736	9 Nov	M	**3:291v**	3:185r	Confession	D
737	10 Nov	Tu	**3:292r**	3:185r	Confession	D
738	11 Nov	W	**3:292r**	3:185r	Confession	D
739	12 Nov	Th	**3:292r**	3:185v	Confession	D
740	13 Nov	F	**3:292v**	3:185v	Confession	D
741	16 Nov	M	**3:292v**	3:185v	Confession	D
742	17 Nov	Tu	**3:293r**	3:186r	Confession	D
743	19 Nov	Th	**3:293r**	3:186r	Confession	D
744	20 Nov	F	**3:293r**	3:186r	Confession	D
745	23 Nov	M	**3:293r**	3:186r	Confession	D
	25 Nov	W			Fast	
746	26 Nov	Th	**3:293v**	3:186v	Confession	D
747	27 Nov	F	**3:294r**	3:186v	Catechism	D
748	30 Nov	M	**3:294r**	3:187v	Catechism	D
749	1 Dec	Tu	**3:294r**	3:187v	Catechism	D
750	2 Dec	W	**3:294v**	3:187v	Catechism	D
751	3 Dec	Th	**3:294v**	3:188r	Confession	D
752	4 Dec	F	**3:295r**	3:188v	Confession	D
753	7 Dec	M	**3:295r**	3:188v	Approving and licensing	A
	9 Dec	W			Fast	
754	10 Dec	Th	**3:295v**	3:189r	Catechism	D
755	11 Dec	F	**3:295v**	3:189r	Catechism	D
756	14 Dec	M	**3:296r**	3:189v	Catechism	D
757	15 Dec	Tu	**3:296r**	3:189v	Catechism	D
758	16 Dec	W	**3:296v**	3:190r	Catechism	D
759	17 Dec	Th	**3:296v**	3:190r	Catechism	D
760	18 Dec	F	**3:296v**	3:190v	Catechism	D
	21 Dec	M	**3:297r**	3:191r	Approving and licensing	A
761	24 Dec	Th	**3:297r**	3:191r	Approving and licensing	A
762	25 Dec	F	3:297v	3:191r	Approving and licensing; Business	A, B

Sess.	Date	Day	Min. folios	Other sources	Main subject(s) of discussion	Subj. class.
763	28 Dec	M	**3:299r**	3:191v	Catechism	D
	30 Dec	W			Fast	
764	31 Dec	Th	**3:299r**	3:192r	Approving and licensing	A
	1647					
765	1 Jan	F	**3:299r**	3:192r	Approving and licensing	A
766	4 Jan	M	**3:299v**	3:192v	Approving and licensing	A
767	5 Jan	Tu	**3:299v**	3:192v	39 Arts.	D
768	6 Jan	W	**3:299v**	3:192v	39 Arts.	D
769	7 Jan	Th	3:299v	3:193r	Confession	D
770	8 Jan	F	**3:300r**	3:192r	Confession	D
771	11 Jan	M	**3:300r**	3:192r	Approving and licensing	A
772	12 Jan	Tu	3:300r	3:193v	Confession	D
773	13 Jan	W	**3:300v**	3:193v	Approving and licensing; Confession	A, D
774	14 Jan	Th	3:301r	3:193v	Catechism	D
775	15 Jan	F	**3:301r**	3:194r	Approving and licensing; Confession	A, D
776	18 Jan	M	**3:301r, 302r**	3:194r	Confession	D
777	19 Jan	Tu	**3:301v, 302r**	3:194r	Confession	D
778	20 Jan	W	**3:301v, 302r**	3:194v	Confession	D
779	21 Jan	Th	**3:301v, 302r**	3:194v	Confession	D
	22 Jan	F	**3:301v, 302r**	3:194v	Approving and licensing; Confession	A, D
	25 Jan	M	**3:303r**	3:194v	Approving and licensing	A
	27 Jan	W			Fast	
780	28 Jan	Th	**3:303r**	3:194v	Confession	D
781	29 Jan	F	**3:302r, 303r**	3:195r	Confession	D
782	1 Feb	M	**3:302r, 303r**	3:195r	Confession	D
783	2 Feb	Tu	**3:302r 303r,**	3:195r	Confession	D
784	3 Feb	W	**3:302r, 303r**	3:195v	Confession	D
785	4 Feb	Th	**3:303v**	3:195v	Approving and licensing; Confession	A, D
786	5 Feb	F	**3:302r, 304r**	3:196r	Confession	D
787	8 Feb	M	**3:302r, 304r**	3:196v	Confession	D
788	9 Feb	Tu	**3:302r, 304r**	3:196v	Confession	D
789	10 Feb	W	**3:302r, 304r**	3:196v	Confession	D
790	11 Feb	Th	**3:302r, 304r**	3:197r	Confession	D
791	12 Feb	F	**3:302v, 304r**	3:197r	Confession	D
792	15 Feb	M	**3:302v, 305r**	3:197r	Confession	D
793	16 Feb	Tu	**3:305r**	3:197v	Approving and licensing	A

Sess.	Date	Day	Min. folios	Other sources	Main subject(s) of discussion	Subj. class.
794	17 Feb	W	3:302v, 305v	3:197v	Confession	D
795	18 Feb	Th	**3:302v, 305v**	3:198r	Confession	D
796	19 Feb	F	**3:302v, 306r**	3:198r	Confession	D
797	22 Feb	M	**3:302v, 306r**	3:198v	Confession	D
	24 Feb	W	Fast			
798	25 Feb	Th	**3:302v, 306r**	3:198v	Confession	D
799	26 Feb	F	**3:302v, 306v**	3:198v	Confession	D
800	1 Mar	M	**3:306v**	3:199r	Approving and licensing	A
801	2 Mar	Tu	**3:302v, 307r**	3:199r	Confession	D
802	3 Mar	W	**3:302v, 307r**	3:199v	Confession	D
803	4 Mar	Th	**3:307v**	3:199v	Approving and licensing	A
804	5 Mar	F	**3:308r**	3:200r	Confession	D
	10 Mar	W			Fast	
805	11 Mar	Th	**3:308r**	3:200v	Confession	D
806	12 Mar	F	**3:308v**	3:200v	Confession	D
807	15 Mar	M	**3:308v**	3:201r	Approving and licensing; Confession	A, D
808	16 Mar	Tu	**3:309r**	3:201r	Confession	D
809	17 Mar	W	**3:309v**	3:201v	Approving and licensing	A
810	18 Mar	Th	3:309v	3:201v	Approving and licensing	A
811	19 Mar	F	**3:310r**	3:202r	Approving and licensing	A
812	22 Mar	M	**3:310v**	3:202r	Confession	D
813	23 Mar	Tu	**3:311r**	3:202v	Confession	D
814	24 Mar	W	**3:311r**	3:203r	Confession	D
815	25 Mar	Th	**3:311v**	3:203r	Approving and licensing	A
816	26 Mar	F	**3:311v**	3:203v	Confession	D
817	29 Mar	M	**3:312r**	3:203v	Approving and licensing; Confession	A, D
	31 Mar	W			Fast	
818	1 Apr	Th	**3:312r**	3:204r	Approving and licensing	A
819	2 Apr	F	**3:312v**	3:204r	Confession	D
820	5 Apr	M	**3:312v**	3:204v	Confession	D
	5 Apr pm	M	**3:312v**	3:204v	Approving and licensing	A
821	6 Apr	Tu	**3:312v**	3:205r	Confession	D
822	7 Apr	W	**3:313r**	3:205r	Confession	D
823	8 Apr	Th	**3:313r**	3:205v	Confession	D
824	9 Apr	F	**3:313r**	3:205v	Confession	D
825	12 Apr	M	**3:313v**	3:205v	Confession	D
826	13 Apr	Tu	**3:313v**	3:206r	Confession	D
827	14 Apr	W	**3:314r**	3:206r	39 Arts.	D
828	15 Apr	Th	**3:314r**	3:206r	Catechism	D
829	16 Apr	F	**3:314v**	3:207r	Catechism	D
	19 Apr	M	**3:314v**	3:207v	Approving and licensing	A
	20 Apr	Tu	**3:314v**	3:207v	?	?
	21 Apr	W	**3:315r**	3:207v	Approving and licensing; Business	A, B

524

Sess.	Date	Day	Min. folios	Other sources	Main subject(s) of discussion	Subj. class.
830	22 Apr	Th	**3:315r**	3:207v	Catechism	D
831	23 Apr	F	**3:315v**	3:208r	39 Arts.; Catechism	D
832	26 Apr	M	**3:315v**	3:208r	Catechism	D
	28 Apr	W			Fast	
833	29 Apr	Th	3:316r	3:208v	Catechism	D
	30 Apr	F	**3:316r**	3:209r	Business; Approving and licensing	B, A
834	3 May	M	**3:316v**	3:209v	Catechism	D
835	4 May	Tu	**3:316v**	3:210r	Catechism	D
836	5 May	W	**3:317r**	3:210v	Catechism	D
837	6 May	Th	**3:317r**	3:211r	Catechism	D
838	7 May	F	**3:317r**	3:212r	Catechism	D
839	10 May	M	**3:317r**	3:212r	Approving and licensing	A
840	11 May	Tu	**3:317v**	3:212v	Approving and licensing	A
841	12 May	W	**3:317v**	3:212v	Catechism	D
842	13 May	Th	**3:317v**	3:213r	Catechism	D
843	14 May	F	**3:318r**	3:213v	Catechism	D
844	17 May	M	**3:318r**	3:214r	Catechism	D
845	18 May	Tu	3:318r	3:214v	Catechism	D
846	19 May	W	**3:318v**	3:214v	Approving and licensing	A
847	20 May	Th	**3:318v**	3:215r	Catechism	D
848	21 May	F	**3:319r**	3:215v	Approving and licensing	A
849	24 May	M	**3:319r**	3:215v	Catechism	D
	26 May	W			Fast	
850	27 May	Th	**3:319r**	3:215v	Approving and licensing; Business	A, B
851	28 May	F	**3:319v**	3:216r	Catechism	D
852	31 May	M	**3:319v**	3:216v	Catechism	D
853	1 June	Tu	3:319v	3:217r	Catechism	D
854	2 June	W	**3:320r**	3:217r	Catechism	D
855	3 June	Th	**3:320r**	3:217v	Catechism	D
856	4 June	F	**3:320r**	3:217v	Catechism	D
857	7 June	M	**3:320v**	3:218r	Catechism	D
858	8 June	Tu	**3:320v**	3:218v	Catechism	D
859	10 June	Th	**3:320v**	3:219r	Catechism	D
860	11 June	F	**3:320v**	3:219v	Catechism	D
861	14 June	M	**3:320v**	3:219v	Catechism	D
862	15 June	Tu	3:321r	3:220r	Catechism	D
863	16 June	W	**3:321r**	3:220v	Catechism	D
864	17 June	Th	**3:321r**	3:221r	Catechism; Approving and licensing	D, A
865	18 June	F	**3:321v**	3:221v	Catechism	D
866	21 June	M	**3:321v**	3:222r	Catechism	D
867	22 June	Tu	**3:321v**	3:222v	Catechism	D
868	23 June	W	**3:321v**	3:223r	Catechism	D
869	24 June	Th	**3:322r**	3:223r	Catechism	D
870	25 June	F	**3:322r**	3:223v	Approving and licensing	A
871	28 June	M	**3:322r**	3:223v	Catechism	D
	30 June	W			Fast	
872	1 July	Th	**3:322r**	3:224r	Catechism	D
873	2 July	F	**3:322v**	3:224v	Catechism	D
874	5 July	M	**3:322v**	3:225r	Catechism	D

Sess.	Date	Day	Min. folios	Other sources	Main subject(s) of discussion	Subj. class.
875	6 July	Tu	**3:323r**	3:225v	Catechism; Business	D, B
876	7 July	W	**3:323v**	3:226r	Catechism	D
877	8 July	Th	**3:323v**	3:226v	Catechism	D
878	9 July	F	**3:323v**	3:226v	Catechism	D
879	12 July	M	**3:323v**	3:227r	Catechism	D
880	13 July	Tu	**3:324r**	3:227r	Catechism	D
881	14 July	W	**3:324r**	3:227v	Approving and licensing; Catechism	A, D
882	15 July	Th	**3:324r**	3:228r	Catechism	D
883	16 July	F	**3:324v**	3:228r	Catechism	D
884	19 July	M	**3:324v**	3:228v	Catechism	D
885	20 July	Tu	**3:325r**	3:229r	Catechism	D
886	21 July	W	**3:325r**	3:229v	Catechism	D
887	22 July	Th	**3:325r**	3:230r	Catechism	D
888	23 July	F	**3:325r**	3:230r	Catechism	D
889	26 July	M	**3:325v**	3:230v	Catechism	D
890	29 July	Th	**3:325v**	3:230v	Catechism	D
891	30 July	F	**3:325v**	3:231r	Catechism; Fast	D
892	2 Aug	M	**3:325v**	3:231r	Business	B
893	3 Aug	Tu	**3:326r**	3:231v	Business	B
894	5 Aug	Th	**3:326r**	3:231v	Business; Catechism	B, D
895	6 Aug	F	**3:326v**	3:232r	Catechism	D
896	9 Aug	M	**3:326v**	3:232r	Catechism	D
897	10 Aug	Tu	**3:326v**	3:232v	Catechism	D
898	11 Aug	W	**3:326v**	3:232v	?	?
	12 Aug	Th			Thanksgiving	
899	13 Aug	F	**3:327r**	3:233r	Catechism	D
900	16 Aug	M	**3:327r**	3:233r	Catechism	D

Minutes: Volume III (unrevised sessions continued)

Sess.	Date	Day	Min. folios	Other sources	Main subject(s) of discussion	Subj. class.
901	17 Aug	Tu	3:327r		Catechism	D
902	18 Aug	W	3:327v		Catechism	D
903	19 Aug	Th	3:327v		Catechism	D
904	20 Aug	F	3:327v		Catechism	D
905	23 Aug	M	3:327v		Catechism	D
	25 Aug	W			Fast	
906	26 Aug	Th	3:327v		Catechism	D
907	27 Aug	F	3:327v		Catechism	D
	31 Aug	Tu			Thanksgiving	
908	1 Sept	W	3:328r		Catechism	D
909	2 Sept	Th	3:328r		Catechism	D
910	3 Sept	F	3:328r		Catechism	D
911	8 Sept	W	3:328r		Catechism	D
912	9 Sept	Th	3:328r		Catechism	D
913	10 Sept	F	3:328v		Catechism	D
914	13 Sept	M	3:328v		Catechism	D

Sess.	Date	Day	Min. folios	Other sources	Main subject(s) of discussion	Subj. class.
915	14 Sept	Tu	3:328v		Catechism	D
916	15 Sept	W	3:329r		Fast Business; Catechism	F, D
917	16 Sept	Th	3:329r		Catechism	D
918	17 Sept	F	3:329r		Catechism	D
919	20 Sept	M	3:329r		Approving and licensing; Business	A, B
920	21 Sept	Tu	3:329v		Catechism	D
921	22 Sept	W	3:329v		Catechism	D
922	23 Sept	Th	3:329v		Catechism	D
923	24 Sept	F	3:330r		Catechism	D
924	27 Sept	M	3:330r		Approving and licensing; Catechism	A, D
	29 Sept	W			Fast	
925	30 Sept	Th	3:330r		Approving and licensing; Catechism	A, D
926	1 Oct	F	3:330r		Catechism	D
927	4 Oct	M	3:330v		Catechism	D
928	5 Oct	Tu	3:330v		Catechism	D
929	6 Oct	W	3:330v		Approving and licensing; Catechism	A, D
930	7 Oct	Th	3:330v		Catechism	D
931	8 Oct	F	3:331r		Catechism	D
932	11 Oct	M	3:331r		Catechism	D
933	12 Oct	Tu	3:331r		Catechism	D
934	13 Oct	W	3:331r		Catechism	D
935	14 Oct	Th	3:331v		Approving and licensing	A
936	15 Oct	F	3:331v		Catechism	D
937	18 Oct	M	3:332r		Approving and licensing	A
938	19 Oct	Tu	3:332r		Approving and licensing; Business	A, B
939	20 Oct	W	3:332r		Catechism	D
940	21 Oct	Th	3:332r		Catechism	D
941	22 Oct	F	3:332v		Catechism	D
942	25 Oct	M	3:332v		Catechism (shorter)	D
	27 Oct	W			Fast	
943	28 Oct	Th	3:332v		Catechism (shorter)	D
944	29 Oct	F	3:332v		Catechism (shorter)	D
945	1 Nov	M	3:332v 333v		Catechism (shorter)	D
946	2 Nov	Tu	3:333v		Catechism (shorter)	D
947	3 Nov	W	3:333v		Approving and licensing; Business	A, B
	5 Nov	F			Powder plot anniversary	
948	8 Nov	M	3:333v		Catechism (shorter)	D
949	9 Nov	Tu	3:334r		Business	B
950	10 Nov	W	3:334r		Catechism (shorter)	D
951	11 Nov	Th	3:334v		Catechism (shorter)	D
952	12 Nov	F	3:334v		Approving and licensing	A
953	15 Nov	M	3:334v		Catechism (shorter)	D
954	16 Nov	Tu	3:335r		Catechism (shorter)	D
955	17 Nov	W	3:335r		Catechism (shorter)	D
956	18 Nov	Th	3:335v		Catechism (shorter)	D
957	19 Nov	F	3:335v		Catechism (shorter)	D
958	22 Nov	M	3:335v		Catechism (shorter)	D
	24 Nov	W			Fast	
959	25 Nov	Th	3:336r		Catechism (shorter)	D

Sess.	Date	Day	Min. folios	Other sources	Main subject(s) of discussion	Subj. class.
960	26 Nov	F	3:336r		Business	B
961	29 Nov	M	3:336v		Approving and licensing	A
962	30 Nov	Tu	3:336v		Catechism (larger)	D
963	1 Dec	W	3:337r		Catechism (larger)	D
964	2 Dec	Th	3:337r		Catechism (larger)	D
965	3 Dec	F	3:337r		Approving and licensing	A
966	6 Dec	M	3:337v		Business; Approving and licensing	B, A
967	7 Dec	Tu	3:337v		Catechism (larger)	D
968	8 Dec	W	3:337v		Catechism (larger)	D
969	9 Dec	Th	3:337v		Catechism (larger)	D
970	10 Dec	F	3:337v		Catechism (larger)	D
971	13 Dec	M	3:337v		Catechism (larger)	D
972	14 Dec	Tu	3:338r		Catechism (larger)	D
973	15 Dec	W	3:338r		Catechism (larger)	D
974	16 Dec	Th	3:338r		Approving and licensing	A
975	17 Dec	F	3:338v		Catechism (larger)	D
976	20 Dec	M	3:338v		Catechism (larger)	D
977	21 Dec	Tu	3:338v		Catechism (larger)	D
978	22 Dec	W	3:339r		Catechism (larger)	D
979	23 Dec	Th	3:339r		Catechism (larger)	D
980	24 Dec	F	3:339r		Approving and licensing	A
981	27 Dec	M	3:339r		Catechism (larger)	D
	29 Dec	W			Fast	
982	30 Dec	Th	3:339v		Catechism (larger)	D
983	31 Dec	F	3:339v		Catechism (larger)	D
	1648					
984	3 Jan	M	3:339v		Catechism (larger)	D
985	4 Jan	Tu	3:339v		Approving and licensing	A
986	5 Jan	W	3:340r		Catechism (larger)	D
987	6 Jan	Th	3:340r		Catechism (larger)	D
988	7 Jan	F	3:340r		Catechism (larger)	D
989	10 Jan	M	3:340r		Catechism (larger)	D
990	11 Jan	Tu	3:340r		Catechism (larger)	D
991	12 Jan	W	3:340v		Approving and licensing	A
992	13 Jan	Th	3:340v		?	?
993	14 Jan	F	3:340v		Business	B
994	17 Jan	M	3:341r		Catechism (larger)	D
995	18 Jan	Tu	3:341r		Catechism (larger)	D
996	19 Jan	W	3:341r		Approving and licensing	A
997	20 Jan	Th	3:341v		Catechism (larger)	D
998	21 Jan	F	3:341v		Catechism (larger)	D
999	24 Jan	M	3:341v		Approving and licensing	A
	26 Jan	W			Fast	
1000	27 Jan	Th	3:341v		?	?
1001	28 Jan	F	3:342r		Approving and licensing	A
1002	31 Jan	M	3:342r		Catechism (larger)	D
1003	1 Feb	Tu	3:342r		Catechism (larger)	D
1004	2 Feb	W	3:342r		Approving and licensing	A
1005	3 Feb	Th	3:342v		Approving and licensing	A

Sess.	Date	Day	Min. folios	Other sources	Main subject(s) of discussion	Subj. class.
1006	4 Feb	F	3:342v		Approving and licensing	A
1007	7 Feb	M	3:342v		Approving and licensing	A
1008	8 Feb	Tu	3:343r		Approving and licensing	A
1009	9 Feb	W	3:343r		Business	B
1010	10 Feb	Th	3:343r		Catechism (larger)	D
1011	11 Feb	F	3:343v		Approving and licensing	A
1012	14 Feb	M	3:343v		?	?
1013	15 Feb	Tu	3:343v		Approving and licensing	A
1014	16 Feb	W	3:343v		Approving and licensing	A
1015	17 Feb	Th	3:344r		Approving and licensing	A
1016	18 Feb	F	3:344r		Catechism (larger)	D
1017	21 Feb	M	3:344v		Approving and licensing	A
	23 Feb	W			Fast	
1018	24 Feb	Th	3:344v		Approving and licensing	A
1019	25 Feb	F	3:344v		Approving and licensing	A
1020	28 Feb	M	3:345r		Sects	D
1021	29 Feb	Tu	3:345r		Approving and licensing	A
1022	1 Mar	W	3:345r		Catechism (larger)	D
1023	2 Mar	Th	3:345r		Catechism (larger)	D
1024	3 Mar	F	3:345v		Catechism (larger and shorter)	D
1025	6 Mar	M	3:345v		Catechism (larger and shorter)	D
1026	7 Mar	Tu	3:345v		Approving and licensing	A
1027	8 Mar	W	3:345v		Catechism (shorter)	D
1028	9 Mar	Th	3:346r		Catechism (shorter)	D
1029	10 Mar	F	3:346r		Catechism (shorter)	D
1030	13 Mar	M	3:346r		Catechism (shorter)	D
1031	14 Mar	Tu	3:346r		Business	B
1032	15 Mar	W	3:346r		Catechism (shorter)	D
1033	16 Mar	Th	3:346v		Catechism (shorter)	D
1034	17 Mar	F	3:346v		Approving and licensing; Business	A, B
1035	20 Mar	M	3:346v		Catechism (shorter)	D
1036	21 Mar	Tu	3:346v		Approving and licensing in Grand committee; Catechism (shorter)	A, D
1037	22 Mar	W	3:347r		Catechism (shorter)	D
1038	23 Mar	Th	3:347r		Approving and licensing	A
1039	24 Mar	F	3:347r		?	?
1040	27 Mar	M	3:347r		?	?
	29 Mar	W			Fast	
1041	30 Mar	Th	3:347r		Catechism (shorter)	D
1042	31 Mar	F	3:347r		?	?
1043	3 Apr	M	3:347v		Approving and licensing	A
1044	4 Apr	Tu	3:347v		Approving and licensing	A
1045	5 Apr	W	3:347v		Approving and licensing	A
1046	6 Apr	Th	3:347v		Approving and licensing	A
1047	7 Apr	F	3:347v		Approving and licensing	A
1048	11 Apr	Tu	3:347v		Business; Approving and licensing	B, A
1049	12 Apr	W	3:347v		Catechism (shorter)	D
1050	13 Apr	Th	3:347v		Church gov. (*jus divinum*)	C
1051	14 Apr	F	3:348r		Approving and licensing	A
1052	17 Apr	M	3:348v		Approving and licensing; Catechism (shorter)	A, D

Sess.	Date	Day	Min. folios	Other sources	Main subject(s) of discussion	Subj. class.
1053	18 Apr	Tu	3:348v		Church gov. (*jus divinum*) in Grand Committee	C
1054	19 Apr	W	3:348v		Church gov. (*jus divinum*)	C
1055	20 Apr	Th	3:348v		Approving and licensing	A
1056	21 Apr	F	3:349r		Approving and licensing	A
1057	24 Apr	M	3:349r		Approving and licensing	A
	26 Apr	W			Fast	
1058	27 Apr	Th	3:349r		Approving and licensing	A
1059	1 May	M	3:349r		Approving and licensing	A
1060	2 May	Tu	3:349r		Business	B
1062[8]	? May	?	3:349v		?	?
1063	5 May	F	3:349v		Business; Church gov. (*jus divinum*)	B, C
1064	9 May	Tu	3:349v		Church gov. (*jus divinum*)	C
1065	10 May	W	3:350r		Church gov. (*jus divinum*)	C
1066	11 May	Th	3:350r		Church gov. (*jus divinum*)	C
1067	16 May	Tu	3:350r		Approving and licensing	A
	17 May	W			Thanksgiving	
1066[9]	18 May	Th	3:350v		Approving and licensing	A
1067	23 May	Tu	3:350v		Approving and licensing	A
1068	24 May	W	3:350v		Approving and licensing; Business	A, B
1069	25 May	Th	3:351r		Church gov. (*jus divinum*)	C
1070	27 May	F	3:351r		Approving and licensing; Church gov. (*jus divinum*)	A, C
1071	29 May	M	3:351r		Business	B
	31 May	W			Fast	
1072	1 June	Th	3:351v		Approving and licensing	A
1073	2 June	F	3:351v		Business	B
1074	5 June	M	3:352r		Business	B
1075	6 June	Tu	3:352r		Business	B
1076	7 June	W	3:352r		Business	B
1077	8 June	Th	3:352v		Approving and licensing	A
1078	9 June	F	3:352v		Approving and licensing	A
1079	12 June	M	3:353r		Approving and licensing	A
1080	13 June	Tu	3:353r		Approving and licensing; Church gov. (*jus divinum*)	A, C
1081	14 June	W	3:353v		Church gov. (*jus divinum*) in committee	C
1082	15 June	Th	3:353v		Church gov. (*jus divinum*) in committee	C
1083	16 June	F	3:353v		?	?
1084	19 June	M	3:354r		Church gov. (*jus divinum*) in committee	C
1085	20 June	Tu	3:354r		Church gov. (*jus divinum*) in committee	C
1086	21 June	W	3:354r		Church gov. (*jus divinum*)	C
1087	22 June	Th	3:354v		Approving and licensing	A
1088	23 June	F	3:354v		Approving and licensing	A
1089	26 June	M	3:354v		Approving and licensing	A
	28 June	W			Fast	
1090	29 June	Th	3:355r		Approving and licensing	A
1091	30 June	F	3:355r		?	?
1092	3 July	M	3:355r		Approving and licensing	A

[8.] Scribal error?

[9.] Scribal error

Sess.	Date	Day	Min. folios	Other sources	Main subject(s) of discussion	Subj. class.
1093	4 July	Tu	3:355r		Approving and licensing	A
1094	5 July	W	3:355r		Approving and licensing	A
1095	6 July	Th	3:355v		Business	B
1096	7 July	F	3:355v		Approving and licensing	A
1097	10 July	M	3:355v		?	?
1098	11 July	Tu	3:355v		Approving and licensing	A
1099	12 July	W	3:355v		Approving and licensing	A
1100	13 July	Th	3:356r		Approving and licensing	A
1101	14 July	F	3:356r		Approving and licensing	A
	19 July	W			Fast	
1102	20 July	Th	3:356r		Approving and licensing	A
1103	21 July	F	3:356r		Approving and licensing	A
	26 July	W			Fast	
1104	27 July	Th	3:356r		Approving and licensing	A
1105	28 July	F	3:356v		Approving and licensing	A
1106	31 July	M	3:356v		Approving and licensing	A
1107	1 Aug	Tu	3:356v		Approving and licensing	A
1108	2 Aug	W	3:356v		Approving and licensing	A
1109	4 Aug	F	3:357r		Approving and licensing	A
1110	7 Aug	M	3:357r		Approving and licensing	A
1112[10]	11 Aug	F	3:357r		Approving and licensing	A
1113	? Aug	?	3:357r		Approving and licensing	A
1114	16 Aug	W	3:357v		?	?
1115	17 Aug	Th	3:357v		Approving and licensing	A
1116	22 Aug	Tu	3:357v		Approving and licensing	A
1117	23 Aug	W	3:357v		?	?
1118	24 Aug	Th	3:357v		Approving and licensing	A
	30 Aug	W			Fast	
1119	31 Aug	Th	3:358r		Approving and licensing	A
1120	1 Sept	F	3:358r		Approving and licensing	A
1121	4 Sept	M	3:358r		?	?
	7 Sept	Th			Thanksgiving	
1122	8 Sept	F	3:358r		Approving and licensing	A
	12 Sept	Tu			Fast	
1123	14 Sept	Th	3:358r		Approving and licensing	A
1124	20 Sept	W	3:358v		Approving and licensing	A
1125	21 Sept	Th	3:358v		Approving and licensing	A
	27 Sept	W			Fast	
1126	28 Sept	Th	3:358v		Approving and licensing	A
1127	4 Oct	W	3:358v		Approving and licensing	A
1128	11 Oct	W	3:358v		Approving and licensing	A
1129	12 Oct	Th	3:359r		Approving and licensing	A
1130	13 Oct	F	3:359r		Approving and licensing	A
1131	18 Oct	W	3:359r		Approving and licensing	A
1132	19 Oct	Th	3:359r		Approving and licensing	A
1133	20 Oct	F	3:359r		Approving and licensing	A
	25 Oct	W			Fast	
1134	26 Oct	Th	3:359v		Approving and licensing	A

[10.] Scribal error

Sess.	Date	Day	Min. folios	Other sources	Main subject(s) of discussion	Subj. class.
1135	27 Oct	F	3:359v		Approving and licensing	A
1136	31 Oct	Tu	3:359v		Approving and licensing	A
1137	3 Nov	F	3:359v		Approving and licensing	A
1138	9 Nov	Th	3:360r		Approving and licensing	A
1139	10 Nov	F	3:360r		Approving and licensing	A
1140	16 Nov	Th	3:360r		Approving and licensing	A
1141	17 Nov	F	3:360r		Approving and licensing	A
1142	23 Nov	Th	3:360r		Approving and licensing	A
1143	24 Nov	F	3:360v		?	?
	29 Nov	W			Fast	
1144	30 Nov	Th	3:360v		Approving and licensing	A
1145	1 Dec	F	3:360v		Approving and licensing	A
1146	6 Dec	W	3:360v		Approving and licensing	A
1147	7 Dec	Th	3:360v		Approving and licensing	A
	8 Dec	F			Fast	
1148	13 Dec	W	3:360v		Approving and licensing	A
1149	14 Dec	Th	3:361r		Approving and licensing	A
1150	20 Dec	W	3:361r		?	?
1151	21 Dec	Th	3:361r		Approving and licensing	A
	22 Dec	F			Fast	
	27 Dec	W			Fast	
1152	28 Dec	Th	3:361r		Approving and licensing	A
	1649					
1153	3 Jan	W	3:361v		Approving and licensing	A
1154	10 Jan	W	3:361v		Approving and licensing	A
1155	11 Jan	Th	3:361v		Approving and licensing	A
1156	17 Jan	W	3:361v		Approving and licensing	A
1157	18 Jan	Th	3:362r		Approving and licensing	A
1158	24 Jan	W	3:362r		Approving and licensing	A
1159	25 Jan	Th	3:362r		Approving and licensing	A
	31 Jan	W			Fast	
1160	1 Feb	Th	3:362r		Business	B
1161	8 Feb	Th	3:362r		Approving and licensing in committee	A
1162	15 Feb	Th	3:362v		Approving and licensing	A
1163[11]	22 Feb	Th	3:362v		Approving and licensing	A
	28 Feb	W			Fast	
	1 Mar	Th	**3:362v**		Approving and licensing	A
	8 Mar	Th	**3:363r**		Approving and licensing	A
	15 Mar	Th	**3:363r**		Approving and licensing	A
	23 Mar	F	**3:363r**		Approving and licensing	A
	29 Mar	Th	**3:363r**		Approving and licensing	A
	6 Apr	F	**3:363v**		Approving and licensing	A
	13 Apr	F	**3:363v**		Approving and licensing	A
	19 Apr	Th			Fast	
	20 Apr	F	**3:363v**		Approving and licensing	A
	26 Apr	Th	**3:363v**		Approving and licensing	A
	3 May	Th			Fast	
	4 May	F	**3:364r**		Approving and licensing	A

11. The scribe(s) stop numbering plenary sessions after this date.

Sess.	Date	Day	Min. folios	Other sources	Main subject(s) of discussion	Subj. class.
	10 May	Th	**3:364r**		Approving and licensing	A
	18 May	F	**3:364r**		Approving and licensing	A
	25 May	F	**3:364v**		Approving and licensing	A
	1 June	F	**3:364v**		Approving and licensing	A
	7 June	Th			Thanksgiving	
	8 June	F	**3:364v**		Approving and licensing	A
	14 June	Th	**3:365r**		Approving and licensing	A
	15 June	F	**3:365r**		Approving and licensing	A
	22 June	F	**3:365v**		Approving and licensing	A
	29 June	F	**3:365v**		Approving and licensing	A
	6 July	F	**3:365v**		Approving and licensing	A
	11 July	W			Fast	A
	13 July	F	**3:366r**		Approving and licensing	A
	20 July	F	**3:366r**		Approving and licensing	A
	27 July	F	**3:366r**		Approving and licensing	A
	3 Aug	F	**3:366v**		Approving and licensing	A
	10 Aug	F	**3:366v**		Approving and licensing	A
	17 Aug	F	**3:366v**		Approving and licensing	A
	24 Aug	F	**3:367r**		Approving and licensing	A
	29 Aug	W			Thanksgiving	
	31 Aug	F	**3:367r**		Approving and licensing	A
	7 Sept	F	**3:367r**		Approving and licensing	A
	14 Sept	F	**3:367r**		Approving and licensing	A
	21 Sept	F	**3:367v**		Approving and licensing	A
	28 Sept	F	**3:367v**		Approving and licensing	A
	5 Oct	F	**3:367v**		Approving and licensing	A
	12 Oct	F	**3:368r**		Approving and licensing	A
	19 Oct	F	**3:368r**		Approving and licensing	A
	26 Oct	F	**3:368r**		Approving and licensing	A
	1 Nov	Th			Thanksgiving	
	2 Nov	F	**3:368r**		Approving and licensing	A
	5 Nov	M			Powder plot anniversary	
	9 Nov	F	**3:368r**		Approving and licensing	A
	15 Nov	Th	**3:368r**		Approving and licensing	A
	22 Nov	Th	**3:368v**		Approving and licensing	A
	29 Nov	Th	**3:368v**		Approving and licensing	A
	6 Dec	Th	**3:368v**		Approving and licensing	A
	13 Dec	Th	**3:368v**		Approving and licensing	A
	20 Dec	Th	**3:368v**		?	?
	27 Dec	Th	**3:368v**		Approving and licensing	A
	1650					
	3 Jan	Th	**3:368v**		Approving and licensing	A
	10 Jan	Th	**3:369r**		Approving and licensing	A
	17 Jan	Th	**3:369r**		Approving and licensing	A
	24 Jan	Th	**3:369r**		Approving and licensing	A
	31 Jan	Th	**3:369r**		Approving and licensing	A
	7 Feb	Th	**3:369r**		Approving and licensing	A
	14 Feb	Th	**3:369r**		Approving and licensing	A
	21 Feb	Th	**3:369r**		Approving and licensing	A

Sess.	Date	Day	Min. folios	Other sources	Main subject(s) of discussion	Subj. class.
	28 Feb	Th			Fast	
	1 Mar	F	**3:369v**		Approving and licensing	A
	7 Mar	Th	**3:369v**		Approving and licensing	A
	14 Mar	Th	**3:369v**		Approving and licensing	A
	21 Mar	Th	**3:369v**		Approving and licensing	A
	28 Mar	Th	**3:369v**		Approving and licensing	A
	4 Apr	Th	**3:370r**		Approving and licensing	A
	11 Apr	Th	**3:370r**		Approving and licensing; Business	A, B
	18 Apr	Th	**3:370r**		Approving and licensing	A
	25 Apr	Th	**3:370r**		Approving and licensing	A
	2 May	Th	**3:370r**		Approving and licensing	A
	9 May	Th	**3:370v**		Approving and licensing	A
	16 May	Th	**3:370v**		Approving and licensing	A
	23 May	Th	**3:370v**		Approving and licensing	A
	30 May	Th	**3:370v**		Approving and licensing	A
	6 June	Th	**3:371r**		Approving and licensing	A
	13 June	Th	**3:371r**		Approving and licensing; Fast	A
	20 June	Th	**3:371r**		Approving and licensing	A
	27 June	Th	**3:371r**		Approving and licensing	A
	4 July	Th	**3:371v**		Approving and licensing	A
	11 July	Th	**3:371v**		Approving and licensing	A
	19 July	F	**3:371v**		Approving and licensing	A
	24 July	W	**3:372r**		Approving and licensing	A
	26 July	F			Thanksgiving	
	1 Aug	Th	**3:372r**		Approving and licensing	A
	8 Aug	Th	**3:372r**		Approving and licensing	A
	15 Aug	Th	**3:372r**		Approving and licensing	A
	22 Aug	Th	**3:372r**		Approving and licensing	A
	29 Aug	Th	**3:372r**		Approving and licensing	A
	5 Sept	W	**3:372v**		Approving and licensing	A
	26 Sept	W	**3:372v**		Approving and licensing	A
	3 Oct	W	**3:372v**		Approving and licensing	A
	8 Oct	M			Thanksgiving	
	10 Oct	W	**3:372v**		Approving and licensing	A
	17 Oct	W	**3:372v**		Approving and licensing	A
	24 Oct	W	**3:372v**		Approving and licensing	A
	31 Oct	W	**3:373r**		Approving and licensing	A
	5 Nov	M			Powder plot anniversary	
	7 Nov	W	**3:373r**		Approving and licensing	A
	14 Nov	W	**3:373r**		Approving and licensing	A
	21 Nov	W	**3:373r**		Approving and licensing	A
	28 Nov	W	**3:373r**		Approving and licensing	A
	5 Dec	W	**3:373v**		Approving and licensing	A
	12 Dec	W	**3:373v**		Approving and licensing	A
	19 Dec	W	**3:373v**		Approving and licensing	A
	26 Dec	W	**3:373v**		Approving and licensing	A
	1651					
	2 Jan	W	**3:373v**		Approving and licensing	A
	9 Jan	W	**3:374r**		Approving and licensing	A

Sess.	Date	Day	Min. folios	Other sources	Main subject(s) of discussion	Subj. class.
	16 Jan	W	**3:374r**		Approving and licensing	A
	23 Jan	W	**3:374r**		Approving and licensing	A
	31 Jan	Th	**3:374r**		Approving and licensing	A
	13 Feb	W	**3:374r**		Approving and licensing	A
	20 Feb	W	**3:374v**		Approving and licensing	A
	27 Feb	W	**3:374v**		Approving and licensing	A
	6 Mar	W	**3:374v**		Approving and licensing	A
	13 Mar	W			Fast	
	14 Mar	Th	**3:374v**		Approving and licensing	A
	20 Mar	W	**3:375r**		Approving and licensing	A
	27 Mar	W	**3:375r**		Approving and licensing	A
	3 Apr	W	**3:375r**		Approving and licensing	A
	10 Apr	W	**3:375r**		Approving and licensing	A
	17 Apr	W	**3:375r**		Approving and licensing	A
	24 Apr	W	**3:375v**		Approving and licensing	A
	1 May	W	**3:375v**		Approving and licensing	A
	8 May	W	**3:375v**		Approving and licensing	A
	15 May	W	**3:375v**		Approving and licensing	A
	22 May	W	**3:376r**		Approving and licensing	A
	4 June	Tu			Fast	
	5 June	W	**3:376r**		Approving and licensing	A
	12 June	W	**3:376r**		Approving and licensing	A
	19 June	W	**3:376r**		Approving and licensing	A
	26 June	W	**3:376v**		Approving and licensing	A
	3 July	W	**3:376v**		Approving and licensing	A
	10 July	W	**3:376v**		Approving and licensing	A
	17 July	W	**3:377r**		Approving and licensing	A
	23 July	Tu	**3:377r**		Approving and licensing	A
	31 July	W	**3:377r**		Approving and licensing	A
	7 Aug	W	**3:377v**		Approving and licensing	A
	14 Aug	W	**3:377v**		Approving and licensing	A
	21 Aug	W	**3:377v**		Approving and licensing	A
	26 Aug	M			Fast	
	5 Sept	Th	**3:378r**		Approving and licensing	A
	11 Sept	W	**3:378r**		Approving and licensing	A
	23 Sept	M			Fast	
	2 Oct	W	**3:378r**		Approving and licensing	A
	9 Oct	W	**3:378r**		Approving and licensing	A
	16 Oct	W	**3:378r**		Approving and licensing	A
	24 Oct	Th			Thanksgiving	
	30 Oct	W	**3:378v**		Approving and licensing	A
	5 Nov	Tu			Powder plot anniversary and thanksgiving	
	6 Nov	W	**3:378v**		Approving and licensing	A
	13 Nov	W	**3:378v**		Approving and licensing	A
	20 Nov	W	**3:379r**		Approving and licensing	A
	27 Nov	W	**3:379r**		Approving and licensing	A
	4 Dec	W	**3:379r**		Approving and licensing	A
	11 Dec	W	**3:379v**		Approving and licensing	A
	25 Dec	W	**3:379v**		Approving and licensing	A

Sess.	Date	Day	Min. folios	Other sources	Main subject(s) of discussion	Subj. class.
	1652					
	1 Jan	W	**3:379v**		Approving and licensing	A
	8 Jan	W	**3:379v**		Approving and licensing	A
	15 Jan	W	**3:380r**		Approving and licensing	A
	22 Jan	W	**3:380r**		Approving and licensing	A
	5 Feb	W	**3:380r**		Approving and licensing	A
	12 Feb	W	**3:380r**		Approving and licensing	A
	? Feb	?	**3:380v**		Approving and licensing	A
	4 Mar	W	**3:380v**		Approving and licensing	A
	11 Mar	W	**3:381r**		Approving and licensing	A
	18 Mar	W	**3:381r**		Approving and licensing	A
	25 Mar	W	**3:381r**		Approving and licensing	A

Contributors

Robert C. Cannada, Jr., DMin, is Chancellor of Reformed Theological Seminary which has US campuses in Jackson, Mississippi; Orlando, Florida; Charlotte, North Carolina; Washington, DC; and Atlanta, Georgia.

Robert J. Cara, PhD, is a Professor of New Testament at Reformed Theological Seminary / Charlotte and the Chief Academic Officer for Reformed Theological Seminary. He is an ordained minister in the Associate Reformed Presbyterian Church.

Ligon Duncan, PhD, is the Senior Minister of the historic First Presbyterian Church (1837), Jackson, Mississippi, and Adjunct Professor of Theology at the Reformed Theological Seminary (RTS). He was formerly the John R. Richardson Professor of Systematic Theology at RTS. He is President of the Alliance of Confessing Evangelicals.

J. V. Fesko, PhD, is the pastor of Geneva Orthodox Presbyterian Church in Woodstock, Georgia and an adjunct Professor of Theology at Reformed Theological Seminary in Atlanta, Georgia.

David C. Jones, PhD, is Professor Emeritus of Systematic Theology at Covenant Theological Seminary, St Louis, Missouri.

Donald Macleod is Principal of the Free Church of Scotland College, Edinburgh.

William M. McMillan, MDiv, is the Managing Editor for the Matthew Henry Project and resides in Houston, Texas.

Robert M. Norris, PhD, is Senior Pastor of Fourth Presbyterian Church, Bethesda, Maryland. He has served as adjunct professor at Reformed Theological Seminary and has also taught history and doctrine in seminaries in Ukraine, Malta, Japan, and Sudan.

Jerry F. O'Neill, PhD, is President and Professor of Theology at Reformed Presbyterian Theological Seminary, Pittsburgh, Pennsylvania.

W. Duncan Rankin, PhD, currently serves as Senior Pastor of Christ Church Presbyterian, Evans, Georgia. He is an Adjunct Professor of Systematic Theology at Reformed Theological Seminary.

J. Nicholas Reid, MDiv Candidate, is Assistant to Ligon Duncan and Associate Editor of Reformed Academic Press. He has served as a teaching assistant in the Old and New Testament Departments at RTS.

Guy M. Richard, PhD, is senior minister of the First Presbyterian Church in Gulfport, Mississippi. He has taught classes in systematic and historical theology at seminaries and universities in the U.S. and abroad.

Mark E. Ross, PhD, is Associate Dean and Associate Professor of Systematic Theology at Erskine Theology Seminary in Columbia, South Carolina.

Valdeci Santos, PhD, is a professor at the Andrew Jumper Graduate Center, Mackenzie University in Sao Paulo, Brazil.

Wayne R. Spear, PhD, is Professor Emeritus of Systematic Theology and Homiletics at the Reformed Presbyterian Theological Seminary, Pittsburgh, Pennsylvania. He serves as a ruling elder in the Grace Reformed Presbyterian Church in Gibsonia, Pennsylvania.

Derek W. H. Thomas, PhD, is the John E. Richards Professor of Pastoral and Systematic Theology at Reformed Theological Seminary. He is also Minister of Teaching at the First Presbyterian Church in Jackson, Mississippi.

William C. Traub is a pastor in the PCA and serves as Coordinator of Theological Education and Training for MTW Europe.

Chad B. Van Dixhoorn, PhD, serves as associate pastor of Grace Orthodox Presbyterian Church in Vienna, Virginia and as a senior research fellow at Wolfson College (University of Cambridge). He is the general editor of the minutes and papers of the Westminster assembly.

Rowland S. Ward, ThD, is minister of Knox Presbyterian Church of Eastern Australia, Melbourne. He has written extensively on historical and doctrinal issues, particularly those related to the Westminster Assembly.

Index

541

V

Van Til, Cornelius ... 223–224, 261, 280
Variata 82
Vermigli, Peter Martyr 238–241
Vines, Richard 402–404
virtues, theological 332, 451

W

Warfield, B.B. 272–274, 329
Warren, Rick 447
Westminster Assembly
   and Lord's Supper 369–382
   committees 31–43
   epistemology 165–167
   formation of 19–23
   journals of 22–23
   journals of - subject classification,
   .... 23–31, 503–536
   minutes 24–26
   organization of 145–148
   plenary sessions 27–31
Westminster Confession of Faith
   .... 85, 91
   amending 125–129
   relation to Scripture 130–131
   ch.1 / 183–184, 252
   ch.2 / 289
   ch.3 / 191–193, 271–276,
   ....285–289, 372-373
   ch.5 / 193–194
   ch.7 / 194–196, 444n, 450n
   ch.8 / 286, 288
   ch.9 / 196–197
   ch.10 / 199–200, 252
   ch.10-20 / 197–199
   ch.11 / .74–75, 200, 303, 312, 423
   ch.12 / 200–201
   ch.13 / 201-202
   ch.14 / 202, 327ff
   ch.15 / 203
   ch.16 / 203–204, 442n
   ch.17 / 205–207
   ch.19 / 207–208
   ch.20 / 208, 252, 420n

   ch.21 / 209–210, 252–253
   ch.25 / 210
   ch.26 / 211
   ch.27 / 409, 426, 428n
   ch.29 / 369n, 370n, 371n,
   .... 372n, 409–410
Westminster Larger Catechism ... 465
   history 415–419
   timeline aspects 63–68
   q.2 / 252–253
   q.6-196 / 63
   q.6 / 64
   q.12-14 / 74
   q.14-15 / 64
   q.18 / 64
   q.20-22 .... / 64
   q.26 / 64
   q.27 / 64
   q.30-35 / 64
   q.31 / 65, ... 74
   q.32 / 452
   q.36 / 65
   q.38 / 64
   q.42-56 / 65
   q.47 / 65
   q.51 / 65
   q.52 / 66
   q.57 / 422
   q.60 / 252
   q.64 / 75
   q.65 / 422
   q.65-90 / 62, 66, 72–73, 75
   q.66 / 422
   q.67 / 74
   q.69 / 423
   q.75 / 425, 436
   q.77 / 453
   q.78 / 64
   q.87 / 74
   q.92-94 / 64
   q.97 / 465
   q.99 / 465
   q.101 / 66
   q.102-148 / 66
   q.151 / 252

Z

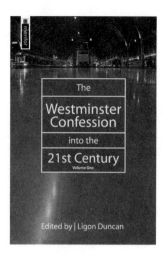

VOLUME 1
ISBN 978-1-85792-862-4

'...a most worthy undertaking...that is quite timely not only because of the anniversary of the Assembly but also because of the clear need in Presbyterian and Reformed circles for scholarly work on the Reformed tradition and its confessions.'

RICHARD A. MULLER

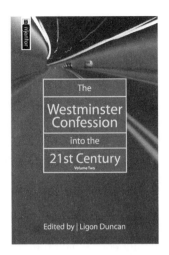

VOLUME 2
ISBN 978-1-85792-878-5

'If the historic confessions are to be preserved for the future, it will take the kind of sympathetic historic description and effective doctrinal argumentation displayed in this book...'

MARK A. NOLL

Christian Focus Publications

publishes books for all ages

Our mission statement –
STAYING FAITHFUL
In dependence upon God we seek to impact the world through literature faithful to his His infallible Word, the Bible. Our aim is to ensure that the Lord Jesus Christ is presented as the only hope to obtain forgiveness of sin, live a useful life and look forward to heaven with Him.

REACHING OUT
Christ's last command requires us to reach out to our world with His gospel. We seek to help fulfill that by publishing books that point people towards Jesus and help them develop a Christ-like maturity. We aim to equip all levels of readers for life, work, ministry and mission.
Books in our adult range are published in three imprints.

Christian Focus contains popular works including biographies, commentaries, basic doctrine and Christian living. Our children's books are also published in this imprint.
Mentor focuses on books written at a level suitable for Bible College and seminary students, pastors, and other serious readers. The imprint includes commentaries, doctrinal studies, examination of current issues and church history.
Christian Heritage contains classic writings from the past.

Christian Focus Publications, Ltd
Geanies House, Fearn,
Ross-shire, IV20 1TW, Scotland, United Kingdom
info@christianfocus.com

For details of our titles visit us on our website
www.christianfocus.com